Teaching mildly handicapped children

METHODS AND MATERIALS

Teaching mildly handicapped children

METHODS AND MATERIALS

A generic approach to comprehensive teaching

GEORGE E. MARSH II, Ed.D.

Department of Special Education, University of Arkansas,
Fayetteville, Arkansas

BARRIE JO PRICE, Ed.D.

Department of Special Education, University of Arkansas,
Fayetteville, Arkansas

TOM E.C. SMITH, Ed.D.

Department of Special Education, University of Arkansas,
Fayetteville, Arkansas

with **70** *illustrations*

The C. V. Mosby Company

ST. LOUIS • TORONTO • LONDON 1983

MOSBY

A TRADITION OF PUBLISHING EXCELLENCE

Editor: Julia Allen Jacobs
Assistant editor: Catherine H. Converse
Manuscript editor: Joan M. Lange
Book design: Jeanne Bush
Cover design: Diane Beasley
Production: Kathleen L. Teal, Carol O'Leary

Printed in the United States of America

The C.V. Mosby Company
11830 Westline Industrial Drive, St. Louis, Missouri 63141

Library of Congress Cataloging in Publication Data

Marsh, George E.
Teaching mildly handicapped children.

Includes index.
1. Handicapped children—Education. I. Price, Barrie Jo, 1947- II. Smith, Tom E.C. III. Title.
LC4015.M36 371.9 82-3440
ISBN 0-8016-3177-7 AACR2

AC/VH/VH 9 8 7 6 5 4 3 2 1 05/C/640

To

Kama, Meredith, and **Jake**

PREFACE

The emphasis in *Teaching Mildly Handicapped Children: Methods and Materials (A Generic Approach to Comprehensive Teaching)* is on programming for handicapped children who are to be served cooperatively by special *and* regular educators. The focus is generic, or noncategorical, because of the lack of consensus about labeling and classification and, more importantly, because of the fact that the majority of handicapped children can be served in mainstream classes. *The term mildly handicapped has been applied in this text to a large group of students to include any handicapped child who differs from nonhandicapped children in cognitive-academic, sensoriphysical, or socioemotional characteristics to such a degree that special education and related services are required, but not to such an extent that segregated special class placement is essential for such services.*

Although many authorities will continue to consider the traditional categories separately for purposes of research and scholarly interest, the pragmatic concern of the special and regular educators is the child for whom they will have a shared teaching responsibility. *Ordinarily this will be a child who is labeled in the traditional categories of mental retardation, learning disabilities, or emotional disturbance or behavioral disorders. However, it may also include many other children who may benefit from regular class instruction, such as those having hearing and vision loss and those with physical and health conditions that do not preclude regular class placement.*

The majority of handicapped children may reasonably be served in a regular classroom, to some extent, depending on the nature and severity of each child's unique needs and characteristics. There may be many types of special education support, but regular class placement for the vast majority of mildly handicapped students is the common factor. Children who can participate in the mainstream classes are mildly handicapped; programming that places greater emphasis on each child's needs rather than on the official label of the child is noncategorical in nature.

A mildly handicapped child is functionally defined as one who may participate in and benefit from regular classroom placement because there are no severe limitations imposed by cognitive-academic, socioemotional, or sensoriphysical handicaps. Thus, at a practical level this becomes a team decision made by the placement committee. Children with intellectual handicaps have, in the past, been barred from regular class placement because of attitudes and school regulations that worked against them. Children with behavior disorders have been placed in special education classes because of the inability of teachers to work effectively with such children in large group settings. Children with a variety of sensory and health conditions have been unable to participate in regular classes because of poorly equipped buildings and inadequate technological aids. However, as attitudes have changed, school policies have changed through lawsuits, behavioral management techniques have become a part of teacher-training programs, and technological advancements have been made; many children are now able to benefit from regular classroom placement who would have otherwise been restricted in their educational options.

In general, we are employing the term mildly handicapped to refer to the large group of children traditionally classified as mentally retarded, emotionally disturbed or behaviorally disordered, and learning disabled. However, as society changes its attitudes and former prejudices alter, as legislation and litigation changes school policies, as teachers develop a common body of management skills, and as medical and technological advances develop, educators must reevaluate their position and permit a broader view of the mildly handicapped child to emerge. Whether, for example, a child with muscular dystrophy is thought to be severely or mildly handicapped cannot simply be determined by the medical condition alone. The field of special education is currently undergoing tremendous change. Although the issue of a severe versus a mild handicap has complicated the conceptualization of this text, our emphasis is that teaching children in regular and special classes is a practical necessity facing most special and regular teachers in the field today.

We envision the roles of special and regular educators as interactive. To the extent that this can be realized the services to handicapped children will be improved, and the nature of each discipline, regular and special education, also will be improved. As the differences and similarities of special and regular classroom programming become more clearly defined, the roles of each type of teacher also will be more clearly defined. We hope that this text will be regarded as a contribution to the field because of the emphasis on shared educational responsibility and cooperative planning. Inclusion of considerable amounts of material dealing with daily program planning is an effort to provide practitioners with information that is of more than just theoretical value.

The arrangement of *Teaching Mildly Handicapped Children* is based on the systems approach. The first section, Chapter 1, provides an overview of various issues and sets the focus of the text. The general rationale of noncategorical and mainstream programming is presented, and the problems involved in it are identified. The remaining chapters of the text deal with the many issues confronting educators who are attempting to conceptualize shared educational responsibility.

The second section, Chapters 2 and 3, deals with the learner. Chapter 2 concerns assessment in much greater detail than commonly covered in a methods textbook. The reason for this arrangement is that the basis for all special education planning must begin with assessment. The textual coverage is limited to the major types of educational instruments usually administered by the teacher, and the instruments are categorized, according to the model included in this chapter, into the areas of cognitive-academic, socioemotional, and sensori-physical functioning.

The fundamental plan in special education is the individualized education program (IEP). Chapter 3 is presented as a comprehensive description of the IEP, a description of the means by which assessment information may be used in developing specific parts of the IEP, and a description of the problems associated with the IEP.

The third section, Chapters 4 through 12, deals with the school program. Chapter 4 is a description of the elementary school and its organization and administration and a discussion of the many issues that pertain to the education of handicapped children. From a systems viewpoint, understanding the elementary school is important for the special educator, who will need to be able to anticipate problems in the school that are defined generally by the roles of various persons in the school environment.

Chapter 5 concerns the role of the special education teacher under the prevailing conditions of contemporary special education. Various issues and roles are described in relation to the practical problems of designing and delivering services to handicapped students.

Chapters 6 to 10 provide coverage of topics in

teaching under the cognitive-academic, socioemotional, and sensoriphysical areas of need. Chapters 6 to 8 deal with reading, expressive language, and arithmetic. Chapter 9 is a comprehensive coverage of various approaches to meeting the socioemotional needs of handicapped students. Chapter 10 provides the regular and special educator with information important for aiding in the adjustment of children who have any of a variety of impaired sensory or health conditions or who require prostheses and special equipment. Chapter 11 includes a discussion of the competencies of the regular classroom teacher, examples of strategies to be used in accommodating the regular education environment to meet a variety of needs of handicapped learners, and suggestions for the special educator who may initiate compensatory approaches.

The final chapter of the textbook, Chapter 12, deals specifically with coordination of the program and effectively implementing the strategies outlined in the first several chapters. A comprehensive approach to implementing the IEP, described in the chapter, draws on the many issues, concepts, and approaches of the previous chapters.

We wish to acknowledge the support, advice, criticism, and contributions of our dean, Fred Vescolani, who has supported special education programming at the college level to such an extent that we are certain that special education need not be an isolated discipline. We are also indebted to the many regular classroom teachers who participated in a federally supported in-service training project over a 4-year period and who were able to shape our thinking and field-test many of the ideas that are recommended. We are especially indebted to Anna C. McFadden for her support as critic and experimenter with many of the techniques that are suggested for regular classroom approaches. Finally, we are grateful to the helpful suggestions of the reviewers, Anna Gajar and Henry A. Goodstein, who assisted us in preparation of the final manuscript.

George E. Marsh II
Barrie Jo Price
Tom E.C. Smith

CONTENTS

SECTION ONE

INTRODUCTION

Special education is at a crossroads. During the last decade significant advances have been made to secure rights for handicapped children through legislation and litigation. The uniform regulations subsequent to the Education of All Handicapped Children Act (Public Law 94-142) provided a foundation for determining basic equality for all handicapped children in the United States, regardless of a school district's wealth or breadth of services. Systematic educational programming would be available by means of the individualized education program (IEP). Perhaps many educators failed to recognize that the implications of P.L. 94-142 would affect the entire field of education, not just a minority of handicapped students. Underlying the mandates of P.L. 94-142 was a clear direction for all of education. It would be possible to transform the field from a system of group expectation and normative comparison to a system of mastery learning based solely on educational criteria. The promise could be made that no school or child would be denigrated because of differences in relative standing on group norms. Each child would be provided with instruction leading to the sequential acquisition of skills regardless of the pace of other students. The degree and conditions of supplemental support would be determined only by the needs of the student and not because of a label or existing administrative arrangements.

Unfortunately the promise may be broken, and the hope for the future put off for many years. There are two reasons. First, the initial reaction of many educators to the mandates of this legislation ranged from anxious concern to serious criticism. In effect the law has only required schools to plan and specify what might reasonably be expected of a school program. However, many educators have regarded the placement of handicapped students in their classrooms and the requirements of P.L. 94-142 to be an unreasonable burden. Procedures pertaining to due process, assessment, and the IEP have been criticized for creating extra expense and demanding excessive time. Many schools have accommodated to the mandates and only lack sufficient time to systematize these innovations, when it may reasonably be expected that school personnel will be able to adjust to a new work norm. Second there is a changing mood in the country that has been characterized as a conservative trend. This conservative mood, which is related to a troubled economy and shifting political trends, may cause schools to be purged of "frills," innovations, and, in particular, "governmental interference." If states and schools are to be granted more autonomy, the battle to secure rights for handicapped students may have to be renewed in state legislatures and the courts. There are signs that funds for schools will be diminished at every governmental level and that organizational and control structures of education will be more loosely organized or decentralized. However, the real danger is that P.L. 94-142 may be changed or weakened. For a group of persons such as the handicapped, removal of rights so recently gained and briefly held would be devastating. No one can be certain what directions the field will take in the future, but doubt and confusion surrounding a field still unsettled from the impact of sweeping changes makes effective educational planning and teaching a necessity. Therefore, the focus of Section One is on the many issues within the field that must be considered in order to deliver effective programming, issues which may not be resolved for many years, but which will affect special education teachers.

1 OVERVIEW

The roles of special and regular classroom teachers are expanded and complicated by the mandates of P.L. 94-142 primarily because handicapped children will not necessarily be educated in accordance with traditional categorical concepts. The old system has changed under the weight of litigation, legislation, and social activism. In every state there are variations on the mandate to place handicapped children into the least restrictive environment, differences in the nature of teacher training programs and licensure standards, and wide variations in the ways that school programs are organized and services delivered.

As Smith and Neisworth (1975) so aptly stated in the middle of the last decade, and which remains true today, "If you are, or are preparing to be, a special educator, you are involved in a profession that is undergoing rapid change. Advances in social philosophy, learning theory, and technology have produced a continuing revolution which makes it difficult but exciting to be a special educator" (p. 6).

To meet the needs of handicapped children under new regulations, according to Charles and Malian (1980), a number of changes in school programs will be necessary:

1. *Student clientele*. Teachers will work with students, such as the deaf, blind, mentally retarded, health impaired, and orthopedically handicapped, who require unusual accommodations in the regular classroom.

2. *Curriculum*. Regular classrooms will need to expand, reduce, or alter the curriculum to meet the needs of each student.

3. *Physical environment*. The physical environment of the school and the space of the regular classroom will need to be changed to accommodate special equipment, materials, and wheelchairs.

4. *Social environment*. Special attention will have to be given to the social interactions of handicapped and nonhandicapped students in regular classrooms.

5. *Teaching methods*. Teachers will need to develop truly individualized education to include educational diagnosis, objectives, and instructional prescriptions. Teaching will shift from presenting information to diagnosing, prescribing, and tutoring. Classroom management techniques (e.g., behavior modification, contingency management, flexible scheduling) will be necessary; teachers will need to work with the full range of disabilities by having some knowledge of special teaching techniques for the deaf, blind, mentally retarded, health impaired, and orthopedically handicapped.

6. *Evaluation*. Standardized tests will have limited use in evaluating individual instruction; criterion-referenced assessment will be essential with a greater emphasis on observation of students by teachers and other specialists, and samples of student work.

7. *Parental involvement*. Although it will be difficult to achieve, parental involvement in placement, planning, and evaluation will be needed.

8. *Other*. Additional issues, such as class size and resources, will need to be considered as the field is changed by the impact of P.L. 94-142.

NORMALIZATION

The changes in the preceding list are directly attributable to the impact of P.L. 94-142, but the law itself became possible because of substantial changes in the society. The essence of this change is *normalization,* a philosophy maintaining that all handicapped persons should enjoy the privileges and opportunities of nonhandicapped persons (Nirje, 1969). Professionals, handicapped persons, parents, and lay persons, aware of the intense discrimination suffered by handicapped persons in our society, pressed for change. In many respects, the normalization effort for the handicapped was a civil rights movement. The major advances of the movement were secured through litigation and ultimately through passage of federal and state legislation, issues that will be discussed more fully in the next section.

In education, the equivalent of normalization is *mainstreaming,* a term which means that handicapped children should have access to public education and should not be limited in such an opportunity because of their handicaps. In a more legal sense, although it is certainly not an equivalent term, the *least restrictive environment* defined in P.L. 94-142 is a normalization concept. In accordance with a child's specific needs, educational experiences will be provided through an IEP, which is ordinarily interpreted to mean that most children should be educated along with nonhandicapped children.

In order to conceptualize this process, schools have been prompted to provide a continuum of services for inclusion of handicapped children according to individual needs. The famous "cascade of service" model (Deno, 1973) is a list of service options ranging from the most segregated to the most integrated, permitting the appropriate setting to be selected by educators. Generally, this continuum of services is thought to include the following options: (1) regular class placement with indirect support from a special educator or consulting service to the teacher, (2) itinerant services whereby the child is served periodically by a mobile teacher, (3) regular class placement with resource room support, (4) special class placement with part-time placement in special education, (5) full-time special class placement, and (6) other arrangements outside the mainstream setting.

In reality, most schools do not actually provide such an array of options. For economic and other reasons, schools have increasingly tended to provide resource rooms and/or self-contained special classes for most children. For the most part the "mildly handicapped" are served through resource room programming. Mildly handicapped children are designated by the following categorical labels: educable mentally retarded (EMR), learning disabled (LD), and emotionally disturbed or behaviorally disordered (ED/BD). Combined, such children comprise the largest group of handicapped students. The more severely handicapped are ordinarily provided with special class placement or limited access to association with nonhandicapped peers. Many children, such as the deaf, blind, health impaired, and orthopedically handicapped, attend regular classrooms throughout the country. Expectations about their abilities to function in regular classrooms are highly variable from one district to another.

EMERGING ISSUES

The changes that have occurred or are still developing are related to a few distinct issues in contemporary special education. The most succinct list of these issues is provided by Lilly (1979), who identifies them as follows:

1. Litigation in special education
2. Free and appropriate public education for all handicapped children
3. Positive and negative aspects of the use of traditional categorical labels in special education
4. Appropriate educational placement
5. Role of the federal government in special education
6. Role of parents in special education
7. Cooperation between special and regular educators

These issues are interrelated and difficult to separate. For example, litigation has caused a redefinition of school policies and defined rights of students, elements that have been adopted in legislation. Concerns of professionals about testing have been similarly addressed in litigation and legislation. Landmark court cases (e.g., *PARC* v. *Commonwealth of Pennsylvania,* 1971, and *Diana* v. *State Board of Education,* 1970) and subsequent cases have established the rights of handicapped children to a free, appropriate public education, the right to fair assessment, and the right to due process and have defined students' rights in regard to punishment and expulsion.

P.L. 94-142, which will be described more fully in a later section, and companion legislation of the states, have incorporated principles of court decisions to assure a free, appropriate public education for all handicapped children, nondiscriminatory testing practices, appropriate educational placement, due process procedures, parental involvement, and other rights.

Of particular concern today is the role of the federal government in special education. A number of writers have carefully detailed the role of federal support for special education (e.g., LaVor, 1976), which dates from 1827. Federal support has been profoundly important in developing materials and teaching methods, stimulating program development, and supporting teacher training. However, the most significant legislation has been P.L. 94-142.

Recent change in the political leadership of the congressional and executive branches of the federal government has threatened the status of special education support. At present there is a significant reduction by Congress in the financial support of the schools. An even more serious threat is the possibility that the mandates of P.L. 94-142 may be weakened or eliminated. Nonetheless, it is clear that litigation remains in place and will continue to unfold, and laws in most states mirror the federal law in some respects. In any event, P.L. 94-142 has already transformed the schools greatly, and it may optimistically be expected that gains already made will be defended.

The other two major emerging issues mentioned previously will be a major focus of this chapter and of following sections of the text, namely, traditional categorical labels in special education and cooperation between special and regular education.

THE ISSUE OF CATEGORICAL LABELS IN SPECIAL EDUCATION

At the heart of all of the change in special education that most directly influences special and regular classroom teachers and which impacts directly on teaching methodologies, is the issue of categorical labels. The significance of this issue can be outlined in two major points. First, prior to P.L. 94-142, teacher training, teacher certification, assessment practices, delivery of services, funding, and teaching methodologies were tied directly to the categorical labels. The special education field was precisely defined and separated by each category. Second, since P.L. 94-142 and other changes in the field, the categories have been altered or deemphasized in many states. Therefore, generic programs affect teacher training, certification, delivery of services, assessment, and teaching methodologies, which do not necessarily coincide as they have in the past.

Generic or noncategorical special education is defined loosely as any approach to the preparation of teachers, certification of teachers, or delivery of services that combines, eliminates, or ignores categories of handicapped children. The generic and mainstreaming trends combine to create many changes in public education. In many states generic special education refers to the traditional categories of EMR, LD, and ED/BD, which have been combined into single categories recognized by such terms as ''mildly handicapped,'' ''educationally handicapped,'' or ''learning and behavior disordered.'' There is also a group consisting of the traditional categories of severely/profoundly handicapped, mentally retarded, emotionally disturbed, and crippling conditions (Lilly, 1979).

Much of the emphasis in this book will be on teaching children in regular and special classes without particular reference to some specific definition, cluster of categorical traits, or classification system. Inclusion of the more severe categories in this text does not imply that we are advocating a single generic or noncategorical approach. Rather, this is a practical necessity in an effort to address a broad audience of teachers who may encounter many variations of service delivery. In many schools, regular classroom teachers will be required to deal with the placement of children who have a full range of problems—visual impairments, hearing impairments, reading disorders, special health problems, and specialized equipment needs. This places a responsibility on the special and regular teachers who must work cooperatively to meet educational needs of students (Lilly, 1979; Reynolds & Birch, 1977).

Beginning with the influence of Dunn (1968), although previous writers had made similar assertions, special educators began to seriously question the efficacy of special education programs for the mentally retarded and ultimately other categories, on the grounds that self-contained classes did not appear to benefit students academically. The controversy grew and culminated in an indictment of the entire categorical system, even though the categorical system remains superficially intact in legislation and in the literature. The major points of criticism have been discussed by many writers; and Smith and Neisworth (1975, pp. 8-9) list them as follows:

1. The categories are educationally irrelevant.
2. Categorical groupings overlap, since children do not fit neatly into single categories.
3. Categories label children as "defective," implying that the cause of the educational or developmental deficiency lies only within the child.
4. Special educational instructional materials and strategies are not category-specific.
5. Preparation of teachers along traditional categorical lines results in redundancy of course work and barriers within the profession.
6. Finally, patterns of funding for special education have perpetuated the categorical approach.

Lilly (1979) addresses the same issues as Smith and Neisworth and also notes that categories ignore the interactive nature of instruction; they discriminate against minority groups and the poor because of the use of culturally biased tests and tracking of children based on test results; they set special education apart from regular education; and they create stereotyped public images of various types of exceptionality.

For these and other reasons, there has been a shift from formulating definitions of exceptional children solely to serve as eligibility criteria for placement to an emphasis on definitions that can be used for instructional planning (Meyen, 1978). This emphasis was partly stimulated in the early 1970s by the leadership of the Bureau of Education for the Handicapped, which, according to Lilly (1979), called for interrelated or generic training programs for special teachers. Since then, many colleges and universities have designed noncategorical (generic) teacher training programs, especially for educable mental retardation, learning disabilities, and emotional disturbances or behavior disorders. Many states have adopted generic certification of teachers. Categorical programs have persisted in the more severe areas of exceptionality, where differences seemed somehow more unique and training techniques more specialized, such as for blind, deaf, and deaf-blind children.

Hallahan and Kauffman (1978) discuss *two* interpretations of *noncategorical,* or generic, special education:

1. Children of all areas of exceptionality, except the gifted, have such common educational needs that they should not be separated for instruction.
2. Only the learning disabled, mentally retarded, and mildly disturbed should be considered as the focus for noncategorical planning.

The basic position for supporting the second viewpoint, according to Hallahan and Kauffman, rests on the grounds that these three categories (EMR, LD, and ED/BD) have similar psychological, educational, and behavioral characteristics, and the teaching methods used with one group are employed with the others.

In traditional programs, the label determined all aspects of teaching training, certification, and methodologies. The teacher of the EMR would receive EMR certification and would be trained in college to use EMR methodologies. Once employed, the teacher would be assigned to teach EMR children in an EMR class, which would be funded by the EMR label, either as a unit or by the type of teacher serving the unit.

In a generic approach the effect is much different. Each component can be independent. The certification may be different than the way the teacher is prepared, the methods of teaching may be at variance with the roles expected in the school, and the service delivery system or funding pattern may be influenced by factors different than assessment and definitional criteria. A district may, under state guidelines, assess children within the traditional categories but be also required to serve them in noncategorical special education programs. The implications for teaching methodologies and for relationships with regular classroom programming may not be apparent. In fact, the mainstreaming trend has created a situation in which some of the traditional remedial approaches cannot be easily implemented because there is not sufficient time (with children in regular classes for great portions of the day) or the approaches are significantly at variance with programming goals and objectives of the regular curriculum.

Cautions have been noted about the noncategorical trend. Weiderholt, Hammill, and Brown (1979) assert that the noncategorical approach must not be considered a substitute for special (categorical) education for certain children. They believe that the noncategorical approach is useful for most handicapped children and that the resource room approach seems to be the most promising service delivery model for these children. However, they state that blind, deaf, disturbed, and language-disordered children should also be served in categorical programs.

CHARACTERISTICS OF HANDICAPPED STUDENTS

Even in many noncategorical programs it is still true that labels are initially assigned and characteristics are used to define educational and other needs. This happens as a result of the assessment process. This text has devoted considerable attention, perhaps an inordinate amount, to assessment. However, it is an inescapable fact that the special educator will have to deal with assessment issues. Even in settings in which labels are virtually ignored and instructors have a noncategorical philosophy, it is still necessary that children be officially labeled as handicapped. This requires some definition, some set of characteristics, a battery of tests, and certification by one or more examiners that the student has a recognizable handicapping condition according to a state regulatory definition.

The findings of examiners, based on assessment data, will be used to characterize a child in terms of a current level of educational functioning, presumed needs, and presumed reasons for academic or adjustment disorders. For children who are traditionally regarded as EMR or LD, the characteristics will be some combination of intellective, perceptual, language, or conceptual disorders. For children who are primarily regarded as emotionally disturbed or behaviorally disordered the characteristics will be expressed in such terms as conduct disorders, tantrum behavior, withdrawal, hyperactivity, phobias, anxiety, and aggression. Children with severe physical, peripheral-sensory, or health disorders will be characterized in medical terminology so as to include visual impairments, hearing disorders, brain damage, orthopedic conditions, epilepsy, motor deficits, and health impairments.

The issue of characteristics is controversial. Some writers, such as Lilly (1979), take the position that characteristics, at least for children with learning and behavioral problems, tend to be inaccurate in individual cases and divert attention from a careful assessment of individual strengths and needs. Hallahan and Kauffman (1978) list psychological and behavioral characteristics, but emphasize that they are derived from research studies comparing groups of children and may not typify individual children. Of course, there are many texts which list specific characteristics for certain categories, maintaining that they have diagnostic significance.

According to Reynolds and Birch (1977), important characteristics of a child are those which relate to or interact with instruction; thus, they are variables. This position is taken in this text; the planning matrix recommended later is an attempt to permit better identification of such interactive variables. Classificatory or prognostic characteristics are of little use in the classroom. Poor vision, attention disorders, or spina bifida explained in etiological terms are not very helpful in planning instruction. In general, the operant behavioral approach is useful here because it stresses observation of the child, instructional treatments based on observation, and measurable outcomes.

The following general points are made to emphasize the important issue of characteristics in special education:

1. The similarities among handicapped students of various categories are greater than their differences. Characteristics associated with one condition or another overlap significantly, and many of the teaching approaches, methods, and materials useful for one diagnostic category are also appropriate for another. In the same vein it can be said that the differences among children labeled within one category are greater than their similarities. Characteristics are significant only as they are applied to a particular student.

2. Teaching should be based on what the student can and cannot do, on what the curricular sequence should be in response to specific individual objectives, and on what the teacher should or should not do to effect change and learning in the student.

3. Instructional methods and materials should be selected to meet the needs and characteristics of an individual learner rather than those that seem to be appropriate for a label or certain type of group assignment deemed appropriate for children who share certain theoretical characteristics.

COOPERATION BETWEEN REGULAR AND SPECIAL EDUCATORS

Within the context of noncategorical and mainstream programming, the problem of teaching handicapped children is defined by two general problems. First, the regular teacher may be uncertain about how to provide for the handicapped learner in an environment that was once thought to be inappropriate for handicapped children. Second, the special educator is confronted with the task of interpreting assessment data and modifying special education approaches for use in the regular classroom environment. The question is, what are the instructional responsibilities of mainstream and special educators?

In recent years, the most widely used conceptualization of teaching handicapped children has been the diagnostic-prescriptive teaching (DPT) approach. Many special educators have attempted to use DPT for aiding the regular teacher in mainstreaming. Originally proposed by Peter (1965), the approach has been elaborated on by a number of special education writers and is recognized by various names (Charles, 1980; Haring & Schiefelbush, 1976; Lerner, 1976; Smith, 1974; Stephens, 1977). DPT and the IEP tend to mirror one another. The basic steps in the process are well known:

1. Determine instructional objectives.
2. Determine instructional strategies.
3. Select appropriate materials.
4. Implement the program.
5. Determine the progress of the learner.
6. Revise the program according to evaluation.
7. Revise or erect new objectives.

Under clinical or self-contained teaching designs, DPT is conducted by implementing some classical types of methodologies. The teacher, who is supposed to have a thorough knowledge of instructional methodologies and materials and who also knows the needs of a student, is theoretically capable of matching student needs with instructional options. However, many of the approaches that may be used do not translate easily into regular classroom methodologies, and the approaches may actually conflict with goals of the regular classroom teachers. If a special teacher provides training in the special classroom, it is essential that it not interfere with instruction in the regular classroom where most handicapped children will spend the greater part of the school day. The strategies employed in both environments must be coordinated in order to benefit the student.

Application of the DPT approach to the regular class may be difficult for reasons other than incompatibility. Diagnostic-prescriptive teaching can only be as effective as the validity of the "diagnosis" and the efficacy of the "prescription." In the medical field there are many clear examples of diagnosis of disease and effective treatment with the correct, prescribed medication. In special education, however, there are many writers who criticize the validity of psychoeducational diagnosis. The arguments, which will be covered in detail in Chapter 2, attack this process on the grounds that characteristics of students, such as process disorders (visual perception and visual-motor integration), are not necessarily causally related to academic disorders, that tests used with students to measure such traits are invalid, and that treatment approaches based on remediation of underlying processes do not result in improved functioning or significant academic gains. Similarly, specific methods approaches to reading, arithmetic, and other basic skills may not necessarily be more effective for academic deficiencies than other approaches available to the teacher. Thus, the most common approach to special education, DPT, is difficult to translate into use in the regular classroom. The implication of this is far reaching: the special educator must now search for a new approach that is more compatible with the mainstream setting or for ways to alter traditional strategies so that they mesh with mainstream instruction.

This text includes many of the traditional methods approaches to special education because of their popularity and acceptance in the field and the usefulness elements of each approach may have for particular students. However, the emphasis is on observing students in learning environments to determine instructional approaches. Reynolds and Birch (1977) have stated as follows:

> Educational decisions require attention to variables of characteristics that interact with instruction, that is, that help educators to make a difference rather than a simple prediction. This requirement is far beyond the content of psychological reports written in simple terms of capacity, expectation, or underachievement, all of which are prognostic in orientation. (p. 68)

If the most important characteristics of children are those which interact with instruction, it will be the challenge of the regular and special teacher to alter instruction dramatically rather than simply permit handicapped students to attend regular classes. A major focus must be on the teaching behaviors of the classroom teacher, as indicated by some conclusions of Dunkin and Biddle (1974), who reviewed hundreds of studies in the regular classroom:

1. The teacher is the central figure and conducts all activities.
2. Most class time is spent by the teacher verbalizing about subject matter.
3. The typical class involves considerable time in whole-class activities, particularly prolonged, unvaried seatwork.
4. Teachers criticize children a great deal. Criticism is especially prevalent in the lower grades and is directed more frequently at boys.
5. Teacher praise is directed primarily at those whom teachers like and admire, the higher-functioning students.
6. Better-achieving students are seated in the front and center of the class in close proximity to the teacher.
7. Students are expected to be passive; interactions between students and significant interactions between the teacher and students are limited.

Other problems with mainstreaming are listed as follows:

1. Special education programs for students involved in mainstreaming are poorly designed (Bullock and Rigg, 1980).
2. There is a lack of coordination between regular and special educators.
3. Students are confronted with competing sets of instructional goals.
4. Rather than concerns about instructional methodology and individualized programming, problems created by mainstreaming have surfaced as concerns about the attitudes of teachers and peers toward the handicapped student, the difficulty of the regular curriculum, self-concepts of students, and many other factors not necessarily related to direct teaching events (Evans, 1980; Goodman & Miller, 1980; Palmer, 1980).

Analyzed as learning conditions, this environment does not appear to be very promising for most handicapped students. The special educator must assist the regular classroom teacher in making a transition from group instruction to individualized approaches based on student data. The special educator must deal with alterable teaching variables that interact with instructionally relevant characteristics of the learner.

Bloom (1980) regards alterable variables as important in the new generation of educational research. He refers to the creation of favorable learning conditions that can enable virtually all students to learn to a high standard. He notes that many variables cannot be changed, such as the amount of time available during a school day, age of the teacher, personality of the teacher, and IQ of the student. However, those which can be changed are time-on-task (the amount of time a student is engaged in learning during the available time), cognitive entry (the specific knowledge and abilities that a student has as prerequisites to further learning), and formative rather than social or economic status of the student's parents. Bloom contends that as the educator searches for more variables that can be changed, learning can be improved by moving from an emphasis on prediction and classification to a concern for causality and the relationship between means and ends in teaching and learning. The educator's search for the reasons a child fails in the learning environment in terms of teaching events (attention, presentation, responding, and feedback) will be more fruitful than dealing with classificatory characteristics of children.

The suggestions in this text are largely based on alterable variables. These suggestions will be presented in the following parts of this chapter, which deal with a comprehensive educational model and with classroom teaching variables. To recognize alterable variables one must make observations. As applied to children, this approach has long been stressed in special education (Lovitt, 1967). However, if the teaching and learning variables are to be considered as interactive, it also becomes necessary to observe the teacher, to observe the classroom interactions of students, and to consider related variables dealing with the curriculum, types of materials, skill level of the student, and the manner by which the student receives, organizes, and retrieves information.

The role of the special educator as consultant has become widely accepted as part of the concept of shared responsibility for serving handicapped students (Reynolds, 1978), although it may not be widely practiced or well done. Consultation can have a significant impact because of the broadened scope of services beyond the individual classroom (Montgomery, 1978).

Following are some of the advantages of the consultant role of special educators:

1. Increased cost and time effectiveness (Montgomery, 1978)
2. Comprehensive services (Reynolds, 1978)
3. Prevention (Cantrell & Cantrell, 1976)
4. Help for students without the need to label (Newcomer, 1977)
5. Sharing of benefits with more students (Swift & Spivack, 1975)

The goals of consultation may be viewed differently among educators, and it is certain that some would object to the concept entirely, but generally there are two major approaches:

1. Increase the competence and confidence of the regular teacher in serving handicapped students.
2. See that services to a particular student are coordinated.

Much of the orientation of this text is based on the practical, field-based experience of mainstream teachers who have attempted to employ a wide range of approaches to teaching children in the mainstream setting. These issues will be addressed at various points in the text. It is important to note at this point that the greatest impact of the special educator on mainstream education is through the cooperative role the educator plays; not only is individual programming designed for a particular student, but major alterations in the organization of the classroom and management of students are also achieved. The conditions for this level of involvement include the ability of teachers to view consultation as a process that takes place between peers, to recognize that special education is not the sole responsibility of the special educator, to see that specific teaching competencies are added to the repertoire of the regular classroom teacher, and to view consultation as a continuing process. The two major approaches to be stressed in the remainder of this book will deal with the classical approaches to special education and means of assisting the regular classroom teacher.

A COMPREHENSIVE EDUCATIONAL MODEL

Considering the many issues and problems just discussed, the following model is an attempt to articulate and expand on various components in contemporary special education. The comprehensive model addresses three major concerns (Fig. 1-1):

1. Educational responsibilities of the mainstream teacher
2. Educational responsibilities of the special teacher
3. Interaction between the special and regular programs

Major sections of this text primarily concern the responsibilities of the mainstream teacher, some parts address the responsibilities of the special teacher, and other parts deal with interactions. Even in sections dealing with reading approaches or arithmetic instruction, problems of implementing one approach or the other are discussed in terms of shared responsibilities.

Determining the needs of an individual student is the first and most important step. This text considers the student in terms of the following broad categories of need:

1. Cognitive-academic
2. Socioemotional
3. Sensoriphysical

Tests are administered, of course, but other sources of data are used to collect important information that can be used to plan an IEP. Aspects dictated by the IEP include appropriate placement, teacher responsibilities, educational goals, types of materials, and related services. The teaching approaches of special educators may be drawn from the large body of techniques available. Decisions about teaching approaches unique to the regular classroom are determined by the same process. However, the environment of the regular class creates different circumstances and conditions for

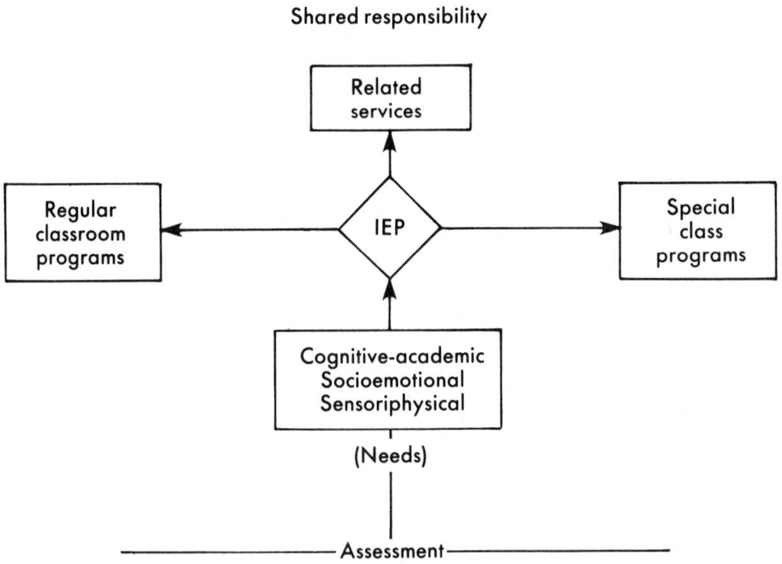

Fig. 1-1. A comprehensive education model for shared instruction in mainstream programs.

learning. In either the special or regular environment the following teaching events must occur:

1. Attention of the learner
2. Presentation of information
3. Response of the learner
4. Feedback

Each step in the sequence of teaching events may be affected by many factors, including learner characteristics, actions of the teacher, and events in the learning environment. To assist the teacher in adjusting to meet the needs of the learner through effective classroom teaching, 12 variables in classroom teaching are presented below.

CLASSROOM TEACHING VARIABLES

As indicated previously, and discussed throughout this text, the problems in selecting educational strategies for any student, handicapped or nonhandicapped, are complicated by the lack of empirical evidence to support any one approach. The overwhelming conclusion of Joyce and Weil (1980) is that no one reliable, multipurpose teaching approach can be identified. The same conclusion may also be used to explain research in special education. No one particular approach can be identified as superior to another. Therefore, the 12 variables below and the recommendations in this text are based on a broad spectrum of methodologies defined by the following factors:

1. A systems framework (from systems theory) was used to identify the instructional problems of teachers and the educational needs of students.
2. The demands on regular and special teachers were isolated within the context of the classroom environment.
3. An approach was sought that would have broad application to the classroom whether the classroom was located in a comprehensive, small, urban, rural, wealthy, or poor district. Instructional elements that are common to these districts would be essential for inclusion rather than those which might ap-

TWELVE CRITICAL VARIABLES IN GENERIC TEACHING STRATEGIES

Direct teaching variables

1. Control of the student's attention and time-on-task learning
2. Organizational control of information (input) to be learned with objectives
3. Redundancy of instructional cues
4. Alternative informational access
5. Alternative responding
6. Reinforcement and feedback

Ecological variables

7. Environmental climate of the classroom
8. Time and space utilization
9. Participation-interaction of students

Curricular variables

10. Sequence and rate of presentation of skills to be learned
11. Uses and adaptation of materials and equipment
12. Accommodation and compensatory teaching

ply in only the most "ideal" environments.

4. An approach was sought that could be used to coordinate the activities that might occur between the regular and special classrooms and that could be associated with the IEP and DPT approach, which is so predominant in special education.
5. Pertinent research was reviewed to aid in the selection of strategies, and to justify the use of these strategies.

From this effort a list of 12 teaching variables was identified and the list divided according to direct teaching, ecological, and curricular variables. These serve for planning cooperative instruction on a broad basis with a primary emphasis on mainstream instruction. Justification for many of the instructional variables may be found in the review of research reported by Gephart, Strother, and Duckett (1981). Conceptually, these 12 variables may also be fitted to major learning models reviewed by Joyce and Weil (1980): information-processing, personal, social, and behavioral. Moreover, flexibility is made for adjusting to or accommodating for the learner depending on needs apparent in the cognitive-academic, socioemotional, and sensoriphysical areas of assessment. There is no attempt to offer a simple prescription for the needs of children or for the behaviors of a "good" teacher. As Gephart et al. indicated, teaching and the context in which it is embedded are too complex for simple applications or remedies. Rather, a framework is provided with guiding principles that may be used by teachers for the improvement of instruction through planned approaches to integrating teaching and learning behaviors that may maximally benefit a particular student. Further discussion of these variables will be made throughout the text.

The basic components of the framework are concerned with principles of mastery learning (Carroll, 1963). It is absolutely necessary that the available time of the school year be organized so that time, as a variable, can be manipulated so that each handicapped student may reach mastery on criteria in each of the curricular areas of the school. Under current circumstances in many typical classrooms the regular teacher holds time constant for the group and permits learning levels to vary among the students. The lower-functioning students, as a result, learn less, reach lower levels of mastery, and receive poor grades. By letting time vary and holding mastery as an expectation for each student, the educator allows handicapped students to be more fairly treated in the mainstream classroom. Handicapped students will not necessarily need to be compared with higher-achieving students because achievement will be measured in terms of individual progress, time will be specifically divided between group and individualized instruction to address the needs of each learner, specific skills in the curriculum will be used so that each student can be placed on a learning continuum, teachers will be free to use a variety of educational approaches and materials, and diagnostic-prescriptive teaching can be altered so that it focuses on sequential skills measured by summative and formative tests.

In summary, the problems inherent in planning cooperative educational efforts between regular and special education under normalization philosophy can be solved by effective utilization of the IEP as a process instrument. If all conceivable needs of the learner are identified as individual rather than categorical characteristics, and if plans are made to meet each need within the school as necessary, the goals directing these plans must be as follows:

1. To organize the interactions between special education and other programs of the school
2. To coordinate teaching methodologies reflecting curricular goals of the school for the handicapped student
3. To articulate the resources of the school to effect a unique pattern of programmed environments for each handicapped student

THE PLANNING MATRIX

Mainstreaming requires the selection and incorporation of methodologies, strategies, and materials from among the universe of those formerly associated with traditional categories, as they seem appropriate to meet the needs of a particular student in an instructional plan. In that labels narrowed the choices considerably, the former process was very often sequential and *pro forma*. Moreover, the process also focused the attentions of the teacher on one aspect according to the label that was assigned: namely academic concerns were elevated with learning disabled, behavior or self-concept with emotionally disturbed, and so forth. The deemphasis of labels, as in noncategorical programming, leaves the teachers either without initial guidelines or with the task of adapting categorical approaches to the mainstream setting. The result is that teachers must start by examining all areas of student development—cognitive-academic functioning, socioemotional development, and sensoriphysical functioning. Under these conditions, the selection of strategies is guided by the distinct profile of information about each student in each of these areas. Traditional models in education (ability/deficit, skill/content, and teaching models) must be superimposed on the student data to generate a unique IEP and instructional plan.

The conceptual model in Fig. 1-2 provides the foundation for depicting teaching as conceived within this text. To actually implement teaching based on an IEP, it is necessary to scrupulously gather all relevant data about a child. The planning matrix in Fig. 1-2 aids in this conceptualization. The matrix forces the teacher to target major areas of interaction between the student's profile and approaches to instruction. The grid design of the matrix produces data on which a functional IEP can be developed because, in addition to student areas of need, information is produced that guides in the selection of strategies, materials, and other forms of placement and teaching decisions. This may be approached as diagnostic-prescriptive teaching, although education must be based more on assumptions than prescriptions because of the lack of any one "best" approach or array of "best" approaches for several problems.

To truly individualize the education of a particular student, it is necessary to focus on the unique needs of the student and to arrange all instructional elements around those traits. The predominant practice of assigning students to "the special education program" cannot be the basis for planning. The IEP must be viewed as a *process* tool rather than a *product*. It is necessary to narrow the focus of planning on the idiopathic characteristics of a

		Services				
		Teacher variables	Instructional procedures	Placement	Referral services	Other
Needs	Cognitive-academic functioning					
	Socioemotional functioning					
	Sensoriphysical functioning					

Fig. 1-2. Individualized education program (IEP): a model for data collection.

particular student and not the label, test scores, or predetermined treatment approaches (e.g., those designated by types of service models built into the system for special education). Educational plans should be erected *only* according to individual needs and characteristics.

The following general description of the components of the model in Fig. 1-2 for planning individual programs are elaborated on at other points in the text. The purpose here is to provide explanations of the use of each part in the matrix. The utility of the planning matrix is that it can serve as a uniform and systematic basis for the identification of needs and educational plans. Thus, we would ignore any predetermined plans associated with a label or with types of program alternatives in a continuum of services because attention only to the label or the continuum may cause predisposed planning to occur. Specific instructional approaches and precise needs of a student may be masked by a diagnostic category that only implies the student's needs.

The IEP process is all too often *pro forma* in many settings. IEPs are developed on the basis of group characteristics, assignments to a specific type of service model are determined by the label of the student, and methodologies are used by teachers who develop group programs. There is frequently little planning to account for the learning experiences of the student in the mainstream setting. The IEP is developed on the basis of convenience from the institutional point of view. Attention to more subtle and important aspects such as the nature of the curriculum, the teachers, teaching styles, peers, instructional techniques, and other factors are overlooked. This may be due to the fact that the assessment process and IEP development are formal procedures viewed by schools as required administrative functions. It is also true that team behavior in many settings is beset by personal and professional discord. The process should be *dispositional,* with planning decisions based on as many characteristics and needs of the student as may be feasibly met in the total school environment and beyond, if necessary. Moreover, the plans for the child should be changed as frequently as necessary because, as students grow and learn, their needs change.

Data collection

There are two general forms of collecting data for the purpose of planning. One, of course, involves the use of familiar tests that play a prominent part in school assessment programs. These are standardized and informal measures of a wide range of skills. The other, and in our view the most important, is the use of direct observation of the student in learning environments. Through observation it is possible to determine coping styles of behavior of the student and to assess the interactions of the student with peers and teachers. This permits the collection of ecological data essential to planning and daily instruction. Many of the techniques in behavioral modification approaches are also used for more detailed analysis of specific behaviors and for daily instructional purposes.

Needs and services components

Reference to the planning matrix (Fig. 1-2) shows 15 cells in a 3 × 5 table with *Needs* along the left (rows) and *Services* across the top (columns). This is a graphic representation of the broad assessment categories for students and possible services and responses of the school as determined in an IEP. In reality, we are advocating the assessment of both the student and the services in order to make a proper match.).

The categories for collection of needs data are (1) cognitive-academic functioning, (2) socioemotional functioning, and (3) sensoriphysical functioning. The significance of these components is obvious. The major activity of the school is to conduct assessment procedures—to collect useful assessment information in each of the components to determine educational and related needs. Formal tests, informal tests, observations, records assessment, case histories, medical reports, screening activities, and all other sources of data typically used in assessment and placement decisions can be organized within these three categories. However, many times the assessment process is routine, and specific tests are administered in accordance with a referral problem, which may cause many important areas of assessment to be overlooked. At the time of developing an IEP and pursuing the development of daily instructional activities, undoubtedly it will be necessary to provide essential information. These components will be described in detail in the following chapters.

Programming is concerned with instructional methodology, learning environments, interactions of the learner with other persons in the environment, events in the curriculum, and feedback to the learner and teacher. Direct teaching through teacher-controlled variables is the fundamental framework. A planning matrix is necessary for designing each conceivable treatment or interaction necessary to plan the instructional design. The learner's needs are addressed by the school's resources rather than having the school fit the student into a service slot or force the use of certain materials based on perceptions associated with a label.

The purpose of programming is to assist the student to achieve, according to the factors of individual aptitude and individualized instruction, under conditions unique to the student. Each decision, such as the type of classroom(s), choice of teachers and materials, type of related services, nature of interactions, and all other treatments would be determined by careful examination of the student's needs and examination of the existing resources. Verification of the student's progress is determined on a daily basis through monitoring. This is contrary to random mainstreaming, categorical placement, curricular tracking, and fixed-time arrangements.

SUMMARY

The following major points have been made in this chapter:

1. The roles of special and regular classroom teachers are expanded and complicated by the mandates of P.L. 94-142.
2. The normalization trend in society and mainstreaming in public education have been supported by litigation and legislation, which have secured the rights of handicapped children to have access to public education.
3. Of the many issues affecting education of the handicapped, cooperation between special and regular education is an important issue that is complicated by a lack of clarity about the responsibilities of regular and mainstream teachers.
4. Noncategorical, or generic, special education is any approach that combines, eliminates, or ignores the traditional categories of handicapped children in preparation of teachers for delivery of services.
5. A comprehensive educational model addresses the issues of the responsibilities of the mainstream teacher, the responsibilities of the special educator, and the interaction between special and regular programs.
6. Educational needs of students must be determined on the basis of individual characteristics that are categorized generally within the areas of cognitive-academic, socioemotional, and sensoriphysical functioning.
7. The teaching act can be simply outlined but is extremely complicated by a variety of variables. Twelve teaching variables were identified as important in mainstream education of handicapped children because they can be manipulated to address needs determined by an IEP in a regular classroom environment.
8. The planning matrix permits the collection of numerous pieces of information to design a unique IEP for each handicapped student.

Regular and special teachers must be prepared, theoretically, for the possibility of designing, implementing, and evaluating individualized educational programs for any handicapped child who may, under current trends, have mild to severe handicaps. Such programs must address cognitive-academic, socioemotional, and sensoriphysical needs of each student in a cooperative, coordinated program bridging the mainstream setting and special education program. Plans must, therefore, be based specifically on the IEP developed by the teachers, parents, students, and other professionals.

REFERENCES AND SUGGESTED READINGS

Bloom, B.S. The new direction in educational research: alterable variables. *Phi Delta Kappan,* 1980, *61,* 382-385.

Bullock, L.M., & Rigg, W.C. Relationship of individualized instruction to placement of exceptional children. *Exceptional Children,* 1980, *47,* 124-125.

Cantrell, R.P., & Cantrell, M.L. Preventive mainstreaming: impact of a supportive services program on pupils. *Exceptional Children,* 1976, *41,* 381-386.

Carroll, J.B. A model of school learning. *Teacher College Record,* May, 1963, pp. 723-733.

Charles, C.M. *Individualizing instruction* (2nd ed.). St. Louis: The C.V. Mosby Co., 1980.

Charles, C.M., & Malian, I.M. *The special student: practical help for the classroom teacher.* St. Louis: The C.V. Mosby Co., 1980.

Deno, E. *Instructional alternatives for exceptional children.* Reston, VA: The Council for Exceptional Children, 1973.

Diana v. State Board of Education, No. C-70 37 RFP, District Court of Northern California (February 1970).

Dunkin, M.S.T., & Biddle, B.J. *The study of teaching.* New York: Holt, Rinehart & Winston, 1974.

Dunn, L.M. Special education for the mildly retarded: Is much of it justifiable? *Exceptional Children,* 1968, *35,* 5-22.

Evans, S. The consultant role of the resource teacher. *Exceptional Children,* 1980, *46,* 402-404.

Gephart, W.S., Strother, D.B., & Duckett, W.R. (Eds.). Practical applications of research. *Phi Delta Kappan,* 1981, *3,* 1-4.

Goodman, L., & Miller, H. Mainstreaming: how teachers can make it work. *Journal of Research and Development in Education,* 1980, *13,* 45-57.

Hallahan, D.B., & Kauffman, J.W. *Exceptional children.* Englewood Cliffs, NJ: Prentice-Hall, Inc., 1978.

Haring, N.G., & Schiefelbush, R.L. *Teaching special children.* New York: McGraw-Hill Book Co., 1976.

Joyce, B., & Weil, M. *Models of teaching* (2nd ed.). Englewood Cliffs, NJ: Prentice-Hall, Inc., 1980.

LaVor, M.L. Federal legislation for exceptional persons: a history. In F.J. Weintraub et al., (Eds.), *Public policy and the education of exceptional children.* Reston, VA: The Council for Exceptional Children, 1976, pp. 96-112.

Lerner, J.L. *Children with learning disabilities* (2nd ed.). Boston: Houghton Mifflin Co., 1976.

Lilly, M.S. *Children with exceptional needs: a survey of special education.* New York: Holt, Rinehart & Winston, 1979.

Lovitt, T.C. Assessment of children with learning disabilities. *Exceptional Children,* 1967, *34,* 233-242.

Meyen, E.L. *Exceptional children and youth.* Denver, CO: Love Publishing Co., 1978.

Montgomery, M.D. The special educator as a consultant: some strategies. *Teaching Exceptional Children,* 1978, *10,* 110-112.

Newcomer, P. Special educational services for the mildly handicapped: beyond a diagnostic and remedial model. *Journal of Special Education,* 1977, *11,* 11-12.

Nirje, B. The normalization principle and its human management implications. In R.B. Kugel & W. Wolfensberger (Eds.), *Changing patterns in residential services for the mentally retarded.* Washington, DC: U.S. Government Printing Office, 1969, pp. 231-240.

Palmer, D.J. Factors to be considered in placing handicapped children in regular classes. *Journal of School Psychology,* 1980, *18,* 163-171.

PARC v. Commonwealth of Pennsylvania, 334 F. Supp. 1257 E.D., PA (1971).

Peter, L.J. *Prescriptive teaching.* New York: McGraw-Hill Book Co., 1965.

Reynolds, M.C. Staying out of jail. *Teaching Exceptional Children,* 1978, *10,* 60-62.

Reynolds, M.C., & Birch, J.W. *Teaching exceptional children in all America's schools.* Reston, VA: The Council for Exceptional Children, 1977.

Smith, R.M., & Neisworth, J.T. *The exceptional child: a functional approach.* New York: McGraw-Hill Book Co., 1975.

Smith, R.M. *Clinical teaching: methods of instruction for the retarded.* New York: McGraw-Hill Book Co., 1974.

Stephens, T.M. *Teaching skills to children with learning and behavior disorders.* Columbus, OH: Charles E. Merrill Publishing Co., 1977.

Swift, M.S., & Spivack, G. *Alternative teaching strategies: helping behaviorally troubled children achieve.* Champaign, IL: Research Press, 1975.

Weiderholt, J.L., Hammill, D.H., & Brown, V. *The resource teacher: a guide to effective practices.* Boston: Allyn & Bacon, Inc., 1978.

SECTION TWO

THE LEARNER

The second section of the text is devoted to a consideration of the characteristics and assessment of handicapped students that would culminate in an IEP. Although most mildly handicapped students are generally regarded as mildly retarded, learning disabled, or emotionally disturbed or behaviorally disordered, it is now necessary to view students within many contexts for determination of needs and educational planning. For example, many children who are said to be mentally retarded also display emotional conflict and secondary health conditions. Also, many children who have such conditions as spina bifida, limited vision or hearing, or other health disorders might be placed in the regular classroom. Whether or not a child should be placed in a regular classroom depends on the viewpoint one has about severity of the handicap.

It is not the purpose of this text to enter into this debate; rather, it is apparent that any child who may be regarded as handicapped will have highly individual needs and characteristics. Whether or not the child should be placed in a regular classroom for programming depends on each unique set of needs and characteristics. If a child can be placed in the mainstream environment and benefit from it, the school will probably regard the child as having a mildly handicapping condition. For example, many children with cerebral palsy can attend regular classes because they also have the cognitive ability to benefit from such placement. However, some children, who are otherwise academically capable, have such extensive physical impairment that it is necessary to resort to total special class placement. There is no formula for making such determinations easily. Each case must be considered on its own merits. Thus, instead of focusing on labels or service delivery systems, it is necessary to focus on three broad areas of assessment for each child: cognitive-academic, socioemotional, and sensoriphysical functioning.

The two chapters in this section deal specifically with the following: (1) assessment practices, (2) specific instruments commonly used in special education, (3) a model for collecting assessment data, (4) means by which data may be interpreted, (5) educational planning, and (6) development of the IEP. The validity of educational planning is determined by the quality of the data collection effort and the suitability of the IEP as a planning tool in educational programming.

2 FOCUS ON THE LEARNER: DATA COLLECTION

The assessment process in special education seems to consume a disproportionate amount of human and fiscal resources of the school budget in terms of its apparent efficiency and effectiveness. Assessment is, obviously, very expensive, but the most common disappointment for teachers is that it culminates in very little useful information for teaching. This can be explained in terms of what testing and assessment practices accomplish and what different groups expect. Test scores have long been used for a variety of purposes to satisfy legal and administrative needs of schools. Interpretations of test data permit decisions to be made about the effectiveness of teaching materials, teaching programs, teaching personnel, and about the quality of education or the suitability of students for different lines of professional endeavor.

Assessment has been very important in special education programming, and nowhere has it been more controversial. Although psychologists and other assessment personnel make recommendations about the education and treatment of children on the basis of test data, the primary function of the assessment program is to satisfy the legal requirements for placement of children in special education classes. However, many classroom teachers, administrators, and parents view assessment and subsequent labeling as a diagnostic procedure similar to the identification of disease in the medical field. It seems reasonable to many that the logical consequence of assessment, after it is known what is "wrong" with a child, is that specialists should be able to immediately and effectively introduce the appropriate intervention based on the diagnosis.

The value of test scores and diagnostic profiles depends to a great extent on what one believes about tests. Some professionals search for a certain profile or typical pattern of test response in the belief that accurate diagnostic information can clearly indicate the existence of a particular condition and its effect, like a "psychoeducational litmus test." Other professionals believe that tests are merely useful as a general guide in uncovering trends in a subject's performance, a better procedure than making subjective observations or informed guesses. Still others would totally abandon the use of standardized tests in the belief that they are virtually worthless and can harm children because of the interpretations that are made by well-meaning but misguided professionals.

Testing is required to meet the legal requirements of P.L. 94-142 and state regulations for identification and placement of handicapped students. Unless major changes are made, the required assessment process will continue to be a part of special education. Therefore, regardless of the objections a teacher may have to tests, a practical view of the required assessment program would deal with the legal requirements and the teacher's role in the process, a process that is legally bound to special education screening, placement, programming, and evaluation.

Purposes of assessment

Most writers take the position that assessment is a comprehensive program of which testing is but one component. Discussion here is limited primarily to test instruments, test data, types of evaluation, uses of test data, cautions about test interpretation, and the role of the teacher. The purposes of assessment are usually viewed as screening, placement, program evaluation, and student progress.

Screening. Specific instruments, procedures, and data from routine assessment of students with group tests are used to identify children who may be suspected of deviating significantly from age peers in some way, warranting more intense evaluation because of the possibility that special education, medicine, therapy, or some other intervention may be required. Ideally, screening is an active process in which teachers and parents attempt to locate children, rather than waiting until the problems cause them to identify themselves. Hearing, vision, motor development, speech, language, and academic functioning are included in the screening process. Behavior is also included in many screening batteries. A variety of formal tests may be used in screening, as well as data from classroom performance and group tests administered to entire classes of students. More active, informal methods are generally used in screening and include the following types:

1. Teacher-made tests
2. Checklists
3. Rating devices
4. Interviews
5. Inventories
6. Records review
7. Sociometric ratings
8. Observation

Placement diagnosis. A variety of formal and informal tests are used to determine the eligibility of children for special education in accordance with state laws and regulations. Some states have specific criteria for determination, such as specific cutoff scores. Other states have very vague definitions, but it is still expected that decisions made by a committee will be based on test data.

The basis for the testing program concerns evaluation for placement because it is required that students be evaluated with instruments by qualified examiners. The initial structure of the IEP, placement, and related services are based on this part of the assessment process. Whether such information can be used in *planning* educational programming beyond the IEP is entirely dependent on the breadth and scope of evaluation, the nature of the available information, and the qualifications of examiners and teachers who use such data.

Program evaluation. Tests are also used for determining the effectiveness of programs. Pretest and posttest scores are collected on students, and decisions are made about overall progress. Gain scores on student achievement at the beginning and end of the school year are of limited value (Tallmadge & Horst, 1974) because of the error in instruments, the mismatch between a test and the curriculum, and a variety of problems in test characteristics.

Student progress. Tests are also used to chart the progress of individual students, to determine programming changes, and to communicate student achievement to parents, administrators, and other consumers of test information. Individual student gain scores are frequently used, based on normative test data. As stated previously, such comparisons are of little value. There is no way to determine the acquisition of skills or effectiveness of instruction.

Types of tests

Literally hundreds of tests may be used in special education, although a few popular instruments seem to be used universally. The types of tests may be generally categorized as follows.

Norm-referenced tests. Norm-referenced tests are instruments with an objective scoring format that permits the comparison of a person with others of the same age and characteristics (norms) on some trait or traits. The relative standing of the individual (how the person ranks with others) is determined. We can know very little about how much a person actually knows or has achieved—only the relative ranking, expressed in some type of score. This procedure enables global determination of ability and is useful in screening because it accounts for the relative deviation of a subject's performance from the performance of others in the standardization sample. Thus, a subject's relative standing can be influenced by who else took the test and by the nature of items on it. Minority children, who may not have had similar experiences or familiarity with items on a test as those who comprise the standardization group, will have scores that may be affected by factors of acculturation.

Criterion-referenced tests. A criterion-referenced test is based on the sequence of skills in a particular area of the school curriculum and is used to determine a student's mastery of skills without any reference to norms. The performance of other students is inconsequential. Tests of this type are only as sound as the accuracy of the skill sequences comprising them. Most skills are arranged logically or by expert opinion. Skills are usually presented to students in a manner that makes sense to the teacher, not necessarily in a way that is best for the learner. If there is criticism of criterion-referenced tests, it is criticism of the nature of the underlying sequence of skills. A superior approach is the use of scaled items, a method that is yet to be widely adopted in education. For most practical purposes in planning educational programs for students, the criterion-referenced test is much more suitable than norm-referenced instruments. Unfortunately the traditional assessment process relies heavily on norm-referenced data; in fact, most states require norm-referenced tests to be used in diagnosis and placement decisions. Much of the criticism that teachers have about the evaluation of students is that they "know no more about the student than they did before testing." Their expectations are at variance with the purposes of assessment in most settings. The inclusion of criterion-referenced tests would be extremely useful.

Informal tests. An informal test is typically one that is devised by teachers or others in a particular setting for evaluating student behaviors in many domains. An informal test does not have norms, is not scaled, and does not have other properties (validity, reliability) carefully determined in test construction. An informal test may be in the form of a checklist for behaviors. Ordinarily the purpose of an informal test is to elicit specific information about how a child performs problem-solving tasks to determine why the child is experiencing difficulty. The Independent Reading Inventory is an example. The objective is to determine error-pattern analysis and learning approaches that will be directly useful in teaching, not just skills which the student has not acquired.

Observation. Observation is the systematic examination of a student in natural settings for the purpose of eliciting useful information in order to develop educational plans. The best observational approach is one that is reliable—all raters agree on what they observe. A predetermined scoring system is used. Time sampling, event sampling, rating scales, checklists, and measurement of target behaviors (baseline/treatment) are examples of observations that do not necessarily concern comparisons with other subjects. In operant conditioning techniques the use of observation is essential. Checklists and rating scales are the least useful because rater bias can invalidate the observation. Reliable instruments and measurement of target behaviors are much less subject to bias.

• • •

Tests may also be classified as *group* or *individual*. A group test is administered to a large number of students and requires that the subjects read and interpret directions in order to perform tasks. An individual test is designed for one-to-one administration with virtually all directions explained and all tasks organized by the examiner. The use of group tests with handicapped students is unsatisfactory because there are complications involving the ability of the student to understand the directions, the range of items suitable for handicapped students, and the number of random responses that may be made. In most states the use of group intelligence tests for purposes of diagnosis and placement is not permitted.

In addition, tests may be classified as *power* or *speed*. A power test allows the subject to respond without a time restriction; a speed test requires a limited time for completion of a task and may provide additional points if a subject completes a task quickly. Tests may also be classified as *diagnostic*, indicating that the instrument is designed to permit analysis of a student's processes during performance. Rather than concentrating on the response, one examines a student's behavior during the act of performance.

Classification by domain. Tests may be classified by the domain or area in which assessment is made. The principal categories of tests are as follows:

1. Intelligence
2. General achievement
3. Reading
4. Arithmetic

5. Spelling and written expression
6. Language
7. Perceptual
8. Sensory
9. Behavior and personality
10. Specialized

In the discussion that follows, emphasis will be placed on the various tests under the categories in the planning matrix (Fig. 1-1). This structure, superimposed on the various tests, provides a method of classifying instruments and test data for easier understanding and communication.

Statistical properties of tests

The most important properties of standardized instruments are the various statistics associated with them because their worth as tools for making significant decisions can be partly determined by these properties. Descriptive data pertaining to tests are of particular usefulness to teachers in understanding test data and the performance of students. Other characteristics of tests, such as reliability and validity data, also are of great significance, but many consumers often ignore this information.

The teacher should be thoroughly acquainted with statistical concepts—mean, median, standard deviation (SD), standard error of measurement—and should be able to use and interpret scores reported in various forms. The teacher should also examine the *reliability* and *validity* of instruments that may be used with particular children because these test characteristics are specifically addressed in legislation and have been the major points of contention in litigation.

Reliability. The reliability of a test is expressed as a correlation coefficient or the relationship between a test-retest or split-half administration of an instrument to the same subjects. For example, in determining the reliability of a test the developer will administer the test to a group of subjects and readminister it at a later date. The test may be split into two tests, perhaps by taking every odd-numbered item out to make the second test form. Subsequently each half of the test for each subject will be treated as two equivalent tests, and a reliability coefficient will be derived. In essence, the reliability is the consistency of the test to provide stable results. If a subject were to take the test one day and receive a certain score, the examiner would theoretically want to be able to get the same score on the next day or on repeated administrations. The reliability coefficient provides this estimate. The more reliable a test, the more confidence the examiner can have that the obtained score is not a random measure comprised of error. The less reliable a test, the more the examiner could expect the subject's score to change over repeated administrations, and the less confidence the examiner could have in measurement.

It should be noted that there are different reliability coefficients on tests appropriate to different age or grade levels. Thus, a test may be more reliable on certain subtests than others and more reliable at certain grade levels. The user should examine the manual when making decisions about students because tests have a tendency to fluctuate in reliability and in the standard error of measurement.

Validity. Validity of a test refers to the degree it actually measures what it is purported to measure by the developers. *Content validity* refers to the relationship between test items and the purpose of the test. *Concurrent validity* refers to the test's ability to measure the subject's current level of functioning on specific tasks. *Predictive validity* refers to the ability of the test to predict the subject's future functioning. Validity is established by the test developer. If an examiner uses a test in a manner inconsistent with the recommendations of the test developer, the examiner is responsible for establishing the validity of the unique approach. It is not uncommon in special education assessment for some examiners to have unique ways of aggregating scores or "teasing out" certain profiles that supposedly have significance in the identification of a particular type of problem. If this is so, the examiner must be prepared to demonstrate the validity of the approach if it is contested. Many tests used in special education assessment have poor or no validity data at all.

Norms. The norms of a test, or the normative sample, consist of the persons who took the original test and their responses. Thus, a person who takes the test afterward will be compared with the individuals who were initially in the normative sample. If a subject's background and experience are markedly different from the persons in the normative sample, the responses of the subject may appear disparate, and erroneous interpretations of the test performance may ensue. This, of course is the major concern about minority students who have been required to take examinations in which no persons of comparable background, experience, or minority membership were included in the normative sample. Much of the litigation in special education has concerned minority children who lack the experiences or language of persons in normative groups on whom standardized tests are based.

Most of the criticism has been directed at intelligence testing. Sattler (1974) has considered a number of arguments against the use of tests:

1. Standardized instruments have a strongly white, Anglo-Saxon, middle-class bias.
2. Minority children are handicapped in taking tests because of differences in motivation, test practice, and reading.
3. Rapport problems exist when the examiner is of a different ethnic group.
4. Intelligence tests are more related to nonschool problem-solving experiences of middle-class children than to minority (lower-class) children.
5. Minority children are characterized by test scores in such a way that schools expect the children to be unsuccessful in their performance.

Recommendations for statistical properties and uses of tests

Salvia and Ysseldyke (1978) make recommendations about the minimum values of tests required for a more confident use in assessment. Although group tests should not be used for important decision-making purposes, a reliability of .60 should be the minimum standard if the test is used for reporting group data. A value of .90 on an individual test is required for placement decisions and .80 for screening.

Types of scores

A variety of scores may be derived from assessment instruments. Some of them are associated with certain types of tests, and others may appear regardless of the type of test. The following discussion presents scores representative of those which may be reported in assessment documents and test profiles.

Percentile. The percentile, one of the most common and easiest to interpret scores, simply provides the standing of an individual's performance in terms of all subjects who theoretically take the test or, more appropriately, in comparison with the norms. The percentile tells how a person ranks with other subjects, but it shows little else about the person's performance. The 90th percentile can be interpreted to mean that the subject's score was equal to or greater than 90 percent of the scores. It should be remembered that percentiles form an ordinal scale and consequently the intervals between two points on the scale are not equal. Differences between the 85th and 90th percentile ranks are greater than between the 55th and 60th.

An interesting use of the percentile is that by which an examiner will convert a standard score, such as an IQ to a percentile in order to disguise it from consumers. Although teachers and parents may be capable of dealing with true IQ reports, and parents have a right to know such information, some examiners believe that IQ scores will be interpreted literally and misused. By using the appropriate formula or obtaining a text with a table showing the relationships among various types of scores, the percentile can be directly transformed into the IQ equivalent.

Developmental scores. The major types of developmental scores are age equivalents, mental age

(MA) equivalents, and grade equivalents. An age equivalent is expressed in terms of years and months (e.g., 6-5) and is found on various types of tests that purportedly measure age-related skills. A grade equivalent is the most common developmental score. Literally it means that a child's raw score is equivalent to the score of children in the normative sample who were of a certain grade level. There are variations on these scores, such as a developmental quotient that is similar to the intelligence quotient. An age comparison is relatively meaningless because it does not relate to skill acquisition and does not represent equal intervals on the scale (Tallmadge & Hart, 1974).

Standard scores. Although it is rarely used and infrequently reported, the basic standard score is a Z score, which is obtained by subtracting an obtained score from the mean of a distribution and dividing it by the standard deviation. The value will bear a positive or negative sign and can be interpreted in terms of standard deviation units. The Z score distribution is transformed into other types of scores that are all used to some extent in assessment. These include T scores, deviation IQ scores, and stanine scores. The deviation IQ and stanine are probably the most common scores in education. A deviation IQ of 85 ($\overline{X} = 100$; SD = 15) would be interpreted as 1 SD below the mean (Z value = −1) and would be equivalent to the 16th percentile. A deviation IQ of 115 is 1 SD above the mean (Z value = +1) and is equivalent to the 84th percentile.

Stanine scores (standard nine scores) are arranged on a scale from one to nine, with each score representing an interval or category that is 0.5 SD in width, except at the ends. Inspection of the stanine on a comparison table will show an associated percentile rank.

Assessment process

In accordance with federal and state regulations, a school is bound to a set of procedures in the assessment of children who may be handicapped. Ordinarily the process is initiated with screening, after which a referral is made, or it may originate with referral if no active program of screening is available or if the student was not detected during screening. Subsequently, with appropriate procedures the student will be submitted for evaluation by a number of examiners and data may be collected within the categories listed previously. After analysis of data is complete, a placement conference may be held and a decision rendered determining whether the student meets eligibility criteria for special education. Finally, the student may be placed in special education programming. Conferences must be held at each juncture, and assurances of due-process procedures must be maintained. The conclusion of this process is the development of the IEP.

It is our contention that the most important function of the assessment process, as it currently exists, is to assure that proper procedures are followed in the placement decision. Test instruments commonly used are norm referenced. As a rule little attention is given to more educationally relevant assessment. The teacher must conduct additional assessment after the placement decision has been made in order to acquire sufficient information for understanding the actual educational abilities and needs of the student. This constitutes the basis for the misunderstanding and ill will that surrounds assessment. Many teachers and parents want precise answers to their questions, immediate resolution of their concerns, and precise information about how to proceed with assisting the student. Since the greatest body of test data is primarily comprised of global scores showing relative standing on various measures, there is not much information of practical value to teachers and parents; of course, this is not necessarily the purpose of evaluation for placement.

The teacher can be prepared to be a contributor and consumer in the assessment process by thoroughly understanding the following points:

1. Legal requirements in the state
2. Local requirements determined by the school administration
3. Kinds of tests that are required and those which are optional

4. Requirements of the teacher in providing information to the assessment team or committee
5. Teacher's responsibility after the placement decision is made
6. Types of tests administered by the teacher during and after the assessment
7. Requirements for reevaluation of the student

The examiner

Qualifications. To comply with federal regulations pertaining to assessment, the examiner should be qualified to administer any test or examination he or she employs and must adhere to the guidelines for administration as indicated in test manuals. Otherwise, the qualifications of examiners are governed by state laws, regulations, certification, and licensure standards. Ordinarily certain types of tests require administration by an examiner with specialized training, such as a psychologist or psychometrist, although this could vary from state to state. A test should never be administered by a teacher who is not qualified to give it, and the teacher should comply with test administration, scoring, and interpretation standards on instruments for which the teacher is qualified. The teacher should not hesitate to learn as much about each test instrument as possible, even those within the professional domain of another examiner. Historical abuses and misuses of tests have been made by otherwise qualified persons. The teacher should assume an active role in discussing the merits of instruments and the interpretations of test data, especially if educational recommendations are made on the basis of such data. The teacher should not be intimidated by other assessment personnel, should protect the rights of children at any point in the assessment process, and should ensure that educational planning is reasonably determined.

Actions. Qualified examiners should use tests for making important educational decisions. Tests are expensive, and assessment takes time from other important duties. Therefore, testing should be employed only when necessary and useful. Most functions of assessment are to ensure that students are identified in accordance with regulations. However, no matter what the purpose of assessment is, the examiner must follow the directions in the manual precisely, score the test accurately, adhere to standardization principles, and interpret results in accordance with recommendations in the manual. A user of tests or consumer of test information should examine each test manual to determine all statistical properties of the test (validity, reliability, and so forth) and should be critical of tests that are poorly designed.

Quality of instruments

The quality of educational assessment can be determined by the validity it has in making educational decisions. The more removed the data from the actual behavioral characteristics of a student in a learning environment, the more suspicious we should be about implications for teaching or treatment. Educational assessment data are derived from many sources, but there is a significant emphasis on standardized instruments. In general there are only two broad types of data in terms of quality—*indirect/theoretical* and *direct/observable*.

The uses of data may vary according to the experience, composition, and philosophical orientation of the team of examiners and the guidelines imposed on schools for classification of children. Except in clear-cut medical categories, in which there is still a surprising amount of guesswork, most conditions recognized in special education are taxonomic inventions. In other words, each category consists of characteristics agreed upon by authorities and formalized through regulations. The guidelines, the nature of the team, and the types of data determine the outcome of the assessment. The following points summarize the problems confronting examiners:

1. Assessment involves the collection of data to determine the performance skills of a child to see what the child can and cannot accomplish.
2. Specific treatments or programs are to be de-

signed or prescribed to promote more normal functioning.

3. Standardized tests are used to determine performance skills.
4. Strengths and deficits as indicated by the tests are used to determine the disorders of the child and to suggest remediation.
5. The majority of standardized tests lack validity, reliability, or a relationship to disorders of the student.
6. The major strength of standardized tests is the ability to show the rank of a student in contrast to normative data, assuming that the norms and items of the tests are appropriate for comparison.
7. The tests do not necessarily provide any information about why a student is not performing skills appropriate for a specific age group.

It is here that the guesswork begins with theory filling the gaps. To reveal this circumstance more graphically, the following listings of qualitative aspects of assessment data are included:

Indirect/theoretical data

Case history. Case histories, interviews, and cumulative records are indirect and outdated. Such data may depict the student's status in the past or may indicate current concerns or notions about present functioning, but largely such data are not necessarily accurate, relevant, or important. Many schools require a case history or social history, and guesswork is used to explain what is perceived as a current problem. For example, one case history indicated that the child, who was otherwise normal except for a moderate reading problem, "may have minimal cerebral dysfunction" because of the possibility that his mother had measles. Moreover, much of the data in case histories that might reveal sensitive information about family members can become school gossip and can hold no particular benefit for any legitimate educational purpose.

Standardized tests and personality measures. Most standardized tests provide data that are of limited use in educational planning because the measures are global, are limited to relative standing of a score, and are indirect indicators of performance. For example, visual-motor problems have failed to be supported by research as being factors in problems of reading and arithmetic. Nonetheless, tests and programs are specifically used based on the presumed significance of visual-motor deficits. The true quality of such data is unknown, as are the implications.

Rating scales and checklists. Believing that behavioral observation is much more direct and useful, a user of certain instruments can be misled by the name, such as behavioral rating scale. Many of the behavioral rating scales, checklists, and other devices are based on opinions of someone who has observed the student in a setting and who may use categories that are not necessarily behavioral. A teacher may not be able to give an objective evaluation of a student, a parent may be biased, and categories such as *ego strength* are open to interpretation. Indirect measures of behavior, although based on the context of knowledge about behavior, are not necessarily unbiased.

Direct/observable data

Criterion-referenced tests (CRTs). A criterion-referenced test may be useless if the underlying curriculum experience of the student is not reflected in the instrument. Otherwise, information from this approach to assessment is much more direct and is superior to standardized test data. Very direct and meaningful measures can be obtained. The quality of such data is good because it indicates what a student can and cannot do, as well as giving clues about why the student performs in certain ways.

Observation. A variety of observational and behavioral techniques may be employed in watching a student. Such data are of good quality. As with any type of data, interpretations by users of the information may be erroneous. However, the chances for misinterpretation are less because there is less guesswork in the assessment process. Depending on the system that is used, a great deal of time may be involved in collection of such information, but it is worth the effort because the results are superior and the quality of data is excellent.

Normative data are primarily *summative,* whereas process data are *formative*. Formative data can be used to immediately alter instructional techniques and to approach desired outcomes. Summative data may tell whether or not the examiner "hits" or "misses the mark," but not the reason for it, and it will be too late to change an approach if the examiner is not satisfied with it. The assumptions of normative data conclude in the general notion that students do not learn tasks in school because of defective processes of cognitive functioning. Assumptions of observational, behavioral data lead to the conclusion that a task is not learned because prerequisite skills were not learned.

REVIEW OF THE PLANNING MATRIX

Chapter 1 (Fig. 1-1) presented a general description of a planning matrix to be used in organizing and interpreting data for decisions in the assessment process. This model will be further described in Chapter 3. It has been stressed that the major endeavor of the assessment process is to make diagnostic or placement decisions, although teachers and other consumers of test data may wish to obtain more practical benefit from the process. By convention and regulation, the primary tests required or permitted during the referral and evaluation process are standardized. Although some informal information will be used, especially during screening, the foundation of assessment is based on standardized test data. The limitations of such instruments naturally result in global descriptions of behavior and relative standing of the student on various measures. The administrative focus of assessment is to find significant deviation, to ensure that the student meets criteria for placement, and to reach consensus among a group of professionals that deviations and definitional criteria are supported by test data. Criterion-referenced measures and informal data are not inconsequential to examiners but are of limited usefulness in making placement decisions. The planning matrix is particularly useful for organizing the assessment data into systematic components.

The outcome of assessment will be to determine (1) a primary handicapping condition, (2) the least restrictive environment, and (3) the goals for the IEP, which are all based on the current level of educational functioning and related data. These points essentially reflect the *needs*. How the school responds to the needs through execution of the IEP *services* is based on accurate planning, available resources, and expertise of teaching personnel. Chapter 3 will provide a more thorough consideration of planning and use of the matrix in planning. The purpose of this chapter is to focus on the common assessment instruments and procedures used to collect data for determination of needs. The broad areas of student needs, as detailed in the planning matrix, are cognitive-academic, socioemotional, and sensoriphysical functioning.

As we have indicated, the process of assessment in most states is systematic and sequential. Usually it is comprised of the following steps: screening, referral, evaluation, analysis, placement, and programming. It may be extended to a follow-up evaluation in which the student and the program are evaluated. Screening and referral may occur more or less simultaneously, depending on how the process is set up in a particular district. There are certain tests which, by their nature, are screening instruments, others which are designed particularly for that purpose, and others which should only be used for screening but are employed as assessment tools during evaluation and placement decisions. Screening should be an active process in which there are two objectives: (1) to obtain global measures in all areas of current levels of functioning and (2) to obtain indications of a need for more intense evaluation. Thus, a child may be functioning poorly in academic areas according to an achievement screening test, but poor performance during a hearing or vision evaluation may determine that the reason could be explained by sensory deficits. A more intense evaluation would be indicated in an area of sensory functioning. However, if the student passes all screening in areas of health, vision, hearing, and so forth, the evaluation team would be able to proceed more confidently with traditional assessment in academic areas using diagnostic tests in the belief that the problems presented by the student probably are not explained by the status of sensory processes.

A variety of teacher-made tests, observations, checklists, rating devices, inventories, and other approaches are used in many schools to conduct a "child find." The most valuable contributor to screening is the classroom teacher who, by experience, is able to detect children who may have physical, learning, and behavioral problems.

COGNITIVE-ACADEMIC FUNCTIONING

Included within this classification are tests used to evaluate students in the areas of intelligence, process abilities, and academic functioning. Tests mentioned here are those frequently used in assessment batteries. Many other tests might be included, but emphasis is placed on those which are currently popular. The placement of certain tests in this category may be somewhat arbitrary, and the reader might argue that certain tests should be placed under a different category. Tests are described under appropriate classifications and by type. Reference to Table 2-1 will provide the reader with a brief description of the most common instruments in this category. Other tests that are not listed in the table will also be described. The most important aspects of any instrument are the validity, reliability, and usefulness. Table 2-1 includes a brief overview of the technical adequacy of each instrument.

Intelligence tests

Group intelligence tests, although used in many schools, should not be used for placement decisions because they are of questionable validity and usually have poor reliability. Individual tests are much more acceptable as long as the normative sample matches the characteristics of the subject. Undoubtedly, the Wechsler Intelligence Scale for Children–Revised (WISC–R) is the most popular instrument. The Stanford-Binet Intelligence Scale has fallen into disuse because the WISC–R provides a measure of nonverbal ability and a profile analysis. The profiles of the WISC–R have become popular among certain schools of thought for determining process abilities of students. Another test that enjoys some popularity, because of its brevity, is the Slosson Intelligence Test (SIT). The SIT, however, is characterized by unclear validity and reliability data, and the normative sample is inadequately described. The SIT may be used as a screening instrument, but using this test for placement decisions might lead to complications if the quality of the evaluation is challenged, especially in the case of minority students.

The WISC–R is technically adequate and much more defensible, although use of any intelligence scale with minority students can be challenged. The major criticism of the WISC–R is in the use of profile analysis by some examiners in the "diagnosis" of process deficits. Significance is attached to discrepancies between the Verbal and Performance scales; subtests, with a mean of 10 and standard deviation of 3, are used in the profile.

Scatter, or profile, analysis is used by examiners in an attempt to identify specific process deficits or strengths, to identify minimal cerebral dysfunction, anxiety, impulsivity, and other traits. It is common for learning disabilities to be verified on the basis of a discrepancy between the scales of a certain number of IQ points. If the verbal IQ or the performance IQ is higher, or if there is a lot of scatter (subtests scores that deviate from one another), certain interpretations tend to be made. Differences on the order of 10 IQ points between scales is quite common. About 20 out of every 100 tests yield deviant subtest scores, also very common. Subtest scores should not be used to diagnose learning disabilities or process disorders, neither should subtest patterns be used to classify students (Kauffman, 1976; Tittle, 1975). Even a difference of 11 to 15 points between scales may be statistically significant but have no real meaning or practical significance for the evaluation of the student. It is startling to find the high number of reports that confirm learning disabilities on the

Table 2-1. Characteristics of some common instruments used in special education assessment programs: cognitive-academic functioning

Test	*Description*	*Technical adequacy*
Intelligence tests		
Stanford-Binet Intelligence Scale	Individual test that is not as widely used as in the past because of the increasing popularity of the WISC–R. It yields an MA with a deviation IQ of 100 having an SD of 16.	The 1973 revision reports no demographic data; validity and reliability are based on the prior standardization. Thus, the use of the test is risky because comparison of a subject's response to the norms of a different instrument is problematic.
Wechsler Intelligence Scale for Children–Revised	Consists of three scales: verbal, performance, and full scale. There are a total of 12 subtests, each with a mean of 10 and SD of 3. The mean for each scale is 100 with an SD of 15, a deviation IQ. The three scales and scatter of subtests are used for various interpretive approaches.	It was standardized on a large representative, stratified sample. The validity and reliability are considered very acceptable. Many uses by examiners to identify groups or process problems by profile or scatter analysis are not valid.
Slosson Intelligence Test	Short-form test comprised of items taken from other instruments. No age range is reported for the test.	The test yields a ratio IQ. Reliability and validity are unclear; the user can have no clear idea of who comprised the normative sample. The best use is for screening.
General achievement tests		
Wide Range Achievement Test (WRAT)	Comprised of three tests: reading, spelling, and arithmetic. Reading requires the identification of words, spelling involves writing words from dictation, and arithmetic is strictly computational. An evaluation may be quickly administered and scored. Grade equivalents, standard scores, and percentile ranks are provided. It is used for profile analysis comparison with the WISC–R, although no correlations or standard errors of the difference are reported.	The best use is for screening, especially because the test is too brief to indicate diagnostic information and may not reflect the actual skills taught by a school. Thus, the validity may be questioned.
Peabody Individual Achievement Test (PIAT)	Provides measures of mathematics, reading recognition, reading comprehension, spelling, and general information. It is arranged for easy presentation in a spiralbound book format that permits multiple choice pictures for response selection.	Test validity is a concern for the user depending on the nature of the actual curriculum. Reliability measures are low enough to recommend its use as a screening instrument. Standard error in some subtests at certain levels is large. Grade equivalents, percentile ranks, and normalized standard scores are available.

Table 2-1. Characteristics of some common instruments used in special education assessment programs: cognitive-academic functioning—cont'd

Test	*Description*	*Technical adequacy*
Reading achievement tests		
Woodcock Reading Mastery Tests	Consists of five separate tests: letter identification, word identification, word attack, word comprehension, and passage comprehension. The test was designed to serve as both a criterion- and norm-referenced instrument. There are two forms.	Normative sample is representative, and the validity is enhanced by the use of a criterion-referenced format. Reliability is weak in some subtests. The test yields age and grade scores, percentile ranks, standard scores, and mastery scores. Depending on the curriculum and the approach in assessment, the test may be used for placement and evaluation decisions.
Spache Diagnostic Reading Scales	Consists primarily in reading passages of increasing difficulty to examine reading comprehension and silent and oral reading. Supplementary tests are used for consonants, vowels, blends, syllables, and letter sounds.	There is no description of the consistency of the standardization group; the validity and reliability data are not adequate. Normative comparisons would be difficult to defend.
Arithmetic tests		
KeyMath Diagnostic Arithmetic Test	The authors base the test on developmental theory and include more skills than computation. There are 14 subtests within three process areas: content, operations, and applications.	The test is best used as a criterion-referenced instrument. Normative scores must be used with caution. The user can obtain scores in process areas, profiles of subtests, and behavioral statements.
Written expression		
Picture Story Language Test	Provides a basis for examining spontaneous written responses of a subject required to create a story about a picture. The response is examined in terms of productivity (length), correctness, and meaning.	Test is unique because it emphasizes actual production rather than recognition. Because of the undifferentiated nature of the written responses and questionable statistical properties, it is best used as an informal measure.
Language		
Illinois Test of Psycholinguistic Abilities (ITPA)	Consists of ten subtests, two of which are supplementary: it measures auditory-vocal and visual-motor modes of communication (channels); receptive, organizing, and expressive ability; and representation and automatic levels of language organization. The test has generated considerable controversy. The test yields a standard comparison profile, with a mean of 36 and a deviation of 10 considered to be remarkable. Age scores and quotients may be obtained from the test.	Norms are criticized because they are convenient rather than random and stratified. They also exclude minority and handicapped children. Validity has been questioned by a number of writers; there is considerable variability in the reliability. The greatest criticism has been of examiners who use the test to verify the existence of learning disabilities on the basis of subtest profiles not considered to be valid.

basis of a discrepancy of no more than 10 points. Perhaps the most interesting subtest pattern is the one identified by Rugel (1974) who found that disabled readers tended to perform poorly on arithmetic, coding, and digit span. Typically, students who show lower scores than their averages on arithmetic, coding, information, and digit span (the so-called ACID factor) may have attentional disorders or poor learning strategies. However, to conclude that such performance indicates a different type of processing disorder and to explain the cause as a cognitive or neurological deficit is at best theoretical. In fairness, the scatter of scores on the WISC–R can give an examiner information that can be used in generating hypotheses about the performance of a subject. Unfortunately the WISC–R may not be used to clearly separate students into various diagnostic groups.

Achievement tests

NORM Referenced Tests

There are many problems with the most popular general achievement tests. The Wide Range Achievement Test (WRAT) lacks adequate norms and validity studies. The possible differences between an actual curriculum and the items of the WRAT, and the limitations of actual academic skills examined, detract from its usefulness. It cannot be easily used as an index of individual growth or of program success for groups of students, although it is employed for these purposes. The WRAT and the Peabody Individual Achievement Test (PIAT) are both widely used to identify students and to chart growth. Unless they are carefully correlated with the actual school curriculum, and unless statistical aspects of each test are respected, the results will be misleading.

Specific achievement tests in curricular areas may provide better information, especially if the purpose of the tests is to go beyond screening. The Woodcock Reading Mastery Tests are appealing because of a criterion scale and superior technical characteristics. Other popular tests, such as the Spache, are more useful for informal, diagnostic purposes because of concerns about normative data. Other tests that have been very popular should be used with extreme caution. For example, the normative data of the Gray Oral Reading Test have not been updated since 1960, and the Durrell Analysis of Reading Difficulty has no norms. Criterion-referenced tests, such as the Brigance, are very appealing, but care must be taken to ensure that the curriculum is matched with the criteria. Some criterion programs, such as the Fountain Valley Teacher Support System in Reading, are only useful if the entire school adopts the curriculum. The Independent Reading Inventory, developed by the teacher, is very powerful because it is curriculum based and forces attention to specific reading behaviors.

Another approach, the Reading Miscue Inventory, has become popular in the last few years as an alternative to traditional norm-referenced and informal approaches. The concept is based on the theory that oral reading errors (miscues) are grammatical substitutions that may reflect cultural or regional differences or the idiosyncratic pattern of the child. Oral and silent reading are different behaviors entirely and require different responses from the reader. Thus, the oral evaluation may not actually reflect silent reading efficiency. Even though the natural language pattern of the child may be at variance with standard English and might be expected to influence the decoding task, the theory of miscue analysis is interesting. However, the validity of the approach has not been determined, and practical applications have yet to be developed. Knowing the kinds of errors a student makes that may be attributed to imposition of the child's language pattern on the reading process may provide useful information to the teacher. Otherwise the test is of limited value for referral and placement or for follow-up.

In the area of arithmetic, choices are limited by what is available. The subtest scores on general achievement tests are not suitable for placement decisions. The KeyMath Diagnostic Arithmetic Test is the most popular instrument. The KeyMath is useful because it has both norm- and criterion-referenced information available to the examiner.

Moreover the KeyMath provides measures that are not often found in arithmetic assessment because most attention is typically directed at computational ability.

Language tests

Tests that have been used to assess language are similar to intelligence tests, and it is not surprising that they correlate highly with intelligence tests. Unfortunately language has not been investigated as extensively as other aspects of school-related behaviors. Language production (e.g., rate of development and frequency of words at different age levels) constitutes the basic interest of most researchers. Therefore, language assessment is not well organized, and remedial approaches are not well founded. Popular instruments, such as the Utah Test of Language Development and the Houston Test of Language Development have limited normative information and are highly questionable for use with minority students. Both the Utah and Houston test instruments are limited to a screening function. The best known test in the area, the Illinois Test of Psycholinguistic Abilities (ITPA), has come under severe attack in recent years primarily because it has been used to diagnose learning disabilities and process-training programs have been based on it. The norms have been criticized because only middle-class white children were used, and the validity and reliability of the data are questioned. A number of writers have indicated that these processes have a doubtful relationship to academic achievement and to language growth (Hammill & Larsen, 1974; Larsen & Hammill, 1975; Newcomer & Hammill, 1976). This is a disappointing conclusion with implications for theoretical orientations to treatment of learning disorders. The validity of any use of a test is the responsibility of the examiner, unless the test specifically includes validity data for that purpose. Many tests have no claims about esoteric uses, but the lack of validity does not deter examiners from such applications. Despite the lack of proof about modality training and aptitude treatment, entire schools of remedial training are based on these concepts, and the appeal to teachers and examiners is great.

Perceptual tests

The ability models used in special education have accepted explanations of academic deficiency in terms of etiological factors, which are broadly described as perceptual problems. The extent to which a perceptual disorder may actually contribute to academic disorders is debated by some professionals and ignored by others. However, the usefulness of training programs based on techniques to improve the perceptual functioning of a child is another matter. The relationship between these traits and academic performance is questionable. The amount of time a teacher decides to devote to such classical problems is determined by the teacher's theoretical orientation to intervention. Many perceptual measures are derived from subtests of various instruments, while many others are determined from specific tests developed for such purposes. Of particular interest are the perceptual-motor tests of which Salvia and Ysseldyke (1978) have stated: "What the majority of the research *has* shown is that most perceptual-motor tests are unreliable. We do not know what they measure, because they do not measure anything consistently. . . . And for the most part they are neither theoretically nor psychometrically sound" (p. 303).

It should be recognized that perceptual-motor theories constitute the major theoretical foundation of the field of learning disabilities. If the basic tenets of this field are so faulty, it will be necessary for teachers to carefully consider alternatives, especially those based on a skill sequence. Thus, the etiological-treatment interaction (diagnostic-prescriptive teaching) models that currently exist cannot be used with confidence if assessment and planning are primarily based on perceptual disorders. Discussion here will be limited to a few prominent instruments.

Bender Visual-Motor Gestalt Test. The Bender Visual-Motor Gestalt Test has been used to diagnose brain damage, emotional disturbance, and learning disabilities. The test requires the examiner to present a series of nine geometric designs to the subject, who may copy the items freely or reconstruct them from memory. Various interpretative approaches are used based on a scoring system that accounts for distortions, perseveration, integration, and rotation of designs. There is little evidence to justify placement of children in specific categories for treatment based on this test. The test is inadequate for its uses because it was not designed as a measure of intelligence, predictor of achievement, or measure of emotional disturbance or minimal brain dysfunction (Salvia & Ysseldyke, 1978).

Developmental Test of Visual Perception. More commonly known as the Frostig test, the Developmental Test of Visual Perception has been used to measure eye-hand coordination, figure-ground perception, form constancy, position in space, and spatial relations. Presented in a booklet, the test items require the subject to produce certain fine motor tasks with a pencil. The subject must draw lines, identify embedded figures, recognize shapes in different sizes and orientations, identify reversal of a stimulus figure among choices, and copy complex figures using a dotted matrix. Factor analytic studies have demonstrated that the five subtests are not independent. Although the reliability is highly variable at different age levels, the greatest concern should be in the use of the instrument as a global measure of visual perception and the use of visual-perceptual training activities with children.

Purdue Perceptual-Motor Survey. The Purdue Perceptual-Motor Survey is not a normative-based test; it is intended as a guide in making a survey of specific skills. The subject is required to demonstrate balance and posture, show knowledge of body parts, engage in blackboard writing activities, reveal oculomotor pursuit in following a penlight, and reproduce geometric designs. As a screening instrument, the test may be used to identify children who reveal inadequate perceptual-motor skills. The extent to which the teacher uses such information in teaching is based on what one believes about the theory.

Goldman-Fristoe-Woodcock Test of Auditory Discrimination. The Goldman-Fristoe-Woodcock Test of Auditory Discrimination is used to assess the ability of a subject to discriminate sounds under quiet conditions and with background noise. Standard presentation uses a tape recording. The subject's task is to discriminate between words that are highly similar in sound. It is best used as an informal measure of auditory skills because of its limited validity.

Auditory Discrimination Test. The Auditory Discrimination Test has long tenure in special education, and it is used to assess the subject's ability to discriminate between sounds in similar-sounding words. There are no norms.

• • •

There are numerous other tests that might be used for tapping the same areas of behavior. The user of a test should inspect the manual for technical data and take into account the arguments about perceptual functioning in academic success to the uses of such data.

Discussion

The reader will recognize the fact that most of the tests reviewed in this section have serious limitations: reliability, validity, and normative inadequacies are common. The relationship between many of the deficits in psychological processes and academic functioning is expressed as a correlation. With each new research endeavor new correlates may be found. However, until specific etiologies are clearly identified, treatment approaches are validated, and academic functioning is unquestionably improved as a result, the time and expense of assessment will be justified in terms of classification and placement decisions. It is imperative that educators wisely use standardized achievement and intelligence tests because of the continuing controversy over such instruments and the potential for harm to children. To the extent that they are required by law to use certain tests, special educators must also be aware of the cautions and limitations of them.

SOCIOEMOTIONAL FUNCTIONING

Assessment of socioemotional functioning has traditionally been based on psychoanalytic interpretation of subjective test data for the purpose of classifying children as emotionally disturbed, socially maladjusted, psychotic, neurotic, or autistic. The psychoanalytic approach has lost popularity. Behavioral assessment has become more prominent in assessing socioemotional functioning because behavioral data are more useful in making educational decisions than are the interpretations of a psychotherapist. Behavior can be seen by all observers; hence, it is defensible as an assessment technique. The impact has been dramatic because many schools now prefer the term "behavior disorders." However, when used with minority and poor children, behavioral data can be abused just as easily as standardized test data. Behavior is always interpreted in terms of social standards of acceptability. Thus, children who swear or present negative attention-getting behaviors may be classified as emotionally disturbed or behaviorally disordered.

The values of the predominant culture and of the rater are also significant. Merely because children differ from implicit social standards of dress, mannerisms, social amenities, and interpersonal behaviors does not justify considering them to be emotionally disturbed. However, this happens with some frequency on the basis of apparently objective behavioral measures. The fact that a child does not stay in the seat or pay attention in class a significant amount of time, compared with peers, may be interpreted as hyperactivity, emotional disturbance, behavioral disorder, or any other label the school may see fit to apply to a behavioral description. Here is the danger in the use of behavioral data, the interpretation. We have found (Marsh & Price, 1980) that the off-task behavior of mainstreamed handicapped students was very high in comparison with nonhandicapped peers in the same classes. Although the off-task behavior could be observed and measured by common agreement (interrater reliability) and was evidently detrimental to learning, it could be explained, depending on one's point of view, as an indication of an underlying disorder(s) in the child or as behavior created and reinforced by the mainstream environment (group instruction). How the school chooses to use behavioral data is an important consideration. The behavioral approach to assessment should at least be defensible, and the interpretation must account for implicit and explicit criteria. The school should be careful in the interpretation of such data as they apply to a minority student because behavioral differences may not be pathological but either culturally different or a result of differential treatment by school personnel.

Many schools use locally developed rating scales and behavioral checklists for observation of children. These instruments may be based on a wide variety of behaviors, may use a Likert scoring system (1 to 5), and may be highly unreliable and invalid. Such instruments may be best suited to screening. Methods that require the observation of students are superior to checklists and rating scales, especially if a normative basis exists for the instrument. Observation can be a time-consuming activity. The approach used should be sufficient and efficient. Some schools use videotape recordings of classroom behavior and others require an observer to sit for long periods of time in a classroom watching a particular student. Neither of these approaches is efficient, although the output may be sufficient for assessment. Checklists and rating scales are highly efficient, but may not provide a valid or sufficient data base. Informal methods concerned with specific target behaviors (e.g., movement cycles, event recordings, and duration recordings), which are commonly used in behavior modification procedures, are of value in assessment for placement but may be too narrow for most general purposes. If a predetermined behavior is to be observed and recorded, other behaviors of interest may be ignored, and a great deal of time will be devoted to the collection of a small piece of information.

Classroom behavior

The observation of the classroom environment can involve the examination of the student's behavior with the teacher, with other students, and in handling curricular materials. The general categories of behavior are as follows:

1. Measures of acceptable or unacceptable behavior
2. Interpersonal interactions
3. Work habits
4. Attitudes

The first three areas can be directly observed, but the last area, attitudes, must be assessed through some form of interview or written test. The nature of unacceptable or acceptable behavior must be determined within the context of a particular school and classroom because some behaviors might be tolerated in one setting and not in another. Generally, the more rules a teacher has, the greater the degreee of unacceptable behavior that might be observed. The more private or inconsistently enforced a teacher's rules, the more confusion there will be about measurement. For example, an observer may find that some teachers require students to raise their hands before asking a question. Favored students will find that they need not always do this, calling out questions and making remarks that result in a response from the teacher rather than a reprimand. The unfavored students may be punished for the same behavior. Such unfairness may prompt some students to become negative, unmotivated, and troublesome, while others will withdraw because they know they are not well liked.

Observation in mainstream classrooms can be threatening to teachers, especially if the examiner is known to be specifically observing the teacher. Use of certain instruments may cause the teacher to be resistant or hesitant because it is known that teacher behavior is being observed. Although many examiners may not be visiting classrooms for the expressed purpose of observing and evaluating the teacher, the belief that such classroom observation may reflect negatively on the teacher may be a complicating factor. The instruments that are listed in the following discussion are primarily used for assessment of classroom behavior of the student, but it should be stressed that such behavior is primarily determined by what occurs in the environment under the direction of a teacher.

Burks' Behavior Rating Scales. Burks' Behavior Rating Scales were developed for use by parents and teachers with children in grades 1 through 9. The instrument is based on a Likert scoring system (1 to 5) for the rating of 110 items in 19 categories, such as excessive self-blame, excessive anxiety, poor ego strength, and poor anger control. There is no assurance that raters can agree on what they see in these categories because items such as ego strength may be different according to the rater's understanding and use of such terms.

The standardization group consisted of only 200 children in one state, the procedures were not fully described and the reliability and validity of the instrument are unclear. Category scores in excess of 11 are considered important. Arbitrary ranges for the categories are established as "not significant," "significant," or "very significant." Only summative scores are available showing total score values and ranges within groups labeled as "significant" for each category.

Because of concerns about standardization, questionable validity and reliability, and subjective terms such as anxiety, ego strength, and persecution, this instrument should be used only as a tool for screening. Placement decisions, especially with minority children, would be difficult to defend.

Walker Problem Behavior Identification Checklist. The Walker Problem Behavior Identification Checklist was designed for use by teachers with children in the fourth, fifth, and sixth grades. The teacher checks 50 statements concerning behavior, if they have been observed in the student. There are five scales (acting out, withdrawal, distractibility, disturbed peer relations, and immaturity.)

The standardization procedure of the test is

sketchy. A total of 21 teachers rated 534 children in the three grades. Otherwise little is known about the sample. Total scores and scale scores can be obtained by summing and plotting on a profile form. T scores can be obtained by sex, but not by age or grade level. The manual indicates that a total score value or standard score value may indicate a problem. Scale scores above 1 SD are significant.

This instrument is probably best used as a screening tool. Great care must be exercised in using it with minority children, especially if it is used for purposes other than screening.

Devereux Elementary School Behavior Rating Scale. The Devereux Elementary School Behavior Rating Scale was designed for use by teachers with children in grades 1 through 6. Teachers rate their agreement with statements that are descriptive of behaviors. There are 11 behavioral factors, including disrespect-defiance and external reliance.

The standardization group included black and white children, a total of 800 subjects in the six grades. All students were enrolled in the same school district. Reliability ranged between .71 and .91 on test-retest administration. Validity of the test is not mentioned. Ratings of teachers are assigned to statements descriptive of behavior. The sum of ratings is plotted on a profile. There are no age or sex norms available to the user of the test. Comparison is made with the performance of the standardization group. This instrument would be most useful as a screening device.

Adaptive behavior

In recent years adaptive behavior tests have been retained in assessment batteries primarily because of the problems associated with assessment of students referred for possible mental retardation and because of the question of acculturation. These are two related concepts. Adaptive behavior roughly means that a subject is able to adapt to the demands of the environment. For the most part, tests of adaptive behavior have been based on self-help and social skills, many of which are related to items on intelligence tests. The logical connection between a low IQ score and poor adaptive behavior as an index of mental retardation is undermined by the fact that in some studies a high correlation between adaptive measures and IQ scores reveals the possibility that both types of tests are actually assessing the same domains; different cultural experiences of children require differential assessment of adaptation (e.g., rural-urban or suburbs–inner city).

AAMD Adaptive Behavior Scales (public school version). AAMD Adaptive Behavior Scales consist of two parts. Part 1 has 56 items to assess behaviors in independent functioning, physical development, economic activity, language development, understanding of numbers and time, vocational activity, self-direction, responsibility, and socialization. Part 2 has 39 items to rate behaviors characterized as violent and destructive, antisocial, rebellious, withdrawn, and stereotyped behavior; odd mannerisms; inappropriate interpersonal manners; unacceptable vocal habits; unacceptable or eccentric habits; hyperactive tendencies; psychological disturbance; and uses medication.

This scale was standardized on 2,600 children in California and is appropriate for use with children between ages 7 and 12. The breakdown of norms is characterized by the subject's age, sex, socioeconomic status, demographic location, and ethnic class and by the type of service model used. No reliability data are reported.

The informant (usually the teacher) provides information to the examiner, who completes the form and totals the scores within each part of the test. Percentiles are used to compare a subject's rating with the norms as follows: age, sex, educational placement, and ethnic status. Although the AAMD Adaptive Behavior Scales are widely used in public school programs, the limitations of the instrument are such that it is not possible to accurately make placement decisions.

Cain-Levine Social Competency Scale. The Cain-Levine Social Competency Scale is used to elicit information from an informant about children between the ages of 5 and 14 who are suspected of having trainable mental retardation. There are 44 items available to gather information about self-help, initiative, social skills, and communication skills.

The scale was standardized on 414 males and 302 females with variable IQ scores at each age level. The validity is adequate, and reliability is high for instruments of this type. Scoring is accomplished by rating each item on a Likert scoring system; the test yields percentile ranks. This is one of the few tests for use with lower-functioning students that has sufficient technical adequacy for confidence in screening.

System of Multicultural Pluralistic Assessment (SOMPA). The SOMPA is a combination of existing tests and new tests developed into a battery with statistical manipulations of data used to erect unbiased norms for different ethnic groups (white, black, and Hispanic). There are sociocultural scales, a medical model, a social system, and a pluralistic measure. The sociocultural scale is a method of weighting scores for each ethnic group to determine how different a subject may be from the American core culture. The factors are family size and structure, socioeconomic status, and urban acculturation. Individual tables are used to transform raw scores to difference scores. These scales are not validated and have no reliability data. Within the social system model the WISC–R and the Adaptive Behavior Inventory for Children (ABIC) are used. The ABIC is a new instrument developed for the SOMPA.

The distinctive feature of SOMPA is the use of various norms to eliminate differences between ethnic groups on obtained measures. Because tests are not culturally fair, the SOMPA attempts to eliminate cultural bias against black and Hispanic children by means of statistical manipulation of scores. Although a school may wish to employ this instrument and system in procedures used with minority children, there are many cautions. The potential user will have to acquire specific training from the developer and will need to consult the advice in the manual about attempts to develop local norms.

Direct observation

The majority of tests used to determine classroom performance or adaptive behavior are based on informants or on indirect measures of behavior (memory from experience), which are all subject to bias. For example, it is difficult for a teacher who has daily confrontations with a child, whom the teacher may perceive as posing a threat or a serious problem, to be truly objective. Many of the tests culminate with global information that only confirms what a referring agent might have known, just as in the case of achievement tests. However, it is easier to determine discrepancy in information from a reading level than from sociobehavioral standards. Thus, direct observation by a trained observer who uses a system of objective measurement will provide relevant information about how a student functions and about how to change the behavior. Antecedent events can be identified, and consequences can also be delineated. This is much more helpful than the process of determining a child to be anxious or defiant. Many behavioral approaches can be useful for this purpose and will be described in another part of this chapter. One standardized instrument, we believe, is superior to the rating scales, checklists, and other instruments reviewed here because it provides efficient and sufficient descriptions of objective behavioral measurements that may be included directly in assessment, the IEP, and daily instruction. It is described next.

Coping Analysis Schedule for Educational Settings (CASES). CASES was developed by Dr. Robert Spaulding, who is currently at San Jose State University. CASES is designed to be used in public schools and other educational settings to evaluate the process of socialization. Its focus is on students, and the categories it incorporates are theory based. Nineteen categories are used to code samples of behavior of a subject over a period of time; individual profiles or group norms can be obtained.

To use the instrument an observer must be trained to interrater reliability. Styles of behavior are determined by transforming raw data into coping styles based on factor analysis of data taken from 2,000 case studies of children in public school classrooms. Style scores (coefficients) are standardized to reflect the visibility of a coping behavior. When the value of a style coefficient reaches a value of 1.0, the behavior pattern (e.g., aggressive, peer dependent, or compliant) is dominant and visible to observers. Style coefficient data were obtained on 2,700 pupils. Immediate scores are possible through direct observation. Style coefficients, an overall coefficient, and percentages of time may be obtained. The primary scores are standard coefficients and percentages of time.

CASES is an excellent tool for quick, valid, and efficient observational data that can be directly related to each environment in which the child is observed. Teachers and consultants trained to use the instrument can facilitate communication between the classroom teacher and support personnel attempting to design better learning environments. Behaviors of students are directly measured and changes can be plotted over time by means of the style coefficient and percentages of time. The data can be used in referral, placement, IEP, instructional activities, and follow-up evaluation. Use of style scores must be tempered because of the lack of information in the manual about the demographic characteristics of the normative sample. Interrater reliability and percentages of time in certain behaviors or styles are defensible. This approach is similar to other behavioral designs based on time sampling, but it is much more inclusive and specifically related to classroom behavior.

SENSORIPHYSICAL FUNCTIONING

Many aspects of the sensoriphysical functioning of children may affect educational programming. Conditions that might be considered when planning and implementing programs for handicapped children are as follows: visual or hearing impairments; disorders of the musculoskeletal system, central nervous system, and internal organs; and other health factors such as asthma and diabetes. These may be primary or secondary conditions for some handicapped children. Although many of the diagnostic procedures used to assess sensoriphysical functioning are outside the purview of the school, a knowledge of the procedures is important (formal evaluations are reviewed in the appendices). Teachers can assist in identifying and managing these disorders by being aware of manifested symptoms, referring children to appropriate persons, and working with allied health professionals.

Visual impairment

Children who are visually impaired range from those who are totally blind, with no light perception, to those with significant residual vision, who need only minor educational accommodations. Whereas medical professionals use visual acuity for legally defining a visual handicap, educators use more practical criteria, such as whether or not the child can read printed material.

Screening. Screening for visual handicaps is based on observation for manifested symptoms and the use of wall charts and machines to determine visual acuity and other visual functions. Symptoms include appearance of the eyes, including swollen or red-rimmed eyelids; frequent sties; watery eyes; different-sized pupils and drooping eyelids; visual behavior, including complaining about aches or pains; squinting and blinking; undue light sensitivity; holding reading material extremely close; and stumbling over objects. The two most widely used screening methods are charts and machines, primarily the Snellen Wall Chart and the Keystone Telebinocular. Although currently expensive, available laser technology permits the direct examination of acuity without the need for a response from the subject. This reduces the error in screening and permits accurate assessment of nonverbal or uncooperative children.

Snellen Wall Chart. The Snellen Wall Chart is the most frequently used screening test to measure visual acuity. The chart contains letters of decreasing size that individuals must read from a distance of 20 feet. For young children who do not recognize letters, the test can be modified to have the child indicate the orientation of the letter E.

Scoring. Ratios such as 20/20, 20/70, and 20/200 indicate a person's visual acuity. These ratios correspond to the size of letters on the chart that individuals with normal visual acuity can read comfortably. A person who can read the 20-foot symbols at 20 feet is considered to have normal visual acuity (20/20). A person with a measured visual acuity of 20/70 can read the symbols at 20 feet that a person with normal visual acuity can read at 70 feet. Referral is indicated for children in kindergarten through third grade if acuity is less than 20/40 in either eye and for older persons if acuity is less than 20/30 in either eye.

Discussion. The Snellen chart measures only distance visual acuity and not near-point acuity, which would be required for reading. Variations in testing environment, such as glare, illumination, and position of the examinee's head, might affect scores. Persons with the same measured visual acuity may manifest considerably different functional vision. The Snellen chart also does not measure peripheral visual acuity: a person might have a measured visual acuity of 20/20 and have tunnel vision. At best, this is merely a screening device.

Keystone Telebinocular. This instrument measures 14 different visual skills. Children sit in front of the telebinocular unit, view slides, and tell the examiner what they see. Visual functioning in each eye separately and both eyes together is determined. Near and far visual acuity, depth perception, lateral and vertical phorias, and color discrimination are all measured.

Scoring. With minimal training, school personnel can easily score the responses of a student.

Discussion. The Keystone, like other machines, is superior as a screening device because presentation procedures are always standard. Although not all kinds of visual disorders can be detected, this method is worthwhile because it is quick and relatively inexpensive.

Hearing impairment

Hearing impaired children are classified as deaf and hard of hearing. The distinction between the two groups is based on whether the individual can understand speech through the ear alone, with or without the assistance of a hearing aid (Moores, 1980). Hearing loss is frequently measured by the amount of decibel (dB) loss; however, this information has very little functional value for educators.

Screening. Although there are several group auditory screening tests, most of these instruments have lost popularity because of their low validity and reliability as compared with individual measures. Most screening is individualized using informal measures, including observations for symptoms indicative of hearing loss: straining to hear, asking for questions and statements to be repeated, speech inaccuracies, frequent confusion, running and aching ears, scratching at ears, apparent daydreaming, and difficulty following directions. The pure tone audiometer is a formalized method of screening for hearing loss.

Pure tone audiometer. The pure tone audiometer determines the degree of hearing loss by producing a series of calibrated tones, which vary in tone and pitch, through a set of headphones. The results are charted on a graph (audiogram) depicting loudness and frequency of hearing ability.

Scores. An audiometer indicates the degree of hearing loss in decibels. The greater the decibel loss, the greater the hearing loss. For example, a person with a 75-dB loss has a greater hearing loss than someone with a 50-dB loss. Using decibel loss as the criterion, the following categories indicate the degree of hearing loss:

Mild	27 to 40 dB
Moderate	41 to 55 dB
Moderately severe	56 to 70 dB
Severe	71 to 90 dB
Profound	91 dB and above

Discussion. Children who fail an audiometric examination should be referred to an otologist or audiologist for additional testing. A failure is considered a hearing level in one or both ears of 25 dB or greater at any one of the frequencies of 500, 1,000, 2,000, and 6,000 or 30 dB or more at the 4,000 frequency. Caution must be exercised when interpreting audiometric results. Students with similar losses may function very differently, and there is no agreement on the relationship between the amount of hearing loss and the type of special education program required (Gearheart & Weishahn, 1980).

Disorders of the central nervous system

Many disabilities are associated with disorders of the central nervous system. Among the more common are cerebral palsy, epilepsy, Huntington's chorea, Parkinson's disease, multiple sclerosis, meningitis, and encephalitis. Diagnosis of these conditions is primarily the responsibility of the medical profession.

Screening. Teachers involved in screening may suspect disorders by using checklists indicating certain neurological signs. Items that are monitored include hyperactivity, hypoactivity, nystagmus (rapid eye movement), perseveration, speech and language problems, and clumsiness.

Special considerations. Epilepsy is one condition related to disorders of the central nervous system frequently encountered by teachers. There are several types of epilepsy, including grand mal, jacksonian, and petit mal. Whereas a grand mal seizure, which is characterized by jerking muscles and frequent loss of consciousness, is unmistakable, petit mal seizures can go unnoticed by teachers. Children who suffer from petit mal seizures may manifest the following characteristics: temporary loss of consciousness, rhythmic movements of the eyelids, loss of posture control, loss of balance, apparent daydreaming, fixed staring, and rapid swallowing. Teachers may think the student is not paying attention or is lethargic. Students who persist in these manifestations should be referred to health personnel for examination.

Muscular dystrophy

Muscular dystrophy is a progressive, diffuse weakness of all muscles, characterized by fat and fibrous tissue replacing degenerated muscle cells. There is no known cure for muscular dystrophy.

Screening. Symptoms include poor posture, clumsiness, tiptoeing, protruding abdomen, enlargement of muscles (because of replacement of muscle with fat), obesity, and curvature of the spine.

Arthritis

Arthritis includes a variety of conditions that cause inflammation of the joints. Juvenile rheumatoid arthritis occurs in children before the age of 16. The condition may be sporadic or constant; severity also varies. There is no known cure, but spontaneous remission may occur (Mullins, 1979).

Screening. Symptoms include swelling, redness, hot, and painful joints, and stiffness of the joints; fatigability; and weight loss.

Cardiovascular system disorders

The cardiovascular system can be a primary or secondary condition for school-aged handicapped children. There are many types of heart disease, including congenital, coronary, chronic pulmonary, and hypertensive heart disease and arterial disorders.

Screening. Some manifestations of heart disease are weakness, shortness of breath, fainting, abdominal pain, chest pain, cyanosis (blueness in the fingers, toes, nose, lips, and ears), edema (fluid accumulation in the legs, and ankles, abdomen, and lungs), and abnormal blood pressure.

Respiratory disorders

Disorders of the respiratory system affect oxygen intake and carbon dioxide expulsion. Allergies, asthma, and chronic bronchitis are common in children, although allergies may also involve the eyes, ears, and skin. Problems in this area include periods of malaise, missing school, and medications that create drowsiness.

Asthma and bronchitis. Asthma and bronchitis interfere with the flow of air because of the diseased walls of the bronchial tubes and the presence of sputum. Symptoms include coughing, wheezing, mucoid secretions, constriction of the chest, headaches, and nasal blockage.

Allergies. Coughing, sneezing, nasal blockage, iritated eyes, affected skin, and ear infections may result from allergies to dust, pollen, animals, food, and many other agents in the environment. The care and concern afforded children with respiratory disorders can often result in "learned helplessness" or "being sick" to avoid responsibility. It is easy to create reinforcement contingencies that cause the child to use chronic illness as an excuse to avoid attending school or doing assigned work.

Internal organ disorders

Disorders of the internal organs include diabetes, hepatitis, kidney disease, ulcers, hernias, colitis, and cirrhosis. Teachers should be aware of any internal organ disorder, since it may have implications for educational programming.

Diabetes mellitus

Diabetes mellitus results from the body being unable to metabolize glucose into energy because the pancreas cannot produce ample amounts of insulin. The condition may begin any time from childhood through late adulthood and can result in severe disability, including blindness.

Screening. Symptoms include increased food consumption, increased thirst and intake of fluids, increased urine volume, loss of weight, weakness, fatigue, and frequent itching.

Hepatitis

Hepatitis is a disorder of the liver that prevents the complete removal of bilirubin from the blood. It may be transmitted by a blood transfusion or unsterilized needle or by contaminated food and water. Certain types of this disorder may be caused by viruses.

Screening. Symptoms include loss of appetite, jaundice, and loss of energy.

Kidney disease

The major purpose of the kidney is to regulate the volume and composition of body fluids. Disorders of the kidney prevent this function.

Screening. Symptoms include loss of strength, vigor, and mental alertness; irrational behavior; twitching; pains in the extremities; muscle cramps; loss of appetite; nausea; vomiting or diarrhea; and high blood pressure.

Cystic fibrosis

Cystic fibrosis is often misdiagnosed as bronchitis or asthma. This condition is a chronic disorder that interferes with the glands' secretion of mucus, saliva, and perspiration.

Screening. Symptoms include a dry, hacking cough, shortness of breath, and fatigue.

Discussion

The sensoriphysical conditions of the child may require special management or adaptations in the classroom environment. Although in the past many blind, deaf, or physically handicapped children were placed in special classrooms, this practice was based more on the attitudes of the school personnel than on the needs of the children. Many thousands of blind children, for example, are raised in institutions merely because local school districts do not provide specialized service. The fact that blind children are capable of attending regular schools has been established many times, but the tradition is difficult to break. A principal or teacher may simply reject the notion, thinking that the child belongs somewhere else. The same circumstances are true for the hearing impaired, physically handicapped, and many other children with disabling conditions. For the most part, children will be given special service if they are categorized primarily by cognitive-academic or socioemotional characteristics. However, the less numerous group of children with physical handicaps or sensory impairments is of specific importance under the newer approaches to special education. The variety of health-related conditions have a significant influence in the classroom setting because of their implications for learning. Although the teacher may not be expected to directly treat what are obviously medical problems, the interactions of medical problems with teaching and learning are the responsibility of the educator, who should seek assistance, advice, and direction in meeting the needs of such students.

INFORMAL ASSESSMENT

Tests assess a small fraction of the responses children make in or out of school. As Brandt (1975) stated, "Teachers often evaluate as they interpret, with setting and contextual forces" (p. 15). Data collected in the naturalistic setting can prove to be the most revealing for educators because they provide a more sound basis for the inferences about processes and learning, which are required for educational programming. Thus, informal assessment as compared with standardized measures produces more relevant information for the persons designing the instructional program.

There is a wide variety of informal assessment techniques that the teacher is capable of conducting and that should be considered part of the comprehensive assessment program. Each strategy has its own distinct condition for use and advantages and disadvantages, which are presented in the following discussions under these headings: informal tests, commercial games and other materials, teacher-made activities, observation, and other informal measurement activities.

Informal tests

Typically, informal tests are administered by the classroom teacher during the course of daily instruction to obtain performance data not produced by standardized tests or to supplement information resulting from more formal procedures (Otto, McMenemy, & Smith, 1973). Informal tests, therefore, may be used for a variety of purposes including assessment of skills, knowledge competency, or readiness levels. Informal tests are designed to provide information on student performance from which the teacher can plan instruction and select appropriate materials.

Informal tests have several advantages for the teacher including the following:

1. Informal tests have a more direct relationship and similarity to classroom activities than do standardized tests (Strang, 1969).
2. Teachers are more involved in the assessment process, which is certainly appropriate since they are responsible for instruction and are in a better position to conduct educational assessment (Smith & Neisworth, 1969).
3. Informal tests are comparatively easy to administer and interpret, are time efficient (Heilman, 1972), and are less threatening to the student (Wallace & Larsen, 1978).
4. Informal tests are inexpensive, since they do not require the purchase of costly profiles, kits, or other test materials.

Prospective users of informal tests should be aware of several factors (Wallace & Larsen, 1978):

1. Test development requires precision in item selection and sequencing.
2. Interpretation of results should be conducted carefully.
3. Results should be compared with data produced by other assessment procedures before major planning decisions are made.

Informal survey tests. This type of informal test is considered one of the most common. The primary example is the Informal Reading Inventory (IRI). These surveys are designed to cover broad ranges of a particular academic area, encompassing numerous skill areas within the overall topic. In the case of the IRI, items included in a test of reading comprehension might be related to the various types of comprehension, such as inferential or literal. Survey tests are designed to sample the level of skill performance within areas to target more specifically the various abilities or problems the student might demonstrate. A strength of the test is that it is based on actual classroom materials.

Informal skill tests. In this type of test a specific skill is targeted. The test is designed to provide data on which instruction for that specific skill is planned (Wallen, 1971). Such tests are typically developed from a sequenced skill list found in a textbook manual, curriculum guide or other list of instructional objectives, and, thus, can be constructed for most subject matter areas. The teacher who plans to develop an informal skill test is cautioned to be certain that the items included measure the skill intended. Often skills can be so closely related that performance ability is compounded, making item selection important.

Suggestions for developing informal tests. Informal tests can be developed by the classroom teacher with minimal time and effort, particularly if these guidelines are followed (Charles, 1972):

1. Be sure the test directions are clear.
2. Do not include questions on trivial matters.
3. Use simple wording, language, and sentence structure.
4. Do not include more than one problem in an item.
5. Try to include items that have only one correct answer.
6. Do not use tricky statements or double negatives.
7. Use true-false items that are clearly either true or false, not yes or no, maybe, or sometimes.
8. Do not use words that give hints about correct answers, such as *all, always, none, never, totally, exactly,* or *completely*. Avoid *a* and *an* and singulars and plurals before blanks, such as ''Toby rode *an*____, a large animal of India.''
9. Be sure that one item does not give the answer for another item. (pp. 333-334)

Commercial games and other materials

Inventories of elementary classrooms invariably include a number of commercially prepared games. These are usually secured through two means: (1) *school budget*—each teacher may be given a small amount of money annually to be used to purchase materials for the classroom; and (2) *personal resources*—teachers frequently purchase materials for the classroom, an expense that is tax deductible; donate personally owned items; or request that parents and acquaintances donate ''used'' games and toys. Individual classroom inventories and sources of acquisitions will vary, but the typical classroom might be equipped with a number of common materials, including the following:

Bingo (in various forms)
Dominoes
Blocks and patterns
Stringing beads
Pegboards
Puzzles
Board games
Card games

Teachers seem to use the games primarily for instructional diversity in drill practice and free time or as rewards, which are both valid uses. We recommend that the special educator use games extensively to reduce the effect of compounding variables such as the student's inability to write and negative attitudes toward traditional school activities. The creative special education teacher can teach a vast number of concepts in certain content areas by using commercially prepared games rather than worksheets; for example, word puzzles requiring the student to assemble a sentence from word chips may produce more direct results related to understanding the sentence as a unit that conveys an idea than would requiring the child to write a sentence. The latter activity is more complex and may prove too difficult. The ability to *write* a sentence differs significantly from the ability to *construct* a sentence. In addition, the child may have experienced repeated failures with traditional pencil-and-paper tasks, which can greatly color the attitude and level of motivation with which the student approaches the assignment.

Games can also be used effectively in informal assessment in the classroom. Whether individually or in group situations, students can engage in games that aid the teacher in various aspects of analysis. Such evaluative data collection procedures that use games have several advantages including the following:

1. The games do not provoke undue anxiety.

Table 2-2. Examples of the use of commercial games in informal assessment

Title of material	*Age range*	*Description*	*Sample skill*
Tell Time Quizmo	Grades 1 to 4	Bingo format	The student will tell time to the minute.
Fractions and Fractional Numbers	Grades 3 to 4	Puzzle	Given a fraction such as $^4/_{10}$, the student can provide the simplest form (i.e., $^2/_5$).
Math Facts Games (Level 5)	Grades 1 to 2	Board game	Given problems with missing addends, the student can perform subtraction to derive the missing value.
Consonant Match	Grades 5 and up	Card game	The student is able to identify consonant sound-symbol relationships and initial-final positions.
Sullivan Reading Games	Grades 2 to 4	Puzzle	The student is able to recognize and understand compound words.
DLM Homonym Cards	Grades 3 to 5	Card game	The student is able to define and recognize homonyms.

2. It is a format or activity with which the children are familiar.
3. They do not require that special materials be purchased.

The list of games presented here is not exhaustive but rather representative. Although all areas of concern cannot be examined through the use of games, several skills and potential deficit areas can be scrutinized as shown in Table 2-2.

Technological innovations. Microcomputers, electronic games, and calculators should be considered for possible use in classroom evaluation and instruction. As the price of technology decreases, these commercial products will become more accessible for classroom use. These products have a number of advantages including the following:

1. Students are highly motivated to use the equipment and to engage in the activities.
2. Performance data may be produced in the form of number of items done correctly, scores attained, and so forth.
3. Dependence on pencil-and-paper skills is further reduced.

Workbooks and activity books. These materials are available from discount stores, drug stores, and some department stores. They may include connecting dot-to-dot, tracing, word and math problems, cutting, and Rebus reading stories, which can be used as enrichment and assessment strategies. The use of comic strip–like characters and format heighten motivation and reduce the association with school-type activities. The worksheets can also save teachers time when used in lieu of teacher-made sheets. Activity pages may allow the use of markers and crayons rather than pencils, possibly another positive factor for students.

An efficient teacher who wishes to use such activities will want to develop a storage and retrieval system for the items to reduce preparation time and to ensure maximum use and accessibility. Based on our classroom experience, we suggest two possible organizational systems that were found to be helpful in accessing the desired workbook sheet or activity:

1. In this system the teacher follows these steps:
   a. Set up a file cabinet or storage bin with dividers identifying the various skills or deficit areas for which sheets might be used: decoding, comprehension, tracing, addition, self-concept, or whatever categories the teacher might identify. Possible categories may be based on practical experience of the teacher, subtests of vari-

ous standardized tests frequently used, and skills included in the curriculum or area of major concern to the teacher.

b. Scout various sources for such workbooks to secure several books covering an array of skills included in the categories, as well as a broad range of student capabilities. The workbooks should require a variety of responses and include diversity in format to maintain the interest of students.

c. Remove all sheets and activities from the workbooks, and file them according to the categories included in the organizational system.

2. In this sytem the pages are not removed; instead, the books are kept intact and a file card system is used. The teacher follows these steps:

   a. Identify an organizational system of skills or areas as described in system 1. A code is assigned to each category rather than to a file folder or bin; for example, decoding materials might be coded as a color (blue), number (10), or letter (a). Any symbol may be used; a color-coded system is easier for primary-aged students to comprehend.

   b. Scout all possible sources for material to fit into the categories. When appropriate material is found, its identification information is recorded under the appropriate code. For example, decoding activities would be listed on a blue card, including the name of the workbook and the page number. A blue dot would be placed on the front of the workbook.

   c. File all cards containing the identification information in a file box under the appropriate code. Locating a specific sheet or activity simply means sorting through the file cards under the proper code. The teacher or student then knows to go to a certain page of a particular workbook.

The major concern of some teachers using such workbooks is that they must constantly try to replace or reproduce the various sheets or activities. One solution we offer is to prepare an acetate sheet kit. Instructions for the kit are as follows:

1. Secure an acetate sheet for each student. These may be purchased.
2. Use a piece of heavy-duty construction paper for each student, printing the student's name in large letters on the paper.
3. Place the acetate on top of the paper so that the student's name can be seen through the acetate.
4. Tape down the *right side,* taping the two pieces together. Durable masking tape works best.
5. Issue the student a personal acetate kit to use on any workbook assignment. The student slips the assigned page between the construction paper and the acetate and writes with wax crayons or pens whose marks can be wiped off.

The teacher or an assigned student grades the worksheet from the acetate before the student proceeds to the next assignment.

Teacher-made activities

Teachers traditionally seem to be creative people with a great deal of resourcefulness when it comes to developing materials for the classroom. As the old saying goes, "necessity is the mother of invention." Many teachers simply do not have the funds, either institutional or personal, to purchase a vast inventory of materials. They design original games and materials, copy commercially produced items, and endlessly share ideas through professional exchanges, newsletters, and word of mouth. Observation of teachers attending professional meetings reveals that they often can be found clustered around various booths in the exhibition hall, furiously copying ideas on a note pad!

Many of the most innovative commercially prepared materials began as an idea in a teacher's head. Although often crudely produced, teacher-made materials typically meet a specific need, offer creative use of existing materials, employ sim-

Table 2-3. Examples of teacher-made activities for informal assessment

Title of activity	*Age range*	*Materials needed*	*Description*	*Sample skill*
Let's Tell Time	Grades 1 to 4	Old clock Flash cards showing various times (e.g., 1:10 and 3:40)	Give the child the clock to use during the game; the child draws a card and then, using the clock, illustrates the time shown. As long as the clock is set correctly, the student retains the turn, getting 1 point for each correct clock. When the child misses, the teacher or another child takes the turn, similarly drawing from the stack of cards. The first student to reach 12 points wins.	The student will tell time to the minute.
Bake-a-Pie	Grades 3 to 4	Two envelopes per child, each containing "pie" pieces made of colored construction paper One envelope contains whole "pies"; the second one contains wedges Paste One sheet of paper per child	Give each student an envelope containing colored circles with dividing lines drawn. Then give each child a second envelope containing different-sized wedge-shaped pieces. The student will "make pies" from the second envelope to match the "baked pies" in the first envelope. After the student has correctly matched the "pies," the "pies" can be glued to a sheet of paper and labeled ½, ¼, and so forth.	Given a fraction such as $^4/_{10}$, the student can provide the simplest form (i.e., $^2/_5$).
Say It–Write It	Grades 2 to 5	List of homonyms for teacher Blackboard Chalk	Select teams. The teacher pronounces a homonym. Each team member in turn attempts to spell the word and write it on the blackboard to earn 2 points for the team. If the next team member gives the correct spelling for the second word and writes it on the board, another 2 points are earned. An additional point can be earned by any team member who can use both words correctly in a sentence. If an error is made at any point, the team retires, and another team goes to the board.	The student is able to define and recognize homonyms.

Continued.

Table 2-3. Examples of teacher-made activities for informal assessment—cont'd

Title of activity	*Age range*	*Materials needed*	*Description*	*Sample skill*
"Wrong Sound" Old Maid	Grades 1 to 4	Flashcards with letters Flashcards with pictures from magazines	Prepare consonant flashcards using heavy poster board and then cut two sets of cards the same size. Have each child select a letter card, cut out a picture of something beginning with that letter and something ending with the letter, and then glue each picture on another card. *Ending Old Maid:* In this variation only the letter cards and the pictures cards of items with the matching final consonants are used. The teacher takes out one picture, leaving an odd letter as the Old Maid. *Beginning Old Maid:* In this variation only the letter cards and the cards with pictures of items with the matching initial consonants are used. Again one picture or letter is removed to leave an Old Maid.	The student is able to identify consonant sound-symbol relationships, and initial-final positions.

ple instructions, and have a high degree of student appeal. Obviously it would be impossible to list all materials, since the possibilities are endless. However, several types are commonly found in classrooms:

Bean bags
Worksheets
Card games
Board games
Team games and activities (including ball games)
Art and construction projects
Blackboard activities

Teacher-made activities present a wonderful opportunity for informal assessment in a setting identical or similar to that in which instruction will take place. In these activities the teacher has direct and total control, the student functions in a group, in which comparable performance is expected in achievement, and the environment is the same, thereby reducing the difference between assessment and daily performance that might be attributed to environmental distractions and other such variables. An additional benefit gained in informal assessment by teacher-made activities is that the effects of peer interactions are consistent between evaluation and instruction. Table 2-3 illustrates some applications of teacher-made activities for evaluation in the classroom, the activities presented are examples from which the teacher can gain ideas for other applications in informal assessment.

Sociometric techniques

According to Stanley and Hopkins (1972) "sociometry is the study of interrelationships among members of a group—that is, its social structure: how each individual is perceived by the group" (p.

403). Sociometric techniques are used by teachers to measure the social organization of classrooms and for the social appraisal of individuals and groups. Such information is often considered a desirable part of the screening process for children with learning problems. In addition, sociometric information can prove beneficial for the following purposes:

1. Assigning instructional groups and peer tutors.
2. Planning affective development activities.
3. Identifying potential social groups.
4. Predicting interpersonal difficulties within the group.
5. Measuring change in social adjustment.

Reliability of sociometric data appears to be consistent for elementary school students (Gronlund, 1955). As Bonney (1960) stated, "it seems fair to conclude that there is indeed a strong tendency for the members of a group to maintain quite similar sociometric ranks over several weeks or several months" (p. 1321). The validity of sociometric data is heavily dependent on the group's conviction that information produced will be confidential and on a high degree of familiarity existing between the group members. When these requirements are met, immediate validity of sociometric data seems satisfactory (Mouton, 1955), especially for elementary classes.

Sociograms. One of the most common sociometric techniques employed by teachers is the sociogram. Teachers ask students to respond to questions such as "With which student would you prefer to study?" "Which three students do you like best?" "Which two students do you prefer to play with at recess?", and "Which three students are your best friends?" A more complex approach is the hypothetical student sociogram. A personality sketch of a hypothetical student is presented to the class, and each student is asked to name three persons in the class who most closely, in their opinion, match the descrition, listing first, second, and third choices.

The *graphic sociogram* (Fig. 2-1) appears to be a popular type of sociogram to determine interpersonal relationships in the classrooms. Typically "most chosen" students are assigned letters at the beginning of the alphabet (A,a,B,b); therefore, a quick glance at the chart reveals the most chosen student by alphabetical label and location in the center of the chart. "Isolates" or "less often chosen" students appear around the outer edges. The arrows indicate first or second choices, and double-headed arrows indicate mutual selection by both parties. Although easy to produce and read, this particular sociogram has two pertinent limita-

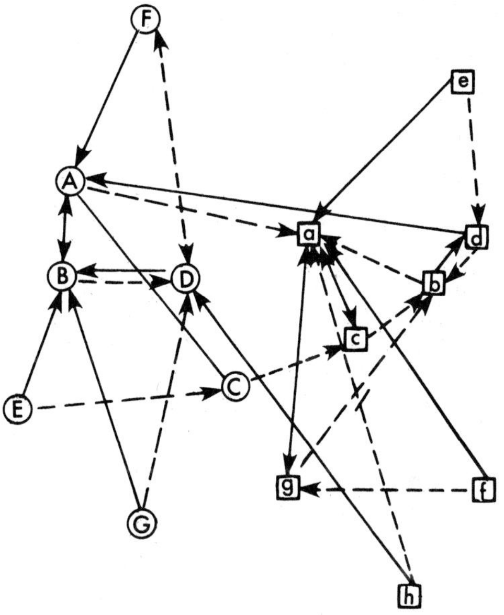

Fig. 2-1. Graphic display of sociometric data. ***Circles,*** **Girls *A* to *G;*** ***squares,*** **boys *a* to *h;*** ***solid arrows,*** **first choices;** ***dotted arrows,*** **second choices.** ***Interpretation of data:*** **Girl *A* is quite popular as indicated by having been selected as first choice by three other girls and one boy. Boy *a* is also very popular, having been selected as first choice by four other boys and as second choice by two boys and one girl. A mutual relationship appears to exist between girls *A* and *B*, since each chose the other as first choice; the same appears to be true for boys *a* and *c*. Examination of data reveals that girls *G* and *E* and boys *h* and *f* might be considered isolates, since no student selected them during the sociometric process.**

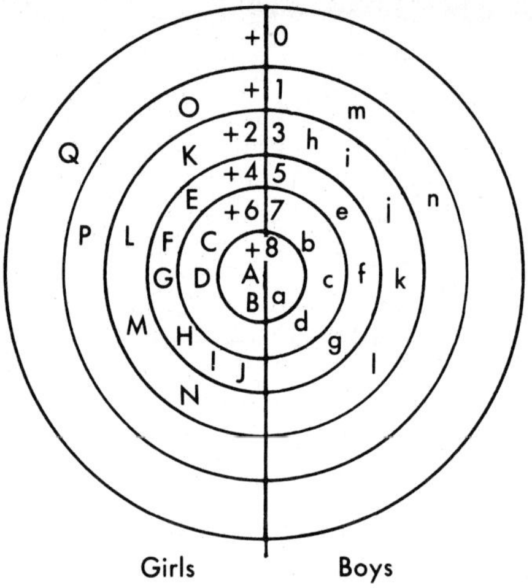

Times chosen	Girls	Boys	Total
>8	2	1	3
6-7	2	3	5
4-5	6	3	9
2-3	4	5	9
1	2	2	4
0	1	0	1

Total class size: 31

Fig. 2-2. Target sociogram data. ***Interpretation of data:*** **Girls *A* and *B* and boy *a* are quite popular, having been chosen eight or more times by their peers. Girl *Q* was not selected at all by her classmates.**

tions (Bonney, 1960; Stanley & Hopkins, 1972); (1) for groups of 30 or more, the chart becomes extremely complex to read, and (2) effective placement from such a chart necessitates some trial and error.

Another type of sociogram is the *target diagram* (Fig. 2-2). Although less common than the graphic sociogram, the target diagram produces data that may be more useful to teachers with large classes (Stanley & Hopkins, 1972). Concentric circles are used to delineate placement choices, with "students characterized as "stars" located in the center and "isolates" on the outer edges. For easier interpretation the circles can be divided in half, as shown in the figure, with girls recorded on one half and boys on the other. Arrows may be added to the chart if the teacher wishes.

Guess who. One of the most easily used techniques is the *guess who* approach (Hartshorne & May, 1928). Playing the "guessing" game with classes produces insightful information concerning peer judgments. Each child lists the classmate or classmates who match a set of brief descriptions, which can be positive or negative in nature. Responses to each description are optional; in other words, the child may elect not to match any student to a statement. Data produced by such a game include the identification of "quiet" students and happy students (Fig. 2-3). Stanely & Hopkins (1972) list the advantages of the "guess who" technique as (1) easy administration, (2) time-efficient tabulation of results, and (3) multidimensional results.

Q-sort. This technique, developed by Stephenson (1953), has sometimes been used for measurement of interests, attitudes, or other affective vari-

Student	Positive characteristics									TOTAL	Negative characteristics									TOTAL
	Most liked	Nicest manners	Neat	Best friend	Best to work with	Best at games	Makes me happy	Good team captain	Messy		Unhappy	Messy	Talks too much	Bossy	Cheats	Not fun to play with	Never finishes work	Causes trouble	Has bad manners	
A	5	4	2	5	4	1	4	1	5	31		1	1	1						3
B	3	3	1	3	2	1	3	1	2	19				2						2
C	1		4		2	2	1	2	2	14								2	2	4
D	1	1		1			1		1	5						3				3
E	1	1	1	2			1			6							2			2
F		1	2							3							1			1
G	1			1	1		1		2	6									1	1
H		1			1					2		5				1		1		7
I		1			1					2	3	2				1				6
J					1	4		3		8						2			3	5
K					1					1	2	1		8		2			1	14
a	4	2	5	4	2	5	3	6	3	34										0
b	3	2	2	3	1		4		3	18										0
c	1	1	2	1	2		1		2	10						2				2
d			1							1				1					4	5
e										0			7		4	3				14
f		1					1			2						1				1
g					2					2						2	3	4		9
h						3		4		7		7	4				6	5	7	29
i		1				4		3		8		4		2	4		8	8	2	28

Fig. 2-3. Data produced by the "guess who" technique. *A* to *K*, Girls; *a* to *i*, boys. *Interpretation of data: Girl A* appears to be positively perceived by her peers, as indicated by 31 positive ratings, whereas girl *K* is perceived as bossy by eight of her peers, receiving a total of 14 negative ratings by her peers. Boy *a* is obviously a "star," whereas boy *i* is perceived as having several negative traits.

ables. A set of cards containing descriptions, statements, character traits, pictures, and other items is presented to the student, who then sorts them into piles representing a continuum. The continuum may range from categories such as "like me" to "not at all like me," best to worst, or most to least. The number of cards to be expected in each pile is determined before beginning the game to approximate a normal frequency distribution. The sorted piles are then compared with the normal distribution. In addition, this technique can be used to compare perception of self with the "ideal" self by having the student sort the cards to reflect the ideal and then sort the cards to reflect the current self-perception. This is a much less commonly used technique, but it is one which teachers might consider in affective investigations.

Checklists and rating scales

It is important to distinguish between these two common types of affective measurement strategies. Checklists are just what the name implies, instruments on which the presence or absence of a behavior or characteristic is recorded, whereas rating scales enable the user to rate the *degree of presence* of the frequency of the trait. Both instruments are used to obtain and report the judgments of teachers or students, but, as stated previously, the nature of the judgment differs.

Obviously checklists are easier to prepare, but they also produce less specific information than rating scales. Data produced by rating scales allow examination of the social relationships found in the classroom, whereas the checklist is most appropriately used as an initial means to give a broad profile of a trait or ability, which usually leads to identification of areas requiring closer investigation. Cartwright and Cartwright (1974) indicate that checklists and rating scales help focus attention on particular behaviors while facilitating precision in recording.

Several researchers have listed advantages of rating scales and checklists (Smith, Neisworth, & Greer, 1978). These advantages include (1) direct observation toward specific and clearly stated behavior, (2) provision of a common ground for comparing children, (3) provision of a convenient record, (4) a system addressing the issue of accountability, and (5) actual measurement of behavior, not just a description of it.

In preparing rating scales the teacher must be precise in identifying the characteristics to be rated, the conditions under which the ratings will be taken, and the design of the form itself. Gronlund (1976, pp. 444-445) lists six principles that are of major significance in the use and development of rating scales:

1. Characteristics should be educationally significant.
2. Characteristics should be directly observable.
3. Characteristics and points on the scale should be clearly defined.
4. Between three and seven rating points should be provided, and raters should be permitted to mark at intermediate points.
5. Raters should be instructed to omit ratings concerning areas they feel unqualified to judge.
6. Ratings from several observers should be combined, wherever possible.

Wallace and Larsen (1978) suggest that three types of rating scales are appropriate for use in an educational setting: numerical, descriptive, and graphic. All three types use a continuum that requires a judgment by the rater concerning the degree of presence or absence of the trait in an individual, but each type of scale differs in the way in which the traits are described.

Numerical scales require the rater to indicate the degree of presence, as in the following example adapted from Ryans (1960, p. 86):

Student behavior:

Apathetic 1 2 3 4 5 6 7 N Alert

Descriptive scales consist of a list of illustrative phrases representing the continuum. The rater elects the most appropriate descriptor, as in the following example:

Is the student motivated? (Check most appropriate response.)

- __ Motivated and eager in all situations in the classroom
- __ Usually motivated; participates most of the time
- __ Not usually motivated
- __ Usually unmotivated; only participates now and then
- __ Unmotivated; never participates

Graphic scales consist of a line representing the continuum, with the degree indicated by specific marks along the line as illustrated by the two examples from Stanley and Hopkins (1972, p. 289):

	A	B	C	D	E
Motivation:	Excellent	Good	Fair	Poor	Lacking

The second example illustrates the use of descriptive components or phrases along the scale:

Motivation:

Purposeless	Vacillating	Usually purposeful	Effectively motivated	Highly motivated

This latter type is most satisfactory for school use (Gronlund, 1976), since it more specifically describes the type of behavior included.

Observation

Behavior is considered an indicator of processes involved in the development of an organism. These processes can only be inferred from the overt behavior of the organism in its natural environment. Behavior must be seen, heard, or measured. Mayr (1970) states that behavior is exhibited by organisms as a means of dealing with the environment. Cartwright and Cartwright (1974) agree that inferences can be made from behavior, but they temper this statement with the following caution: "It is possible to increase the probable accuracy of inferences by using more than one behavior as evidence. Patterns or clusters of related, similar behaviors will emerge, and these sets of behaviors are much preferred to using a single behavior for the purpose of making inferences" (p. 8).

Cartwright and Cartwright (1974) also note that "observation is a process of systematically looking at and recording behavior and can be used for the purpose of making instructional decisions" (p. 3). Observation of behavior has been employed as a tool in psychology and other disciplines for many years. In the early 1920s Piaget used child observations to formulate developmental stages of cognitive development, and more than a century ago Charles Darwin used ethological methods (Charlesworth & Spiker, 1975). Although observation has had successful application in many fields of scientific inquiry, until the 1960s only 8 percent of empirical studies in the child development literature appeared to be based on observational data.

The most frequently identified research need is for identification and understanding of the basic learning processes, which implies a need for increased systematic behavioral study. In the 1960s individual subject designs characterized much of the research with children in school settings (O'Leary, 1975); some rating scales derived from factor analysis and checklists appeared later (O'Leary & Kent, 1974). Simon and Boyer (1970) reported that by 1970 some 79 systems for collecting behavioral data existed, reflecting a heightened interest in systematic observation. The trend then began to diminish.

The collection of observational data in the natural setting has become particularly attractive to special educators. Sechrest (1969) has noted the inconsistencies between human behavior under testing and laboratory conditions and in ordinary life situations, a disparity long lamented by classroom teachers. Charlesworth and Spiker (1975), in the following statement, note the differences between artificial and natural environments: "Making observations and descriptions of behavior in natural environments, rather than in controlled or experimental settings, is the most meaningful point of departure if one wants to know the function of the behavior in the individual's real world" (p. 167).

Most of the original observation systems were used by behavior modification researchers and were designed to evaluate one or two critical problem behaviors, such as temper tantrums, crying, or isolated play (Bijou, 1965). Target behaviors were identified in advance of observation, and data collection was limited to these targets. The use of observers for recording the occurrence of units or classes of behavior as the basis for planned behavioral intervention was extended to public school classrooms by Becker, Madsen, Arnold, and Thomas (1967) and investigators at the University of Kansas (Bushell, Wrobell, & Michaelis, 1968; Hall, Lund, & Jackson, 1968).

Special educators have turned more and more to observational methodology, partly as a result of disenchantment with standardized tests and because of the influence of behaviorism. Observation is conducted in the classroom for several purposes:

1. To obtain information concerning student outcomes on cognitive and affective variables, which are not measured effectively by traditional tests (Brandt, 1975, p. 11)
2. To produce information about behaviors in areas such as social interactions, behaviors on the playground, and oral reading situations (Cartwright & Cartwright, 1974, p. 16)
3. To provide comprehensive diagnosis or assessment through a combination of achievement tests and direct, systematic observation of the child
4. To provide data from direct naturalistic observation that can be used in designing individualized intervention programs
5. To measure entry-level performance (Smith, Neisworth, & Greer, 1978)
6. To measure student outcomes (Cartwright & Cartwright, 1974)
7. To measure important classroom variables such as student-teacher interaction, peer interaction, attitudes, behavior in groups, and individual instruction (Pasanella & Volkmor, 1977)
8. To measure transfer or application of skills to other situations (Cartwright & Cartwright, 1974)

Observation in the classroom has several important advantages when compared with other types of assessment strategies: (1) it can be conducted as part of the regular instructional plan for the class, (2) it provides a sample of performance taken in the setting in which instruction will be conducted, (3) it allows an opportunity for the teacher to develop "hunches" and to experiment with instructional design to ascertain the impact on student performance, and (4) it can be conducted continuously without interfering with the program and without the concern for "overtesting." However, observation is not without problems or weaknesses. Brandt (1975) listed weaknesses that include halo effects, ambiguous trait definitions, and global ratings. Cartwright and Cartwright (1974) list the following problems associated with the observation process as a whole: inefficiency, subjectivity, unreliability, difficulty in interpretation, poor economy, and inaccuracy. Other types of problems identified include "drift" (failure to maintain consistency of definition of target behavior) and observer bias (O'Leary, 1975). Cartwright and Cartwright offer the following suggestions for reducing and controlling error in the observation process:

1. Use observation when and only when a definite purpose has been determined for gathering information about the learner.
2. Select observation methods suited to that purpose.
3. Be systematic; collect meaningful, useful information on which instructional decisions can be made.
4. Collect information or samples over time, possibly using videotape or other aids.
5. Be aware of rater biases and check for objectivity in rater reliability.
6. Summarize information and interpret carefully.

The classroom teacher has more opportunity to observe the student's learning behavior than do other members of the assessment team and is, perhaps, the greatest consumer of assessment results. Therefore, the teacher who conducts classroom observation is integral to the planning and placement process. Teachers' observations have been found to be consistent in detecting behaviors associated with learning and behavioral problems (Bryan & McGrady, 1972; Keogh, Tehir, & Windeguth-Behn, 1974; McCarthy & Paraskevopoulos, 1969; Myklebust, Boshes, Olson, & Cole, 1969; Swift & Spivack, 1969).

The effectiveness of the observation depends on a number of items, as pointed out in the preceding list of suggestions by Cartwright and Cartwright. One of the major factors is the skill level of the observer. Pasanella and Volkmor (1977, pp. 86-87) suggest the following steps to improve observer skill:

1. Select and define the target behavior.
2. Observe the setting for and events following the demonstration of the target behavior.
3. Be thoroughly informed about the purpose underlying the observation.
4. Be as unobtrusive as possible.
5. Try to collect a large amount of observation data.
6. Select or design appropriate data-recording procedures.
7. Experiment with the procedures and forms.
8. Be precise.
9. Perform a reliability check (have another person observe the student and later compare notes).

The potential benefits to be gained from including observational data in the assessment process can best be demonstrated with the following example adapted from Cartwright and Cartwright (1974, pp. 19-20):

1. *Information generated from assessment strategies other than observation*
   a. Objective: given a series of 50 flashcards of vocabulary words at the second-grade level, Sarah pronounces only 10 percent of the words correctly.
   b. Sarah cannot orally read simple sentences from a basal reader for the first grade.
   c. After listening to a sentence read orally by the teacher, Sarah cannot find a picture to match the sentence from a collection of pictures.
2. *Information generated from comprehensive assessment (reading behaviors plus socio-emotional behaviors)*
   a. Objective: when sitting with a group of children during story time, Sarah "bothers" other children by actions such as touching, poking, talking, and kicking.
   b. When her desk is moved away from others, Sarah draws a picture. She attends to this task for 5 minutes.
   c. When an adult sits with her and immediately rewards her appropriate behavior with raisins, Sarah attends to reading tasks for at least 10 minutes.

CONCLUSIONS: Sarah's instructional program must be delivered individually; she is not able to function within a reading group. Thus, observational data resulted in a major change in the instructional design, if not the instructional content. Without the information concerning Sarah's ability to perform in a group, the instructional program more than likely would have failed, not because of the content or skills included but because of the instructional mode employed.

Types of observational techniques

Frequency recording. This is a technique used to record high-rate behaviors when we simply wish to know how often a particular behavior occurs. The only requirement is that the target behavior must be a discrete unit that can be counted, for example, hitting another child, walking to the pencil sharpener, asking the teacher for help, and leaving the seat. In frequency recording, the teacher merely tallies the results of the observation (Fig. 2-4).

Duration recording. Some behaviors do not lend themselves well to frequency counting, since they are not separate and distinct units; examples

Continuous recording

	Monday	Tuesday	Wednesday	Thursday	Friday

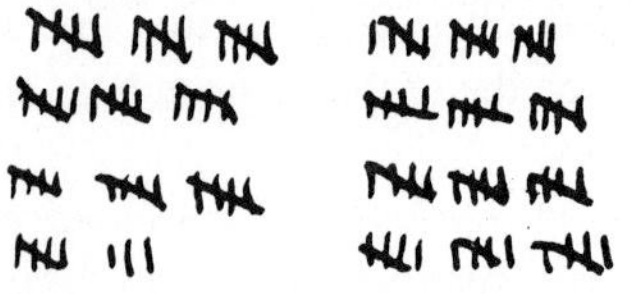

	Monday	Tuesday	Wednesday	Thursday	Friday
TOTAL	53	60			

Time sampling

Time period	Wednesday	Thursday	Friday	Total for time period
8:15- 8:30	|||	||	||	7
9:15- 9:30	||||			|||	8
10:15-10:30	||	|||			6
11:15-11:30			|||	|||	7
12:15-12:30	||			|||	6
1:15- 1:30	|||	||			6
2:15- 2:30							3
Total by day	16	13	14	

Fig. 2-4. Sample frequency recording, continuous and time sampling, of Donnie's light switch flipping behavior. By Tuesday afternoon the teacher had decided Donnie's light switch flipping behavior was occurring so frequently that time sampling was required.

are crying, screaming, laughing, staring off into space, and tantrums. In these cases, the teacher should use duration recording to collect information about the target behavior. The teacher should note the beginning and ending time of each occurrence of the behavior or time the actual duration of the behavior and record it (Fig. 2-5).

Time sampling. This technique allows the teacher to record behaviors at certain times rather than continuously. Time sampling is typically used if behavior occurs 25 or more times per day, occurs only in a certain setting, or is difficult to observe (Wallace & Kauffman, 1978). The teacher selects certain periods of time during which data are to be collected. It is often a good idea to select periods during which the behavior is of most concern, as well as times when it is not so important. Suggested schedules for data collection might include the first few minutes of the hour, 15-minute periods every 2 hours in the morning and afternoon, or 5 minutes in the middle of each instructional block. According to Cartwright and Cartwright (1974) "the teacher should make the decision on the basis of previous experiences with the behavior and should be sure that the time periods chosen coincide with a variety of activities" (p. 87). The occurrence of the behavior outside the selected time periods should not be recorded. An example of recording data from time sampling is shown in Fig. 2-4.

Interval recording. This is another alternative to continuous recording. A specific block of time is chosen by the teacher and then divided into equal, brief intervals (commonly 10 seconds). Next, as

Duration Recording

Day	Time: Begin	Time: End	Total time (minutes)	Total number of occurrences	Average duration (minutes)
1	8:20	8:29	9		
	9:08	9:16	8		
	12:13	12:23	10		
			27	3	9
2	8:09	8:20	11		
	10:03	10:15	12		
	11:19	11:29	10		
	12:01	12:12	11		
			44	4	11
3	8:17	8:27	10		
	8:51	8:59	8		
	10:12	10:24	12		
	11:46	12:00	14		
			44	4	11
4	8:03	8:17	14		
	9:08	9:19	11		
	10:28	10:42	14		
			39	3	13
5	9:01	9:10	9		
	9:54	10:05	11		
	10:42	10:52	10		
			30	3	10

Fig. 2-5. Sample duration recording of Buddy's screaming behavior.

Martin and Pear (1978) elaborate, "a specified behavior is then recorded a maximum of once per interval throughout the observation period, regardless of how many times the behavior might occur during each interval and regardless of the duration of the behavior" (p. 293). The teacher simply records the presence or absence of the behavior during the interval, and results are usually graphed in terms of the percentage of intervals in which the behavior was observed.

Charting and graphing data. Interpretation of data may be accomplished more easily if the frequency or duration of behavior is presented as a chart or graph. It is common practice for the *ordinate points* (behavior's frequency, duration, and percent of occurrence) to be located on the vertical axis of the chart, and the *abscissa points* (hours, days, and sessions of observation) to be located on the horizontal axis (Axelrod, 1977). Fig. 2-6 illustrates the use of bar and line graphs to display data.

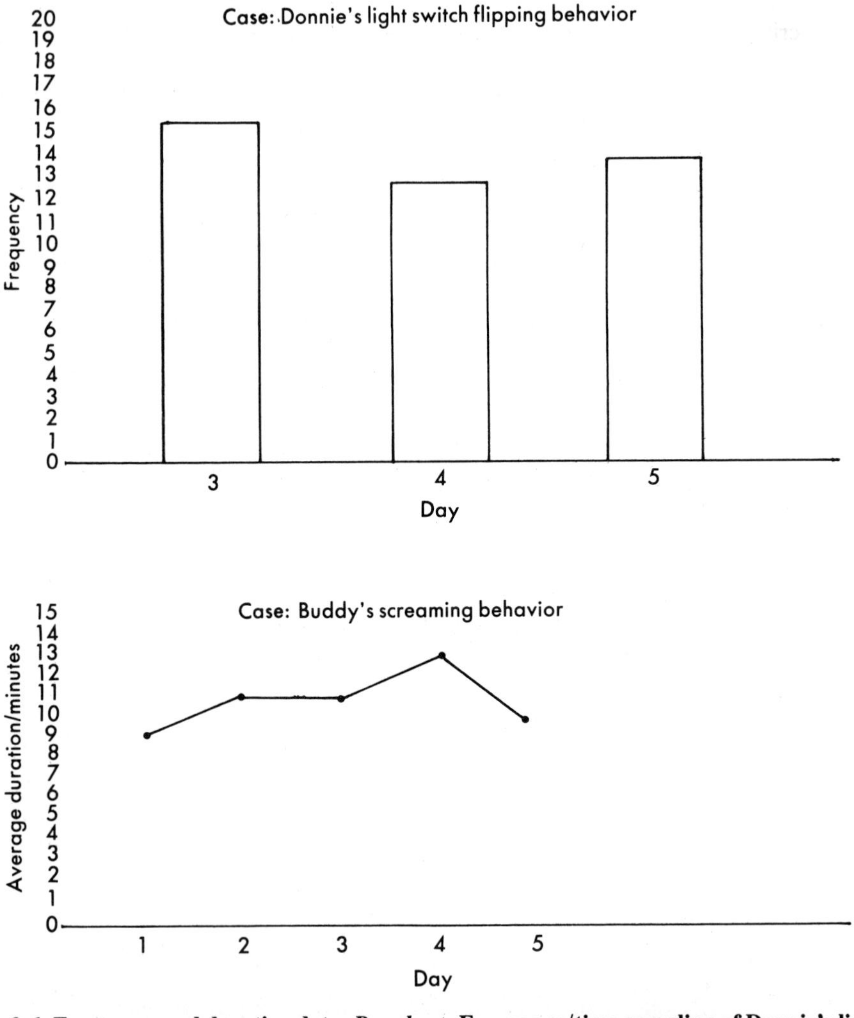

Fig. 2-6. Frequency and duration data. *Bar chart,* Frequency/time sampling of Donnie's light switch flipping behavior. *Graph,* Duration of Buddy's screaming behavior.

Stages in data collection

Baseline data collection. Baseline data are information collected before any efforts to change behavior. They are descriptive data used as the foundation for determining whether behavior needs to be changed and, if so, for planning the type of intervention. In addition, baseline data aid the teacher in determining whether any change has occurred after the intervention or treatment. Baseline data should be taken for a period of 1 to 2 weeks (Reinert, 1980).

Intervention data. Although this aspect of data collection is not critical in the assessment process, it is introduced here to explain the relationship between baseline and intervention data. The teacher continues to collect data on the student during the treatment or intervention period, using the same target behavior and method begun in the baseline period (Fig. 2-7). From a comparison of the baseline and intervention data the effectiveness of the intervention can be measured; that is, it can be determined if the child's behavior has changed as desired by the teacher. This is the typical behavioral design—*A* is the baseline period, and *B* is the intervention period. There are other more complex types of designs, but these are not typically used by a classroom teacher in public schools.

Anecdotal records. An anecdotal record provides a factual description of an event recorded immediately after the event occurs. Such an informal observation technique is most appropriately used with low-frequency behaviors, behaviors occurring in a unique context, or unanticipated, spontaneous behaviors. The only preparation required of the teacher using an anecdotal record is the selection of a format. Thorndike and Hagen (1955, p. 486) state that a properly maintained anecdotal record would have the following characteristics:

1. It provides an accurate description of a specific event.
2. It describes the setting sufficiently to give the event meaning.
3. If it includes interpretation or evaluation by

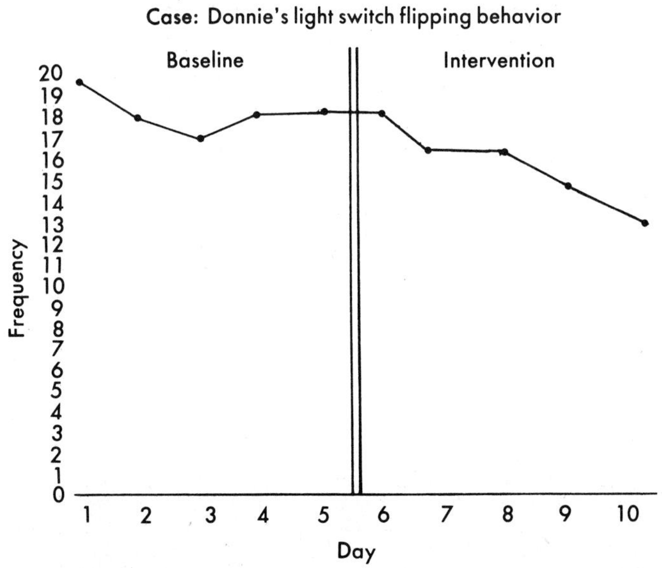

Fig. 2-7. Recording baseline and intervention data using frequency/time sampling data of Donnie's light switch flipping behavior. Double lines separate baseline and intervention data, a convention in recording behavioral data.

Anecdotal Records Summary

Observer ______________________ Student: ______________________

Room: ______________________

Dates observed: ______________________

____

____

Total number of observations: ______________

Settings in which observations were conducted: ______________________

____

____

____

Is any relevant supportive information available? ______________________

Indicate location: ______________________

____

Summary of findings:

Recommendations:

Signature of observer: ______________________

Date

Fig. 2-8. Sample summary form for reporting anecdotal information.

the recorder, this interpretation is separated from the description and its different status is clearly identified.

4. The event it describes is one that relates to the child's personal development or social interactions.
5. The event it describes is either representative of the typical behavior of the child or significant because it is strikingly different from the usual forms of behavior. If it is unusual behavior for the child, that fact is noted.

The following general admonitions can be given to the teacher before using anecdotal records (Cartwright & Cartwright, 1974): the teacher should (1) be factual; (2) avoid overemphasizing atypical behavior; (3) select the behaviors to be observed carefully to avoid, as much as possible, selecting behaviors that merely reflect the teacher's values or biases; (4) use only statements that concretely describe what is seen, rather than words which reflect what the teacher *thought* about what was seen (e.g., the difference between "the child hit another student" and "the child took his anger out on another student" is significant); (5) include samples of work and other supporting evidence relevant to the behaviors being observed; (6) be purposeful, observing the student for a reason; and (7) be systematic, keeping the record on a regularly scheduled basis, rather than just as a reaction to a situation or an impulse.

Formats for anecdotal records vary, but basic information included is the student's name, date, observer's name, time of observation, setting, and description of the incident. Cartwright and Cartwright (1974) suggest the use of mimeographed index cards or pages containing the format, because the use of blank cards or sheets encourages the observer to record less systematically. The cards or sheets can be filed under a number of systems, including student's name or dates. Regardless of the format selected, we urge the teacher to be consistent in order to facilitate storage and organization for retrieval of information. Cartwright and Cartwright (1974) also suggest the use of an anecdotal record summary (Fig. 2-8) to increase ease of examination and interpretation of data collected.

Other informal measurement activities

The teacher may engage in a number of other activities to produce information concerning student performance in any of the three areas of functioning—cognitive-academic, socioemotional, or sensoriphysical. These activities typically consist of actions taken by the teacher to further specify the performance level of the student, describe the nature of the problem, and identify instructionally relevant information.

Task analysis. Wallace and Kauffman (1978) state that "task analysis may be viewed as a sequence of evaluative activities that pinpoints the child's learning problem and guides the teacher in planning an effective remedial sequence of instructional tasks" (p. 105). *Theoretically,* the teacher would break the target task into successively simpler steps and use them to identify the precise location of the child's difficulties in performing the skill. Once the errors have been "analyzed," the teacher designs a remedial program directed toward correcting the deficits. *Pragmatially,* task analysis falls far short of the ideal for the following reasons:

1. Underlying the concept of task analysis is the belief that the teacher can identify the hierarchical set of skills involved. This leads to difficulties because there is still widespread disagreement in many curricular areas as to what constitutes the skill sequences. As long as these skill lists are developed by "expert opinion," differences can be expected to continue.

2. Many areas of the elementary school curriculum do not lend themselves readily to task analysis. The special educator may not be able to secure a list of skills and may not have the required expertise in all areas to properly break the skill into subskills. Certain behavioral tasks are also much more difficult to analyze because of their subjective nature.

3. It is easy for the teacher to become overly involved with the *process* of task analysis, there-

by neglecting the product or outcome. The procedure can become time consuming, since the teacher devotes time to designing elaborate task ladders and other instruments, with the teacher passing the point of diminishing returns in terms of instructionally relevant information.

4. Most of the examples provided in books emphasizing the task-analytic approach focus on a limited range of behaviors such as the number of words read per minute, number of movements demonstrated, and number of problems completed or percentage of correct responses. Some important considerations missing in these examples follow: What are the words? How were the problems selected? and What, if any, relationship existed between the various samples of work included in the comparison? Teaching cannot be simply stated in terms of percentages or numbers of correct responses without consideration being given to decisions such as what is taught, when it is presented, and how it is presented.

5. The methodology associated with the task-analytic approach appears to be more appropriate for clinical instruction (one-on-one) than for the type of group instruction found in public classrooms. Teachers often do not have the time for such strategies and view them as somewhat impractical for their use. Teachers do not consider six-line drum paper standard teaching equipment and have difficulty envisioning its use in a regular classroom.

Task analysis may be of great use in some types of instructional settings with specifically identified types of curricula. However, its application cannot be generalized to all areas of the elementary classroom. The teacher should examine the task, the setting, and the outcomes expected from the process before making the decision to use task analysis. In time, as skill sequences become more logically determined via statistical methods, the classroom use of task analysis may become more viable.

Case histories and case studies. *Case histories* appear to be a fairly consistent part of the referral and evaluation process in most schools. A standard form is usually used to record information in such areas as family history, medical background, birth history, child development, educational history, and psychological history. The questionnaires may be completed through interviewing or self-report, depending on the complexity of the information required and the qualifications of the person from whom information is sought. Case histories should be considered useful as screening instruments; however, teachers must be careful in using case history information to maintain confidentiality, respond as objectively as possible to data included, and resist the tendency to weigh such information too heavily when making educational decisions. An appropriate admonition is that the case history should be examined to reveal information pertinent to programming, not to try to identify cause or to lay blame.

Case studies consist of information gained from all available sources, including test results, observational data, daily class performance, school records, and home and health records (Beatty, Madden, & Gardner, 1966). Although the format and depth of the case study will vary greatly according to the time available, the types of cases, the professional who assumes primary responsibility for its development, and the nature of the problem, the following guidelines are suggested by Ekwall (1976, pp. 377-378):

1. Use a type of outline form that will make sections and subsections clearly visible.
2. Include important information, but exclude any information that would be of no value in working with students.
3. Where subjective observations are stated they should be identified as such.
4. List specific test scores and the sources of each score.
5. List specific skills needing remediation.
6. Give a brief interpretation of the results of each test that may not be familiar to the person or persons reading the report.
7. Keep sentence structure simple.
8. Use the third person when referring to oneself.

9. Make a specific recommendation for the remediation of various difficulties noted.
10. Give exact dates of the administration of each test.
11. Show a summary of significant strengths and weaknesses.
12. Include possible causes for weaknesses of the student.

Typically information included is very broad in nature and should only be used to contribute to an overall profile evolving from other types of investigative efforts. Realistically teachers will not be expected to prepare many case studies but may provide input for them. In specific situations, case studies may be needed, as in cases with a major medical focus or behavioral concerns.

Interviewing. Interviewing is considered an informal assessment technique that is useful because of its efficiency and almost unlimited scope *if* it is conducted for a specific purpose. Following are examples of the types of information to be gained through interviewing, according to Pasanella and Volkmor (1977, p. 103):

1. Assessment of teacher concerns about student behavior
2. Assessment of parental concerns regarding student behaviors in the home and classroom
3. Assessment of student motivational variables (interests, reinforcers, fears, expectations, cooperation, etc.)
4. Assessment of attitudes
5. Informal evaluation of attempts to remediate behavioral problems or performance

Ekwall (1976) suggests that the teacher use a general outline of major points to be covered in the interview to ensure that it proceeds smoothly and with purpose. Interviews may be *open* with the interviewer using open-ended questions and other strategies to encourage conversation and sharing or highly structured with the interviewer asking specific questions and carefully recording the responses.

The following are for the teacher interested in using interviewing as part of the informal assessment of students:

1. Communicate your genuine desire to gain information.
   a. Listen carefully.
   b. Encourage communication through verbal and nonverbal cues.
   c. Avoid "roadblocking" of sharing efforts (don't "take the conversation away" from the respondent).
2. Be aware of all aspects of the informant's communication, including nonverbal or body language (posture, eye contact, and voice quality).
3. If possible, make the purpose of the interview clear to the respondent to reduce any anxiety or concern that there might be a hidden agenda.
4. At strategic points or particularly critical points summarize or restate what you believe you have heard; this gives the respondent an opportunity to clarify or modify any aspect of the response.

A properly conducted interview takes time and a good deal of practice. The suggestions included in Chapter 5 for conducting parental conferences should be studied by the teacher considering interviewing. Interpretation of information gained through interviewing must be examined with care, and the teacher should attempt to refrain from making judgments and premature conclusions (Strang, 1969).

Expressive methods. The elementary school curriculum offers much instructional flexibility for the creative teacher. Such a teacher may wish to employ one or more expressive methods of obtaining informal assessment information, such as those suggested by Lister (1969):

1. Drama
2. Role playing
3. Artistic productions

All of these provide opportunities for the teacher to gain insight into one or more of the areas of functioning—cognitive-academic, socioemotional, and sensoriphysical. Our primary concern here is that the teacher must remain objective; Pasanella and Volkmor (1977) state that teachers must not use such approaches to support their own beliefs about the child's problem.

Record analysis. In this informal strategy, the teacher simply examines the student's records to determine additional information accrued through other experiences. Types of relevant information might include the following:

1. Record of previous referrals and/or assessments
2. Chronological outline of evaluative history
3. Historical information on health and familial factors
4. Achievement data

If any information is integrated into the evlauation report or educational plan, the teacher should record the source and date of the information. A valid precaution is to examine the continuing status of the information before incorporating it into current services.

Error pattern analysis. During the assessment process, it may become obvious to the teacher that the student cannot perform the desired skill. The teacher may elect to examine the student's performance to see if some type of pattern is observable in the errors made. Hawisher and Calhoun (1978) comment that "the child's mistakes, especially if a pattern can be discerned, give clues about the subtasks the child has not yet mastered" (p. 57).

The teacher should consider the following steps in employing error pattern analysis:

1. Examine the student's work in comparison with the work of another student committing the same errors; the comparison may aid the teacher in spotting trends or patterns.

2. Present the task to the student in a variety of forms (worksheet, blackboards, orally, etc.) to ascertain the effect of the instructional medium.

3. Allow the student an opportunity to attempt the task at different times during a period of several days.

Job samples or work analysis. The teacher can very carefully plan and orchestrate activities through which job samples or work analyses are possible. Two major types of information can be generated through these planned activities: skill performance and behavioral styles or patterns. Skill performance can be revealed through activities such as the following:

Skill	*Job samples*
1. Count money.	Count real or play money.
	Play Monopoly.
2. Write sentences.	Write a friendly letter.
	Write instructions on the blackboard.
3. Tell time.	Be the monitor to tell the class when it is time for physical education.
	Set paper plate clocks at the time requested by the teacher.

Social or behavioral data can be produced through a vast collection of activities, such as the following:

1. Discussion groups and other leaderless groups
2. Field trips
3. Games such as "Simon Says," "Mother May I?," and "I Spy"
4. Team games

Obviously many of the activities can produce information simultaneously about skill and behavioral patterns, a definite benefit of this type of informal assessment. The student's work habits and approaches to problem solving can also be observed through these carefully structured activities. The two most obvious advantages are the direct relationship to programming that is possible and the "non-testlike" appearance of such strategies.

Informal assessment plans

The example of Sarah, mentioned previously, underlines not only the importance of observational data but also the overall role that informal assessment can play in diagnostic-prescriptive procedures and instructional design. Sample informal assessment plans shown in Table 2-3 demonstrate how the teacher might conduct informal assess-

Table 2-3. Sample informal assessment plans reflecting a variety of strategies

	Informal assessment strategies						
Problem description	*Inventories*	*Commercial games*	*Teacher-made activities*	*Observation*	*Socio-metrics*	*Activities*	*Results (problem validated?)*
Case no. 102 A							
Math performance problems	X	X	X	X		X	No
Reading difficulties	X	X	X	X		X	No
Poor peer relations			X	X	X	X	Yes
Low self-concept		X	X	X	X	X	Yes
Physically aggressive				X		X	Yes
Case no. 103P							
Lack of word attack skills	X	X	X	X		X	Yes
Low-reading comprehension	X	X	X			X	Yes
Good peer relationships			X	X	X	X	Yes
Particular preference for certain materials		X	X	X		X	Yes

ment through the use of one or more of the strategies discussed in this chapter.

Norms and criteria in teaching

Most handicapped students are viewed as deviant because they do not meet common classroom expectations. The normative test and normal curve are used for comparisons of students or are used to determine their relative standings, but these also cause fixed expectations to be recognized as standards. As long as normative tests serve this function, those who fall below expectations in achievement, behavior, and other dimensions will fail. The educational response has been to use *ability models* (process training and diagnostic-prescriptive teaching); *aptitude treatment,* wherein a specific set of materials is used to match the learner's style (visual, auditory, kinesthetic, and tactile sensations and modality preference); and *best methods,* wherein a particular approach is used because research tends to support better gains for classes of students. Thus, determining what to teach is based on global assessment and theoretical constructs, an approach that cannot be supported scientifically (Cronbach & Snow, 1969).

Criteria, rather than relative standings, are used

in skill models, task analysis, and criterion-referenced tests. The premise is that handicapped students are unsuccessful because they have not mastered entry-level skills necessary for the performance of a task. The problems with this approach are that mastery criteria (competency tests) will be used to discriminate against students in the same manner as normative tests. On the positive side, attention can be devoted to the independent rate of development of each student.

There are advantages and disadvantages to both approaches. The teacher should recognize the following points:

1. Norm-referenced tests are primarily used to classify students; they neither determine what to teach nor tell what skills a student has mastered.

2. The normal curve or minimal competencies will ensure that some students fail in a competitive academic environment.

3. As long as there is no focus on the teaching process itself, the student can be totally blamed for failure under either normative or criterion-referenced systems.

4. Standardized tests cannot precisely measure aptitudes, abilities, or deficits.

5. Educators cannot scientifically select specific treatments, materials, or programs that can interact with aptitudes and abilities. Further research in this area may provide a rational approach for instruction, but this is not currently available.

6. Training aptitudes or abilities separately as a means of improving academic functioning has not yet been proven to be successful.

7. Treating children based on process-oriented approaches cannot be supported by research.

8. Classification and prediction cannot be satisfactorily accomplished with available assessment tools.

9. Any given task may actually require different abilities at different points during the learning process. One type of presentation (modality) or material (e.g., whole word versus phonics) will not remain stable over a period of time. Many tasks may require a general ability initially, followed by specific abilities later. The rate of development may be affected by initial general abilities and subsequent specific abilities, materials, practice, instructional design, and numerous other variables that are not recognized or considered in simplistic modality or aptitude-treatment designs. Most so-called auditory or visual learners are not discrete in their preferences, neither are the methods used to teach them discrete.

10. The most important variables in teaching are those over which the teacher has the greatest control, including presentation, time-on-task, attention, and reinforcement.

11. Scaled sequences of measured skills can be used to determine what to teach, and progress can be measured in terms of achievement along the sequence.

12. Skill sequences enable handicapped students to follow the basic curriculum design of the school.

13. Criterion-referenced tests will facilitate more reasonable expectations for development of a particular student since normative comparisons are deemphasized.

14. Curricula that are selected by the school and based on a skill sequence determine how students will be expected to learn despite the type of service or delivery model.

15. What to teach will be predicated on the curriculum and the needs of the students in terms of entry skills. How to teach will be based on presentation variables and reinforcement theory.

SUMMARY

In this chapter we have considered the evaluation tools commonly used in assessment of children who are referred for special education. Tests in formal assessment were categorized under the major headings of the planning matrix used in the text—cognitive-academic, socioemotional, and sensoriphysical functioning. The primary emphasis in assessment is placement. Tests for this purpose are generally standardized. Because standardized tests are limited to providing global information, it is impossible to know what a student can and cannot do. These tests can only determine whether a student is typical or atypical in terms of some measure contrasted to normative data. The most significant problem in the use of standardized tests is that examiners may use theoretical approaches to ''diagnose'' conditions that do not really exist and to recommend treatments based on test data that may have no empirical or rational basis. Many tests commonly used in special education have poor validity, reliability, and limited information about normative data. Decisions made on the basis of such information are only as correct as the precision of the obtained data and the accuracy of the constructs used to explain human behavior.

Informal assessment is much more direct and therefore more useful to the teacher in instructional design. It was recommended to the teacher that testing during the placement process will not yield much information but that it should not be expected to do so. Informal assessment will satisfy the needs of the teacher and the student if the data are tied to appropriate instructional designs. Criterion-referenced systems will permit the use of individualized programming for all students and not just the handicapped because the necessity for comparisons will be eliminated.

The challenges to assessment currently in litigation concerning minority students may generally reshape assessment for all students. If standardized tests are deemphasized in the process and observational approaches combined with criterion-referenced testing systems are employed, a significant change in American education can be anticipated.

TESTS

AAMD Adaptive Behavior Scales
American Association on Mental Deficiency
Washington, D.C.

Auditory Discrimination Test
Language Research Associates
Chicago, IL.

Bender Visual-Motor Gestalt Test
American Orthopsychiatric Association
New York, NY

Burks' Behavior Rating Scales
Arden Press
El Monte, CA

Cain-Levine Social Competency Scale
Consulting Psychologists Press
Palo Alto, CA

Coping Analysis Schedule for Educational Settings
San Jose State University
San Jose, CA

Developmental Test of Visual Perception
Consulting Psychologists Press
Palo Alto, CA

Devereux Elementary School Behavior Rating Scale
Devereux Foundation
Devon, PA

Durrell Analysis of Reading Difficulty
Harcourt Brace Jovanovich, Inc.
New York, NY

Goldman-Fristoe-Woodcock Test of Auditory Discrimination
American Guidance Service
Circle Pines, MN

Gray Oral Reading Test
The Bobbs-Merrill Co., Inc.
Indianapolis, IN

Houston Test of Language Development
Houston Press
Houston, TX

Illinois Test of Psycholinguistic Abilities
University of Illinois Press
Urbana, IL

KeyMath Diagnostic Arithmetic Test
American Guidance Service
Circle Pines, MN

Peabody Individual Achievement Test
American Guidance Service
New York, NY

Picture Story Language Test
Grune & Stratton, Inc.
New York, NY

Purdue Perceptual Motor Survey
Charles E. Merrill Publishing Co.
Columbus, OH

Reading Miscue Inventory
Macmillan Inc.
New York, NY

Slosson Intelligence Test
Slosson Educational Publications
East Aurora, NY

Spache Diagnostic Reading Scales
McGraw-Hill Book Co.
Monterey, CA

Stanford-Binet Intelligence Scale
Houghton Mifflin Co.
Boston, MA

System of Multicultural Pluralistic Assessment
Institute of Pluralistic Assessment Research and Training
Riverside, CA

Utah Test of Language Development
Communication Research Associates
Salt Lake City, UT
Walker Problem Behavior Identification Checklist
Western Psychological Services
New York, NY
Wechsler Intelligence Scales for Children–Revised
Psychological Corp.
New York, NY
Wide Range Achievement Test
Guidance Associates
Wilmington, DE
Woodcock Reading Mastery Tests
American Guidance Service
Circle Pines, MN

REFERENCES AND SUGGESTED READINGS

Aiken, L.R., Jr. The grading behavior of a college faculty. *Educational and Psychological Measurement,* 1975, *23,* 319-322.

Axelrod, S. *Behavior modification for the classroom teacher.* New York: McGraw-Hill Book Co., 1977.

Bateman, B.D. *Educational implications of minimal brain dysfunction.* Paper presented at a conference on minimal brain dysfunction, New York Academy of Sciences, New York, March 20-22, 1972.

Beatty, L.S., Madden, R., & Gardner, E.F. *Stanford diagnostic arithmetic test manual.* New York: Harcourt Brace Jovanovich, Inc., 1966.

Becker, W.C., Madsen, C.H., Jr., Arnold, C.R., & Thomas, D.R. The contingent use of teacher attention and praise in reducing classroom behavior problems. *The Journal of Special Education,* 1967, *1,* 287-307.

Bijou, S.W. Experimental studies of child behavior, normal and deviant. In L. Kresher & L.P. Ullman (Eds.), *Research and behavior modification.* New York: Holt, Rinehart & Winston, 1965, 56-81.

Blake, K.A. *Educating exceptional pupils.* Reading, M.: Addison-Wesley Publishing Co., Inc., 1981.

Bonney, J.M. Sociometric methods. In C.W. Harris (Ed.), *Encyclopedia of educational research* (3rd ed.). New York: The Macmillan Co., 1960, pp. 1319-1324.

Brandt, R.M. An historical overview of systematic approaches to observation in school settings. In R.A. Weinburg & H. Woods (Eds.), *Observation of pupils and teachers in mainstream and special education settings: alternative strategies.* Leadership Training Institute, Minneapolis: University of Minnesota Press, 1975.

Bryan, T.S., & McGrady, H.J. The use of a teacher rating scale. *Journal of Learning Disabilities,* 1972, *5,* 199-206.

Bushell, D., Wrobell, P.A., & Michaelis, M.L. Applying "group" contingencies to the classroom study of behavior of preschool children. *Journal of Applied Behavioral Analysis,* 1968, *1,* 55-61.

Cartwright, C.A., & Cartwright, G.P. *Developing observation skills.* New York: McGraw-Hill Book Co., 1974.

Charles, C.M. *Educational psychology: the instructional endeavor* (2nd ed.). St. Louis: The C.V. Mosby Co., 1976.

Charlesworth, W.R., & Spiker, D. An ethological approach to observation in learning settings. In R.A. Weinburg & F.H. Wood (Eds.), *Observation of pupils and teachers in mainstream and special education settings: alternative strategies.* Leadership Training Institute, Minneapolis: University of Minnesota Press, 1975.

Cronbach, L.J., & Snow, R.E. *Individual differences in learning ability as a function of instructional variables* (Final report). Stanford, CA: Stanford University, March, 1969.

DiVesta, F.J., & Dick, W. The test-retest reliability of childrens' ratings on the semantic differential. *Educational and Psychological Measurement,* 1966, *26,* 605-616.

Edwards, A.J. *Individual mental testing: research and interpretation* (Pt. 3). New York: Intext Educational Publishers, 1975.

Ekwall, E.E. *Diagnosis and remediation of the disabled reader.* Boston: Allyn & Bacon, Inc., 1976.

Gallagher, J.J. (Ed.). *The application of child development research to exceptional children.* Reston, VA: The Council for Exceptional Children, 1975.

Gearheart, B.R., & Weishahn, M.W. *The handicapped student in the regular classroom.* St. Louis: The C.V. Mosby Co., 1980.

Gronlund, N.E. *Measurement and evaluation in teaching.* New York: Macmillan Inc., 1976.

Hall, R.V., Lund, D., & Jackson, D. Affects of teacher attention on study behavior. *Journal of Applied Behavior Analysis,* 1978, *1,* 1-12.

Hammill, D. Evaluating children for instructional purposes. *Academic Therapy Quarterly,* 1971, *4,* 341-353.

Hammill, D., & Larsen, S.C. The effectiveness of psycholinguistic training. *Exceptional Children,* 1974, *4,* 455-459.

Hartshorne, H., & May, M.A. *Studies in deceit.* New York: The Macmillan Co., 1928.

Hawisher, M.F., & Calhoun, M.L. *The resource room: an educational asset for children with special needs.* Columbus, OH: Charles E. Merrill Publishing Co., 1978.

Heilman, A.W. *Principles and practices of teaching reading* (3rd ed.). Columbus, OH: Charles E. Merrill Publishing Co., 1972.

Heilman, A.W. *Phonics in proper perspective* (3rd ed.). Columbus, OH: Charles E. Merrill Publishing Co., 1976.

Kauffman, A.S. A new approach to the interpretation of test scatter on the WISC-R. *Journal of Learning Disabilities,* 1976, *9,* 160-168.

Keogh, B.K., Tehir, C., & Windeguth-Behn, A. Teachers' perceptions of educationally high-risk children. *Journal of Learning Disabilities,* 1974, *7,* 367-374.

Larsen, S.C., & Hammill, D.D. Relationships of selected visual perceptual abilities to school learning. *The Journal of Special Education,* 1975, *9,* 281-291.

Lister, J.L. Personal-emotional-social skills. In R.M. Smith (Ed.), *Teacher diagnosis of educational difficulties.* Columbus, OH: Charles E. Merrill Publishing Co., 1969.

Marsh, G.E., II, & Price, B.J. *Methods for teaching the mildly handicapped adolescent.* St. Louis: The C.V. Mosby Co., 1980.

McCarthy, J., & Parakevopoulos, J. Behavior patterns of learning disabled, emotionally disturbed and average children. *Exceptional Children,* 1969, *35,* 69-74.

Martin, G., & Pear, J. *Behavior modification: what it is and how to do it.* Englewood Cliffs, NJ: Prentice-Hall, Inc., 1978.

Mayr, E. *Population, species, and evolution.* Cambridge, MA: Harvard University Press, 1970.

Moores, D.F. *Educating the deaf: psychology, principles, and practices.* Boston: Houghton Mifflin Co., 1978.

Mouton, J.S. The validity of sociometric responses. *Sociometry,* 1955, *18,* 7-48.

Mullins, J.B. *A teacher's guide to management of physically handicapped students.* Springfield, IL: Charles C Thomas, Publisher, 1979.

Myklebust, H.R., Boshes, B., Olson, B., & Cole, C. Final report: U.S.P.H.S. Contract 108-65-142. Evanston, IL: Northwestern University Press, June, 1969.

Newcomer, P.L., & Hammill, D.D. ITPA and academic achievement: a survey. *The Reading Teacher,* May 1976, pp. 731-741.

O'Leary, K.D. Behavioral assessment: an observational slant. In R.A. Weinburg & H. Woods (Eds.), *Observation of pupils and teachers in mainstream and special education settings: alternative strategies.* Leadership Training Institute, Minneapolis: University of Minnesota Press, 1975.

O'Leary, K.D., & Kent, R.N. *A behavioral consultation program for parents and teachers of children with conduct problems.* Paper presented to the American Psychopathological Association, Boston: March 7, 1974.

Osgood, C.E., Suci, G.J., & Tannenbaum, P.H. *The measurement of meaning.* Urbana, IL: University of Illinois Press, 1957.

Otto, W., McMenemy, R.A., & Smith, R.J. *Corrective and remedial teaching* (2nd ed.). Boston: Houghton Mifflin Co., 1973.

Pasanella, A.L., & Volkmor, C.B. *Coming back . . . or never leaving.* Columbus, OH: Charles E. Merrill Publishing Co., 1977.

Reinert, H.R. *Children in conflict: educational strategies for the emotionally disturbed and behaviorally disordered* (2nd ed.). St. Louis: The C.V. Mosby Co., 1980.

Rugel, R. WISC subtest scores of disabled readers. A review with respect to Bannatyne's recategorization. *Journal of Learning Disabilities,* 1974, *1,* 48-55.

Rundquist, E.A., & Sletto, B.F. *Personality in the depression.* Minneapolis: University of Minnesota Press, 1936.

Ryans, D.G. *Characteristics of teachers.* Washington, D.C.: American Council on Education, 1960.

Salvia, J., & Ysseldyke, J.F. *Assessment in special and remedial education.* Boston: Houghton Mifflin Co., 1978.

Sattler, J.M. *Assessment of children's intelligence.* Philadelphia: W.B. Saunders Co., 1974.

Sechrest, L. Nonreactive assessment of attitudes. In E.P. Williams & H.L. Reush (Eds.), *Naturalistic viewpoints in psychological research.* New York: Holt, Rinehart & Winston, 1969.

Simon, A., & Boyer, E.D. (Eds.), *Mirror for behavior: an anthology of observation instruments* (Pt. 2). Philadelphia: Research for Better Schools, 1970.

Skydell, B., & Crowder, A.S. *Diagnostic procedures: a reference for health practitioners and a guide for patient counseling.* Boston: Little, Brown & Co., 1975.

Smith, R.M., Neisworth, J.T., & Greer, J.G. *Educating educational environments.* Columbus, OH: Charles E. Merrill Publishing Co., 1969.

Spodick, D.H. Diseases of the heart and peripheral blood vessels. In J.D. Meyers (Ed.), *An orientation to chronic disease and disability.* London: Collier Macmillan Limited, 1965.

Stanley, J.C., & Hopkins, K.D. *Educational and psychological measurement and evaluation.* Englewood Cliffs, NJ: Prentice-Hall, Inc., 1972.

Stephenson, W. *The study of behavior: Q-technique and its methodology.* Chicago: University of Chicago Press, 1953.

Strang, R. *Diagnostic teaching of reading* (2nd ed.). New York: McGraw-Hill Book Co., 1969.

Swift, M., & Spivack, G. Clarifying the relationship between the academic success and overt classroom behavior. *Exceptional Children,* 1969, *35,* 99-104.

Tallmadge, C.K., & Hart, D.P. A procedural guide for validating achievement gains in educational projects. Washington, DC: U.S. Department of Health, Education and Welfare, Office of Education, 1974.

Thorndike, R.L., & Hagen, E. *Measurement and evaluation in psychology and education* (2nd ed.). New York: John Wiley & Sons, Inc., 1955.

Tittle, K.R. Wechsler Intelligence Scales for Children-revised. *Journal of Educational Measurment,* 1975, *12,* 140-143.

Walike, B.C., Marmor, L., & Upshaw, M.J. Rheumatoid arthritis. In D.D. Peterson (Ed.), *The physically handicapped: a book of readings.* New York: M.S.S. Information Corp., 1969.

Wallace, G., & Kauffman, J.M. *Teaching children with learning problems* (2nd ed.). Columbus, OH: Charles E. Merrill Publishing Co., 1978.

Wallace, G., & Larsen, S.C. *Educational assessment of learning problems: Testing for teaching.* Boston: Allyn & Bacon, Inc., 1978.

Wallen, C.J. Informal testing. In B. Bateman (Ed.), *Learning disorders* (Vol. 4). Seattle: Special Child Publications, 1971.

3 APPLICATION OF DATA ANALYSES

In the first parts of this chapter we describe the general requirements, obligations, and responsibilities for the development of the individualized education program (IEP). The IEP can be a genuine innovation in education because it can serve as the framework for individualized education if it is used as a process instrument. The conditions for this circumstance involve acceptance of a skill model in teaching and particular attention to environmental variables that interact with learning. If programming is based on categorical concepts only, teaching becomes an attempt to remediate unknown or theoretical processes that cannot be clearly defined, that have unknown correlations with academic achievement, and that have no clear indices of improvement. Nonetheless, the ability model is the basis for categories in special education and the structure of diagnostic evaluation. Examiners are required to make some disposition about the handicapping conditions of students, and this invariably relates to test interpretation. Regardless of the many constructs and apparent psychological evidences of deficits and disabilities, the labels applied to children are convenient educational conventions and do not define handicapping conditions in a clinical sense. Only the medical conditions recognized in special education would meet clinical criteria.

Examiners search for some pattern or typical response of students on test performance to diagnose handicapping conditions. Test patterns only demonstrate variance and may suggest unique differences in a global manner. The WISC–R, Stanford-Binet, or any other combination of test instruments cannot diagnose any condition. However, a number of research efforts have been made to find typical test profiles for specific conditions such as learning disabilities, minimal brain damage, delinquency, dyslexia, reading disability, and many other conditions. People are still searching. Although certain group characteristics are suggested, which may be partly explained by the fact that initial selection of subjects for research builds in differences, the diagnosis becomes a matter of making a decision based on broad criteria. Test patterns, although not validated, are frequently applied in data analyses.

Using and interpreting standardized tests in accordance with federal guidelines and professional standards would seem to assure that tests would be used appropriately. There is good evidence that this is not true. In fact, using certain instruments at all would seem to be a clear violation of regulations. Tests that have no norms or that have poor reliability or questionable validity simply should not be used to make important decisions about children; but they are. Not knowing who comprised the norms prevents the examiner from knowing if the test is appropriate for a specific subject who may be different in terms of many variables, such as acculturation, and is not really useful for any subject because it is not possible to know what the comparisons mean. Norms with known characteristics, such as "2,000 middle-class children," might make the instrument just as unsuitable for a particular subject, for example, one who is clearly from a poverty background. The statistical properties of tests, such as poor reliability, will make a test unsuitable for important decisions because of the great amount of error. However, these facts tend to be ignored by many examiners. A test to measure a specific skill, such as perceptual-motor ability, tends to be accepted at face value even though it may have no available norms and validity. Nonetheless, a student may be said to have evidence of minimal brain damage or to be dyslexic because of a low score on such an instrument. Classifying children as mentally retarded is much more serious in our culture because of the social implications. However, any erroneous classification cannot be defended even if it is rather innocuous in our culture. The following conclusion of Edwards (1975) serves to clarify this point:

> Decisions depend upon scores obtained on tests, hopefully along with other forms of information related to the referral problem. The scores of the tests themselves depend upon aspects of examiner procedures as well as the degree of intuition which may or may not be employed. The more subjective the approach taken both in scoring and in interpreting, the more possibility for

instability among examiners and consequent effects upon persons tested. . . . Despite the institution of training programs in major universities and colleges throughout the United States, there continues to be great idiosyncratic behavior in test administration and interpretation. (p. 20)

The test, the examiner, and the interpretation of test results can culminate in greatly different conclusions, depending on which test and which examiner is involved. Add to this the variables of which students are involved, prevailing philosophies or regulations in a district, and a number of less evident variables and it becomes clear why wide differences may exist. The following discussion focuses on IEP development as more than a testing program.

THE IEP PROCESS

Services for handicapped students are generally described and defined in P.L. 94-142. This law requires that all handicapped students shall have a free and appropriate public education, includes specific procedures to be followed in assessment, specifies due process procedures protecting the student's rights, and includes other major aspects of services. The most significant component of the act is the requirement of a written IEP for each student who receives special education.

Abeson and Weintraub (1977) describe in detail the meaning of the term *individualized education program:*

> *Individualized* means that the program must be addressed to the educational needs of a single child rather than a class or group of children. *Education* means that the program is limited to those elements of the child's education that are specifically special education and related services as defined by the act. *Program* means that the individualized education program is a statement of what will actually be provided to the child, as distinct from a plan that provides guidelines from which a program must subsequently be developed. (p. 5)

While the individualized education program may represent the ideals or goals of education for all students (Pasanella & Volkmor, 1977), it also represents a demand for a level of teaching excellence by local districts that, in many cases, exceeds the ability of the school to deliver. The simplicity of the concept of an IEP belies the major changes it implies in public education, for example:

1. Development of an IEP requires that new skills be added to the professional repertoire of teachers (Cartwright & Cartwright, 1972; Mann, 1974).
2. Increased cooperative interaction among all sectors of the school system must be established (Abeson & Weintraub, 1977).
3. A continuum of programs and services, some of which were not previously available, must be provided by individual districts or by groups of districts involved in cooperative planning (Beery, 1972).

Preservice and in-service training programs have addressed the teaching skills required, such as writing behavioral objectives, conducting informal assessment, collecting observational data, and altering instructional patterns; however, such changes take time to impact the field as required by law. Orchestrating the interactions of the various components of school programming, such as physical education, content-area classes, speech therapy, and special education, has often proved to be a difficult task for teachers or administrators to accomplish. Unfamiliarity with other areas of the profession and lack of understanding about the cooperative relationships required by the IEP have been major barriers to comprehensive programming. Finally, the addition of a full range of services has been slowed by budget constraints, administrative resistance, and lack of interdisciplinary cooperation; however, these problems are gradually being overcome as the IEP becomes an accepted part of education.

Although many teachers may treat the IEP as a single event that is finalized once a form is completed, this is far from the intent. Development of an IEP should encompass a vast range of activities that are undertaken by several professionals and that culminate in the provision of comprehensive services to a handicapped student. Although the

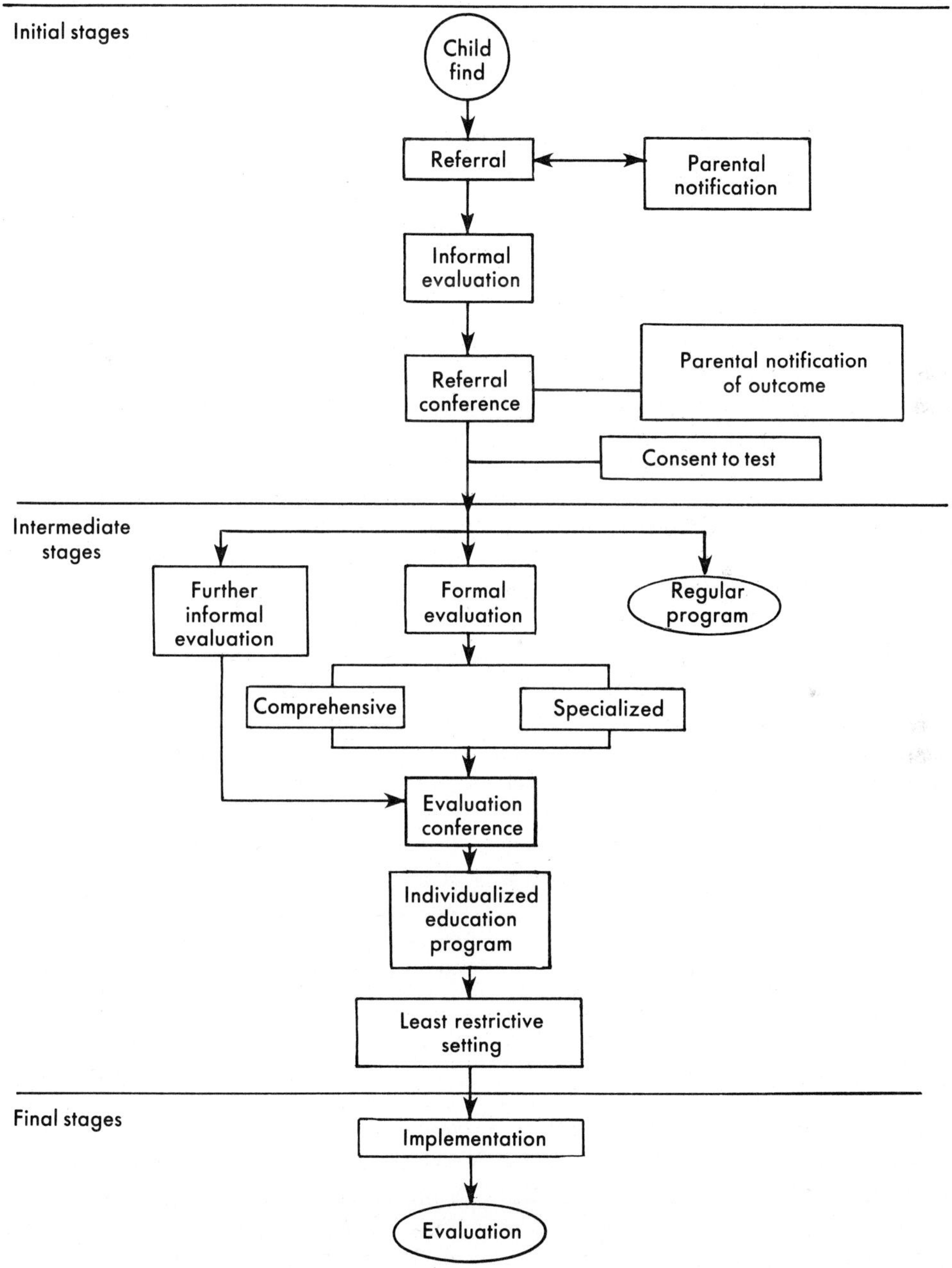

Fig. 3-1. Stages and events in the development of an IEP as required by P.L. 94-142.

IEP may actually be finalized in written form at a single meeting, preparations for this activity begin with screening and child-find procedures that were initiated much earlier. Understanding the IEP's purposes and role in education requires knowledge of the total placement procedure (Fig. 3-1). An understanding of the sequence of events enables the special educator to accomplish the activities required to properly execute the IEP itself, as well as provide the best educational practices.

INITIAL STAGES

Child find

P.L. 94-142 specifically requires school districts to assume responsibility for locating students who may be eligible for services under state and federal laws. Included in the child-find activities is a school screening program, which is designed to identify children who have problems that may interfere with their school performance and success. The child-find activities consist of the following elements:

1. *Screening programs* typically include various achievement tests and other group measures, as well as questionnaires distributed to teachers that ask them to identify students exhibiting certain types of behaviors and/or problems. Formal and informal screening must be conducted when the children enter the district in either kindergarten or first grade.
2. *Public awareness* campaigns are designed to inform the community about the availability of educational services for handicapped children. Additional public information concerning the rights of handicapped children and their families is provided to encourage parents to seek assistance for their children.
3. *Surveys* are often distributed to community leaders, health specialists, and other groups in an effort to reach previously unserved or poorly served children.
4. *Cooperation* with other agencies, such as welfare agencies and human services groups, can aid the school in child-find activities.
5. *Interaction* with the regular teaching faculty is one of the most valuable means for locating high-risk children. As in-service efforts continue and knowledge of special education services grows, regular classroom teachers will become better informed about the type of student eligible for services. Cooperation and understanding between the regular and special educators will reduce inappropriate referrals as well as failure to refer students who are in need of assistance.

Referral

The completion of the required referral form is typically considered the first step of the referral process. Referral actually begins when the initiating party suspects that a child is having a problem of such magnitude that it is interfering with achievement or adjustment. The total referral process (Fig. 3-2) proceeds from recognition of a *potential* problem to validation of the referral problem.

Initiation. Referral can be initiated by parents, teachers, administrators, or other parties. However, the typical referral agent is the regular classroom teacher. This discussion will focus on the teacher's role and responsibilities in referral.

As indicated in Fig. 3-2 the first phase of the referral process is the confirmation of a concern that the child is not achieving, adjusting, or functioning at a level commensurate with the perceived potential. The teacher may proceed to *explore* the area of concern through various activities such as the following:

1. Examination of school records for information relevant to the concern
2. Scrutiny of daily work to more precisely define the problem
3. Reduction of the complexity of the instructional task to measure entry-level skills
4. Experimentation with alternative materials for teaching the same skill

The exploratory actions and the resulting information aid the teacher in two ways: (1) to more precisely define the initial concern, and (2) to elucidate the nature of the behavior precipitating the

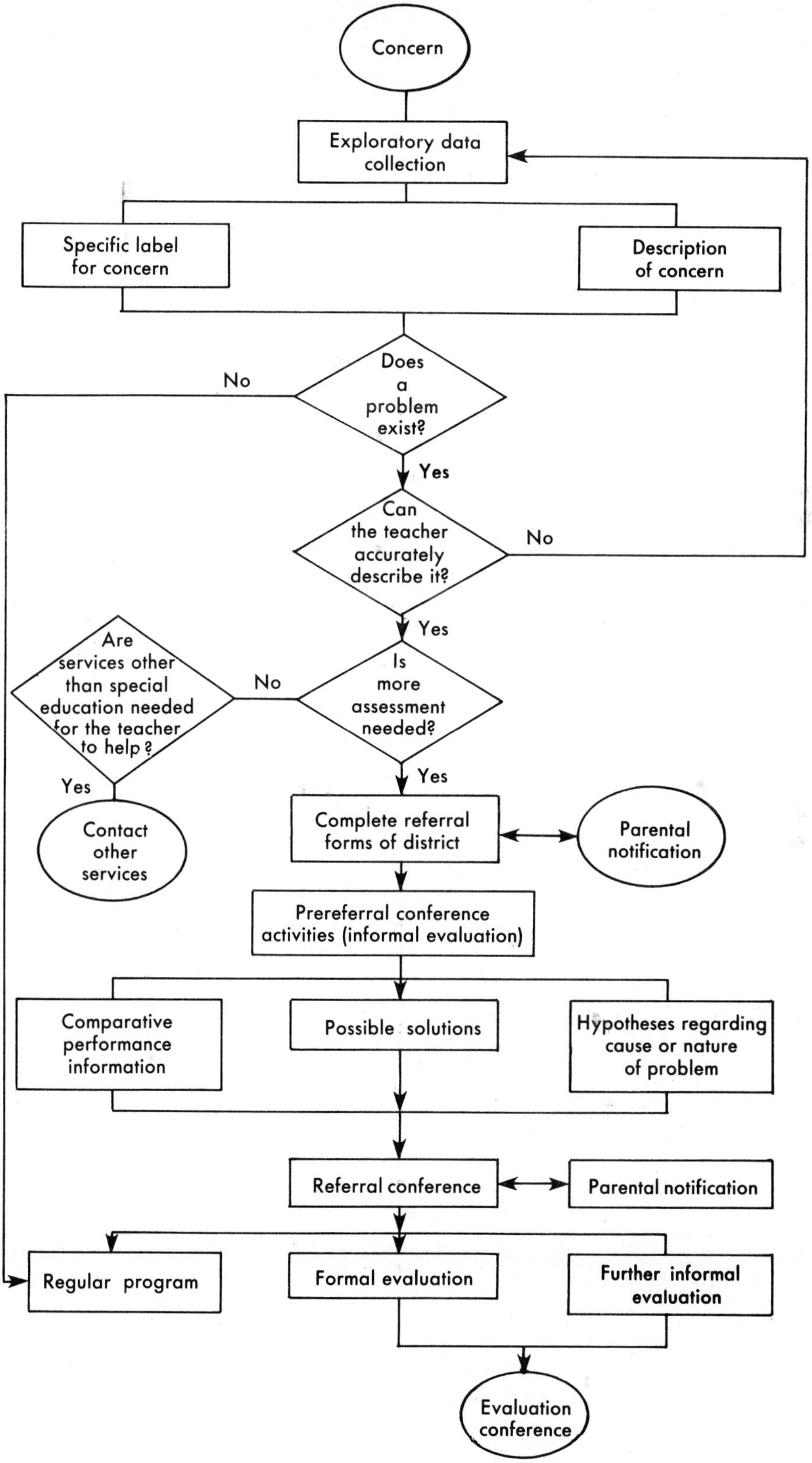

Fig. 3-2. Events comprising the total referral process.

Table 3-1. Case examples of exploratory data collection conducted by regular classroom teachers before actual referral

Case	*Action by teacher*	*Resulting information*
Jake: This third-grade student is not doing well in any of his subjects, thus attracting the attention of his teacher.	Checks school records Talks to previous teachers	Jake was at or above the achievement level for his class, K-2.
	Carefully looks at daily work, examining missed items rather than overall scores Observes work habits	Jake fails to complete most work assignments and appears to have large blocks of time during which he is not working at all.
	Gives him easier work sheets during seatwork period	Jake's performance fails to improve; he still completes only a portion of the work, which, although correct, is well behind his class in terms of rate of production.
	Moves him nearer to teacher's desk and away from peers considered potentially distracting	His performance does not change; long periods are still spent in total inaction.
Marilyn: This fourth-grade student is a severe behavior problem.	Checks school records Talks with previous teachers	Marilyn had trouble with all her previous teachers. The records indicate that her parents have been involved in a number of conferences concerning her aggressive behavior on the school bus.
	Observes her and keeps notes concerning her disruptive behavior	Anecdotal notes seem to reveal that she engages in an inordinate number of physical interactions with her peers.
	Alters daily seatwork assignments for her and puts her in a lower-level reading group	Physically aggressive behaviors continue at an accelerated rate.

teacher's concern. Examples of exploratory efforts in a classroom are shown in Table 3-1. In the case of Jake, the exploratory actions allowed the teacher to move from a general concern ("He isn't doing well") to a more specific identification ("He isn't completing his work, although he should have the required skills to do so"). In the case of Marilyn, the teacher conducted exploratory activities that resulted in moving from a general description, "severe behavior problems," to a more specific description, "peer-directed, aggressive behavior."

As the cases of Jake and Marilyn demonstrate, the primary outcome of such investigations is to provide information to aid the teacher in determining whether the child has a problem and, if so, to assist the teacher in describing the problem in concrete terms. It is necessary that the teacher be specific about the problem to determine whether a referral is the appropriate action to be taken (Fig. 3-3).

Unfortunately many teachers are unaware of the problem-solving potential of such exploration and experimentation. As a result, a teacher's vague concern about a child's condition is presented as a problem to the referral committee with the unrealistic expectation that completion of the referral form will culminate in a solution provided by

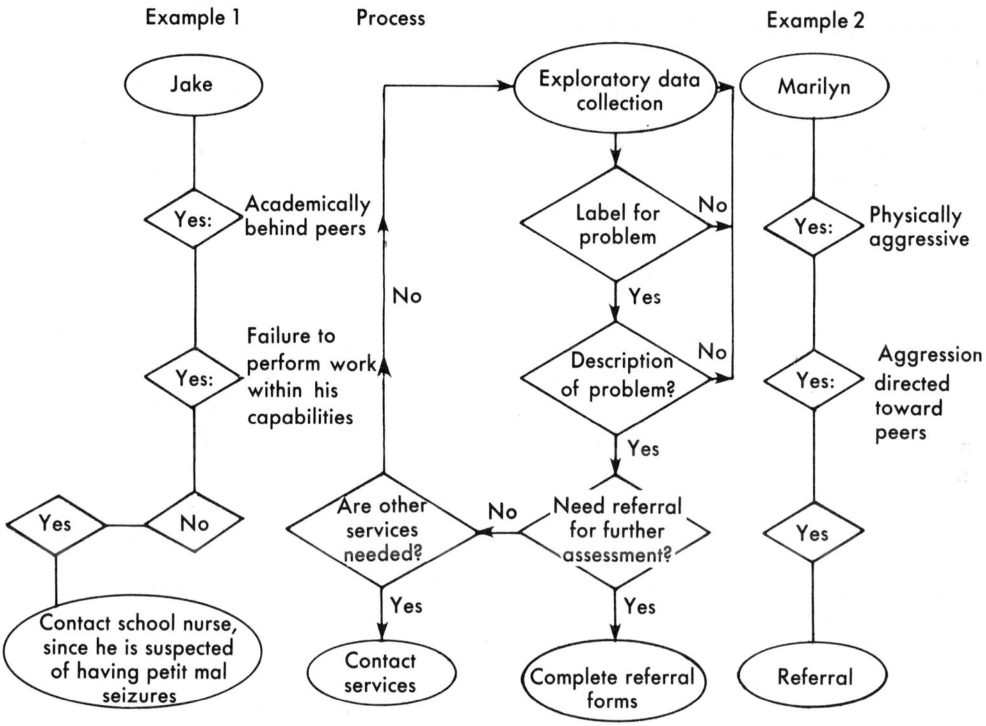

Fig. 3-3. Two examples using the decision-making process in problem identification.

others. Unless the teacher, as the initiating party, has completed the investigative activities needed to properly define this concern as a problem appropriate for referral, the effectiveness of the referral procedure is greatly reduced. Poorly conceived referrals may prove extremely unsatisfactory for teachers because the outcome may be equally nebulous. An additional difficulty fostered by premature referrals is that the referral process itself may be unnecessarily lengthened as specialists attempt to clearly state the problem, a factor which is often irritating to classroom teachers. Classroom teachers must elucidate the concerns that attract their attention to a particular child. Studies concerning the use of referral forms indicate that some common difficulties are encountered in teacher-initiated referrals:

1. Lack of specific terms for describing the behavior
2. Lack of understanding about the purpose of referral
3. Unrealistic expectations about the benefits to be gained from testing

Teachers appear to complete the forms in such a fashion as to communicate only the general fact that the student is not "doing well." The precise nature of the behavior should be identified.

Common reasons. Based on our examination of several forms, the following is a list of reasons commonly cited by teachers on referral forms explaining why a child presents a concern:

1. Inability to complete classwork
2. Difficulty getting along with peers
3. Poor reading performance
4. Short attention span
5. Level of learning far below grade level

Referral forms. The referral form may represent the first communication between special education personnel and the regular teacher that concerns a particular student (Pasanella & Volkmor, 1977). As indicated earlier, teacher effort should have been expended before completing the referral form. Ideally the regular teacher would informally discuss the child with the special educator, perhaps to seek suggestions for further investigative efforts. In reality it is often difficult for the two educators to find time for such discussions, and, therefore, the referral is the first contact between the two.

Forms should be as concise as possible to reduce the amount of time required to complete them and yet useful enough to convey the essential information about the student. A few basic components should be in the referral form; Hammill and Weiderholt (1972) suggest the following:

1. Level of performance in basic skills
2. Classroom behavior
3. Ability to benefit from group instruction

Most districts have some type of referral forms available, but in-service training in completing the form proves beneficial. The special educator may be expected to provide training and assistance to the regular faculty in completing the referral forms, thereby ensuring that the information is specifically stated to facilitate the referral process (Marsh & Price, 1980). Sample referral forms (Figs. 3-4 and 3-5) illustrate the commonalities and the differences that exist among referral forms used by different districts.

Referral conference

Once initial exploratory actions have been taken and the referral form completed, in cases in which it is deemed appropriate to process a referral, the next step is the referral conference. The purpose of the referral conference is to bring together professionals previously or currently involved with the referred student in order that all available information might be aggregated and considered. Ideally the referral conference provides the forum for collective decision making concerning the student and the future actions to be taken to assist the student.

Referral committee or team. The composition of the referral committee may vary somewhat, depending on state guidelines and/or the district's perception of the purpose of the conference. A typical team might consist of the following persons:

Building principal or designee
Special education supervisor or administrator
Special education teacher
Referring teacher
Parents
Child (if appropriate)

Additional professionals who attend might include any other teachers or professionals involved in services or with relevant information about the child. Guidelines include the requirement that a minimum number of persons (three) attend the conference. This assures the intent and integrity of the referral conference. The purpose of the referral conference would be greatly limited if it were reduced to simply a meeting between the special education teacher and the principal or other professional.

Responsibilities of team members. A *chairperson* assumes responsibility for arranging the meeting, including location, time, and parental notification. The chairperson also assumes responsibility for orchestrating the meeting so that all parties have ample opportunity to participate. The following suggestions for the chairperson might facilitate the meeting:

1. Notify everyone in writing well in advance of the meeting. (More will be said later on documentation and parental involvement.) The notices should include the following:
   a. Beginning and ending time of the meeting
   b. Exact location
   c. Purpose of the meeting
   d. Instructions (e.g., "Bring relevant materials")
   e. List of participants
2. Maintain a record of the events of the meeting including the following:
   a. List of participants
   b. Summary of information presented by each participant

Student referral

Student's name: ________ Parent/guardian: ________

Address: ________ Phone no.: ________

Birthdate: ________ Date of referral: ________ Grade: ________

Teacher: ________ School: ________

- -

Reason for referral:

Social adjustment in classroom:

Areas of strength:

Description of academic performance:

Materials being used in academic areas:

Comments on general health-related conditions:

Other comments:

Fig. 3-4. Student referral form sample 1.

Student Referral

Date:______________________ School:______________________

Student:______________________ Address:______________________

Age:____ Birthdate:________ Parent/guardian:____________ Phone no.:_____

Grade:________ Room:________ Teacher:______________________

Recent test scores:

Name of test	Date given	Primary results

Specific area of academic weakness:

Subject	Description of problem

Remedial assistance and approaches tried:

Check the space beside the statements that best describe the student:

Adjustment

___ poised ___ tense ___ moody ___ lazy ___ at ease ___ anxious

___ hostile ___ shy ___ depressed ___ sensitive ___ excitable ___ easily upset

___ cries often ___ unhappy ___ cheerful ___ cooperative ___ needs frequent reassurance

Responsiveness

___ alert ___ hyperactive ___ indecisive ___ deliberate

___ prompt ___ impulsive ___ withdrawn ___ daydreams

___ industrious ___ confused ___ hesitant ___ irrelevant or bizarre responses

Teacher opinions and behavior observations (please comment on the student's personality and general adjustment as you know him or her):______________________

____

____

Fig. 3-5. Student referral form sample 2. (Adapted from *The resource room: an access to excellence*. South Carolina Region V, Educational Services Center, 1975, pp. 167-169.)

Relations with others:

___outgoing, good natured ___friendly ___tolerant ___jealous ___tactful

___independent ___patient ___has many friends ___seeks attention

___has few friends ___enjoys group activities ___plays alone

___conscientious ___very peer conforming

Effort and application:

___careful ___careless ___distractible

___spontaneous ___creative ___readily fatigued

___gives up easily ___works at fast pace ___works at slow pace

Self-criticism:

___extremely critical of self ___boastful ___downplays own inadequacies

___healthy recognition of own mistakes ___does not seem bothered by poor effort

Attention:

___listens carefully ___inattentive to most instructions

___seems to understand most instructions ___waits until instructions are complete

___begins to work impulsively without listening to instructions

Perseverance:

___works constructively on long tasks ___easily distracted after short periods

___does not complete many tasks ___distracted only by unusual events

Motivation:

___eager ___resistant, sullen ___guarded, suspicious

___indifferent ___apathetic ___excessive concern with results

Verbalization:

___talkative ___expresses self well ___difficulty in expression

Self-concept:

___seems self-centered ___forceful ___submissive

___seems self-confident ___lacks self-confidence

How do you see this child?____

____

Signature of referral party: ___________________________

Fig. 3-5, cont'd. Student referral form sample 2.

c. List of concerns or questions
d. List of additional actions recommended by the group
3. Introduce all team members, identifying their positions.
4. Summarize all information leading to the current meeting.
5. Retain leadership of the meeting so that team members present only relevant information, thereby avoiding the tendency for the meeting to become counterproductive and lengthy.
6. Terminate the meeting when closure has been reached by the team.

Additional responsibilities of the chairperson include seeing that all procedural safeguards are followed, the required forms completed, and the desired outcome achieved.

The *special educator* participates in the referral conference to provide information concerning service alternatives and possible assessment strategies. The *referring teacher* should play a central role in the referral conference because he or she has, at this point, the greatest amount of information concerning the student's school performance. Many identifying characteristics of handicapped children are associated with performance within the school setting, making teachers perhaps the first to recognize various potential problems. The role of the referring teacher is to accurately and objectively specify the nature of the problem. The following activities can aid the teacher in performing that function more professionally:

1. Clearly stating the exact nature of the problem rather than simply saying the student "is not doing well"
2. Examining any test data available on the student to see if the problem observed has already been investigated through other means
3. Setting up specific situations in the classroom to probe the perceived difficulty
4. Asking a specialist to observe these staged situations and other examples of student behavior, as well as having available professionals review the situation
5. Reviewing school records to see if a situational explanation may be given to the problem, such as a medical problem or change in family structure
6. Generating various hypotheses about the nature and cause of the difficulty, and considering causes within the behavioral context of the regular classroom

Parental responsibilities in the referral conference include the following:

1. Providing information about their perception of the problem
2. Providing information concerning the student's behavior at home, as it is related to the problem at school
3. Learning about educational objectives and services
4. Asking any questions in order to gain a comprehensive understanding of the problem
5. Participating in the decision-making process

Responsibilities of other professionals. Other professionals attending the conference will vary somewhat depending on their particular discipline and reason for attending. Generally their responsibilities are as follows:

1. Providing any relevant information concerning the student
2. Providing pertinent information concerning a particular intervention, strategy, or environment being considered
3. Suggesting assessment strategies appropriate to the identified problem in the event that additional investigation is needed
4. Fulfill any legal requirements specified for members of the team, such as signing the appropriate forms

Student participation. If the student participates, no formal or informal data should be gathered from the student during the conference. Information secured from the student might include personal interests, opinions concerning the problem, and possible solutions considered viable. The major responsibility of the student is to participate in the decision-making process of the team.

Text continued on p. 89.

Referral conference decision

I.D. no.: ____________________

Referral conference outcome

Student: ____________________

Birthdate: ____________________ CA ____________________

School: ____________________ District ____________________

Referral conference: Date ____________ Location ____________________

Attendees: ____

____

Referral conference decision:

Programming or review recommendations:

Professional(s) designated responsible: ____________________
(Date)

Signature of principal designee: ____________________
(Date)

Fig. 3-6. Sample referral conference decision form.

Parental notification of referral conference decision

Date:________________________

Dear ____________________:

The possibility of special education services for your child, ____________

__________________________, was discussed at a referral conference on

__________________________.

The following decision was reached:

This decision was based on:

____________________ has been designated as responsible for seeing that the referral conference decision is carried out. Please contact this person if you have any questions or concerns. The telephone number is __________.

You have the right to a hearing if you disagree with this decision, and you have the right to review all relevant records maintained on your child. However, if you feel that different or additional services may be appropriate, or if you wish to bring further information about your child to us, please contact

_________________.

Sincerely,

____
(Principal)

____
(School)

Fig. 3-7. Sample parental notification form (referral conference decision).

Parental notification of referral

Date: ____________________

Dear ____________________:

Your child, ____________________, has been referred as possibly being able to benefit from special services. Such special services would provide extra assistance to help your child learn.

We are holding a referral conference to discuss the educational needs of your child. We would like you to be there so that you can provide us with information about your child and also learn more about our services.

We have scheduled a referral conference on ____________________
(Date)

at ____________________ in ____________________
(Time) (Room)

of ____________________.
(Building)

Since we are required to see that children are best served as soon as possible, we will need to go ahead with the referral conference by ____________________ if we do not hear from you.

Please feel free to contant ____________________ if you have any questions. The phone number is ____________________.

We are looking forward to hearing from you.

Sincerely, ____________________

____
(Principal)

____
(School)

Fig. 3-8. Sample parental notification of referral form.

INFORMED CONSENT—RELEASE OF RECORDS

Student: ______________________________ Birthdate: ______________

Address: ______________________________ School: ______________

(Mark one or more boxes.) Authorization is hereby granted to ______________ for:
(Name of district)

1. ☐ Conducting a formal evaluation of my child:

____
(Purpose of evaluation)

____
(Agency or person approved for conducting evaluation procedures)

2. ☐ Releasing the following information to a third party:

____
(Description of information)

____
(Name of third party)

____
(Address)

____
(City, state, zip code)

____
(Purpose)

3. ☐ Using the following information for other purposes:

____
(Description of information)

____
(Purpose)

I have read and I understand "Information for Parents or Guardians" on the first page of this form. I understand the purpose(s) for which my consent is being requested.

Signature of parent: ______________________________
(Date)

Fig. 3-9. Sample informed consent–release of records form.

Tasks

Several responsibilities must be assumed by the referral committee, all of which center around making a decision concerning the problem of the student and future actions that should be taken. These tasks include the following:

1. Validating the existence of a problem that is interfering with the student's school performance
2. Precisely identifying the nature of the problem
3. Aggregating all relevant data
4. Identifying all areas requiring additional examination or in-depth assessment
5. Identifying further actions to be taken

Outcomes of referral

There are three possible outcomes of the referral conference:

1. *Further informal assessment.* The school personnel would conduct further evaluation to obtain more information about the problem. Following this extended data collection procedure, an evaluation conference would be held to make decisions about whether to provide services.

2. *Formal evaluation.* A comprehensive assessment would be conducted by special assessment personnel. When all additional data have been collected, an evaluation conference would be held to determine further actions and services.

3. *No evaluation or services required.* The student may return to the regular class to receive other types of assistance, or the teacher may receive additional support from administrative staff in dealing with a problem that is outside the domain of special education.

An additional task of the committee is to provide a detailed explanation of the decision of the referral committee (Fig. 3-6) and complete the referral conference decision form (Fig. 3-7). If the team elects to employ further evaluation, the student may be placed in a temporary setting, one agreed on by the team and parents. A time period (60 days) is set at the time of the referral conference, thus establishing a deadline by which the required evaluation must be completed. Any additional planning associated with future actions should be done in the meeting and reported. Formal notification to the parents and team members must be provided by the team chairperson.

Parental involvement and notification. The law very specifically states that parents, parental surrogates, or guardians are to participate in the decision-making process. This participation must be documented carefully to ensure that rights are not violated. The parents must be notified of the referral and the scheduled time of the referral conference (Fig. 3-8). It is imperative that the time of the conference be scheduled to accommodate the parents.

If the decision made by the team at the referral conference is to seek formal evaluation data, the parents must complete the informed consent form (Fig. 3-9) for the release of student records and parental consent to the evaluation. This form is required by federal and state law before further assessment can be conducted. Parents must also be officially notified of the outcome of the referral conference (Fig. 3-7).

INTERMEDIATE STAGES

Evaluation

Evaluation is the next phase of the investigative process delineated in P.L. 94-142. In this context, according to the *Federal Register* (1977), evaluation is a term that describes the procedures used to ascertain

> whether a child is handicapped and the nature and extent of the special education and related services the child needs. The term means procedures used selectively with an individual child and does not include basic tests administered to or procedures used with all children in a school, grade, or class. (p. 42494)

The purpose of evaluation is to examine the various aspects of the child's performance to document the existence of a handicapping condition. Evaluation must be conducted before placing or denying placement to a student in a special education program. The evaluation precedes the student's transfer or denial of transfer from a special class into a regular class.

Procedural safeguards. Before evaluation, as indicated in the referral stage, the parents must document consent for testing in order for the child to be evaluated and the resulting information to be shared among the professionals involved in the case. The evaluation itself, according to the *Federal Register* (1977, pp. 42496-42497), must conform to the following guidelines:

1. Tests are provided and administered in the child's native language or by some other mode of communication, unless it is not feasible to do so.
2. Tests have been validated for the specific purpose for which they are used.
3. Tests are administered by trained personnel in conformance with the instructions provided by their producer.
4. Tests and other evaluation materials include those tailored to assess specific areas of educational need and not merely those which are designed to provide a single general IQ.
5. Tests are selected and administered to ensure that when a test is administered to a child with impaired sensory, manual, or speaking skills, the test results accurately reflect the child's aptitude, achievement level, or other factors the test purports to measure rather than only reflecting the child's impaired sensory, manual, or speaking skills (unless these skills are the factors that the test purports to measure).
6. No single procedure is to be used as the sole criterion for determining an appropriate educational program for a child.
7. The evaluation is made by a multidisciplinary team or group of persons, including at least one teacher or other specialist with knowledge in the area of sensory disability.
8. The child is to be assessed in all areas related to the suspected disability, including (if appropriate) health, vision, hearing, motor abilities, social and emotional status, general intelligence, academic performance, and communicative status.

The school is responsible for adhering to these regulations and must develop evaluation policies designed to ensure that all requirements are met; this is typically a responsibility assigned to a special education administrator or other administrative personnel. Special educators should be provided with a copy of the school system's *written policy* concerning the evaluation procedure because they must share some responsibility for seeing that the policies are followed. Classroom teachers may or may not be given a copy of the policy, but it is recommended that such information be provided to regular teachers because, when classroom teachers refer students for evaluation, the teacher is automatically placed in a responsible position for seeing that legal requirements are followed (Turnbull & Schulz, 1979, p. 64). State and local educational agencies must assume responsibility for test selection and administration, making certain that procedures are not racially or culturally discriminatory.

Assessment procedures for specific learning disabilities. For cases in which the suspected condition is specific learning disabilities, *additional* procedures are required, intended to augment the procedure described in the previous section. These additional procedures include the following aspects:

1. *Composition of evaluation team.* The team members include (a) the student's regular teacher, a regular classroom teacher qualified to teach a student of that age and grade if the child does not have a regular teacher, or a teacher qualified to teach kindergarten if the child is preschool age and (b) at least one professional qualified to conduct individual diagnostic examinations of children.

2. *Observation.* The student must be observed in the regular classroom by a team member other than the child's regular teacher. In the case of the preschool child, the observation must be conducted by someone qualified to teach that age group in an environment considered appropriate for a child of that age. The observational data are

to include information relevant to the child's behavioral and academic performance.

3. *Criteria for determining a specific learning disability.* The evaluation team must provide information demonstrating that the child is not achieving at levels commensurate with expectations for his or her age and ability, thus validating the existence of a severe discrepancy between performance and potential. This severe discrepancy must not result from a hearing, visual, or motor handicap; emotional disturbance; mental retardation; or cultural, environmental, or economic disadvantage. The areas examined by the team include written expression, oral expression, listening comprehension, reading skill, mathematical calculations, mathematical reasoning, and reading comprehension.

4. *Written report.* At the conclusion of the evaluation the team must prepare a written report that states whether the child has a specific learning disability, describes the basis on which the determination was made, includes any medical information with implications for educational programming, and describes the behavioral data collected and the relevance of these behavioral data to educational programming. In addition, assurances must be given in the written report that the assignation of the label for a specific learning disability is not the result of cultural, environmental, or economic deprivation and that the problem (discrepancy in performance) cannot be alleviated through services other than special education. All team members disagreeing with the label must submit their dissenting opinion in a written report.

Evaluation procedure. The evaluation procedure results in the assignation of a label and produces relevant information for educational placement. Thus, it is imperative that the assessment be conducted very carefully and thoroughly. Certain general guidelines are provided in Part B of P.L. 94-142 and are as follows:

1. A broad scope of information must be produced from sources such as teacher recommendations and aptitude and achievement tests and should include physical condition, adaptive behavior, and social or cultural background.
2. Information must be documented and interpreted carefully.
3. The evaluation team should include individuals knowledgeable about the child, assessment procedures and interpretation, and placement options.

The components of the evaluation should include all measures necessary for determining, as precisely as possible, the nature of the problem interfering with the child's performance. The minimum components are as follows:

1. *Measures of academic performance.* These include tests and measures that evaluate the level of academic skill attainment or educational achievement of the child. Such measures should result in a specification of the child's academic strengths and weaknesses, indicate specific skill deficit areas, and provide information on which to make recommendations for the child's educational program. All testing should be done by certified school personnel and/or other appropriate professional personnel certified or licensed by the state. Individual achievement tests are included in this area.

2. *Measures of intellectual skills.* Intellectual ability of the child must be measured by an individual intelligence test *appropriate to the child.* Such testing must be done by a certified educational examiner, licensed psychologist, or licensed psychological examiner.

3. *Measures of adaptive behavior and social functioning.* Adaptive behavior refers to the effectiveness with which the child copes with the natural and social demands of his or her environment. Measures include an evaluation of the degree of the child's independent functioning, ability to communicate, perceptual-motor development, and socialization and self-help skills. Behavioral observation techniques, interviews of both the child and others, and adaptive behavior scales are employed. Data should come from several sources.

4. *Language assessment.* This assessment determines the level of receptive and expressive lan-

guage development and the presence of language and auditory disabilities. Such assessments must be conducted by certified school personnel and/or other appropriate professional personnel certified or licensed by the state. If disabilities are indicated, further assessments must be conducted by a licensed or certified speech and hearing therapist.

5. *Child history*. The history should include existing pertinent data such as the child's medical records, reports of previous evaluations, reports from other provider agencies, the cumulative school records, and family information. Contact with the parents should be made to gain data on the child's developmental history and home behavior. Such data should be gathered or coordinated by the professional designated responsible in the referral conference.

6. *Additional components*. Additional components of the comprehensive evaluation should be included as necessary by the team to provide further information useful in educational programming for the child. An additional component may be a licensed physician's evaluation of the child's current health, ophthalmological, audiological, neurological, and psychiatric status.

The precise tests comprising the evaluation procedures are not specified in the law. Instead the selection of tests is the responsibility of qualified examiners unless specified by state or local agencies. Each state has its own plan for meeting the requirements established to guarantee that the student's evaluation is conducted in an appropriate manner. The plans include more specific guidelines for test selection. Typically it consists of a battery of tests from which the team and/or examiner makes selections.

Test selection itself is dependent on the course of action determined in the referral and screening process. The decision of the referral team to pursue either a comprehensive or specialized evaluation is predicated on a data-based hypothesis that a handicapping condition exists and is impeding the child's performance. The committee may suspect that a particular handicapping condition is present and, therefore, will provide some general direction for those involved in the evaluation. Most of the handicapping conditions are indicated by definite characteristics that emerge during the referral process, thus simplifying the evaluation selection somewhat. The most difficult conditions to document appear to be specific learning disabilities and emotional disturbances. Almost all evaluations will include an intelligence test. The continuity between referral and evaluation is highly desirable for the assessment process to be appropriate for the student and time efficient for the evaluation team.

Evaluation conference

Once evaluation activities have been completed, an evaluation conference is held to document whether a handicapping condition exists. The data produced by the evaluation process should be presented and analyzed by the team with careful consideration given to definitions of handicapping conditions as specified by the state agency. The definitions and eligibility criteria serve as the criteria for the team as the team aggregates information to produce a collective decision.

Evaluation committee or team. The team may be determined to some degree by the type of suspected handicap and the type of evaluation conducted. Participation of *specific* professionals with training in areas considered relevant to the condition may be required. For instance, students suspected of having a significant medical problem may require a team that includes a physician or at least has access to transmittal of medical information. The team or committee may include the following:

1. Chairperson
2. Special education personnel
3. Parents
4. Child
5. Child's present teacher or other appropriate trained personnel if child is not in school
6. Personnel who conducted the components of the evaluation
7. Other professionals deemed appropriate

Responsibilities of team members. The *chairperson* plays a vital role in the evaluation conference by insisting that all parties clearly and succinctly present relevant data resulting from the various assessment procedures employed. The chairperson should coordinate the team in analyzing the results of the standardized tests that form the core of the typical evaluation process. In addition, the chairperson should lead the team to view the whole child and the environment in which the child must function in order to produce a comprehensive picture of the child in the classroom. The team can easily focus on standardized test results, thus omitting important information to be gained from those involved with the child on a daily basis. When this happens, interpretations may be distorted.

Although not always involved in the conference, *special educators* can play an important role because they may provide professional information concerning the service alternatives available to handicapped students, unless labeled students are automatically assigned. Once the team has identified and documented the existence of a particular handicapping condition, a placement decision must be made, an action that can be greatly facilitated by the participating special educators.

The participation of *parents* may not be quite as great in the evaluation conference as in the referral conference, since their role in assessment is limited. This can be a stressful meeting for them. They should be welcomed to ask questions of all members present and to interject anecdotal information as they deem it appropriate.

Regular classroom performance should figure in the assessment process, thus making participation by the *regular classroom teacher* important. The regular classroom teacher's responsibilities might include the following:

1. Being able to report achievement information that reveals how the student functions in a group setting with fellow students. This requires reporting objective data, such as scores on any group tests given, daily grades, and specific strengths and weaknesses observed in the classroom. In some cases behavioral data concerning the learning style of the student and other sociometric data may be considered integral to the decision-making process.

2. Bringing samples of the work of the student if it is thought such data will contribute to the knowledge of the decision-making body. For instance, if the student is having particular difficulty with a certain subject or type of academic activity, an example or explanation of the task might help the group.

3. Understanding who the participants in the group are and their roles in the process. This helps the teacher direct the most relevant information to the proper person.

Other professionals who administered various assessment instruments and conducted any type of evaluation activity should participate in the conference to ensure that all data are accurately interpreted within the context of the educational environment and disciplinary viewpoints. Objective presentation of test results and explanations of their educational implications is necessary so that those in attendance who may be unfamiliar with test data will understand the implications.

Tasks. The major tasks that must be accomplished by the team include the following:

1. Examination of assessment data to identify patterns of student performance
2. Documentation of the presence of absence of a handicapping condition
3. Certification of the primary handicapping condition
4. Selection of the least restrictive placement

The two possible outcomes of the evaluation are (1) the decision that the student does not have a handicapping condition requiring special education and (2) the decision that special education is required. The latter outcome necessitates that the team consider the type of services and select the most appropriate educational setting for the student. Larsen and Poplin (1980) state that "evaluation for placement is primarily administrative in orientation and is not necessarily intended to yield

Evaluation conference decision

I.D. no.: ______________________

Evaluation conference outcome

Student: ______________________________________

Birthdate: ________________________ CA ____________________

School: __________________________ District ________________

Evaluation conference: Date ___________ Location ________________

Attendees: ____

Student eligibility for special education is certified by the establishment of the primary handicapping condition, _________________________.

Signature of evaluator: ______________________________________

The above categorical statement is a requirement of Public Law 94-142 if a student is to receive special education services.

This is not a statement of the student's general ability but only involves the narrow area of public education.

This statement will be used only for determination of eligibility for special education services. There will be no further reference to this categorical statement during the delivery of educational services.

This categorical statement will be destroyed as soon as special service delivery is terminated.

Evaluation conference decision:

Programming recommendations:

Professional(s) designated responsible: ___________________________

____

Signatures of attendees: ______________________________________

Fig. 3-10. Sample evaluation conference decision form.

Parental notification of evaluation conference

Date:____________________

Dear ____________________:

Your child, ____________________, has been referred as possibly being able to benefit from special services. Such special services would provide extra assistance to help your child learn. The evaluation that you consented to has been completed.

We are holding an evaluation conference to discuss the educational needs of your child. We would like you to be there so that you can provide us with any additional information about your child and serve as a team member in making appropriate educational decisions concerning your child.

We have scheduled an evaluation conference on ____________________ (Date), at ____________________ (Time) in ____________________ (Room) of ____________________ (Building).

Since we are required to see that children are best served as soon as possible, we will need to go ahead with the evaluation conference by ____________________ if we do not hear from you.

Please feel free to contact ____________________ if you have any questions. The phone number is ____________________.

We are looking forward to hearing from you.

Sincerely,

____
(Principal)

____
(School)

Fig. 3-11. Sample parental notification form (evaluation conference).

Parental notification of evaluation conference decision

Date: ______________________________

Dear ________________________:

An evaluation of the learning needs of your child, ____________________________

____________________, has been conducted to determine whether special education services would be beneficial. The results of the evaluation were reviewed at a conference, and the following decision was reached:

This was based on:

The recommended services for your child include __________________________________

____.

(Type of placement)

The detailed information that was used to arrive at this decision is available for your inspection.

__________________________ has been designated as responsible for seeing that the decision reached as a result of your child's evaluation is carried out. Consent is required for initial placement of your child in a special education program.

You have the right to obtain an independent evaluation of your child. You have the right to a hearing if you disagree with this decision. We feel that the decision made represents the most appropriate educational services for your child at the present time. However, if you feel that other services may be more suitable, or if you wish to provide us with additional information about your child, please contact ________________________.

Sincerely,

____
(Principal)

____
(School)

Fig. 3-12. Sample parental notification form (evaluation conference decision).

instructionally relevant data'' (p. 73). Ideally the evaluation process could lay the foundation for planning daily services rather than just concluding with label and placement decisions. As understanding of the relationship between evaluation and the development of the IEP grows among educators and administrators, it may become apparent that maximum benefit can be derived from the professional time, effort, and expertise committed to student evaluation.

Reporting. The decisions of the evaluation team are reported on an evaluation conference decision form (Fig. 3-10) and signed by all participants. A description of the services selected should be included, and the team should develop long-term goals to be addressed in the IEP.

Parental involvement. The individual who assumes administrative responsibility for seeing that the evaluation is conducted in accordance with procedural safeguards must make sure that the following acts are carried out:

1. Send written notification of the evaluation conference so that the parents may attend (Fig. 3-11).
2. Have the parents participate in the meeting as much as possible and understand the purpose of the conference.
3. Send written notification of the outcome and decisions of the evaluation conference committee to the parents (Fig. 3-12).
4. Have the parental release form completed before initiation of services.

Increased understanding of the evaluation process and active participation by the parents will increase the chances for support of the decision and the recommended services. All efforts should be made to have parents attend and participate, as specified in the regulations. Even telephone communications must be recorded, as well as indications of mailed communications.

Some states have experienced difficulty in getting parents to participate. It must be remembered that meetings can be very stressful for parents, who will be anxious about the problems of their child, confused by the terminology, and uncomfortable in a room filled with a variety of professionals, many of whom may be strangers. Some parents may react by denying that there is a problem, and others may be hostile or defensive. The school personnel should understand the feelings of the parents and attempt to handle each situation with diplomacy.

THE INDIVIDUALIZED EDUCATION PROGRAM

Once an evaluation team has documented the existence of a handicapping condition that requires special education and has selected the least restrictive environment in which services are to be delivered, an IEP must be developed. The IEP must reflect the needs of the student that were indicated in evaluation and provide a guide to a comprehensive education designed to alleviate or circumvent the handicap considered a barrier to the child's efforts to obtain an education. The IEP must also serve as a plan for monitoring the effectiveness of the program. Criteria and deadlines are established for each of the objectives included in the program, and responsibilities for implementation and evaluation are specified at this time. Thus, the format and process of the IEP are crucial in provision of services to the student.

Description of the IEP

The IEP is the heart of P.L. 94-142, but its form and content vary somewhat from one district to another. However, regardless of the form used, the IEP must contain the following elements:

1. Statement of the present levels of educational performance of the student
2. Statement of annual goals, including short-term instructional objectives
3. Statement of the specific educational services to be provided to the student, and the extent to which the student will be able to participate in the regular educational programs
4. Projected date of initiation and duration of services
5. Appropriate objective criteria, evaluation procedures, and schedules for determining, on at least an annual basis, whether instructional objectives are being achieved.

P.L. 94-142 also requires states to provide assurances that handicapped students will be served in the least restrictive environment, one which is integrated with nonhandicapped students to the maximum extent practicable.

The overall procedure leading to the development of the IEP requires an understanding of the components of the written plan for the data collection process to be completed properly. Kaufman, Gottlieb, Agard, and Kubic (1975) call the total procedure the "educational planning and programming process" and define it as "an ongoing cyclical process consisting of two elements—planning and programming." In the six steps they identify in this process, writing the IEP is step four. Kaufman et al. (1975) employ the same concept we wish to promote: that writing the IEP or completing the form requires extensive understanding of the referral process, effective assessment and interpretation of data, and creative instructional approaches. The actual writing of the IEP is the synthesis of all data from collection procedures initiated and conducted by all parties, including the older student. The IEP can be one of the most innovative procedures in education, if it is not handled in a *pro forma* manner.

IEP forms and format (Figs. 3-13 and 3-14). The IEP itself is a written commitment of intent that includes the objectives deemed appropriate, instructional strategies and services, and materials to meet the student's needs. The following discussion presents suggestions for development of each of the required components—current level of functioning, long- and short-term goals, behavioral objectives, educational services, projected dates and duration of services, and evaluation criteria.

Current level of functioning means that the school must conduct assessment for the purpose of describing the current level of functioning exhibited by the student. This is done for several reasons, including (1) to clearly state the nature of the present performance and clarify the exact nature of the problem, (2) to accurately describe the present performance level to aid the team in properly selecting placement for the student, (3) to comprehensively examine the present overall functioning of the student to ensure that the student's condition will be viewed as a whole rather than in a fragmented manner, and (4) to establish standards against which the objectives are designed to meet the evaluation criteria.

Typically an assessment of current level of functioning includes both formal and informal assessment approaches as well as the collection of observational and behavioral data. Data collection may be completed by classroom teachers, special educators, administrators, and other professionals involved in services for handicapped students. The exact areas examined are identified through the referral process, and the specific assessment approaches used are the decision of the various professionals following the guidelines of the particular state plan. Examination of IEPs reveal that this component frequently contains grade-level equivalency or other such scores on various tests. In the case of IEPs for students with behavioral disorders, the description of current level of functioning may be stated in forms such as percentage of time the student demonstrates a targeted behavior. Two examples of statements are as follows:

1. Meredith demonstrated resistant, nonconforming behavior 35 percent of the time sampled during a teacher-directed activity conducted by a reliable rater (.85 or above interrater reliability) using an observational instrument (e.g., CASES).
2. Kama exhibited aggressive behavior 8 percent of the time during a behavioral sample conducted by a reliable rater using an observational instrument in accordance with instrument guidelines.

The current level of functioning must be stated in terms that allow specific description and comparison, such as scores, percentages, and grade-level equivalency; assessment incorporates information gained from standardized tests, criterion-referenced tests, and various other instruments, which were described in Chapter 2.

Long-term goals are specifically required in

Text continued on p. 105.

INDIVIDUALIZED EDUCATION PROGRAM SAMPLE # 1

Student's name or I.D. no.: 103 P School: Haven Elementary School

Principal: Larry May Date plan was developed: 10/15/80

Description of student's participation in regular educational program (do not include lunch or recess): Student will participate in regular class for 3 hours per day for instruction in science, social studies, and math.

Special education services provided: Student will participate in a special education resource room 3 hours per day.

Long-range goals:

Description of present level of functioning: The student demonstrates performance in basic word attack skills that is at least 2 years below grade expectancy, as measured by the WRAT and informal reading inventories administered by the teacher.

Objective: The student will read orally from a third-grade basal reader with a minimum of 50 words per minute with no more than three errors.

Date initiated: 10/18/80 Date completed:

Short-range goals:

1. The student will decode the words of CVC (consonant-short vowel-consonant) pattern, as measured by a teacher-made inventory, with 90% accuracy.

   Date initiated: 10/18/80 Date completed:

2. The student will demonstrate the ability to decode the following sound patterns with the indicated criteria, using a language chart approach:

   Consonants (35 per minute)

   Consonants and digraphs (35 per minute)

   Consonant blends (35 per minute)

   Consonants and vowels (35 per minute)

   Vowels (long and short) (35 per minute)

   Total number of errors allowable: 2

   Date initiated: Date completed:

Continued.

Fig. 3-13. IEP sample 1.

3. The student will read a language chart story, prepared by the teacher and comprised of at least four words from each CVC pattern, with 100% accuracy on the pattern words.

   Date initiated: Date completed:

4. The student will decode the pattern words found in a teacher-selected sample from a second-grade reader with 90% accuracy.

   Date initiated: Date completed:

Long-range goals:

Description of present level of functioning: The student demonstrates reading comprehension 1.5 years below grade expectancy, as measured by informal reading inventories administered by the teacher.

Objective: The student will demonstrate improved comprehension skills by scoring 90% or above on a Distar Mastery Test.

Date initiated: 10/18/80 Date completed:

Short-range goals:

1. The student will answer comprehension questions concerning teacher-designed paragraphs that focus on major aspects of the content, such as characters and actions, with 90% accuracy.

   Date initiated: Date completed:

2. The student will complete short-answer worksheets, prepared by the teacher and covering teacher-designed paragraphs with 90% accuracy.

   Date initiated: Date completed:

3. The student will complete the activities and stories of Distar II with 100% accuracy.

   Date initiated: Date completed:

Fig. 3-13, cont'd. IEP sample 1.

Least restrictive setting:

1. Circle the placement (service setting) that is least restrictive for this child based on data obtained during his/her evaluation and on components of this plan:
   a. Regular class—indirect services
   b. Regular class—direct services
   c. Regular class—maximum three periods per day in resource room
   d. Some instruction in regular class—minimum ½ day in self-contained room
   e. No instruction in regular class—self-contained class
   f. No instruction in regular class—special day service facility
   g. Residential school facility
   h. Hospital program
   i. Homebound instruction
2. Describe nonacademic services in which the child is participating:
   Physical education, art, music, and intramural sports.

Parental participation:

Describe the involvement of the parents in the development of this plan:

The student's mother participated in a 45-minute IEP conference and made the following suggestions for her own involvement with the IEP: (1) participating in sports program, and (2) attending a class taught by a male teacher.

Signatures:

Agreement to and acceptance of this individualized education program is so indicated by the signature of the persons involved in the development of this plan:

____________ (Principal or designee)	____________ (Evaluation personnel)
____________ (Special education supervisor)	____________ (Parent)
____________ (Regular class teacher)	____________ (Counselor)
____________ (Special educator)	____________ (Other)

Fig. 3-13, cont'd. IEP sample 1.

INDIVIDUALIZED EDUCATION PROGRAM sample #2

Student's name or I.D. no.: 102 A School: ________

Date plan is developed: ________ Assigned classroom: ________

Long-range goals:

Summary of present levels of performance: The student exhibited aggressive behavior 11% of the time during a behavior sample conducted by a reliable rater (0.85% interrater reliability), using an observational instrument in accordance with instrument guidelines.

Objective: The student will demonstrate aggressive behavior 4% or less of the time as measured with an observational sample taken by a rater, with 0.85% or higher interrater reliability, during a teacher-directed activity that uses a valid observational instrument (e.g., the Coping Analysis Schedule for Educational Settings).

Short-range goals	Person responsible	Beginning date	Ending date
1. The student will demonstrate noncontact behavior in the special class for periods of 5 or more minutes consistently for at least three periods per day for 5 days.	Special teacher		
2. The student will demonstrate noncontact behavior in the special class when placed in a group with two other students under teacher supervision for three or more 5-minute periods per day for at least 5 days.	Special teacher		

Fig. 3-14. IEP sample 2.

3. The student will demonstrate aggressive behavior in a highly structured regular classroom situation 6% or less of the time as measured by a reliable rater using the Coping Analysis Schedule for Educational Settings.	Special educator
4. The student will demonstrate nonaggressive behavior in the regular classroom during a controlled lecture setting for at least a 15-minute period per day for 5 days.	Special educator and regular teacher

Percentages of time:

Regular classroom: 16%   Special classroom: 84%

Specific procedures, techniques, materials, and motivational factors:

1. Use the treatment plan for style A (aggressive behavior) of the Coping Analysis Schedule for Educational Settings.
2. Establish a reinforcement program for noncontact behavior, using tangible rewards.
3. Use programmed workbooks on the grade level. These workbooks are both well-liked by the student and compatible with the rewards system.
4. Provide frequent and immediate feedback on appropriate behavioral events.
5. Begin intervention in a 1:1 arrangement, gradually increasing the ratio to include two peers in the highly structured environment of a resource room.
6. Continue to include academic material being taught in the grade-level class so that the student can return to that placement more often as behavioral adjustment is accomplished.

Continued.

Fig. 3-14, cont'd. IEP sample 2.

Least restrictive setting: Student is to be placed solely in a resource room for the first phase of intervention. When short-range goal #2 is achieved, the student is to be integrated into the regular classroom for one period (16% of the day) under special teacher supervision. Participation in the regular class can be gradually increased as nonaggressive behavior is exhibited.

The student will participate in extracurricular activities with the special education program until nonaggressive behavior is consistently demonstrated in structured situations; integration into nonstructured situations is gradually accomplished until total participation with peers is exhibited.

Parental involvement in IEP development: The student's mother and father attended the conference of 1 hour and 5 minutes. They specifically requested that the student not be allowed to interact with peers until such time as physically aggressive conduct reached the desired level. They stated a desire to continue the rewards program at home to reduce some of their own difficulties with the student. They specifically requested that the student not be placed with Ms. Thomas in the future.

Signatures:

Agreement to and acceptance of this individualized educational program is indicated by the signatures of the persons involved in its development:

(Principal or team leader)	(Parents)
(Regular class teacher)	(Special education teacher)
(Special education supervisor)	(Support personnel)
(Evaluation personnel)	(Other)

Fig. 3-14, cont'd. IEP sample 2.

legislation and represent a major component of the IEP. The determination of long-term goals is obviously central to the provision of appropriate education for handicapped students. These goals must not be developed in terms of a single class or group, but rather they must be developed for the individual student, based on his or her unique needs. The National Association of State Directors of Special Education (1976, p. 30) suggests that the following crucial areas be considered in developing long-term goals:

1. What concerns have priority with the parents?
2. What concerns have priority with the teacher?
3. What are the appropriate developmental sequences of skills or behaviors that the child would be expected to progress through?
4. What are the behaviors that appear to be the most modifiable as determined from baseline assessment data, which includes the child's strengths, weaknesses, and learning style?
5. Are any other crucial considerations needed to select areas of educational need, such as any problem areas that are truly dangerous for the child or injurious to his or her health or others?

The decision about which areas will be addressed in the long-term goals is probably one of the most complex issues encountered by the placement group, yet it is the area receiving the least attention from professional writers. At best, discussions of the long-term goals consist of lists of possible areas for programming, such as basic skills, body coordination, health and hygiene, self-concept, community adjustment, and vocational and career development (Pasanella & Volkmor, 1977), or the suggestion that the curricular areas of the school program be used, such as reading, arithmetic, perceptual-motor activities, and language arts (Hayes, 1977).

One of the most common errors found by monitoring teams seems to be an overdependence on academic areas as content for the long-term goals. In cases in which the primary handicapping condition is emotional disturbance, it would be expected that at least the first long-term goal would address some behavioral aspect of the student's performance rather than academic progress. Other correlates of poor academic performance that might be addressed in the long-term goals include (1) failure to complete assignments, (2) extreme peer dependency, (3) out-of-seat behavior, and (4) aggressive behavior.

If areas such as those listed previously in the discussion of the assessment of current level of functioning are to be included, they should be carefully scrutinized, and present levels described in the IEP. Thus, if the special educator and the placement team wish to focus on behavioral aspects of performance in long-term goals, appropriate attention must be given to such areas in the assessment process. Presenting all aspects of the current-level-of-functioning data in terms of academic performance and then targeting behavioral performance in long-term goals misses the mark intended for the IEP.

Turnbull and Schulz (1979) suggest including the student in the determination of long-range goals. The law includes the child as a participating party when appropriate, and this is certainly beneficial with regard to the IEP. Inclusion of the student may result in the development of a more appropriate set of long-term goals, if appropriateness is measured in terms of the student's relationship to the real world.

The range of content and depth of the goals are as varied as the students themselves (see p. 106). The difficulty, as expressed by teachers involved in the determination of long-term goals, is in "knowing how much is enough for a year." Resolving this difficulty depends on the collective experience and knowledge of the placement group, as well as the thoroughness of the data collected on the particular student. That this difficulty exists so extensively indicates the impreciseness of common assessment and teaching methods. Without a clearly defined skills list as well as some information

EXAMPLES OF GOALS FOR THE IEP

1. Meredith will exhibit resistant, nonconforming behavior 14% or less of the time as measured with an observational sample taken by a rater with .85 or above interrater reliability during a teacher-directed activity and using a valid observation instrument (e.g., CASES).

2. Jake will identify from visual and auditory stimuli words belonging to the following sound groups:

   ___ an ___ it
   ___ at ___ and
   ___ in ___ ip

3. Kama will solve with 85% accuracy two-digit multiplication without the use of concrete aids as measured with a teacher-made test (without a time limit).

about the rate of progression expected of handicapped students, committees must continue to rely on experience and "best guesses."

One of the major concerns expressed by teachers about this aspect of the IEP is whether teacher effectiveness will be measured against the attainment of the long-term goals. Obviously, given the imprecision of estimation in education and the innate variance of human performance, teachers cannot be held totally accountable for failure of the student to attain goals. Teachers should strive to see that students achieve the goals, but teachers cannot assume total responsibility for this task. If all goals are achieved, new ones must be set, and the process continued; if the goals are not achieved, instructional procedures and other aspects involved in learning should be examined to see if the goals or the procedures are inappropriate. The basic fact to be kept in mind by those designing the IEP is that the purpose of the entire procedure is to provide a better, more appropriate educational program that will culminate in an increased likelihood that the handicapped student can function as normally as possible in society; the focus is not to distinguish between good or bad teachers, since other, more appropriate means exist to do this.

Determination of the long-term goals for any individual student may represent the major task of the placement team and will probably require extensive deliberation about information generated by the assessment procedures. For this reason we advocate the use of the planning matrix described in Chapter 1. This matrix superimposes organization on the collected information and aids the group in targeting major areas of concern or need, as well as preventing the group from focusing on one narrow aspect of the student's profile. Specific examples of the use of the planning matrix can be found later in this chapter.

Short-term objectives make up the next required element of the IEP. Once the long-range goals are determined by the committee or team, the specific short-range goals must be developed to ensure that daily and weekly activities build toward the attainment of long-range goals. Attempting to write short-range objectives to cover all areas of need will probably prove too unwieldy for both the teacher and student (Turnbull & Schulz, 1979; Van Etten & Adamson, 1973). It is more realistic and practical to select needs of the highest priority that will have the greatest impact over the long term. Selecting the proper objective can be accomplished by the teacher; assistance in making the selection might be gained through one of the following strategies:

1. Examining state or local curriculum guides for listings of objectives associated with the long-term goals identified for the student
2. Scrutinizing the teacher's guide of various textbooks in the area of the targeted long-term goals; these often list objectives or skills subsumed under major goals
3. Requesting a skills list from the publisher of various instructional materials that is directed at the goals

Behavioral objectives. Once the teacher has selected the precise skill to be included in the IEP, it must be written so as to conform to the requirements of a *behavioral objective*. Mager (1962) presents a list of questions that must be answered in planning effective instruction: (1) What must we teach? (2) How will we know when we have taught it? and (3) What materials and procedures will work most effectively to teach what we want to teach? The objective must communicate the precise behavior expected of the learner, any conditions associated with the performance of the behavior, and some specifications as to what constitutes "good" performance.

Components of behavioral objectives include *conditions* (materials the student will use and any specific instructions as to how the student will perform the task) and the *criteria* (the minimum behavior that will be accepted as satisfactory). Criteria statements are the standards against which the behavior will be measured and may consist of one or more of the following (Pasanella & Volkmor, 1977, p. 157):

1. *Number* of behaviors
2. *Time* a behavior takes
3. Characteristics of the *process* of performing a behavior
4. Characteristics of the *product* of a behavior

The difference between the following objectives emphasizes important aspects in a well-written behavioral objective:

1. The student will demonstrate a thorough knowledge of the anatomy of an ant.
2. The student will list all major parts of an ant's body.

In the first objective there are no indications as to what constitutes a "thorough knowledge" or how it will be measured. On the other hand, the second objective provides specific guidelines for what the student must do.

The sample IEPs provided in this chapter and the behavioral objectives on pp. 99-104 should be examined. Examination of these objectives should reveal both the commonalities of objectives and the unique differences that can be written into them. One point must be stressed: objectives should not be regarded as a teaching script. Some teachers make the error of writing objectives in terms of their own behavior rather than that of the learner, for example, "The teacher will teach the parts of speech." Examination of the sample objectives included in this section will underscore the fact that the specified behavior must be that of the learner.

Including the short-term objectives in the IEP represents the culmination of the process of selecting the proper instructional sequence and writing the objectives required to identify the sequence for the learner. As with long-term goals, teachers frequently ask the question, "How much is enough?" An examination of IEPs reveals that the scope of the short-term objectives varies from teacher to teacher and district to district. The "rules of thumb" that follow may aid the teacher in selecting short-term objectives:

1. Remember the IEP will be used primarily by you and other teachers familiar with the various instructional areas; some of the smaller subskills can be omitted.

2. Have colleagues examine the cluster of short-term objectives you selected to see if the sequence of skills and distance between skills appear logical and appropriate to the goals.

3. Maintain copious notes on the progress of

students to aggregate some information regarding the appropriateness of the objectives; this might help in future years.

4. Take into consideration the anticipated rate of progress of the individual student; even though over the years you may validate the clustering of objectives for various long-term goals, the rate must be varied to reflect the unique learning rate of students.

Specifying educational services. Services may include special class placement; speech, physical, and occupational therapy; counseling; transporation; and various other related types of support. The primary determinant of these services is the particular need of the student and not the availability of these services. Completing this aspect of the IEP may be difficult, since the required services may not be present in the local education agency (LEA), which creates a problem at the local district (Greer & Torres, 1977). Parents and advocacy groups will be instrumental in resolving this problem if it arises.

Services described must also include a description of the extent to which the student will participate in the regular classroom. Most IEP forms have a continuum of services description or a specific grid to show the level of participation, typically a percentage of time or number of hours.

The decision as to how much time a student should be in a regular class should be based on the unique characteristics of the individual student and the particular nature of the classrooms in which he or she will be integrated. A particular label does not reflect any reliable standard of the student's ability to handle the demands of the regular classroom. In other words, two EMR students with identical IQ scores and achievement records may vary greatly in their respective ability to function among their nonhandicapped peers. The use of the planning matrix described later in this chapter can facilitate this decision by providing some systematic means of examining the mainstreaming environment in light of the particular abilities of the student and teachers and the responsiveness of the student to various environments.

Projected dates and duration of services. This is a relatively easy component of the IEP to complete. The forms include specific places for the initiation dates of the required services, as well as the initiation and completion dates for short-term objectives.

Evaluation. Evaluation of the IEP is addressed in the regulations of P.L. 94-142. As a minimum requirement the educational agency must examine the IEP and its effectiveness on an annual basis. The central concern of the annual review meeting is whether the child is achieving the objectives identified in the IEP; therefore, during the meeting progress is reviewed, changes are made in the objectives, and/or the instructional process is altered. Although such annual evaluation meets bureaucratic needs, it is obvious to professional educators that it is not sufficient to ensure appropriate programming on a daily basis. Continuous evaluation and monitoring are necessary and will be addressed later as a distinct responsibility of the district.

IEP conference. Within a reasonable time after completion of the evaluation process an IEP conference must be held to complete the IEP document. Annual goals, short-term objectives, and placement must be finalized. All aspects of services to be delivered, as well as monitoring activities, should be discussed so that all parties understand their responsibilities in implementation. The conference should be approached as an opportunity to establish communication lines between home and school that will continue to allow interaction beyond the conference itself, since parental involvement in the educational process can have a positive effect on the child's achievement (Edgerly, 1975, Locke, 1976).

IEP team or committee. The IEP team consists of (1) school representatives, (2) the child's teacher, (3) the child, when appropriate, (4) parents, and (5) any other professionals deemed appropriate by the parents or the school. In cases in which the child is being placed for the first time, the student and one or more members of the evaluation team who conducted various tests may also participate.

The composition of the team can be expanded

beyond the minimum group mandated by the regulations of P.L. 94-142. The membership of the team is determined by the type of handicapping conditions identified because each condition may require the expertise of different professionals.

Responsibilities of members. The *school's representatives,* typically a special education administrator or building principal, should play a major role in the IEP conference by performing the following duties:

1. Handling arrangements for the conference including the following:
   a. Notifying all parties
   b. Arranging the time and place
   c. Preparing required documents
2. Conducting the conference in such a manner so as to ensure the following:
   a. That all parties understand the purpose of the IEP
   b. That participants are allowed to contribute to the developmental process
   c. That the IEP is properly developed
   d. That all participating parties understand the roles they are expected to play in implementation
   e. That all forms are completed and signed
3. Completing follow-up activities such as the following:
   a. Completing all required forms
   b. Monitoring implementation stages
   c. Assisting the teacher and child in initiating services

Child's teacher. The *child's teacher* obviously has major responsibilities in the development of the IEP because, as an educator knowledgeable about the student as well as the curriculum, the teacher is in a unique position to mesh the child's needs with required services. The evaluation team determines the general areas of concern and initiates the IEP process by delineating the general goals. However, the teacher is in the best position to assume leadership in the development of short-term objectives for instruction. The teacher has knowledge and training in instructional design and materials, thus being able to provide information pertinent to the task of the team. This requires that the regular classroom teacher contribute the following elements to the design process:

1. Assisting in the development of the long- and short-term goals because classroom experience and the knowledge of what is expected there can be meshed with the specific performance data gathered on the individual student
2. Making recommendations concerning placement in specific classrooms and with certain teachers, keeping in mind the individual characteristics of the student and the regular classroom
3. Suggesting certain types of learning activities or commercial materials that might be incorporated into the instructional plan
4. Scrutinizing the plan for points at which you might aid in making the evaluation and contribute to the modification of the plan as the student progresses or fails to do so
5. Sharing in the responsibility for making mainstreaming work by probing your own resources and those which you know exist within the school, because providing support to ensure success is at the heart of the meaning of mainstreaming

Responsibilities of other professionals. Nonteaching personnel have the responsibility of listening to the recommendations for educational programming made by other team members and augmenting these plans with suggestions relevant to their particular area of speciality. In some cases the other professionals may include representatives from agencies cooperating in services, in which case their roles would be to provide information concerning the interface of the two service providers.

Tasks. Collectively the team must accomplish the following tasks in the IEP meeting:

1. Finalizing a written IEP for the disabled student
2. Establishing clear guidelines for implementing the IEP
3. Delineating responsibilities for all parties involved in implementing the IEP
4. Finalizing review plans

5. Establishing communication among parties sharing responsibility for education of the child
6. Complying with all state and federal regulations, including signing the completed document

Parental involvement

The child may participate in the development of the written IEP when appropriate, but *parental participation* is mandatory. The law states specifically that extensive effort must be made to see that the parents, guardian, or parental surrogates attend the IEP conferences. As in other conferences at the various stages of the developmental process, parental input concerning the child is vital, but the major factor to be considered in parental participation in the IEP conference is the fostering of future support and assistance in attaining the goals and objectives. The interface of home and school has long been acknowledged by educators, and the merit of such cooperation is intensified in the education of handicapped children.

The primary procedural safeguards afforded to parents include the following components:

1. *Prior notice.* Written notice must be provided to the parents within a reasonable period before any change of status, evaluation, or placement; in addition, any school refusal of parental requests must also be communicated in writing.

2. *Parental consent.* This must be obtained before placement of the child and initiation of services. Examples of the parental consent form are shown in Fig. 3-9.

3. *Opportunity to examine records.* Parents may examine all files maintained by the school and may also request explanation or interpretation of information contained in the files. Parents who suspect that inaccurate or misleading information is included may request that the school alter the files. If the school refuses, due process proceedings may be initiated.

4. *Independent evaluation.* Parents may wish to have their child evaluated by an outside professional, typically in cases in which the parents disagree with the results of the previous evaluation and the resulting decision of the school. In some cases this independent evaluation may be paid for by the school. If the school refuses the independent evaluation, due process proceedings may be initiated. The results of the additional evaluation must be used in any new decisions made concerning the student.

Parental involvement should be viewed as a beneficial element for its own merits rather than as compliance with federal law. However, regardless of the motivation, parental involvement is required and must be handled in accordance with the regulations of P.L. 94-142.

PRACTICAL REALITIES

Unfortunately, the IEP conference as it occurs in reality may often fall far short of the desired ideal. Rather than a forum for cooperative planning, the IEP conference is basically treated by school officials as a "performance procedure" (National Education Association, 1978, p. 36). The experience of the authors in working with special education and regular classroom teachers tends to be consistent with the following findings concerning the actual placement and IEP process:

1. The IEP conference is viewed as a meeting during which the completed IEP is shown to the parents (Goldstein, Strickland, Turnbull, & Curry, 1980).
2. Most of the actual writing of the IEP is done by the special education teacher at home on personal time (Price & Goodman, 1980). This study revealed that of the group of teachers sampled, 32 percent of the time required to actually complete the IEP, including diagnostic data collection and writing the program, was done on personal time at home, with most of the time devoted to actual construction of the plan.
3. A common procedure for making placement decisions and planning instructional programs is for the special educator to share information with the classroom teacher on an informal basis rather than as part of a true

planning conference (National Education Association, 1978).

4. Parental involvement tends to be limited to receiving information from the special educator (Price & Goodman, 1980). This seems to be consistent with feelings of professionals, as indicated by a survey which revealed that the majority of those responding believed parents could contribute in the initial stages, such as referral and evaluation, but would have little or no input in IEP development (Yoshida, Fenton, Kaufman, & Maxwell, 1978).
5. Team decision making is difficult to achieve for reasons including the fact that team members "are neither fully aware of nor in agreement about their placement team duties" (Fenton, Yoshida, Maxwell, & Kaufman, 1979).
6. Following are other important findings of Goldstein et al. (1980):
   a. Classroom teachers attended fewer than 50 percent of the conferences.
   b. No real communication existed among members.
   c. Only 36 percent of the conferences were attended by the required representative of the LEA, and in these cases the administrator played only a passive role.
   d. Minimal attention was given to placement, since the parents were merely informed of the placement, and little or no discussion was given about related services.
   e. No attention was given to the evaluation plan or review of the IEP, a definite requirement in the regulations.
   f. The average length of time devoted to the conference itself was 36 minutes, indicating that little time was provided for interaction to take place and implying that it is a *pro forma* act.

It may be anticipated that these errors and shortcomings may continue to exist in school districts until such time as all professionals have received in-service or preservice training in performing the various roles associated with services to the handicapped. The problem also may attract the attention of state agencies who have responsibility for monitoring services. In the initial stages of the implementation of P.L. 94-142 the emphasis has been on gross aspects of the law, such as the presence or absence of the IEP for each child; in time it is expected that agencies will begin to scrutinize the process in terms of quality. We hope that the IEP process can be brought to fruition through training rather than enforcement. As professional educators learn how to effectively and time-efficiently perform the roles specified for them, improvement can be anticipated.

However, different theoretical viewpoints of professionals about causes and treatment of disorders, personality clashes, and various administrative elements are likely to have an adverse effect on the process at specific schools. These problems are not easily overcome. Strong leadership of key personnel is necessary to ensure that the best interests of children are not undermined by local politics.

Major competencies in the IEP process

The IEP developmental process, from referral to the actual writing of the IEP, requires a vast number of skills on the part of all those participating. However, two major competencies seem to be prominent: (1) the ability to function as part of a group decision-making team and (2) the ability to handle volumes of information produced by the referral and evaluation procedures and to synthesize it into an individualized education program. The attainment of the ideals set forth in the regulations and remediation of the errors in the process identified previously are dependent on these two competencies. These competencies are recent and only newly emphasized, making experienced and new teachers unprepared for the task.

Practical experience gained through the conduct of training and case consultation in public schools and the adaptation of information gleaned from a review of literature from fields dealing with information-handling and group interactions have led us to the development of several strategies designed to aid professionals in the acquisition of the two skill clusters. The first set of strategies addresses the problem of facilitating group interaction, which is applicable to the required conferences as well as to continued cooperation among the professionals of the school involved in implementation of services. The second set of strategies centers around the use of the individualized planning matrix introduced in Chapter 1. The matrix provides a means of superimposing some structure on the body of information that evolves throughout the investigative process, thereby aiding the teacher and others in establishing priorities and targeting the most immediate interventions needed.

Suggestions for effective group planning. Listing the reasons why group decision making is difficult can be quite lengthy; time is better spent here identifying the means through which group decision making can be made less difficult and more applicable to educational planning:

1. The goals of the group should be concrete and easily identifiable to all participants; participants should be given advance notice and precise instructions as to what will happen in the meeting. An agenda might be provided at the beginning of the meeting to impose a direction on the group.

2. A manual might be prepared that identifies each state-defined responsibility of the team, including specifics from the law itself.

3. Time might be provided at the beginning of the meeting or before the meeting for all members of the team to examine test results and other information produced during the evaluation period; it has been shown that in some cases varying perceptions of the goals of a group may be caused by members of the group possessing different amounts and types of information (Katz & Kahn, 1966).

4. Specific instructions should be provided to each team member before the meeting as to the role that is expected of them; explaining the role of the individual in this particular group increases identification with the placement team and reduces the likelihood that identification with another group might impede team operation (Delbecq, 1965). The problem most frequently observed in this context is that team members feel compelled to identify with their own professional group (speech therapists, psychologists, classroom teachers, etc.) rather than with the small group or team. This results in a very fragmented team with individuals and/or professions competing for superiority or defending positions rather than meshing knowledge and experience from all fields.

5. The school representative, such as the principal, counselor, or special education supervisor, designated to assume responsibility for group actions can enhance the group's performance through the following strategies:

a. Asserting leadership in keeping the group "on task"
b. Reiterating the expectations for the group
c. Periodically summarizing during the meeting the efforts and/or consensus of the group up to that point
d. Studying the state regulations and due process guidelines carefully before the meeting, and reminding the group of the obligations dictated by these documents

The implementation of P.L. 94-142 is dependent on the ability of professionals to cooperate and communicate effectively, which unfortunately requires skills and a philosophy not traditionally included in training programs. We believe that the next stage of examination in the field will concern the quality of services and the process through which the services are developed, including the ability to function together as members of a decision-making team.

The special educator can play a vital role in making the group conferences work effectively to the advantage of the child, family, and school by carefully monitoring his or her own performance in the group. It is quite easy for the teacher to assume responsibility for the conference and take on a prominent role, as indicated by the Goldstein et al. (1980) study, which revealed, in the sample of conferences observed, that most of the talking was done by the resource room teacher and directed at the parents. The focus of the talk was found to be curriculum and evaluation performance, assuming more the character of a mild, informative lecture rather than an opportunity for two-way interaction. To avoid such a dialogue, the following suggestions should be considered:

1. Briefly discuss plans with the administrator or school representative before the meeting, reinforcing his or her own role as chairperson.
2. Listen attentively to the information presented by other team members.
3. Draw others into the discussion as often as possible when appropriate.
4. Provide as much information as possible to the school representative before the meeting.

Using the individualized planning matrix. The distinction should be made between the two major purposes of assessment: labeling and programming. The "typical" assessment process culminates in assignation of a label. Contrary to the medical model, the presence of a label (ED, EMR, or LD) does not directly imply a treatment or educational program. The total assessment program should produce, in addition to a label, information on which an instructional plan can be founded. The exact *learner profile* as seen in the *learning environment* provides more instructionally relevant information; the special educator, having primary

		Services			
	Teacher variables	Instructional procedures	Placement	Related services	Other
Student needs: Cognitive-academic functioning					
Student needs: Socioemotional functioning					
Student needs: Sensoriphysical functioning					

Notes:

Fig. 3-15. Individualized planning matrix.

responsibility for developing the instructional plan, must take into consideration all aspects of the information provided and identify priorities. The process of evaluation produces tremendous amounts of information, making the task of organizing the information into appropriate and useful categories or units quite difficult.

The individualized planning matrix shown in Fig. 3-15 is a useful instrument as well as a conceptual guide in the decision-making process. The special educator can use the matrix to record and organize information as it accrues through the various assessment phases and numerous conferences. The major steps involved in use of the matrix are shown in Table 3-2.

The special educator initially uses the matrix in the referral conference, as Table 3-2 indicates. The teacher can identify the child with a number or other coding system so that all information will remain confidential; the matrix is kept in a folder in the classroom, making important information readily available for teacher use. The matrix should be

Table 3-2. Chronological steps in use of the individualized planning matrix

Step	*Procedure*	*Description*
1 Referral conference	Recording information on student produced by referral/screening procedures	To categorize data
2 Formal or informal evaluation procedures	Identifying areas overlooked in previous investigative efforts/recording data in proper cells of matrix	To aid the teacher in targeting areas within ecological assessment that might otherwise be overlooked; assisting in organization of results as they accrue
3 Evaluation conferences	Completing cells in matrix to reflect data presented by other professionals; asking for pertinent information from others to obtain complete student and environment profiles	To facilitate structuring of data to reveal deficits addressed in the IEP
4 IEP development	Establishing priorities for long-range goals and instructional objectives; identifying least restrictive environments; selecting appropriate materials and instructional procedures	To assist the teacher in identifying instructionally relevant information to aid in designing daily programming; to aid in decision making in finalization of the IEP and implementation
5 Programming	Coordinating the daily program for individualized instruction for each student	To aid in scheduling students; to target areas appropriate for group instruction or unit study
6 Evaluation	Monitoring daily programming/assessing total program interaction	To allow the teacher to make daily changes in instruction without having to reexamine total folder; to aid the teacher in judging progress in terms of student's success within the environment

viewed as a working tool, retained throughout the service process. The components of the matrix and examples of typical information included within each component are shown in Table 3-3.

Figs. 3-16 and 3-17 are examples of the applications of the matrix developed from actual cases by special education teachers and reflecting the types of information recorded on the matrix form. It is apparent that interaction may not occur between variables, and it is not necessary to develop a program element for each cell. It should be apparent that there is vertical interaction (e.g., behavioral or personal interaction with physical interaction). Teachers have found the matrix useful as a record sheet, and time has been saved because of the following characteristics:

1. Provides a succinct, coded means of retaining student information within the classroom for daily use in planning
2. Facilitates scheduling during the initial days of the school year, since scrutiny of the single form is more time efficient than sorting through the entire folder of each child
3. Aids in any grouping for the use of a particular unit of instruction and/or piece of equipment
4. Saves time in monitoring activities, since students are followed through related services, the related services column on the form readily identifying such services

Use of the matrix results in more comprehensive decision making, more time-efficient planning of services, and the establishment of instructional priorities. These actions take the assessment process beyond labeling into programming, the primary concern underlying the IEP. Teachers who are competent in the use of the matrix find designing and implementing the IEP a much less awesome task.

FINAL STAGES

Programming

Implementation of the IEP appears to be the one area not directly addressed in the regulations associated with P.L. 94-142. A number of assumptions must be made, including the following:

1. Programming automatically proceeds smoothly and consistently.
2. Most educators possess a sound foundation in learning theory and instructional design.
3. Successful mainstreaming automatically occurs if the IEP is completed.
4. Close cooperation develops among the various persons involved in serving handicapped students.

Comprehensive programming for handicapped students requires that teachers must coordinate their efforts to ensure consistency and progress toward collectively established goals. This task is complicated by the fact that a prototype for mainstreaming beyond the writing of the IEP is neither available nor even a possibility because of the unique characteristics of each child and school district. Thus, even though two students may bear the same label, other variables considered in planning may result in the development of totally different IEPs with different programming and environments.

Special education services consist of a combination of cognitive-academic, socioemotional, and sensoriphysical programming, as dictated by the unique characteristics of each child within the unique setting of a particular learning environment. Thus, it is not feasible to propose that "packaged" or "mass produced" IEPs be used by teachers, unless these documents are going to be considered irrelevant to daily instruction, leaving all professionals involved in service delivery with tremendous responsibilities in program implementation.

Responsibilities

All parties involved in education of the child share in the responsibility for ensuring that services provided to handicapped students are appropriate. Although the specific nature of the responsibilities vary with each case, some general suggestions can be made concerning the responsibilities of the professionals involved.

Special educators. Primary responsibility for implementing and monitoring the education of handicapped students ordinarily falls to the special

Text continued on p. 120.

Table 3-3. Information typically recorded on the individualized planning matrix

Component	*Typical information*	*Use*
Services		
Teacher variables	Content area or grade taught Special training or area of interest Personality or temperament Willingness to accept handicapped students Instructional style, such as use of lectures, learning centers, and amount of student interaction Types of evaluation used	Inclusion of this information in decision making makes the selection of the least restrictive environment more meaningful; teachers should be, as much as possible, matched to a student in terms of identifying student needs rather than simply assigning a student to a class.
Instructional procedures	Nature of content, such as science lab or composition course Use of instructional media—type and frequency Use of group instruction to allow peer interaction Types of instructional materials used Variety of strategies used as opposed to strict reliance on lecture and reading Skills covered Types of management used, such as punishment, positive reinforcement, or token economy	Examination of these variables in decision making can produce vital information in selecting mainstream courses and designing special class instruction, since a particular student may be able to perform with certain types of instructional material (programmed text) when functioning in a class using a token economy. This information would greatly aid in assignment to a content class, as well as targeting the type of instruction that might work in the special classroom. Another example is placement of a child who is very peer dependent in a classroom that allows peer interaction as an instructional medium.
Placement	Grade level Type of special program recommended Content areas identified as need areas Amount of special programming suggested Type of classroom suggested, such as teacher or program directed Special considerations such as the need for special seating arrangements Milieu	Selection consideration should include physical attributes of the classroom as well as content concerns; certain students might need to be at a particular grade level, but the individual factor might be proximity of the room to the restroom if a physical problem is involved or if a student is a behavior problem in the hall; this component would also reflect recommendations such as grade-level placement, open classroom, and other location factors.

Table 3-3. Information typically recorded on the individualized planning matrix—cont'd

Component	*Typical information*	*Use*
Services		
Related services	Physical conditions such as allergies, braces, or other accompanying problems Extreme difficulties with self-concept or other interpersonal relationships Medical interventions employed, such as medication Family provided therapeutic services Specialized transportation requirements	Any legally defined related service such as physical therapy or counseling may be very important to a particular student as an aid to the major special education activities, and any such service may have an impact on personal and interpersonal functioning of a student. Services being provided to the family under auspices of the school should be included here.
Other	This cell of the matrix would include relevant information that is not encompassed by other components; examples include information about familial services being provided outside the school, any special interests of the child, and, if considered important, attendance record.	
Needs		
Cognitive-academic functioning	Standardized test results Achievement test data Criterion-referenced test information Informally acquired information Suggested materials Instructional procedures shown to be effective or particularly ineffective Analysis of preference for content area of instruction Recommendation for percent of time to remain in special classroom Areas of weakness associated with the handling of classroom information (e.g., difficulties with arithmetic workbook)	Component concerns level of educational functioning and displays interaction across the service aspects of the matrix; it aids team in selecting a particular teacher, type of program or material, and most appropriate instructional mode.
Socioemotional functioning	Personality measures Sociometric data Observational data collected in class Peer relationships observed Behavioral strategies found successful or unsuccessful with student Counseling services needed Familial concerns Relationship to adults	Information provided is crucial to comprehensive programming, yet it is often overlooked; consideration of the ability to function within interpersonal relationships, personality variables, and social supports is important in making sound programming decisions.
Sensoriphysical functioning	Sensory or physical conditions such as deafness, blindness, or orthopedic conditions Medical supervision requirements Medication Counseling Transportation requirements Special handling	These aspects of the learning and teaching process might have implications for the overall success of mainstreaming; these factors aid in decisions regarding placement, daily service materials, and related services.

Individualized planning matrix

Teacher's name: Ms. McFadden   Student code no.: 103 P

	Services				
	Teacher variables	Instructional procedures	Placement	Related services	Other
Cognitive-academic functioning	Needs teacher who uses Distar and other approaches and who is well trained in reading instruction	Reading and arithmetic are about 2 years behind Poor comprehension Appears to like Distar materials Previous teacher stated that student has auditory perception problems. Lacks word attack skills	WRAT: Reading — 1.3 Spelling — 1.1 Arithmetic — K.9 LD placement		
Socioemotional functioning	Has stated a preference for the one male teacher the student has ever had	Short attention span Disorganized work habits Requires considerable reinforcement Works better when assigned with a peer		Consider setting up a peer tutoring program through counselor or regular teacher	
Sensoriphysical functioning	Consider placing with Mr. Smith, since he is familiar with student's allergies			Possible auditory problem; testing suggested Slight allergies require medication in certain seasons	

Fig. 3-16. Example 1 using the individualized planning matrix.

Individualized planning matrix

Teacher's name: Ms. McPhail　　Student code no.: 102 A

Student needs	Services: Teacher variables	Services: Instructional procedures	Services: Placement	Services: Related services	Services: Other
Cognitive-academic functioning	Spent 6 unsuccessful weeks in Ms. Thomas' classroom; had personality clash with her Has difficulty with authoritarian teachers	Produces less work when placed in peer groups Works well in programmed workbooks	WISC-R: 121 PIAT: on grade level and above		
Socioemotional functioning		Very physical behavior Short attention span Poor work habits Poor peer relations Responds best to tangible rewards	Coping Analysis Schedule profile: 11% in aggressive style Sociometric data reveal isolated role	Parents have requested help from counselor	
Sensoriphysical functioning		Often hides glasses, but they are absolutely necessary for student to function		Wears glasses, very nearsighted Needs frequent checking since glasses must be changed often because of changes in eyes	

Fig. 3-17. Example 2 using the individualized planning matrix.

educator. Aspects of this responsibility are as follows:

1. Seeing that daily instruction is consistent with the goals and objectives in the IEP
2. Observing student behavior in order to alter daily instruction as needed
3. Noting any particular difficulties that might indicate that the IEP needs modification
4. Providing personal support to the student and family as instruction proceeds
5. Serving as a "first line" of information and support for others involved in services to the student

Mainstream teachers. The degree of involvement of mainstream teachers will vary in each student's case, but the regular teacher must share in the responsibility of serving the student. Often mainstream teachers mistakenly perceive the special education student as the sole responsibility of the special educator, believing that their only responsibility is to "allow" the student to attend their class. Instead the mainstream teacher should have a very active role in programming, including the following actions:

1. Selecting instructional tasks commensurate with the IEP of the student and without isolation from the peer group
2. Accommodating instruction for the student within the classroom to maximize content learning despite particular learning impairments
3. Observing student functioning within the context of the regular classroom and peer group
4. Providing personal support as the student copes with adjustments to the mainstreaming process
5. Communicating with the special educator, sharing pertinent information on student performance

Administrators. The role of administrators in programming may not be as obvious. However, administrative support and involvement have been listed as a major factor in fostering a beneficial climate for the mainstream effort (McFadden, 1980). The principal or other administrator with direct responsibility for special education programming can facilitate mainstreaming by performing the following tasks:

1. Sharing specific points of agreement in development of overall goals or expected outcomes of the special program
2. Becoming personally acquainted with all teachers involved in mainstream services
3. Visiting special and regular classrooms to provide support, rather than limiting visits to only those required for teacher evaluation
4. Showing an open attitude of acceptance of handicapped students and support for teachers
5. Instituting administrative practices to ensure compliance with policy
6. Supporting all teachers and students involved in mainstreaming
7. Facilitating communication among professionals

Related service personnel. Persons from various disciplines involved in serving handicapped students may be actively involved in the child's daily education. Professionals who provide transportation, counseling, or medical support have some responsibilities associated with their role in comprehensive education, including the following:

1. Viewing related services as a part of total programming rather than in isolation from other aspects of education
2. Communicating with the special educator rather than assuming that the specialist is aware of significant events involved in service for which they are responsible
3. Supporting the student in coping with mainstreaming

The extension of shared responsibility beyond the required meeting associated with the finalization of the written IEP is the basic intent of P.L. 94-142. All professionals must perform cooperatively for an appropriate education to be provided, necessitating that each professional assume a measure of responsibility for making mainstreaming a success for each student.

A discussion of individualized education, in addition to a discussion of content in the curricular areas (Chapters 6 to 8), must also include specific implications for teaching, which can be gleaned from examination of applied learning theory. Although such specific implications for teaching comprise the major focus of Chapter 12, the topic of implementation of programming is not complete without making note of the importance of the teaching act itself. Comprehensive programming is not ensured for each student through the specification of a set of goals or objectives; instead these must be viewed as the content for instruction addressed through teaching strategies and based on knowledge of the learner and learning process. A number of ways exist to teach a skill or concept; selection of the "best" approach is a complex process that requires examination of the research on learning and scrutiny of the learning patterns of the particular student to be taught. Chapter 12 provides a synthesis of the content and the learning and teaching process.

MONITORING AND PROGRAM EVALUATION

The IEP process ends neither with the finalization of the written IEP nor even with its implementation; rather the process should be viewed as cyclical. The connective aspect in the process is the monitoring or evaluation function, conducted intermittently to ascertain the effectiveness of the current IEP. P.L. 94-142 mandates the inclusion of an evaluation plan for measuring the objectives developed for the student, thus requiring the monitoring of student progress toward the stated educational goals. The major requirements of the evaluation plan are as follows:

1. Appropriate criteria must be identified.
2. Evaluation procedures must be employed.
3. Responsibilities of those involved must be delineated.
4. Schedules for evaluation activities must be developed.
5. Results must be reported.

The subtleties of fulfilling the evaluation requirements are not clearly delineated, leaving to the local district the primary responsibility for meeting these requirements. The lack of specific details of the monitoring plan has resulted in enormous differences among the various evaluation strategies used and reports prepared. However, some general comments should be made about each of the major requirements of the evaluation plan.

Criteria

Evaluation cannot be conducted unless there is some standard against which to measure the attribute or performance. That is, the ideal or desired level of performance must be stated in such terms as to permit comparison. For instance, to describe a student's behavior as "good" has no utility unless some definite standard is identified as "good." The nature of the standard may vary, but typical examples include the following:

1. Average, determined statistically
2. Percentage figure
3. Model or example to be replicated
4. Skill level (performance) specification to be duplicated

It seems common practice for criteria to be written into the objectives of the IEP, as shown in the examples in Fig. 3-15. The key to proper specification of criteria is to have the desired behavioral standard stated in observable and measurable terms; such specificity is necessary when developing the objectives and goals of the IEP.

Procedures

Lovitt (1980) states that "when it comes to selecting a means for measuring student performance, there are too few choices available." The constraints of reality, such as limited teacher time, group management requirements, and lack of knowledge of assessment strategies beyond standardized tests, produce an extremely narrow menu of measurement approaches for use in monitoring student progress. Most procedures in a typical school dictate the convenient use of standardized tests, which is more satisfactory to the administration than the needs of the student. The discussion presented here will include not only standardized tests but also the use of criterion-referenced tests, direct observation, and a sequenced-skills list in an effort to expand the scope of evaluation strategies that may be employed.

Standardized tests. Standardized tests appear to be a very popular means of measuring student progress for the following reasons:

1. They appear to be the preferred method of administrators and others responsible for services, as well as state department officials.
2. They are perceived to be the easiest method of testing.
3. Teachers seem to gain some sense of security from the use of standardized instruments despite questionable validity and reliability of many tests.
4. Reporting is considered easier when using tests results.

It is at this point that the purpose and implementation of evaluation seem to divorce. The regulations stipulate that only short-term instructional objectives be examined, a purpose for which standardized tests seem inappropriate. These tests have two disadvantages when used to monitor student progress on short-term objectives:

1. *Directness*. This term denotes the relationship between the test item and what is being taught. The degree of relationship or directness between the curriculum and materials and the test used is more clearly reflected in the test score than actual student progress. In other words, rather than measuring overall gain in knowledge, the measurement reveals progress on the items tested. On tests with poor norms the score may reflect only test error.

2. *Frequency*. Tests are typically administered annually or at the end of a 9-month period. Evaluation of short-term goals should be continuous rather than based on isolated test administration. The opportunity for feedback and modification is lost, thus reducing the flexibility of programming to reflect student changes and producing a very staid program (Lovitt, 1980).

The use of standardized tests may be appropriate when the purpose is to evaluate the degree to which the annual goals have been addressed. Although it is true in theory that the evaluation should investigate the overall effectiveness of the IEP including its annual goals, in reality minimum effort is put into evaluation; most of this effort is directed toward test administration at the beginning and the end of the year, distancing the implementation from theoretical practice. Standardized tests may be appropriate in some instances, but the professionals involved should carefully scrutinize the expected outcomes to ascertain that the purpose for which the tests are being used is consistent with the task of the review committee or team.

Criterion-referenced tests. Criterion-referenced tests consist of items that reflect the material being taught, thus avoiding the lack of directness found to be a potential problem in using standardized tests. The following advantages have also contributed to the growing popularity of this method of monitoring:

1. The availability of criterion-referenced tests is increasing.
2. The number of items on these tests is usually smaller than standardized tests, making them faster to administer.
3. The frequency of administration is teacher determined, allowed for more frequent monitoring.
4. This method produces results more closely related to the curriculum than the global score or grade-level equivalent produced by standardized tests.

Because of the relationship between criterion-referenced tests and the skills comprising the curriculum, these tests can be used effectively to measure attainment of short-term goals and to revise instructional sequences based on the results, thus reducing the likelihood that evaluation of progress will be conducted only once per year. Annual goals can also be examined by this method if the evaluation committee desires to do so.

Direct observation. Observation is a process of systematically looking at and recording behavior and can be used for the purpose of making instructional decisions (Cartwright & Cartwright, 1974).

The collection of observational data in the natural setting has become particularly attractive to educators. Sechrest (1969) has noted a number of inconsistencies between human behavior under testing and laboratory conditions and in ordinary life situations, a disparity long lamented by classroom teachers. Direct observation is increasingly being viewed as a tool with potential for evaluation in the IEP for reasons that include the following:

1. The "sample" is taken in the exact environment in which the child must function rather than in one of isolation; this factor makes observation particularly useful for evaluation if the evaluation team really desires some indication of the success of the mainstreaming effort and other measures of progress.

2. The data collection process does not require that the child be interrupted; rather the observation is conducted during the regular activities of the day.

3. The simplicity of observation, in terms of teacher and student time required, makes it easier to encourage teachers to routinely collect evaluative data.

4. IEPs seem to be broadening the scope of the goals and objectives to include a more extensive picture of the child than that provided by IEPs limited to academic objectives only; IEPs including objectives specifying behavioral changes must be monitored through techniques that include observation.

Sequenced-skills list. The other monitoring strategies discussed have varying degrees of direct relationship to the actual teaching process in daily use. Use of a sequenced-skills list is appropriate for all levels of evaluation, short-term objectives, general goals, and annual goals, and has direct relationship to the curriculum. The list should be compromised of all the required skills or competencies that make up a particular subject or skill area and should be stated in behavioral terms to facilitate instruction and evaluation. The student's progress would be charted along the skills continuum, which reflects both daily and annual progress. Instructional sequences could be planned using the skills continuum as a reference, thus reducing the likelihood that the daily curricular content would be removed from the material on which evaluation is to be focused.

Use of a sequenced list of skills should be acceptable to teachers, since it greatly clarifies teaching and evaluation. Some teachers use a skills list as a tool to guide daily instruction, but, as the following reasons suggest, such lists are not frequently employed as evaluation instruments:

1. Skills lists may vary a great deal if teachers extract them from various commercial sources or curricular guides. Comparisons would be difficult and invite criticism that skills are inappropriate.

2. Most skill sequences are developed through "expert opinion," which contributes to variance among lists, and the lack of a statistical foundation contributes to a lack of confidence in the lists. The absence of norms may make state agency personnel and administrators reluctant to accept them as valid evaluation instruments.

One effort to establish a scaled sequence of skills is underway in schools in Portland, Oregon, in which each track of the curriculum has been subjected to statistical analysis. The attributes of this approach include the following:

1. Each skill sequence is independent of the influence of subjects who took the tests, a problem with norm-referenced instruments.
2. The difficulty of items is graduated on a logarithmic scale, making item difficulty an unimportant factor in assessment.
3. Students can be directly assessed in terms of which skills they have acquired and which they should achieve.
4. A test of a few items is individually developed for each student, and progress can be predicted over a year.
5. Measures reflect only the students' performance against the scale and are not affected by the performance of other subjects or item differences.
6. Skills are directly related to activities that are taught in the curriculum.
7. Measures are valid; there is no confusion about acculturation or other experiential fac-

tors, and comparisons with other students is unnecessary.

Responsibilities

Theoretically evaluation is conducted daily or at least weekly by the teacher, as reflected through the written record of the accomplishment of the short-term objectives, and by a team or committee, who have responsibility for the annual evaluation or annual tasks. The responsibilities should be shared among the teachers serving the child, support personnel involved, supervisory representatives of the local agency, and the parents; when deemed appropriate the child participates. Ideally professionals who originally participated in the placement and IEP development conferences would also participate in the review meeting.

Unfortunately typical practices in the school vary from the ideal. Major responsibility for the review of objectives and goals seems to fall to the special educator rather than a committee or team. This is not a totally unsound practice, since the special educator is the professional who probably has the most involvement with the child on a day-to-day basis. However, if such teacher evaluation is the only effort, the evaluation will be little more than a superficial compliance with the regulations, and most of the potential value of evaluation will be lost.

Schedules for evaluation

The regulations for implementation of P.L. 94-142 specify that progress in the area of short-term goals must be reviewed at least on an annual basis; thus, typical practice is for an annual review conference to be held. Although this would be in compliance with the regulations, it would be something less than ideal if that is the only time the student's progress is examined. Larsen and Poplin (1980) state that "consequently, it is inconceivable for one year to pass prior to evaluating a given youngster's attainment of those short-term instructional objectives that constitute the bulk of all direct teaching activities. To do so would almost certainly result in an individualized education program that is poorly managed and does not serve to provide the youngster an appropriate education" (pp. 331-332).

Reporting evaluation results

As the team or committee examines the student's progress to that point, a number of other factors besides short-term objectives should be scrutinized, including appropriateness of placement, need for related services, and progress in terms of annual goals. Reporting should be conducted in the committee meeting with the professionals reporting in much the same manner as in earlier conferences. Since some writers recommend that the professionals originally participating in the placement and IEP conference should also participate in the evaluation conference, a great deal of continuity should be expected.

It is a common practice for the annual review, which is the minimum period required by law, to be scheduled to coincide with the anniversary of the formation of the IEP. Unfortunately, it is also common practice for this to be merely a superficial effort of compliance rather than a genuine attempt to solicit information for the purpose of making group decisions about the future of a handicapped child. Results reported consist of scores on standardized tests and the teacher's recommendation for continued placement or altered placement.

More appropriately the evaluation meeting would include reports of results of investigative efforts, such as the following:

1. Indication of the student's progress on a sequenced-skills list
2. Observational data collected during handicapped student's participation in the mainstream and special education classes
3. Grades earned
4. Teachers' reactions and input
5. Parental input
6. Descriptive information on related services provided
7. Descriptive information on placements previously used

The reporting of an extensive collection of information can result in more appropriate decision making, thus reaching far beyond a facade of compliance with regulations. All aspects of the student's placement, including the variables comprising the individualized planning matrix, should undergo examination. The matrix might even be used in the evaluation process as a means of recording and summarizing information in much the same way as it was used in the referral and placement process. The outcome of the evaluation should be an altered or modified IEP that includes a reevaluation of all of its component parts to ensure that the student's education is continuous and appropriate.

SUMMARY

In this chapter the reader has been presented with specific information about the development of an IEP. It has been noted that the IEP is a document that can serve as the process tool in guiding and evaluating individualized education. If conceived and implemented accurately, the IEP can be the most significant innovation in American education. Unfortunately the IEP tends to be developed routinely, is not actually used in guiding the teaching process, and is viewed as a burdensome task.

The initial steps in development seem to be addressed adequately by schools. Assessment is conducted to determine the current educational status, goals and objectives are erected, instructional and service requirements are defined, the degree of mainstreaming is recorded, and other clerical details are handled. However, implementation of the program and its evaluation tend to be ignored in practice.

The assignment of students to predetermined special programs and convenient mainstream classrooms to coincide with administrative schedules interferes with the opportunity to actualize the IEP and define specific environments and educational experiences for each student. The school is in a position to effect these processes. Curricula that are based on sequences of identified skills permit teachers to engineer effective teaching methodologies. Curricula that are not effective obstruct the use of an IEP because educational activities are viewed less directly as accumulating events that lead to short-term, intermediate, and long-term outcomes, the basic framework of the IEP.

REFERENCES AND SUGGESTED READINGS

Abeson, A., & Weintraub, F. Understanding the individual education program. In S. Torres (Ed.), *A primer on individualized education programs for handicapped children*. Reston, VA: Foundation for Exceptional Children, 1977.

Beery, K. (Ed.). *Models for mainstreaming*. Sioux Falls, SD: Dimension Books, Inc., 1972.

Cartwright, C.A., & Cartwright, G.P. *Developing observation skills*. New York: McGraw-Hill Book Co., 1974.

Cartwright, G.P., & Cartwright, C.A. Gilding the lilly: comments on the training based model. *Exceptional Children*, 1972, *39*, 231-234.

Delbecq, A.L. Managerial leadership styles in problem-solving conferences (Pt. 2). *Journal of Academy of Management*, March 1965, pp. 32-43.

Edgerly, R.F. Effectiveness of parent counseling in treatment of children with learning disabilities. *Dissertation Abstracts*, 1975, *36*, 1301.

Edwards, A.J. *Individual mental testing*. New York: Intext Educational Publishers, 1975.

Federal Register. Washington, D.C.: U.S. Government Printing Office, August 1977, pp. 42494; 42496-42497.

Fenton, K.S., Yoshida, R.K., Maxwell, J.P., & Kaufman, M.J. Recognition of team goals: an essential step toward rational decision making. *Exceptional Children*, 1979, *45*, 638-644.

Goldstein, S., Strickland, B., Turnbull, A.P., & Curry, L. An observational analysis of the IEP conference. *Exceptional Children*, 1980, *46*, 278-285.

Greer, J., & Torres, S. Arranging specific educational services to be provided. In S. Torres (Ed.), *A primer on individualized education programs for handicapped children*. Reston, VA: Foundation for Exceptional Children, 1977.

Hammill, D., & Wiederholt, J.L. *The resource room: rationale and implementation*. New York: Grune & Stratton Inc., Buttonwood Farms Division, 1972.

Hayes, J. Annual goals and short-term objectives. In S. Torres (Ed.), *A primer on individualized education programs for handicapped children*. Reston, VA: Foundation for Exceptional Children, 1977.

Kaufman, M.J., Gottlieb, J., Agard, J.A., & Kubic, M.B. Mainstreaming: toward an explication of the construct. *Focus on Exceptional Children*, 1975, *7*(3), 1-12.

Katz, D., & Kahn, R. *The social psychology of organization*. New York: John Wiley & Sons, Inc., 1966

Larsen, S., & Poplin, M.S. *Methods for educating the handicapped: an individualized education program approach*. Boston: Allyn & Bacon, Inc., 1980.

Locke, W.W. The effect of frequency of home visits on parent behavior and child achievement. *Dissertation Abstracts*, 1976, *37*, 4217.

Lovitt, T. *Writing and implementing an IEP: a step-by-step plan*. Belmont, CA: Fearon Education, 1980.

Mager, R.F. *Preparing instructional objectives.* Palo Alto, CA: Fearon Education, 1962.

Mann, P.H. (Ed.). *Mainstream special education: issues and perspectives in urban centers.* Reston, VA: Council for Exceptional Children, 1974.

Marsh, G.E., II, & Price, B.J. *Methods for teaching the mildly handicapped adolescent.* St. Louis: The C.V. Mosby Co., 1980.

McFadden, A.C. *Internal and external factors contributing to "burn-out."* Paper presented to Council for Exceptional Children, Topical Conference on Behavior Disorders, Minneapolis, MN, August 1980.

National Association of State Directors of Special Education. *Functions of the placement committee on special education.* Washington, DC: Author, 1976.

National Education Association. *Education for all handicapped children: consensus, conflict, and challenge.* Washington, DC: Author, 1978.

Pasanella, A.L., & Volkmor, C.B. *Coming back . . . or never leaving: instructional programming for handicapped students in the mainstream.* Columbus, OH: Charles E. Merrill Publishing Co., 1977.

Price, M., & Goodman, L. Individualized education programs: a cost study. *Exceptional Children,* 1980, *46,* 446-454.

Sechrest, L. Nonreactive assessment of attitudes. In E.P. Wilems & W.L. Raush (Eds.), *Naturalistic viewpoints in psychological research.* New York: Holt, Rinehart & Winston, 1969.

Turnbull, A.P., & Schulz, J.B. *Mainstreaming handicapped students: a guide for the classroom teacher.* Boston: Allyn & Bacon, Inc., 1979.

Van Etten, G., & Adamson, G. The fail-safe program: a special educational service continuum. In E. Deno (Ed.), *Instructional alternatives for exceptional children.* Reston, VA: Council for Exceptional Children, 1973.

Yoshida, R.K., Fenton, K., Kaufman, M.J., & Maxwell, J.P. Parental involvement in the special education pupil planning process: the school's perspective. *Exceptional Children,* 1978, *44,* 531-533.

SECTION THREE

EDUCATION: A SHARED RESPONSIBILITY

For much of its history special education has been a separate, somewhat isolated part of public education. In recent years, the trend has been for handicapped children to be reintegrated into public schools and into mainstream classrooms. The success or failure of this effort will be determined more by the acceptance of teachers and the design of regular education curricula than by any direct service of the special educator. It is essential that the special educator be reintegrated into mainstream education if the goals of the program and needs of each student are to be met. This places an extraordinary responsibility on the special educator, who must provide students not only with direct services but also with indirect services by affecting the attitudes and skills of teachers and the policies of the school. The special educator must understand the administration of the school, informal power, school polices, political realities, pressures on colleagues, and many other issues. Special education must be a functional part of the school that is articulated among the various components.

Chapter 4 provides a description of the elementary school and the regular classroom with consideration of various issues as they relate to the special education program. Chapter 5 continues this process with an analysis of the roles of the special educator, who may be expected to perform many duties under different circumstances depending on the prevailing policies and regulations of the state and school district. The remaining chapters in this section, 6 through 11, pertain to instructional methodologies that may be used in reading, arithmetic, written and expressive language, and affective development. These chapters also contain elements to support the student and the classroom teacher, support services, accommodation, compensatory approaches, and relationships with collateral fields. The preparation of this section was conducted with recognition that services will vary greatly from one setting to another. The special educator may be expected to manage a self-contained program in some schools or to operate a multicategorical resource room in others. In each type of service the focus should be placed on the needs of each learner, although certain arrangements will interfere with such planning. However, some teachers will be constrained by certain factors that, although undesirable, may not be readily altered. The significance of Section Three is that any teacher should be able to find direction in the implementation of a program regardless of the type of organization or extent of resources. Proper planning and shared educational responsibility between the special educator and other teaching personnel will help ensure that children do not become victims of their own childhoods. In our society, elementary school is the foundation of adulthood and the scene of the most important initial experience in the process of socialization. The special education teacher has a significant responsibility, which we hope to support by our suggestions.

4 THE ELEMENTARY SCHOOL

The goals and activities of schools are established by professional educators to reflect the demands of society. Unfortunately the society is not always clear about what it expects, and its attitudes about the mission of schools can change suddenly, with criticism and faultfinding directed at educators. As economic, political, and social conditions change, so will the view of public education. Throughout history periods of economic distress have resulted in criticism and demand for reform of public education. For example, during 1973 the public opinion poll conducted by George Gallup revealed generally favorable opinions of the effectiveness of schools. By 1979, attitudes had changed dramatically; the public was overwhelmingly critical of schools for lack of discipline, low standards, irrelevant subject matter, and lazy, uninterested teachers. Surely the schools had not actually deterioriated that much during the short span of 5 or 6 years. Nonetheless, public attitude had changed. It is interesting that 1973 was the year of the oil embargo, a serious recession, and the beginning of high inflation that continues to be a problem affecting the American life-style, satisfaction with governmental agencies, and prospects for the future.

The back-to-basics movement and criticism of the "frills" in education were reactions to what had been progressive views of education in the 1960s, views that had been incorporated into education by the 1970s. Schools responded to critics and reform movements of the 1960s by implementing new systems of humanistic discipline rather than corporal punishment, by changing the curriculum to reflect innovative concepts rather than merely basic skills, and by experimenting with new organizational arrangements such as the open school. However, by the time schools attempted to satisfy public demand by switching from traditional to progressive approaches to education, the public's mood and attitude changed again. Now it would be incumbent on schools to eradicate irrelevant topics from the curriculum, to vigorously discipline children, and to get back to basics. Within half a decade the schools were graded by the public as inferior and had to undo what the public had wanted. At present the trends portend a continuation of the demand for stern discipline of students, better teaching, competency-based education of students, competency examination for teachers, and critical exchanges between teachers' organizations and administrators and college professors. Everyone will likely be criticized: families and television will be blamed, administrators and textbooks will be criticized, and colleges of education will be judged as out of touch with the realities of teaching. Once again, as we noted in Chapter 1, few will look at how teaching is actually conducted on a daily basis. No one will develop a simple set of expectations for student outcomes. There will be a lot of suffering, but the issues are not likely to be clearly identified. A political realignment in the future may result in local districts regaining more direct control of functions that were assumed by federal and state agencies. There may be a softening of the stand on the rights of handicapped children as governmental regulations and regulatory agencies are weakened or removed by the federal government.

It is impossible to accurately predict the future, but it seems certain that the current and future problems of special educators will be defined by the problems of the schools in general and without firm support from governmental regulations. Understanding the nature and problems of schools is important to the special educator for defining the role of special education. As a part of the system, special education will experience the influence of each factor that affects the school. If, during a period of reexamination and retrenchment, the local school is able to assume more control of its policies and future directions, the special educator may need to function even more effectively to ensure that the gains made on behalf of special programs and handicapped children will not be lost, especially if the federal role to aid special education throughout financial and regulatory support is weakened.

Such matters as high standards, an emphasis on traditional academic achievement scores, strict discipline policies, grading, and course content have significant implications for special education and mainstreaming. Understanding the elementary school, its organization, and the pressures on it are important to the special educator. Planning IEPs for handicapped children must account for the influence of the entire school environment. From a realistic and systematic viewpoint it is necessary to consider educational methodologies beyond the scope of mere remedial programming. The purpose of this chapter is to provide the reader with a discussion of topics that have a bearing on special education:

1. Role and function of school administration
2. Organization and philosophy of the elementary school
3. Curriculum of the elementary school
4. Attitudes, teaching practices, and role of the regular classroom teacher
5. Extracurricular activities of the elementary school

Knowledge of these areas will enable the special educator to prepare to deal effectively with such contingencies as negative attitudes, an inflexible curriculum, an unsympathetic administration, and problems associated with traditional organization of the school.

THE ADMINISTRATION

The theory and practice of school administration is a subject that is rarely covered in texts for teachers but one which should be of particular interest to teachers in special education because the attitude of the school administration can directly and indirectly influence special education. Many special education problems are also administrative problems; understanding the administrative structure and demands on administrators provides the specialist with knowledge that can be useful in maintaining an efficient program and preventing complications; in addition, the specialist may be able to find ways to secure the support of the administration under circumstances that might otherwise culminate in turmoil.

One way to appreciate the importance of administration is to envision the public school as a social system with separate parts, each one specialized for the purpose of contributing to overall goals of the institution. At the apex is the principal, who is vested with the official authority to adhere to specific policies and to make discretionary decisions about administering, supervising, interpreting policies, and distributing resources. The principal is the key individual in the establishment of a climate that can promote and support special education programs. The special educator may find that, whereas some principals are extremely supportive, others are frankly antagonistic to special education. Thus, the educator must modify the management of planning and activities according to the conditions.

Tasks of administration. As have other aspects of institutions, administration has become increasingly complex in the last two decades. Since the 1960s the amount of federal support for school programs has increased dramatically. Each federal program has also increased the amount of record keeping and accounting necessary for reporting and evaluation. In addition, the school has been the focus of controversy. The principal is no longer the leader of a placid group of teachers who quietly educate children. Teachers' unions, strong community pressure groups, student activists, and many other problems complicate administration. Litigation has risen in public education to new levels of activity, and each policy or action of the school must be weighed against possible effects and outcomes. With dwindling financial support, dropping enrollments, and a continuation of power struggles between teachers' organizations and school administrators, it seems certain that the 1980s will continue to be a difficult time for administrators.

The many varied and complex tasks of principals in elementary schools may be categorized as follows:

1. Supervision of instruction and curriculum development
2. Pupil personnel procedures
3. Staff personnel procedures

4. Community-school relations
5. Physical plant and school transportation matters
6. Organization and structure of school activities
7. School finance and business management

Role of administrators in special education. The recent emphasis on special education has added to the principal's responsibilities. In addition to routine matters dealing with the regular education program, principals must now devote particular attention to the special education program (Robson, 1981). For example, Raske (1979) surveyed school administrators in 29 school districts in Michigan and discovered that administrators claim to spend an average of 14.6 percent of their time on activities related to education, with the greater portion of this time involved in attending IEP meetings and completing special education forms (Table 4-1). Although 14.6 percent of administrative time on approximately 10 to 12 percent of the school population would not seem to be inordinate, it adds to the administrator's burden and may cause negative attitudes. Support of the principal is essential to the success of the program and morale of the teacher. Understanding the principal's role is helpful to the teacher in planning.

Additional duties and responsibilities related to special education indicate a need for school administrators to possess specific new competencies identified by Nevin (1979) as follows: (1) ensuring due process, (2) interpreting federal and state laws, (3) using appropriate leadership styles, (4) showing that records comply with confidentiality and due process, (5) resolving conflicts among program personnel, (6) using evaluation data to make program revisions for exceptional learners, and (7) determining staff functions and qualifications for special education programs. Administrators who possess these competencies and who support special education should be able to provide for effective special education programs. The problem is that few administrators receive training in these areas. Stile and Pettibone (1980) determined that only 12 states require special coursework related to special education for general administrator certification. Without adequate preservice training, administrators must acquire the competencies indi-

Table 4-1. Percent of time spent on specific special education duties*

Duties	*Percent*
Participating in IEP meetings	18.2
Filling out forms	16.7
Reviewing referrals for services	8.3
Supervising and coordinating the annual review, IEP, and follow-up system processes	8.1
Providing special education communication, either written or by telephone	7.3
Attending special education staff meetings outside district	6.8
Attending special education staff meetings within district	5.9
Preparing and monitoring the special education budget	5.1
Observing special education instruction within the district	5.0
Interviewing prospective special education personnel for employment	3.8
Developing the special education curriculum	3.8
Reviewing special education purchase orders, conference and field trip requests, etc.	3.7
Arranging special education transportation	3.7
Evaluating the special education staff	2.2
Arranging special education in-service programs	1.4

Modified from Raske, D.E. *Exceptional Children,* 1979, *45,* 645-646.

*This breakdown refers to the portion of time administrators spend on special education matters, which is 14.6 percent of total administrative tasks.

rectly or through in-service training. However, few states have made a priority of in-service training for school administrators.

Legislation and legal concerns

Public Law 94-142. Public Law 94-142 is the most important federal legislation affecting public school programs for handicapped children. Unless it is revoked or altered, local school administrators must be knowledgeable concerning this law if they are to be able to carry out its provisions. The following areas concern school administrators:

1. Child identification program
2. Provision of services to "first"-priority children
3. Full educational opportunity timetable
4. Provision of appropriate service
5. Provision of services in the least restrictive setting
6. Adherence to due process procedures
7. Use of nondiscriminatory assessment

In addition, administrators must also deal with state laws pertaining to the education of handicapped children. Along with P.L. 94-142, state mandates form the legislative requirements administrators must understand to provide appropriate educational programs for handicapped children.

Buckley Amendment. The Family Education Rights and Privacy Act of 1974, commonly referred to as the Buckley Amendment, requires schools to have a written policy concerning privacy and access to students' records. This act accords parents, as well as students of the age of majority, the right to view all of the following information:

1. All test scores, including IQ scores
2. Teachers' evaluation of the student's progress
3. Grades
4. Counselors' records
5. Any other information recorded about the student's behavior and the student's family

Parents may request that all inaccurate or irrelevant information be removed from students' records. The Buckley Admendment simply protects the rights of parents and students to privacy concerning sensitive information about the child. However, the procedures involved are the principal's responsibility.

Tort liability. Another legal concern of school administration is tort liability. Teachers and other school personnel may occasionally be defendants in lawsuits filed by parents of children allegedly injured as a result of negligence. Actions that involve negligence or that may lead to bodily injury include (1) asking students to do something that is dangerous, (2) sending students off campus to perform errands or for disciplinary reasons, (3) transporting students in a private vehicle, and (4) administering first aid. Handicapped students, because of a greater incidence of health problems, physical limitations, epilepsy, and behavioral misconduct, are a great source of concern to the school because of the increased likelihood of bodily injury. A greater degree of care is required, and the principal may regard the handicapped as an extra burden.

Special education supervisor or administrator. Many schools employ one or more persons who have some degree of administrative responsibility for aspects of the special education programs of the district. In smaller districts there may be one district-wide staff member for this purpose; in large districts the duties may be assumed by an assistant superintendent who directs one or more supervisors in managing various special education components. Sometimes the lines of authority are unclear. Some supervisors exercise a degree of actual administrative control with authority to manage budgetary and personnel matters. Others are strictly limited to a support position and perform routine procedural duties. Some are experienced, qualified special educators, whereas others are specialists in related fields or have no experience with the handicapped. The unclear nature of the position, varying degrees of responsibilities, and overlap with principals and other administrative positions sometimes causes conflict. As a result the special education teacher must be wary, especially in a new job, being careful to determine the actual responsibilities of the supervisor and ensuring that the principal, who has direct control over the building program, is fully informed of all activities. Some principals may be content to relinquish control of all special education matters to a supervisor; others may not. The special education teacher may sometimes be caught between conflicting authority and clashing personalities. The informal power structure of the school will greatly shape the influence of a particular supervisor or principal. The most important key is to determine who evaluates the teacher's performance and makes tenure and salary decisions.

General duties of the special education supervisor include the following (Gearheart, 1974):

1. General administrative duties
2. Supervisory duties
3. Research and continued professional duties
4. Public relations
5. In-service training

Since implementation of P.L. 94-142, the supervisor has assumed the burden of extra administrative duties including monitoring due process, participating in IEP and placement meetings, curriculum development, interaction with parents, materials selection, staff development, and consulting.

PHILOSOPHY AND SCHOOL POLICIES

The philosophy, codes, and policies of schools greatly affect the special education program. Because many children who "get into trouble" with authorities are likely to be handicapped, special education teachers must be aware of and attempt to understand the school's philosophy and policies concerning these areas and attempt to influence them.

Discipline. The policies a school implements in the area of discipline are of utmost concern to the special education teacher. The style of discipline practiced by a school reflects the values and wishes of the community, school board, and administration and is affected by the legal system in which laws and lawsuits reinforce or challenge the code. The person with primary responsibility for discipline is the principal. Special educators should be aware of any written policy the district has about discipline as well as the informal policy typically practiced by other teachers. Many schools are returning to corporal punishment. Children who misbehave most often are likely to be physically punished more frequently. Attempts should be made to encourage the development of positive reinforcement, which is more effective than punishment. Special education teachers should work diligently with regular classroom teachers to educate them about the effective uses of isolation, nonreinforcement through ignoring actions, and reinforcement, rather than punishment and intimidation. If teachers learn to cope more effectively with discipline problems and to prevent confrontation, the incidence of corporal punishment can be reduced and successful methods of teaching can be fostered. Rigid disciplinary codes will continue to be controversial and of particular concern to special educators. Some courts are preventing schools from punishing handicapped children if their behavior is caused by their handicapping condition. This has implications for great controversy. Any management strategies that reduce misconduct reduce the need for controversy.

Expulsion and suspension. One method of dealing with students who have discipline problems has been to expel them from school for a particular legnth of time. Courts have tended to reject expulsion and suspension policies because they are used to deny poor and handicapped children access to schooling. In some instances schools have been required to provide alternative education during the time children are forced to be absent from school. Courts have protected the rights of all children to an appropriate education. Such decisions maintain that a free public education cannot be disrupted through suspension or expulsion (Lipham & Hoeh, 1974). Special education teachers need to be aware of the district policy concerning expulsion and suspension, especially as related to the normal length of time, activities with the child during this time, and any alternatives to disciplinary action.

Dress codes. Dress codes are more important at

the secondary level but can also be a concern in elementary schools. Before the 1960s, school codes were not challenged. Most communities and schools agreed that a causal relationship existed between grooming and student conduct. However, as part of the demand for freedom of expression and increased civil rights, several cases concerning student dress and grooming went to the courts. The courts have generally been consistent in upholding the rights of students in their dress and grooming preference, so long as appearance or hair length does not disrupt the learning environment or constitute a hazard. Dress codes are not likely to pose problems for most young children. A greater concern may be that handicapped children dress in a manner similar to their peers and maintain standards of grooming to improve social acceptance.

Due process issues. Although primarily a concern in secondary schools, searching lockers for drugs, cigarettes, overdue library books, and other contraband has also been an issue in elementary schools. Students are protected from shakedowns and locker searches without due process. The Fourth Amendment to the Constitution prevents unlawful search and seizure, and students have used this guarantee to protest such actions. After reviewing litigation in this area, Olson (1971) suggested that a search by a responsible school authority is legal under the following circumstances:

1. The search is based on reasonable grounds for believing that something contrary to school rules or significantly detrimental to the school and its students will be found in the locker.

2. The information leading to the search and seizure is independent of the police.

3. The primary purpose of the search is to secure evidence of student misconduct for disciplinary purposes, although it may be contemplated that in appropriate circumstances the evidence would also be made available to the police. If evidence of a crime or grounds for a juvenile proceedings is lawfully obtained by school personnel, it may be turned over to police and used by them.

4. The school has keys or combinations to the lockers and the students are on some form of prior notice that the school reserves the right to search the lockers.

In any event, school authorities must adhere to procedural due process regarding search and seizure, and they should make sure that any searches and seizures conducted have a legal basis. The special educator would be well advised to refrain from such searches, since they are obviously more appropriate as an administrative duty. Unfortunately the trend for younger children to have drugs and weapons may cause this to be an issue of concern in some elementary schools.

The Fourteenth Amendment to the Constitution prevents the deprivation of life, liberty, or property to any person without due process of law. The basic elements of due process include written charges, hearing notice, preparation time for hearing, and opportunity to confront witnesses and stay pending appeal. These must be followed before any act of expulsion, exclusion, dismissal, or lengthy suspension of students and matters pertaining to special education placement. In the past, students would be suspended, dismissed, or otherwise punished summarily without receiving appropriate due process. Litigation emphasizing the rights of students to due process has prompted school administrators and teachers to be more cautious about punitive actions. Special education teachers should be aware of all requirements of due process and ensure that all procedures are carried out. Due process related to special education includes (1) advance notice of change in placement, (2) advance notice of evaluation, (3) right to an independent evaluation, and (4) right to a due process hearing.

Drugs. Our children are currently growing up in a drug-oriented culture. Drugs are increasingly a problem in elementary schools. Special education teachers must be aware of the availability of drugs, proper drug education, and ways to deal with students suspected of using drugs. Wood, Nicholson, and Findley (1979, p. 241) suggest the following actions when drug use is suspected:

1. The foremost concern should be with the physical welfare of the student. Judgments as to

whether the student is "drugged" or ill from some other cause should be made by someone qualified by training to make the judgment.

2. It should be determined whether the student is taking prescribed medication.

3. Psychological help should be made available to the student through a drug crisis center or through a school or community counseling service.

4. It should be determined whether this is the first time the student has been involved with drugs.

5. If lockers are to be searched, the student should be present if physically able.

6. An appeal procedure should be established to handle the cases in which students are suspended or expelled from school for the use of drugs.

Drug abuse is a problem for all teachers and school administrators in secondary and elementary schools. As a result, all school personnel should be aware of the potential problems associated with drug use and know appropriate steps to take in case of suspected abuse.

Tenure and dismissal. Teachers are usually employed under the terms of one of three types of contracts; term contracts for a single school year; continuing renewal contracts; and tenure contracts, whereby a teacher's job is secure from year to year unless dismissal occurs for valid reasons or there is a reduction in the number of teachers employed by a district. Teachers can be dismissed for incompetence, cruelty, negligence, insubordination, and immorality. These charges are difficult to prove without meticulous record keeping on the part of the administration. As a result of liability insurance, teachers' organizations, and a better general understanding of individual rights, the dismissal of teachers is a very difficult undertaking. The best protection for teachers is a thorough understanding of the local district's policy on contracts and dismissal procedures. Understanding one's rights as well as having the backing of a professional organization makes it very difficult to be unfairly dismissed. Special education teachers especially need to understand this procedure because of the sensitive position in which they find themselves as they balance the responsibilities associated with due process and advocacy for handicapped children. For example, in a due process hearing, a teacher may be required to respond to a question that sheds negative light on the school district. The teacher's competence may be called into question over matters pertaining to special education under rare circumstances. Teachers may need to take extra care in managing and supervising handicapped children to reduce the chances of criticism or vulnerability to dismissal charges. This is not a major concern but one which should be recognized.

Informal power structure. If special education teachers attempt to be maximally effective in school, they must understand the power structure of the school and the district. The formal structure is obvious because administrators are given authority to conduct the affairs of the organization. The informal power structure is similar in effect but loosely organized with no clear leadership. The formal power structure can be characterized by the traditional hierarchical design by which power flows proportionately from top to bottom (Wood et al., 1979). The informal power structure is invisible. The head of the formal structure in the school is the building principal. Although principals have considerable control over curricular innovations, budgets, pupil behavior, and other aspects of the school, recent developments such as the rise of teachers' unions and organizations, growing emphasis on student rights, implementation of federal and state legislation, litigation, and growth of parent groups have tended to erode some of the principal's traditional power. Even with the reduction of the principal's power, the role as head of the formal power structure makes it important as a central aspect in program development, morale, and effectiveness.

The informal power structure is very important in the functioning of the school. An informal organization appears to be essential to an organization's functioning and usually possesses great power of influence (Owens, 1970). The informal organization is composed of relationships among members of the faculty and community. The informal organization differs significantly from the formal organization, as pointed out by Lipham and Hoeh (1974, p. 102):

1. The formal organization consists of a set of structured roles; the informal one is characterized by interpersonal interactions.

2. Whereas the principal may exert formal authority, prestige is essential to the use of power.

3. Whereas the formal structure prescribes decision-making responsibility, the informal structure regulates the degree and quality of decision-making involvement.

4. The formal organization has well-defined lines of communication; the informal one has grapevines that are perhaps equally effective.

5. The formal organization may invoke positive or negative sanctions, pay, and promotions; the informal one may give or withhold favors and rewards.

Administrators heed the informal power structure because it aids in the accomplishment of group goals. For the same reason, special educators must be aware of this structure. If special educators are to be successful in gaining the support and collaboration of regular educators, they must court this power source. For example, if a regular classroom teacher has been at the local elementary school for 22 years and has the respect of most of the teachers in the building, it would behoove the special education teacher to gain his or her support in the mainstreaming movement or other innovations. Indeed, "it is the informal primary group, to a very large extent, which sets behavioral 'norms' for those who occupy teacher roles" (Owens, 1970, p. 50). Although these "significant" individuals within the informal structure hold no official status or rank, they may be able to cause innovations to succeed or fail. Without their cooperation, the special educator's role can be ineffective. The informal organization must be considered as important to special education as is the formal organization.

Those who have contact with decision makers in the power structure have influence. This can be nurtured by persons in the school or in the community. Husbands, wives, and friends of school administrators can wield influence and express opinions about the curriculum, departments, and personnel—opinions that might affect the operation of the school. The teacher should assess the local setting; try to identify the persons who have influence; find out how rewards and punishment are dispensed in the informal structure; avoid conflict with especially important persons, who, out of spite, might undermine the special education program; establish rapport with these persons; and, if necessary, take protective measures in the event that self-defense would be necessary in a public forum or in internal confrontations of the school.

The following points may assist the teacher in understanding the implications of the informal power structure:

1. Although a teacher may be the most qualified, best prepared, and most thoroughly dedicated person on the faculty, even a minor difficulty with important persons in the formal power structure may be sufficient to have serious implications for the program and the teacher's tenure, salary, and reputation. If the unhappy sentiment of the invisible informal group communicates negatively about a teacher along the grapevine of the school, the consequences can be devastating.

2. Not all administrators and teachers have positive attitudes toward handicapped students and special education.

3. Mainstream teachers may resent what they regard as extra duty, that is, an appeal for cooperation with the special education program.

4. The special education teacher is likely to have a concentration of problems and needs that is out of proportion to that of the rest of the school because of the nature of the students. Regular teachers are likely to resent the problems and disruptions. Principals may view special teachers as complainers and troublemakers unless problems are handled efficiently.

5. Feelings of ill will about the extra "burdens" of P.L. 94-142 can affect teachers and administrators and may be transferred to the specialist.

In most settings the special education program will represent a major source of change in the operation of the school. Change is unsettling to most organizations and disruptive to each individual. Some persons will be actively resistant. The special educator may have many sources of criticism, which maximizes the need for a command of good sociopersonal skills, efficient planning, and public relations abilities.

Another part of the informal power structure with which special educators must contend comprises pressure and advocacy groups, including parents acting independently, parents acting as members of parent groups, and other advocacy bodies such as professional organizations. Just as special educators must take into consideration the actions and attitudes of the informal organization within the school, they must also be sensitive to the influence of external pressure groups. In many ways P.L. 94-142 has promoted the cooperation of special educators and advocacy groups by requiring parental participation and consent. This indirectly assists special education teachers in working with a part of the informal power structure. Teachers can enhance the provision of services to handicapped children by gaining the support of parental groups and professional organizations but must be careful to balance the position between the school and power groups. If teachers have the support of the informal organization within the school, individual parents, and parental and professional groups, their chances of success are greatly improved.

There is considerable danger to the teacher who is caught between the school and one group or another over some issue or concern. Potential problems include the following:

1. Giving the wrong advice to parents may prompt them to act against the school. If a hearing is requested, the principal may accuse the teacher of inciting the parents.
2. Within a given context facts may be misperceived by parents as having a meaning that the teacher did not intend.
3. Using other children as examples to parents may cause distrust or may start gossip about the child, which can reflect unfavorably on the teacher.
4. Failure to inform the administration of requests or concerns of parents may lead to (a) dissatisfied parents who may "spread the word" that the teacher is incompetent or unsympathetic or (b) an awkward position for the administration.
5. Criticism of school personnel, policies, or curricula may lead to discontent of parents or key teachers in the school.

In a public relations context the special educator must attempt to be evenhanded in all dealings with parents and colleagues. Although others in the school may complain, the special educator must be much more cautious about engaging in this kind of behavior because of its possible implications for the program. In addition to many fine persons in each school are those who are unhappy and critical. The specialist needs to be able to deal with each personality, recognizing greater responsibility of actions that may damage or enhance the special education program.

ATTITUDES OF SCHOOL PERSONNEL

Attitudes are predispositions to behavior. The way a person feels about a concept, group of people, or practice will affect the person's behavior. Rokeach (1968, p. 112) defines attitudes as "a relatively enduring organization of beliefs around an object or situation predisposing one to respond in some preferential manner." Because attitudes affect behavior, it is important to understand educators' attitudes toward handicapped children. Several studies have shown a relationship between teachers' attitudes and their classroom behavior (Reid, 1967; Silberman, 1969).

How educators view the handicapped is important to mainstreaming. Studies have determined that teachers prefer some types of handicapped children over others (Kingsley, 1967; Murphy, 1960; Smith, 1979), principals perceive that some types of handicapped children will be more successful than others in mainstream classrooms (Davis, 1980), and principals' attitudes toward handicapped children are related to the effectiveness of the special education programs (McGuire, 1973; Smith, 1977).

Dismantling the categorical, or labeling, process may ultimately reduce the negative attitudes of some regular classroom teachers. Labels such as mental retardation may have the effect of providing a mechanism for bias to exist. Special education teachers should do everything possible to affect positive attitudinal changes among school personnel. Although change is a long process that succeeds only when teachers feel competent to deal with handicapped students in regular classrooms, following are approaches to initiate changes in attitudes:

1. In-service training based on the needs of handicapped students and reasonable classroom goals
2. Visits to the special education classroom and explanations by special education personnel about means of achieving integration
3. Direct, successful experiences with handicapped children
4. Demonstration of methods and materials useful with handicapped students in regular classrooms

Negative attitudes toward the handicapped are similar to prejudice toward others in terms of sex, race, or religion. On a daily basis the special educator may attempt to reduce bias toward children who fail to meet the educational expectations of teachers by avoiding stereotyped or negative comments, politely countering irresponsible remarks and policies, publicizing the improvement and success of handicapped children, and reinforcing desirable changes in regular classroom teachers.

THE REGULAR CLASSROOM

Currently the majority of handicapped children are being integrated into mainstream classrooms for some portion of the school day. This practical, if not philosophical, change in education has thrust the regular classroom into the forefront as a vital part of the educational environment for handicapped children in public education. The special educator must have a working knowledge of the organization and function of the regular classroom to fulfill responsibilities associated with special education planning and programming.

The classroom teacher

Attitudes and skills. The attitudes and skills of regular teachers are important to the successful management of handicapped children in the school environment. The chances of success are certainly minimized if regular teachers do not want handicapped children in their classrooms or have no skills to deal with them.

Of particular concern to the special educator is the fact that the regular classroom teacher is unlikely to have had much training or experience with handicapped students. Although efforts have been made to provide inservice education to regular classroom teachers, most of these teachers remain unprepared. This can be correlated with attitudes. Persons who feel poorly equipped to deal with a situation are likely to have a negative attitude, especially because regular teachers have been previously led to expect that the handicapped would be the responsibility of a specialist. Another complicating factor is that regular classroom teachers are essentially skill oriented. They teach groups of children to acquire facility with skills that are presented methodically in a reading or arithmetic curriculum. Most educators currently perceive special education to involve highly sophisticated special training devoted to correcting the problems of handicapped learners (process training). Regular teachers may think that they are incapable of dealing with handicapped students in the regular classroom because they neither understand the characteristics and needs of handicapped students nor have the specialized training necessary to conduct process-oriented learning activities.

Larrivee and Cook (1979) studied the various institutional variables affecting regular teachers' attitudes toward mainstreaming and determined that the single most important variable was that of teacher perception of degree of success in dealing with handicapped children. Teachers were found to be more accepting of mainstreamed children if they could rely on necessary support from special educational personnel. In another study, Kavale and Rossi (1980) surveyed regular teachers to determine their attitudes and perceptions of resource room programs. Results indicated that the majority believed the resource room program was beneficial to both handicapped students and regular educators.

Some teachers are accepting of handicapped children, are very flexible in their instructional procedures, and attempt to accommodate various learning styles. It is also apparent that some teachers are totally unsympathetic toward handicapped children, some use teaching styles that are rigid and unyielding, some value a strong and uncompromising set of academic standards, and some will not permit even slight modification of their instructional procedures. These teachers should be avoided when decisions are being made regarding the placement of handicapped children in regular classes. Placing handicapped children in classes with teachers who are not perceptive of their presence will only harm their educational performance. However, every effort should be made to alter their attitudes by providing direct support and offering concrete suggestions.

Training is a major concern of the special educator. Since the level of state and federal support for in-service training is expected to dwindle and it may be anticipated that most regular classroom teachers will be older persons who did not receive appropriate preservice training, the special educator will be expected to fill the gap of training and attitudinal change. Two surveys support this contention: only 15 states require that all preservice educators receive some type of training in special education (Smith & Schindler, 1980), and only 34 percent of teacher training institutions require elementary teachers to have some kind of special education coursework (Vacc, 1978).

Roles. The roles of the elementary teacher have been dichotomized into psychological and instructional roles (Jarolimek & Foster, 1976). The psychological roles include social model, evaluator, encyclopedia, moderator, morale builder, parent substitute, and friend.

Instructional roles include planning for instruction, facilitation of learning, and instruction, and evaluation of learning and instruction. These roles must be performed by regular classroom teachers when dealing with both nonhandicapped children and mainstreamed handicapped children. Unfortunately teachers tend to favor and praise certain children, especially those whom they perceive to be more talented. They need to plan for instruction for both groups of children. Although one can conclude that the roles performed by regular classroom teachers for nonhandicapped children will apply to handicapped children, this may not always be true. In addition, mainstreamed handicapped children require a few additional roles of the teacher:

1. *Team member*. Regular teachers and special education teachers must work collaboratively to effectively implement IEPs for handicapped children. Although being a team member is important for teachers who deal only with nonhandicapped children, it is vitally important when handicapped children are in the classroom. Without this team effort, it is possible that (a) actions by one teacher might duplicate actions by the other, (b) actions by one teacher might confuse children as a result of their receiving different forms of instruction, or (c) activities needed by children might be entirely overlooked as a result of a lack of communication.

2. *Advocate for the handicapped*. As a result of having handicapped children in regular classes, classroom teachers should become advocates for these children. Regular teachers should do everything in their power to ensure that handicapped children in their classrooms receive all services necessary to achieve success in school. They should seek administrative support.

3. *Parent counselor*. Although regular classroom teachers should maintain a dialogue with parents of nonhandicapped children, communication with parents of handicapped children is even more critical. This requires teachers to (a) understand the needs of parents of handicapped children, (b) assist parents in extending programming into the home environment, (c) assist parents in understanding the needs of the child, and (d) communicate concerns about the progress of the child.

4. *Instructional designer*. Individualized instruction is an important goal for all children. For handicapped children in regular classes, it is a necessity. Therefore, classroom teachers must be able

to design and implement individualized programs or the success of handicapped children in regular classrooms will most likely be limited. This is an area of emerging legal concern.

5. *Compliance consultant*. As a result of federal and state laws requiring that handicapped children be afforded due process, teachers who deal with these children have specific responsibilities to ensure the proper implementation of these safeguards. Teachers should know how to gain permission for placement and program changes, as well as what steps are necessary to develop and implement individual educational programs.

6. *Innovator*. Classes may include 25 nonhandicapped children and several handicapped children, thus requiring teachers to be creative in their teaching. Philosophically, mainstreaming is easy to accept; however, its implementation can be extremely difficult. Effective teachers in mainstream classes must be innovative, well organized, and committed.

Milieu

Most of a child's day is actually spent in a classroom with peers and teachers. For students in kindergarten and the first three grades the majority of contacts will be with one teacher and the same peer group. Beyond the third grade, depending on the organization of the school, students will encounter several teachers and students. The primary concern of the elementary teacher is to effectively orchestrate learning activities in accordance with the curriculum of the school district. The major emphasis of the special educator in assisting the classroom teacher is on learning activities. This includes the skills to be taught, the environment under which learning activities must occur, and the methods of presentation and reinforcement used. The classroom can be divided into two sections of major importance: milieu and curriculum.

The nature of the learning environment is totally controlled by the teacher, who establishes a climate, arranges space and materials, sets the tone, and manages the affairs of students. Certainly through the third-grade level, or when students are approximately 8 years of age, the teacher is one of the most significant adults in the lives of children. The standards, definitions of "good" and "bad," codes of conduct, and self-image of students are greatly affected by the teacher's verbal and physical conduct. The teacher communicates many attitudes to children that are difficult to measure in isolation because so many aspects of behavior are interwoven into a social fabric. The teacher's attitude, style of teaching, method of management, and personality characteristics contribute to the observed pattern of adult behavior that creates the environment in which each child will find acceptance or rejection, encouragement or frustration, and success or failure.

Of interest to special educators, especially when placement decisions are being made or when inservice or consulting activities are conducted, is the process of classroom interaction, which includes the following general dimensions:

1. Means by which approval and disapproval are conveyed to students
2. Manner in which teachers use their authority with students
3. Emotional tone of the classroom
4. Means by which teachers prefer to receive student information
5. Types of behavior that elicit approval or disapproval

In considering the issues, the specialist may reflect on the nature of the child in the classroom. Teachers who are directive, demanding, and task oriented may create a structured learning environment that is beneficial to all students. However, if teachers are also highly critical and punitive, the child who fails may develop any of a variety of feelings and undesirable behaviors. Teachers who are accepting, child oriented, and supportive may have beneficial effects on the personality development of all children but not necessarily on academic achievement. Such teachers must also be demanding of achievement or have expectations that all students will progress. The means by which any teacher may achieve growth is through appropriate reinforcement of learning, that is, feedback, appropriate reinforcements, and monitoring. The nature of classroom rules, the amount and nature of student-teacher interactions, and the kind of student-student interactions shape the milieu. This is the major context of the classroom environment in which learning occurs and students succeed or fail. Use of direct observation in this environment is essential to determine how to maximize teaching effectiveness in general as well as learning for a particular student.

Organization

Movement of pupils in elementary schools is both vertical and horizontal; the curriculum patterns of the school are organized vertically and horizontally.

Vertical organization. "Vertical organization is the plan of the school for identifying when and who is ready to enter, as well as the procedures for regulating pupil progress through the elementary school to a completion point" (Ragan & Shepherd, 1977, p. 109). Vertical organization permits planning for movement of students to higher curricular areas and for completion of a program. Although there are many vertical organizational strategies, most can be dichotomized as graded and nongraded.

Graded schools. The most common arrangement in the elementary school is to move groups of students through the school in a series of graduated steps or grades. Each grade conforms to the 9-month academic year. Following are basic features of graded schools (Ragan & Shepherd, 1977):

1. The graded school recognizes chronological age as the primary determinant for entry. Chronological age and number of years in school are the major factors fixing the child within the vertical sequence.
2. The graded school curriculum is based on a body of skills and knowledge distributed according to the grade level.
3. Decisions governing vertical movement of pupils through the sequence are made at the end of the school term. Some variations have been introduced to provide for quarterly or semester promotions. Promotion from one position to the next within the sequence usually depends on the completion of work at the preceding position.
4. Graded schools may employ horizontal organizations, such as the self-contained classroom, departmentalization, the platoon, or the team.
5. Gradedness is essentially a lockstep system.

Nongraded schools. Nongraded schools allow progression through a curriculum at an individual rate. The advantages to the student are obvious. Some students can progress through two or more traditional grade levels in one academic year. Students who progress at a slower rate are not stigmatized by having to repeat a grade or being passed on to the next grade without having mastered the required competencies. Nongraded schools are not common. Following are features of nongraded programs:

1. Continuous progress for students is provided throughout the school year.
2. Skills and knowledge in content areas, not length of time, are central to curriculum articulation.
3. Pupils are placed in the sequence based on competencies rather than number of years in school.
4. Successful experiences are provided for students regardless of their position along the sequence.

The implications of graded and nongraded programs for mainstreaming are apparent. In a nongraded approach the integration of handicapped students would be facilitated. Social considerations take prominence because students are encouraged to achieve maximal growth without comparison to other students. Most programs, however, are graded causing mainstreaming to have a full-range of potential problems for the handicapped student. Table 4-2 summarizes organizational patterns and possible implications for special education programs.

Horizontal organization. The two basic types of horizontal organization are self-contained classrooms and departmentalization. In self-contained organization, students are assigned to a classroom in which they receive the majority of their instruction under the direction of one teacher. Advantages of the self-contained organizational approach are that (1) teachers have an opportunity to learn a great deal about their pupils, (2) teachers are in a position to manage the relationship of subject areas, (3) pupils have a better opportunity to participate in group activities, (4) time is more flexible, (5) subjects in elementary schools are not so complex that teachers cannot teach several areas, and (6) teachers who are weak or uninterested in specific areas can exchange classes with other teachers (Ragan & Shepherd, 1977).

Limitations of the self-contained organization are apparent: pupils and teachers are isolated from other classes; students are primarily forced to interact only with students in the same classroom; cliques are easily established with some children being ostracized and isolated; some teachers are not capable of effectively teaching all subjects; and teachers may have a tendency to spend more time on subjects with which they feel comfortable and competent, ignoring those for which they have little interest.

In departmentalized schools, teachers specialize in particular curricular areas. One advantage of the departmentalized approach is that teachers become very knowledgeable about the content, methods, and materials of one or two subjects. Disadvantages include the following:

1. Teachers do not have an opportunity to get to know pupils well, an especially important factor in primary grades.
2. Unit teaching across several subjects is difficult.
3. Teachers may have a tendency to regard themselves as subject-matter specialists, and not teachers of children.

Other horizontal organizational alternatives include the platoon school and team teaching. The platoon school attempts to blend the self-contained and the departmentalized approaches. Students spend half the school day with homeroom teachers, and the remainder with teachers who specialize in particular subject areas. Advantages include those associated with the self-contained and departmentalized approaches.

Team teaching attempts to use various talents and experiences of several teachers. Although schools differ in approach, most employ a combination of large group learning situations and opportunities for individual projects. The composition of the team also varies greatly: some teams are composed of two teachers who share equal responsibility; others may consist of several teachers with one filling the role as team leader. Regardless of the team composition, effectiveness requires good rapport, common planning, flexible abilities, and support. Teachers who are forced into teams or who compete for leadership inevitably experience frustration and conflict.

As with vertical organization, various horizontal organizations provide different implications for the special education program. Table 4-2 summarizes these implications.

Cooperatives. Many schools are not large enough to provide comprehensive services to handicapped children. One way to circumvent this problem is for schools to join together in a cooperative effort enabling them to provide services they otherwise would not be able to afford. Although special education services are most often the preferred services provided through cooperatives, other programs such as vocational education are also frequently included.

Intermediate educational unit. Another organizational arrangement found in some states and rural areas is the intermediate educational unit (IEU), which is defined as "any public authority, other than a local education agency, which: (a) is under the general supervision of a State educational agency; (b) is established by State law for the purpose of providing free public education on a regional basis; and (c) provides special education and related services to handicapped children within that State" (Office of Education, 1977). Although special education services are easily suited to IEUs, other services such as computer services,

Table 4-2. Organizational patterns and possible implications for special programs

Organizational arrangements	*Relevant characteristics*	*Possible implications for special programs*
Graded school	Curriculum is strongly tied to grade level. Progress is measured against grade level standards.	Skill instruction may have to be carefully structured to mesh with grade-level content so that program is viewed as compatible. For example, special teacher would need to secure copy of a curriculum guide, content area skills list, or teacher's manuals to attempt to integrate skills taught in special program with those emphasized in regular classroom. Materials selected for special program may need to be similar to those used in some classrooms yet not exact duplicate. For example, child mainstreamed in second-grade classroom may be aware of type of workbook used in first grade. Thus, special educator will want to select a different set of workbooks or other materials that are compatible yet not clearly identified with a grade. Assignation of grades may be a important issue, requiring special educator to deal with pressure to conform to strict grading policy based on test results. It may also be more difficult for special teacher to reconcile individual focus of program with group standards emphasized in school.
Nongraded school	Curriculum is viewed as total body of skills through which students progress at individual rate. Recording and reporting of student progress is done more frequently and on more individual basis. Instructional experiences are varied.	Mainstreaming may be more easily accomplished because of absence of grade-level concern when searching for "appropriate" mainstream placement. A comprehensive skills list comprising all content to be taught should be more readily available. Special educator should secure list, thus making it easier to make content consistent between special class and regular classroom.

Table 4-2. Organizational patterns and possible implications for special programs—cont'd

Organizational arrangements	*Relevant characteristics*	*Possible implications for special programs*
Nongraded school—cont'd		Participation in IEP process may be more easily achieved because of individual focus of school; teachers may be more receptive to interaction with special teacher.
		Special educator may have more instructional flexibility in terms of materials used and objectives addressed. Social experience designed to foster learning and emotional growth may be more acceptable.
Self-contained classroom	One teacher has primarily instructional responsibility.	Instructional interface may be more difficult to achieve because teachers are unaccustomed to coordinating their program with other instructional components.
	Students form peer groups within their own class.	Mainstreaming may require more effort from special educator, since students may not be easily accepted by regular class students and may face more social barriers.
	Teachers generally appear to form strong personal bonds with students in their classes.	Teachers can provide detailed information on regular students, such as interests, attitudes, and abilities, thus aiding special teachers because of almost total instructional control of classroom teacher.
Departmentalized	Teachers tend to have subject-matter emphasis.	Special educators may find less support and interest in area of student social growth.
	Teachers deal with more students.	Handicapped students may be under greater pressure to perform to group standards in handling course content.

media services, curriculum consultation, and assessment are also provided.

EXTRACURRICULAR AREAS

Play activities. In addition to the regular classroom environment, several other sites and activities related to the school are important to the handicapped student. Interpersonal relationship of handicapped students and their peers in nonclass situations are important for the development of attitudes and self-concept. The experiences of students in social situations free of significant adult supervision or direction will foster relationships that will be carried into the teacher-directed learning environment.

Recess, an activity that most elementary children look forward to, is a period when they are free to run and play in a relatively unstructured atmosphere unless organized games are used. During this period, handicapped children need to feel accepted by their nonhandicapped peers and to be included in the daily activities because recess can be a very trying situation for children who are ostracized by their classmates. Whereas teachers can structure classroom situations to ensure participation by handicapped children, they cannot always structure the recess period. As a result, many handicapped children are overtly rejected by their nonhandicapped peers or ignored entirely. In these situations, teachers need to organize games and activities that will enable the participation by handicapped children. These activities should be such that handicapped children can participate without emphasizing their disabilities.

To attempt to correct or prevent such situations, the regular classroom teacher might consider employing one or more of the following strategies:

Organized games, planned to allow participation by handicapped students.

A unit of study on recreation, providing a broader menu of activities than the typical playground fare and emphasizing the ability of different types of persons to participate.

Bibliotherapy, using stories about various handicapped persons or individual's feelings about being included in group activities.

Platoon play, a system in which the students group themselves into four or five "platoons" each week. The "platoons" then select from a number of activities in which they participate as a group.

These strategies can have great impact on play activities without emphasizing the disabilities of handicapped students.

Assemblies. Also occurring outside the structured classroom are assemblies. Although not totally unstructured, assemblies still present an opportunity for handicapped children to be ostracized. Again, teachers should attempt to prevent rejection by such actions as the following:

1. Subtly inserting handicapped children in line so they will be sitting next to "accepting" children.
2. Arranging for handicapped children to be called on to perform acts within their capability.
3. Being present at assemblies to prevent aggressive actions on the part of nonhandicapped children toward their handicapped classmates.

Lunch period. During lunch period, handicapped children again face the possibility of overt rejection by their peers. Children like to mingle and form groups during the eating period. Teachers can reduce rejection by being present and by requiring children to eat at particular locations. In making these assignments, teachers should avoid placing handicapped children with children who invariably will abuse them.

Bus. Handicapped children are often the object of abuse from aggressive and older children on buses. Bus drivers should be provided in-service training in managing disruptive behavior, as well as the needs of handicapped children who may be riding their buses. Teachers should make sure that bus drivers are aware of any facts that may be important in dealing with handicapped children on the bus, such as health conditions and special handling needs.

SUMMARY

In this chapter we have presented the reader with a broad overview of the elementary school, including the role and function of the elementary school administration, the organization and philosophy of the elementary school, the role and function of the regular classroom teacher, and extracurricular activities that occur in the elementary school. The administration is a vital element in the special education program. Special education teachers must gain the support of both the formal organization, consisting of the administration, as well as the informal organization, consisting of important teachers and the members of the community, if special education programs are going to be optimally effective. The major purpose of teachers in elementary schools is to teach the basic skills. Special education teachers must support these efforts by working with students, as well as assisting regular classroom teachers if they are requested to do so.

We discussed the organization of the curriculum as it relates to the special education program. Traditional teaching and grading methods create difficulties for handicapped children, and special education teachers should circumvent these practices to enable handicapped children to be successful. Practical strategies were included for special education teachers to use with regular educators.

REFERENCES AND SUGGESTED READINGS

Behrens, T., & Grosenick, J.K. Deans grants projects: supporting innovations in teacher education programs. In J.K. Grosenick & M.C. Reynolds (Eds.). *Teacher education: renegotiating roles for mainstreaming*. Reston, VA: Council for Exceptional Children, 1978.

Berkowitz, J., & Sheridan, M. Group composition and use of space in a preschool setting. *Teaching Exceptional Children*, 1979, *11*, 154-157.

Boland, S.K. Instructional materialism—or how to select the things you need. *Teaching Exceptional Children*, 1976, *8*, 156-158.

Davis, W.E. Public school principals' attitudes toward mainstreaming retarded pupils. *Education and Training of the Mentally Retarded*, 1980, *15*, 174-178.

Dixon, B., Shaw, S.F., & Bensky, J.M. Administrator's role in fostering the mental health of special services personnel. *Exceptional Children*, 1980, *47*, 30-36.

Faber, C.F., & Shearron, G.F. Elementary school administration, theory, and practice. New York: Holt, Rinehart, & Winston, 1970.

Fain, S.M., Shostak, R., & Dean, J.F. *Teaching in America*. Glenview, IL: Scott, Foresman & Co., 1979.

Gearheart, B.R. *Organization and administration of educational programs for exceptional children*. Springfield, IL: Charles C Thomas, Publisher, 1974.

Goldhammer, K., Rader, B.T., & Reuschlein, P. *Mainstreaming: teacher competencies*. East Lansing: Michigan State University, 1977.

Goodman, L. Meeting children's needs through materials modification. *Teaching Exceptional Children*, 1978, *10*, 92-94.

Jarolimek, J., & Foster, C.D. *Teaching and learning in the elementary school*. New York: Macmillan Publishing Co., Inc., 1976.

Kavale, K., & Rossi, C. Regular class teachers' attitudes and perceptions of the resource specialist program for educable mentally retarded pupils. *Education and Training of the Mentally Retarded*, 1980, *15*, 195-198.

Kingsley, R.F. Prevailing attitudes toward exceptional children. *Education*, 1967, *87*, 426-430.

Kohfeldt, J. Blueprints for construction. *Focus on Exceptional Children*, 1976, *8*(5), 3-4.

Larrivee, B., & Cook, L. Mainstreaming: a study of variables affecting teacher attitudes. *Journal of Special Education*, 1979, *13*, 315-324.

Lipham, J.M., & Hoeh, J.A., Jr. *The principalship: foundations and functions*. New York: Harper & Row, Publishers, 1974.

Marsh, G.E., Gearheart, C.K., & Gearheart, B.R. *The learning disabled adolescent: program alternatives in the secondary school*. St. Louis: C.V. Mosby Co. 1978.

Murphy, A.T. Attitudes of educators toward the visually handicapped. *The Sight-Saving Review*, 1960, *30*, 157-161.

National Education Association. *The elementary school principalship in 1968: a research study*. Washington, DC: Department of Elementary School Principals, Author, 1968.

Nevin, A. Special education administration competencies required of the general education administrator. *Exceptional Children*, 1979, *45*, 363-365.

Office of Education. Implementation of Part B of the Education of the Handicapped Act. *Federal Register*, 1977, *42*(163), p. 42479.

Olson, E. Student rights—locker searches. *National Association of Secondary School Principals Bulletin*, 1971, *55*, 49-50.

Owens, R.G. *Organizational behavior in schools*. Englewood Cliffs, NJ: Prentice-Hall, Inc., 1970.

Ragan, W.B., & Shepherd, G.D. *Modern elementary curriculum*. New York: Holt, Rinehart & Winston, 1977.

Raske, D.E. The role of general school administrators responsible for special education programs. *Exceptional Children*, 1979, *45*, 645-646.

Reid, M. *The relationships of identified teacher concerns and personality characteristics and attitudes of teachers of disadvantaged children.* Unpublished doctoral dissertation, Texas Tech University, 1967.

Reynolds, M. Some final notes. In J.K. Grosenick & M.C. Reynolds (Eds.), *Teacher education: Renegotiation roles for mainstreaming.* Reston, VA: Council for Exceptional Children, 1978.

Robson, D.L. Administering educational services for the handicapped: Role expectations and perceptions. *Exceptional Children,* 1981, *47,* 377-378.

Rokeach, M. *Beliefs, attitudes and values.* San Francisco: Jossey-Bass, Inc., Publishers, 1968.

Ryan, K., & Cooper, J.M. *Those who can, teach.* Boston: Houghton Mifflin Co., 1980.

Salvia, J., & Ysseldyke, J.E. *Assessment in special and remedial education.* Boston: Houghton Mifflin Co., 1978.

Silberman, M.L. Behavioral expression of teachers' attitudes toward elementary school students. *Journal of Educational Psychology,* 1969, *60,* 402-407.

Smith, J.E., Jr., & Schindler, W.J. Certification requirements of general educators concerning exceptional pupils. *Exceptional Children,* 1980, *46,* 394-396.

Smith, T.E.C. *Principals' attitudes toward the handicapped and the work-study program.* Unpublished doctoral dissertation, Texas Tech University, 1977.

Smith, T.E.C. Attitudes of principals and teachers toward mainstreaming handicapped children. *Journal for Special Educators,* 1979, *16*(1), 89-95.

Stile, S.W., & Pettibone, T.J. Training and certification of administrators in special education. *Exceptional Children,* 1980, *46,* 530-533.

Theragarajan, S. Designing instructional games. *Focus on Exceptional Children,* 1976, *7*(9), 26-28.

Vacc, N.A. Preservice programs deficient in special education courses. *Journal of Teacher Education,* 1978, *29,* 42-43.

Wiederholt, J.L., Hammill, D.D., & Brown, V. *The resource teacher: a guide to effective practice.* Boston: Allyn & Bacon, Inc., 1978.

Wood, C.L., Nicholson, E.W., & Findley, D.G. *The secondary school principal: manager and supervisor.* Boston: Allyn & Bacon, Inc., 1979.

Yaffee, E. Experienced mainstreamers speak out. *Teacher,* April 1979, *4,* 62-63.

5 THE SPECIAL EDUCATION TEACHER

Judgments about the complexity of specific roles within the teaching profession are difficult to make objectively because of the variability of responsibilities at one level or another. The elementary classroom teacher who spends virtually every minute with children providing instruction, supervising, and planning is not to be persuaded that teachers at other levels work any harder. In fact, there has always been a certain resentment among classroom teachers about specialists who seem to have more "free" time to relax, have a cup of coffee, and use the telephone. This resentment has been directed at speech therapists and counselors and is increasingly associated with special education teachers who do not have a teaching role, such as the consulting teacher. This perception of classroom teachers has even been associated with special educators in self-contained classrooms primarily because they have "fewer" students in class. The acceptance and attitudes of regular classroom teachers will increasingly determine the effectiveness of special educators as long as the requirement for mainstreaming exists. Without any doubt the emerging role of the special education teacher is one of the most taxing, demanding, and stressful teaching positions in American education. This can be demonstrated not only by the nature and scope of responsibilities but also by the significant turnover and "burnout" among special education teachers.

As we noted in Chapter 1, the demands on the special education teacher are myriad and poorly defined because of changes in education of the handicapped. These are not changes primarily defined by colleges, universities, or experts in the field but rather by school districts as a result of alterations in the policies, regulations, and philosophies of officials in state and local education agencies. This text is written with these realities in mind. Even though a special education teacher may receive a degree and specific type of training on completion of college studies, the type of job and role expectations that await in a particular school may differ from that anticipated during preparation. There will be many variations from self-contained, multicategorical special classes to multicategorical resource rooms in which a teacher may be expected to assist children who have such labels as learning disabled, emotionally disturbed, mentally retarded, visually impaired, and hearing impaired.

Whether this requires a "super teacher" is debatable among writers in the field. As observed previously, the debate seems to exist between the behaviorists on one side, who focus on individualization and deny the importance of labels or group characteristics, and the traditionalists on the other side, especially some learning disabilities writers, who wish to maintain the categorical approach to save LD children from mixing with other "categorical types" in the belief that the approach of well-prepared LD specialists who use LD strategies with LD children will be most effective.

Various published opinions about what should be done to organize special education and group children for instruction do not necessarily relate to what is happening in the field at the building level. The angry opponents of mainstreaming have complained for more than a decade, but mainstreaming is a reality. Those who would argue for self-contained, categorical classes will have to present data-based arguments demonstrating the effectiveness of these approaches before they can be taken seriously. Even then, if the schools wish to employ other approaches, and despite research evidence to the contrary, the reality will be that the special education teacher must assume the roles and responsibilities defined by the school in which he or she is employed. Therefore, we will not suggest that any one approach is superior to others because there is no evidence to support such a statement; there are only opinions. Moreover, such assertions are not meaningful or purposeful because the trend in public schools is clearly fixed, and teachers must be prepared to grapple with the realities of the job, which are neither like they once were nor the way that a number of writers would wish them to be. Our position is that, in addition to any special competencies implied by the categorical training of teachers, special education teachers must possess generic skills to be used in regular and special classes, regardless of the arrangement.

Because of changes in special education during the last decade and the lag time of training programs to respond to the daily practical needs of teachers, many special educators are unprepared for certain aspects of their jobs and unclear about what is actually expected. This not only leads to confusion and anxiousness but also to role conflict and interpersonal problems with other faculty members and administrators. The purpose of this chapter is to provide a description of the range of responsibilities of the special educator at the building level that have developed because of the dramatic changes in school management and placement of handicapped children. The field is chaotic because of the many different ways in which children will be educated. The clear pattern is a generic approach, but the way in which generic programming is handled varies widely from one district or another; in addition, a number of districts will not use generic programming, although they require students to attend regular classes for some portion of the school day. In the midst of this chaos the only way to impose order is to look at the generic needs of handicapped students regardless of the placement and the generic competencies of teachers who will serve in a variety of settings under different models of management and placement. Basically the roles of the special educator are similar to those of all teachers, with the additional responsibility of performing a number of roles and tasks not expected of others.

Not long ago it would have been possible to accurately describe special education teachers in general terms by the areas of specialization that happened to coincide with the categories, for example, visually handicapped, hearing impaired, mentally retarded, and learning disabled. Some states had classifications that many others did not have, such as orthopedically handicapped, and some had names that differed but which really meant the same thing, such as perceptually handicapped instead of learning disabled. For the most part, the traditional categories defined the field of special education, each with its own literature, methods, and specialists. However, as the trends of normalization, mainstreaming, and generic programming have grown stronger, the labels have been deemphasized; in some states they have been combined, and many states have provided for special education by the development of generic teaching certification. Even in states in which teachers are still certified by categorical areas, many teachers find themselves in consulting or resource room positions that require them to provide services that are essentially generic.

The reality is that most handicapped children will be attending regular classrooms, a contingency for which the students and teachers must be fully prepared. A teacher who is involved in almost any public school program in special education will find that there will be similar demands regardless of whether the program is categorical, cross-categorical, or generic. There will be a need to provide instruction in academic and social areas and to deliver some degree of services in the sensoriphysical area. Most children can be integrated into the regular program. Thus, the service requirements for the children in school dictate the role of the specialist more than does the type of training or certification of the teacher.

Reynolds and Birch (1977) have described these emerging roles as ''collaborative models'' and indicate that the key is the degree of collaborative efforts or interaction that exists between regular and special teachers. They describe five models: the diagnostic-prescriptive teacher model in which specialists are trained to work with handicapped children who are not assigned categorical labels, the resource teacher model in which one or more specialists serve a variety of labeled children (cross-categorical), the consulting teacher model, the crisis teacher model, and the early intervention collaborative model. Reynolds and Birch summarize these models as follows:

> In a sense, each of these models proposes a solution to the problems of knowledge dissemination and of role coordination. From the broad domains of knowledge

> relevant to the education of exceptional children are drawn the knowledge and skills that are most useful in school practice. Instead of mediating the knowledge and skills through a variety of narrowly categorized specialists, attempts are made to mediate through generic workers who have been selected and prepared with great care and who, themselves, engage in continuing training efforts. (p. 451)

Evidence that the general trend is growing and that it divides professionals into opposing camps is detected in the results of two surveys. Belch (1979) reported that half of the states had adopted or were considering the adoption of some form of generic certification, a circumstance that was viewed as an agreeable sign of change from categorical programming. In 1981 Sparks and Richardson were able to affirm that the generic trend was continuing, but they greeted this discovery with alarm as a distortion of the concept of the least restrictive environment and an indication that teachers would be ill prepared to meet the needs of diverse groups of students. The argument essentially reduces to whether one believes that categories are meaningful. At present these are merely academic concerns because teachers must engage in a considerable amount of activity with regular classroom teachers because of IEPs which expressly state that students will be integrated. Therefore, generic competencies and strategies, far from being theoretical notions, are consequential components of a teacher's skills in all settings, even those which are very traditional and categorical. Multicategorical resource rooms or categorical self-contained rooms require the interaction of teachers and programs as never before.

TRAINING

Teachers who enter the field of special education discover that preparation is not necessarily based on a common core of accepted experiences and training objectives. States have maintained the right to govern certification or licensure standards and vary widely. Some states require generic certification, others require categorical certification, and some have requirements for classroom organization that differ from those for teachers. For example, in the same state, a teacher may earn a degree with categorical training but enter a classroom that is multicategorical. Many states that have categorical programming for teachers have colleges that elect to require generic training in their degree coursework. Otherwise, each state primarily relies on coursework rather than competencies for certification.

Because state certification requirements of a state agency may not satisfy trainers of teachers who wish their graduates to acquire certain skills and attitudes, various colleges and universities have infused unique philosophies, attitudes, and skills in coursework, depending on the orientation of the faculty. There have been two major approaches to training: *course*-based training and *field, competency*-based programs. In the former approach a variety of content is presented through lecture and reading assignments. Students are judged according to factors such as attendance, performance on written examinations, class participation, and written work. In the latter approach specific competencies or skills are identified and students are partly, if not totally, judged by the ability to demonstrate uses of skills in laboratory settings and student teaching or practicum experiences. Competency-based teacher training has been heralded as a significant innovation in teacher training because specific skills and standards are established for the content of instruction and teachers must be able to acquire them before they are permitted to teach. This is said to be superior to the more traditional approach in which teachers are able to pass pencil and paper tests demonstrating knowledge of a body of information but not necessarily the ability to apply it in a teaching setting.

The competency-based approach is now the center of an emerging controversy because of research conducted by Coker, Medley, and Soar (1980), who have concluded from classroom research that there is little evidence to show a relationship between mastery of a given set of competencies and effective teaching. The implication is that competency-based training is no better than more traditional approaches. This leaves the profession with the age-old concept that teaching is more an art than a specified science or technology.

Whether a teacher completes training in a 4- or 5-year degree program that is based on coursework or competency, the ultimate requirement is to meet certification or licensure standards of the state. Although many universities are empowered to award certification automatically on completion of a degree, in some states the candidate must present credentials to a state agency for evaluation. In certain states a teacher may receive only a degree and certification in special education, whereas in others the teacher may receive dual certification in the elementary grades and in special education. Depending on the state, special education may be categorical or generic. In categorical certification the teacher is permitted to teach only in areas of training and certification, such as LD, ED, or EMH. In generic certification the approach may involve serving children who are labeled in several categories in resource or self-contained rooms. The most efficient way to consider the roles of a special educator is to consider the various expectations that might exist at a local school district under the regulations of P.L. 94-142.

ROLES

The special education teacher may assume various roles. These may not all apply at specific schools because of local variation in the responsibilities of teachers and the resources available to the school. In general, the following role descriptions are appropriate for any teacher operating under the new trends in special education.

Advocacy

Advocacy is the assumption of responsibility to actively seek the acquisition of rights for handicapped students. Many special education teachers are committed to child advocacy and believe in the value and dignity of every child. As an advocate in the school and the community, the teacher must temper zeal with reality and supplant emotional reactions with rationality. Often the teacher, as advocate, becomes incensed by what the "system" does to children and tends to react suddenly and angrily. It is necessary to blend teaching responsibilities with advocacy postures in a manner that reduces conflict between the teacher and the school and yet benefits children.

To be an advocate one must know the laws, the regulations, and the limits. A list of key personnel and resources pertaining to advocacy should be maintained. The teacher should have at least general knowledge concerning the following areas:

1. State laws pertaining to rights, education, and training
2. State procedures and regulations
3. Specific federal regulations and legislation
4. Particular groups, organizations, and individuals that can be helpful

In addition, the teacher should have specific knowledge about education policies of the school district, parental and student rights, institutional rights, transportation, related services, and due process procedures.

In most situations the teacher should handle each inquiry or request from parents in a uniform manner. If parents are dissatisfied with services or unaware that other options may exist, they should be encouraged to work out their differences with the appropriate principal or other school administrator. The teacher can always give the following information to parents:

1. Their rights according to P.L. 94-142 and local procedures pertaining to grievances and due process
2. Appropriate procedure for registering a complaint
3. Resources in the community that may benefit them

In each situation in which a dispute, misunderstanding, or overt conflict may exist, the parents must first make their position known to the school, usually the building principal. The school should always have an opportunity to respond before any other action is taken. The teacher as an advocate and representative of the school must make this known to parents. This communication reduces the chances that the teacher will be viewed as a malcontent by the administration.

Teachers should be cautious about involvement with parents and patrons of the school who crusade independently or in small groups to exert pressure on school administrators. Although many of these pressure groups have legitimate aims, others seem to be interested in petty faultfinding. For example, one teacher remarked that she had difficulty getting materials for her resource room. What she meant to say but had not precisely communicated was that there had been a delay in receiving them from the manufacturer: the school had purchased them but not yet received the shipment. She was surprised and embarrassed when a parent who had heard her remark introduced the issue at the school board meeting and charged the administration with not supporting handicapped children.

Advocacy groups exist in networks throughout the country. In some locations there are strong organizations usually under the sponsorship of interested parents. These groups can provide parents and other interested parties with support and information such as the following:

1. Explanation of legal rights and provisions
2. Legal assistance
3. Contact with attorneys and surrogate parents
4. Referral
   a. To agencies for special services and evaluations
   b. To volunteer groups for counseling, tutoring, and so forth

An advocate will attempt to provide appropriate, accurate information to assist parents in making decisions about their children in the educational setting or will assume responsibility for representation of a child who has no parents or active surrogate. Advocates are careful to communicate with parents about their rights and options rather than to incite them.

The teacher will undoubtedly receive many requests and inquiries from parents about different aspects of special education. The teacher will be in the position of representing the school to parents and parents to the school, neither of which is useful or productive if managed improperly. The teacher should communicate to the parents that as an employee of the school system he or she is unable to assume certain obligations. It is the parents' responsibility to communicate their concerns and dissatisfaction directly to the school through the proper channels. The teacher should take care to ensure that misunderstandings or misinterpretations do not exist because the teacher does not want to be in the position of being blamed for disputes or used as a scapegoat.

The best approach is to have general information in a written form that is shared with the building principal. Such information should include facts about the laws, rights, and procedures. The parents should be advised about how to approach the school directly if they have problems with the child's status or educational program. The teacher's role should be to attempt to resolve disputes if at all possible by providing information, discussing facts, and seeing that all information and appropriate personnel are brought into the discussion. If the dispute continues, it may be resolved in a hearing, but the teacher will be viewed negatively by neither the parents nor the school for assuming the role of mediator. Resolution is always in the best interest of the child.

Direct pupil services

Teaching responsibility is the most direct and obvious role of special education, and much of this text is devoted specifically to this function. The emphasis of this discussion is on general consideration about direct services in special education.

The organization of the school, the organization of the curriculum, and the type of service delivery models dictate how teachers in special education provide direct pupil services. In programs involving self-contained classes or isolated resource rooms the child's activities in the special program may have little relationship to the regular classroom activities. In more integrated approaches the key is to follow instructional goals and objectives that are mirrored in both the mainstream class and the special education class. The following possible interactions must be considered:

Regular class	*Special education*
Graded	Self-contained
Nongraded	Resource room
Departmentalized	Itinerant
Self-contained	Consulting
Team teaching	Categorical
Open schools	Cross-categorical or multi-categorical
Open class	Generic

To simply describe a program as self-contained or resource room does not communicate what must be done to accomplish delivery of direct services. The variables associated with the regular classroom must also be considered. For example, a graded, self-contained regular third-grade class presents different options to the teacher who works in a resource room for special education than does a regular classroom that is departmentalized, employs team teaching, or is an open class. Three general models of organization and development affect the actions of the teacher in direct pupil services as follows:

1. Organization of the curriculum and regular classes
2. Expectations of the district and building principal for the special education program
3. Nature of the child being served

General observations may be made about the interactions of each type of service delivery with regular classroom organization:

Self-contained class. A self-contained class, whether it is categorical or noncategorical, is somewhat insulated from the regular class. There is ordinarily little interaction between the teachers or integration of teaching techniques, curricula, and so forth. Children may attend classes under the guise of mainstreaming for some insignificant activity. Thus, the teacher is free, unless otherwise required, to implement any type of instruction based on any special curricula. Whether this is to the advantage of students in another matter. This type of programming has diminished significantly.

Resource room. The resource room (categorical, noncategorical, multicategorical, or generic) should be more responsive to the regular classroom and curriculum, although we have seen many that are operated much like the self-contained classroom to the great jeopardy of the children. It makes little sense to place a child in a basal series in the regular classroom and have the child subjected to an unrelated reading approach in the resource room. The unrelated activities are detrimental to the child's learning. Unless the resource teacher becomes actively involved with the regular curriculum and regular classroom, the activities of the resource room will be at best unproductive and at worst counterproductive. The resource room holds great promise as a means of interrelating the special and regular curricula using a common skill sequence, compatible learning activities, consistent methods of instruction and application of teaching technology, and consistent evaluation techniques. Interactions of the resource room with nongraded, team teaching, open school, and open class arrangements permit the greatest flexibility. Self-contained regular classes seem to provide better interaction and more time for interactions between the two programs than do departmentalized programs. Most schools do not departmentalize below the third-grade level. This is advantageous because of the great number of skills introduced during these early years and the need for younger children to have a more stable environment.

Consulting and itinerant models. In a sense the consulting teacher does not provide direct services to students in regular classrooms, but the nature of the itinerant and consulting models are such that they bear remarkable similarity. The teacher may attend the class, interact with the student, observe the student, and make recommendations to the regular classroom teacher. This requires that the visiting special educator be accepted and regarded as having something to offer. The specialist must be competent and must deliver what is promised. As in all interactions of specialists with regular classroom teachers, lack of assistance and practical, daily problem solving will soon lead to a breakdown between the two types of educators. The consulting and itinerant teachers, if they have workable strategies, can be very effective in the mainstream class regardless of its organization.

Special education content. In most schools the content of the special education program will be determined by local curriculum committees. In other districts it may be undefined. Teachers may be expected to provide (1) ability or process training, (2) remedial training, (3) training to augment the activities of the child in the regular class, (4) instructional support, and (5) affective education. This lack of definition can be a source of concern. Some teachers who have not been trained to provide ability or process training may be expected to do so. Teachers who have devotion to particular approaches, such as perceptual-motor training, may be frustrated because the school expects primary help in direct skill instruction. Although some teachers may attempt to blend process training and skill models as advocated by certain writers (e.g., Lerner, 1981), this has the appearance of forcing antithetical systems to fit together so that old theories need not be abandoned. Regardless of the logical problems in supporting this approach, the teacher must ascertain how the progress of each student will be monitored and how the program will be evaluated.

Administration

The special educator is often expected to perform administration functions as related teaching tasks. The number of such duties will be determined by the effectiveness of the special education administrator and the degree of involvement of the building principal. Following are some administrative functions:

1. Supervision of volunteers, tutors, and aides
2. Managing a variety of forms and documents
3. Making decisions about uses of resources
4. Coordinating activities of classroom teachers and other professionals
5. Developing and altering student schedules
6. Preparing data or program effectiveness
7. Maintaining files of important records
8. Collecting data pertinent to the cost-effectiveness or cost-benefit ratio of programs
9. Providing input about decisions involving the overall school system
10. Representing the school officially in parental and community contacts

Many of these functions will be performed by administrative officers of the school, but the teacher will, to some extent, be involved in them. This can present a number of problems that should be considered before the teacher enters these roles.

The fact that the special education teacher may assume more administrative responsibility lays the foundation for potential conflict. The teacher should be cautious about exceeding the bounds of the loosely defined administrative role or to assume responsibility for accountability in areas that clearly belong under the supervision of an administrator. Role conflict can jeopardize the program and the teacher's status. Great care must be taken to clearly establish the lines of authority and to protect oneself from faultfinding and blame in the event that errors are made or conflict arises. If the teacher is employed in a school in which the principal exerts little leadership and leaves most details to others, the mistakes that might be made will be attributed to someone involved. In a program in which the principal is authoritarian, any appearance of challenging the principal's authority may result in direct conflict and criticism.

A significant step toward maintaining good relations with the administration is to keep supervisors and principals informed. This can have additional benefits because teachers who function smoothly and never encounter problems with the administration are apt to be overlooked and taken for granted. Reporting can be accomplished by submitting a quarterly, written document with appropriate copies sent to other significant individuals. In other words, sending a report directly to an assistant superintendent without a copy to the principal is inviting problems because the "chain of command'' has been interrupted. In the same vein, sending a copy to the principal without informing the special education supervisor may cause problems. Reports may be made on the following subjects (Knight, 1976):

1. Program tests, scores, and conclusion
2. A current roster of students receiving services including demographic information and comments about progress or special problems
3. Suggestions and plans for in-service workshops to facilitate teacher consultation
4. Special problems requiring administrative attention
5. Needs of the program and the future scope

Nothing is more upsetting to an administrator than to be blind-sided by a problem. An irate parent, a newspaper reporter, or a complaining classroom teacher who appears in the office with a problem that the principal has not heard about is unsettling. If the teacher knows about the problems in advance, he or she should communicate it to the principal immediately. This will ensure the good graces of the principal, who will learn to trust the teacher because being forewarned is being forearmed. It should be remembered that the special education teacher has more opportunity to become embroiled in conflict than any other teacher because of the nature of the children that are served and related problems. Also, the teacher has significant opportunity to interact with the administration and other individuals outside the school to develop favorable attitudes toward special education.

The school principal and special education administrator will rely on the special education teacher for assistance in managing all details of procedures in special education: referral, evaluation, placement, programming, and annual review. Although such matters can be regarded as routine procedures in the general administrative load of the school, the legal significance of many special education matters requires that extra care and scrutiny be taken. The teacher may frequently be asked to review records of each handicapped student to determine that all necessary actions have been taken and proper forms are in place. The teacher who knows the system well will be a valuable resource to the administrators. Only in schools in which teachers' unions exist will there be specificity in such matters and the teacher's role delimited by agreement between the district and the union.

The special educator must realize that, from the principal's point of view, special education programming may present a variety of problems, among which are the following:

1. Many administrators have only the most basic understanding of special education and may resent the amount of time that must be devoted to a part of the program that accounts for only about 10 percent of the students.
2. Concerns about due process hearings and lawsuits may be stressful, as will the pressures of parents and advocacy groups.
3. The mandated involvement of parents complicates administrative procedures.
4. Modification of the curriculum, scheduling, and budgetary consideration at the local level are perceived as additional complications.

Anything that can be done to encourage the administrator to view special education more positively should be attempted. To do this it is necessary to look at the process from the principal's perspective and determine how the problems can be anticipated or ameliorated. Each role can greatly facilitate the other and lead to improved programming and services. Table 5-1 is a summary of possible administrative tasks.

Curriculum specialization

Under the previous self-contained model of special education the special educator could implement any of a variety of loosely constructed process-training programs, most of them having more theoretical orientation than curricular substance, or use classical remedial programs, commercial materials, or some other curriculum specifically designed for the handicapped. The demand to integrate handicapped students in the regular classroom creates circumstances in which the teacher must

Table 5-1. Administrative responsibilities in services to handicapped students and types of supportive input needed from the special educator

Areas of administrative responsibility	*Types of assistance from special educator*
Referral/diagnosis	
Implementation of referral process	Parental liaison
Student assessment	Assistance in securing services of other professionals in diagnostic process
Implementation of diagnostic process	Setting up meetings and staffings
Parental participation	
Programming	
Personnel development	Leadership in IEP development
Enrollment	Input in school policy affecting handicapped
Pupil progress	Providing direct student services
Physical provisions for program	Aid in materials/equipment decisions
Parental reporting	Parental liaison
	Input in staff development/in-service
	Providing teacher consultation
Program evaluation	
Pupil progress	Maintaining student progress data
Cost-benefit analysis	Record keeping on parental contact
	Keeping inventories on materials and equipment
	Collecting summary data on mainstreaming support activities
	IEP review

carefully coordinate the curricula of the regular and special programs or modify the regular curriculum in some way. Teachers who do not coordinate the curricula (two unrelated teaching approaches) cause significant frustration for the children and for themselves. If the purpose of the program in special education is only to engage children in process training such as perceptual-motor activities, there will be little conflict. The teacher simply needs to find a convenient time to schedule the child for such training. The perceptual-motor activities will be additional activities to the regular curriculum and will not necessarily have any degree of relationship to the major academic tasks conducted in the regular classroom. Nonetheless, there remain a number of special programs that will involve students in perceptual-motor training or some other type of ability training for the purpose of attempting to improve underlying developmental skills or for the presumed impact on later academic skill acquisition. However, most contemporary approaches are influenced more by remedial approaches, direct skill training, or operant models. These will require that the regular curriculum and the special class efforts be coordinated to prevent confusion for the students and the teaching personnel.

The responsibility of the special teacher for assuming leadership in such coordinative functions seems to be greater than that of other teaching personnel. Despite the impact of federal and state laws, special teachers appear to be leaders in cooperative or shared roles. Thus, the role of curriculum specialist is one that is implied if not directly required in special education. As a curriculum specialist the teacher will need to perform the following functions:

1. Analyze curriculum taught in regular classrooms.
   a. Request a curriculum guide.

b. Get copies of teachers' manuals.
c. Secure scope and sequence charts from book publishers.
d. Talk with grade teachers about curricula.

2. Examine curricular-related variables derived from student analysis.
   a. Determine grades/classes in which students are mainstreamed.
   b. Ascertain preference for certain types of curricular materials or approaches.
   c. Review IEP.
3. Design special program to ensure interrelatedness.
   a. Base instruction on skills common to child's needs and regular curriculum.
   b. Use similar but not identical materials.
   c. Identify ways to introduce aids in the daily instruction of the student in mainstream classes.
   d. Ensure that materials, activities, and approaches in the special class are correlated with the skills and needs of the student in the regular classroom.
   e. Determine a fair system of grading skills; criterion-referenced and mastery-based approaches are most acceptable.

Consultation

Unlike most teachers, who may close the door to the classroom and proceed with the instruction of children, the special educator's effectiveness is greatly determined by professional contacts with teachers, parents, and support personnel. This is only true because of the dramatic shift from self-contained special classes to integrated models. Many believe that the regular classroom teacher, as well as others, should possess the appropriate attitudes and skills to deal with handicapped youngsters. However, many teachers who had accepted the fact that handicapped students belong in special education classes are not necessarily in favor of the changes. They may have negative attitudes, skill deficiencies, and little notion of how to assist handicapped students. This seems to be the primary reason that some writers in the field and some states support the use of consulting teachers. A minor movement in the field would have all teachers possess a common core of competencies that would include the education and management of handicapped children. Regardless, in any setting the special education teacher will be viewed as a source of information and instruction even if that is not a specific job responsibility. Currently, resource room teachers spend less than 5 percent of their time consulting (Evans, 1980).

The role of the teacher as consultant has become an accepted part of the concept of shared responsibility for serving handicapped students. The primary advantages of the consultant model are as follows (Cantrell & Cantrell, 1976; Montgomery, 1978; Newcomer, 1977; Reynolds & Birch, 1977; Swift & Spivack, 1975):

1. Cost and time effectiveness
2. Comprehensive services
3. Prevention
4. Reduction of the need to label students
5. Sharing the benefits of special techniques with more students and classrooms

Whether these advantages are realized depends on a number of important factors that act as variables in a particular setting. For example, special education teachers who are consultants or who act part time in a consulting role will not be permitted to deliver services directly or indirectly to students who have not been actually identified and evaluated. If a child is in a regular classroom and appears to have problems that warrant intervention, changing the child's status by providing something under the heading of special education services involves legal implications. Regardless of whether this is an important consideration, it should be remembered. If a state agency monitored a program to find that nonlabeled students were "receiving services," the program might be cited for a deficiency with the possible outcome of a reduction of state fiscal support. It may be ideal to conceive of services wherein the consultant is free to deliver services to classroom teachers that affect special nonlabeled students, but administratively this may not be possible.

Contacts with teachers. The primary goals of the consultant in dealing with classroom teachers are to increase the competence and confidence of the regular teacher and to ensure that services for a student are coordinated. In any setting certain assumptions and conditions must exist before consulting can be effective. These have implications for each consultant and each setting.

Consultation takes place between peers. Rapport between the special educator and the regular classroom teacher must exist. If there are personality clashes or a feeling of threat and coercion, the process will not succeed. Viewing the special educator as a consultant implies that the special educator possesses expertise and specific competence that the regular classroom teacher does not have. The style and manner of the consultant can create the climate for effective consultation; however, the behavior and degree of acceptance of the classroom teacher can create immediate obstacles. Generalizations do not apply because each interaction will be different. The consultant must be aware of the informal power structure of the school and avoid direct confrontations with influential teachers. The special teacher must be able to communicate ideas, approaches, and teaching strategies effectively without threatening the recipient or causing feelings of hostility. Pompous, arrogant people, no matter how skilled, are invariably rejected as consultants. People who are sincere and earnest but who have no skills are just as ineffective. One of the problems that can be anticipated because of the large numbers of younger special educators and high turnover is that mature, confident classroom teachers may find it difficult to accept advice from a "rookie."

It is logical that the special education teacher serve as a consultant. However, for this to happen the role must be developed to the extent that a mutual exchange of information exists as part of a collaborative endeavor. Under current conditions the special educator is the one who must make the most effort and who must struggle for acceptance.

Consultation requires a shared view of the student. As indicated before, the change from self-contained special education to integration has been difficult for classroom teachers who had grown accustomed to viewing the handicapped child as someone else's responsibility. The attitude may still prevail even under mainstreaming models. Regular classroom teachers may not believe that specialists have anything to offer, that the condition of handicapped students can be remedied, or that consultation is valuable. This is an area of concern to the special educator for which there are no easy answers.

Consultation must be based on the presumption of specific competencies of the classroom teacher. In this text we have identified specific skills or competencies that teachers must possess to manage the handicapped student effectively in the regular classroom. These have nothing to do with knowledge competencies in related fields; rather, they deal with instructional strategies. If the special educator and the classroom teacher can agree on specific instructional approaches, consultation is facilitated. The special educator may find that, even though a classroom teacher is willing to cooperate, the teacher may have a number of weaknesses in behavior management, task analysis, and techniques of individualization.

Consultation should be viewed as continuous. Consistent, positive interactions between the consultant and classroom teachers ensure the consulting role in the process of education. These interactions should occur even in the face of persistent sarcasm and rejection by uncooperative teachers. Nothing can be gained by acting in kind. Being a genuine help to teachers, developing a proven "track record," and demonstrating effectiveness to cooperative teachers will permit program growth and development. If most teachers view the consultant positively, it will be possible to work around those who would be obstructionists. After time passes and the successes become evident, the consultant's value as a professional will enhance the possibility of success in other less satisfactory interactions.

A considerable amount of stress can be anticipated in the special education role. There is a great deal of turnover and burnout. Burnout is a loose term used to describe job dissatisfaction and disaffection. The primary characteristics in special education are loss of interest in the job, a tendency to give up trying to deal with the problems because they seem to be hopeless, and submitting to depression. Many teachers ask for reassignment, seek jobs elsewhere, or change professions for the following reasons (McFadden, 1980):

1. Lack of administrative support
2. Lack of agreement about desired outcomes or goals of the program
3. Difficulties with aides or support personnel
4. Difficulties with classroom teachers
5. Clash between the teacher's training or expertise and realities of the job's requirements

Most of these points seem obvious. The last point might need some elaboration. Essentially, clashes between job expectations and actual job requirements relate to the type of training a person has and the scope of the job. Some teachers are trained in a very narrow focus such as the "Hewett" approach. They may find that for a variety of reasons they are unable to use this method because the school's organization and administration cannot adjust to it. We have known many teachers who were extremely limited in their ability to use certain applications of behavior modification because administrators and teachers were opposed to the concept. Obviously, if a teacher is equipped to go into a classroom with certain skills and competencies, the inability to use them will affect job satisfaction quickly. To perform the consulting role and to conduct direct services, the teacher must have the freedom to perform as trained or be able to adjust or accept limitations. These are factors the teacher should consider during the interview process when seeking a position.

Following are some facts to consider about the consulting role:

1. Clarify your training and experience as they relate to the consulting role.
2. Examine areas of potential weakness in which you may need assistance.
3. Anticipate resistance from teachers and expect criticism as a natural part of the role.
4. Expect doubts about the ability to help children perform more efficiently.
5. Remember that consultation takes place between peers.

Initiating the consulting role can be a difficult, exploratory period. It is somewhat different with each new teacher. Certain considerations must be regarded as they pertain to consulting. For example, the classroom teacher must be able to trust the consultant. Requesting any assistance is threatening because the teacher is essentially admitting a lack of ability to deal with a situation. A number of thoughts like the following might be unexpressed:

1. If I ask for assistance, will it appear that I am incompetent?
2. Will the administration learn about my classroom from the special educator?
3. Will my request for help merely result in more work for me?
4. Can anything be done to actually help these students?
5. Does the specialist really know anything that can make a difference?
6. How much experience does the specialist have? Has he or she ever been in a regular classroom?
7. Is the specialist paid more than other teachers? Does the specialist have similar responsibilities?

Many of these concerns will disappear with time. A number of steps can help establish good rapport:

1. The specialist should treat each encounter professionally and never say anything about another teacher.
2. Services can be described in handouts and during meetings.
3. The specialist should become acquainted with each person on the faculty and should spend some time in casual conversation when the time is available and appropriate.
4. When a request is made, it is essential that the specialist make every effort to respond as

Special needs of parents of handicapped children	*Possible strategies*	
	Direct services	*Referral*
Need to communicate about a problem	Individual counseling	Parent organization
Explanation of cause	Providing facts	Medical specialists
Help with correlates of handicapping condition	Group sessions	Specialists
Assistance in planning student's future	Career information	Agencies

quickly as possible. Delays and problems should be explained promptly.

5. Schedules of services should be developed in cooperation with the teachers. This avoids conflict.
6. Reports and communications to teachers should be problem related, clearly stated, and brief.
7. The specialist should invite visitation and sharing of ideas and materials.
8. All interactions of the specialist should be conducted in a professional, patient, and positive manner.

Contacts with parents. *Parent counseling* falls within the domain of the school guidance counselor and special education teacher. All teachers, especially elementary teachers, have frequent contacts with parents. Parents of handicapped children are likely to have more contacts than others and will contact special education teachers at school and at home. Briefly, some needs of parents and types of strategies that might be employed are shown at the top of the page.

The school counselor, special education teacher, classroom teacher, and others may be involved to some degree in parental contacts. The roles may not always be clearly defined. Parents may contact the person who is of the most help. Special education teachers are likely to have contact with parents when a referral is made and during evaluation and placement, IEP conferences, annual reviews, and other official meetings. Parents of students placed in the special education program will also contact the teacher about progress. If a school is departmentalized in the later elementary grades, the parents may contact the special education teacher rather than a number of classroom teahers whom they know little about or see infrequently. The special education teacher should be able to handle meetings with parents effectively and efficiently because of the need to serve parents and the need to function as a member of the school team.

Representing the school to the families of handicapped youngsters is a special responsibility that has certain disadvantages, including the following:

1. Role conflict with other professionals, especially the counselor
2. Possibility that parents will misunderstand communications, causing difficulty and concern for the family and child or the school
3. Vulnerability in knowing sensitive information about children and their parents
4. Possibility that some parents will depend on the teacher for assistance, even important family decisions that have nothing to do with school or the child's problem
5. Possibility that parents will be chronic complainers, calling on weekends and evenings to talk
6. Possibility that some parents will be dissatisfied and complain to others about perceived faults of the special teacher

Parents provide a wealth of information about children that can be helpful during assessment and teaching or treatment. Behavioral observations and reports, perceptions of strengths and weaknesses, educational concerns, and management ideas are among the areas in which parents can provide information (Escovar, 1976). Parents may range from fully cooperative to resistant or interfering. Each case must be managed differently and in accordance with the problems that are presented. If extreme difficulty exists, the teacher may require the assistance of the counselor and the principal. Teachers should encourage parent participation

Table 5-2. Interactive roles of parents and special educators

Input from parents	*Input from special educator*
Referral/diagnosis	
Provide observational data	Make parents aware of their rights, and provide clear, precise information
Cooperate with school and members of team	Arrange conferences at times and places convenient for all
Attend conferences	Notify parents well in advance of meetings
Share relevant information from other evaluations	Share reports and information
	Provide samples of student's work
	Explain the purpose of conference in advance
Programming	
Share concerns about educational goals	Clearly explain program curriculum
Study placement options, including visiting programs	Facilitate classroom visits
Read pertinent literature	Point out similarities and differences in various placements
Attend conferences	Share samples of activities, materials, and strategies
Observe student's behavior	Identify specific ways parents can help
Cooperate in placement decision	Provide information about parent groups
Participate in parent organizations	Provide reading materials and sources of materials for interested parents
Support the program	
Reinforce child's positive behavior	
Program evaluation	
Observe behavior	Encourage continuous contact between parents and school
Provide feedback	Provide feedback
Provide feedback	Support parent groups
Be realistic	Provide anecdotal information as well as grades
Participate in parent groups	

and open channels of communication because of the benefits to students.

Parent conferences constitute the major official meetings to be held. Communication skills of the teacher will be important in initial meetings to establish a basis of trust. Most conferences are held to satisfy the legal requirements of legislative mandates. Regardless of the reason for a conference, it should be conducted in a manner that is mutually beneficial. Table 5-2 delineates the major interactive roles of the special educator and parents.

Meticulous attention to details before a meeting is scheduled will help accomplish the purposes of the meeting. Meeting preparations, conduct, and conclusion are important (Kroth, 1975; Long, 1976). Planning should include the following details:

1. Selecting an appropriate site for the conference; making certain that nothing else is scheduled for the same period
2. Making sure that all necessary records, materials, equipment, or other items are available
3. Sending advance notice to all participants listing the place, time, date, purpose, and length
4. Examining the student's record
5. Making particular note of any information about the student such as reports from other teachers, grades, and scores, depending on the purpose

6. Making certain that the purpose of the meeting is clear
7. Collecting work samples of the student if they would contribute to the meeting
8. Always collecting some positive information about the student to be communicated to the parents, even if the purpose of the meeting is to discuss negative aspects

Conducting the conference is an important process that is no less significant if only the parents and the teacher attend:

1. The conference site should be comfortable, private, informal, and arranged so that parents and professionals are not separated by the table.
2. Materials used in the conference should be neatly arranged and easily accessible. A pile of materials is unsightly, and inability to quickly find what is needed communicates inefficiency.
3. Opening the meeting with casual talk may set a friendly tone. Clearly stating the meeting's purpose, expected outcomes, and length will assist all participants in dealing with the task. If notes are taken, the parents should be informed about the purposes and should be given the opportunity to see them.
4. Ending the conference is as important as is preparing for it. Setting a definite ending time is important because it communicates the need to come to a conclusion and enables persons to meet other obligations without having to leave the meeting early. Summarization of themeeting assists in determining that all have the same perception of the issues at hand. If follow-up is required, the end of the meeting is a good time to make such plans if possible.

Depending on the nature of the conference, a number of follow-up activities will need to be conducted: (1) each conference should have a written report, the length and details ranging from simple notation to full documentation; (2) a summary should be filed and copies sent to the participants; (3) specific actions required by the conference should be attended to; and (4) after additional actions are completed, the participants should be informed.

Written communications should be on approved stationery of the school, and copies should be provided to the principal. No notes or forms should be used unless they are approved by the administration. No written communications should be sent to parents unless they are explained. A prior personal communication might be helpful. Communications should be in clear, concise, accurate language. All communications must be copied and placed in files for future reference. Telephone communications should be logged with a simple notation of the date, time, and general nature of the conversation. Anything of substance that transpires during the phone conversation should be described in greater detail and kept in the records.

Contacts with support personnel. Consulting with *nonprofessional support personnel* is also a very important but overlooked activity. Encounters of students with bus drivers, clerical staff, food services personnel, paraprofessionals, and tutors can be significant to the student for a number of reasons and can have implications for the program. The general points of importance are as follows:

1. Nonprofessional support personnel can affect the self-esteem and peer attitudes of handicapped students.
2. Nonprofessional support personnel are extremely important to the operation of the school and contribute to success of programs.
3. Nonprofessional support personnel are involved in the communications network of the school and in the informal power structure.
4. Attitudes of staff members can affect the attitudes of professional employees.

Obviously bus drivers, custodians, and secretaries are more important to the physical maintenance of the building, transportation of students, and management of phone calls and records. If a teacher is ill, a substitute is called. If the secretary is ill, the school may seem to shut down. The principal relies on these individuals for aspects of the job that are important on a daily basis. The activities of a teacher in a closed classroom are relatively more remote. The principal is likely to have more personal contact with staff members than with the faculty. Their information and attitudes will help the principal's view of different teachers and students. If the custodian says that certain teachers or students leave the rooms dirty and unsightly, the principal will be influenced. If the secretary finds consistent errors in records turned in by teachers or considers certain teachers to be rude or incompetent, the principal may develop the same attitude.

Some teachers may tend to treat nonprofessional persons differently. If a teacher presents an air of superiority or unfriendliness to the secretary or cook, the teacher's behavior will be described to other teachers and to the principal. Word that a special education teacher spends a lot of time drinking coffee and that the children just play games in the resource room is likely to come from support staff in the school. The importance of these people to the functioning of the school cannot be underestimated. They are integral to its operation and can have a significant impact on key personnel in the school and on persons in the community. The special education teacher should treat them with dignity and respect and should attempt to develop friendly relationships with them. Also, bus drivers, custodians, secretaries, and food service personnel should not be overlooked in in-service programs because, if they understand the purpose of the special education program, the image of the program can be greatly enhanced. These nonprofessional personnel see children in various environments. They can provide a valuable source of information about the behavior of a student in different contexts, about interpersonal interactions, and can provide information to assist the teacher in preventing problems of children that may exist in the halls and to and from school.

Public relations

Increasingly in special education it is becoming important for teachers to acquire skills in public relations. As it has become necessary to change the image of special education and to seek acceptance and support from other educators and the community, the marketing concept has been applied to special education; that is, the special educator has a product to sell to consumers, and efficient sales techniques require good interpersonal skills and a product image. As with so many other aspects of special education in the emerging roles, this area has not been stressed in most training programs but is certainly important to the systematic view of methodology. The role has developed as the realities of dealing with teachers and patrons have forced its recognition by some writers in the field (D'Alonzo & Wiseman, 1978; Marsh, Gearhart & Gearhart, 1978; McNutt & Heller, 1978). Although it may be viewed as unfortunate that the special educator is burdened with another responsibility that other teachers do not contend with, it is no less an important role function if services are to be appropriately delivered.

Public relations may be conceived within three broad categories: (1) teachers, (2) administrators, and (3) parents and patrons. Each of these publics have different degrees of impact on special education. Much of the concern about dealing with teachers and administrators has been expressed, as have relationships with parents. But, special education teachers are also likely to be involved in public speaking engagements such as in-service training, presentations at school functions, and addresses to clubs and organizations. Following is a list of suggestions for preparing presentations:

1. Any presentation should be prepared in advance with good public speaking actions: eye contact, appropriate gestures, and use of audiovisual aids.

2. Most presentations should range between 15 and 45 minutes in length, which dictates the amount of information to be communicated.

3. One or two major points should be presented.

4. Technical terminology should be avoided to enable the audience to easily grasp the message.

5. Certain topics should be avoided, such as

''diagnosing'' a child's potential problems in public based on limited descriptions of behavior.

6. Nothing should be said that would communicate dissatisfaction with the school district, a particular administrator, or colleagues.

7. Real names and locations should be avoided because of the potential for embarrassment.

8. Positive aspects should be discussed more than negative ones.

9. Referral information should be available.

10. Oversimplification should be avoided so that the audience will not be misled.

11. Discussions of medical aspects and conditions should be presented with cautions about the speaker's background and expertise. Any detailed discussion should be left to qualified professionals.

12. The speaker should be prepared to answer inquiries about services.

13. Complaints about the school or personnel in it may be expressed by members of the audience on some occasions. The speaker should be prepared to either defend the school or to refer the complainer to a source for clarification. It is important to not let sessions degenerate to personal issues and griping.

14. The speaker should be prepared to deal with an occasional heckler.

15. The speaker should be prepared to deal with controversies that may exist between members of certain political groups or organizations, such as between learning disabilities groups and the International Reading Association.

16. Any donations from clubs and organizations should be approved by the administration. The speaker should not seek donations as a member of a school.

If numerous presentations are made, the teacher as speaker will want to develop a complete record of all meetings and the topics and jokes or anecdotes used. If invited to speak to the same group, the teacher will be reminded by the record to avoid repetition. A file might be developed specifically for presentations to include the following information:

1. List of films
2. List of resources in the community
3. Materials suitable for distribution to the community
4. Outlines of previous presentations
5. Complete list of anecdotes, stories, and jokes
6. List of reading materials suitable for public consumption
7. Overhead transparencies, samples, and models for use in presentations

These materials can be accumulated and used as a valuable resource in presentations. This aspect of the public relations role might be important to teachers.

Relationship with other professionals

The special educator must coordinate activities with other professionals within the school district. Depending on its size and resources, the district may have many types of support personnel such as psychologists, speech pathologists, curriculum specialists, occupational and physical therapists, counselors, and social workers. In many districts many support services, especially those involving assessment, are contracted outside the district. In any case the special educator is required to coordinate different aspects of the roles of support personnel as they impact on the student. The distinctive features of relationships with support personnel are similar to those with other professionals such as teachers and administrators: (1) each type of specialist has some kind of involvement with handicapped students and their programming; (2) each discipline has a certain set of skills to bring into the school setting; (3) there is potential for ''turf'' problems to exist, since different professionals may argue about their roles and responsibilities; and (4) special teachers often function as the major link between services and parents, which raises the possibility that information will be erroneously communicated to parents that was not intended by the various professionals.

Responsibilities of the special education teacher and other professional personnel obviously overlap.

A comfortable working relationship must be developed in each instance. It must be anticipated that not all relationships will be harmonious, however. All these professionals have contact with students, teachers, and parents, and it would be best if the efforts were coordinated. Whether and how this is done depends entirely on local circumstances. A strong, efficient principal clearly identifies all roles and responsibilities. Other principals simply let the various professionals sort things out for themselves. Before assuming responsibility for any particular service that may seem to be partly the responsibility of others, the special educator should determine if these functions involve policies and procedures. If not, the special educator should seek approval of the administration to avoid the possibility of future recriminations. Points of interest common to support personnel and the special educator follow:

1. Student progress data
2. Parental contacts
3. Sociopersonal development of students
4. Teacher consultation
5. Contact with community agencies and professionals

Greater efficiency and improved results obviously result from cooperation rather than competition. If duties are not specified, the teacher should seek out each professional and determine a common ground and operating rules that they can all live with. The full range of personality types exists among these persons just as in any other occupational group. Some relationships work smoothly, whereas others are difficult and uncomfortable.

Personal characteristics

Earlier in this chapter we briefly discussed teacher burnout. It should be obvious that tremendous responsibilities that are unlike those of other professionals fall on the shoulders of the special educator. In many ways the job of the special educator is like that of any teacher who must provide direct pupil services and deal with the problems associated with teaching. However, the special education teacher is also burdened with numerous other responsibilities of a different degree and kind. While fulfilling job requirements, the special teacher is required to perform duties similar to those of school psychologists, counselors, and other nonteaching specialists who do not have to spend time in direct teaching. They have more time to conduct their specialized roles, time that is specifically defined for that purpose. The special educator must attempt to fit everything into a full day, which creates pressures that can cause frustration, depression, fatigue, and dissatisfaction with the job.

The key to good mental health is defined differently by various professionals who write about the subject. In general it appears that the ability to plan carefully, to relax, and to have a balanced lifestyle is important. To perform effectively as a special education teacher requires expenditure of a great deal of energy. The job itself can be taxing; in addition, personal concerns such as family affairs and outside obligations associated with church or community groups must be considered, and the tendency to become overloaded increases feelings of anxiety and frustration.

The special education teacher may feel isolated and alone and may need to seek support and outlets to maintain a sense of equilibrium. The ability to succeed in teaching may be more a matter of learning how to cope than having command of a variety of teaching techniques. It should be evident that teaching, particularly in special education, is all-encompassing and not simply limited to classroom instruction. The teacher must expect frustration, disappointment, and conflict and learn how to deal with them maturely. Some suggested coping strategies are as follows:

1. Admit that you can neither accomplish everything nor solve all problems.
2. Set lower goals that are reasonable to accomplish, and select a time frame or deadline for completion.
3. Identify precisely what seems to cause an

emotional change or sudden feeling of defeat, and plan to ignore, change, or circumvent it.

4. Refrain from self-condemnation; seek creative alternatives.

Tolerance for frustration seems to be related to goal setting. Persons who attempt to do more than they can accomplish are creating the circumstances for failure. Balancing the many roles of teaching requires planning and concentration. If every day is filled with a hectic routine, the nights with meetings, and the weekends with catching up on paperwork, it is only a matter of time before a cycle of frustration, fatigue, and failure set in. This failure can be avoided by realistic goal setting and planning. One helpful suggestion is to find a friend or another special educator to talk with about professional problems. Venting one's feelings is good therapy with the added benefit of being able to share alternatives to mutual problems.

The approach the special education teacher uses with students and other teachers is greatly colored by individual disposition. A personality that might be described as positive, easygoing, and personable can be a great asset. Anticipating resistance from parents, teachers, administrators, and students is realistic behavior. Role reversal, looking at a situation from another's point of view, can be instructive and calming in the face of adversity. It may be possible to remain calm if one understands why others seem to be so difficult.

Willingness to acknowledge efforts and shortcomings of regular teachers rather than assuming "it is just their job" to cooperate is important. Reinforcing and rewarding small gains in relationships with colleagues is as important as is teaching children. Realistic expectations and a willingness to accept others as they are will earn for the teacher the same privilege. Feelings must be accurate, and care taken to develop and sustain rapport. Most problems have solutions, and most people cooperate. A certain amount of worry about keeping everyone happy may be natural but is as unrealistic as is dwelling on setbacks, criticisms, and rejections that emanate from a few sources. Time and effort would be more productively spent identifying the nature of a problem and looking for ways to change it or selecting a new strategy.

Professional organizations offer one source of support to teachers. Professional groups such as the Council for Exceptional Children and the American Association on Mental Deficiency provide many direct and indirect benefits. Professional journals provide substantial information that can be helpful in teaching and dealing with daily problems, important research publications can be of assistance, and some organizations provide liability and health insurance to members. Special education teachers are urged to consider membership in these and other organizations because of personal and professional rewards and professional growth.

SUMMARY

Teaching, in the traditional sense, is only one role of the special education teacher. For teaching to be effective, especially because of the demand for mainstreaming, it is necessary for the teacher to engage in many activities that traditionally have been within the scope of other professionals in the school setting. The generic trend has impacted on all modes of service delivery, even those which appear to be self-contained because nearly all handicapped children experience some type of integration. Clearly, the trend is toward generic competencies, although training institutions may still be preparing teachers under older concepts. The teacher will discover that the demands of the job are greatly expanded and still evolving.

The special education teacher's roles include advocacy, direct services, administration, curriculum specialization, consultation, public relations, relationships with other professionals, and personal characteristics. Truly the role of the special educator is complex and demanding; it must be conceived beyond the limits of classroom activities if excellence is to be achieved.

REFERENCES AND SUGGESTED READINGS

Belch, P.J. Toward noncategorical teacher certification in special education: myth or reality? *Exceptional Children,* 1979, *46,* 129-130.

Cantrell, R., & Cantrell, M. Preventive mainstreaming: impact of a supportive services program on pupils. *Exceptional Children,* 1976, *42,* 381-386.

Coker, H., Medley, D., & Soar, R.S. How valid are expert opinions about effective teaching? *Phi Delta Kappan,* 1980, *62,* 131-134.

D'Alonzo, B.J., & Wiseman, P.F. Actual and desired roles of the high school LD resource teacher, *Journal of Learning Disabilities,* 1978, *11,* 390-397.

Escovar, P.L. Another change for learning: the assessment class. *Teaching Exceptional Children,* 1976, *9,* 2-3.

Evans, S. The consultant role of the resource teacher. *Exceptional Children,* 1980, *46,* 402-403.

Knight, N. Working relationships that work. *Teaching Exceptional Children,* 1976, *8,* 113-115.

Kroth, R. *Communicating with parents of exceptional children.* Denver, CO: Love Publishing Co., 1975.

Lerner, J. *Learning disabilities* (3rd ed.). Boston: Houghton Mifflin Co., 1981.

Long, A. Easing the stress of parent-teacher conferences. *Today's Education,* 1976, *65,* 84-85.

Marsh, G.E., Gearheart, C.K., & Gearheart, B.R. *The learning disabled adolescent: program alternatives in the secondary school.* St. Louis: The C.V. Mosby Co., 1978.

McFadden, A.C. *Internal and external factors in teacher burnout.* Paper presented at the Fourth Annual Conference on Severe Behavior Disorders, Council for Exceptional Children, St. Paul, MN, November 1980.

McNutt, G., & Heller, G. Services for learning disabled adolescents: survey. *Learning Disability Quarterly,* 1978, *1,* 101-102.

Montgomery, M.D. The special educator as a consultant: some strategies. *Teaching Exceptional Children,* 1978, *10,* 110-112.

Newcomer, P.L. Special educational services for the mildly handicapped: beyond a diagnostic and remedial model. *Journal of Special Education,* 1977, *11,* 36-39.

Reynolds, M.C., & Birch, J.W. *Teaching exceptional children in all America's schools.* Reston, VA: Council for Exceptional Children, 1977.

Sparks, R., & Richardson, S.O. Multicategorical/cross-categorical classrooms for learning disabled students. *Journal of Learning Disabilities,* 1981, *14,* 60-61.

Swift, M.S., & Spivack, G. *Alternative teaching strategies: helping behaviorally troubled children achieve.* Champaign, IL: Research Press, 1975.

6 TEACHING READING

Of all the academic skills a child might acquire in American schools, reading is the most valued in our culture. Verbal ability is highly prized. People who are able to read, write, and express themselves effectively are regarded as intelligent and educated. An intelligent person who, for some reason, is deficient in these skills will be subjected to intense culture discrimination and prejudice. Teachers consider their "best" readers to be their "best," most capable, better adjusted, and bright students. Since reinforcement and a sense of self-satisfaction may be acquired through academic success, it is not surprising that students who do not master reading tend to have more adjustment problems, less satisfaction, and conflict later in life. The school does not reward poor readers. A poor reader who experiences persistent failure and disapproval from teachers and peers and who consequently lacks self-esteem will have a different future than a good reader who almost incidentally acquires academic skills. Regular and special educators have devoted many resources to the challenge of improving reading for students who do not meet school expectations.

CHARACTERISTICS OF DISABLED READERS

Regardless of the special education label that might be applied to a child, reading may be a major consideration of the team in placement and programming. Moreover, children who are classified as learning disabled or mentally retarded tend to have reading as an elevated concern because this academic skill is involved in the placement-decision process. With many LD students, the referring problem is reading that is confirmed during assessment, and some explanation of it is offered on the basis of psychometric data to justify placement and programming decisions. However, reading disorders are pervasive, affecting children who are considered under all diagnostic categories and children who are never labeled. The teacher will find a label to be of little help in either explaining the problem or determining an individualized approach.

Numerous characteristics and correlates of reading disabilities have been associated with the heterogeneous population of students who fail in reading. There is no clear understanding of the reading process itself; neither is there a clear understanding of a cause and effect relationship in reading disorders. One aspect that is rarely examined is how children are taught. We may know the grade a student is in, whether it is self-contained or departmentalized, the kinds of materials used, whether it is individualized or rooted in a basal series, and so forth. However, unless the child is directly observed, it is not possible to determine how the child is taught and how the classroom environment may be contributing to the child's failure. Thus, most of the assessment process is devoted to personological characteristics derived secondhand from various instruments and professional opinions. Table 6-1 presents the most common factors related to reading disorders. Most of these characteristics are only correlates with no clear relationship to reading performance.

Regardless of the actual label that may be applied to a student, the following general considerations may be used in considering a student with a reading disability (Kirk, Kliebhan, & Lerner, 1978, pp. 13-14):

1. Children with various labels (e.g., mentally retarded, learning disabled, borderline intelligence, slow learner, and disabled reader) deviate from the norm in the manner in which they learn.
2. The same diagnostic procedures and tests are used for all students.
3. Preferred treatment approaches overlap regardless of the label or diagnostic group.
4. Correlates of reading failure found in one group are also found in the others.

Depending on the view and philosophy a teacher has about reading disabilities, the approach to remediation will be based on either the student's learning characteristics or the curriculum. In general, the following categories can be used to classify approaches:

1. *Ability models*. Diagnostic-prescriptive teach-

Table 6-1. Factors related to reading behavior

Factors	*Presumed effects on reading behavior*
Central nervous system damage	Slight damage or dysfunction of the central nervous system is thought to interfere with learning and processing of information, thus impeding normal reading development.
Motoric abnormalities	Faulty motor development is thought to interfere with later learning; perceptual-motor deficits are thought to account for problems experienced by children who cannot make stable reproductions of symbols and forms.
Hyperactivity	Hyperactivity is viewed either as a structural or learned behavioral pattern that interferes with attention, responses to the environment, strategic planning, and organization. However, it has recently been referred to as an attention deficit disorder.
Attention disorders	Disorders of attention—distractibility, selective attention, and other constructs—have been used to explain learning disorders. Students may not be able to attend to instruction, engage in sustained attention to a task, or follow directions.
Perceptual disorders	Auditory discrimination, sound blending, visual perceptual, speed, and other perceptual constructs are used to explain a variety of basic disorders. Perceptual disorders are inabilities to organize sensory stimuli and data necessary in the reading process at its most elemental level.
Memory disorders	Disorders of memory—short-term memory (auditory, visual, and kinesthetic) and metamemory (awareness of one's own memory strategies)—are thought to interfere with reading.
Language disorders	Although moderate to severe language disorders have always been implicated because language serves as the basis for all verbal skills in school, subtle language problems are becoming a more popular explanation for reading difficulty.
Mixed dominance	Problems of dominance and laterality have long been associated with reading disorders. Despite long-standing interest in this characteristic, the problem of dominance lacks research evidence to demonstrate a cause and effect relationship. However, some specialists still consider it an important correlate to reading disabilities and it cyclically emerges as a matter of diagnostic interest.
Intermodal, transfer disorders	The inability to integrate modalities—the changing of visual and auditory stimuli into equivalents of another modality—or to transduce information, has been associated with reading disabilities; this has led to varying theories about process training, aptitude-treatment interactions, and learning styles.

ing, test-based systems such as ITPA or the Frostig, visual-motor perceptual training, auditory perceptual training, the Kephart approach, and many others are included here. Previously we discussed the limitations and poor research base for such approaches. Despite their drawbacks they remain popular, in the belief that underlying processes can be assessed with instruments, weaknesses and strengths can be identified, training can improve the weak processes, and reading will advance as a result of improved basic processes and appropriate remedial instruction in the basic skills.

2. *Skill/content models.* Theoretically a skill model is one in which the major emphasis is on the skill or content to be taught. The application of task analysis, which is also used in a number of other approaches, is part of the behavioral orientation to teaching. The basic premise is that the student must be assessed to determine entry-level skills and then taught subsequent skills based on reinforcement theory. One problem with many of the task-analytic approaches is that tasks are not seen as linearly related. Also reading may be simplified to the extent that the number of words presented and read per minute (a ratio of correct words called to amount of time) is the index of improvement. Reading is a much more complex task than word calling, and variation in instruction must use more than word lists and reinforcement as the substance of instruction.

3. *Teaching models.* Teaching models include any reading approach that does not attempt to change the learner but rather accepts weaknesses or strengths in determining the preferred teaching approach. Such models include learning styles, aptitude-treatment interaction, preferred modalities, the Fernald and VAKT approaches, and other methods that match presentation to a profile of abilities.

In general, no compelling evidence supports the process-training approaches or aptitude-treatment interaction methods; preferred modality approaches are also suspicious. The best discussion about the suspicious validity of these approaches can be found in Haring and Bateman (1977). Many practitioners have zealous dedication to these methods and are convinced that they are valid and supported by research. The fact that there is more mythology than substance to the methods will not prevent their use. Nonetheless, most factors associated with reading development (e.g., attention, memory, visual-motor integration, and auditory and visual discrimination) have relatively low-positive correlations with achievement (Samuels, 1973). Training based on such characteristics is not empirically justified.

READING PROCESS

If it is not possible to base reading instruction on the deficient characteristics of learners, it seems logical to accept the reading tasks per se as the steps for concentration in remediation. Unfortunately considerable controversy surrounds the reading process itself. Reading has been considered under various models as follows:

1. Taxonomic
2. Psychometric
3. Psychological
4. Cognitive
5. Information processing
6. Linguistic
7. Psycholinguistic

The greatest single impact on reading instruction is the basal series of textbooks. Most schools use one or another basal series. Although the stories, pictures, and associated activities differ, they share a similar basic format. Examination of various series indicates that essentially the same skills are introduced with remarkable consistency. The process is comprised of word recognition, comprehension, effect on the learner, and application of skills to personal needs. In its simplest form the reading process is regarded as the recognition of printed symbols that denote meaning and transmit information. In other words, the reading process involves *decoding* and *comprehension*.

Decoding

At its most elemental level, the reading process is disputed among authorities. Major approaches to decoding have been based on the following methods of transforming printed symbols into spoken equivalents:

1. *Meaning emphasis.* The word is used as the basic unit of meaning. Children are taught to memorize a basic sight vocabulary, after which the rate of reading development is expected to grow as the child practices with familiar words and gradually learns newer ones. The whole-word approach to reading was very popular in the United States for many decades until the 1960s.

2. *Code emphasis.* A code-emphasis approach rejects the whole-word approach to beginning reading by stressing the tasks that are demanded in reading. The student is expected to scan a sequence of graphemes and respond with a verbal (phonemic) equivalent, accurately reproduce phonemes in the proper sequence, and pronounce proper words. Arguments about the nature of code emphasis exist among its proponents. Some reject phonics because students are expected to make unnatural sounds that do not exist as phonemic equivalents in the spoken word; others maintain that common patterns or groups of phonemes should be stressed along with their visual distinctiveness; and still others maintain that a controlled word list should be used to eliminate irregular orthography.

Basal series have tended to incorporate a blend of both general approaches: common and irregular words are taught with the whole-word method while phonics are also emphasized, primarily during the first year of reading instruction. Pure types of linguistic approaches and programmed texts are used, but more often they only supplement a basal text. Examination of relevant research on the topic would be helpful. Unfortunately there are no clear answers, as the following review might indicate.

Significant research on decoding. Since the 1920s reading instruction has changed and improved primarily because the reading process became recognized as a language-based system and a method of reasoning and problem solving rather than simply word calling (regardless of the approach to decoding). There was also a change in the trend from oral to silent reading; inclusion of a greater variety of instructional materials with content of particular interest to children; measurement of the difficulty of reading matter; and recognition that reading instruction should be adapted to the language of the country and appraisal of worldwide problems in literacy (Burns, 1975).

A few studies provide significant research on decoding. Durrell (1958) concluded that the majority of reading problems among first-grade children may be *prevented* by early instruction in letter names and sounds with subsequent applied phonics and a meaningful sight vocabulary. Furthermore, a minimum sight vocabulary would not be necessary before word analysis could begin.

Another significant study was actually a compilation of several studies known as the United States Office of Education (USOE) First-Grade Reading Studies (Bond & Dykstra, 1967) in which it was concluded that (1) phonic instruction is necessary, although there was little agreement about how much was needed and when instruction should occur; (2) initial reading should be based on a balance between phonetically regular words and high-utility words; (3) word-study skills should be emphasized in instruction and (4) basal programs are superior to single approaches. This study concluded that the teacher is the most important factor in the teaching/learning process. Furthermore, an eclectic approach is warranted, and there is no one best method.

Lastly, the work of Chall (1967), who examined the reading process thoroughly by examining an incredible amount of research spanning many decades, is of importance in understanding current views of the reading process. She concluded as follows:

1. Reading methods with a code emphasis (sound values of graphemes) tend to promote better reading achievement than methods with a meaning or whole-word emphasis.
2. Code emphasis demands accuracy, which lays the foundation for better acquisition of

word-attack, vocabulary, and comprehension skills, although early reading gains may be slow to develop.
3. Direct teaching of code-breaking techniques, that is, letter and sound relationships, is superior to less direct teaching methods.
4. Students with poor aptitude and below-average abilities tend to perform better with a code-emphasis method.

Comprehension

Comprehension is the other major facet of the reading process. Controversy has surrounded the importance of comprehension and the teaching of comprehension strategies. It is usually thought of as comprised of three types: literal, interpretive, and critical. Opinions about comprehension vary from one extreme to the other. Some contend that reading comprehension cannot be taught. It is a simple matter of language or intellective ability acquired once a student has learned to decode; to improve comprehension one should improve language and reasoning abilities. Others maintain that comprehension can and should be directly taught as part of the reading process because it is the heart of reading.

Significant research on comprehension. Durkin (1966) has contributed to research on comprehension by stressing that early learning experiences of children are an important foundation for later reading development. Prereading skills are recognized as important to ultimate development, as evidenced in preschool curricula and materials. Strickland (1962) has demonstrated the importance of reading as a language process. This is yet an increasing influence on education of handicapped and nonhandicapped students. The stilted, artificial reading materials of the past have been replaced by content that fits the spoken language patterns of children. A notable exception is the linguistic approach that uses controlled words with regular orthography. Guzak (1967) investigated comprehension and demonstrated that a child may engage in thinking behavior according to the type of questions asked by the teacher. Analysis of teachers' questioning reveals that literal questions are asked throughout the elementary grades. The USOE First-Grade Studies and the work of Chall, mentioned previously, also indicate that comprehension is related to teaching style. Teachers who use the DRTA (Directed Reading-Thinking Activity), which is now a part of the basal series, produce better student outcomes. Chall specifically indicates meaning-emphasis approaches for developing comprehension and vocabulary.

Most of the research indicates that results of the teaching act are more likely to produce desired or undesired behaviors in the student, not simply the approach that is used. The eclecticism of reading approaches is probably related more to the enthusiasm and managerial skills of a particular teacher than to a specific approach or set of materials. It is also clear that certain approaches, despite a teacher's enthusiasm, may be inappropriate for instruction of children, in general, and handicapped students in particular.

Most handicapped students who experience difficulty in the acquisition of reading have significant problems with decoding. A smaller number have problems with comprehension. The greatest concern of special educators has always been to teach decoding. If it was difficult in the self-contained classroom, it is exacerbated by the mainstreaming trend in which it will be necessary to coordinate regular and special class activities to maximize the learning experience of the student. This forces special education to recognize the importance of the developmental reading program, the regular classroom environment, and the teacher's style.

Depending on which side one decides to support (code versus meaning emphasis), certain assumptions are made about how each relates to meaningful reading or to comprehension. Most agree that comprehension is the outcome desired in reading instruction. However, if problems in reading comprehension are viewed as caused by the type of reading matter presented to students, the issues may be brought into focus. If the content of any material (''Dick and Jane'' or ''The fat cat on a mat'') is considered, it becomes important to recognize that the grammatical, lexical, syntactical, and conceptual content of many types of reading material are beyond the experiential backgrounds of many readers who are still adjusting to the physiological demands of the reading process. Reading comprehension can be improved by increasing the experiences and language abilities of students, rather than simply inducing children to read and answer comprehension questions. The reading matter presented to them should be matched closely to their experiences, interest, environment, and language. As the language base expands, the content may vary accordingly. However, the underlying foundation for early reading is unquestionably the ability to break the code of reading. As a metamemorial process (i.e., the child being aware of his or her own attention and memory skills) the act of reading requires the child to become aware of the fact that spoken language is comprised of words and sounds that are represented by written symbols. Language is a sequence of sounds that can be represented by visual symbols. This is the task of decoding. Comprehension will be possible after decoding is mastered, so that the sensoriphysical act of reading is automatic, facile, and unencumbered by the guessing and hesitations of beginning reading. As the language experience increases, comprehension of increasingly difficult reading matter also increases. The learner who has not mastered decoding confronts the impossible task of memorizing every word.

Whether or not special educators elect to use hypothetical and apparently irrelevant teaching methodologies (e.g., process training) is a matter of personal preparation, interest, philosophical orientation, and professional commitment. Some teachers attempt to blend processing and skill approaches. We will describe all types in this section but will primarily emphasize the acquisition of skills as they are currently understood in the literature. For general purposes of discussion the reading process can be classified within the following major components:

1. Readiness or prereading
2. Word recognition
3. Comprehension
4. Study
5. Applied reading

DEVELOPMENTAL READING

Developmental reading has a number of approaches. In general, regardless of the specific skills or materials that are stressed, the developmental program encompasses the preceding basic reading process components. The following discussion presents the major types of developmental reading programs.

Language-experience approach

The language-experience approach is primarily limited to preschool, kindergarten, and the first part of the first grade. In the past it was a popular approach in self-contained special classroom. Generally the purposes of the language-experience approach are as follows:

1. To stimulate language development as a basis for reading
2. To promote thinking behavior
3. To direct interactions of children
4. To base activities on children's interests
5. To diagnose reading needs
6. To teach appropriate reading and vocabulary skills

The purposes of this approach closely resemble perceptual levels of training and are compatible with traditional special education approaches. The major perceptual or process areas that would be affected are listening skills, oral language, auditory and visual perception, and visual-motor functioning.

The language-experience approach is relatively unstructured and highly dependent on the individual teacher. This can be a strength and a weakness. If the approach is used beyond the first grade for developmental reading, some critics fear that its unstructured nature may permit poor instruction and uneven development to occur. The *steps* of the approach and the advantages and disadvantages are as follows:

1. The teacher engages the children in a concrete experience dealing with something in their environment—a field trip is usually involved.
2. A discussion of the experience unfolds over a period of time as the children talk about various ideas and listen to one another.
3. The class plans a chart on which sentences and paragraphs may be written to depict the experience.
4. Each person reads the story after it is completed.
5. Title, sentences, and other components of the structure are identified.
6. Specific attention is devoted to "new" words in the story.
7. Review activities are based on the words in the story.
8. After initial unison reading, each child is expected to read the story individually.
9. Each child may be provided a copy of the story to be taken home and shared with the family.

Advantages of the approach. The advantages generally recognized are as follows:

1. The approach is child oriented and based on group motivation and interests.
2. It can be tailored to a particular culture and neighborhood with experiences relevant to a particular group of children.
3. It accepts the children's language rather than imposing other language forms on them.
4. It meshes the various components of language arts.
5. Children, having created the story, are expected to have a high degree of interest.
6. Children are familiar with the ideas and words expressed in the story.
7. The teacher is keenly aware of individual needs and behavior because the teacher is forced to attend to behaviors that would otherwise be masked and ignored by instruction with commercial materials.

Disadvantages of the approach. The major disadvantages are as follows:

1. The unstructured nature of the approach is apt to ignore important developmental activities.
2. Commercial materials are better designed and prepared to integrate language arts experiences and introduce appropriate vocabulary.
3. Use of the approach is limited to beginning reading; children must rapidly adjust to a structured approach.
4. This approach places a tremendous demand on the teacher to create all of the necessary instructional materials.
5. Effective commercial materials can provide all advantages of the language-experience approach while ensuring proper vocabulary control.

Basal reading programs

The basal reading program is the most common form of reading instruction used in public schools because schools have elected to secure a thorough and comprehensive approach to the instruction of reading. Surveys have consistently shown that over 90 percent of teachers use basal programs. Because of the expense, public schools or state committees select programs. The basal program consists of a complete teacher's manual, associated skill book, graded readers, additional teaching aids, diagnostic and placement tests, and a skills list.

Advantages of the approach

1. Each basal program is a complete program.
2. Opportunity for overlearning is built into the program.
3. The mechanism is available for careful monitoring of student progress along a recognized skill sequence.

Disadvantages of the approach

1. The program's structure can cause children to become disinterested.
2. The program is predictable; the sameness causes a limitation in interest and motivation.
3. Graded texts cause methodical planning in which all materials must be introduced within a given time period; children who do not keep pace are left behind because the curriculum sequence is paramount.
4. The format encourages the teacher to engage in group instruction to the detriment of children who deviate from the group.
5. Teachers tend to use accompanying worksheets and other materials as fillers to take up time.
6. Vocabulary is too controlled.
7. Children from minority backgrounds are confronted with middle-class values, concepts, and vocabulary that differ from their experiential backgrounds.
8. The content is sex biased.
9. Children do not have ample opportunity to engage in word-recognition activities.

ALTERNATIVE SYSTEMS

Schools with the freedom to organize programs that are self-contained or departmentalized may also vary the organization of the curriculum. Some schools compartmentalize instruction so that each subject is taught separately. Others combine several subjects. Language-arts programs may consist of reading, spelling, writing, and other content areas. Reading, although emphasized, will also be an instructional component with other activities, rather than being singled out as a separate skill. Schools that base reading instruction primarily on a basal series will be limited in the amount of flexibility for incorporating extraneous books and other reading matter. Use of an individualized reading program provides for maximum flexibility. The more open the system used, the more likely that the school will be attracted to a number of approaches which are not complete enough to serve as a comprehensive program but which are more thorough than supplementary aids. A number of approaches that have waxed and waned are listed here as alternative systems; more appropriately they would be supplemental systems. The only exception is in the case of linguistic programs that are sometimes used by schools as the primary reading program.

Eclectic or individualized approaches

Some schools, by design or neglect, permit the development of eclectic approaches. If it is a planned approach, the instruction of children can be as effective as any approach; however, if it is happenstance, the good effect can be serendipitous. In an individualized approach there is (1) a wide variety of reading matter (e.g., library books, paperback books, newspapers, and magazines), (2) acknowledgment of the skill sequence in a basal program but no reliance on it, and (3) programming tailored to a particular student's interests and level of development. Theoretically the approach is individualized and child oriented. Thus, in an eclectic or individualized approach, elements of any or all basal series, supplemental aids, individual experience activities, and any other materials may be incorporated.

Advantages of the approach

1. The approach is child centered.
2. Multimedia materials can be used.
3. Each child has an opportunity to find an area of interest.
4. Boring activities can be avoided because there is no routine.

Disadvantages of the approach

1. The system is too unstructured, possibly causing the teacher to ignore proper evaluation of students.
2. There is not necessarily any common design or purpose.
3. The teacher can lose control of the program.

4. Too much is expected of the teacher, who does not have the time, resources, or sufficient equipment to effectively manage the reading growth of each child.
5. Games, kits, activities, audiovisual materials, and so forth may not contribute to a cohesive program. Record keeping is impossible.

Linguistic approach

Linguistic approaches to reading have been guided by principles that have been presented in the research of Durrell, the USOE First-Grade Reading Studies, and Chall, all of which were discussed earlier. These principles state that initial reading experiences of the child should stress phoneme/grapheme correspondences without the additional burden of attempting to find meaning in what is read. The earliest reading behavior of a child is nothing more than a mechanical process of code breaking, which is facilitated by practice, controlled sound-symbol associations, and delay of a heavy comprehension load until the first basic skills are fully mastered. Although there are many differences of opinion among linguists who have an interest in reading, the following general factors apply to such approaches:

1. An emphasis on learning letters, graphemes, and clusters of graphemes
2. A stress on words with regular orthography
3. Irregular words presented last

Over time a child may be expected to develop a stable relationship of sounds to symbols. The taxing requirements of thinking about the written passage, drawing inferences, extrapolating, and so forth are spared until the child's automatic skill with decoding is firmly in place. The most well-known linguistic programs are the *Miami Linguistic Readers* and the *Merrill Linguistic Readers,* which have been adopted in place of basal series by some schools. Many basal series have incorporated linguistic concepts into the instructional format. However, linguistic approaches remain controversial. Basal series, which are complete programs reducing the preparation responsibilities of teachers, will not be threatened by them; however, the contributions of linguistic theory to the field may continue the improvement of basal texts.

Behavioral approach

Although some of the most significant gains in reading achievement have been documented through behavior modification, the materials and approaches that have been used have represented many other approaches. The element of reinforcement has been the significant factor applied to a wide variety of instructional designs. Behaviorists, many of whom are not teachers, tend to be concerned only with the rate of word calling expressed as a ratio of words read per minute. Otherwise, programmed approaches have been highly developed, based on the behavioral principles.

The programmed approach is based on the continuous, incremental presentation of interrelated reading matter, with feedback as the most important aspect. The *Borg-Warner Systems 80* and the *Sullivan Readers* are the best-known examples. Teaching is determined by specific learning objectives and outcomes for the learner. After each response of a learner in the program, feedback is immediately forthcoming. The primary emphasis is on word recognition. These materials are often viewed by teachers as supplemental to a more traditional reading program. They may not be related to what is happening in the regular curriculum, different conflicting skills may be simultaneously introduced, and the reading experience can become confused. A better approach would be a complete program that is cross-referenced to the exact skill sequence used in the school. Such programs are not likely to be forthcoming until computers and scaling techniques are better received in education and teachers learn how to program and use them as instructional support. Otherwise, programmed and other behavioral schemes in reading must be infused into the existing program for maximum effectiveness.

Eadmark Reading Program

The Eadmark Reading Program is a behaviorally engineered program that is based on task analysis of reading skills and presented through programmed instruction. Although specific steps are identified and clearly defined, learning activities are associated with each step. The program consists of a total of 150 words. For children who have experienced failure it may be an excellent program choice; however, it would not be used in a developmental, mainstreamed program. The nature of instruction is sound because of the behavioral design: discrimination learning, cuing, shaping, fading, and reinforcement are designed conspiciously in each sequence of learning. A great deal of research has been conducted with the Eadmark program, indicating that its success is primarily with children labeled as mentally retarded. The distinguishing feature of the program is that it is based on an identified skill sequence and presented through carefully controlled behavioral approaches presented by classroom teachers; it is not surprising that success can occur. Undoubtedly, if classroom instruction could approach the level of sophistication of this and other behaviorally based materials, many students who now fail under ordinary instruction would experience achievement.

DISTAR

The DISTAR program, Direct Instruction Systems for Teaching Arithmetic and Reading, is a highly structured system of teaching that is based on an identified skill sequence and that uses a behavioral design. Students are required to master each step in a sequence before progressing. The teacher's manual is explicit, and the freedom to engage in enrichment activities, which is a common characteristic of other approaches, is not permitted in the design.

Except for initial learning experiences that involve a unique alphabet, all activities in the DISTAR system are similar to other traditional learning activities in reading. The major difference is that any activity involving sound-symbol association, blending, syllabication, word recognition, and so forth is directly supervised by the teacher. Feedback is immediate, and mastery of the skill before progression to the next skill is an absolute requirement. This aspect has made it either attractive or unattractive to particular teachers, depending on their attitudes about reading instruction. The program has also been controversial because of its use with black children. This system has been referred to as "cultural genocide" because the child is expected to make standard English a part of classroom verbal behavior, and no allowances are made for nonstandard English forms. On the whole, however, the system has been very successful, and children have made incredible gains. The structure, feedback, and reinforcement undoubtedly account for the success because the content is not necessarily unique. As in other instances, this approach would be most difficult to use in a mainstreaming effort, unless, of course, the regular classroom were also employing the DISTAR method.

Color-coded phonetic approach

Some investigators have used color as a means of introducing concepts to children. Some students are attracted to color as a distinctive feature in the learning process. However, the teacher should not use color haphazardly because if students cue by color they can become confused. If color is to be used in reading or arithmetic, it should have a purpose and be consistent.

One system in reading is the Psycholinguistic Color System (Bannatyne, 1971), which was developed for learning-disabled students. The major elements of the approach are as follows:

1. Linear sequencing of sound-symbol associations is to be learned, as well as structured grapheme/phoneme correspondences.
2. The words used are meaningful, unlike some "nonsense" activities of some linguistic approaches.
3. Sensory input is organized for desired motor responses.
4. The individual letter element is learned as a

grapheme with a particular phonemic association.
5. Color codes serve to cue particular sounds.
6. Color can be faded after initial learning experiences.

Associated phonemes for letters are learned, consonants and vowels are mastered, irregular words are introduced, and individual stories are constructed. Teachers who do not use this particular system, but who employ color, should be aware of the natural attraction to color, its limitations, and proper fading techniques. As such, this would fit well into a behavioral design for instruction.

Code-emphasis approaches

Some rather complete programs exist that heavily stress decoding skills for initial teaching of reading, such as the phonics and linguistics series. Although phonics are included in all basal series to some extent and the teacher may employ a variety of supplemental aids, a few programs are dedicated to phonics instruction and can stand singly as complete programs similar to basal texts. These programs emphasize instruction in sound-to-symbol associations, applications of rules, and perceptual activities. Three types of programs that use this method are the *Open Court Correlated Language Arts Program, Basic Reading,* and *Keys to Reading.*

Reading growth is slower in these systems, as in all systems with a heavy phonics emphasis; however, the redundant skill practice for young children is considered to be a strength by some authorities. Considerable multisensory activities are used. Activities, games, and other language-arts experiences are tied together by a structure involving multisensory training. If a school system does not adopt these programs for use in regular classrooms, teachers may employ parts of the approaches for support as long as such activities are carefully planned.

A number of critics do not favor these programs because they maintain that phonics rules are of little value, initial reading is too slow and tedious, and children may become word callers rather than readers. This relates to the long-standing debate in the field about finding a proper balance between word and code-emphasis approaches.

Peabody Rebus Reading Program

The Peabody Rebus Reading Program is well known in special education because it has been used for several years. The popularity of the approach was probably at a high level when special education programs were self-contained. The Rebus program could serve as the basis for group instruction of all students in a class. Since mainstreaming, however, this and other programs do not necessarily fit into the plans of schools. There is an expense involved, and the approach may be antithetical to the one used in regular classroom. Having children involved in two types of reading programs can be confusing, especially if the methods are quite different.

The Rebus program may be used as an alternative for children who have failed to grasp early learning in traditional approaches. Essentially a picture word story can be used. A child can theoretically gain the experience of reading a sentence or story without having to decode because of the rebuses.

Skills or skill-management approaches

Along with the back-to-basics movement and the recent emphasis on task-analytic approaches, some schools are attempting to use skills in the learning sequence as the framework for all planning and teaching. This is highly recommended, especially for handicapped students. However, the use of criterion-referenced systems, such as the Fountain Valley Teacher Support System in Reading and the Wisconsin Design for Reading Skill Development, requires a heavy financial commitment of the school. These systems are not special education programs. Skills systems are not likely to be used in a school. The basal series or another approach will be used without much attention to the underlying skill sequence. The advantage of a skills system is that criterion-referenced tests, accurate record-keeping systems, and other devices are used to pinpoint development. This is not typically true of other systems.

Some critics are concerned that important skills will be omitted, unnecessary skills will be taught, and focusing on skills will somehow diminish the importance of the reading act through compartmentalization of skills. These apparently romantic arguments are made by persons who are not convinced of the importance of skills.

Other approaches to a skills emphasis concentrate primarily on decoding in the initial stages of reading. Analytic and synthetic instruction of phonetics, combined with some sight-word development, are managed in a skill sequence. The contention is that students who are able to decode will be capable of better reading growth. Although basal series commonly include these elements, some schools carefully identify basic decoding skills and attempt to ensure that students master them in sequence before the students are expected to engage in more complicated reading acts.

CLASSICAL REMEDIAL PROGRAMS AND APPROACHES

It is interesting that the preoccupation of special education with process-training approaches to remediation has caused a lack of interest in the development of specialized reading techniques, except as they may have been related to a process theory. Little research has been conducted on specific approaches with students who have specific psychological characteristics. A handful of classical remedial approaches are available, none of which is supported by much research. Examination of the approaches reveals a similarity that can be attributed to the early work of Itard, Sequin, and Montessori.

Most of these approaches are based on some system of presentation to sensory channels. The visual, auditory, kinesthetic, and tactile senses (VAKT) are used for some unique methods of reading instruction. It is impossible to escape the input of these channels in any learning activity, and the acquisition of any skill or concept is enhanced by means of multiple stimulation. Nonetheless, the tedious overemphasis of reading skills through VAKT systems has resulted in progress for some students because the system provides redundant and slowly paced concrete learning activities. The fact that learning is organized for input, details are isolated and made apparent to the learner, and progress is carefully monitored may explain the success of such approaches with certain students.

Multisensory approaches

One traditional multisensory approach is the VAKT, a classical remedial approach designed by Fernald (1943). It is a method similar to the concepts of Itard, Sequin, and Montessori. Basically this program is used with older students who are nonreaders. The approach has four basic elements: the teacher selects words the student wants to learn and follows the basic sequence of (1) tracing—the student traces a word until it becomes automatic; (2) writing—the student looks at a word and writes it without tracing; (3) recognition—the student looks at, hears, says, and writes the word from memory; and (4) generalization—the student is taught to generalize familiar parts of a word in the process of identifying new words. This process is not used frequently because it requires a great deal of work on the part of an instructor who may find more direction in commercially available materials.

Other approaches are based on the VAKT concept. Although some have praised this approach, success does not necessarily result because specific modalities are stimulated; rather, it is achieved because the student is motivated and induced to overlearn. Ultimately, conventional reading materials are introduced. Some teachers, critics, and students find this approach too tedious and uninteresting.

Gillingham approaches

A number of Gillingham approaches are available as multisensory alternatives to ordinary developmental instruction for pupils who experience failure in reading. The Gillingham approach, although a VAKT system, is different from the Fernald technique in that it stresses phonics, is highly structured, has accompanying materials, and requires at least 2 years to complete. Like the Fernald technique, it gradually builds on overlearned skills until the student is able to function with automatic responses. Progress is not left to chance. Phonograms and associated sounds are introduced; later, instruction in writing is introduced. The student must see, say, trace, and write the phonograms. Accompanying drill cards with key words and pictures are used to reinforce learning. After a series of phonetically compatible sounds are learned and can be organized into simple words, stories are presented that use these words. Obviously this approach would not be a first choice. Its use would have to be carefully considered against the backdrop of mainstreaming because simultaneous instruction in both a Gillingham approach and a common classroom developmental approach would be unsatisfactory.

Neurological impress method

Although it is not a classical approach and it is not much used, the neurological impress method has gained recognition as a unique remedial approach. Based on the simple proposition that a student can model the reading behavior of a good reader, unison reading is used. The student simply follows along in a reading passage and imitates the teacher. The teacher points at words and attempts to read at a fairly fast pace. The teacher may fade in and out, and the eventual goal is to have the student acquire reading behavior independently.

Hegge-Kirk-Kirk remedial reading drills

The Hegge-Kirk-Kirk remedial reading drills have been in existence for many years, although it is not known if they have been in widespread use. It is customary to include the approach in textbooks. The purpose is to establish sound-symbol associations, closure, and left-to-right progression in the reading act. There are four parts: (1) training begins with associating sounds with common consonents, short vowels, and regularly occurring consonent blends, diphthongs, and digraphs; (2) the drills proceed with combinations of sounds learned in phase 1; (3) the drills introduce more advanced and uncommon sounds included in whole words; and (4) the drills concentrate on word-building exercises and training in nonphonetic, sound-symbol associations and letters that are easily confused.

This method is recommended for use with students who have failed to learn after several years of conventional teaching. It is not recognized as a general method of instruction; rather, it is a method of assisting students who are functioning at low levels of reading development but who need a system to make rapid gains. This method provides structure, rapid movement to meaningful content, and measurable progression through a hierarchy of skills.

PROCESS-TRAINING APPROACHES

The controversial process-training approaches that have been used in special education, primarily with children who have learning disabilities, are still significant in planning for handicapped students because of their extreme popularity with practitioners. Discussion of the limitations and nonsupportive research was made earlier. Nonetheless, it is clear that many practitioners view such approaches as helpful. Many teachers implement process training as a total or partial aspect of the special education program. A brief discussion of the most popular approaches is required at this point to create a perspective for planning in special education.

Perceptual-motor approaches

Popularized primarily by Kephart (1960), a number of perceptual-motor approaches have been used in special education with the implicit assumption that reading achievement and other academic gains could be ultimately realized by stressing perceptual-motor development. In the belief that many reading disorders are caused by inadequate perceptual-motor development, a premise which has not been established, the therapist would implement a program to directly treat perceptual-motor deficits. However, the program ignores the fact that perceptual-motor characteristics of disabled readers are only correlated with reading failure. The remedial approaches are based on intuition rather than on sound empiricism. A variety of gross motor and fine motor activities may be beneficial to children, especially young children, in development of motoric patterns and generalizations, receipt and propulsion, perceptual-motor match, laterality and directionality, and oculomotor control. However, no empirical evidence is available that justifies the use of such programming as a primary emphasis in special education for improving reading (Hammill, Goodman, & Weiderholt, 1974). Similarly, the approach of Frostig and Horne (1964), which maintains some of the same principles as Kephart, may be criticized. Visual perception is stressed in the Frostig approach, although it has not been clearly demonstrated what relationship visual perception has to the reading process or more specifically its relationship as a causative factor in reading disorders. The complete set of training materials used in the Frostig approach may not have any direct benefit in reading achievement but rather may be detrimental if this is the only focus of the special education effort. These aspects of development may or may not play a significant role in learning and readiness for reading, but the evidence is lacking at the present time.

Neurological approaches

Two approaches that have had a profound impact on special education are related in principle because they accept neurological disorders, or brain damage, as the basis for reading disabilities. The most famous approach is the work of Strauss and Lehtinen (1947) which postulated that certain children could be characterized by disorders of perception, concept formation, and behavior that resulted from brain damage. The syndrome, which is recognized generally as the Strauss syndrome, has become important in the field because of the many branches of development resulting from the original work. Perceptual, linguistic, and motoric theories and behavioral control approaches emanated from their work through various students and proponents of the theory regarding brain damage as the cause of learning disorders. The work of Goldstein (1939), which concerned brain-damaged adults, was applied by Strauss to the study of children. The concept of brain damage, or the neoneurological approach (minimum brain damage), has been rejected by many authorities. However, practitioners are greatly influenced by Strauss' work either directly as an educational view or indirectly through other approaches that have been developed for use with handicapped children. For example, Strauss observed that children with reading difficulties had visual-perceptual problems, poor auditory-perceptual ability, and disorders in sequencing, all of which developed into pronounced approaches subsequent to his work. The approach to reading was surprisingly more direct than the approaches of followers.

Remedial methods were direct, sharing a similarity with the approaches of Itard and Sequin, and unique because of the insistence on control of environmental distractions. Control of attention was the central consideration in the environmental control scheme. The scheme was structured by eliminating extraneous stimuli, screening windows, placing materials and supplies out of sight, controlling sound intrusions, and having the teacher dress simply and without distracting adornments. Reading readiness activities were not unlike developmental activities used today; perceptual development, language experiences, visual exercises, and motoric training, and auditory-perceptual training were emphasized. An initial sight vocabulary was stressed, and phonics instruction was introduced later. The use of colors to highlight certain sounds has become an alternative approach in some complete systems of today. A language-experience approach to reading was used, building on the words children acquired through training. The theories underlying the view of causation were independent of the remedial approaches because these methods were not unique—Itard, Sequin, and Montessori, had used them. The theories might have justified the approaches. No attempt was made to change or alter an underlying process except in the readiness stages of reading development. More emphasis was placed on how information would be presented to children, which might be described as a modality preference or aptitude-treatment/interaction approach.

A more recent neurological approach is the work of Johnson and Myklebust (1967). They developed a more extensive theory emphasizing a hierarchy of learning integrities and stressing that at any point in the hierarchy a problem might interfere with reading. The perceptual levels, according to them, are overemphasized. Most problems of children can be attributed to disorders at higher levels in a sequence of sensation, perception, imagery, and symbolization. Moreover, they attributed problems in learning to types of input-organization-output processing. Intraneurosensory disorders are considered to be problems in one mode or process, such as auditory, and interneurosensory disorders are problems in which two modes do not function in unison; that is, the child is unable to transduce one form of information (e.g., visual) into another (e.g., auditory).

Johnson and Myklebust regard these disorders as dyslexia (a symbolic deficit within a wide category of learning disabilities). Failure to read may be the result of auditory, visual, or integrative disorders. Teaching is based on examination of the input-integration-output paradigm of information processing. If the child cannot learn to read in an ordinary manner, the manner in which information is processed should be examined. There are theoretically a large number of permutations, or ways in which information may be introduced, stored, and retrieved, depending on the child's idiosyncratic characteristics. However, their theory contains two broad categories of dyslexics: auditory and visual, requiring different approaches for teaching. A meaning-emphasis approach to reading would be used with the auditory dyslexic, and a code-emphasis approach would be used with the visual dyslexic. The modality preference is determined by examination. According to the view, children are not necessarily pure types. Therefore, careful planning, which is not well described, is required to find the best approach for mixed types.

The recommendations of Johnson and Myklebust are untested by research, as are many approaches in special education. The most problematic issue here and in approaches that recommend a diagnostic-prescriptive or clinical approach is that the theory, assessment procedures, and analyses are not explained to help in identification of differential treatment (approaches, reading matter, learning strategies, etc.).

READING AS INFORMATION PROCESSING

The increased use of computers in education has caused a number of writers to examine the psychology of learning within the same context as information handling in computer programs. In general, the tasks facing the learner in reading may be similar to the tasks of a computer in classifying, storing, and processing information for various purposes such as decoding and comprehension; insight about the learning requirements of these components can be gained by superimposing an information-processing framework on them.

Decoding has primarily been approached by special educators as a problem of aptitude treatment or preferred modality. Because of notions about process deficits, teachers may induce children to improve their underlying perceptual processes or submit to a specialized type of instruction. The child who is said to be an "auditory learner" will be given an intensive phonics approach. The "visual learner" will be given a meaning-emphasis approach. From an information-processing view all successful learners arrive at the same point and possess essentially the same skills, or they would not have succeeded. However, the additional activities that are recommended in teaching both types of children may be counterproductive.

Teaching children to read by attending to configurations of words is apparently a waste of time; shapes of words are not meaningful in the reading process. However, in the decoding process the combinations and shapes of letters are important. Covering the top half of a line of print reduces recognition of the line to nearly zero. Covering the bottom half does not interfere substantially with decoding the line, since the bottoms of letters are less distinctive than the tops. Shapes of letters are essential to decoding, and the most distinctive features of the letters are above the median.

Stable and instantaneous recognition of words is the outcome of a great deal of practice. The requirement of this task is that the learner must continue to make finer and finer discriminations, visually and auditorily, between letters that are similar. The most confusing aspect for children is letters and/or sounds that are the least discriminable. The shapes of the letters *b* and *d* are the same; their significance comes from the fine discrimination of proper orientation in space. Letters such as *M* and *W* are also difficult for the same reason. Moreover, most of the early speech problems that children have are the result of inadequate discrimination. The basic task of the teacher is to ensure that students are given sufficient instruction so that they can automatically recognize elements of words as a decoding strategy.

Children who have not mastered decoding strategies have difficulty with comprehension because they are attending to decoding and not the meaning of a sentence or paragraph. Until decoding becomes automatic for them, they will continue to have difficulty with comprehension. Many children can listen to a passage and answer literal and inferential questions accurately but are unable to read efficiently enough to comprehend the passage. Like any other skill, decoding requires that the student practice, stay on task, and receive feedback and reinforcement. Children who are presented with unreasonable demands, are unmotivated, and do not practice reading skills are likely to fail.

Attention disorders

It has long been maintained that many children with serious learning problems have significant attentional deficits. The most notable of these authorities is Ross (1976) who explains the problem as an inability to use attention selectively. However, Ross contends that some children are apparently unable to focus attention appropriately. Elaboration of this theory indicates that some children are overselective: by attending so carefully to an item or object, they miss other elements of the instructional process. In a further elaboration, Hallahan, Gajar, Cohen, and Tarver (1978) have found that some students attend to incidental but not central elements in a learning task. Metamemory theory, which is discussed in detail later, explains attentional problems within a framework of information processing. The ability to apply attention strategies depends on one's experience and development. Being aware of how to process information—what is important, what is unessential, and how to organize—are learned skills that need to be deliberately taught to some children to enable them to perform efficiently. Some research indicates that the apparent deficits of children disappear when information is presented in a different form, if distinctive cues are highlighted and organization is apparent.

Some of the perceptual disorders attributed to children can be explained in the same way. The fact that a student confuses *b* and *d* is important depending on one's theoretical attitude. If this is viewed as a perceptual disorder, the student may be subjected to perceptual-motor training. If this is viewed as an information-processing disorder, the finer discriminations and orientations of the letters will be emphasized.

Memory disorders

Memory disorders have long been associated with poor reading performance. Most reading specialists tend to consider short-term memory deficits (visual and auditory) as a plausible explanation. The child may appear to have a disorder as indicated on a test and evidenced from the act of reading. Many children have been induced to repeat strings of digits or to extend visual memory through tachistoscopic or pencil-and-paper exercises; however, little evidence supports that such training is directly helpful or incidentally related to improved reading. The research of Morsink, Cross, and Strickler (1978) and Gibson (1970) indicates that such problems are developmentally related to inappropriate instructional planning. Disabled readers have more difficulty with meaningful than nonmeaningful tasks when required to recall them after a brief exposure. From an information-processing point of view such difficulty may be explained as an instructional problem. The students may not know how to simplify such recall tasks by grouping information in a meaningful way. This skill can be taught, and most students seem to automatically acquire it during learning activities. In some respects memory problems may be mislabeled as attentional problems. The students are not aware of what information is important or how to group and classify information for storage. Recall is unrelated to performance on a memory task if the input is disordered.

Transfer

Another deficit commonly used to describe poor readers is the inability to transfer information. However, Guthrie (1973) has shown that the reading subskills of good readers are interrelated. Good readers are aware of the relationships of reading skills. Poor readers are not. Each subskill may need to be taught independently and deliberately. Organization may need to be imposed by the teacher to show the students relationships that are not obvious to them. Again, this can be considered an information-processing skill similar to the concepts presented under the heading of attentional disorders. If the learner knows what is expected and why it is important, the task will be more meaningful.

INSTRUCTIONAL GOALS FOR READING

In our opinion the most important aspect of instruction deals with identifying the exact skills that a student is supposed to learn in a skill or content area. We have observed that teachers sometimes become overinvolved in the process of developing games, materials, activities, and other experiences for children and are unable to relate them to any specific skills. The games or activities seem to be so engaging that teachers worry about the quality of the presentation rather than determining the practical value of such activities in contributing to the acquisition of skills in reading.

Undoubtedly many arguments exist about the importance of skills in teaching. Some writers contend that skills do not exist in a natural hierarchy, whereas others maintain that they do. The importance of particular skills, the sequence of skills, and the nature of activities to be associated with teaching skills can all be debated. Nonetheless, we maintain that an underlying skill sequence is absolutely essential if we are to ensure that students are learning. Knowing the skills, the sequence, and what skills a student has or has not mastered dictates what should be taught next. A skill sequence will permit the use of a variety of programs and materials. Therefore, a language-experience approach, basal series, or individualized approach can be used confidently with any other supplemental activities as long as the teacher is confident about the skill sequence. This aspect is built into the few existing criterion-referenced systems of reading. Regardless, if a skill sequence is already available in the materials, is created by logic and expert opinion, or is identified statistically, as in the Rasch model, a skill sequence is necessary for effectively implementing designs of instruction that are based on feedback and reinforcement. The more teaching is regarded as an art, the more the student is required to actively impose order on the materials. Handicapped students should not be expected to approach reading in such a haphazard manner.

A skill sequence is absolutely essential for special educators if they are to be effective in assisting classroom teachers and students. Special educators cannot allow students to drift in and out of regular classrooms and be subjected to highly divergent reading activities. If a basal series is used in the regular classroom and the student receives reading instruction in the regular classroom, the supportive activities of the special educator must match the regular curriculum. The use of DISTAR, Rebus, or some other approach in this case cannot be justified. If the student is not expected to receive reading instruction in the regular classroom, the teacher may be free to employ any instructional system. In either event, we maintain that a skill sequence must be identified.

For the purpose of this text we have identified a comprehensive sequence of skills for the first six grades (pp. 189 to 198). This was accomplished by examining five of the most popular basal series and extracting each skill that was introduced at any particular grade level. The order of skills was remarkably similar, with only minor variations at specific grade levels.

Using this skill sequence the teacher can approach the development of criterion-referenced tests, monitoring systems, and integration of reading activities between special and regular classrooms. The goals for reading instruction can also be identified by the skill sequence. This process reduces the system of teaching to a manageable system rather than a random presentation of activities. The sequence can be used as a guide in planning activities, games, supplemental aids, and associated experiences by cross-referencing such activities to each skill level.

We would suggest that diagnostic-prescriptive approaches, if they are to have any merit, must be based on a skill sequence. In most textbooks the reader will find a statement similar to the following: "The teacher must have a thorough knowledge of the needs of the student and the ability to match the student to appropriate reading approaches." There are a lot of gaps in this logic. Unless the teacher can actually identify what a student is to learn, a task analysis or diagnostic-prescriptive teaching is a hollow term. To accomplish this the teacher will have to meet the following criteria in planning:

1. A sequence of skills must be identified; the actual sequence used in the school must be listed in the order in which the skills are introduced. The sequence presented in this chapter should not deviate too far from what is used in most programs.
2. Assessment practices, probe sheets, progress checks, and other informal approaches to evaluation must be related to each skill level in the sequence.
3. Any and all materials (basal, individualized, language-experience, supplemental, and remedial activities) must be cross-referenced to each skill level.
4. A comprehensive record keeping system must be developed. It should meet the needs of the school and be reduced to a manageable level so that records do not consume the instructional time of the teacher.
5. Directed reading activities should be based on the skills a student is expected to master at any one time. Any program, system, or element of a program must be determined on the basis of the student's current instructional needs as determined by the skill sequence and any personological information that may contribute to planning.

COMPONENTS FOR PLANNING

Aside from the general skills lists and the discussion about planning just presented, the foundation of reading development is comprised of the components of skills in reading. These components are readiness, word recognition skills, comprehension, and study skills. Most of the reading skills are introduced by the end of the third grade. Therefore, early learning experiences of the child are very important, as is planning at this level. Children who do not acquire skills rapidly, such as the handicapped, are quickly penalized in a program in which the teacher moves rapidly to new skills. This is an important area of planning for the special educator. The skills of the first three grades should receive special attention.

Text continued on p. 199.

TYPICAL SEQUENCE OF SKILLS INTRODUCED IN THE ELEMENTARY SCHOOL READING PROGRAM

First-grade skills

I. Decoding

A. Word recognition (sight recognition)

1. Student is able to identify and discriminate between capital and lowercase letters.
2. Student is able to use context clues in decoding to include using picture and/or object clues and sentence clues.
3. Student is able to identify distinguishing characteristics of words to include length differences, double letters, and configuration.

B. Phonetic analysis

4. Student is able to identify rhyming patterns from a visual stimulus and/or an auditory stimulus.
5. Student is able to identify consonant sound-to-symbol relationships and initial and final positions:

   b, d, f, g, h, j, l, m, n, p, r, s, t, w, y
   hard "c," soft "c," and z
   k, q, v, x

6. Student is able to identify consonant-digraph patterns in initial and final positions, including the following:

ch-	-ch	-ss
sh-	-sh	-ng
th-	-th	
wh-	-ll	

7. Student is able to identify consonant blends in the initial and final positions, including the following:

st	fr	cl	sm
tr	bl	fl	sp
br	pl	gl	
gr	sl	pw	

8. Student is able to identify (recognize) short-vowel sounds: a, e, i, o, u.
9. Student is able to identify (recognize) final vowels in one-syllable words and long-vowel sounds:
   a, e, i, o, u.
10. Student is able to identify (recognize) *r*-influenced vowels, including the following:

    ar   ur

11. Student is able to identify the following vowel digraphs:

    ai, ee, oa, ea, oe, igh oy

Continued.

TYPICAL SEQUENCE OF SKILLS INTRODUCED IN THE ELEMENTARY SCHOOL READING PROGRAM—cont'd

12. Student is able to identify syllables by the following clues:

    -er
    -le

C. Structural analysis

13. Student is able to recognize root words.
14. Student is able to recognize words containing grapheme bases, including the following:

an	ike	ate	ill
ame	old	ell	ook
all	ack	ear	
et	and	ick	

15. Student is able to recognize word endings and suffixes, including the following:

-ed	-ing	double consonant + ing
-s	-y	drop e + ing
-er	-ly	drop e + -ed
		-'s

16. Student is able to recognize and understand compound words.
17. Student is able to identify the following contractions:

can't	let's	he'll	I'm
don't	that's	I'll	
isn't	what's	she'll	
didn't	here's	we'll	
wasn't	there's	you'll	

II. Comprehension

A. Word meaning or vocabulary skills

18. Student is able to recognize antonyms when they are presented visually or orally.
19. Student is able to define and recognize homonyms.
20. Student is able to define and recognize synonyms.
21. Student is able to identify the proper pronoun referent.
22. Student is able to identify relationship words that include time and place phrases.
23. Student is able to identify special words that include words reflecting specific sensory impressions.

B. Literal comprehension

24. Student is able to recall details in written material.

25. Student is able to identify main ideas including the following:
    a. Identifying central thought and main events
    b. Relating sentences and pictures
    c. Relating the title to the main idea
    d. Distinguishing between relevant and irrelevant information
26. Student is able to recognize and identify sequential events central to comprehension, including the following:
    a. Sequencing events in a story presented in the modes of pictures, text, and pictures and text
    b. Identifying key words for recognizing story sequence in written text that include sequences of logical, spatial, and chronological events and events of importance
    c. Organizing major ideas and events in the story endings when the story is presented pictorially, orally, or with accompanying text
27. Student is able to predict story endings when the story is presented pictorially, orally, or with accompanying text.
28. Student is able to identify cause and effect relationships when the story is presented orally and with pictures and/or text.

C. Critical and analytic comprehension

29. Student is able to distinguish facts from fantasy and/or opinions.
30. Student is able to identify relationships in text read orally and/or pictures, including such elements as cause and effect and people and actions.
31. Student is able to draw conclusions from text read orally and/or pictures and make inferences including generalizing; identifying characteristics of the characters; interpreting motives and feelings; stating implied conversation; using clues; and speculating about events and outcomes.

III. Study skills

32. Student will be able to locate information to verify statements, use content pages, use maps and globes, and find pictures that correspond with written phrases.
33. Student will be able to classify information by classifying objects, events, and characters in a written selection and by categorizing words and phrases.
34. Student will be able to outline by relating story and unit titles.
35. Student will demonstrate ability to summarize by making charts and recording and recalling important facts.
36. Student is able to follow written directions, such as instructions to complete a given task.
37. Student is able to alphabetize.

Second-grade skills

I. Decoding

A. Word recognition

B. Phonetic analysis

38. Student is able to decode words with double consonants:

-ff -bb- -dd- -ff- -gg- -ll- -mm- -ss-

Continued.

TYPICAL SEQUENCE OF SKILLS INTRODUCED IN THE ELEMENTARY SCHOOL READING PROGRAM—cont'd

39. Student is able to recognize vowel digraphs and diphthongs:

ow	ou	ue	ie	au
ew	oo	ough	ey	oi
ay	aw	augh	eigh	

40. Student is able to identify *r*-influenced vowels:

err	are	ir	orr	urr	ore	ire	ier
or	ear	er	our	air	arr	eer	

41. Student is able to identify consonant blends and digraphs in final and initial positions:

ld	dr	st	sn	sw	squ
mp	kn	str	thr	spr	spl
nch	pr	wr	tch	shr	lt
ft	qu	mp	sc	scr	ct
cr					

42. Student is able to identify the following consonants:

ph-	g-	-mb	-v-
-gh-	-ge	kn-	-ve
gu-	-dge	-se	gh-
wh-			-ze

43. Student is able to identify syllables using the following clues:

a-	en-	-it
-ar	be-	-ent
-al	al-	-ic
-el	to-	per-
-on	-or	in-
-et	-ain	-age
-kle		

C. Structural analysis

44. Student is able to recognize the following word endings:

-es	-y to i + -es	-double consonant + -er
-drop e + -ed	-y to i + -ed	-double consonant + -est
-drop e + -er	-s'	
-drop e + -est	-est	

45. Student is able to recognize the following suffixes:

-y	-en	-or	-ly	-full	-er	-ness

46. Student is able to identify the following contractions:

are	aren't
have	I've, haven't
has	hasn't
had	hadn't
would	he'd, I'd, you'd

47. Student is able to identify word patterns such as consonant–vowel–consonant–final e.
48. Student is able to recognize words containing grapheme bases that include the following:

ight	ank	ind
ock	end	ump
ound	ent	

49. Student is able to identify the following prefixes:

a-	un-

II. Comprehension
  A. Word meaning or vocabulary skills
  B. Literal comprehension
    50. Student is able to identify *who, what, where,* and *when* phrases.
    51. Student is able to identify time and place phrases.
    52. Student is able to identify logical response in phrases.
  C. Critical and analytic comprehension
    53. Student is able to identify clues to answer riddles.
    54. Student is able to interpret feeling and emotions.
    55. Student is able to identify implied meaning.
    56. Student is able to predict future events.
    57. Student is able to recognize faulty assumptions.

III. Study skills
    58. Student is able to organize words in alphabetical order.
    59. Student is able to make pictures and maps.
    60. Student is able to skim for information.
    61. Student is able to prepare summaries including main ideas and facts.
    62. Student is able to use the library.

Third-grade skills

I. Decoding
  A. Word recognition

Continued.

TYPICAL SEQUENCE OF SKILLS INTRODUCED IN THE ELEMENTARY SCHOOL READING PROGRAM—cont'd

B. Phonetic analysis

63. Student is able to identify the following consonants:

    -ch-
    sc-

64. Student is able to identify the following vowels:

    i as long e
    e as short i
    y as short i

65. Student is able to identify the following digraph:

    -th-

66. Student is able to identify syllables when they appear between two unlike consonants, between single consonants between two vowels, and between two vowels; and by the following clues:

de-	pre-	-tion	-teen
ex-	dis-	-ous	pro-
con-	e-	-sion	sub-
re-			

C. Structural analysis

67. Student is able to identify the following word endings:

    f to *v* + *es*
    y to *i* + *er*
    y to *i* + *est*

68. Student is able to identify the following suffixes:

-ry	-th	-ward	-ish	-eth
-ist	-less	-ness	-some	-ship
-hood	-able	-ment		

69. Student is able to identify the following prefixes:

un-	mis-	in-
re-	dis-	

70. Student is able to identify words with these grapheme bases:

eak	eam	ank	ate	ill	old
eal	amp	ame	ell	ink	

71. Student is able to identify the following contractions:

doesn't	what's	you're
there's	mustn't	

II. Comprehension
  A. Word meaning and vocabulary
  B. Literal comprehension
    72. Student will demonstrate the ability to locate details to validate inferences.
    73. Student will demonstrate the ability to determine appropriateness of titles.
  C. Critical and analytic comprehension
    74. Student will demonstrate the ability to identify information explaining moods.
    75. Student will demonstrate the ability to locate details used for making conclusions and generalizations.
    76. Student will demonstrate the ability to identify details needed for problem solving.
    77. Student will identify facts and details for making comparisons.
    78. Student will identify details relating to characters' feelings and attitudes.

III. Study skills
    79. Student will employ skimming skills to obtain central ideas.
    80. Student will demonstrate the ability to use a glossary.
    81. Student will demonstrate the ability to use information in report writing.
    82. Student will construct a simple outline.
    83. Student will make summaries using important facts.
    84. Student will interpret diacritical markings.

Fourth-grade skills

I. Decoding
  A. Word recognition (sight recognition)
  B. Phonetic analysis
    85. Student is able to identify the following consonant blends and digraphs:

shr   thr

    86. Student is able to recognize accented and unaccented syllables.
  C. Structural analysis
    87. Student is able to recognize the following suffixes:

-ian	-ous	-ern	-ant
-ence	-ion	-ier	-ure
-age	-ation	-ite	-ance
-al			

    88. Student is able to identify the following contractions:

couldn't   she'd   he'd   weren't   they'll

Continued.

TYPICAL SEQUENCE OF SKILLS INTRODUCED IN THE ELEMENTARY SCHOOL READING PROGRAM—cont'd

89. Student is able to recognize the following prefixes:

counter-	al-	tri-	de-
ex-	pre-	en-	over-
non-	sub-	im-	under-
ad-			

90. Student is able to recognize words containing the following grapheme bases:

ast	oost	are	int	idge	odge
ale	um	oss	edge	ift	udge

II. Comprehension
  A. Word recognition
    91. Student will identify similes and make comparisons.
    92. Student will recognize foreign words, special phrases, and specialized vocabulary.
  B. Literal comprehension
    93. Student will use details to identify aspects of a story.
  C. Critical and analytical comprehension
    94. Student will recognize contrasting points of view.
    95. Student will demonstrate the ability to make deductions.
    96. Student will identify unusual phrases.
    97. Student will predict logical outcomes.
    98. Student will contrast cultures based on comprehension of material.
    99. Student will determine statements of probability.
    100. Student will identify elements of exaggeration.
    101. Student will identify irrelevant sentences.
    102. Student will demonstrate the ability to extend the author's thoughts.
    103. Student will demonstrate comprehension of materials employing codes.
III. Study skills
    104. Student will prepare topical outlines and study outlines.
    105. Student will employ dictionary skills including using guide words, reading pronounciation keys, and using multiple meanings.
    106. Student will use the index of a text correctly.
    107. Student will use an atlas to locate information.
    108. Student will use encyclopedias for locating information.
    109. Student will use diagrams and interpret information presented in diagram form.
    110. Student will locate and interpret data from tables.

Fifth-grade skills

I. Decoding
  A. Word recognition
  B. Phonetic analysis
    111. Student will identify the following consonant blends in initial and final positions:

phr-	-sk	-nt	-ft	-sp

  C. Structural analysis
    112. Student is able to recognize words with the following suffixes:

-eth	-some	-ity	-ic
-est	-ish	-ive	

    113. Student is able to identify the following contractions:

he's	here's	where's	we're	they're

    114. Student is able to identify the following prefixes:

pre-	pro-	out-	mid-	be-	a-	trans-	con-
intra-	anti-	fore-	tele-	come-	des-	com-	

II. Comprehension
  A. Word meaning
    115. Student will identify analogies.
    116. Student will interpret dialects and colloquialisms.
    117. Student will interpret figurative language.
  B. Literal comprehension
    118. Student will identify introductory and concluding remarks.
    119. Student will recognize the use of flashback techniques.
  C. Critical and analytic comprehension
    120. Student will identify elements of suspense.
    121. Student will identify themes of jealousy, sarcasm, and flattery.
    122. Student will demonstrate the ability to identify elements judging ideas and acts.
    123. Student will identify with the character's feelings.
    124. Student will identify words that create humor.
III. Study skills
    125. Student will use the phone directory to locate information.
    126. Student will locate bibliographic references.
    127. Student will take notes.
    128. Student will use the almanac to locate information.
    129. Student will use the *Reader's Guide* to locate information.
    130. Student will use time lines.
    131. Student will interpret cartoons.
    132. Student will make inferences from illustrations.
    133. Student will use appendices and listings.

Continued.

TYPICAL SEQUENCE OF SKILLS INTRODUCED IN THE ELEMENTARY SCHOOL READING PROGRAM—cont'd

Sixth-grade skills

I. Decoding
  A. Word recognition
  B. Phonetic analysis
  C. Structural analysis
    134. Student will identify words with the following suffixes:

    -ent -ize -ary -ire -ar -aye -ible

    135. Student will identify words with the following prefixes:

    in- hecto- kilo- centi- deca- milli- deci- ir- post-

II. Comprehension
  A. Word meaning
    136. Student will recognize and interpret acronyms.
    137. Student will recognize origins of words.
  B. Literal comprehension
    138. Student will recognize episodes.
  C. Critical and analytic comprehension
    139. Student will generate hypotheses.
    140. Student will identify supportive evidence.
    141. Student will determine reliability of sources.
    142. Student will judge author's qualifications.
    143. Student will support hypotheses.

III. Study skills
    144. Student will use the card catalogue.
    145. Student will use reference books to locate information.
    146. Student will use catalogues.
    147. Student will use community resources to locate information.
    148. Student will prepare outlines, including topics and subtopics.
    149. Student will use cross-indexed sources to locate information.
    150. Student will prepare book reviews.
    151. Student will keep records, using consistent form and format.

Readiness skills

The basic skills of reading are readiness, or pre-reading, skills. The majority of children come to school equipped with these skills, but many handicapped students and students from minority backgrounds are not well equipped to engage in reading activities because their readiness is extremely low. The elements of skills in this component are those familiar to most special educators: visual perception, auditory perception, listening comprehension, visual-motor integration, and language development. Although a teacher may not expect to "improve" the process of a child in any of these areas in the remedial sense, the skills of these areas may be directly taught. In general, the teacher will attempt to orient children to reading by developing a reading interest, developing attitudes about reading, and improving the experiential background. Language-experience charts have already been discussed, but they are of particular value in this stage of development. Activities that engage children, field trips, discussions, play, and so forth, are used to develop intellectual processes.

Visual perception. Although there are programs for the development of visual perception (e.g., the Frostig), cautions about using such programs in the expectation of improving a process have been noted previously. More importantly a training program might be dedicated to actual experiences with manipulable, concrete objects necessary for visual discriminations and concepts in reading. Activities for matching, discriminating, determining likenesses and dissimilarities, and other tasks should be used. Specifically, games, puzzles, and activities that teach the following skills should be developed:

1. Matching shapes
2. Matching letters
3. Matching words with similar letter characteristics
4. Matching letters to words that have specific patterns of letters

Auditory perception. Auditory training exercises are important for children who require development in auditory perception, especially minority students. The typical activities and games used address the following needs:

1. Developing rhyming ability
2. Determining sounds and words that begin and end with the same sounds
3. Making "same" or "different" distinctions between similar-sounding words
4. Developing memory games that extend the process of retaining units of verbal information, such as "I'm going to the circus and I'm going to take a ______."
5. Discriminating between phonemes

Listening comprehension. The language of a child can be expanded by direct experience in readiness training. Listening comprehension is an important aspect of this development. Stories and incomplete stories can be used to help develop listening comprehension abilities. In essence, the teacher can encourage children to answer literal and inferential questions, propose possible alternatives in a story line for discussion, guess what might happen next or what might happen if some element in the story had been changed, and recall the essential story line. The sequence and scope of events is important in listening comprehension.

Visual-motor integration. The major factors in visual-motor integration concern the use of directionality in the reading process. Children must be directly taught that letters have specific meanings (sound associations) in specific orientations. Many children are confused by the letters *b, d, p,* and *q* because each is actually the same and only has significance in a particular spatial attitude. Thus, sequencing, left-to-right order, and letter identification are important. The fact that good readers have a knowledge of letter names probably is not as significant as the fact that they also learn orientation of letters and other discriminations.

Teaching children to distinguish between letters that are highly similar in shape causes difficulty because the discriminations are really fine distinctions. Teaching highly dissimilar letters causes less confusion. Therefore, many of the Kephart-type activities and other perceptual-motor programs are suitable for developing sequencing and orientation skills in young children.

Language development. Obviously, the language base of the child is the foundation for reading. The entire curriculum of the school is language. The earliest attempts at training should encompass the concepts of language development. The many programs and materials ordinarily used for language growth would be recommended, but language should not be seen as a separate ability that is compartmentalized for training. Even the activities in visual, auditory, and perceptual-motor areas should be directed by language.

Word recognition skills

As noted previously, word-recognition skills are of two basic types; meaning emphasis and code emphasis. *Context clues* are also included in some programs, but this strategy encourages guessing rather than developing a basis for actual word attack.

Structural analysis is also included as a word-recognition skill in which a student uses contractions, word compounds, prefixes and suffixes, root words, and other characteristics to recognize a word. However, basic decoding is the major problem confronting most handicapped students, and meaning and code-emphasis approaches will be discussed here.

Meaning emphasis. Any of the variety of games and activities discussed in this chapter may be adapted to provide instruction in meaning emphasis. It should be noted that some approaches specifically avoid the development of a sight-word vocabulary. Other approaches blend sight words with phonics instruction. Basal series attempt to combine both approaches and reach some balance. The activities used to teach sight words are varied, and are familiar to most elementary school educators. Determining which sight words to present may sometimes be a problem, if deviation from a basal approach occurs. For the most part, lists such as the Dolch 220 word list and other lists of high-utility words are used. Most approaches limit sight words to those which are meaningful to a student, have practical utility, and are regular. Irregular words are usually taught later.

The specialist should attempt to engage the student in activities that are directly related to the content of the regular classroom. Meaningful sight words that are required in a series of skill sequences in the basal program should be the focus of the special education program. As in other aspects of instruction, the task of the teacher is to identify the specific skills the students are to learn, use varied approaches to introduce and reinforce the skills, use overlearning, keep the student on task, and provide feedback and reinforcement.

Code emphasis. Phonics instruction concerns the following elements: consonants, single consonants representing several sounds, consonant sounds that are represented by various graphemes, long- and short-vowel sounds, the schwa sound, vowels controlled by the *r* sound, digraphs, diphthongs, and syllabication. Most programs emphasize initial consonants and long vowels. If students make significant progress, instruction in other phonic elements is found to be unnecessary. Phonics are very important for first-grade reading but are of much less importance by the fourth grade. Students who continue to experience difficulty with decoding are given more intensive practice in phonics instruction. However, rules or phonics generalizations typically are not taught to young or handicapped children because even if they can remember the rules, they cannot apply them in attacking words. The order of instruction is as follows:

1. Consonants
2. Consonant digraphs
3. Consonant blends
4. Short vowels
5. Long vowels
6. Vowel digraphs
7. Diphthongs
8. Silent e

One approach that has gained popularity in the learning disabilities literature is the Glass analysis technique (Glass, 1973), which is a method of recognizing common letter clusters in decoding. The basic element is not the consonant or the vowel but the common patterns of letters that combine naturally in English orthography. Although commercial materials are available, the teacher can use simple teacher-constructed flash cards. The purpose of the Glass analysis technique is to support perceptual learning by means of increased auditory and visual memory through association of redundant letter clusters of sound-symbols (Miccinati, 1981). According to Miccinati the following exercises may be used:

1. Students write letter clusters within words either kinesthetically or by common spelling.
2. Contrived stories are made using words with the cluster patterns.
3. Bingo games are used for reinforcement of patterns.
4. Flip cards are used for practice.
5. A commercial game, Ends and Blends, is used for reinforcement of many skills of the Glass system.

The ultimate shift is from the Glass system to common single phonemic elements. Ordinarily, those who use this approach believe that phonics instruction is too difficult for students and that meaning-emphasis approaches are also inappropriate.

Another distinction made in the code-emphasis approach is between *analytic* and *synthetic* approaches to phonics. The analytic process is used to teach a child sounds as they naturally occur in words. The synthetic approach refers to isolated methods of teaching sound-symbol associations before applying skills to words.

Comprehension

Almost every textbook in reading carefully includes a statement similar to this: "Decoding is merely a means of unlocking the sounds of words, but true reading requires comprehension." This may be true, but in fact it too is a debatable point among authorities. Nonetheless, few would argue with the notion that reading is a process by which the reader acquires information from the written passage. Similarly, listening is another verbal skill by which a person should be able to derive meaning from the spoken word of another person. This analogous process is not stressed much in school. The greatest concern of most teachers in regular classrooms and of special educators is to teach children decoding skills. The primary skills introduced in the first three grades are decoding skills. Little attention is devoted to teaching comprehension, and, as we have demonstrated, most teachers only ask literal, concrete questions at any grade level. How seriously the profession attempts to teach comprehension is a debatable point when one examines what actually happens.

For the most part it seems that educators expect children to continue to make progress in reading on an individual basis through practice after the children have acquired basic decoding skills. Many children are capable of doing this if the reading process does not become boring and aversive to them. Rewarding children for reading, making reading interesting, and increasing the amount of reading that children do will undoubtedly improve comprehension for most of them as an incidental factor. However, the field is devoted to the concept that comprehension should and must be taught as an independent skill.

Comprehension can be no better than the language ability of the reader. Messages and nuances may be lost on a reader who, although able to decode, is unable to understand the language and uses of the writer. Therefore, comprehension is a language skill. Much of what is attempted in teaching reading comprehension may be thought of as language training. The elements of comprehension are as follows:

1. Meaning of words (vocabulary development)
2. Meanings of sentences and phrases
3. Meanings of paragraphs and longer written units (chapters, themes, etc.)
4. Literal, inferential, and critical comprehension skills

These elements are familiar and self-explanatory. Most teacher's manuals have voluminous information and exercises devoted to teaching comprehension in these areas. Other rather specific techniques have become popular for use in assessing the readability of particular material for a given student and for increasing comprehension skills. These techniques are listed as follows:

1. *Cognitive organizers* (prereading and postreading questions). A useful method for organizing thought processes is to limit the focus of attention to specific elements. Depending on the content, the teacher orders a body of information by erecting cognitive organizers, or prereading questions, before the act of reading. The student is encouraged to read for specific content; there is no need to read an entire passage and then attempt to extract what may have been important. This is an evaluative skill that takes years to develop. Reading in content areas is enhanced by the process.

2. *Key elements*. The approach to comprehension stressed in basal programs and classroom instruction is that of identifying facts, finding main and subordinate ideas, predicting outcomes, drawing inferences and conclusions, and considering cause and effect relationships.

Teachers in content areas who attempt to have students acquire *concepts* and *vocabulary* provide important assistance in reading development. The student's disability requires compensation. If the student can still learn the content of a subject area, there will be learning and a sense of achievement. Students who have limited reading ability, who are required to engage in significant amounts of reading in all subject areas, and who attempt to learn to read simultaneously will simply be overwhelmed. Teachers who do not accommodate such students may not be aware that this practice is similar to handing a textbook to a blind student and expecting him or her to read it!

Study skills

At the apex of reading development in the elementary school are study skills. Beyond the fourth grade most of the remaining reading skills are study skills. Study skills are functional reading abilities or specific reading competencies that enable a student to study the content areas of the curriculum. Reading in textbooks is quite different from reading that students typically encounter in basal series and other developmental materials. Most reading books are attractively displayed, have uniform type, are interspersed with colorful pictures and photographs, and are relatively predictable. Textbooks are expository, include many changes in typeface, are filled with technical words and uncommon uses of words, have many unfamiliar concepts, and are usually boring.

Texts are heavily weighted with facts and concepts, and they complicate the task of the learner and deny the joy of reading that is promised. Study skills are essential for effective learning because reading in the subject-matter areas is much more difficult than in the reading class, where students learned to read about puppies, picnics, and the fun-filled pastimes of children.

Study skills typically include using the dictionary and reference materials, locating information, and organizing information through note taking and outlining. We have organized study skills into mechanical and critical reading skills, which differentiate between reading in organized reading classes and reading in subject-matter areas. Although both types are necessary for efficient learning in school subjects, the tasks are different:

Mechanical	*Critical*
Recalling main ideas	Perceiving relationships
Locating main ideas	Drawing conclusions
Retelling a story	Making inferences
Recalling sequences	Interpreting feelings
Classifying information	Making judgments
Skimming	Comparing
Outlining	Contrasting
	Making generalizations
	Summarizing

In Table 6-2 we have provided a graphic representation of the applications of study skills. Primary skills for study assignments and for products encompass most of the required school activities. Assignments and the creation of products are the major endeavors of homework, laboratory work,

Table 6-2. Study skills and their applications

Primary skills	*Learning activities for application of skills*
Study assignments	Study and reading assignments
Reading	
Technical vocabulary	Textbooks
SQR3	Workbooks
Outlining	Fiction and nonfiction
Note taking	Reading notes
Graphics	Responding to questions and solving problems
Charts	
Tables	
Maps	
Graphs	
Diagrams	
Products	Study products
Locating information	Book reports
Dictionary	Themes
Atlas	Oral and written reports
Encyclopedia	Projects and experiments
Library	Maps and charts
Computer retrieval	Models
Other references	Other
Specific information	
Alphabetizing	
Book parts	
Cross-reference	

and in-school study. Both types are used by students to meet the demands of course requirements on a daily basis, and they contribute significantly to successful completion of units and earning passing grades. Simple decoding skills will not give the student this status of achievement in the middle and secondary grades.

Technology

The greatest source of direct support for teachers lies in the capabilities of various electronic information-handling systems, especially the microcomputer. Unfortunately these devices are not in widespread use in education. The application of computers in teaching reading could be a tremendous benefit to handicapped students. Motivation, feedback, reinforcement, and a structured skill sequence could be easily managed by means of electronic hardware. The influence of the teacher could be greatly extended beyond the limitations of current instructional practices. The time-on-task of students would be effectively maximized, which is a critical concern for handicapped students. Teachers who take the time to become acquainted with computers and other teaching machines, who learn how to develop software (until such programs become commercially available), and who can integrate such technology into the instructional program will be able to transcend the current state of reading instruction. Gradually, teachers will emerge from college preparatory programs possessing these skills. Until colleges change the undergraduate curriculum to incorporate these innovations, the potential impact of technology will be limited.

Behavioral applications

Applied behaviorism is the most promising approach to teaching reading and other areas of the curriculum. The behavioral approach is a medium, not the content of instruction. As such it can be used to improve reading through motivation and reinforcement of students. Essential elements for effective instruction are the skill sequence (knowing what to teach), components of instruction, and reinforcement. Some applications, such as the ratio of words read to time, seem simplistic in view of what is known about reading instruction. However, the science of behaviorism cannot be denigrated. Effectively blending knowledge of the skills of the reading process with reinforcement theory can have an agreeable result in learning.

ESTABLISHING A PROGRAM

Some steps need to be taken by the specialist in developing a new program. There are many considerations that will be more fully discussed in Chapter 12. We are interested here in establishing general guidelines for beginning and coordinating the reading program in a school setting. The steps

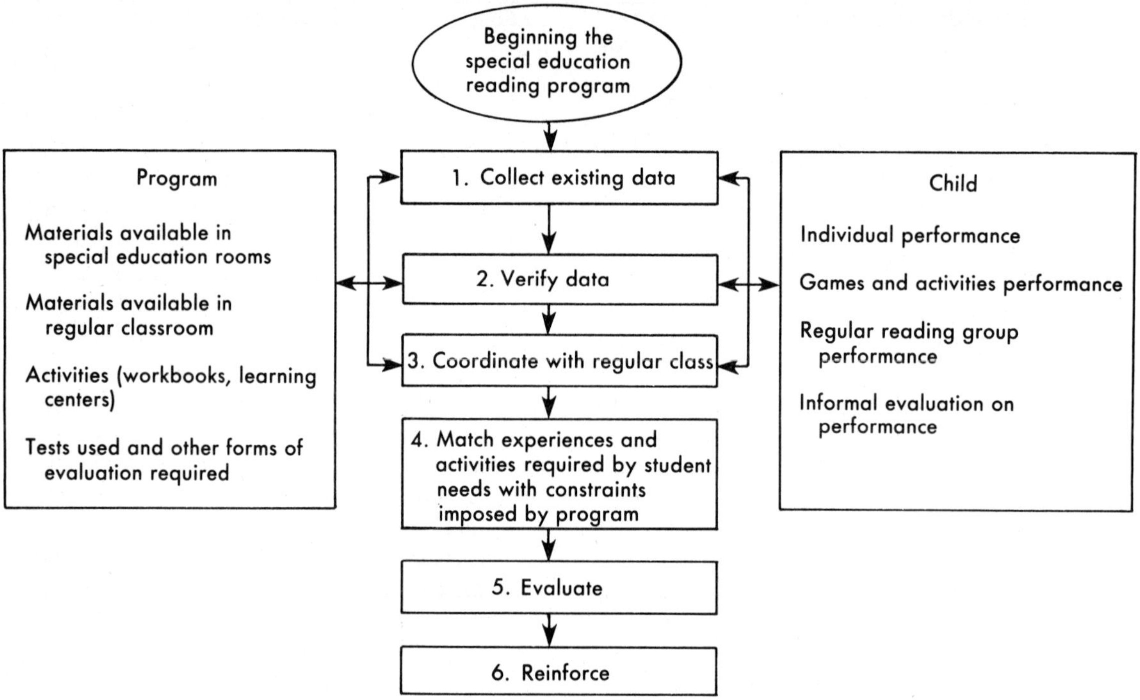

Fig. 6-1. Steps involved in initiation of the reading program.

in establishing a special program are graphically depicted in Fig. 6-1 and are outlined as follows:

1. Collect existing data
   a. *Child*. Determine the availability of records on the students to be served in the program. This can be done by requesting the folders, identifying previous teachers, and noting any reading personnel who might have provided services to the students. Informal information concerning the performance level of students should include some background on student interests and preference for materials.
   b. *Program*. Find out what materials are included in the special reading program. Request a copy of the room inventory from the principal. In addition, request a list of the adopted texts used in the district and any listing of old books that are stored. Scout the building, taking note of the various types of reading books and materials seen on shelves in the regular classrooms, and ask teachers if they use any special activities in connection with reading. Check with the administrator concerning the type of reading achievement tests administered in the district, and request a copy of the materials.
2. Verify data
   a. *Child*. Once the children arrive and begin reading instruction, use informal assessment strategies to ascertain the accuracy of information gained in step 1. This is important because students may respond differently because of growth, a new environment, or modified teaching ap-

proaches. Experimentation with various methods and materials to best match learner preference with skill needs will pay big dividends in terms of student achievement and motivation.

b. *Program.* You may find that items listed on the inventory no longer exist or are beyond use! In addition, you may discover that some materials listed for building use are difficult to obtain for the program because they are already scheduled for use by other teachers. Materials observed in regular classrooms may or may not be available, depending on the cooperation of other teachers. It is essential to establish good rapport with the teachers, so if borrowing materials or activities, be certain to use them properly, return them intact, and return the favor in some fashion. Teachers who are willing to share various teacher-made skill games can be an asset to your reading program. Talk with the various teachers concerning their reading evaluation program, and ask if they administer any other reading tests besides those required by the system.

3. Coordinate with the regular class

a. *Child.* Keep in mind the expectations of the regular classroom when planning for individual students. Even if the special education program is self-contained, we have found through experience in such programs that close coordination in terms of similar activities and student goals facilitates cooperation among the teachers, aids students in peer interactions outside the classroom, and makes parent communication easier. We have found it imperative that the decision concerning which of several needed skills should be taught in the resource room should be made with regard for the sequence in which these skills are taught in the mainstream class.

b. *Program.* Coordinate the selection of materials and approaches with other aspects of the school program; that is, the regular teacher may be using a specific material and may allow you to use it in the special education class. On the other hand, the mainstream teacher may prefer that the special program *not* include the material. In this case, you should identify materials that are different but still address the same skills being taught in the mainstream. The degree of coordination possible at this point of programming will be greatly determined by the closeness of the relationship between you and the regular faculty.

4. Match experiences and activities

This step is critical because it is at this point that the degree of interrelationship between regular and special programming is determined. Ideally the skills taught in the special classroom will parallel and augment those taught in the mainstream class. However, some students will receive instruction in reading exclusively in the special class, either as a result of the IEP or because the regular teacher views such instruction as a substitute for reading instruction in the mainstream setting. It is not satisfactory when the student receives instruction in both settings without any attempts on the part of the teachers to match the instructional sequences. The student in this situation may, on any given day, receive instruction in short vowels in the special class and in consonant blends in the regular class. Rather, we would urge that the skills addressed be consistent, but the experiences and materials be varied. For instance, if the child is taught the short i in the regular classroom using a reading group and workbook approach, we would suggest that you support the objective for the short i on the same day by using games, blackboard activities, and alternative workbook sheets. Table 6-3 provides sample activities and games to illustrate this type of instructional planning.

Table 6-3. Examples illustrating the use of commercial games to assess or teach basic skills

Material	*Skill*
Blend Bingo (Sullivan Reading Games, Behavioral Research Laboratories)	Student is able to identify consonant blends in initial and final positions.
Consonant Match (card game) (Sullivan Reading Games, Behavioral Laboratories)	Student is able to identify consonant sound-to-symbol relationships and initial and final positions.
Mr. Rabbit, Mr. Snake, and the Egg That Wouldn't Break (kit) (Singer Education Division)	Student is able to predict story endings when story is presented pictorially, orally, or with accompanying text.
Written Language Cards (flashcards) (Developmental Learning Materials)	Student is able (from text read orally or pictures) to draw conclusions and make inferences.
Vocabulary Development (contractions) (Milton Bradley)	Student is able to identify contractions.

5. Evaluate
   a. *Child.* Assessment of the student's achievement progress is probably the primary means of measuring the effectiveness of a reading program. The evaluation should include both formal and informal measures.
   b. *Program.* Program evaluation would also include feedback as to how the regular teachers view the reading program and the student's progress. Obtain this type of feedback informally through casual discussions or through direct requests for feedback from the cooperating teachers. The evaluation results may require that the student's programs be altered or that the approaches being used in the special reading program be modified to better fit in the overall school program.
6. Reinforce
   Once student progress is noted, reinforce it through definite means, either a formal, structured reinforcement system or informal teacher rewards. Of equal importance, reinforce any cooperative or sharing efforts from the regular faculty. This reinforcement may take the form of sharing special education materials, performing tasks as a favor for the teacher, and providing social reinforcement such as praise for assistance given to ensure further student progress.

SUMMARY

It is evident that despite the general approach used in teaching developmental reading, with the exception of the most extreme linguistic approaches, a common skill sequence underlies instruction. The most common approaches are basal series, the eclectic or individualized approach, and the language-experience approach. Throughout the early grades most schools will use basal series, although individual teachers or schools may use a variety of approaches in addition to basal texts. The major components of reading instruction are readiness, word recognition, comprehension, and study skills. By the end of the fourth grade most reading skills have been introduced. Throughout the early grades the majority of handicapped students have difficulty maintaining pace with most nonhandicapped students. Some are incapable of engaging in beginning reading at the same time as their peers, and others cannot develop as quickly and will vary from a few weeks to several months in skill acquisition. This aspect of development has not been accurately studied in education; however, it is clear that students can pass through the same sequences of development but at different rates.

The skills of reading become the focus of instruction more than any other theoretical correlate of learning failure that is attributed to the learner. The best approach to integrating resource room and regular class instruction is to ensure that the skills presented in the regular curriculum are respected. The regular teacher must accept varying levels of performance among students. Activities of the special educator must support the major learning activities of the student rather than supplant them. In programs in which highly specialized approaches or a self-contained or modularized approach to reading is employed, students would not be mainstreamed for reading in the regular program. In any content area of the curriculum, such as social studies, the student's reading problems should be circumvented, and the reading requirement should be diminished because it is the content of the subject that the teacher is emphasizing, not just the process of reading.

Task-analytic and diagnostic-prescriptive approaches have been popularized in special education. However, such approaches should be guided by the sequence of skills identified in the school. If there is no agreement about what the sequence is, a group of teachers must reach a consensus about what they are teaching and in what order. This would clarify the goals of instruction in any school. Subsequently the task analysis would be related to decoding and comprehension skills, when appropriate, for a particular student at a specific level of skill. The use of observation, monitoring, and frequent review is necessary for effective instruction. Data-based methods (behavioral models) are appropriate; however, reading cannot be viewed merely as a rate of word calling. The demands on the learner must be considered in keeping with the tasks or skills that are being introduced. Criterion-referenced testing is superior to any norm-referenced method of evaluation. In its most basic form, learning to read is an information-processing problem in which the learner must make increasingly finer discriminations; as a result, these skills can be identified and evaluated on a linear basis. The following conclusions can be drawn:

1. The skill sequence ties the regular and special class programs together, as expressed in the IEP.
2. In the early grades a skills-management approach to teaching is superior; implementing special self-contained or modularized reading instruction is a last resort for students who are clearly not succeeding.
3. As soon as content or subject matter emerges as a distinct element (reading to learn versus learning to read), support must be implemented to ensure that the student's knowledge acquisition is not sacrificed in the interest of intensive remediation.
4. A record-keeping system is imperative.
5. Communication must exist between teachers concerning progress of each student.

REFERENCES AND SUGGESTED READINGS

Bannatyne, A. *Language, reading and learning disabilities.* Springfield, IL: Charles C Thomas, Publisher, 1971.

Bond, G.L., & Dykstra, R. *Final report* (Project No. X-001). Washington, DC: Bureau of Research, Office of Education, U.S. Department of Health, Education, and Welfare, 1967.

Burns, S. *A study of sequential memory skills in reading disabled and normal children.* Unpublished doctoral dissertation, Northwestern University, 1975.

Chall, J. *Learning to read: the great debate.* New York: McGraw-Hill Book Co., 1967.

Durkin, D. *Children who read early.* New York: Columbia University, Teachers College Press, 1966.

Durrell, D.D. First grade reading success study: a summary. *Journal of Education,* February 1958.

Fernald, G.N. *Remedial techniques in basic school subjects.* New York: McGraw-Hill Book Co., 1943.

Frostig, M., & Horne, D. *The Frostig program for the development of visual perception.* Chicago: Follett Publishing Co., 1964.

Gibson, E. Learning to read. In H. Singer & R. Ruddell (Eds.), *Theoretical models and processes of reading.* Newark, DE: International Reading Association, 1970.

Glass, G. *Teaching decoding as separate from reading.* Garden City, NY: Adelphi University Press, 1973.

Goldstein, K. *The organism.* New York: American Book Co., 1939.

Guthrie, J. Models of reading and reading disability. *Journal of Educational Psychology,* 1973, *65,* 9-18.

Guzak, F.J. Teachers' Questions and levels of reading comprehension. In T.C. Barrett (Ed.), *The evaluation of children's reading achievement.* Newark, DE: International Reading Association, 1967.

Hallahan, D., Gajar, A., Cohen, S., & Tarver, S. The learning disabled as an inactive learner. *Journal of Learning Disabilities,* 1978, *11,* 231-236.

Hammill, D.D., Goodman, L., & Weiderholt, J.L. Visual-motor processes: can we train them? *The Reading Teacher,* 1974, *27,* 469-478.

Haring, N.G., & Bateman, B. *Teaching the learning disabled child.* Englewood Cliffs, NJ: Prentice-Hall, Inc., 1977.

Johnson, D., & Myklebust, H. *Learning disabilities: educational principles and practices.* New York: Grune & Stratton, Inc., 1967.

Kephart, N.C. *The slow learner in the classroom.* Columbus, OH: Charles E. Merrill Publishing Co., 1960.

Kirk, S.A., Kliebhan, J.M., & Lerner, J.W. *Teaching reading to slow and disabled learners.* Boston: Houghton Mifflin Co., 1978.

Miccinati, J. Teaching reading disabled students to perceive distinctive features in words. *Journal of Learning Disabilities, 1981, 14,* 140-142.

Morsink, C., Cross, D., & Strickler, J. *How disabled readers try to remember words.* Reading Horizons, 1978, *18,* 174-180.

Ross, A.O. *Psychological aspects of learning disabilities and reading disorders.* New York: McGraw-Hill Book Co., 1976.

Samuels, S.J. Success and failure in learning to read: a critique of the research. *Reading Research Quarterly,* 1973, *8,* 200-239.

Strauss, A., & Lehtinen, L. *Psychopathology and education of the brain-injured child.* New York: Grune & Stratton, Inc., 1947.

Strickland, R. The language of elementary school children: its relationship to the language of reading textbooks and the quality of reading of selected children. *Bulletin of the School of Education,* 1962, *37,* 21-28.

7 TEACHING EXPRESSIVE SKILLS

Expressive language includes gestures, oral expression, and written language. The obvious importance of these skills in social and vocational functioning justifies the emphasis of the elementary curriculum on teaching verbal skills. The child's progress in all aspects of the curriculum is evaluated through these responses. Since language arts are emphasized in the mainstream class, it is necessary for the special educator to plan supportive activities that are coordinated with the goals of mainstream education. These activities should be designed to assist the child in coping with deficits in expressive language, to aid in developing corrective interventions, and to augment the services of the regular classroom teacher. In self-contained classes and other arrangements in which integration is deemphasized, the special educator will have primary responsibility for these aspects of the curriculum. For most handicapped children it is necessary for the special educator to deliver services that neither interfere with nor supplant activities of the regular classroom. The special educator is concerned with expressive language in three forms—oral speech, handwriting, and spelling. The stimulation of spoken language is a primary concern; subsequently, handwriting, spelling, and applications of these skills are developed.

ASPECTS OF LANGUAGE

There are essentially two major schools of thought on language and its development. The study of language has been deterred significantly because of the popularity of behaviorism in America. Not being able to look into the brain and observe its development and functioning, the behaviorist is content to observe data that can be measured and leave conjecture about language processing to others who have less constraining empirical guidelines. As a consequence, there is considerable information concerning the rate of development of specific sounds, words, sentence structures, and other aspects that can be directly observed and counted. Psycholinguistics has taken longer to emerge. If behaviorism were included as a third school of thought, language would be explained, as are other behaviors, in terms of reinforcement.

The two primary schools of thought are biological and developmental. The biological view (Lennenberg, 1964) maintains that the infant is predisposed to language development; an inborn ability exists for its rudimentary and ultimate development. The developmental view interprets language development as normal stage theory. Although both views have similarities, they have been antagonistic in the literature.

Lennenberg emphasizes three aspects that are found in all languages: (1) phonology, (2) semantics, and (3) syntax. Morphology is usually included as a major aspect in most discussions.

Phonology

Phonology is the science of sounds. Sounds are called phonemes, and the English language has 45 phonemes. Consonants are categorized according to three types of characteristics:

1. *Method of articulation:* plosives, fricatives, glides, nasals, laterals, and retroflexives
2. *Oral location of articulation:* bilabials, labiodentals, dentals, alveolars, palatoalveolars, palatals, velars, and glottals
3. *Voiced or unvoiced articulation:* sounds made with or without the resonance of the larynx

Phonological aspects of language are the first to be learned by a child. This essentially involves repetition, reinforcement, and discrimination learning. As the child is able to make finer discriminations between sounds and to produce them appropriately, the basic command of language is ensured. The first attempts of the infant to imitate language reflect the melodious quality of the language and patterns of inflections. Many abilities are important for normal acquisition of language; vision, hearing, and discrimination abilities are required for the child to learn.

Specific sounds seem to develop at certain ages. By the time a child is 8 years old, most of the sounds of the language have been mastered. The most common errors of children in this category are substitutions of sounds, usually ones that sound similar or are articulated in close proximity of the oral cavity. With finer discriminations, immature errors are ultimately overcome by most children. Substitutions are errors of discrimination learning. More serious problems involve distortions and omissions.

Semantics

Semantics deals with the meaning of words, sentences, and the characteristic combinations of concepts that are conveyed in language. The meaning of a word relates to the experiences of the speaker. Thus, semantics is really concept development. The child must have many experiences with words to determine appropriate uses in the expression of ideas; these experiences must be rooted in concrete exposures to words.

Syntax

Syntax dictates the serial order and relationships of words according to the rules of a language necessary to convey meaning. The child must acquire flexibility and facility with a variety of nouns, kernel sentences using a noun and a verb, and elementary grammatical rules. The child must learn to transform basic sentences to indicate tense, use complex and compound sentences, use negation, and substitute pronouns accurately. For a child who is beginning to speak, verbs are especially difficult because they must be employed with various tenses. Nouns are learned more easily because they are simpler and can be associated immediately with concrete objects. Language development is evidence of substantial intellectual activity. The child must perform an incredible amount of classification and discrimination, not only at the perceptual level, as in phonology, but also at increasingly complex levels of development in terms of meanings, multiple meanings, idiomatic expressions, and numerous patterns, rules, and complex syntactical structures.

Language is the basis of social activity. It continues to exist because it serves social needs. The child's ability to develop language depends greatly on the ability to superimpose acquired motor responses over the larynx and breathing system, to engage in increasingly complex discrimination learning, to receive feedback and reinforcement, and to actively refine the process.

Language and academic skills

Development of basic skills in reading and arithmetic are aided by the acquisition of language. Piagetian theory relegates language to a much less significant status than most educators would accept, contending that language is not necessary for the development of logical, abstract reasoning; in fact, this has been demonstrated among adult deaf persons who have no linguistic system. However, language can also aid in the child's development as a verbal mediator for control of behavior and social interaction and can facilitate learning in all areas of the curriculum. An interesting contention is that basic arithmetic may not be well served by spoken language, as we shall describe in Chapter 8. For the most part, in our culture verbal ability is equated with intelligence; most intelligence tests have a heavy "verbal load." An interesting trend in the literature, especially in the category of learning disabilities, is the correlation of subtle language deficits with reading disabilities.

In an arduous review and discussion of relevant literature, Vellutino (1979) has dismissed the literature that attributes reading disorders to visual perception, visual memory, intersensory integration, and temporal-order recall. His conclusion is that these process dysfunctions are symptomatic of a verbal processing disorder. Vellutino maintains that reading disorders may be explained as deficits in phonologic, semantic, and syntactic abilities; perceptual disorders are only secondary manifestations of verbal mediation deficiency, possibly associated with basic language problems. Although an alternative view explains reading disorders as a learner deficiency in basic encoding strategies, this concept has been growing in popularity, and, since speech pathologists are becoming more involved in this field, it may be expected that research and remedial programs will increase. No one disputes the importance of language abilities in relationship to school performance. However, specific deficits of language may have an etiological connection with some disorders of basic skills, and adequate or superior language abilities may have little relationship to fundamental spatial and arithmetical skills.

SPOKEN LANGUAGE

Children who have oral language disorders will require the support of classroom teachers and special educators. These children will receive direct service from a speech therapist or pathologist; however, teachers who provide indirect and supportive services should consider the following conditions associated with correcting a special or language disorder:

1. A speech disorder can have an impact on a child's self-concept and interpersonal relationships.
2. The teacher can assist in reducing embarrassment and stress.
3. The teacher can follow the leadership of the speech pathologist and reinforce therapy in the classroom, as well as emphasize the importance of follow-through activities to parents.

The types of speech problems are articulation, stuttering, voice disorders, and cleft palate. Other areas of concern to the pathologist include hearing handicaps, cerebral palsy, and aphasia.

Articulation disorders

Following are the major articulation disorders:

1. *Substitution errors.* Errors in substitution are usually made by children who have not mastered the discriminations necessary to make appropriate sounds. Usually an error is similar to the correct sound and is repeated consistently in all speech productions, for example, saying "toofbrush" or "birfday cake."
2. *Omissions.* This type of problem is exemplified by consistent omissions of particular sounds. The more sounds omitted, the more difficult the child's speech will be to understand.
3. *Distortions.* The most typical sound distortion is the lisp, which results from the incorrect product of the *s* sound.
4. *Additions.* Some children add sounds that do not occur in words, such as "dogd" for dog.

Articulation disorders and other problems of speech and language are treated by speech pathologists who employ a variety of formal and informal tests to determine the nature and degree of deviancy in speech. The child who is suspected of having articulation disorders will be examined by use of one or more standardized instruments and will have samples of speech included in the evaluation. The production of sounds is examined in the initial, medial, and final positions of words. If it is determined that the child's speech production attracts attention and deviates significantly from age peers, and if the errors are not explained in terms of regional speech patterns, the child may be included in therapy.

Voice disorders

A relatively small number of children have voice disorders. Most estimates indicate that about 1 percent of children are affected. There are three kinds of disorders that interfere with communication and that direct the listener's attention to how the individual talks, and they are as follows:

1. *Disorders of pitch.* Some people have a voice quality that is too high or too low in pitch. Although this is a social problem in some cultures for adolescents and adults, the concern during childhood may be about a high or low pitch, or more likely it will be about the lack of pitch variation.
2. *Disorders of loudness.* For organic and psychological reasons, some children develop conditions of speaking in which speech volume is inordinately loud or so soft that it is difficult to hear the child under quiet conditions.
3. *Disorders of quality.* In a more subjective

area, a child's voice that is too harsh, breathy, nasal, or denasal may sometimes be a cause for concern.

Fluency disorders

Although dysfluency is common for young preschool children as a normal matter of development, in our culture disorders of fluency stigmatize school-aged children and adults. Relatively few children, usually boys, fall into this category, and the etiological factors are less clear than in other speech disorders. Treatment approaches have been many and varied. For the classroom teacher it is important to recognize that stressful situations can induce dysfluency; reinforcement of dysfluency can create acquisition of the dysfluent behavior; and adults, who set explicit and implicit standards of behavior, can create circumstances in which children feel hesitant to speak.

Although this condition, known as stuttering, stammering, and cluttering, is considered to be pathological in a minority of children, it has attracted a disproportionate amount of attention in our culture. The value system is important in understanding this condition. Many therapies have been developed with varying claims to success. Nonetheless, there is little agreement among therapists about the causes of the condition and the treatment approaches that should be used. The classroom teacher's greatest role will be in the encouragement of speech production, acceptance of dysfluency, and the creation of an accepting environment wherein the dysfluent speaker need not fear embarassment or recrimination from the teacher or peers.

Role of teachers

Children who manifest disorders of spoken language are usually served by speech pathologists who (1) ensure communicative competence for all children, (2) provide direct or indirect service to children, and (3) work intensively with children whose language disorders interfere with their academic achievement or social adjustment (Freeman, 1977). Wood (1969) suggests the following ways in which teachers can play a supportive and collaborative role in the process:

1. Working with children at their own level of language
2. Lessening the demands of speech
3. Translating gestures into simple, concrete words
4. Allowing children to demonstrate what they mean
5. Giving children the sense that their speech is important and interesting
6. Attempting to eliminate gestures
7. Working from concrete to abstract
8. Taking advantage of strengths of children
9. Using stimulus materials from children's environments

The mutual support and cooperation of teachers and speech pathologists is vital for children who manifest spoken-language disorders. They must follow specific guidelines and ensure that procedures in therapy and in the classroom are not contradictory.

In addition to these general guidelines, a number of common classroom activities may be used to stimulate speech and language development. With the cooperation of the speech pathologist, the special education teacher and the classroom teacher can evaluate classroom activities with the purpose of determining ways of incorporating more direct activities to benefit children who require intervention. Some suggested activities are as follows:

Action activities

- Charades
- Role playing
- Acting out simple stories
- Extemporaneous speaking
- Puppetry

Sharing

- Show and tell
- Experience chart development
- Describing a personal art project
- Telling about vacations and trips
- Participating in group planning

Games and activities

Collective or group stories
Singing
Games with kernel sentences such as "I spy. . . ."
Taping stories and other media productions
Choral reading and riddles

A number of commercial kits and materials are available for language development. It should be recognized that many of the activities may be less expensively developed by using available materials and objects in the school or those which can be easily acquired. The teacher would carefully analyze the materials, consider the advantages, consider the expense, and determine the cost-benefit and cost-effectiveness ratios of purchases. Table 7-1 provides a summary of commercial materials for language development and brief descriptions of their uses. Their value and quality would have to be determined by the potential user. Some materials are actually complete programs. They are expensive and might not relate to the general goals and objectives of the school.

Table 7-1. Common commercial materials and their uses in language-development programs

Material	*Primary use*
DISTAR I, II, III	The program may be used for preschool children and elementary school children; it is highly structured and emphasizes phonological, semantic, and syntactic elements.
Peabody Language Development Kits	The kits are mainly concerned with oral expression and would be highly developed for semantical aspects. The packaging, lesson plans, and associated materials facilitate uses by the teacher.
Fokes Sentence Builder Kit	This is a structured kit emphasizing syntax.
Monterey Language Program	This is a programmed plan based on a behavioral design that includes evaluation instruments.
MWM Program for Developing Language Abilities	Influenced by the ITPA, these materials are used by the teacher to develop areas of deficit that may be evaluated in terms of the psycholinguistic process theory of the ITPA.
GOAL	Also based on the ITPA, these lessons are conceived within a game format. No specific skills are associated with developmental stages.

HANDWRITING

Disabilities of written language may be classified as disorders of (1) handwriting, (2) spelling, and/or (3) written expression. All three may be manifested in children as primary or secondary disorders. Handicapped children should receive assistance in developing useful skills important for daily functioning and vocational adjustment. Much less interest and research has been evident in this aspect of language.

In handwriting, the initial skill to be mastered is the ability to execute the motor acts involved in forming letters, numerals, and words. The development of handwriting usually follows an ordered sequence, although a specific sequence of strokes, circular movements, and other patterns have not been verified.

The causes of handwriting problems are not clear, with the possible exception of a lack of practice or corrective intervention. Good handwriting has not been correlated with such factors as eye-hand coordination, IQ, race, or chronological age; the first area to examine for causes and to seek direction for treatment would be in the teaching process (Graham & Madan, 1981). Teaching specific skills is important, and as Graham and Madan note, only a few letters (a, e, r, t) account for 50 percent of the problems in letter formation.

Speed, accuracy, and neatness are important qualities. Slow, tedious, and sloppy handwriting causes students to spend more time completing assignments, which makes the process a drudgery and may increase dissatisfaction with school. Neatness affects the teacher's attitude toward the student and grading.

Sequence of skills

The sequence of skills in handwriting begins with a variety of prewriting exercises and ends with proper uses of punctuation in written expression. In general, the order is as follows: using crayons and paint brushes; grasping and holding a pencil; orientating or slanting the pencil; moving the pencil in random patterns; and reproducing meaningful patterns, such as manuscript form, copying letters and words, writing letters and words, cursive writing, and writing sentences and paragraphs. In the educational experience, attention is devoted to size and spacing and ultimately to the neatness of the product. Identifying the sequence of skills may aid in determining the errors that are made by the student. The following inquiries might be useful:

1. Is the child right or left handed?
2. Are the child's motor activities adequate? Can the child grasp, slant, and move the pencil and position the head, arm, and body appropriately?
3. Is the physical arrangement of the learning environment suitable? Other than general comfort and mood of the class, it is important to determine that the lighting, size of desk or table, and size of writing instrument are appropriate.
4. Is the child attempting to use manuscript or cursive writing?
5. How much time does the student spend on the writing task each day? Does the student practice often? Is it supervised and is feedback provided?
6. Does the child have difficulty forming random movements on paper or forming letters, words, sentences, or paragraphs?
7. Does the child have difficulty with size, spacing, speed, and neatness?

To assess handwriting problems, the teacher should address each of the preceding concerns. Determination of problems should begin at the lowest level. If, for example, a child has been writing for a number of years and has a number of problems, starting at the lowest level of development will be important and attempts should be made to ignore problems higher in the hierarchy until the basic problems are resolved. More specifically, at any level the teacher should determine the subskill problem the student presents (Linn, 1970):

1. Improper construction of letters
2. Corners turning at irregular angles
3. Gaping lines
4. Letters of improper size
5. Difficulty with letters that go above or below a line
6. Reversals of letters or words
7. Improper spacing
8. Improper placement

Assessment and teaching objectives

Because of the specific hierarchy of skills in handwriting, it may be beneficial to consider the following list for both assessment and teaching. Although the available commercial tests may provide some information, it is more direct to conduct informal assessment. The student should be able to demonstrate the following skills:

1. Grasping the pencil
2. Holding the pencil at the proper slant
3. Making random marks
4. Making free-form (controlled) marks
5. Imitating line and wave patterns and variant strokes

6. Reproducing nonmeaningful patterns

7. Reproducing meaningful patterns appropriate for manuscript or cursive writing

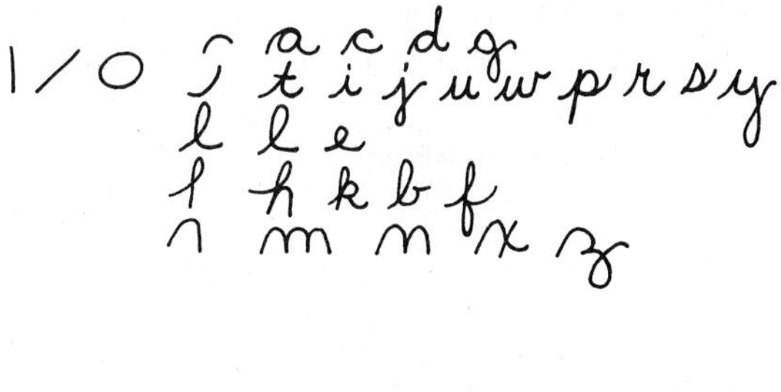

8. Copying letters
9. Writing letters
10. Copying words
11. Writing words
12. Copying sentences
13. Writing sentences
14. Identifying different types of sentences
15. Determining subject-verb agreement
16. Using capital letters
17. Using correct pronouns
18. Identifying common irregular plurals
19. Identifying comparative and superlative adjectives
20. Spacing, aligning, using margins, and preparing neat products
21. Indenting
22. Writing answers to simple questions
23. Composing two or more related sentences
24. Transforming manuscript into cursive style
25. Independently writing a variety of sentences and paragraphs
26. Using vivid modifiers
27. Organizing information into an outline
28. Writing reports on chosen topics
29. Initiating and recording research to support self-generated theories
30. Recording and evaluating personal experiences

Teaching handwriting

According to Graham and Madan (1981), a variety of instructional and motivational procedures for teaching letter formation may be used:

1. Modeling
2. Critical analysis (target letter is compared to similar letters)
3. Prompts and cues (arrows and colored dots can be used for forms)
4. Tracing
5. Copying
6. Repetition
7. Self-correction
8. Corrective feedback
9. Reinforcement

There is a certain similarity between these steps and the techniques originally used by Fernald. Drill, overlearning, and feedback are the key ingredients.

Many different approaches are used to improve handwriting skills. The first issue that must be decided in remediation of handwriting is whether to teach cursive or manuscript writing. Although the majority of elementary schools teach manuscript writing before cursive writing, some research supports teaching cursive initially. The following points are cited by Larson (1970) as advantages of cursive versus manuscript writing for children:

1. Lowercase letters begin on the same line and never "out in space."
2. Words hold together, even with irregular spacing between letters.
3. Words are still separated, even with small spaces between words.
4. Cursive writing provides rhythm, continuity, and wholeness.

In a study investigating the relationship between cursive handwriting, reading, and spelling achievement, it was determined that exclusive cursive writing in the first grade did not adversely affect reading and spelling achievement and had a positive effect on reversals and transposition errors (Early, Nelson, Kleber, Treegoob, Huffman, & Cass, 1976).

Regardless of whether manuscript or cursive writing is taught, certain prehandwriting skills must be mastered first. If children do not possess these skills, handwriting instruction should begin at this point. A list of skills and activities are reported as follows:

Skills	*Activities*
Fine eye-hand skills	Stringing beads one at a time and then making a particular color or shape pattern (Payne, Polloway, Smith, & Payne, 1977); playing games such as jacks
Awareness of figures	Walking in circle or straight line that has been marked on a surface

Skills	*Activities*
Concepts of left to right, forward and backward, and start and stop	Walking in circle or straight line that has been marked on a surface; making lines with finger paint (Madison, 1970); playing games in which child has to touch or point to objects on left- or right-hand side (Payne et al., 1977)
Movement along guided line	Tracing a circle, half circles, and lines; tracing figures on blackboard; tracing over dots
Movement in groove	Tracing grooves made in clay and with templates
Movement with resistance	Making letters in wet clay using templates, fingers, or sticks
Movement without solid guide	Connecting dots to form geometrical figures and letters; tracing figures and letters
Making figures without guide	Making figures and letters in sand, with finger paints, on blackboard, and on paper while looking at a pattern
Making figures without pattern	Making figures and letters in sand, with finger paints, on blackboard, and on paper from memory

Proper pencil grip. An important prehandwriting skill is proper pencil grip. After observing children with handwriting difficulties, Kahn (1970) determined that in *all* cases of improper pencil grip the fingers obstructed the line of sight from the pencil grip to the eye. This further aggravated the writing problem by requiring the student to tilt the head to the side or closer to the page. After age 7, pencil grip habits are more difficult to change.

Proper pencil grip, according to Mendoza, Holt, and Jackson (1978), requires the following actions:

1. Holding the pencil by the thumb, index, and middle fingers at approximately 1 inch above the pencil point
2. Resting the pencil primarily on the near (proximal) side of the middle finger, just below the first joint
3. Placing the end of the thumb on the other side of the pencil opposite the middle finger
4. Resting the end of the index finger on the top surface of the pencil between the other two fingers
5. Resting the remaining portion of the pencil in the rounded space between the second joint of the thumb and index finger

Many methods are used to teach proper pencil grip, including using large pencils, which some researchers believe is ineffective and unnecessary; modeling the proper technique for the student, which may be time consuming (Mendoza et al., 1978); placing a rubber band on the end of the pencil where the grip should be; and using the Grip-Ease, a triangular gripper made of soft plastic that slides on the pencil (Kahn, 1970).

Another method uses drawn circles and colored tape (Mendoza et al., 1978). In using this method, teachers draw different-colored circles on the pencil-contact points of the writing hand. Colored tape that matches the colors on the pencil-contact points is applied to the pencil. This method allows students to monitor their own grip, thus reducing teacher supervision while providing constant feedback to the students.

Manuscript writing. After the students acquire prehandwriting skills and proper pencil grip, teachers must teach or remedy proper manuscript and/or cursive writing skills. Although there are many different methods, the following instructions should be helpful to students with poor handwriting abilities:

1. Be accurate; speed is not as important.
2. Trace letters and/or words with the index finger and then with a writing instrument.
3. Trace letters on the blackboard; ensure proper direction and sequence.
4. Connect dot letters.
5. Make letters in the air.
6. Complete letter fragments.
7. Copy letters from a written copy.
8. Write letters from memory (without a copy of the letters).
9. Combine letters to form simple words.
10. Copy words from a written copy.
11. Write words from dictation (without a copy of the words).

12. Trace words on the blackboard and on paper.
13. Write experience stories.

Cursive writing. The following are general points for the student concerning cursive writing:

1. Be accurate; speed is not as important.
2. Practice rhythm writing; trace and copy increasingly difficult rhythmic patterns. (Fig. 7-1 gives examples of these patterns.)
3. Trace cursive letters on paper, on the blackboard, and in the air.
4. Write letters from copy and dictation.
5. Connect cursive letters to form words.
6. Trace words.
7. Connect dots to form written words.
8. Write words with and without copy.
9. Write experience stories.

Steps in teaching or remedying writing should be encompassed in games and activities that motivate students. The following activities are enjoyed by students and facilitate the development of good writing skills:

1. *Mazes*. Begin with simple mazes. This activity helps the child gain good hand-eye coordination and fine motor skills with a writing instrument.
2. *Dots*. Draw several rows of parallel dots, and have children play "dots," a game in which whoever connects the last side of a dotted box wins the box. This activity helps develop pencil control in drawing vertical and horizontal lines.
3. *Kinesthetic writing*. Have children write letters and words in sand and with finger paints.
4. *Between the lines*. Have children draw a line between two parallel lines. Begin with widely spaced horizontal and vertical lines, and move lines together with decreasing space and elaborate curves.
5. *Alternate letters*. Make letters on the board, and have students add or take away a portion of the letter to create a new letter (Payne et al., 1977).

Special considerations for physically handicapped students

For many children who manifest primary or secondary physical limitations, specific accommodations must be made to facilitate handwriting:

Disability	*Modification*
Inability to grasp pencil because of cerebral palsy, arthritis, or other musculoskeletal disorders	Obtain a pencil holder. It can be a commercial holder or one made by pushing a pencil through rubber ball or molding clay around pencil, making a perpendicular grasp (Fig. 7-2).
Weak grasp	Tie pencil or writing tool to student's hand or fingers (Bigge, 1977).
Amputee	Modify writing tool to fit student's prosthetic device.
Inability to hold arm and/or hand steady because of poor motor control	Attach a magnet to student's wrist, and make a writing pad with a metal base; use wrist weights; use cutout to write between; or use raised lines (Bigge, 1977).
Limited vision	Make a cutout to write between; use paper with raised lines or wide, dark lines; use felt-tip marker or pencil that makes dark lines. Use slant boards to provide correct angle to reduce light reflection and use nonglare paper; use magnification equipment to allow child to enlarge words.

Handwriting for left-handers

Since many handicapped children are left handed, teachers need to be aware of ways to improve the handwriting skills of left-handed writers. A child who writes with the left hand should not be expected to write like a right-handed child because the left-handed child is pushing while the right-handed child is pulling across the page; the slant for left-handed writers should not be the same as

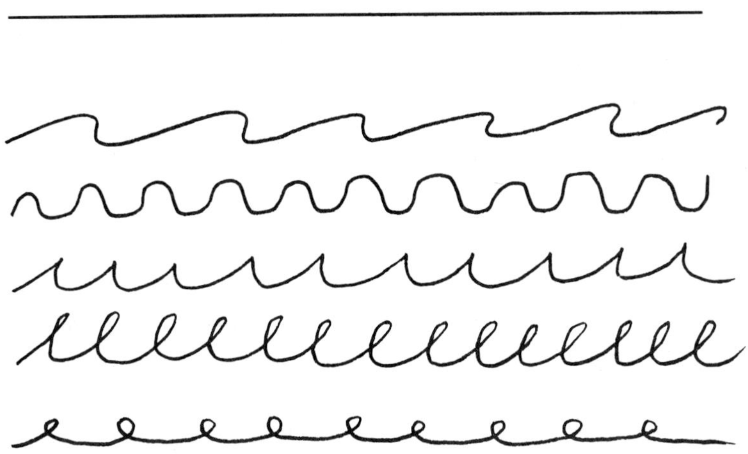

Fig. 7-1. Patterns of rhythmic writing.

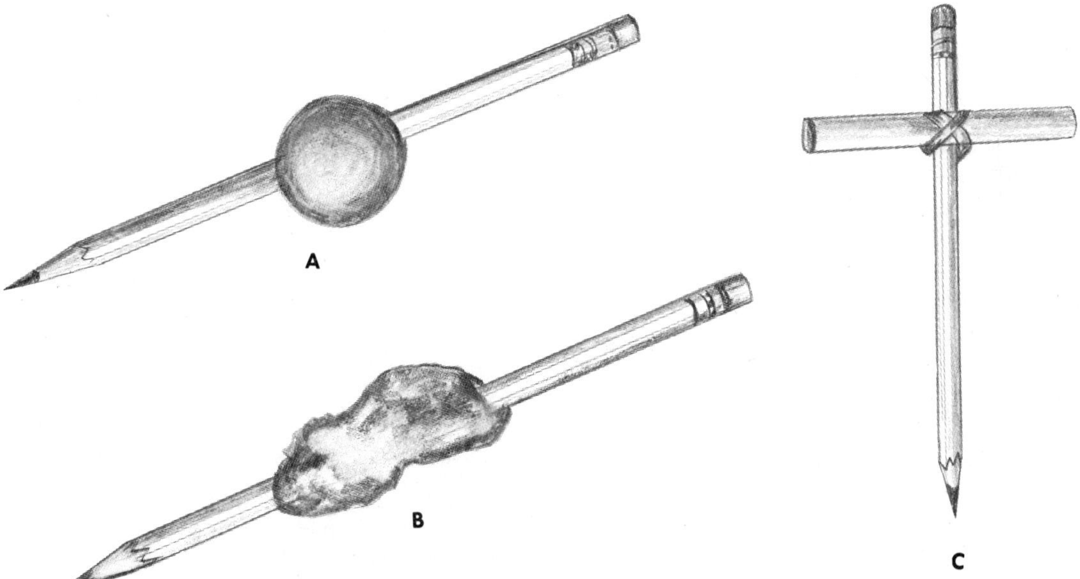

Fig. 7-2. Devices to aid persons who cannot hold handwriting tools: *A*, ball of sponge rubber; *B*, clay; *C*, cross stick. (Redrawn from Bigge, J.L. *Teaching individuals with physical and multiple disabilities*. Columbus, OH: Charles E. Merrill Publishing Co., 1977, p. 204.)

for right-handed writers (Ramos, 1970). Harrison (1981) suggests the following guidelines when teaching or remediating the writing of left-handed children:

1. Group left-handed children together for handwriting instruction.
2. Provide them with a good left-handed model—a teacher, aide, parent, or another student.
3. Give them readiness exercises to develop left-to-right directionality.
4. Encourage a fuller movement of the writing arm by having them practice at the blackboard.
5. Teach them to hold their pencils about 1½ inches from the point, slant their papers to the right, and turn their bodies to the right when they write.
6. Encourage them to eliminate excessive loops and flourishes in their writing.
7. Teach them to write vertically or with a slight backhand slant; do not insist on a slant to the right.
8. Provide each child with a model cursive alphabet showing left-handed writing. The students can use this instead of the usual right-handed model to evaluate and correct their own handwriting.

SPELLING

Spelling is the act of placing letters in the proper sequence to form words. Spelling has been more or less standardized since the acceptance of dictionaries. Previously there could be an incredible variety in the spelling of words; the orthography of the English language is highly irregular in many instances, and a poor relationship exists between graphemes and spoken language. Perhaps the worst period in the history of the English language was during the Tudor reign in England; there were literally scores of spellings for common words, and the educated class used illegible handwriting intentionally as a social affectation of the time. Today it is socially unacceptable to have poor spelling, even though poor handwriting may be ignored after a person is out of school. Typewriters can eliminate poor handwriting but not incorrect spelling.

Types of errors

The major types of errors have been enumerated by Edgington (1968) as follows:

1. Addition of unneeded letters
2. Omissions of needed letters
3. Reflections of a child's mispronunciations
4. Reversals of words
5. Reversals of consonant order
6. Reversals of consonant or vowel directionality
7. Reversals of syllables
8. Phonetical spelling of nonphonetical words or parts
9. Wrong associations of a sound with a given set of letters
10. Neographisms, or letters that are put in a word but bear no discernible relationship with the word dictated
11. Varying degrees or combinations of these or other possible patterns

Regarding this list of the types of errors, the following questions may be asked: How do these errors relate to instruction in the developmental sequence of learning to spell or in remediation? Can an awareness of these errors aid in the development of spelling instruction? A consideration of the major approaches to teaching and some information about research findings will help answer these questions.

Instructional approaches

According to Lerner (1981) the two types of instructional approaches are linguistic and frequency-of-use. The linguistic approach is similar to the technique used in reading. The teacher carefully introduces children to words that are highly regular and that have stable phoneme/grapheme relationships. The frequency approach emphasizes the most common words in the literature at each grade level and employs drill activities to reach mastery. However, if one carefully considers the distinctions made, it is apparent that the two approaches to spelling use the same approach.

Spelling, under each type of instruction, relies on total recall; it is a matter of overlearning, which requires drill. Learning words by families (man, pan, ran, tan, fan) or by simple lists of drill words results in the same outcome: a list of words stored in long-term memory. Grouping similar words together is a good technique for clustering, but the child must still overlearn. Even in the linguistic approach the child must ultimately commit irregular orthrographies to memory without much assistance from linguistic training.

Encouraging children to use the linguistic or phonetic approach to spelling may result in errors because the child might be accustomed to relying on the "ear" to spell words. In either approach it is the redundancy, or repetition of words, that accounts for success and spelling accuracy; however, this is *not* true in reading because of the many clues available to the reader. One does not need to spell efficiently to be able to read.

It is curious then why some writers recommend the use of reading word-attack skills to analyze spelling errors. Some tests also employ this strategy, but to a questionable end. For example, the Kottmeyer Diagnostic Spelling Test provides the teacher with two lists of words (32 in each) that are purported to be appropriate for examining the spelling of children in two large groups (first through third and fourth through sixth grades). Subsequently the teacher is able to analyze spelling according to the following scheme: words with short vowels; two vowels together; silent *e*, *ou* and *ow* vowels; long and short *oo* vowels; and so forth. However, this analysis does not provide the teacher with useful information. The child may be able to read every word but misspell most of them. The finding that the child misspells words having common elements important in decoding is not useful unless the child also cannot read these words.

Reading is a decoding task that relies on a large number of clues. Spelling is an encoding task that demands total recall. These processes are related but are from two different domains. For further evidence the reader may wish to examine the research of Hanna, Hodges, and Hanna (1971), which was instrumental in the development of the Test of Written Spelling (TWS). A computer was programmed with 2,000 rules of English spelling and required to "spell" 1,700 words. Only 50 percent of the words were spelled correctly. Two interpretations might be made based on this result: (1) only 50 percent of words in the sample, assuming that the sample was representative of the English language, fit the rules of English; and (2) if one knows all the rules (an unlikely event) and does not rely on memory for recall, there is a 50/50 chance of spelling a word correctly. As a result, the developers of the TWS elected to include two types of words in the test, those which conform to rules and those which rely on memory. Most children, especially handicapped children, are unable to remember rules. Even if they know rules, they will not necessarily apply them. The conclusion seems to be that drill to the point of overlearning is essential for correct spelling. Analysis of words in terms of spelling or reading word-attack skills, or emphasizing the meanings of words in teaching is probably not a worthwhile endeavor.

To address the questions asked previously, spelling remediation that is based on additions, omissions, or any other error-analysis pattern will not be helpful because the implication is that the teacher should induce the child to learn rules that can be applied to each dictated word.

It may be concluded that spelling requires total recall of a specific sequence of letters that have been retained by a process of memorization. Some writers believe that spelling is simply a matter of practice; the larger the store of spellings in memory, the better the child's performance on tests. This appears to be true, based on the limited research to date.

Some writers have speculated about what occurs in the process of spelling and have implicated the correlated processes; that is, they speculate that visual memory, auditory memory, and deficits of motor skills cause spelling disorders. No compelling reason substantiates this, especially if one refers to the writing of Graham and Madan (1981). They recommend that teaching spelling should be a direct process rather than concentrating on visual-perceptual or some other indirectly (hypothetically) related exercises.

One of the most extensive reviews of research on spelling is the work of Cahen, Craun, and Johnson (1971) which determined that spelling research has followed three tracks: (1) examination of the speller, (2) investigation of words, and (3) analysis of teaching methods. They were interested in what makes a word difficult to spell, and they generally supported the presumption that exposure to words is more important in learning to spell correctly than is using rules.

Examination of spellers is interesting. Some children can read well but cannot spell. Naturally, some children can do neither well, which is explained by varying interest, motivation, success, and frequency of contact with written material. Words that they see in print may not be used in their conversation. Certain words seem susceptible to misspelling because low-frequency use in reading matter and/or frequent occurrence of graphemes, diphthongs, confusing vowel sounds, and so forth. Certain types of phoneme/grapheme correspondences appear with consistency in the English language, and spelling difficulty may be related to the magnitude of correspondences with a certain word or word types.

Apparently phonics can be helpful in the improvement of spelling to the extent that there is a precise phoneme/grapheme correspondence, but a variety of peculiar misspellings are made by both good and poor spellers. If a child is familiar with English orthographic patterns, a variety of substitutions and additions may occur that make orthographic sense. Reliance on phonics will be satisfactory only if spelling can be uniformly applied to sensible phoneme/grapheme matches. When the word violates the sound, an error can occur, unless the child has total recall. Accurate spelling relies on recall, not the probabilities of guessing.

Spelling accuracy can vary depending on the demand on the child's central nervous system. Oral spelling and spelling from dictation can sometimes be quite different for the same child. In one instance, a child was taught the manual alphabet, which improved his spelling; if finger spelling is an intermediary step between oral and written spelling or another method of forcing the child to drill cannot be determined, the latter effect is more likely.

Another consideration involves the uses of lists in teaching spelling and in its assessment. The most commonly recommended lists are the "100 most common words" (Lerner, 1981) and the "100 spelling demons" (Hammil & Bartel, 1978). The 100 most common words were derived from research studies of language arts materials used by children between 1945 and 1955. Most of these words appear in basal series and spelling books; however, currently diverse approaches to reading and new words are included that may not have been widely used 25 years ago. It might also be inappropriate to test and teach common words if children are involved in a linguistic approach, such as the Sullivan Program, which is phonetically based.

The same can be said of the WRAT, which is used in many special education programs at the beginning and end of each year. Many, if not most, spelling and reading words on the WRAT do not appear in the lessons of children learning to read by means of a linguistic, VAKT, or other controlled approach. To this extent, these tests are not valid, since they are not correlated with the curriculum. The same might be said for the spelling demons, the most often misspelled words. Teaching children to spell these words should relate to a structured logical pattern of development or to a post-hoc remedial approach. Finding that children can do well on one or the other list may or may not be meaningful, depending entirely on the curriculum that is used.

Assessment

The school may employ any number of instruments to assess spelling: the WRAT, TWS, PIAT,

SRA Achievement Series, Iowa Test of Basic Skills, or Kottmeyer Diagnostic Spelling Test, to name a few. We have already made some observations about assessment of spelling. The test should include items that are primarily in the basal reading series or language arts program of the child who is being assessed. If not, it is analogous to giving a child a test in Spanish to assess performance in German; it just does not make sense.

However, the teacher can unwittingly fall into a trap in this regard. For example, we examined the Kottmeyer Diagnostic Spelling Test, recommended by some writers as a tool for determining a data-based remedial program. We compared the items in List I, which includes 32 spelling words tapping the spelling ability of children between second and third grades, with a second-grade reader (Ginn series) and found that 50 percent of the words on the list did not appear in the reader! Even more interesting, only five of the words in the list appeared in the Kottmeyer second-grade spelling book. In addition, the children are introduced to new reading words in basal series that may not appear on this or other tests, and it is evident that for practical purposes informal assessment is mandatory if a fair assessment is to be conducted.

Another approach that is used for assessment and teaching, mentioned previously, is the list of the 100 most common words. Lerner (1981) has one listed in her text, as do Cohen and Plaskon (1980). We compared both lists and found that 24 words (or 24 percent) did not agree. Thus, the list has only 76 most common words if only those which duplicate are counted. Our recommendation, which may seem trite, would be to use word lists derived from the reading matter in the language arts program.

Based on our previous comments, we would also disparage the use of process testing, modality-preference testing, spelling error checklists, linguistic approaches, or reading word-attack skills in the assessment of spelling. This can be best summarized in the following conclusions of Cohen and Plaskon (1980, p. 339):

1. Word lists are the most efficient and effective means of presenting spelling.
2. Spelling must be taught in a direct and systematic manner.
3. Phonics is supplemental to, not a substitute for, spelling.
4. The beginning speller should learn first the most frequently used words.

Assessment and instruction should deal with the words used by the child on a daily basis in the language arts program. The "hit" rate on the Dolch 220 word list or, for that matter, in the 100 most common words list (despite their inconsistencies) will only be as high as the frequency with which the words are encountered in materials read in a particular school. The more narrow the program of reading, such as a highly structured linguistic approach, the more likely the child will not encounter these common words.

A teacher who wishes to use a standardized test that has some relevancy to a school curriculum, providing a strictly linguistic approach is not used, would select the TWS because it was developed on the basis of common spelling words in ten basic programs. It has two general types of items, predictable words and words not governed by rules.

Other tests that are widely used, such as the WRAT, PIAT, SRA, and Iowa Test of Basic Skills, which have already been mentioned, must account for discrepancies between the curriculum and the test items.

Informal assessment techniques provide a rich source of information to the teacher. Consideration should be given to factors such as time-on-task, observation of the student, and other factors discussed in various parts of this text. Since these factors are directly related to spelling, the teacher can consider a number of techniques.

However, we would not suggest that reading word-attack techniques be strongly considered in accordance with the reasoning described previously. A knowledge of root words, digraphs, diphthongs, blends, prefixes, plurals, double letters, silent letters, and contractions will not be especially helpful in planning remediation for spelling. This implies a need for teaching rules for a task that involves overlearning.

Initial steps in planning spelling instruction include examining the individual child's strengths and weaknesses in spelling, studying word samples, studying records for information on previously employed instructional materials and strategies, and analyzing spelling errors based on materials the child is using in various aspects of the curriculum. These activities may prove more beneficial than any formal tests. The teacher must consider the child's performance in the subject areas taught in the regular classroom; therefore, spelling instruction aimed at facilitating this performance should be considered a primary focus. Learning to spell essentially requires the same redundancy and overlearning as in other aspects of the school curriculum. If time is to be spent on learning to spell specific words, they should be words the child is expected to encounter daily.

Spelling assessment activities that would aid the teacher in designing programming might include the following strategies, as suggested by Smith (1969):

1. *Dictated words.* The students write words that are dictated by the teacher or a machine.
2. *Cloze procedure.* This technique involves elimination of every nth word (e.g., fifth or sixth) in a story, which then must be completed accurately by the child. This technique is most useful in the upper grades.
3. *Proofreading.* Some teachers require children to correct misspelled words in a running narrative.
4. *Free writing.* The teacher collects samples of written work generated by themes and examines each word for spelling errors to ascertain the nature and extent of spelling errors.

Table 7-2 consists of examples of the manner in which the classroom teacher might employ the assessment strategies suggested by Smith (1969). The teacher who is interested in assessing spelling skills that are related to daily performance might consider employing the four types of strategies using the word lists from the back of the reading books. Each reading series contains a list of words

Table 7-2. Employing assessment strategies

Dictated words	*Cloze procedure*	*Proofreading*	*Free writing*
Dictate list of words from readers, as demonstrated in Table 7-3. Make spelling tapes using vocabulary from readers. Dictate words to be written on blackboard.	Prepare worksheets with blanks, and require students to complete work. Use vocabulary from readers. Write story on chart tablet or blackboard, leaving spaces, require students to complete word by adding letters. This may also be copied for additional instructional purposes. Read child a story, leaving various blanks, and require child to add letters to complete word.	Select one or more paragraphs from child's reader and type it to create worksheet. Purposely include misspelled words, and require child to identify and correct them. Prepare series of sentences using spelling/reading vocabulary. Ask child to identify sentences with spelling errors and correct them.	Have children create original sentences using selected spelling list. Require children to write stories using list. Assign a written task, without reference to specific list, and examine nature of errors.

Based on data from Smith, R.M. Teacher diagnosis of educational difficulties. Columbus, OH: Charles E. Merrill Publishing Co., 1969.

introduced in a particular book; the teacher's manual of some series includes a list of "decodable" words, words that fit into "sound families" or patterns. We have outlined a procedure by which the teacher, using the reading vocabulary, could design an assessment and an accompanying remedial program in spelling (Table 7-3).

The typical weekly spelling plan consists of a few common activities: introduction of words, analysis of words, activities and games used as drill and practice, and a mastery test. Examination of basal reading series reveals that these same activities are included in the suggested instructional sequence. Therefore, the teacher will find the same basic strategies recommended whether a basal text is employed or spelling is correlated with reading vocabulary. We have included several typical instructional strategies in Table 7-3 to illustrate that the source of words does not affect teaching strategies.

Table 7-3. Examples of spelling strategies for daily programming

Strategy	*Activities*
Visual examination of words	Look for similarities such as words beginning with same letter, containing double letter, or having same ending
	Looking for words based on same root word such as *look, looking,* and *looked*
	Identifying any contractions in list; discussing basic words combined to produce contraction
	Noting any plurals included in list
Auditory analysis of words	Listening to teacher read list
	Reading list with teacher
	Listening and clapping when student hears a word that begins with a consonant (and other such cues)
	Selecting words that have same ending sound (rhyme)
	Circling words that have same vowel sounds
Application of words	Writing words in the blank using word list to complete sentences telling what is happening in pictures
	Completing sentences by adding missing letters in certain words
	Writing a sentence with each spelling word in list
	Finding spelling error in each sentence

Because of the central role drill plays in spelling instruction, the teacher will be faced with the task of designing drill activities that are not too boring to the student. The creative teacher will be able to adapt basic types of games and activities to reflect spelling content. Following are a few samples of drill activities to illustrate this adaptive process:

Games

- Word Bingo (correlated with reading)—bingo cards made using spelling lists
  - *Materials:*
    - 8″ × 11″ pieces of paper or cardboard
    - Marker to draw off squares
    - Chips (beans, buttons, or pieces of paper)
    - Master list of words to be cut into slips for caller's list
    - Jar or container to hold slips
- Scrabble

Activities and worksheets

- Crossword puzzles
- Hidden words (unscrambling letters to make words; making words from a group of letters)
- Rhyming tasks
- Spelling tasks
- Spelling bees
- Spelling games using the computer
- Stories requiring the child to find right letter to complete word
- Producing a newspaper in the classroom

The types of activities and materials reviewed in Chapter 2 as part of the informal assessment process could also be used in spelling instruction.

Table 7-4. Designing spelling instruction based on reading words

Materials	*Teacher actions*	*Outcomes*
Assessment		
Copy of reader the student is beginning Copy of reader previously completed Copies of both teacher's manuals	Select a sample list, consisting of 10 percent of words listed as vocabulary for previously completed reader. A system that might be appropriate would be to select every nth word (e.g., fifth, sixth). Give child the spelling text. If student can spell 90 percent or more of the words, child is ready to continue to next level that is consistent with reading content. If child cannot spell 90 percent or more of the words, remedial work needs to be done with spelling list from previous reading content.	An assessment is made of child's ability to spell words from reading content that theoretically has been mastered. If child does not demonstrate 90 percent accuracy on first list, teacher knows to focus spelling instruction on complete list from which sample was taken. If child demonstrates 90 percent competency on first list, teacher knows to design weekly spelling instruction based on vocabulary words associated with child's reading lessons.
Instruction (remedial)		
Copy of reader from which sample was taken Copy of teacher's manual	Design spelling lessons, using one or more of following types of activities: Completion of sentences Crossword puzzles Completion of words (cloze) Creating sentences Word-analysis activities Rhyming words Games Continue remedial instruction until student can spell 90 percent or more of the words accurately.	Lessons in spelling are related to actual reading content. Student reaches competency consistent with reading level.

Spelling instruction

Many schools use spelling programs in addition to the rest of the language arts curriculum, so that there may be a poor relationship between the words that children find in either program. An integrated program is much more sensible because it will ensure that children frequently encounter the same words. The more exposure and practice, the more likely spelling skill will be achieved. Table 7-4 provides a format for instruction, and lists considerations that should be used in determining the spelling program:

1. The words most frequently encountered in the literature of children in a particular school and grade should be used.
2. Less common words may be delayed until children have sufficient mastery of common words.
3. It should be remembered that children may read words that have apparent cues but may not be able to spell from recall.
4. Feedback in spelling comes from the knowledge of errors. The typical study-test-study cycle is not sound. Having children take tests from dictation, especially if a tape recorder is used, and then having them cor-

rect their own words will facilitate learning. A number of commercial machines like Speak and Spell create motivation for practice that cannot be achieved by traditional drill.

5. Spaced practice is superior to massed practice; children should have small segments of time throughout the day and week to study words. As mastery is achieved in some words, others should be introduced.
6. Spelling activities should be separated from reading. That is, a child learning to spell a word should be taught the word as a whole unit rather than attacking the word, as in reading, by using syllabication.
7. Requiring children to spell words with a pencil or keyboard is probably superior to oral spelling because the child has more cues, input, and linkages.
8. A number of "learning theory" techniques (e.g., the Von Restoff technique, which has a letter in the middle of a word that is darker than the others) may be applied, as explained in Chapter 12.
9. A child should not necessarily be burdened with the meanings of words when learning to spell them.
10. Teachers who are able to employ microcomputers with appropriate software can expect greater overall achievement in spelling, but the student should still be expected to use motor responses with a pencil to ensure input.

One of the difficulties that educators have in conceptualizing mainstreaming is that they think in terms of grouping children for instruction by chronological age or functional level. In typical elementary reading class there are three or four groups of children whose placement is determined by reading level. The major justification for self-contained classrooms in the past was that handicapped children deviated from the norm so much that they could not be classified easily within an instructional group. For example, many mildly handicapped students do not begin to acquire first-grade reading and writing skills until the age of 8. Thus, if they are mainstreamed with chronological age peers for any portion of the day, there will be significant discrepancies between them and their classmates in terms of basic skills.

One problem this creates for the system is that teachers who are unaccustomed to teaching basic handwriting and spelling are frustrated in the third, fourth, or fifth grades when they encounter children who possess essentially primary grade skills. The special educator may employ the best practices to remedy the spelling and writing deficits; however, this still fails to address the problem of performance in the regular classroom. The case example provided in Fig. 7-3 illustrates this situation. Jeff, the special education student, was receiving remedial instruction in handwriting in the resource room. Although he was making progress, his handwriting was still poor. Jeff's poor handwriting was a constant source of difficulty, especially in spelling. The regular teacher in this instance was patient enough to labor through the grading, but this attitude might be the exception rather than the rule. More likely the regular teacher would not take the time, failing to notice, for instance, that in number 5 the word surprise is written upside down *as a surprise!* (See Fig. 7-3.) In most classes Jeff would have received a poor grade in handwriting and spelling.

Jeff's teacher was willing to try to help him with his handwriting, provided that it did not take too much time. The resource room teacher assisted the mainstream teacher in developing a learning center to allow Jeff and other members of the class an opportunity to receive additional instruction in handwriting. The teachers planned a trial schedule of letter lessons to be covered during a 2-week period. The lesson activities consisted of tracing with felt-tip markers on newsprint, writing on the blackboard, copying patterns and letters using markers, and copying words on primary lined paper.

The learning center was required for all students during the 2-week period; it was an excellent review and practice for most of the students and

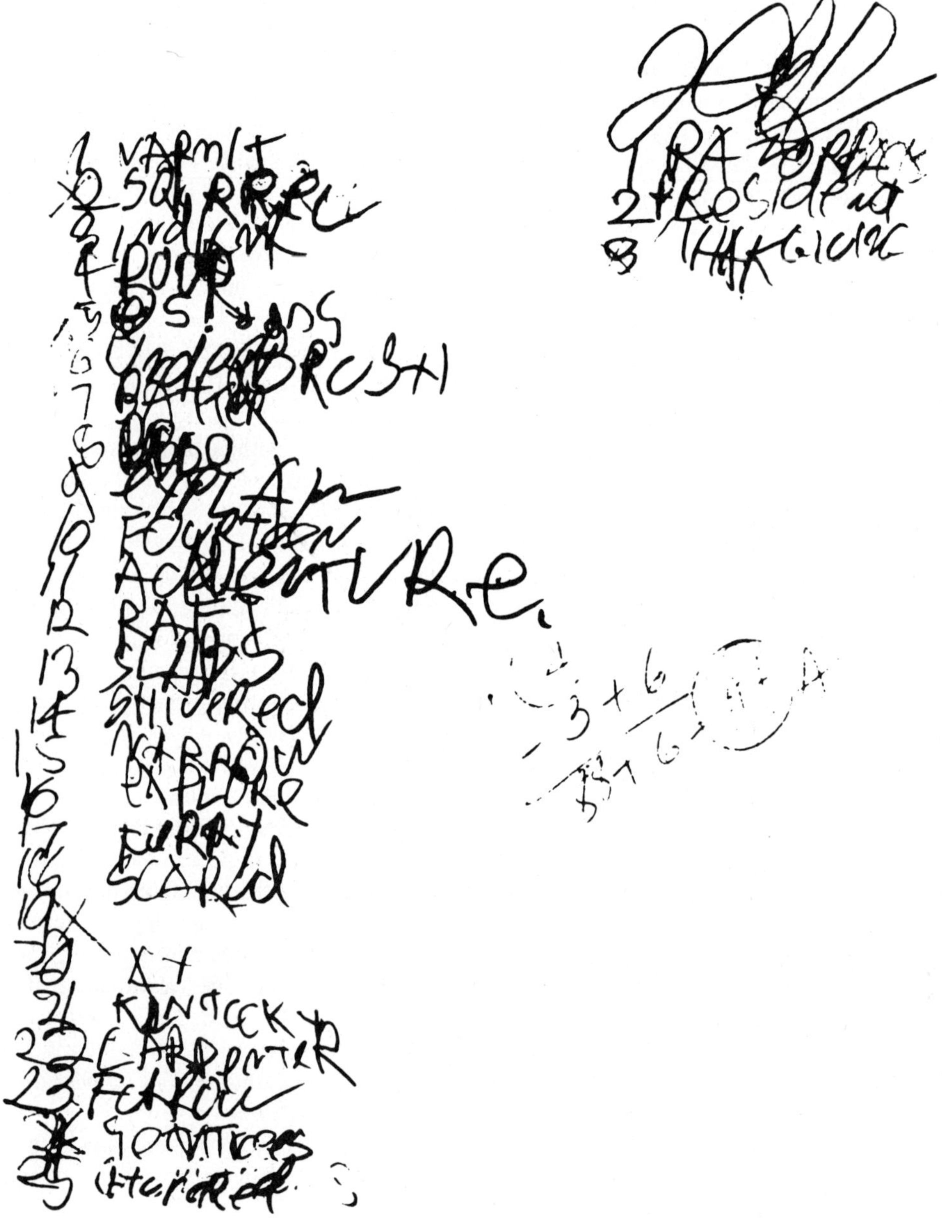

Fig. 7-3. Jeff's handwriting.

necessary instruction for others. For Jeff it was essential! The students took turns going to the learning center as part of the regular language arts period. Jeff's writing improved, partly because of peer involvement and mainstream teacher interest.

Obviously, the use of a learning center for such a short period of time did not solve Jeff's problems with penmanship; however, the combination of interest, motivation, opportunity for practice, and additional instruction accounted for remarkable improvement in a short period of time. Therefore, remedial strategies that are incorporated into existing instructional environments provide individuals with assistance that they would not otherwise receive.

Other strategies suggested in this case include allowing Jeff to dictate the words to other students, type the spelling words, and select the correct word from a list rather than take them from dictation. Although these strategies did not improve his writing directly, they allowed him to perform adequately in the regular classroom.

Structured approaches

Regardless of the spelling program used in public schools, many handicapped children will require highly structured training. They will also have many other problems areas, such as reading and arithmetic. A decision will be made about the amount of time devoted to basic skills, and spelling is likely to have a lesser priority. Because of this, spelling should be correlated to the level of achievement in reading.

Structured systems can be used in training. Gillingham and Stillman (1968) base remediation of spelling disabilities on a multisensory phonetic approach. The system is initiated after sound blending has begun. The following is an example from Gillingham and Stillman of a teacher-directed exercise for learning:

> *Teacher:* "Listen. I am going to say a word very slowly; /map/, /m/-/a/-/p/, /m/-/a/-/p/, /m/-/a/-/p/. What sound did you hear first? . . . Yes, /m/ . . . What letter says /m/? . . . Yes, *m*. Find the *m* card and lay it on the table. What is the second sound? Listen /m/-/a/-/p/" (p. 52).

The students identify each sound and its letter, build on words based on these sounds, and finally write the word. The following sequenced procedure must be followed precisely to prevent loss of associations. After the teacher pronounces the word, for example /bat/, the child proceeds with the following sequence of events:

1. The child repeats the word—/bat/.
2. The child names letters—*b-a-t*.
3. The child writes the word, naming each letter as he forms it—*b-a-t*.
4. The child reads the word—/bat/.

Auditory, visual, and kinesthetic senses are involved in the Gillingham and Stillman approach. The child hears the teacher's voice, hears his or her own voice, feels the speech organs function, hears the sounds of the letters, sees the letters, and, by writing, feels the hand form the letters. The procedure is based on a four-point plan: (1) the teacher pronounces a word, (2) the student repeats it, (3) the student spells it orally, and (4) the student writes it and reads it. Gillingham and Stillman believe that two prerequisites form the basis of their approach: (1) this approach should be taught only to students capable of using it, and (2) emphasis should be placed on applying the words, not memorizing them from repetition. This conflicts with current theories of spelling as a process of recall.

Another multisensory spelling approach was developed by Fernald (1943). This method requires the use of all four modalities—visual, auditory, kinesthetic, and tactile. The following steps should be used in teaching *whole* words:

1. The word to be learned is written by the teacher on the blackboard or on paper.
2. The word is clearly and distinctly pronounced by the teacher and then by the children.
3. An opportunity is established for the children to study the word.
4. The word is written from memory after the children are familiar with the word.
5. The word is written a second time on the back of the page.
6. Arrangements are made so that the word

learned can be used often in the children's written expression.

7. The correct form of the word should be available to the children if they are unsure of its spelling.
8. Spelling contests, if used, should be written instead of oral.

Three other remedial approaches are described by Hammill and Bartell (1978): the sensory approach developed by Montessori, which employs color cuing to aid in memorization of vowels, consonants, and sight words; the phonovisual method developed by Schoolfield and Timberlake, which emphasizes direct training in visual and auditory discrimination; and a visual method developed by Getman, which in theory stresses visual memory.

What all of these systems have in common is redundancy. As children have more experience with spelling words (orally and through writing), they will more likely remember them. The long-term memory of a handicapped child is, in all probability, similar to that of nonhandicapped children. Consequently, encoding strategies and repetition using classical remedial programs or computer technology will be devoted to the same outcome.

WRITTEN EXPRESSION

Although the mechanics of language, such as grammar, spelling, and handwriting, are emphasized along with reading, written expression is at the apex of language development. It can improve over a lifetime. Many educated persons are capable of reading complex material and can understand many abstract words and expressions; however, the ability to write at the same level of comprehension requires considerable effort and practice. Currently there are complaints in the popular press that children do not know how to write as well as children in previous generations. By poor writing it is meant that letters and reports are sloppy and filled with spelling or punctuation errors. This criticism, like so many others made today, is a perception and not necessarily a fact. Professors judge the value of written work in terms of their interests. Book reports, statistical reports, research articles, themes, essays, poems, and prose require different formats and styles. For the majority of high school graduates to function in our society it is necessary for them to be able to write letters, handle personal and official records and forms, and deal with job-specific forms and data-processing systems. In using the term written expression we are not referring to English compositions; for elementary school the emphasis should be on organization, note taking, punctuation, and paragraphs containing simple sentences. The broad goals of written expression include the following abilities:

1. Writing one's name
2. Writing a personal letter expressing simple ideas, feelings, and other personal expressions
3. Writing letters, reports, and verse with abstract repesentations of thoughts, moods, ideas, concepts, and beliefs
4. Using basic study skills such as note taking and outlining

Goals and objectives for individual children will vary, depending on their progress and needs. Unfortunately, since mildly handicapped children seem to be so involved with learning to read and learning arithmetic, teachers may tend to overlook the goals of written expression, especially if the child's skills are developing more slowly than those of peers, and if the child is struggling with handwriting, spelling, and fundamental mechanics.

However, initial writing activities do not need to be masterpieces. It is important that children write, perhaps starting with just a few words or only a sentence. The child should not be subjected to continuous criticism, as in the case of critical teachers who go on a rampage with a red marking pencil.

It seems that most programs tend to select functional writing skills for handicapped students because they want them to be able to fill in official blanks and forms, keep personal records, and function in the adult world of mundane affairs. Creative writing, a favorite subject of many English teachers, is frequently omitted because handicapped children do not seem to show promise as future scholars or novelists. However, creative writing can be a part of the program for these children if one has a liberal view of teaching and tolerance for written work that is not perfectly constructed. Functional writing is necessary, creative writing is enjoyable, and both types of writing skills can contribute significantly to desirable outcomes.

Until writing skills are more clearly defined and formal assessment tools are more extensively refined and/or validated, assessment of written expression will depend on subjective evaluation. To a certain extent the mechanics of written expression can be easily identified and directly assessed because of the conventions about punctuation and style. Otherwise, the evaluation of a poem, story, or theme will depend only on the critic's interests, experiences, and expectations.

Teachers can assess students by analyzing daily written assignments or by orchestrating a written assignment for the purpose of assessing written expression. If teachers choose the latter, they might show a picture to students and have them write stories about it. By relating these pictures to the individual interests of the child, motivation can be more easily achieved than by using pictures that are of little interest.

In written expression it is usually the value of the child's written product that is considered. However, written expression not only includes the ideas and how they are expressed but also the choice of words and punctuation. Handwriting, although based on development of punctuation, is really concerned with the ability of the child to make letters and words. The mechanical reproduction of a sentence and the first generated sentences may also be thought of as handwriting exercises. From then on a child's response to assignments in school or development of written themes is in the realm of written expression. Punctuation is, or should be, taught differently from the recognition of punctuation in reading. In the earliest readers a child encounters quotation marks, but it will be a long time before the child has sufficient skill to use quotation marks in an original story. Thus, the order of using punctuation in written expression is different from its order of recognition in reading. Charting the progress for each child to show when punctuation can be used in writing is unreasonable if it is based on the reading sequence. The order of punctuation in *writing* is as follows:

1. Capital letters
2. Period
3. Question mark
4. Comma
5. Quotation mark
6. Apostrophe
7. Exclamation mark
8. Hyphen
9. Colon

Cohen and Plaskon (1980) recommend that written work be evaluated in terms of the following criteria:

1. Expression of a main idea
2. Expression of a complete thought
3. An adequately developed paragraph
4. A varied and appropriate vocabulary
5. Appropriate use of punctuation
6. Appropriate use of capitalization

It is our position that, until children are able to perform satisfactorily in these areas of written expression, they should be provided with alternative response modes. Many children who are able to pantomime and tell wonderful stories are unable to write well enough to record these ideas. The teacher could permit children to participate by having them tell their stories on tape recordings and grade them for this effort instead. In some schools the teachers permit a transcript to be made and written by another student or typed with appropriate punctuation added. Under these conditions the children are kept from failing and are encouraged to use spoken language in creative ways.

Assessment instruments

If the school elects to use formal instruments, the choices are limited. One of the oldest instruments, the Myklebust Picture/Story Language Test, requires the child to generate a story from a picture stimulus. Its reliability and validity are questioned. Another instrument, the Sequential Test of Educational Progress, uses a contrived writing format. The only test that has been well developed statistically is the Test of Written Language, which yields grade equivalents and standard scores.

Standardized group tests are not necessarily recommended because they do not require the child to write and they have limited items. Informal assessment will be superior in the long run for making important decisions.

A comprehensive informal approach was developed by Poteet (1980) who designed assessment around penmanship, spelling, grammar, and identification. His intent was to allow the teacher to determine the skills of the student and decide which of these needed to be remedied or introduced. Although Poteet's approach lacks research and instruments, it appears to be a significant contribution.

Techniques for improving written expression

Unlike reading and other academic areas, there are few ''canned'' methods for teaching written expression. For the most part, teachers use their own ingenuity in devising methods for improving the written expression of their students. Skills that are based on effective written expression, punctuation, capitalization, vocabulary, grammatical rules, and sentence and paragraph writing can be taught with a variety of methods.

Punctuation and capitalization. Proper use of punctuation and capitalization must be taught to enhance written expression. Hammill and Bartel (1978) suggest using the language-experience approach. The steps include (1) collecting written passages from students that result from an experience, (2) showing them where punctuation and capitalization should occur, (3) discussing why punctuation and capitalization enhance the meaning, (4) demonstrating how to use proper punctuation and capitalization, (5) providing activities for practice, and (6) arranging opportunities for students to demonstrate punctuation and capitalization skills in spontaneous writing. In addition to this method, numerous worksheets and workbooks are available to promote proper use of these skills; however, the teacher should be cautioned about using such materials, as will be discussed later.

Vocabulary and grammar. As with punctuation and capitalization, language arts workbooks and worksheets are readily available to teach vocabulary and grammar. Emphasis should be placed on the functional aspects of these skills and their relationship to the overall goal of adequate expression. Providing a good model for students will enable them to see the application of grammatical rules; emphasizing new words and experiences will enable a gradual growth in their vocabulary. The following activities can assist students in vocabulary development:

1. *Labeled objects in the room.* Labeling should be done not only for concrete objects but also for directions and abstract concepts. When these words are used, regularly point out usage and meaning. A ''road sign'' with directions could also be located in the room. This could include signs with arrows pointing to the appropriate directions indicating where the cafeteria is located and other signs that indicate certain locations outside the room in appropriate groups.
2. *Field trips.* Take advantage of field trips for vocabulary building. Words that are anticipated to come up during a field trip can be discussed the day before, during, and the day after the trip.
3. *A new word per week.* Have a student be responsible for bringing a new word to class each week or daily to teach to the other students. Students should act out or demonstrate the word, not simply relay it orally.
4. *High-interest words.* Allow students to compile words that are of particular interest to them. Students should be given an opportunity to share these words with fellow students.
5. *Word games.* Play word games such as Scrabble and Spill and Spell.
6. *Word-derivative games.* Encourage students to make new words with the addition of a few letters.
7. *Dictionary use.* Teach students the proper use of the dictionary, and develop activities for application.

Sentence and paragraph writing. A key in learning to express ideas and thoughts and convey information in written format is proper sentence development. "Sentence sense" allows students to recognize the different patterns in which ideas can be expressed (Otto, McMenemy, & Smith, 1973). Teachers should not emphasize exact points about sentence structure, that each sentence has a subject and predicate, but instead emphasize clear presentation of ideas, thoughts, and other information. Students are assisted in developing sentence sense by the following methods:

1. Exposing students to model sentences increases their ability to produce them (Otto et al., 1973).
2. Having students read orally increases their recognition of faulty sentences.
3. Establishing teamwork between student and teacher is important to some students; working with students during sentence development minimizes embarrassment and frustration.
4. Allowing students to experiment with sentence construction and encouraging them to arrange various words in several ways to reveal the best sentences should decrease their fear of poor grades or humiliation.

Skills required to write paragraphs include organizing similar content, sequencing events, and making ideas in the paragraph flow. The following activities can be used by teachers to assist students in the development of these skills:

1. Have students divide several sentences into groups dealing with the same subject.
2. Provide several sentences without a particular order, and have the students arrange the sentences in the proper sequence.
3. Have students arrange several pictures of an event in the proper sequence.
4. Give students a paragraph in which sentences are arranged out of order, and have them rearrange the sentences correctly.
5. Use teamwork to develop paragraphs; act as a consultant during paragraph writing rather than simply as a critic.
6. Have students read their paragraphs aloud; ask the questions that will point out areas where improvement is needed.
7. Have students read two paragraphs, one that is well written and one that is poorly written. Discuss the reasons why one paragraph is better than the other and ways of improving the poorly written paragraph.

Once the prerequisite skills to written expression have been mastered, application may be attempted. The following should assist teachers in developing the student's written communication skills:

1. Create an open environment in which students are not fearful of writing. Despite what is written, students should be encouraged and reinforced, not criticized so severely that they will not make the effort again.

2. Provide practical application of writing skills by having students fill out job applications and write letters, biographical sketches, and summaries of stories, books, or discussions. Although some might argue that in elementary school it is too early to begin instruction in filling out job application forms, this activity provides an excellent example of the practical application of writing and can be related to units on career education.

3. Encourage students to write themes with emotional content and about more abstract ideas. This can be an important sharing exercise for children in the mainstream class.

Of all the techniques that might be used to improve spelling and written expression for handicapped students, we prefer the use of proofreading for these important reasons:

1. Proofreading is superior to contrived situations, such as those found in workbooks or standardized tests in which students are dealing with words and language forms that are not their own. Identifying and correcting errors, selecting better word choices, or improving clauses in a multiple choice format is not as interactive or meaningful as proofreading. Proofreading promotes more practice, uses the child's own language and themes, and reinforces conventional rules and mechanics (Poplin et al., 1980).

2. Proofreading can also be more motivating if

word-processing software is used on a microcomputer. By using the keyboard, the student writes faster, stores more items, saves paper, makes corrections more easily, and experiences more enjoyment. If a printer unit is attached to the computer, the student can get a printout of a corrected copy at the push of a button. Software programs compatible with microcomputers are relatively inexpensive.

MINORITY CHILDREN AND EXPRESSIVE LANGUAGE

The two largest groups of children we shall refer to as belonging to minority groups are those whose primary language is Spanish and those who are black. Of course many other minority groups might be considered (e.g., American Indian, Chinese, and Japanese), and some of the issues here will address concerns about these groups as well. However, most schools will be interested in programming for children who are Spanish-speaking or black.

In education there are two basic schools of thought about teaching minority children. The first view, which is espoused by the federal government and influenced by the conservative trend, is government control: English is the language of the country, and all children should learn to speak it fluently. The second view is that bilingual programming should be used. A controversy over the issue of Black English arises in the case of black children: Should children be taught in Black English as a second language, similar to the approach of instruction in Spanish to the Spanish-speaking child? In this instance the dispute surrounds the question of whether Black English is a substandard form of English, an illiterate form, or whether it is a nonstandard dialect. The preponderance of opinion among linguists, as opposed to opinions of lay persons, is that Black English is a nonstandard form of English; it is a separate although similar dialect.

Dillard (1972) notes that English and Black English most revealingly differ in syntax. Phonological differences exist, of course, but the syntactical structure of Black English, which is influenced by African languages, has resulted in a nonstandard form of English that stands alone with its own rules. The differences between Black English and standard English are minor, since one parallels the other, and of such subtle distinctions that the systemic differences and cumulative effects are unnoticed by speakers of standard English, even speakers who are inclined to disdain Black English as a substandard, illiterate form.

We accept the view that children who speak Black English should be treated in the same manner as children who learn English as a second language. It is not surprising to us that disproportionate numbers of black children are identified as handicapped because the cultural attitude toward their spoken language is not the same as it would be toward a monolingual French speaker. Our society disdains the rich and colorful speech of white Americans in the Ozark Mountains and the Appalachians who speak a form of English with the residuals and grammatical forms of Shakespearian England. Our society does not seem to realize that these pockets of communities have been relatively isolated from the transformations the English language underwent in the centers of commerce and industry. If we view Black English or regional speech patterns as illiterate forms of English, we reveal prejudice. Possibly with the impact of television forcing us into a mold in which everyone speaks like someone from Missouri or Nebraska (e.g., Walter Cronkite or Johnny Carson), linguists may someday nostalgically watch videotapes of persons speaking dead forms of our language.

The issues in special education concerning minority children are numerous and complex. Excluding some children from special education because of concerns about misdiagnosis can be as troublesome as including a disproportionate number of minority children in special education classes. The problems with assessment, including litigation and governmental regulations, have stimulated alternative assessment programs such as the System of Multicultural Pluralistic Assessment. However, conceptualization of this system is much simpler than effecting it. No valid or reliable instruments exist that can be used with confidence, and manipulating scores and scoring procedures using existing instruments is unsatisfactory.

Another problem confronting special education in this area is that the current conservative trend in government will influence educational policies pertaining to minority children. Such policies would have all children conform to the language, customs, mores, and values of the predominant Anglo culture in public school. At present, a bill has been introduced in Congress that would declare English as the official national language; funding and regulations for bilingual education have already been largely revoked. If children are held to an "Anglo standard" in school, they will not measure up to the standard in many respects because their cultures, languages, and values are at variance with the standard that might be imposed on them. This could lead to the referral of larger numbers of minority children to special education classes because they do not conform to the Anglo standard.

Even successful programs that have been used with minority children to teach them basic skills, such as the DISTAR, are severely criticized by some who maintain that minority children should be required to forsake their cultural heritage and supplant their speech patterns in favor of the customs and language of the mainstream culture. These are difficult issues for special educators who want to help handicapped minority students.

Although there are probably few answers to these problems, the special education teacher can seek the involvement of other personnel in the school to ensure that there is a consensus about programming. Some suggestions are as follows:

1. The school personnel should be subjected to in-service training, if necessary, to encourage accepting attitudes toward variant dialects and nonstandard forms of English, and they should be equipped to deal effectively with children who are using English as a second language.

2. It is essential that parents be involved in attempts to teach minority students. The IEP would be an excellent instrument for determining the course of programming and to ensure that all parties, including the parents and the student, agree to the proposed measures.

3. The language should be accepted, and the student should not be punished, penalized, or graded unfairly because of the differences in pronunciation, in regional usage, or in syntactical forms.

4. Behavioral and linguistical differences of children should be understood in terms of the cultures that influence them, not in terms of the predominant culture's value system. They should not be interpreted as cognitive differences.

5. Children should be permitted to use their own languages and should understand, as their teachers should acknowledge, that standard English (the language all teachers speak and in which books are written) is another form of communication; thus, as they perform in standard English with difficulty, so most teachers would perform poorly in the students' languages.

6. Teaching minority children (or even mainstream Anglo children) abstract grammatical knowledge is a waste of instructional time. To be able to generate the sentences of a second language, one must be able to automatically use the language forms after having overlearned and internalized them. As Dillard (1972) notes, the ability either to parse sentences or to write rules to generate them is of no practical value.

7. Teachers must recognize that in reading and written expression the written language of standard English is incompatible with the internalized language of one who speaks a nonstandard form. The attempts of these children to succeed in a system that is neither understanding nor sympathetic must be admired.

Commercial materials

Following are some commercial materials that may be useful. They should be evaluated by the teacher.

Materials	*Description*
Bowmar/Noble Handwriting Series (Bowman/Noble Publishers, Inc.)	Complete handwriting program Includes nine workbooks Grades 1 through 8
Creative Growth with Handwriting (Zaner-Bloser Educational Publishers)	Continuous handwriting curriculum Includes eight books
Dubnoff School programs (Teaching Resources Corp.)	Prewriting, manuscript, and cursive writing Grades K through 12
Hancy Lowercase & Uppercase Alphabet (Teaching Resources Corp.)	Trace and team approach Exercises with number, order, and direction of strokes
Handwriting Duplicating Book (Milliken Publishing Co.)	Alphabetic; stroke-by-stroke Self-directing Includes 28 masters Grades K through 3
Handwriting Practice Books (Highlights for Children)	Self-instructional Includes five workbooks Readiness through fourth grade
Help Yourself to Better Handwriting (Educators Publishing Services, Inc.)	Speed and legibility Tracing Right- and left-hand styles Includes guide cards and plain practice pads
SRA Lunchbox Handwriting Kits (Science Research Associates, Inc.)	Manuscript and cursive writing Includes 144 exercise cards Practice overlays to trace before copying Grades K through 4
Writing Manual for Teaching the Left-Handed (Educators Publishing Service, Inc.)	Corrective program Exercises with ovals, spirals, and strokes Individual letter forms
Write Right-or-Left (Walker Educational Book Corp.)	Self-instructional Includes 30 lessons for cursive writing One-to-one remedial
Corrective Spelling Through Morphographs (Science Research Associates, Inc.)	Teaches morphographs One-year remedial Includes 140 lessons and 650 morphographs Grade 4 through adult
Diagnostic and Prescriptive Spelling	Individualized approach Includes three workbooks
Independent Drill for Mastery (Developmental Learning Materials)	Sequential phonetical and morphological structure Based on word frequency Self-study Includes tapes and study sheets
Six Spell Practice Books (Highlights for Children)	Spelling demons Includes six books Grades 1 through 6
Speed Spelling (C.C. Publications, Inc.)	Multisensory approach Includes test and 93 lessons Words and sentences Grades 1 through 6
Spell Well (Pittman Learning, Inc.)	Commonly misspelled words Glossary, diagnostic chart Worksheet masters Primary through sixth grade
Spelling Words in Use (Curriculum Associates, Inc.)	Contextual approach Includes 240 common words Grades 3 through 9
Sound Foundations Program (Developmental Learning Materials)	Spelling phonics Four individual study programs Includes 300 words and 120 lessons
Spelling Words in Use (Curriculum Associates, Inc.)	Contextual approach Includes 240 common words Grades 3 through 9
Working Words in Spelling (Curriculum Associates, Inc.)	Eight series Includes 3,894 basic words Grades 1 through 8
Spelling Mastery (Science Research Associates, Inc.)	Developmental approach Phonemic, whole-word, and morphemic Grades 2 through 6

Materials	*Description*
Target Spelling (Steck-Vaughn Co.)	Consumable books Includes 30 weekly lessons Grades 1 through 4
Basic Writing Skills (B.L., Winch & Associates)	Essay writing, paragraphs, and letter writing Includes four activity books Grades 3 through 6
Creative Writing (Milliken Publishing Co.)	Creative expression Includes two transparency/duplicating books Grades 2 through 6
Creative Writing Activities (Highlights for Children)	Prose and poetry Reusable books Younger children

SUMMARY

In this chapter we discussed issues in assessment and teaching pertaining to expressive language: spoken language, handwriting, spelling, and written expression. The majority of children who have spoken language disorders are primarily affected by articulation disorders. The speech pathologist assumes the primary responsibility for children with speech and language disorders and works cooperatively with teachers and the family in the development of therapy. We presented the subject of handwriting disorders and teaching approaches and included, as major topics, methods of teaching spelling and ways of improving written expression. Issues about the education of minority children were also discussed. To conclude the chapter, we listed a number of materials available to the teacher.

Generally, this area of school behavior has not been investigated to any great extent. Research and program development should occur in all areas, especially in spelling and written expression. The greatest advancement in assisting children in this area will most likely result from acceptance of computer technology and the development of appropriate software to support and extend the skill of the teacher.

PUBLISHERS OF RELATED MATERIALS

Barnell Loft, Ltd.
958 Church St.
Baldwin, NY 11510

Bowmar/Noble Publishers, Inc.
4563 Colorado Blvd.
Los Angeles, CA 90039

C.C. Publications, Inc.
P.O. Box 23699
Tigard, OR 97223

Curriculum Associates, Inc.
North Billerica, MA 01862

Developmental Learning Materials (DLM)
7440 Natchez Ave.
Miles, IL 60648

Educators Publishing Services, Inc.
75 Moulton St.
Cambridge, MA 02238

Highlights for Children
2300 W. Fifth Ave.
P.O. Box 269
Columbus, OH 43216

Milliken Publishing Co.
1100 Research Blvd.
St. Louis, MO 63132

Pittman Learning, Inc.
6 Davis Dr.
Belmont, CA 94002

Science Research Associates (SRA), Inc.
155 N. Wacker Dr.
Chicago, IL 60606

Steck-Vaughn Co.
P.O. Box 2028
Austin, TX 78768

Teaching Resources Corp.
50 Pond Park Rd.
Hingham, MA 02043

Walker Educational Book Corp.
720 Fifth Ave.
New York, NY 10019

Weekly Reader Multimedia
1250 Fairwood Ave.
P.O. Box 16629
Columbus, OH 43216

B.L. Winch & Associates
45 Hitching Post Dr. Building 20
Rolling Hills Estates, CA 90274

Zaner-Bloser Educational Publishers
612 N. Park St.
Columbus, OH 43215

REFERENCES AND SUGGESTED READINGS

Academic Therapy Publications. *Tips on teaching spelling.* Navato, CA: Author, 1975.

Bigge, J.L. *Teaching individuals with physical and multiple disabilities.* Columbus, OH: Charles E. Merrill Publishing Co., 1977.

Cahen, L.S., Craun, M.J., & Johnson, S.D. Spelling difficulty—a survey of research. *Review of Educational Research,* 1971, *4,* 281-301.

Cohen, S.B., & Plaskon, S.P. *Language arts for the mildly handicapped.* Columbus, OH: Charles E. Merrill Publishing Co., 1980.

Dillard, J.L. *Black English.* New York: Vintage House, 1972.

Early, G.H., Nelson, D.A., Kleber, D.J., Treegoob, M., Huffman, E., & Cass, C. Cursive handwriting, reading, and spelling achievement. *Academic Therapy,* 1976, *12,* 67-74.

Edington, R. But he spelled them right this morning. *Academic Therapy,* 1968, *3,* 58-59.

Fernald, G. *Remedial techniques in basic school subjects.* New York: McGraw-Hill Book Co., 1943.

Freeman, G.G., *Speech and language services and the classroom teacher.* Minneapolis, MN: National Support Systems Project, 1977.

Gillingham, A., & Stillman, B.W. *Remedial training for children with specific disability in reading, spelling, and penmanship.* Cambridge, MA: Educators Publishing Service, Inc., 1968.

Graham, S., & Madan, A.J. Teaching letter formation. *Academic Therapy,* 1981, *16,* 389-396.

Hammill, D.D., & Bartel, W.R. *Teaching children with learning and behavior problems.* Boston: Allyn & Bacon, Inc., 1978.

Hanna, P.R., Hodges, R.E., & Hanna, J.S. *Spelling, structure and strategies.* Boston: Houghton Mifflin Co., 1971.

Harrison, S. Open letter from a left-handed teacher: some sinistral ideas on the teaching of handwriting. *Teaching Exceptional Children,* 1981, *13,* 116-120.

Kahn, E.J. Handwriting and vision. In J.E. Arena (Ed.), *Building handwriting skills in dyslexic children.* San Rafael, CA: Academic Therapy Publications, 1970.

Larson, C.E. Teaching beginning writing. In J.E. Arena (Ed.), *Building handwriting skills in dyslexic children.* Academic Therapy Publications, 1970.

Lenneberg, E.H. A biological perspective of language. In E.H. Lenneberg (Ed.), *New directions in the study of language.* Cambridge, MA: The M.I.T. Press, 1964.

Lerner, J. *Learning disabilities: theory, diagnosis, and teaching strategies* (3rd ed.). Boston: Houghton Mifflin Co., 1981.

Linn. S., Remedial approaches to handwriting dysfunction. In J.E. Arena (Ed.), *Building handwriting skills in dyslexic children.* San Rafael, CA: Academic Therapy Publications, 1970.

Madison, B.D. A kinesthetic technique for handwriting development. In J.E. Arena (Ed.), *Building handwriting skills in dyslexic children.* San Rafael, CA: Academic Therapy Publications, 1970.

Mendoza, M.A., Holt, W.J., & Jackson, D.A. Circles and tape: an easy teacher-implemented way to teach fundamental writing skills. *Teaching Exceptional Children,* 1978, *10,* 48-50.

Otto, W., McMenemy, R.A., & Smith, R.J. *Corrective and remedial teaching.* Boston: Houghton Mifflin Co., 1973.

Payne, J.S., Polloway, E.A., Smith, J.E., & Payne, R.A., *Strategies for teaching the mentally retarded.* Columbus, OH: Charles E. Merrill Publishing Co., 1977.

Poplin, M., Gray, R., Larsen, S., Banikowski, A., & Mehring, T. A comparison of components of written expression abilities in learning disabled and non-learning disabled children at three grade levels. *Learning Disability Quarterly,* 1980, *3,* 46-53.

Poteet, J.A. Informal assessment of written expression. *Learning Disability Quarterly,* 1980, *3,* 88-98.

Ragan, W.B., & Shepherd, G.D. *Modern elementary curriculum.* New York: Holt, Rinehart & Winston, 1977.

Ramos, R. Left-handed writing. In J.E. Arena (Ed.), *Building handwriting skills in dyslexic children.* San Rafael, CA: Academic Therapy Publications, 1970.

Reynolds, M.C., & Birch, J.W. *Teaching exceptional children in all America's schools.* Reston, VA: The Council for Exceptional Children, 1977.

Schwartz, M.L., Gilroy, J., & Lynn, G. Neuropsychological and psychosocial implications of spelling deficit in adulthood: a case report. *Journal of Learning Disabilities,* 1976, *9,* 17-21.

Shriberg, L.D. Developmental phonological disorders. In T.J. Hixon & L.D. Shriberg (Eds.), *Introduction to communication disorders.* Englewood Cliffs, NJ: Prentice-Hall, Inc., 1980.

Smith, R.M. *Teacher diagnosis of educational difficulties.* Columbus, OH: Charles E. Merrill Publishing Co., 1969.

Turton, L.J. Education of children with communication disorders. In W.M. Cruickshank & G.O. Johnson (Eds.), *Education of exceptional children and youth.* Englewood Cliffs, NJ: Prentice-Hall, Inc., 1975.

Vellutino, F.R. Toward an understanding of dyslexia: psychological factors in specific reading disability. In A.L. Benton & D. Pearl (Eds.), *Dyslexia.* New York: Oxford University Press, Inc., 1979.

Wood, N.E. *Verbal learning.* San Rafael, CA: Dimensions, 1969.

8 TEACHING ARITHMETIC

Arithmetic has received far less attention in regular and special education than has reading. The stress on mathematics diminished significantly after the intensity of the 1960s and the influence of "new math." In fact, the field of mathematics education currently has a serious shortage of teachers. Mathematics is once again being emphasized because of the economic forces affecting the business, computer, and energy industries. Currently there is a tendency to reevaluate the concepts and presentation of the mathematics curriculum and to emphasize instruction for girls, who have traditionally been discouraged in this area by implicit cultural imperatives.

As a basic skill, arithmetic is introduced according to a developmental scheme. The skills of arithmetic in elementary grades are more easily discernible than are those of reading. Educators clearly understand that certain operations should precede others but have less sensitivity to the developmental needs of individuals. Students in each grade tend to be introduced to new skills in accordance with a curricular plan regardless of whether each child is ready. It seems that most teachers in elementary school are much less interested in teaching mathematics than other subjects. Even with the innovations of new math and discovery approaches, much of arithmetic instruction has been based on rote memorization; remedial programming tends to focus on rote learning and computational facility with algorithms.

For reading instruction, teachers rely on basal series, programs that are highly developed with many planned activities. Basal series are well designed and created by teams of professionals. Mathematics programs, as implemented by teachers, tend to depend on workbooks and seatwork activities. The child may be limited to a narrow range of learning experiences; additional activities may be unstructured and uncoordinated. Many children lack sufficient interactive and concrete experiences necessary for the development of basic arithmetical concepts. According to investigations by Piaget (1958, 1963, 1965, 1974), actual manipulation of concrete objects is essential for alteration of mental structures and development of concepts. Two-dimensional worksheets and verbal instructions fall short of the criteria for optimum learning.

Fortunately, arithmetic materials and activities can be arranged in the classroom to maximize learning through inexpensive concrete learning experiences. Following are general principles for this type of teaching:

1. Use a structured sequence of skills with associated activities appropriate for each task and concept.
2. Use individual and small group instruction for activities at each skill level.
3. Reduce dependence on the use of written materials and worksheets.

Mathematics approaches are generally of two types: (1) the discovery method, a basis for much of modern math, and (2) the behavioral approach. The systems can be blended. Children obviously are not expected to learn division before addition, and no behaviorist would attempt this. However, certain concepts must be introduced in a specific skill sequence for effective learning, and feedback and reinforcement are essential to maximize instructional programs. Montessori programs exemplify the planned approach: the materials permit the child to "discover" planned concepts.

CAUSES OF ARITHMETIC DISORDERS

Although there is no large empirical base for considering the causes of arithmetic disorders, most textbooks in this area seem to accept the causes of reading disorders as also causing arithmetic problems. Many writers include disorders of memory, visual perception, spatial ability, laterality, directionality, verbal ability, and so forth. Consequently, some would also recommend process training to alleviate disorders in this area. A more straightforward approach is to examine the steps or tasks in the skill sequence and the type of instruction. Poor teaching is undoubtedly a major factor; observation of students indicates that in many classrooms students are simply required to complete innumerable worksheets, few concrete aids or manipulable instructional devices are available, and operations are stressed without significant attention to concept development. Because less is known about the causes of arithmetic disorders, relating corrective measures to certain syndromes or emphasizing remediation of hypothetical correlates not actually involved in learning tasks would seem to be illogical. The approach should be to emphasize (1) the developmental process, (2) the tasks, and (3) the necessary concrete experiences, feedback, and reinforcement.

In this chapter, arithmetic is regarded as a branch of mathematics; it is concrete in nature, dealing with concrete entities and primarily with the science of numbers and computation. The primary problems of young children seem to be in computational skill (Otto, McMenemy & Smith, 1973) and, to a lesser extent, the interaction of reading with arithmetic. This is an accepted logical view of arithmetic disorders. When more is known about them, it may be possible to discern that computational errors are symptomatic of more pervasive underlying disorders or deficient concept development.

ASSOCIATION OF ARITHMETIC INSTRUCTION WITH DEVELOPMENT

One useful approach to understanding the connection between the arithmetic curriculum and cognitive development is through the work of Piaget (1958, 1963, 1965, 1974). As a stage theory, certain cognitive abilities are believed to permit the understanding and uses of specific kinds of arithmetic skills within each stage. Rudimentary concepts of time, symbolic thinking, and cause and effect relationships occur in the sensorimotor stage (0 to 2 years); one-to-one correspondence and simple association of sets are managed during the preoperational subperiod (2 to 7 years); and the higher-order skills of subtraction, multiplication, division, fractions, and word problems are developed during the concrete operational subperiod (7 to 11 years). Certain milestones of classical Piagetian theory can be used to determine abilities of students to grapple with certain kinds of problems. The ability to conserve and to demonstrate the concept of reversibility indicates changes in cognitive functioning that may be correspondingly evident in the ability to perform certain arithmetic functions. Although Piagetian theory cannot be used as the basis for a curriculum, it can be extremely useful in determining the nature of learning activities, as well as the order of introduction.

Piagetian theory can be summarized in terms of direct implications for understanding cognitive development. To Piaget, mathematics is a direct extension of logic, so that it is impossible to separate the two. The operational structures of intelligence, being logicomathematical in nature, are neither consciously present in the child's thinking nor objects of conscious reflection. Piaget compares this to being able to sing a tune, although not being able to develop a theory of singing, or being able to automatically generate grammatical forms without being able to enumerate grammatical rules. In arithmetic the child must consciously think about the structures (mental) that are being used. A transition from natural, nonreflective structures to conscious awareness of these structures must occur. Therefore, arithmetic is not computation and rote memorization of tables; it is logic.

Acknowledging the importance of developmental cognitive structures in "thinking" forces the recognition that specific arithmetical skills and concepts must match the child's level of ability. Actually, the process of instruction has always been based on a linear sequence of logical continuity. However, many unique concepts and difficult materials were introduced to children through new math programs that were too difficult for students to manage. For example, the conservation of ratio, a very abstract structure, was introduced to very young children in some programs. Materials should be carefully examined to ensure that a proper skill sequence is maintained and that materials do not violate the order of presentation.

Generally the types of logical thinking that emerge can be classified by chronological age, but this is highly individual. All students apparently pass through the same stages but at different rates. It is useful to match the skill sequence and learning activities with the types of abilities apparent in each stage for a particular student. For the sake of convenience we shall consider the types of concepts that emerge in accordance with Piagetian theory as shown in Table 8-1.

Many of the skills that are introduced in a curriculum are presented to children in a lock-step manner without any attention to the individual abilities of children to understand these tasks. Determining what level of logical functioning a child has attained will aid the teacher in determination of which skills in a sequence should be introduced. Of course, all activities must be concrete and based on interactive events. The wide use of workbooks and worksheets is contrary to good teaching practices unless students have ample opportunity to gain concrete experiences with many kinds of objects in a variety of learning experiences.

It should also be recognized that addition and subtraction are inversely related; multiplication and addition are related concepts that develop simultaneously and are apparent at the age of 8 years. Multiplication and division are inversely related. Until a child can conserve and use reversibility, subtraction is an elusive concept. Addition problems such as $\square + 3 = 5$ are really subtraction problems. Many practices, workbooks, and other commercial materials must be evaluated for consistency with developmental sequences.

In the act of learning to read, the decoding task is a redundant visual-auditory perceptual task that must be overlearned to automaticity. The demand of comprehension is on information processing and language facility. In arithmetic, however, concrete logicomathematical operations and language must have a corresponding relationship. It is a simpler task in reading to rely on stable, overlearned responses (grapheme-phoneme pairs) than it is to apply reasoning in arithmetic. Although the basic computations can be recalled from memory, application does not easily lead to a solution without considerable reasoning. The underlying concepts must also be acquired through concrete experiences so that applications are meaningful. The fact

Table 8-1. Arithmetical concepts that emerge in accordance with Piagetian theory at specific ages

Age	*Concepts*
3 to 5 years	Rudimentary concepts of more, bigger, smaller, etc.
	One-to-one correspondence
6 to 7 years	Cardinality
	Ordinality
	Conceptualization of a set
	Joining sets
	Place value
	Addition
	Concept of equivalency
	Conservation of number
	Reversibility
	Rational counting
	Transitivity
	Subtraction
	Part-to-whole fractions
6 to 7 years—cont'd	Multiplicative relationships
	Mastery of geometrical forms
8 to 9 years	Parallelism
	Three-attribute classification
	Associative property of addition
	Distributive property of multiplication
	Commutative property of addition
	Fractions
10 to 12 years	Percentages
	Proportions
	Probability
	Conservation of weight and volume
	Geometry

that the most common errors of elementary school children are in computation (Otto, McMenemy & Smith, 1973) may reflect the importance attached to computation in the curriculum; older students make significant errors in application. Handicapped students tend to make computation and application errors throughout school. *The most important aspect of teaching is the development of arithmetic concepts.* Remediation should focus on basic facts, computational processes, and application to practical problems. To approach this logically, the teacher should deemphasize the traditional rote activites and arrange concrete learning activities to be associated with the following general areas:

1. *Prenumerical and functional arithmetic.* Arithmetic instruction should be based on the elements of set theory corresponding to logical development:
   a. Sets or classification; basic shapes
   b. One-to-one correspondence
   c. Ordinality
   d. Rational counting
   e. Conservation
   f. Part-to-whole fractions
2. *Basic facts and concepts*
   a. Addition (correlated multiplication)
   b. Subtraction (inverse of addition)
   c. Use of process signs
   d. Algorithms
   e. Basic money and measurement concepts
   f. Multiplication
   g. Division
   h. Proper fractions
   i. Use of higher-order signs and symbols
   j. Advanced time and measurement concepts
   k. Geometrical concepts

The skill sequence that is used in arithmetic is presented more specifically on pp. 243 to 249. These skills are stated in terms that may be adapted for use in behavioral statements. Task analyses and smaller steps may be employed. Use of a skill sequence is essential for assessment and teaching. Basic assessment techniques can be applied at each level in the sequence. The sequence we have provided may or may not match what exists at a particular school. The teacher should verify the sequence; some skills may be out of order, depending on the setting and materials used.

Text continued on p. 250.

SEQUENCE OF ARITHMETIC SKILLS IN THE FIRST SIX GRADES

First-grade skills

1. Given a picture, items, or a description of a set, the student can identify members of a set.
2. Given two equivalent sets, the student can arrange them in one-to-one correspondence.
3. Given two equivalent sets, the student can identify equivalence without matching the sets.
4. Given nonequivalent sets, the student can identify the set with more members through one-to-one correspondence.
5. Given verbal descriptors, the student can demonstrate comprehension of terms such as "more," "bigger," and "less than."
6. Given verbal descriptions of several sets based on one characteristic, the student can identify sets.
7. Given objects of common shapes, the student can identify each shape.

Continued.

SEQUENCE OF ARITHMETIC SKILLS IN THE FIRST SIX GRADES—cont'd

First-grade skills—cont'd

8. Given sets with members down to none, the student can arrange sets in order of size.
9. Given the term "numeral," the student can demonstrate that it represents a number.
10. Given the term "zero," the student can acknowledge that it is associated with a null set. (The student will not comprehend this concept for many years.)
11. Student can count to ten.
12. Student can write numerals through nine.
13. Given nonequivalent sets, the student can identify sets by naming cardinal numbers through nine.
14. Given a numeral, the student can construct a set using available items.
15. Student can order numbers from one to ten.
16. Student can identify the order of an item in a series from one to ten.
17. Student can count to 30
18. Student can write to ten and all two-digit numerals to 30.
19. Given items in print or concrete objects, the student can identify characteristics of a particular item (e.g., length).
20. Given objects varying in a one-dimensional characteristic (e.g., length), the student can order them.
21. Student can name the number of a set with fewer than 30 members.
22. Student can join sets with fewer than nine members.
23. Student can make simple geometrical forms with a pencil or by arranging concrete objects.
24. Student can measure objects with nonstandard units.
25. Given two disjoint sets, the student can name the numeral associated with each and the numeral for the joined sets.
26. Student identifies the meaning of the signs "+" and "−."
27. Student identifies the meaning of the sign "=."
28. Student can identify time by the hour.
29. Given a set, the student can construct a subset.
30. Given concrete shapes, the student can form shapes divided by fractional parts (e.g., ½, ⅓, and ¼).
31. Student can add two one-place numbers totaling less than ten.
32. Student can add two one-place numbers totaling less than ten in the form of an equation.
33. Student can add a one-place number to zero.
34. Student can add two-digit numbers that do not require regrouping.
35. Student can add two-digit numbers totaling ten.
36. Student can add two-digit numbers with regrouping.
37. Given various numbers, the student can name numerals and combinations for each number (e.g., $4 = 2 + 2$ and $4 = 3 + 1$).
38. Student can name numerals for numbers through 99.
39. Student can count to 90 by tens.
40. Student can name components of a two-digit number in expanded notation (e.g., $13 = 10 + 3$).
41. Student can name word names for numbers through ten and write the corresponding numeral.

SEQUENCE OF ARITHMETIC SKILLS IN THE FIRST SIX GRADES—cont'd

First-grade skills—cont'd

42. Student can write an equation for a problem presented in the form of a picture.
43. Given objects in order, the student can identify an object by the "nth" position.
44. Given an ordered set, the student can name the ordinal number for the set by naming the final member of the set.
45. Student can count to 50 by fives.
46. Given concrete materials, the student can name quantities identified as cups, pints, and quarts.
47. Given a two-hand clock placement, the student can identify time to the nearest hour.
48. Given quantities of similarly shaped elements, the student can determine the heaviest and lightest.
49. Student can associate symbols with quantities concepts.
50. Given a model, the student can name the temperature on a scale to the nearest degree.
51. Student can name the common coins.
52. Student can transform values of coins (e.g., five pennies equal one nickel).
53. Student can demonstrate the positions of numbers on a line.
54. Student can demonstrate the ordinal relationship between two numbers on a number line and use appropriate symbols.
55. Student can name odd and even numbers.
56. Student can count to 30 by twos.
57. Given sets of concrete objects, the student can regroup to form new sets by removing members.
58. Given problems with number patterns, the student can complete patterns (e.g., 2, 4, 6, ___, ___, ___).
59. Student can use the vertical algorithm to solve addition problems.
60. Student can use a number line to solve simple subtraction problems.
61. Student can use the vertical algorithm to solve simple combinations of subtraction.
62. Given combinations of numbers to add, the student can demonstrate that the order of addition is unimportant (associative property).
63. Student can solve related addition and subtraction problems with simple combinations.
64. Student can subtract using two one-place numbers.
65. Student can subtract using two one-place numbers in an equation.
66. Student can determine the missing subtrahend in an equation.
67. Student can determine the missing minuend.
68. Student can subtract zero from a one-place number.
69. Student can subtract two two-place numbers with zeros in the ones place.
70. Student can subtract a two-place number with no regrouping.
71. Student can employ the commutative property of addition.
72. Student can use the addition table for problems with missing sums or addends.
73. Student can demonstrate that one hundred is equal to ten tens.
74. Student can count to 100 by tens and fives.
75. Student can write numerals through 100.
76. Student can count to 200 by ones.
77. Student can write numerals through 200.
78. Student can add multiples of ten.

Continued.

SEQUENCE OF ARITHMETIC SKILLS IN THE FIRST SIX GRADES—cont'd

First-grade skills—cont'd

79. Student can add tens and ones using expanded notation.
80. Student can use a vertical algorithm to solve two-digit subtraction problems.
81. Student can read the calendar.
82. Student can tell time to the half hour.
83. Student can use place values to determine larger numbers.
84. Given combinations of simple numbers to subtract, the student can demonstrate that order is important to obtain a specific answer.

Second-grade skills

85. Given models of fractions, the student can name the rational number.
86. Given two-digit numbers, the student can name various combinations (e.g., 52 = 50 + 2 or 40 + 12).
87. Student can name numerals in ones, tens, and hundreds places through 999.
88. Given numbers through 999, the student can give the expanded notation for whole numbers (e.g., 675 = 600 + 70 + 5).
89. Student can state a rule to indicate that a number added to zero will have a product unaffected by the zero.
90. Student can complete number patterns by ones, fives, and tens.
91. Student can name the missing sum or addend in a number sentence.
92. Given an oral problem, the student can write a number sentence.
93. Student can subtract a three-place number with no regrouping.
94. Student can subtract a one-place number from a two-digit number with regrouping.
95. Student can subtract a two-place number from another two-place number with regrouping in the units column.
96. Student can subtract a three-place number from another with regrouping in the units column.
97. Student can subtract a three-place number from a three-place number with regrouping in the tens column.
98. Student can subtract a three-place number from another with regrouping in the ones and tens places.
99. Student can subtract a three-place number from another with a zero in the ones place causing regrouping.
100. Student can subtract a four-place number from another with regrouping in the ones and tens places.
101. Student can tell time by the quarter hour.
102. Student can read calendar dates.
103. Student can measure a line segment to the nearest half inch.
104. Student can multiply two one-place numbers with products less than 10.
105. Student can multiply two one-place numbers totaling more than 10.
106. Using a number line, the student can solve multiplication problems of simple combinations.
107. Student can demonstrate the division of a set by equivalent disjoint sets.
108. Student can multiply a number by zero.

SEQUENCE OF ARITHMETIC SKILLS IN THE FIRST SIX GRADES—cont'd

Second-grade skills—cont'd

109. Student can multiply two one-place numbers in the form of an equation.
110. Student can multiply a two-place number with a zero.
111. Student can multiply a two-place number by a one-place number with carrying.
112. Student can multiply a two-place number by a one-place number requiring regrouping in the tens and hundreds places.
113. Student can multiply two two-place numbers with no regrouping.
114. Student can multiply two two-place numbers with carrying in the hundreds place.
115. Student can multiply two three-place numbers with regrouping.
116. Student can identify division as the dissociation of a set with equivalent disjoint sets.
117. Given a problem requiring measurement by pints and quarts, the student can measure liquid or continuous matter to the required whole unit.
118. Given currency, the student can make change for a dollar in various combinations.
119. Given prices for items, the student can read the prices.

Third-grade skills

120. Given any number from 0 to 9,999, the student can accurately identify the place value of any digit.
121. Given any number from 0 to 9,999, the student can state the expanded notation.
122. Student can demonstrate multiplication as repeated addition, as moves on a number line, or as multiple sets.
123. Student can provide a definition of division as a rearrangement of sets or repeated subtraction.
124. Student can use brackets to contain members in a given set.
125. Student can represent specific sets with other symbols.
126. Student can use the symbol "n" to refer to the members in a set.
127. Student can round numbers to the nearest ten.
128. Student can demonstrate the commutative property of multiplication.
129. Student can demonstrate the inverse relationship of multiplication and division.
130. Student can perform division with a two-place number and no remainder.
131. Student can perform division with a two-place number and a remainder.
132. Student can demonstrate the distributive property of multiplication.
133. Student can identify a ray and a line segment with end points.
134. Student can use the distributive property of division.
135. Student can read and write fractional numbers.
136. Student can name whole numbers as fractional numerals.
137. Student can relate the concept of a fractional part by identifying fractional elements of a set.
138. Given a division problem with a remainder, the student can show the remainder as a fraction.
139. Student can use multiplication to prove division answers.
140. Student can us simple scale measures on maps.
141. Student can use a ruler and yardstick.
142. Student can read a thermometer.
143. Student can read a bar graph.

Continued.

SEQUENCE OF ARITHMETIC SKILLS IN THE FIRST SIX GRADES—cont'd

Fourth-grade skills

144. Given a verbal description of a number from 0 to 999,999, the student can name the place value of each digit.
145. Given a number from 0 to 999,999, the student can provide the expanded notation.
146. Given a fraction, the student can give equivalent fractional names.
147. Student can read major Roman numeral groups.
148. Student can round to the nearest hundred thousand.
149. Student can multiply with four-digit numerals.
150. Student can demonstrate the equivalence of transposed numbers in multiplication.
151. Given two numbers, the student can make equations for all basic functions.
152. Student can determine an arithmetic average.
153. Student can find a quotient named by a three-digit numeral.
154. Student can use multiplication concepts to estimate partial divisors.
155. Student can divide by multiples of ten.
156. Student can order fractional numbers (e.g., ½, ⅓, and ¼).
157. Student can identify coins as fractional components of a dollar (e.g., 5¢ = $^1/_{20}$).
158. Student can add fractional numbers with the same denominator.
159. Student can subtract fractional numbers with the same denominator.
160. Student can reduce numbers stated as fractions to the lowest fraction.
161. Student can write fractional numerals as decimals for fractions with a denominator of 100.
162. Given a problem requiring the measurement of length, weight, area, volume, or temperature, the student can identify the measuring device.
163. Student can tell time to the nearest minute.
164. Student can make change in any combination in amounts less than $5.
165. Student can rename and regroup decimals for subtraction.
166. Student can identify an angle.
167. Student can identify parallel and intersecting lines.
168. Student can identify curves.
169. Student can identify bases of common geometric forms.
170. Student can identify sides of common geometric forms.
171. Student can add weights presented as pounds and ounces.
172. Student can read bar and dot graphs.

Fifth-grade skills

173. Student can develop equivalent fractions.
174. Student can convert improper fractions to mixed numbers.
175. Student can compute sums and differences of decimal values.
176. Student can determine costs, profits, and losses that do not require percentages.
177. Student can convert various measures into equivalencies.
178. Student can name numbers to 1 million.
179. Student can define finite and infinite sets.

SEQUENCE OF ARITHMETIC SKILLS IN THE FIRST SIX GRADES—cont'd

Fifth-grade skills—cont'd

180. Student can use simple algebaic equations to represent vertical algorithms in multiplication (e.g., □ + 4 = 7 is 4 + a = 7).
181. Student can divide by two-digit numerals.
182. Student can state the rule that two lines do not intersect more than once.
183. Student can identify multiple colinear points on a line segment or ray.
184. Student can define a plane.
185. Student can identify a parallelogram, polygon, quadrilateral hexagon, octagon, and trapezoid.
186. Student can identify the diameter, arc, angle, and semicircle.
187. Student can multiply fractional numbers.
188. Student can add and subtract fractional numbers.
189. Student can subtract mixed numbers.
190. Student can divide a whole number by a fractional number.
191. Student can describe units of time in centuries, decades, years, months, days, hours, minutes, and seconds.
192. Student can show the meaning of common metric measures.
193. Student can determine the perimeter and area of common figures.
194. Student can make a graph using broken lines, bars, and pictures.
195. Student can perform division with a two-digit divisor and six-digit dividend.

Sixth-grade skills

196. Student can write numbers in the millions as expanded notations.
197. Student can demonstrate the numerals written in the form of exponents.
198. Student can write names of numbers through the billions.
199. Student can graph a solution set on a number ray.
200. Student can divide with numbers greater than 100.
201. Student can factor numbers.
202. Student can construct a line segment.
203. Student can construct a ray.
204. Student can construct an angle.
205. Student can name the parts of an angle.
206. Student can name three common angles (acute, obtuse, right).
207. Student can determine the reciprocal of a fractional number.
208. Student can divide a fractional number by a whole number.
209. Student can divide a fractional number by a fractional number.
210. Student can apply the ratio concept in solving problems.
211. Student can provide different decimal values for the same fractional number.
212. Student can change ratios to a percentage form.
213. Student can determine percentage names for fractional numbers.
214. Student can construct and interpret all basic tables and graphs.

ASSESSMENT

We addressed assessment in Chapter 2 and noted that the most popular instrument for formal assessment is the KeyMath Diagnostic Arithmetic Test. However, informal procedures provide a rich source of information that can be directly related to everyday classroom functioning. In general, the assessment process involves (1) observing the student's behavior, (2) attempting to have the student verbalize problems as they are attacked, and (3) determining the kind of errors made.

A useful approach to assessment developed by Reisman (1972) has been mentioned in many textbooks. Developmental or remedial teaching cannot begin without a clear understanding of the skills a student has mastered. The sequence of instruction serves as a foundation, task analysis aids in determining specific instructional activities, and informal assessment provides sufficient information to make such decisions. Fortunately the skill sequence in arithmetic is more easily discernible than that in reading. Reisman's approach has been modified as the basic approach to informal measurement. A teacher may implement a variety of problems to examine arithmetical capability. Following are the areas of assessment:

1. *Cardinality*. The student may not have a concept of cardinality, that is, that different sets of objects have different members.
2. *Ordinality*. The student may not have a concept of order, for example, that fourth, fifth, and sixth represent values in a sequence. The child may be able to perform rote counting but not be able to use the concept of order.
3. *Symbol association*. The student may have a concept of cardinality and ordinality but not be able to associate symbols with the underlying concept (e.g., 5 = ●●●●●).
4. *Symbol confusion*. Some students confuse numbers, although they have a concept of numeration. For example, 2 may be confused with 6, or 3 with 8, especially when written by a child.
5. *Inability to group sets*. Given two sets, (●●) and (●●●), the student is unable to merge them into a unity, or new set (●●●●●).
6. *Lack of the concept of place values*. The place values (ones, tens, hundreds, and so forth) are not understood. The student may have a concept of number, but symbolizing numbers as place values may not be learned. A more concrete step is usually required, such as the use of an abacus, sticks, or card pockets.
7. *Inability to dissociate sets (reversibility), or subtraction*. The student may be able to combine sets but unable to reverse the process. The concrete form should be examined before dealing with numerals.
8. *Inability to conceptualize multiplication or division*. Essentially, the same process as in category 7 is involved. The inability to represent multiplication and division in a concrete manner should be examined for concept attainment.
9. *Lack of mastery or appropriate application of computational skills*. A variety of this type of problem require careful analysis to determine the error pattern:

21	27	21
+32	− 14	×4
52	12	74

7 6/36 36 (wrong combination)	(421) +634 213 (subtracts)

21 ×3 64 (adds)	24 ×7 48 (regroups and adds)	24 ×10 24 (ignores 0)

10. *Incompletion of computational functions*. The student may not complete computations:

40 9/364 360	24 ×6 24 (does not carry)

11. *Confusion of null sets or zero*. The student may be confused about null sets or the use of zero:

$\begin{array}{r} 20 \\ -19 \\ \hline 19 \end{array}$ $\quad 8 \times 0 = 8 \quad$ $\begin{array}{r} 26 \\ -10 \\ \hline 10 \end{array}$ $\quad 10\overline{)40}$

12. *Regrouping inaccurately*. Following are examples of inaccuracy in regrouping:

$\begin{array}{r} 26 \\ +14 \\ \hline 31 \end{array} \quad \begin{array}{r} 462 \\ +286 \\ \hline 648 \end{array} \quad \begin{array}{r} 32 \\ +13 \\ \hline 53 \end{array} \quad \begin{array}{r} 43 \\ -8 \\ \hline 45 \end{array} \quad \begin{array}{r} 805 \\ -126 \\ \hline 779 \end{array}$

13. *Inability to translate word problems to basic algorithms*. Some students cannot read; others have difficulty finding the essential mathematics task involved in a problem. Following are factors in the inability to translate:
    a. Unsuitability of text material to reading level
    b. Lack of instruction in reading arithmetic texts
    c. Poor knowledge of vocabulary
    d. Little understanding of graphs and charts
    e. Confusion of symbols

Piagetian tasks may be used to assess levels of development, especially in fuctions related to tasks that can be accomplished at specific transition points in stage development. Simple materials can be used by the teacher to accomplish the informal assessment task as follows:

One-to-one correspondence

Materials: Eight blue chips and eight red chips.

Procedure: Lay the blue chips in a row, equally spaced about an inch apart. Ask the child to remove as many red chips from a container as are placed in the blue row on the table. In stage 1 (5 years of age or younger) the child will put some chips down, unequally spaced, until the end of each line is matched. There may be four, five, or six chips in the row, but each row will end at the same point. Because the length of the rows is the same, the child believes that the rows are equal. In stage 2 (about 6 years) the child will match the rows equally in a one-to-one correspondence. If the teacher spreads out the blue row or the red row, the child will be fooled by the perceptual element of one row taking up more space and will think that the longer row has more chips. In stage 3 (about 7 years) the child will be unconcerned about the length or arrangement of the rows, knowing that they are equivalent.

Conservation of number

Materials: Two containers of blue and red beads.

Procedure: Instruct the child to place blue beads and red beads separately into two containers one at a time using the left and right hands simultaneously. After the containers are full and the child is convinced that an equal number is contained within each group, pour the beads of one container into a much larger container. The same stages as in one-to-one correspondence will be observed. A child of about 7 will be uninfluenced by the peceptual characteristics of the two containers. The child who can conserve number or quantity may be able to deal efficiently with traditional arithmetic tasks.

The preceding tests may be used by teachers who are interested in determining if children have reached a level of development, a milestone, necessary for having initial experiences with numbers. Some children will not reach this level until much later. An 8-year-old who cannot conserve has no real sense of number. Teaching must be altered to accommodate the child. The child cannot be expected to keep pace with youngsters of the same chronological age who are achieving at much higher levels. A review of Piagetian works is useful to teachers who wish to conduct other experiments, especially in projective geometry, conservation of weight and volume, and other skills at higher levels of development.

Although there are a number of other informal assessment approaches and opportunities to observe the behavior of students under conditions in which games are used (e.g., dominoes, dice, and board games), the teacher can employ many direct assessment approaches. The work of Fernald (1943), who is well known for her VAKT approach to reading but little recognized for her work in other school subjects, is of interest in arithmetic. Her approach to assessment and remediation in arithmetic is very direct; it is also, if inadvertently, in keeping with contemporary theories of development.

Fernald worked in a clinic with children who

had experienced considerable school difficulty before being referred. She required students to complete an informal test on combinations of numbers before introducing remedial activities. Although intelligence and achievement tests were also administered, informal tests ("Tests to Determine Nature of Individual's Disability") were the most important. Combined with other informal methods we recommend, we find the recommendations of Fernald to be as relevant today as they were nearly 40 years ago:

1. Tests in simple combinations
2. Tests for skill in complex situations involving simple combinations
3. Tests in problem solving

Fernald contended that many children fail in mathematics because they do not know the simple number combinations that she considered essential to daily needs and ordinary situations. She believed that the student must be able to provide a correct answer immediately for a simple combination rather than relying on some slow, mechanical process to derive a solution. Moreover, she maintained that many children are typically unable to perform certain specific combinations; that is, they may have difficulty adding or subtracting certain combinations but not others. Examination of specific combinations (error pattern analysis) might reveal the underlying problem and reduce the task of remediation to a specific problem or set of problems. Many children in ordinary school situations would be given problems to do, as they are today required to complete worksheets or workbooks. However, they would be given only a score with the numbers correct and incorrect and would not know which problems were correct and which were incorrect. Fernald recommended that children be required to work only on combinations they had missed.

Fernald's test includes 100 addition problems on a sheet with all common combinations of zero through nine (e.g., $3 + 3 = \square$ and $0 + 5 = \square$). The subtraction portion also has 100 problems, but many problems require regrouping (e.g., $16 - 7 = \square$). The multiplication part has 100 problems with the same numbers as on the addition page, and the 90 division problems involve one-digit divisors and one- and two-digit problems. Believing that automatic response is essential in arithmetic, Fernald instructed that the examiner require the student to complete each problem, observe, and inquire how each problem is solved, and keep track of the problems that the student cannot solve rapidly. These become the problems that a student must master as a part of remediation. Children who achieve mastery in use of all basic combinations will have gained much in the ability to perform daily classroom problems and practical life problems.

Students who can perform automatic calculations in the simple combinations may still fail in application because of two fundamental reasons:

1. The lack of concept of the number values involved (similar to word calling in reading)
2. Failure to understand the nature of the operations used

The second skill requires considerable experience with concrete materials. Some children may have no difficulty with problems as long as the sum does not exceed 20, others may have difficulty with sums above 30, and so forth. As experience with the concepts of numbers increases, so too will the child's ability to use operations accurately. The concept of place value, often taught by rote, must be truly understood before it is useful.

TEACHING APPROACHES

Cardinality

Although many children are introduced to numerical concepts through the verbal descriptions of parents and peers about objects (e.g., "big," "little," and "more than"), most authorities recognize counting as the first true arithmetic activity. However, many experiences with numbers precede counting and the basic arithmetic processes. Like most modern arithmetic programs, cardinality is based on set theory. The problems presented to the child should be arranged around concrete experiences and continued throughout the elementary years. The reason is based on the Piagetian theory of equilibrium.

Piaget contended that teaching children a specific response or reinforcing a fact (behaviorism) does not necessarily lead to altered mental states. The mental operations of a child are acquired through considerable direct experience. For example, counting is ''mastered'' by some children as early as the age of 2 years, but they cannot really count anything. They have simply been reinforced for executing a verbal string of numbers. After considerable experience with objects the child acquires the meaning of counting and can use it as a skill in a rational manner. According to Piaget, a new set of mental operations is acquired. The child assimilates new information that gradually interferes with previous operations, a new order is established, and a new equilibrium of mental operations results. The important fact for teaching is that concrete examples should be used liberally and continuously. If a problem can be reduced to a physical model, learning can occur more easily.

The foundation of arithmetic is set theory, which is actually classification of objects by some property. Throughout childhood children continue to refine a classification system for the entire world of experiences that are associated with verbal labels. As a matter of natural logical development and of sound teaching, the student should be given sufficient opportunity to experience arithmetic concepts at a concrete level. Classification of objects should be a classroom activity using the range of features—color, shape, size, and ultimately abstract classification. As Copeland (1974, p. 82) indicates, number presents a challenge to a child because as a property it is not physically present in a class or set of objects as are such apparent characteristics as size and shape.

In developmental and remedial arithmetic activities, classification of concrete objects should be the major emphasis. Cuisenaire rods should be avoided because they are not based on set theory. Fortunately, cardinality, or classification, can be founded on many concrete objects available to the teacher. Many classical Piagetian tasks are appropriate for teaching and testing. Children develop arithmetic concepts through the actions they perform on objects; this is a basic Piagetian principle.

One-to-one correspondence

Part of the process of developing the concept of number involves counting. The coordination of cardinality and ordinality is the first landmark in the acquisition of basic skills. Counting provides a mechanism for knowing the number in a set and the position of items as they are ranked. Rational counting is the ability to truly count; rote counting is a memorized but meaningless activity because the child has neither knowledge of the counting process nor ability to apply it.

Comparison of sets aids in the development of counting. Sets of small units (such as two checkers, two crayons, or two birds) can be compared. Checkers are different from crayons, an obvious concept, but the property of numbers must be developed because it does not exist as a physical characteristic.

An important activity in development of counting and related concepts is one-to-one correspondence, which affords an opportunity to recognize sets and members within them, positions of items, and counting. Motor activities such as clapping, hopping, tapping, and singing in unison with items in a row may be used for early training. Many playground activities can be used. Considerable experience with placing concrete items in rows, matching items with others (set comparisons), and relating each item in one set to items in the other are useful activities. As in the development of other concepts, the child must perform actions on objects to alter mental structures.

Symbol association

Children can be presented with a variety of tasks employing dice, counters, checkers, dominoes, or dots to learn to associate numerals with common patterns in sets. The goal is for children to rapidly recognize patterns, identify the number, and associate the numeral with patterns such as the following:

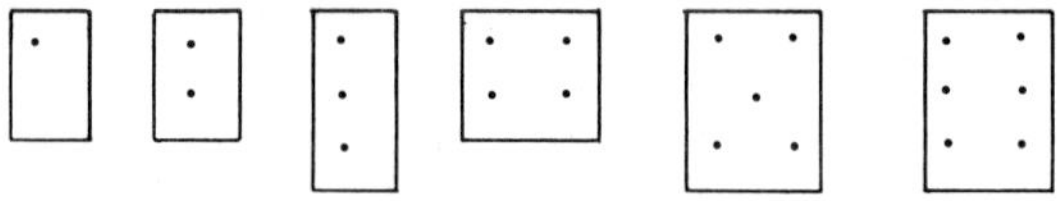

With sufficient exposure and practice, children are able to give the correct number or write the numeral without tediously counting each dot. After stable associations are made, blocks or cards with unusual arrangements like the following can be used:

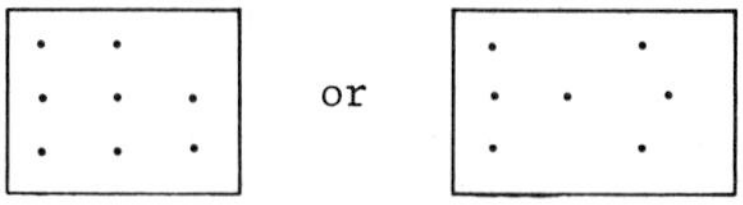

One task of the child in learning the concept of number is to recognize that a unity is invariant regardless of the ways in which its constituent members or addends are arranged. To help teach this concept, the teacher can present all permutations of a number in concrete form. For example, 6 is comprised of six elements in a variety of ways: in pairs (e.g., 1 + 5, 2 + 4, and 3 + 3) and other arrangements such as 1 + 2 + 3 and 1 + 1 + 4. A number of activities can be used to reinforce these concepts for all primary numbers.

Conservation

Although there has been some controversy about whether or not children can be induced to enter the stage of conservation through training, Piaget and classical theorists who support his views believe that stage development cannot be enhanced. Nonetheless, a child must have concrete experiences to develop the mental structures or concepts leading to conservation. Many of the tasks used in testing for stage development in Piagetian theory are actually useful in communicating arithmetic concepts. Montessori and Stern materials may be used for all prenumerical activities such as seriation, sets, and conservations. *The classical tests simply indicate that, when a child is no longer dominated by a specific perceptual characteristic such as size, shape, or length, it is possible for the child to realize that number is not lost or changed by rearrangement of items.* This is the basic foundation of arithmetic. If a child simultaneously understands cardinality and ordinality, the true conceptualization of number is possible. The child is able to simultaneously "hold in mind" the thoughts that an item is both red and wood, that a person can be a father and a son, and so forth. Depending on the criteria, classification with members belonging to more than one set is possible with the concept of number.

Part-to-whole fractions

Conceptualizing proper fractions is a difficult concept that emerges later in the elementary years. However, young children should have experiences with part-to-whole fractions. Young children may refuse to violate the integrity of an item (e.g., cutting up a paper rabbit); a child of 4 years may comprehend halves of geometric shapes. Children of ages 6 to 7 years are able to deal with the division of wholes into thirds. Thus, addition and subtraction of simple fractions with common denominators does not meet with success until about the third grade. Another fractional concept is comparison of wholes in a set, such as half the ducks in a picture or a third of the children in a class.

Process signs

The common process signs (+, −, ×, and ÷) and the signs introduced more recently through modern mathematics can be confusing to children not only because each element must be "read" but also because many children have difficulty using signs when they do not understand the application process. The signs, including numerals, are conventions that represent concepts. However, unlike the symbols in reading, the signs in arithmetic are not based on phonetic elements. If a child makes a mistake such as adding when the sign clearly indicates subtraction, the error may be because the child is not certain of the process, ignores the sign, or is working from a "mind set."

In the past, such errors have been explained as visual-perceptual disorders. As in reading, the treatment has frequently been to attempt to improve the visual-perceptual functioning of the student. It is interesting that most children stop making errors with signs after they have acquired facility with the basic concepts and applications. Our experience has been that signs can be introduced without talking by using a variety of visual exercises. This will be explained in detail later. Engelmann (1969) recommends that signs be introduced to small groups of children by using a blackboard. The sign is used as a verb. Adding is called "plussing." Thus, as children learn to combine addends, they are taught that they are plussing numbers. For example, in the problem 4 + □ = 6, children perform the necessary actions of balancing the equation, and the instructor might say, "Let's write what we did. What did we do? We plussed 2."

Johnson and Myklebust (1964) give special attention to process signs. They recommend that students be given considerable practice in differentiating signs; borders should be drawn around each sign so that they will be perceived as units. A precise mathematics vocabulary should be used each time for a particular sign.

Algorithms

The basic considerations in using algorithms can be listed as follows:

1. Concrete experiences should precede use of numerals.
2. Colored numerals or signs should have a specific coded meaning and not be used haphazardly to avoid confusion in perceptual attraction and meaning.
3. Drill on simple combinations, for example,

$$\begin{array}{r}2\\+1\\\hline\end{array}\qquad\begin{array}{r}4\\-3\\\hline\end{array}\qquad\begin{array}{r}6\\\times 2\\\hline\end{array}\qquad 2\overline{)8}$$

   should be presented only as a method of overlearning responses for practical usefulness after each process is learned at the concrete level.
4. In the beginning, problems should be consistently presented in the same form each time, for example:

$$\textit{either}\quad\begin{array}{r}2\\+2\\\hline\end{array}\quad\textit{or}\quad 2+2=\square$$

5. Provision should be made with card pockets and on paper or the chalkboard to consistently show concrete elements associated with each numeral:

   a. 4 + 2 = □
   |||| ||

   b.

Hundreds	*Tens*	*Ones*
	1	2
	卌 卌	||

or

	Hundreds	*Tens*	*Ones*
		|||	||
		|	|
+		||||	|||

6. It is imperative from the beginning that children learn that an algorithm is based on place values: without this level of knowledge the computational process is meaningless.

Addition

Teaching addition is a matter of both concept formation and computation. Teachers generally attempt to teach computation as an immediate, rote process. According to Fernald and other authorities, this is a desirable objective of teaching. Children should be able to provide immediate answers to simple combinations of addition, as well as other arithmetic processes. Laboring for a long time to derive the answer to 6 + 9 is unfortunate and will interfere with the child's progress because of the lack of facility. However, some children are induced to learn the simple combinations by rote memorization without careful attention to the underlying concept. Children should experience considerable training with concrete objects, being encouraged to use their fingers and other objects.

Initial experience with addition should be based solidly on combining objects (concrete sets). Counters, checkers, or other items that may be easily manipulated should be used. Adding ●● and ●●● leads naturally to 2 + 3. Unfortunately this experience is frequently short lived or absent from training because children are all too quickly confronted with workbooks and worksheets. At the age of 7, most children are capable of dealing with addition as well as rudimentary subtraction. If the first grade of school were spent almost exclusively in handling concrete objects, transformation to the traditional algorithms would be simply a matter of using symbols for concepts that are already understood. However, many children are required to perform computations of simple problems before they have the concepts or processes mastered.

Copeland recommends an interesting approach that is challenging to children. The task is to give a child two sets of counters that are unequal and ask the child to equalize them. If there are 10 in one set and 16 in the other, the task of the child is to form equal sets of 13. The child is required to perform operations on the counters rather than simply develop rote memorization or counting to solve an algorithm. Number is abstract and exists in the mind.

To enhance the development of arithmetic concepts (e.g., cardinality and counting), some teachers encourage children to use their fingers in some meaningful way as a step between the concrete action on objects and symbolization. Others contend that it is important for students to be able to visualize the numerals as associated with objects. Although several approaches can be used, the following recommendations are useful.

''Chisanbop'' is a system of finger counting that fascinates teachers and parents because of the speed of calculation achieved by some students. Except as a method of reinforcing concrete concepts in developing proficiency, use of fingers for counting is not necessarily important because children may also use electronic calculators. Nevertheless, Chisanbop has been popular lately and is most appropriate in beginning instruction of addition and subtraction. It is only useful after place values have been learned, however. It is rather simple: the fingers on the right hand are the ones, and the fingers of the left hand, the tens. With the index finger pressed on the table, counting begins with one. Two is the index and middle finger, and so on. Five is the thumb pressed; with the thumb on the table, six is the thumb and index finger, seven the addition of the middle finger, and so forth until nine is reached with all digits of the right hand depressed. Ten is represented by the index finger of the left hand; twenty is the index and middle fingers of the left hand. Ninety is all fingers of the left hand depressed.

Another method that has been used to reinforce imagery and concrete object–to–symbol association is the overlay of dots on numerals. They may be manipulable numerals or cutout wood, with raised dots or pictures with dots. For example, the numeral 4 would be represented as follows:

This method is really a system of fading: the dots may be faded, or eliminated, after children no longer need the assistance. This technique will be discussed in more specific terms later in the text.

In chalkboard activities, such as those used in the DISTAR approach to arithmetic, children can be taught to place marks of equal length beneath each numeral in a problem. This aids in visualization of cardinality for addition, provides the same information as supplied in a number line except that it is more immediately useful, and it can be faded. Following is an example:

$4 + 2 = \square$
IIII II

Theoretically, most children should not require such prompting if they have acquired the basic concepts that precede computation. The fact that many children are forced into computation before they are ready may explain the popularity of such fading techniques. Some children seem to be able to grasp the concepts of set combination, cardinality, and ordinality but have difficulty associating numerals with quantities.

According to the Piagetian view, addition is not simply the ability to assign numerals to sets of objects, the ability to count all items in two small sets of objects, or the ability to count all items in two small sets to derive one number denoting their unity. Addition is the ability of a child to realize that parts are related to a whole and the whole may be designated or renamed according to the substance of its parts. This is best exemplified by the commutative property of addition.

The commutative property of addition simply means that combining two sets of the same number may be accomplished regardless of the way in which they are joined. For example, 7, expressed as $5 + 2$ or $2 + 5$, is invariant. As introduced later, the associative property simply means that any three numbers may be combined in any order because the whole is invariant and is composed of its parts in any order, for example:

$$\begin{aligned}(4 + 3) + 5 &= 4 + (3 + 5)\\ 7 \quad + 5 &= 4 + \quad 8\\ 12 &= 12\end{aligned}$$

The associative property can be very useful in aiding children with addition problems that require renaming. Concrete materials such as ice cream sticks may be used. Each stick represents one unit, ten combined and wrapped with a rubber band represent a ten, and so forth. Cans or bins supply each place with a container, the units in the right-hand can and the tens in the left-hand. After initial experiences that are successful, the abacus can be introduced. The abacus is an important device for making the transition from concrete to representational arithmetic. The addition of color cues to some abacuses is important because a particular color can represent a place value. This can be accomplished with sticks, but it requires the unwieldy practice of switching to different colored sticks when a bundle of ten is formed through some manipulation. This process is very confusing and should be avoided.

Subtraction

Until a child has the concept of reversibility, addition in a rudimentary form is possible, but subtraction is not. Actually, addition and subtraction are inverse processes. They can be taught simultaneously. Although it is not done in conventional programs, multiplication can also be started at the same time because of its relationship to addition; multiplication is repeated addition.

Addition problems of the type $5 + \square = 7$ are really subtraction problems because the essential requirement in solving the problem is reversibility. Use of a number line is not very helpful if children do not comprehend the underlying concept. Teaching a child to heed the process sign and to add numbers is a relatively useless activity until it is evident to the child that counting is not involved but rather a missing element of the invariant whole number 7.

The child is not as likely to learn the basic, simple combinations of subtraction as in addition. This is true for multiplication and division, also. The difficulty in subtraction is in making the problems concrete and reversing the process in regrouping or renaming. For example, subtracting 12 from 40 in the traditional algorithm

$$\begin{array}{r}40\\ -12\\ \hline\end{array}$$

requires that one ten be renamed as ten ones to be placed in the ones column. This is a difficult procedure. Considerable experience with problems of this type should be provided before a child is required to use an algorithm. Associating sticks with place values is an essential part of the learning process when the child is ready for this skill. A card pocket with pockets corresponding to place values may also be used for subtraction.

A child who understands conservation and reversibility, who knows that a whole is invariant and compromised of elements, and who can reverse the process of addition can master the underlying process. Representing this process with numerals in an algorithm is sometimes difficult because symbols are being used to characterize an actual concrete fact that the child has discovered. A procedure that is similar to the number line but that has advantages because of the relationships of many numbers always evident to the child is the use of the following chart, which has been recommended by many writers:

Addition and subtraction chart

	0	*1*	*2*	*3*	*4*	*5*	*6*	*7*	*8*	*9*
0	0	1	2	3	4	5	6	7	8	9
1	1	2	3	4	5	6	7	8	9	10
2	2	3	4	5	6	7	8	9	10	11
3	3	4	5	6	7	8	9	10	11	12
4	4	5	6	7	8	9	10	11	12	13
5	5	6	7	8	9	10	11	12	13	14
6	6	7	8	9	10	11	12	13	14	15
7	7	8	9	10	11	12	13	14	15	16
8	8	9	10	11	12	13	14	15	16	17
9	9	10	11	12	13	14	15	16	17	18

The child can add any two numbers quickly on this chart by placing the index finger of one hand on the addend in the row and the other index finger on the addend in the column: the answer is where the lines intersect. For example, with the left index finger on the 5 and the right index finger on the 3, the child can converge the fingers at the point of intersection: 8. To subtract, the addends in either the row or column may be used like a number line; in problems presented in the manner of 4 + □ = 6 the child need only find the 4 in the column with the left hand and move across the corresponding row to find the 6. At the top will be the missing number. This chart should be permanently placed on the desk or table.

Multiplication

Although multiplication is related to addition and may be shown as repeated addition (e.g., $3 \times 8 = 8 + 8 + 8$), conceptualization of the process requires recognition of equivalence of multiple sets. This can be concretely represented in the same manner as simple one-to-one correspondence:

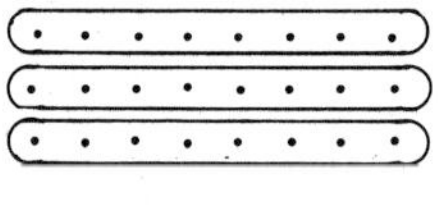

(3 X 8)

Piaget (1964) and Copeland (1974) observed that children who can conserve (about age 7 to 8 years) are able to grasp the equivalence of more than two sets with little difficulty. The classic test is to use a set of vases and two sets of flowers. If the child can use the logic of transitivity (i.e., each set of flowers is matched to a vase), the child will understand that each set is equivalent. Children who are not confused by perceptual features can easily agree to equivalence. Being able to see the relationship of two flowers to each vase (2-to-1 correspondence) is multiplication. Children who struggle with addition are not likely to achieve success in multiplication at a concrete level. Success in addition leads immediately to developing facility with multiplication. Adaptation of the flowers to vases task can be an effective concrete method for teaching rather than resorting solely to computational problems. Any number of experiences can be based on multiple relationships such as $3 \times N$ and $4 \times N$.

The traditional approach to multiplication rests on rote memorization of the tables from ones to nines. If children do not understand the multiplicative relationship (multiple equivalence), they will not find much meaning in the memorized tables. Children who are reinforced appropriately can learn to respond accurately to the tables; however, rote memory of multiplication tables is no more relevant than is rote counting to a young child. It can be boring and frustrating.

Steps in the introduction of multiplication are as follows:

1. Concrete experiences should precede graphical representation.
2. Addition should be related to multiplicative processes.
3. Flash cards, the tachistoscope, games, dice, and worksheets should only be used to establish competency in immediate recall or mastery of the simple combinations after children clearly demonstrate mastery of the underlying process.

After children are presented practical application problems, and until the basic simple combinations are mastered, the following table can be used on all computational problems:

Multiplication table

1	*2*	*3*	*4*	*5*	*6*	*7*	*8*	*9*	*10*
2	4	6	8	10	12	14	16	18	20
3	6	9	12	15	18	21	24	27	30
4	8	12	16	20	24	28	32	36	40
5	10	15	20	25	30	35	40	45	50
6	12	18	24	30	36	42	48	54	60
7	14	21	28	35	42	49	56	63	70
8	16	24	32	40	48	56	64	72	80
9	18	27	36	45	54	63	72	81	90
10	20	30	40	50	60	70	80	90	100

Division

Multiplication and division are inverse processes. Piagetian theorists recommend that both processes should be taught simultaneously. Most traditional school mathematics curricula proceed linearly from addition through division. The relationship of multiplication and division is essentially depicted as

$$xy = Z \therefore x = \frac{z}{y}$$

Division at a concrete level requires that the child distribute numbers of items in terms of a mandatory equivalence or matched correspondence. That is, 16 counters (or pieces of candy) may be distributed among a number of children equally, for example, among 4:

This is graphically the same as

$$\begin{array}{r}4\\4\overline{)16}\end{array}$$

Experience with small numbers should be presented numerous times and associated with the problem presented in traditional form, for example:

$$2\overline{)4} = \bullet\bullet\ \bullet\bullet$$
$$3\overline{)6} = \bullet\bullet\bullet\ \bullet\bullet\bullet\bullet\bullet$$
$$5\overline{)10} = \bullet\bullet\ \bullet\bullet\ \bullet\bullet\ \bullet\bullet\ \bullet\bullet$$

Manipulative activities with concrete materials is the absolute prerequisite to dealing with computation and numerical forms. In Piagetian theory, concrete operational thought is similar to physically performing actions on concrete objects. A rapid departure from the concrete world to symbolism is inconsistent with the child's ability and instructional needs.

Fractions

As noted previously, younger children have great difficulty with the conceptualization of fractions or proportions. Until the age at which conservation occurs, division by halves and thirds of whole objects is possible, but numerical representation or division by other fractional sizes is not. The first experiences with fractions must be part-to-whole transitions:

1. The fractional concept is similar to the understanding of number (conservation). Knowing that a whole is invariant and that dividing it into infinite numbers of fractional parts does not change its unity is essential.
2. Fractionation of a whole must also be equivalent. If a circle, pie, or other object is subdivided into thirds or fourths, each part must be identical. For example, if a child divides an object into thirds as represented in example A, the concept of fractionation is faulty:

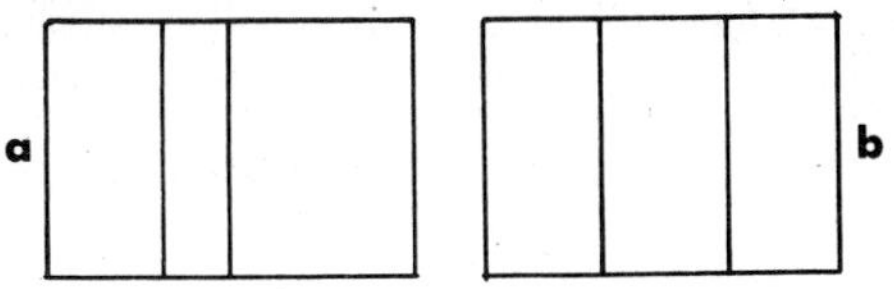

Children must have extensive experience with concrete objects, with verbal and eventually numerical names associated with the model:

With sufficient experiences of this kind, children are less likely to be confused by the size of the fraction as indicated by the denominator. As a whole, eight is twice as large as 4; as a fraction, ⅛ is smaller than ¼, which confuses children who have learned to think of eight as a greater number. Computations with fractions should be carefully introduced after a comprehensive instruction with concrete, part-to-whole activities.

Fractions are frequently depicted in permanent chart form:

<table>
<tr><td colspan="24">1</td></tr>
<tr><td colspan="12">½</td><td colspan="12">½</td></tr>
<tr><td colspan="6">¼</td><td colspan="6">¼</td><td colspan="6">¼</td><td colspan="6">¼</td></tr>
<tr><td colspan="3">⅛</td><td colspan="3">⅛</td><td colspan="3">⅛</td><td colspan="3">⅛</td><td colspan="3">⅛</td><td colspan="3">⅛</td><td colspan="3">⅛</td><td colspan="3">⅛</td></tr>
<tr><td colspan="8">⅓</td><td colspan="8">⅓</td><td colspan="8">⅓</td></tr>
<tr><td colspan="4">1/6</td><td colspan="4">1/6</td><td colspan="4">1/6</td><td colspan="4">1/6</td><td colspan="4">1/6</td><td colspan="4">1/6</td></tr>
</table>

Conceptualizations of proportions, percentages, and probability are based on fractional concepts but are much more difficult. Although the concepts are abstract, it is sensible to present them in concrete form before dealing exclusively with formulas. Our experience has been that undergraduate and graduate students achieve mastery of basic statistical concepts if concrete models are used. If anything is to be stressed in Piagetian theory, it is that concrete experience should precede symbolic representation and that verbalization of arithmetical concepts may aid or may interfere with learning.

Time

Learning to tell time is complicated by an unusual number base, directional confusion, and fractional words to express time-related concepts (e.g., "to," "from," "till," and half "past").

With a traditional clock face, teaching children to tell time is usually done by introducing two-hand placements proceeding with the hour, half hour, quarter hour, 5-minute segments, and finally minutes. Digital clocks, which seem to be rapidly replacing traditional clocks, make "reading" the time a rather straightforward procedure. Although the digital system may be more practical, children should be taught both systems.

Language and arithmetic

The use of language to aid in solving arithmetic problems cannot be denied, but it is also true that language is not entirely necessary and can interfere with learning according to Piaget. In fact, "talking" children through arithmetic problems will not necessarily help in learning; the children can be reinforced to respond verbally, but true learning will not be achieved. "Teacher talk" can be counterproductive.

An approach used by one of us is adapted from the work of Furth (1966), who used nonverbal processing of symbols to examine the symbolic and logical development of deaf persons. Modification of the technique for use in teaching other handicapped children arithmetic is interesting and useful. The procedure is essentially a chalkboard activity, but worksheets can be used for seatwork. There are two general rules: the teacher and students do not talk during the exercise, and all activities use visual symbols but no written words. Actions and requests are pantomimed.

The goal is to convey arithmetic concepts to children without spoken language to capitalize on the symbolism, logic, and concreteness of arithmetic. Initial exercises involve set equivalence in the form of an equation:

○ ○ ○ = ○ ○ ○

Children are required to correct equations like the following:

○ ○ ○ = ○ ○

This is corrected, of course, by adding a circle. A later adaptation could also be to use the negative form, such as $\neq$.

For some children at a prenumerical level, simple activities such as using forms like a house can be used to introduce procedure, concepts, and equation:

The child begins to use the + and = signs inadvertently, becomes acquainted with the equation, and develops the concept of constituent parts of a whole.

Later, children can be introduced with substitutions such as the following:

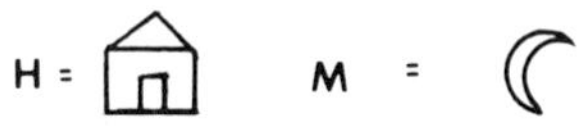

which leads to the familiar forms:

4 = ○ ○ ○ ○

Concepts can be introduced for other signs such as the following:

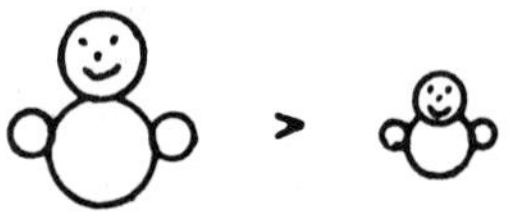

Children can learn that equivalence exists regardless of arrangement:

0 □ 0 = □ 0 0

Teachers can introduce scale activities on the board by using a simple drawing of a seesaw:

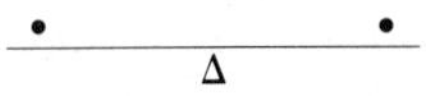

The teacher then asks the student to determine the direction if a large and small child sit on the seesaw:

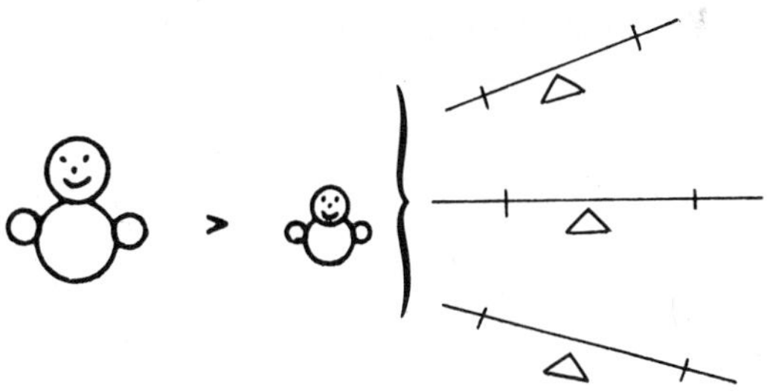

Ultimately traditional algorithms with numerals are introduced; in the beginning a transition is made between more concrete symbols and numerals, a procedure recommended by most authorities. Placing numerals above marks or circles seems to be a natural, easy outcome if sufficient experience is gained with this general approach.

It is surprising how easily children process difficult concepts that they would otherwise not be able to understand or express if restricted to spoken language for instruction and response modes. The nature of these activities can become increasingly more complex, and children can be guided into transition from picture symbols to the use of arithmetic symbols and algorithms exclusively with virtual elimination of spoken language. This approach is in keeping with Piagetian principles.

Games, activities, workbooks, and technological aids

Many teachers have prepared various activities and games to be used in teaching arithmetic. Some textbooks are filled with games and ideas. This is *not* an approach to teaching. Rather, the use of activities such as games, drill, and workbooks must be determined as age appropriate and skill related. Many games (e.g., Monopoly, dominoes, dice games, checkers, and Bingo) are excellent tools but should be used judiciously as the circumstances dictate. Otherwise, such activities may become "busy work" or interfere with learning.

Any college student who has computed a Pearson-product moment correlation coefficient by hand and then used a computer will never resort to pencil and paper again. The savings in time is incredible because computers can ''crunch'' numbers with amazing speed. It makes sense that children should be taught to use electronic calculators and computers because literacy in the use of these devices will be important to this generation. However, children must learn the process first.

Remediation of basic computational skills

Most remedial programs are based on computational skills because examination reveals that children are apparently deficient in this area. If we do not measure anything but computational skills, we should not be too surprised. We teach what we test and test what we teach. Many of the processes that a child learns and uses in arithmetic are not directly taught. If we do not measure underlying processes and skills, as in the use of Piagetian tasks, we are not likely to find any problems there. Thus, if a child is failing arithmetic as indicated by poor performance in computational skills, the plan is usually to give the child more rote training and drill with the skills. Although it is true that a child should have an almost immediate command of the basic computational combinations, the teacher should take a three-step approach:

1. Determine if the child can show evidence of the ability to perform at a conceptual level. Can the child conserve and use reversibility? If so, determine if the child can perform computations in the four basc processes at the concrete level with objects.

2. If the child can demonstrate a function concretely, determine what problems occur in the use of algorithms as indicated earlier in the chapter.

3. Finally, determine if the child can apply the processes of computation in real problems. Ultimately this involves the use of oral and written problems.

Some generalizations are in order about the second step in which nearly all remedial attention has traditionally been captured. It should be remembered that we want children to know the processes and be able to use them meaningfully; many older children who are not handicapped can perform basic computational processes with alacrity but are unable to apply them reasonably in fairly simple problems. Being able to quickly perform simple combinations is desirable and necessary. However, ''marathon'' worksheet performance is not necessary because calculators are available to reduce the chore. Fatigue plays a role in causing errors. If a child knows and understands the basic processes, can do simple combinations, and can apply them reasonably, a calculator should be permitted to ''crunch'' numbers such as in the following example:

$$\begin{array}{r} 469341 \\ 839128 \\ 743621 \\ +439382 \\ \hline \end{array}$$

Many problems of this type invite errors, not because the child does not know the process but because it stifles motivation, creates boredom, makes arithmetic a drudgery, and permits inadvertent errors. Few adults are faced with such problems after the tyranny of arithmetic class is over; if so, they use a calculator or get someone else to do the problem. The basic rule in remediation should be that, if computational problems are considered to be the major problem confronting young children, remedial drills to teach accurate algorithms and simple combinations should be nonpunitive.

Addition. In a problem like

$$\begin{array}{r} 37 \\ 26 \\ +49 \\ \hline \end{array}$$

the teacher should ask the child to perform and explain the process. The following notes should be made:

1. Does the child know the meaning of the process sign?
2. Which column does the child select to begin adding?
3. Does the child know place values?
4. Can the child regroup?
5. Does the child add? If so, is the addition accurate?

6. Is an error pattern evident?
7. Can the child prove an answer?

Knowing how the child performs will determine the procedures to be used in remediation. The child may need to begin with basic concepts and concrete objects. Another child may simply need to work more carefully because simple errors are made; use of a calculator by this child may virtually eliminate errors. In any event, there is no other way to determine what the child can and cannot do except by means of an informal assessment.

Subtraction. Many children who have mastered addition have little difficulty with subtraction because of the close relationship of the two processes. However if a problem is evident, the teacher should observe whether or not the child can use reversible logic. If this is ruled out, it should be the task of the teacher to approach the problem in the same manner as for addition. It goes without saying that, if a child cannot perform addition, there is likely to be trouble with subtraction. Concepts such as place values and regrouping are troublesome here as in addition. The greatest problem in computation will likely be the need for the child to "borrow," or regroup. Sufficient concrete experiences in teaching will reduce the occurrence of this problem.

Multiplication. If the teacher employs the steps in checking the algorithm and the child's performance, the basic questions can be evaluated. Again, it may be necessary to revert to concrete learning experiences rather than to have a child perform page after page of multiplication tables. Ultimately, the simple combinations will have to be learned by a drill method. Drill can be approached in a variety of ways to remove the drudgery. The greatest problem in the algorithm is the function of place values. Partial answers lined up under the problem in multiplication is confusing.

Division. Obviously, knowing the multiplication tables, or simple combinations, is essential for performance in division. However, children who can perform multiplication will sometimes have difficulty with division. Reverting to a concrete process is essential for many children so that they understand that what they are doing is dissociating, or separating, subsets according to a definite procedure. Thus, $21 \div 3$ instructs the child to determine how many members will be in three sets if they are distributed equally: a simple proposition to an adult, but a confusing one to a child who is not permitted to visualize the process and interact with concrete objects. Otherwise, the mistakes that are made by children in division are similar to those in the other basic computations.

ARITHMETIC PROGRAMS

Cawley, Fitzmaurice, Shaw, Kahn, and Bates (1979) contend that children with arithmetic disabilities make little or no progress. The reasons for this may be explained in a number of ways that include poor teaching, ill-prepared teachers, improper materials, and inadequate sequencing. We imagine that the problem for most children is caused by the fact that neither a skill sequence nor proper feedback and reinforcement are used and that most schools are preoccupied with an emphasis on reading. In fact, most children with reading disorders do not seem to make spectacular improvement either. Fitzmaurice (1980) conducted a survey and asked special teachers to rate themselves on mathematics knowledge. Generally, the majority of teachers in the survey rated themselves high in the ability to teach the basic computational skills, rudimentary number theory, monetary systems, and mathematics symbols. They were much less self-assured about teaching concepts involving conversion of bases, determination of the areas of common solid shapes, concepts involved in measurement, the metric systems, different approaches to mathematics instruction, and nontraditional ways of teaching algorithms. Naturally, the conclusion was that specialists are not prepared well in this area and that the college preparatory courses of teachers should be improved. This would be helpful only if teachers also understand the developmental nature of arithmetic as explained in stage theory, if they learn how to provide appropriate instruction for each concept, and if they can employ behavioral principles.

Many teachers rely strictly on rote memorization of tables and computation. Others use mathematics programs as the basis for remediation. However, examination of commercial materials for accord with developmental theory reveals that they are inappropriate without substantial modification. The important fact for teaching arithmetic is to have a clearly defined skill sequence in mind and to carefully coordinate all learning activities around the sequence.

The following programs are included because they are popular and usually recommended for use in some source. However, caution should be used in selecting any program: none is a panacea, and some do not fit well in a mainstreaming model.

Cuisenaire rods. In the truest sense of the term, the Cuisenaire rods and recommended activities do not constitute a program. The rods are of varying lengths and alternating colors to be used in developing concepts based on linear differences. As such, they are not coordinated with most set theory approaches because they use measurement, a difficult concept. In using the rods as a supplement to teaching, great care should be taken to ensure that the basic principles can be taught properly and that the rods do not become the total substance for the arithmetic program.

DISTAR. As mentioned previously, the DISTAR approach is a highly structured program developed for use with small groups of children. There has been general criticism of the program. The group exerts pressure on children to succeed; children who do not do well are likely to receive a great deal of negative attention from peers and the teacher. The program is based heavily on "teacher talk" and is carefully scripted for this purpose. Feedback and reinforcement are built into the program, however. It has been field-tested widely.

Structural Arithmetic. Structural Arithmetic is a very complete, comprehensive program that can be used as a supplement to the school curriculum. The teacher has flexibility. The materials include concrete objects, cubes, and pattern boards. The interactive nature of the program is beneficial. Each lesson is described in the manual so that the teacher can prepare the necessary materials for conducting an activity. Problem solving is sequential and interrelated. The materials can be used repeatedly and, thus, represent a savings to the school.

Project MATH. Project MATH is one of the programs (e.g., Me Now, Me and My Environment, and I CAN) that was developed with federal funds for mentally retarded children. As soon as these specialized curricula were marketed, the mainstreaming trend was in full force. Some programs of this type were originally conveived as curricula for self-contained classrooms. How they can be used in a resource room effectively becomes a problem for the teacher. Project MATH has been extensively field-tested, as were all the federally funded projects. The program is designed for grades kindergarten through six and is built on a multiple-option format. Each of the four kits includes two major sections: one with instructional guides, activities, materials, and an evaluation/recording system and the other with materials for verbal problems.

Sullivan Programmed Math. Based on programmed learning, the eight programs of Sullivan Programmed Math stress acquisition of computational skill. Placement and achievement tests accompany the program. Reading is diminished, feedback is immediate, and materials are consumable. The program cannot be used with children who are at a prenumerical level.

• • •

Many other programs, most of which are not specifically designed for handicapped students, may be acquired and used. Montessori materials are ideal for teachers who wish to design learning activites without the structure imposed by a commercial program. Selection of a program or materials will depend on factors such as the responsibilities of the teacher and the type of program. Teachers who are required to assist children in a resource room will need to coordinate their approaches with those of the regular curriculum. The curriculum will determine the range of programs that might be useful in the special education effort. Obviously, the teacher cannot select a comprehensive program for use with a child who will be receiving instruction in the regular classroom on the same subject, especially if the programs conflict on theory and order of presentation of skills.

Beginning the program

The initial procedures for planning and conducting an arithmetic program are much the same as those identified in Chapter 6 in conjunction with the reading program:

1. Examine the folders of the students to glean information about their performance profiles.
2. Review the inventories for the special program and regular programs to identify existing mathematics programs and materials. Examine the lists for arithmetic-related games, also (Table 8-2).
3. If possible, visit with other teachers in other rooms to see if materials are available that are no longer listed on the official inventories or that teachers have personally made. If you have a strong personal and professional relationship with the other teachers, you might be able to borrow or copy materials.
4. Check other sources outside the school for materials such as those listed in Chapter 2 for informal assessment and programming.

The special educator will have to develop an arithmetic program based on at least three factors (1) students' performance profiles, (2) available materials, and (3) the relationship between the regular and special classrooms. The importance of the first two factors should be obvious, but the role of the latter may not be. The relationship can impact the special education mathematics program in the following ways:

1. If the child receives arithmetic instruction in the regular classroom in addition to that received in special education, it is imperative that the two instructional efforts be coordinated carefully. This type of shared responsibility can be accomplished in two major ways:

Table 8-2. Examples of instructional uses of commercial mathematics games

Material	*Skill*
Board games	
Math Facts Games (level 5) (Milton Bradley)	Given problems with missing addends, student can perform subtraction to derive missing value.
Activity cards	
Goal Program (measurement) (Milton Bradley)	Given a problem requiring determination of length, weight, area, volume, or temperature, student can describe instrument used to measure and corresponding unit of measurement.
Worksheets	
Money Makes Sense (Lear Siegler, Inc.)	Student can identify any coin as fraction of a dollar.
Games	
Dominoes	Student can demonstrate ability to perform basic addition with two-digit numbers.
Going Fishing	Given mixed sets of objects, student can identify members and nonmembers.

a. Both teachers agree to use the same mathematics series. The regular teacher takes the lead, introducing new skills and providing primary instruction by following the manual. The special educator, using the same series and manual, then uses any drill or enrichment activities suggested in the manual and provides additional worksheets needed in coordination with the content being taught in the regular classroom. If the student does not have time to finish in the mainstream class, the work is brought to the resource room to be completed and graded. The special educator has additional opportunity to employ concrete teaching aids and games to assist the child in performing in the regular classroom.

b. The regular classroom teacher prefers that the special education teacher use a series that differs from the one used in the classroom. The special educator then asks for a copy of the manual for the series or a list of skills being taught. Once the list is received, the task of the special educator is to find appropriate materials (i.e., workbooks, games, and worksheets) to teach the same skills that are being covered in the regular classroom. Obviously this is more difficult than is approach a, but it often protects the relationship with the mainstream teacher.

2. In some cases, the attitude of the regular classroom teacher may affect the operation of the arithmetic program. This teacher may believe that mathematics instruction in the special class supplants instruction in the regular classroom and may deemphasize such instruction.
3. Although self-contained special classrooms do not have to be concerned about the content and sequence of arithmetic in the mainstream, they should. Teachers may select total programs. However, if a child is prepared to return to the regular classroom, the following activities should be used to make the student aware of the types of instructional materials and practices used in the mainstream:
   a. Secure a copy of the classroom workbooks so that the child is familiar with the materials.
   b. Demonstrate common instructional approaches used, such as instruction at the blackboard and illustrations with blocks.
   c. Explain to the child any particular expectations (e.g., using items such as rulers) for that class.

   Perform these activities for several days or weeks before actually integrating the child. Ask the regular classroom teacher for any suggestions that would help the teacher and the child make the transition.

If the special educator cannot use the materials from the regular classroom as part of daily instruction, the skills list presented on pp. 243 to 249 will provide the content for mathematics instruction, including assessment and programming. We developed this list by examining major mathematics series; therefore, regardless of the series used by the school, instruction related to this skills list will be appropriate and educationally sound. Reference to Chapter 2 will help the teacher identify instructional materials appropriate for assessment and instruction.

SUMMARY

In this chapter we presented the reader with a comprehensive view of arithmetic development in terms of stage theory, recommended specific teaching approaches to be used at each level, and discussed commercial programs and practical suggestions about establishing a program. Arithmetic receives less attention than do other areas of the curriculum; little is known about the causes of arithmetic disorders. Instruction should be based on a developmental sequence guided by the child's apparent ability to profit from instruction. The development of arithmetic skill is dependent on the ability to grasp underlying concepts rather than to respond with rote answers. However, considerable overlearning will be necessary for most children to gain mastery of basic combinations and computational skills.

PROGRAMS

Cuisenaire rods
  Cuisenaire Company of America, Inc.
  12 Church St.
  New Rochelle, NY 10805

DISTAR (I, II, III)
  Science Research Associates, Inc.
  259 East Erie St.
  Chicago, IL 60611

Project MATH
  EPC Educational Progress
  Educational Development Corp.
  P.O. Box 45663
  Tulsa, OK 74145

Structural Arithmetic
Houghton Mifflin Co.
110 Tremont St.
Boston, MA 02107

Sullivan Programmed Math
Behavioral Research Laboratories
Box 577
Palo Alto, CA 94302

REFERENCES AND SELECTED READINGS

Cawley, J.F., Fitzmaurice, A.M., Shaw, R.A., Kahn, H., & Bates, H. Learning disabled youth and mathematics: some characteristics as gleaned from the literature and from selected data. *Learning Disability Quarterly,* 1979, 1, 29-45.

Copeland, R.W. *How children learn mathematics* (2nd ed.). New York: Macmillan Publishing Co., Inc., 1974.

Engelmann, S. *Preventing failure in the primary grades.* Chicago: Science Research Associates, Inc., 1969.

Fernald, G.M. *Remedial techniques in basic school subjects.* New York: McGraw-Hill Book Co., 1943.

Fitzmaurice, A.M. LD teachers' self-ratings on mathematics education competencies, *Learning Disability Quarterly,* 1980, *3*(2), 90-94.

Furth, H. *Thinking without language.* New York: The Free Press, 1966.

Johnson, D., & Myklebust, H. *Learning disabilities: educational principles and practices.* New York: Grune & Stratton, 1964.

Marsh, G.E. Teaching arithmetic and mathematics to the learning disabled. In B.R. Gearheart, *Teaching the learning disabled: a combined task-process approach.* St. Louis: The C.V. Mosby Co., 1976.

Otto, W., McMenemy, R.A., & Smith, R.J. *Corrective and remedial teaching.* Boston: Houghton-Mifflin Co., 1973.

Piaget, J. *Play, dreams and imitation in childhood.* New York: W.W. Norton & Co., Inc., 1951.

Piaget, J. *The growth of logical thinking in the child.* New York: Basic Books, Inc., 1958.

Piaget, J. *The origins of intelligence in children.* New York: W.W. Norton & Co., Inc., 1963.

Piaget, J. *The child's conception of number.* New York: Humanities Press, Inc., 1964.

Piaget, J. *The child's conception of number.* New York: W.W. Norton & Co., Inc., 1965.

Piaget, J. *The language and thought of the child.* New York: World Publishing Co., 1967.

Piaget, J. *Science of education and psychology of the child.* New York: Grossman Publishers, 1974.

Reisman, F.K. *A guide to the diagnostic teaching of arithmetic.* Columbus, OH: Charles E. Merrill Publishing Co., 1972.

9 SOCIOEMOTIONAL FUNCTIONING

A review of literature reveals significant research supporting the contention that well-developed instructional designs delivered in an *appropriate environment* improve learning and behavior during the teaching process (Brown, 1973; Gardner, 1977; Hewett, 1968; Staats, 1975). Creation of an appropriate environment through management of special education and regular classrooms requires orchestrating more than the content to be taught; such management consists of several important tasks.

1. Designing specific interventions to *treat* "problem behavior" of individual students
2. Developing programs to *prevent* behavioral problems
3. Planning and implementing personal growth programs to *increase* self-understanding and self-concept
4. Performing *support* roles required by the implementation of other interventions such as medical therapies
5. Creating a positive *milieu* for learning as a member of a group

This concept of classroom management extends well beyond the typical focus on discipline and individual treatments of behavioral deficits of students. Classroom management in this sense means attending to the socioemotional functioning of each student as it currently exists and might ideally be, as well as planning for the student as part of an instructional or social group. Most texts emphasize interventions and personal growth. We believe the emphasis should encompass all five areas.

The special educator must view socioemotional functioning of the student's ability to relate to his or her own feelings, the feelings of others, and societal expectations for behavior within a group. Instructional content introduced in an environment that acknowledges socioemotional functioning will produce more satisfactory results (Gardner, 1977; Hamblin, Buckholdt, Ferritor, Kozloff, & Blackwell, 1971; Quay, 1978).

TEACHER COMPETENCIES IN MANAGING SOCIOEMOTIONAL FUNCTIONING

The teacher is in a key position to influence socioemotional behavior, feelings, and attitudes of the learner (Pasanella & Volkmor, 1977, p. 172). While there is no clearly accepted model for achieving such influence, some teachers' competencies and characteristics, including the following adapted from Reinert (1980) and Spinazola (1973), appear to facilitate socioemotional development of students and the teaching-learning process:

1. Group management
2. Ability to share expertise
3. Flexibility
4. Ability to motivate students
5. Professional confidence and competence
6. Ability to plan cooperatively with students
7. Self-evaluation of teaching effectiveness
8. Ability to feel involved with children and the environment

Quay (1978) suggests that teachers be able to use different types of classroom structure, kinds of reinforcement, and types and duration of classroom activities. Leyser and Gottlieb (1980) identify several strategies such as sociometric grouping, classroom discussion, and role playing that might be used by the teacher for improving student acceptance. There appears to be extensive evidence for the contention that teachers can be taught to manage school behavioral problems, given a broad menu of strategies from which to select (Baer & Wolf, 1968; Gardner, 1977; Haring, 1975; O'Leary & O'Leary, 1972; Spaulding, 1980; Worell & Nelson, 1974).

Preparation of the teacher should encompass not only the clinical model of one-to-one intervention but also group activities directed at broad areas of social functioning that include the following competencies:

1. Analysis of the various strategies associated with the major models of human behavior
2. Selection of a particular set of strategies for corrective or preventive use with individual

students that will produce outcomes consistent with program goals
3. Synthesis of strategies into an overall management program for the class as a group
4. Development of a socioemotional program designed to address general adjustment characteristics of the group, increasing self-esteem and understanding of societal expectations

MODELS OF HUMAN BEHAVIOR

The explanation of why behavior occurs, including its frequency and nature, does not have consensus among professionals. Table 9-1 briefly reviews five major models of human behavior, including associated goals and strategies, as an introduction to socioemotional functioning and classroom management. It seemed logical to us to present this overview before introducing the various strategies that might be employed for management purposes. Understanding the goals on which each cluster of strategies is founded should aid the teacher in selecting approaches and synthesizing them within the educational program. Strategies that are expected to produce outcomes consistent with the goals of the program should be selected; approaches implemented without knowledge of the underlying purposes are likely to prove "ineffective" and may prevent the desired effects of the program. In such cases error lies not with the strategies but with the selection process.

Table 9-1. Overview of models of human behavior

Model	*Goals*	*Strategies*
Behavior modification	To identify maladaptive behaviors that interfere with learning To assist child in acquiring new or altered behaviors (Blackham & Silberman, 1980)	Shaping Modeling Token economies Contracting Time-out Satiation Punishment Extinction
Biophysical interventions	To change or compensate for individual's malfunctioning organic mechanisms or processes (Walker & Shea, 1980)	Medications Diet control Other
Psychodynamic interventions	To understand child's behavior in school To communicate acceptance to child To establish secure and meaningful relationship (Hewett, 1968, pp. 17-18)	Milieu therapy Crisis intervention Life-space interviewing Emotional first aid Play therapy Art therapy
Environmental interventions	To modify social situations so that deviants can adjust to social organization and nondeviants can adjust to deviants (Des Jarlais, 1978)	Child-centered strategies Environmentally centered strategies Groups Classroom organizations Class meetings
Ecological interventions	To identify and treat shared process that is occurring between child and microcommunity or communities within which child must function (Rhodes, 1970)	Project RE-ED

BEHAVIOR MODIFICATION

Use in an educational setting

Behavioral management techniques should be developed as part of the special educator's professional training (Stewart, Goodman, & Hammond, 1976). The amount of training needed to reach proficiency in use of behavioral management has not been clearly defined (Hall, 1971), but all special educators should have sufficient instruction and basic experience in application to implement a management system within the special classroom. Behavioral management techniques that reflect a teaching philosophy, as well as aspects of a controlled science, can be used. Unless involved in research, *the teacher may use behavioral management techniques without meticulous collection of base-rate data* (Tomlinson, 1972). If behavioral data are to be used for evaluation purposes such as program evaluation or completion of specific IEP objectives, the collection of base-rate data might need to be more formal to document change. The special educator should make this decision based on program goals.

The teacher who uses behavioral management in the classroom attends to the immediate antecedents and consequences of the student's behavior (Rosenfield, 1979). *Focusing* attention aids the teacher in analyzing the atmosphere of the classroom, the nature of the lesson, and the overall learning environment. *Redirecting* attention produces side effects such as anticipating, avoiding, or increasing the likelihood of events occurring. The teacher notices behaviors of students that would otherwise have gone unnoticed. Self-examination, on the part of the teacher, and an altered view of the student's behavior and performance are important benefits derived from the use of management strategies (Abidin, 1975; Rosenfield, 1979).

In classes with students whose behavior is more disturbed, a complex system of behavioral management is mandatory. With most mildly handicapped students, however, token economies and other less complex systems are adequate. The use of one-to-one, laboratory-based behavioral programs with sophisticated, expensive equipment is neither necessary nor appropriate. Social reinforcement, inexpensive tangible reinforcers, free time, and token economies or check-mark systems tied to contracts are sufficient for most students and can be used with any model or delivery system. The more complex the system, the greater the amount of paperwork and disruption of planning and instructional time.

Legal issues. As the use of behavioral management techniques has become more common among human service professions, concern about the need to protect the human rights of clients has increased (Grambrill, 1977; Martin, 1975; Nay, 1976). Recent litigation has resulted in several judicial decisions concerning the rights of clients and forms of treatments delivered by members of various helping professions identified as behavior change agents. General guidelines appeared in *Law and Behavior* (''Quarterly Analysis,'' 1976) and were summarized by Blackham and Silberman (1980) as follows:

1. The behavior change agent should make a behaviorally specific description of the client's problems and needs.
2. Intervention or treatment goals should also be stated in behavioral terms with a suggested timetable for their attainment. The goal statements should contain sequentially arranged intermediate goals so that progress toward ultimate objectives can be determined before treatment is concluded.
3. The intervention plan should be described in sufficient detail to provide the client with an adequate basis for giving his or her consent. Possible risks, benefits, and side effects of treatment should be clearly indicated.
4. The relationship between each goal and each element of the intervention plan should be carefully explained to the client. This requirement tends to ensure that the intervention plan has been formulated to meet each change objective and guards against the possibility of overtreatment.
5. The intervention plan should describe how individuals from the client's environment will be included. The plan should also describe how restraints or limits imposed on the client will be

withdrawn as the client improves and how the client's significant others will be given increasingly more responsibility for treatment and/or rehabilitation of the client in the natural environment.

6. The person or persons responsible for conducting each element of the treatment plan should be clearly identified. This procedure tends to ensure some degree of accountability to the client and the client's immediate family.

7. The intervention plan should be reviewed and appropriately revised on a monthly basis. Periodic review tends to make the plan relevant and more likely to ensure positive treatment effects.

These suggestions were formulated as guidelines for professionals working with clients in public institutions and might be used by every practitioner in any institution, school, clinic, or private setting.

Misconceptions

Any discussion about the use of behavior modification typically includes concerns and misconceptions. Some of the most common, along with clarifying information for the special educator, have been adapted from Worell and Nelson (1974):

1. *Teachers are supposed to teach, not do therapy*. Although teachers are responsible for instruction in content areas, they must also assume responsibility for assisting their students in obtaining important social skills such as paying attention, following instructions, and other behaviors called "attitude toward learning." Thus, "teaching" can also include activities directed at improving the child's overall ability to benefit from school instruction.

2. *I want him to do his school work because he enjoys it, not because I'm offering him a reward.* This is the ultimate goal for all students, but it is often difficult to achieve. It may be necessary to provide some other incentive until the activity itself becomes rewarding enough to function as a reinforcer. Providing reinforcement along the way as the student demonstrates the appropriate component behaviors for school success can eventually aid the child in reaching the goal of self-motivation.

3. *It's bribery*. The term bribery implies that something illegal or immoral is involved. It is no more bribery to reward student performance than it is for the teacher to give letter grades or for parents to give money for lawn care or housework. This concern is related to the preceding misconception; self-motivation is the ultimate goal and is not incompatible with behavioral techniques.

4. *You can't give him M & M's all his life*. Unfortunately, M & M candies have become symbolic of reinforcers. Reinforcement takes many forms; however, the concern expressed here is not one of dental care but of overdependency on the use of reinforcers. There are several points regarding this concern: (1) all of us receive reinforcement of one type or another daily, (2) social reinforcement coupled with initial reinforcers eventually replaces the need for tangible rewards, and (3) reinforcers only serve as a means to an end.

Obviously, as we indicated at the beginning of this topic, many teachers do not apply behavior modification in the strictest clinical sense, but behavioral management takes place each day within the classroom and can become a useful tool in the daily operation of the class. The educator must balance some of the concerns about using behavioral techniques with the realities of interpersonal functioning. The following points, some of which are adapted from Reinert (1980), should be considered in reconciling the desire to help children with the reluctance to implement behavioral change strategies:

1. Behavior modification is neither the perfect solution nor the sole means of classroom management.

2. The use of behavior modification techniques does not replace the need for good teaching but can aid the teacher in transmitting proper content.

3. Social reinforcement is a component of daily life.

4. Proper application of behavioral principles helps the teacher avoid conflict between those who support the use of token reinforcers and those who

favor only internal controls because the ultimate goal of management is to aid the child in achieving self-control and motivation.

5. Using behavioral strategies does not eliminate the use of common sense in teaching; sometimes changes must be made and plans altered as a result of unpredicted events in the classroom.

6. A common complaint is that behavior management is not fair because one child is reinforced when others are not. The solution is that all students receive some form of reinforcement for good efforts just as adults receive reinforcement in the form of praise, raises, and promotions. Also, high achievers receive many rewards that low achievers do not.

7. A major value is the emphasis on systematic observations of what is actually happening to the child in the classroom.

8. *"Behavior modification is not a panacea that can effectively solve all problems of all children"* (Walker & Shea, 1980, p. 3).

Some educators seem to be reluctant to employ behavior modification strategies, perceiving them to be clinical tools with too much potential for harm to be used in schools. "Most teachers feel a deep obligation to children and are fearful of the ethical implications that manipulation raises. As long as teachers are aware of this powerful tool and desire to help rather than hurt children, there appears to be no real danger of misusing it in the classroom" (Reinert, 1980, p. 92). Armed with proper information, an awareness of the responsibility inherent in teaching, and a genuine desire to properly serve students, a well-trained educator can implement behavioral strategies that will impact socioemotional functioning and academic performance.

Principles

Behaviorists define behavior as any activity of a person that can be *observed, measured,* and *analyzed,* excluding biochemical and physiological processes (Roberts, 1975). This definition is important for special educators to understand. Application of behavior modification requires that the teacher employ precise strategies in observation, measurement, and analysis rather than communicate in general terms that do not consistently convey true meaning, such as "good," "aggressive," or "pleasant." Behaviors of major concern in behavioral strategies are those considered to be *operant.* "Operant behaviors are those which operate on the environment and are changed by subsequent environmental events" (Neisworth & Smith, 1973, p. 44). That is, operant behaviors are those which are learned in contrast to those considered reflexive, occurring automatically in response to a specific stimulus.

Operant behaviors comprise the major part of human behavior (Cohen, 1969), making the potential for behavioral manipulation great. To realize the potential, the educator must be aware that operant behavior is determined by the consequences that follow it. Consequences that *increase* the likelihood that the behavior will occur are called *reinforcers.* Behavioral conditioning has occurred when the operant behavior takes place more frequently as a result of the reinforcing consequence (Blackham & Silberman, 1980).

Reinforcers are of two general types: primary reinforcers and secondary reinforcers. *Primary reinforcers* are those which have biological significance and/or fulfill a basic physiological need, for example, air, water, food, and sex. *Secondary* or *conditioned reinforcers* are those which have become reinforcers through association with primary reinforcers. Any event, item, or action, for example, can become a secondary reinforcer. Following are examples of secondary reinforcers most frequently selected by elementary school children:

Materials

- Tape recorder
- Record player
- Old typewriter
- Microcomputers
- Reading machines
- Felt-tip markers
- Teacher's scissors
- Games
- Special books

Children's magazines
Art materials
Colored chalk on chalkboard
Toy catalogs
Hole punch
Stapler

Activities

Helping clean up
Running errands
Spending time with a friend in classroom
Reading
Time with teacher
Leading the line to special activities
Free time with games
Show and tell
Getting to omit work
Going to library or media center
Selecting certain instructional materials
Special privileges
Art activities

Reinforcers are also classified as negative or positive. *Positive reinforcers* are those which increase the likelihood that the person will exhibit the targeted behavior; if the behavior is followed by something "positive," or desirable, the chances are increased that the person will behave that way again. *Negative reinforcers* also increase the occurrence of the targeted behavior but in a different way. Negative reinforcement means response probability is increased because something is removed or withdrawn (Skinner, 1953); the stimulus that is present is aversive to the person who makes a response. If the response results in the removal of the aversive stimulus, it is usually considered a negative reinforcer, thus increasing the chances that the behavior will occur again in response to the aversive stimulus. More detailed examples of the application of negative reinforcement are presented later; the important point is that negative reinforcement, like positive reinforcement, results in the increased frequency of a behavior.

Decreasing the occurrence of the targeted behavior is accomplished through *punishment* or *extinction*. Both consequences of behavior result in the decreased likelihood that the student will demonstrate the behavior again. The key to understanding behavior modification is to recognize that behavior can be changed by systematic manipulation of its *effect* or *result*. The consequences of behavior (positive reinforcement, negative reinforcement, punishment, and extinction) determine the frequency of behavior.

Positive reinforcement

Positive reinforcement operates on each of us every day. For example, if a student prepares for an examination and succeeds, the consequence is a good grade (positive reinforcement) for studying (behavior). When a student makes a roommate's bed and receives something rewarding, such as a free lunch, the student is likely to make the bed again. The teacher who works diligently and is praised or receives a raise will probably work even harder in the future. Teachers who receive automatic raises may do much less. The existence of positive reinforcement is obvious.

The application of positive reinforcement to the classroom is equally obvious. The teacher who praises the child for a task well done, gives points for an accurate paper, or allows the student 5 minutes of "free time" in return for cleaning the play area has engineered a behavioral consequence known as positive reinforcement. Although positive reinforcement is almost as easy to employ as it appears, the teacher should be aware of some factors identified by Martin and Pear (1978) that influence its effectiveness:

1. *Selecting the behavior to be increased*. The teacher must be specific about the targeted behavior. For instance, the teacher should reward completion of a paper with 100 percent accuracy, putting on gym shoes, replacing books on a shelf, or waiting in line without talking, rather than a broad, general behavioral category such as "being good," "doing well," "socializing," or "working." Without specificity, the process of positive reinforcement becomes confusing to the students (what is "good"?) and makes it almost impossible for the teacher to know when to reinforce consistently.

2. *Choosing reinforcers*. We often hear teachers say that the children "just won't work for re-

wards." The problem lies not in the behavioral system but in the reinforcers selected; the reinforcers simply are not *reinforcing* to the children. Teachers may think the reinforcers are delightful, but that is no guarantee they will have appeal for the children. Reinforcers can be selected by two reliable means: *observing* and *asking* the children. Teachers often experiment with various types of reinforcers, observing those preferred by the children. Regardless of the method of selection, reinforcers must appeal to the children, not the teacher! We agree with the statement of Martin and Pear (1978) that failing to use effective reinforcers is one of the most common errors involved in positive reinforcement. Although candy appears to be a common reinforcer for young children, the teacher must make available a vast array of reinforcers. Time and effort expended in finding reinforcers that are motivating and reinforcing will earn a handsome return for the teacher in terms of student performance and behavioral change.

3. *Employing deprivation and satiation.* Deprivation refers to the time before the instructional session during which the student does not experience the reinforcement. This is very important in positive reinforcement because the child who has been deprived has a higher response rate than does the child who is satiated. Satiation can be important in reinforcement; frequent and lengthy exposure to the reinforcer may result in early satiation, making it necessary for the teacher to allow only brief periods of reinforcement with a particular reinforcer in order to extend its "life" as a positive reward.

4. *Reinforcing immediately.* Reinforcement should follow the behavior immediately. The impact of the reinforcer in terms of eliciting behavior increases as the time gap between reinforcement and behavior is reduced. Adults can delay receiving rewards (e.g., grades at the end of the year or receipt of a paycheck), but many children cannot successfully delay gratification. Another concern, when there is a time lapse between a behavior and a reward, is the possibility that other behaviors may occur in the interim. The student may associate the reward with the wrong behavior, perhaps even an undesirable behavior! Therefore, the reinforcer should be immediate.

5. *Structuring reinforcement.* Several important points are made concerning instructions involved in positive reinforcement: (a) it is not necessary that the individual be able to talk for reinforcement to work; (b) the person need not even understand the process for it to work; (c) however, instructions should be used with the process for those who can understand the relationship between the behavior and its consequence; and (d) instructions for the behavioral consequence must be consistent, and the behavioral consequence following the behavior must always be the same.

6. *Weaning the student from the program and changing to natural reinforcers.* The ultimate goal of the behavioral change program is to make the transition from "working" for rewards to "working" for the intrinsic pleasure or to obtain rewards otherwise available in the natural environment. An excellent example is the case of a student named Collin. Collin was on a point system for completing work assignments correctly in a resource room. Initially, the only reason Collin performed was to earn points that in turn were redeemed for prizes and privileges. However, in a short time the accumulation of points on the chart became more reinforcing than the rewards to be "bought"; finally, the realization of personal goals and accomplishment became the strongest rewards. Collin worked well from a sense of accomplishment and pride, which was maintained by positive social rewards he received from his teachers and peers. Social rewards, such as praise, had been employed at every juncture throughout the process and ultimately became the strongest form of reinforcement.

Extinction

Extinction is the removal of a behavioral consequence that had been increasing or maintaining the occurence of a behavior. It is a method often employed by parents and has been shown to be effective for *decreasing the frequency of undesirable behaviors.* One of the most familiar examples found in the classroom is the "draggy" student who is constantly prodded, reminded, and pushed by the teacher to complete assignments, prepare for physical education class, or assemble materials before going home at the end of the school day. In such cases the undesirable behavior is delaying; the behavioral consequence increasing or maintaining it is the teacher's attention in the form of verbal "pushing." Employing extinction involves ignoring the delaying behavior, thereby removing the consequence that has kept the child exhibiting the behavior. The eventual result will be a decrease in frequency or elimination of the "delaying" behavior when the consequence it produced no longer occurs.

Negative reinforcement

The removal of an operating aversive stimulus is negative reinforcement. Negative reinforcement, like positive reinforcement, results in the strengthening of the behavior, increasing the likelihood that it will recur. The removal of the aversive stimulus "works" because the person no longer experiences the aversive stimulus; whatever behavior resulted from removal is reinforced. Axelrod (1977) provides one of the best descriptions of negative reinforcement in the classroom by saying that it is "an operation in which a student performs a desired behavior and the teacher removes something he dislikes, that he perceives as unpleasant" (p. 8).

A familiar example is the college professor's instructions, "All of you will do a term paper, 35 pages in length." Many students would regard this as an aversive stimulus. However, the professor may add, "Any of you who make 85% or above on the exam do not have to do the paper." Thus, the student who demonstrates the behavior (scoring 85% or more on the test) removes the aversive stimulus (the paper).

Punishment

All of us are familiar with punishment, since it is widely used in the classroom and in society in general, so we know that it is the *addition of an aversive stimulus or the removal of a pleasurable item or activity* (Walker & Shea, 1980). Punishment is used to reduce or suppress a behavior considered undesirable. Examples of punishment in the form of addition of an aversive stimulus are paddling, making the child write a theme, and requiring the student to stay after school (on the assumption that staying over is considered aversive to the child). Punishment in the form of removal of a pleasurable item or activity includes actions such as making the child forego playing at recess time, not allowing the child to sit by friends, and removing the privilege of using the microcomputer. Several concerns are associated with the use of punishment as a means of changing behavior; these are presented in the application section of this chapter. Table 9-2 provides a summmary of the general effects of the consequences of behavior.

Negative reinforcement and punishment. Following are summaries of some of the major differences between negative reinforcement and punishment:

1. Punishment is used to suppress an undesirable behavior, while negative reinforcement is used to strengthen a behavior.
2. Punishment in some instances means *introducing* an aversive stimulus *after* a particular behavior is exhibited; negative reinforcement means *removing* a previously existing aver-

Table 9-2. Summary of consequences of behavior

Consequence	*Action*	*Effect*
Positive reinforcement	Add positive reinforcement	Behavior increases
Punishment	Add aversive stimulus	Behavior decreases
Extinction	Remove positive reinforcement	Behavior decreases
Negative reinforcement	Remove aversive stimulus	Behavior increases

sive stimulus when the behavior is exhibited to encourage the person to exhibit a desired behavior.

Extinction and punishment. Several aspects distinguish punishment and extinction, including the following:

1. Extinction is typically a more systematic, scientific approach.
2. Punishment suppresses behavior, while extinction is considered a method for eliminating behavior.
3. Punishment may mean the addition of an aversive stimulus; extinction is the removal of a reinforcer.

Reinforcement schedules

A schedule of reinforcement refers to the particular pattern in which rewards are presented or withheld when the child exhibits the targeted behavior. In daily life reinforcers are administered or withdrawn in the following patterns.

One-to-one reinforcement schedule. In this pattern, reinforcement is delivered continuously; that is, each time the behavior is exhibited, it is rewarded. This pattern is the quickest way to increase the frequency and strength of a particular targeted behavior. Typically this pattern is used only in the beginning of the treatment to teach a new behavior and is discontinued when the behavior reaches the desired or acceptable level.

Interval schedules. This pattern is based primarily on time intervals as a means of determining reinforcement.

Ratio schedules. Reinforcement is dictated by a certain number of responses being emitted.

Within each of the last two schedules are categories, *fixed* and *variable*. This produces four separate types of schedules as demonstrated by the descriptions and examples in Table 9-3.

Methods and applications of behavioral principles

Modeling. Examination of the professional literature reveals a number of terms for modeling, including observational learning, copying, role playing, social facilitation, identification, and vicarious learning (Bandura, 1969). Modeling, meaning the use of an individual or group to demonstrate behavior to be imitated by the child, is one of the most common means through which learning is achieved. It requires observation and imitation or duplication of behavior.

The prevalence and importance of modeling in our society are demonstrated by the existence of several national groups organized for the purpose of serving as models for children. For example, Big Brothers and Big Sisters provide direct role models to children in the hope that, through imitation, the children will acquire appropriate social behavior. Other examples, such as Scouts and 4-H clubs, use an ideal or abstract model; these organizations present a creed, or code of honor, intended to aid the child in approaching the world with more appropriate behavior. Inherent in modeling is the potential for *prevention,* which is obvious in the activities of the organizations just mentioned. As stated by Blackham and Silberman (1980), "observational learning might effectively promote behavior not already in a person's behavior repertoire, as well as change nonadaptive behavior" (p. 107). Modeling can be a critical strategy for use with handicapped students; if, through effective programming by the regular and special teacher, the handicapped child can observe appropriate behavior of peers, modeling may serve to prevent the acquisition of inappropriate behaviors as well as the attainment of new behaviors.

Blackham and Silberman indicate three types of effects that can result from exposure to a model:

1. Acquisition of a new behavior
2. Inhibitory and disinhibitory effects (The student notes that the behavior, when demonstrated by a model, results in something aversive, so the behavior is inhibited; on the other hand, if the model is rewarded for exhibiting the behavior, the child may elect to exhibit the behavior also. In both instances, the behavior is in the child's repertoire, so it is not a new behavior.)
3. Triggering of existing behaviors that have not been employed in some time

When teachers place students with models or in

Table 9-3. Four reinforcement schedules

Type	*Symbol*	*Description*
Ratio		*Emphasizes completion of tasks*
Fixed ratio	FR	Specific number of tasks or items are identified, and reinforcement is contingent on completing this number. This schedule is very effective in initial stages of behavior change. *Examples:* 3 points for every 10 problems done 10 minutes "free time" per work page
Variable ratio	VR	It is best to maintain levels of performance. Ratio on which reinforcement is provided varies. *Examples:* 1 point given on following ratio to pages worked: For every two pages For every four pages For every five pages For one page Average *ratio* in this example: 1:3
Fixed interval	FI	Time period is specified; first behavior at end of this period is rewarded. *Examples:* 1 point given for each 2 minutes in seat 5 minutes "free time" given for each 10-minute block of work on reading machine
Variable interval	VI	Reinforcement is presented according to varied pattern of time periods. *Examples:* Teacher sets kitchen timer for following intervals: 2 minutes 5 minutes 3 minutes 2 minutes Children who are working at desks when timer sounds receive 1 point; timer is out of sight so that children have no idea as to time period set.

some manner attempt to use modeling, a clear understanding of the processes and effects is necessary. Acquiring a new behavior may take longer than the other two effects. The teacher should be aware that the latter two effects may take place at the same time that the student is acquiring a new behavior. It is important that the teacher select the model carefully and ask the following questions (Walker & Shea, 1980, p. 59):

1. Is the child able to perform the behavior?
2. Is there some reward in it for the child?
3. Is the model "good"?
4. Is the model acceptable to the child?

A review of the literature reveals several other important factors to be considered in using modeling:

1. A model of the same sex seems to produce better results (Goldstein, Heller, & Sechrist, 1966).
2. A child who is incompetent and extremely dependent is a better client for modeling (Zinzer, 1966).
3. The personality characteristics of the model affect the impact of modeling (Blackham & Silberman, 1980).
4. Results are better if the modeled activities

help the learner identify settings in which it is appropriate to exhibit the behavior and those in which it is not (Bandura, 1971).

5. Modeling can be used with groups as well as with individual learners (Ritter, 1968).
6. Modeling can be attempted through the following means:
   a. Films (O'Conner, 1972)
   b. Cartoons (Bandura, 1965)
   c. Puppets (Baer & Sherman, 1964)

Shaping. Shaping is the systematic reinforcement of approximations of the targeted behavior until the behavior occurs. The teacher must employ this technique when the learner does not exhibit the desired behavior or does so infrequently. For example, it is difficult to reinforce "in-seat behavior" when the student never goes near the seat, much less sits in it! The teacher in this situation is faced with the problem of getting the student to sit at the desk so that positive reinforcement can be used.

Shaping consists of the following steps (Walker & Shea, 1980):

1. Selecting a target behavior
2. Obtaining reliable baseline data
3. Selecting potent reinforcers
4. Reinforcing successive approximations of the desired behavior each time it occurs
5. Reinforcing the newly established behavior each time it occurs
6. Reinforcing the behavior on a variable reinforcement schedule (p. 54)

Following are the major errrors teachers seem to make in employing shaping techniques:

1. Rewarding behaviors too far from the targeted skill, which confuses the student and causes behavioral changes that are not desired
2. Failing to reward immediately; this increases the possibility that the learner will misidentify the behavioral stimulus, and, thus, associate the reward with the wrong behavior
3. Not knowing when the intermediate behavior has been rewarded long enough and when it is time to move to the next level of performance

Prompting and fading. In certain situations the learner may require special assistance during the shaping process; such assistance is typically called *prompting*. Prompts may be verbal or manual; for example, the physical education teacher who wishes the handicapped student to walk a balance beam may elect to employ "aids," or "prompts," such as the following:

1. Walking beside the student while holding the student's arm
2. Walking beside the student while lightly holding the student's hand
3. Walking beside the student, not touching but verbally encouraging
4. Providing praise from a stationary position near the beam several steps ahead or behind the student
5. Providing encouragement and praise from the end of the beam

The preceding example illustrates both verbal and manual prompts. This example also demonstrates the technique of *fading,* the process of gradually removing or reducing the amount and frequency of prompts.

Punishment. Punishment may be the most frequently employed method for attempting to modify behavior. As indicated earlier, punishment may be the addition of an aversive stimulus or the removal of a pleasurable event or item. There appear to be two major types of punishment: physical punishment and withdrawal of positive reinforcement, such as "time-out." The current "back-to-basics" movement may be accompanied by a return of more strict rules and disciplinary action in an effort to control student behavior. This rush to employ punishment may result from a common *misconception* that punishment is effective in altering behavior. Punishment is *NOT* an effective intervention because results are typically not long lasting. This should be apparent to anyone who has received a ticket for exceeding the speed limit. The punishment, a ticket and the accompanying costs, may be severe; however, it is rare to find someone who, on receiving one speeding ticket, *never* speeds again. Many people who have numerous expensive tickets, increased insurance rates, and even speed-related accidents continue to speed even at the risk of a suspended license.

Those considering the use of punishment should be aware of the following points:

1. Punishment does not teach; no new behavior is learned as a result of punishment. This can be accomplished only when a desirable, competing behavior is reinforced.
2. Punishment must be *SEVERE* to be even minimally effective; this immediately brings conflict of purposes because the teacher, charged with caring for the child, faces the possibility of using extremely severe punishment.
3. The teacher will probably be identified with the punishment; the student will, of course, associate the teacher with the punishment making it extremely difficult to develop a strong, warm interpersonal relationship.
4. Punishment may have definite negative effects on the emotional state of the child.
5. It has been found that a punished behavior which recurs is exhibited at a higher, stronger rate than before punishment.
6. Children model adult behavior, presenting the possibility for the child to actually incorporate punishment into a behavioral style employed with peers.
7. Punishment can become addictive; it can become a pattern or mode, almost a way of thinking. The implications for students and teachers are obvious.

In some districts punishment may be employed as a standard practice. Whether or not the teacher wishes to engage in punishment as a regular means of behavioral control is an individual decision. Several factors should be taken into consideration: (1) Can withdrawal of positive reinforcement and time-out be employed instead of physical punishment? (2) What are the legal ramifications of employing severe punishment? (3) What emotional aftermath will be produced? and (4) Can the same end be better achieved by another method?

Although we advocate the use of other strategies, we recognize that situations exist in which punishment might be employed. For this reason, we mention the following points:

1. Be sure to identify an avenue through which the student may obtain positive reinforcement, and try to provide reinforcement.
2. Try to identify the stimulus eliciting the undesirable behavior, and attempt to remove it, minimizing the need to punish.
3. Examine the situation surrounding the behavior to identify any reinforcers that might be maintaining the undesirable behavior.
4. Select the punishment carefully (remember the story of "Bre'r Rabbit and the Briar Patch"!). Removal from the class may be just what the child wanted.
5. Realize that gradually building intensity does not work; the effect of severe punishment is lost over time.
6. Punishment must be immediate.
7. Be very careful that punishment is not accidentally paired with positive reinforcement.
8. Deliver punishment *every time* the undesirable behavior is exhibited! It can become time consuming and unpleasant for the person administering the punishment. However, failure to punish each time results in the maintenance of the behavior through the use of random or variable reinforcement. Sometimes the behavior works, so the child will continue to "gamble" and exhibit the behavior.
9. Under current conditions some courts have rendered decisions prohibiting the use of certain kinds of punishment with handicapped students. Examine the state and district guidelines for information pertaining to your students.
10. *Remain very calm;* never administer punishment in anger.

Time-out. Time-out is a form of removal of positive reinforcement in that the child is removed from the reinforcing situation (e.g., the classroom). Time-out may mean going to a specially designed, soundproof room, leaving the classroom, being removed from the instructional group, or sitting on a particular chair out of sight of the activities. Several factors are associated with the use of time-out:

1. The length of time usually should not exceed 5 minutes.
2. The time-out area should not be, in itself, reinforcing.
3. The teacher or some other person should be able to observe the time-out area.
4. Time-out works best with children who really enjoy and prefer being involved in the class or the situations.
5. "Time-out is not a technique that includes lecturing, reprimanding, or scolding before, during, or after the intervention" (Walker & Shea, 1980, p. 82). Only a brief explanation is necessary; if the children know the rules associated with time-out, the learner will simply be told of the violation and sent to the time-out area.
6. If possible, the student should return to the particular situation or task at the point at which time-out was initiated; typically the child should be expected to finish the task.
7. An extremely high rate of time-outs may be indicative of one or more problems: time-out has become desirable or rewarding; the original situation has become unpleasant, and time-out is an escape; or the learner is not aware of the cause of the time-out.

Satiation. Satiation can be best understood by thinking of a particular food that at one time was considered a favorite but that has become less attractive or completely unattractive as a result of overindulgence. This explains why reinforcers lose their appeal. The little girl who constantly asked to wear her mother's perfume was finally permitted to "pour and splash" a much less expensive brand. She totally lost interest thereafter; satiation had occurred. Satiation is defined as providing or allowing such a quantity of a stimulus that its reinforcement value is reduced or eliminated (Ullmann & Krasner, 1965).

Negative practice. Having a person repeatedly perform a behavior is negative practice. The behavior is eventually eliminated because (1) anxiety is no longer associated with the behavior, (2) fatigue makes it unpleasant to repeat it, and/or (3) the person becomes more aware of the successive steps involved in the behavior and the sequence is interrupted (Blackham & Silberman, 1980). Negative practice can be illustrated with the example from the classroom of one of the authors. Jeff, aged 7, whistled loudly during work time, attracting the attention of the teacher and Jeff's classmates. The teacher made no negative remarks but instead asked Jeff to continue to whistle until told to stop. He whistled long and loud for a few moments, but his lips soon became tired, and he had difficulty forming his "whistle." The behavior was quickly eliminated.

Token economies. Token economies are based on earning tokens or tangible units that can later be exchanged for other reinforcers; such systems have been successfully used with groups of elementary students. The tokens have no value outside the controlled economy of the classroom, but they can be exchanged for items or privileges in the same way money and trading stamps are used as tokens in our culture. The student earns the tokens for exhibiting desired behaviors, inhibiting certain behaviors, completing assigned tasks, or in some manner achieving a specific goal.

The important point in token economies is that the token must *not* be available outside the classroom; such availability, among other things, results in an inflated economy! In addition, outside availability reduces the effectiveness of the tokens by permitting counterfeiting, relieving the student of the necessity of demonstrating the desired behavior to obtain the tokens. Typical tokens include checks on a form kept by the teacher, a graph in full view of the class, strings of beads, points, poker chips, and strings of paperclips (remember, they must be made unique in some way). The tokens are exchanged for items or privileges in the "store" at any interval deemed appropriate by the teacher: weekly, daily, or hourly. The length of the period for which the child must delay gratification (shopping and spending the tokens) is determined by the age level of the students, particular schedule constraints, and the children's ability to delay the rewards.

Following are the major components in a token economy:

1. *Tokens.* Tokens should be selected carefully for availability as well as the ease with which they can be provided by the teacher.

2. *Reinforcers.* The items and privileges must be rewarding and worth "buying." A variety must be included for the group, and the selection should be changed frequently.

3. *Cost menu.* The price of reinforcers must be established and posted. The "menu" should list the items and their price; as in any economy, supply and demand determine the current price of things!

4. *List of targeted behaviors.* The students must have some idea as to how tokens are earned. These should be specifically stated, such as completing a worksheet with 90% accuracy, finishing a task within the allotted time, volunteering to clean up milk-break materials, or tying shoes alone. Vague statements such as "being good" make it difficult for the child to understand what to do to earn tokens and for the teacher to operate the economy. Performance criteria must be specific.

5. *Recording procedure.* The teacher may want to "bank" the tokens for the students by using methods such as points, checks, and graphs rather than actually allowing students to hold tokens. Also, the teacher may wish to allow shopping only once a week, perhaps requiring that some storage or recording procedure be instituted to manage the tokens.

Token economies can be used throughout the day or for specified periods of the day. In the self-contained classroom the teacher may wish to use this approach when individual seatwork is being done; a token system increases student performance and eliminates management problems associated with planning for the others while working with one student. Resource room personnel may wish to institute token economy plans with each period or group of students. The latter case will definitely require that some means of recording be used or that immediate shopping be allowed at the end of each period. Initiating a token economy may require time in the beginning, but the returns will be significant. Daily planning will be greatly reduced, management problems will disappear as students become motivated, and the overall atmosphere will be rewarding for all parties.

Contracting. Teachers who use a contracting system simply establish agreements with each student specifying a task or behavioral goal, the rewards to be earned upon completion of the contract, and the allotted time. Contracts have the benefit of student input, which contributes to increased motivation to reach a goal. This factor also reduces misunderstandings about the goal or the criteria for acceptable performance. Following are examples of contracting systems used in special education classrooms.

Example one. The teacher designed a contracting program using verbal contracts, all of which adhered to the following established criteria agreed to by the entire group of students:

1. All aspects of a task will be completed.
2. Written tasks will be properly identified with name and date.
3. Written tasks will be handwritten on full-sized, lined paper or double-spaced and typed.
4. Product tasks (other than written, for example, science charts) will be properly identified with name and date labels.

These criteria were posted in the classroom at the beginning of the program.

The rewards consisted of amounts of free time in the reinforcement area of the classroom or appropriate areas outside the room, such as the gymnasium, canteen, or open hallway. The allotments of earned free time were periods of 5, 10, and 15 minutes. The student and teacher negotiated the value of the contract in terms of amount of free time when the contract was written. The reinforcement area contained items identified by the students as desirable, such as *Popular Mechanics* magazines, a stereo with earphones, and card games. Passes for privileges included time in the

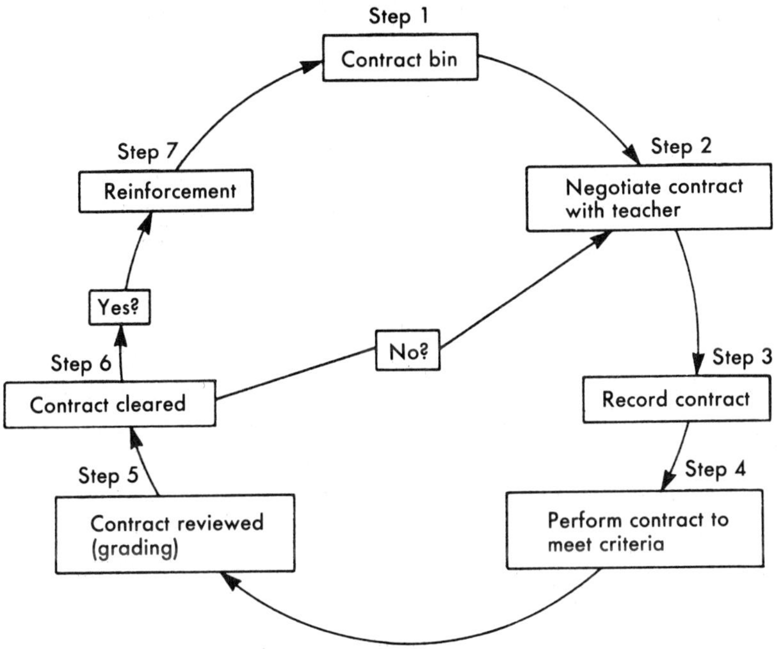

Fig. 9-1. Example of the contracting process. (From Marsh, G.E., II, & Price, B.J. *Methods for teaching the mildly handicapped adolescent.* St. Louis: The C.V. Mosby Co., 1980.)

following areas: gymnasium, media center, courtyard, and library.

The contracting procedure consisted of seven steps through which each student progressed (Fig. 9-1). If a student was at step 4 when the period ended, that was the point at which the student would begin the next session. The amount of time required for each student to complete a contract varied greatly. After a period of experimentation in this particular program it seemed that each student would be able to complete an average of three contracts per period.

Fig. 9-2 shows the data sheet used to record the number and value of contracts. Daily and weekly review of the sheet by the teacher served as a quick means of program monitoring. Failure to complete an average number of contracts was considered indicative of (1) contracts too difficult for the student, (2) reinforcements unmotivating for the student, or (3) necessary materials or equipment unavailable.

Paraprofessionals or volunteers were used at steps 3 (recording contract), 5 (contract review), and 6 (contract clearing) to relieve the teacher; however, this contracting system was also used in a self-contained classroom in which the teacher employed older students at steps 3 and 6. In some cases, when the contract was negotiated, an older student was authorized to review the contract (step 5).

Additional reinforcements included extensive use of social reinforcement from the teacher and other students that took the form of acknowledgment of the number of contracts completed and the frequency of visits to the reinforcement area. Speed in completing contracts was considered secondary to other criteria, but students were highly motivated to perform efficiently to gain time in the reinforcement area. The student completing enough 5-minute contracts to earn, out of the 50-minute period, a total of 25 minutes in reinforcement had obviously applied good work habits.

Date 10/3 10/4 10/5 10/6

Student	Contract (number indicates amount of free time)										
Donald	✓ 5	✓ 10	✓ 5	✓ 5	✓ 15	✓ 5	✓ 10	✓ 10	✓ 5	✓ 5	✓ 5
Betty	✓ 5	✓ 5	✓ 5	✓ 10	✓ 10	✓ 5	✓ 10	✓ 10	✓ 10	✓ 5	✓ 5
Meredith	✓ 5	✓ 10	✓ 10	✓ 10	✓ 5	✓ 5	✓ 5	✓ 10	✓ 15	✓ 15	✓ 10
Kama	✓ 10	✓ 5	✓ 5	✓ 10	✓ 10	✓ 10	✓ 5	✓ 15	✓ 5	✓ 15	✓ 5

Date 10/3 10/4 10/5

Fig. 9-2. One means of recording contracts. ***Check mark,*** **Completed contract. (From Marsh, G.E., II, & Price, B.J.** ***Methods for teaching the mildly handicapped adolescent.*** **St. Louis: The C.V. Mosby Co., 1980.)**

The tasks were kept in contract bins that were actually shirt boxes, each bearing a student's name. Contracts were separated with heavy construction paper so that each bin could contain a large number of contracts at one time. These contracts consisted of worksheets, learning center assignments, and/or task assignments. The student was always required to perform the contract on top; sifting through the bin to locate an easier contract was not allowed! This rule aided the teacher in establishing instructional sequencing in contractual tasks like the following:

1. Complete the science chart and identify the specified parts of the plant; then listen to science tape no. 14 and check the individual chart.
2. Listen to story tape no. 8; complete the accompanying quiz.
3. Complete pp. 35 to 41 in the math workbook provided in your math class.

Contracting can be the basis for establishing *individualized* instruction while also providing *individual* instruction. The teacher designed the learning tasks found in each student's bin based on the IEP and program objectives. Each student also received individual instruction from the teacher on a rotating basis. Thus, the student worked with the teacher at the instructional center each day or every other day for 15 minutes of individual instruction while receiving individualized remedial or accommodative instruction through the contracts and learning centers. This approach had the following effects:

1. Situations requiring disciplinary action were reduced.
2. A competitive spirit evolved around the number of contracts each student completed each period and the amount of free time earned.
3. Attendance problems and tardiness were nonexistent after 6 weeks.
4. Teacher planning was greatly facilitated, and the amount of time required reduced. Contract bins were filled daily for the first month; as the teacher gradually became more familiar with the students, tasks were developed and distributed to the bins monthly or for a period of 6 weeks.
5. Teacher "homework," or grading, each evening was eliminated, since this was accomplished in step 5 (contract review).
6. Students received immediate feedback about their performance (step 5).
7. The teacher had continuous feedback about instructional strategies and student performance.

After 7 months of operation, several students decided that completing the contracts was more reinforcing than the free time and frequently skipped the earned reward time! Student progress and achievement reflected heightened motivation.

Example two. The special education teacher contracted with students individually to complete materials at certain learning centers. For instance, the student would negotiate a blank contract to complete tasks at a particular learning center or set of learning center activities within a certain time frame and to meet established criteria. The teacher would agree to the compensation or reward to be given at the close of the contract, using amounts of free time, tokens, and other rewards. In this case the students and the teacher negotiated the contract from a "menu" of tasks the teacher expected the student to complete. This form of contracting was less individual than that in example 1 but served the same end: increased student motivation and achievement.

Introducing a contracting system requires organizational skills on the part of the special education teacher. Marsh, Gearheart, and Gearheart (1978) suggest the use of a contract checklist in initiating a contracting process. The teachers in examples one and two used such a checklist in the beginning of the program and posted it in the classroom for permanent reference. Both teachers also permanently posted the contracting-process flowchart describing their programs (Fig. 9-1).

Cautions. The teacher who implements a token economy or contracting system must not expect tangible rewards to be reinforcing enough to maintain or eliminate behaviors. For young children praise is powerful. A smile or kind word of sincere praise may be appropriate for many teachers and students. The nature of the social praise varies with the individual personality of the teacher, as well as that of the student. Some teachers have personal styles that yield natural praise, whereas others use humor or mild teasing. Regardless of the method with which the teacher feels comfortable, the message should be clearly given that the student has done well and that the teacher appreciates it!

The teacher must also realize that there will be times when the difficulty of the task has been underestimated and the student has been asked to perform beyond capabilities. In these cases, exceptions should be made or assistance given in completing the contract or task.

The teacher who uses an interactional model and reinforcement techniques must have good organizational skills and a tolerance for frustration. A certain amount of confusion will occur when the program is begun. However, this will dissipate rapidly as the students and teacher become familiar with the system. The rewards to the teacher in terms of increased instructional time, reduced grading time, and improved classroom atmosphere will make the wait worthwhile.

BIOPHYSICAL INTERVENTIONS

Types

Although many of the major biophysical interventions are directed by medical personnel, the educator should have some knowledge of the interventions in order to perform any support activities required during or as a result of treatment. Walker and Shea (1980) identify preventive strategies (genetic counseling, prenatal care, and medical examinations) and corrective strategies (corrective surgery, rehabilitation training, diet and medication therapy). Reinert (1980) discusses three areas of medical intervention related to educational functioning: physical examination, manipulation of physiological functions, and treatment of symptoms through medication. Certain corrective strategies are addressed in more detail in Chapter 10 in relation to sensoriphysical functioning. *Because drug therapy appears to be the major medical intervention in the area of socioemotional functioning, it will receive detailed coverage in this chapter.*

Drug therapy

Decreasing the frequency of inappropriate behavior or changing behavior that interferes with learning appears to be the major purpose underlying the use of medication. The primary assumption appears to be that, if impeding behaviors are altered, learning and achievement will improve. Thus, drug therapy can be considered an intervention directed at behavioral change with the additional possibility of improving cognitive-academic functioning. The exact number of school children receiving medication as a means of behavioral control is not known, but estimates have run as high as 2 million (Offir, 1974). Acceptance of drug therapy in the past is indicated by the statement that more than half of all students with "specific learning disabilities" are administered medications for the purpose of controlling behavior (McIntosh & Dunn, 1973); in 1970 the National Institute of Mental Health reported that nearly 4 million students might benefit from behavior medication (Huntsinger, 1970). Today there is more caution, and educational professionals agree that drug therapy should not be pursued with such enthusiasm (Walden & Thompson, 1981). Although the practice of administering medications to students is widespread, there appears to be some concern about the appropriateness of such extensive applications of drug therapy.

A conference report prepared by the United States Office of Child Development stated that medication is beneficial for *only* about *one third* of the children involved in drug therapy (Freedman, 1971). Johnson and Prinz (1976) expressed concern that "many an inappropriately labeled child is referred to a physician who does not take time to delve into the data presented, but instead starts the child on inappropriate medication" (p. 223). Because of the prevalance of drug therapy and the conflicting views concerning its appropriateness, following is information we consider pertinent to the teacher of students receiving medications.

Concerns related to drug therapy. Educators and medical personnel have some concerns about the use of drug therapy as a means of behavioral management. Although the use of medication has greatly increased in recent years, a scarcity of efficacy studies (Wolman, Egan, & Ross, 1978) and difficulties with methodologies within existing studies (Sulzbacher, 1972) have left a number of unresolved concerns related to use of drugs to control behavior in children, including the following:

1. *Relationship to learning*. "Drugs do not create learning" (Wolman et al., 1978, p. 13). The concern of many professionals is that teachers and parents perceive drug therapy as independent of any other intervention and assume that the administration of a drug will solve the learning problems. Drug therapy, if effective in any sense, must be coupled with appropriate instructional activities and environmental changes in order for the student to learn. Although some writers state that drugs can make learning possible (Eisenberg, 1972; Solomon, 1978), others report conflicting results or data that fail to demonstrate a beneficial effect on learning (Axelrod & Bailey, 1979; Grinspoon & Singer, 1973; Wolman et al., 1978). "Very few studies, however, document objective data revealing change in performance after the medication" (Wolman, et al., 1978, p. 135).

2. *Effectiveness in altering behavior*. The range of "ineffectiveness" is reported by Fish (1971) to be 23 to 100 percent. If this report is accurate, many children are drugged to no good educational or medical purpose. The situation is made even worse when it is realized that the medical profession is unable to identify children who may be expected to benefit from medication. "There are no definite criteria to suggest which children will do well" (Wolman et al., 1978, p. 135). Furthermore, it is our observation that medical research, which is conducted by physicians or pharmaceutical companies, lacks relationship to classroom behavior and learning. The measure of effect typically employed in such research excludes indices of classroom performance. The effectiveness of medication in reducing inappropriate behavior is a point about which researchers cannot reach consensus (Axelrod & Bailey, 1979).

3. *Physiological side effects*. Studies involving medication for behavioral control have revealed numerous possible side effects (Axelrod and Bailey, 1979; Grinspoon & Singer, 1973; Offir, 1974; Millchap, 1973; Safer & Allen, 1975; Safer,

Allen, & Barr, 1972) including inhibition of normal growth, irritability, dizziness, insomnia, and nausea. Concerns frequently voiced in connection with drug therapy include its effects on growth in younger children. Some studies indicate that growth is suppressed during the period of medication (Safer & Allen, 1975; Safer et al., 1972), whereas others have found that medicated youth develop normally while receiving medication (Gross, 1976). Axelrod and Bailey (1979) point out that such side effects may not be found in all cases, but their occurrences cannot be summarily dismissed. Educators should be aware that such side effects are possible.

4. *Psychological side effects.* Some parents and teachers are concerned that drug therapy increases the possibility of drug addiction. However, a higher incidence of drug addiction has not been found in the population receiving medication. Students treated with medication seem to have a reduced likelihood for drug addiction because of an increase in "ego strength," lessened curiosity about drug experimentation, and absences of feelings of elation (Solomon, 1978).

Another concern is that the child will attribute improvement to drugs (Walden & Thompson, 1981), so we suggest that in cases involving medication both teachers and parents emphasize that the student is improving as a result of personal effort, deemphasizing the role of the medication.

5. *Purpose underlying medication.* A major concern of those examining the practice of drug therapy is the purpose behind the decision to employ medication. Safer and Allen (1976) reported concern that some students are drugged for the convenience of the teacher to solve classroom problems rather than because of the belief that the medication will benefit the student. Also questionable is the practice of prescribing drugs to improve peer relationships, since drug treatment may not have an impact on social problems (Walden & Thompson, 1981). In instances in which medication is prescribed in response to the parents' difficulties in management, most drugs are administered in the morning because of side effects such as appetite suppression and insomnia. Since the effects are known to last only a few hours, the parents may not actually see much benefit or change (O'Leary & Pelham, 1978).

6. *Alternatives to drug therapy.* A growing body of professionals are urging that drug therapy not be considered the only avenue of treatment for the purpose of behavioral change and improved performance (Axelrod & Bailey, 1979; Freedman, 1971; Renshaw, 1976; Walden & Thompson, 1981). "Whenever possible alternatives to medication for overactive behavior should be tried with the use of medication coming only after alternatives have been exhausted" (Murray, 1973, p. 25). Axelrod and Bailey (1979) state that school personnel should recognize the potential of classroom or educational strategies in affecting behavior rather than relying on medical interventions. "Teachers and parents who neglect available educational approaches and suggest or readily agree to drug therapy may be abrogating their professional or personal responsibilities to the child" (p. 544).

Walden and Thompson (1981) suggest the following alternatives to drug therapy: (1) home management techniques, (2) classroom management techniques, and (3) self-control techniques. Other suggested alternatives include manipulation of seat arrangements (Axelrod & Bailey, 1979; Burdett-Egner & McKenzie, 1970) and modification of assignments (Krippner, 1978).

Types of medication. The two major types of drugs for behavioral management are dextroamphetamines and methylphenidate hydrochloride. Other types of drugs including chlordiazepoxide and diazepam are used occasionally with students to produce a calming effect. Table 9-4 lists the most frequently used drugs and information about their possible positive and negative effects as summarized from Millchap (1973), Walker and Shea (1980), and Wolman et al. (1978). Possible negative side effects may include one or more of those listed but not necessarily *all* of them. Goodman

Table 9-4. Types and possible side effects of frequently used drugs

Generic name	Trade name	Possible side effects: Positive	Possible side effects: Negative
Psychomotor stimulants			
Amphetamine Dextroamphetamine Methylphenidate Pemoline	Benzedrine Dexedrine Ritalin Cylert	More physical control Reduced impulsivity Increased ability to attend and reduced distractibility Improved personal neatness Better interpersonal communications Improved performance, cognition, and perception	Loss of appetite Loss of weight Insomnia Headaches Abdominal pain Irritability and tearfulness Depression and crying Skin rash Increase of blood pressure and pulse rate Unknown physical impact at adulthood
Neuroleptics (antipsychotics, major tranquilizers)			
Chlorpromazine Triflupromazine Thioridazine Fluphenazine hydrochloride Fluphenazine dihydrochloride Chlordiazepoxide Hydroxyzine Meprobamate	Thorazine, Chlor-PZ Vesprin Mellaril Permitil Prolixin Librium Atarax Miltown, Equanil	Increased calmness Improved functioning	Drowsiness Increased appetite/weight gain Dry mouth/nasal congestion Skin rash Nervousness and/or tremors Nausea Irritability

and Gilman (1975) list more than 40 possible side effects of various drugs. Freedman (1971) points out that children's responses to medication cannot be predicted in advance, making it unlikely that a statement can be made as to the definite outcomes and side effects which will be produced by a drug when taken by a particular child. Table 9-4 should be considered an overview of information generated through examination of current research in the application of drug therapy rather than a definitive description that can be applied to individual cases.

Teacher's role. Obviously the teacher is not in a position to recommend, initiate, or terminate drug therapy, since it is a medical intervention. Medical monitoring of physiological functions must be conducted continuously during drug therapy (Laufer, 1971); even then the teacher has only limited support responsibility. However, the following areas of responsibility seem to be assumed by the teacher.

Referral. The teacher has *no* responsibility for contacting medical personnel concerning possible drug therapy. It is appropriate for the teacher to discuss the child's behavior and performance with the parents, identifying particular examples of difficulties and describing the situation objectively. However, it is inappropriate for the teacher to suggest or recommend drug therapy or to evaluate the practice of drug therapy in general. As noted earlier, medical professionals do not agree as to the appropriateness or effectiveness of drug therapy,

Administration of medication

Student:______________________ Date:__________

Teacher:______________________ Room no.:__________

☐ If a copy of prescription and recommended dosage is attached, indicate with a ✓ in this box.

Physician's statement:

1. Medication prescribed: Dosage:
2. Method of administration:
3. Frequency of administration:
4. Anticipated positive effects on child:
5. Anticipated possible negative side effects or reactions on child:

Signature of physician:______________________
(Date)

Parent's statement:

I approve the administration of the above medication by school personnel in the manner described.

Signature of parent/guardian:______________________
(Date)

Fig. 9-3. Sample parental release form for administration of medication.

so it would be presumptuous of the teacher to attempt to perform this type of evaluation. If parents suggest the possibility of medication, the teacher might provide them with general information, but the teacher definitely should not make recommendations.

Administration of medication. The school should have specific written policies concerning the administration of prescribed medication by school personnel during school hours. The Council for Exceptional Children recommends that a record of medication administration be kept on file for each student receiving medication (Fig. 9-3).

Following are some of the aspects of drug administration of which the teacher should be aware:

A. Permissions or releases to administer drugs
   1. The drug administration form (Fig. 9-3) should be completed by the parents and *physician* and returned to the building administrator's office before administration of medication by school personnel.
   2. This form must be completed each year and when the prescription is changed by the physician.
   3. A copy of this form should be kept in the student's files, housed in the building administrator's office. An additional copy should be retained by the nurse or the personnel designated to administer the medication.
   4. If medical personnel (physician or nurse) are not available, Walker and Shea (1980) suggest that, instead of dismissing the child from school, the teacher obtain permission to administer the medication.

B. Dispensing medication
   1. A record should be kept reflecting each time the child takes the drug. This log should be stored with or near the medication, preferably at the administration location. Included in the record are the child's name, room number, date and time of administration, type of medication given, and person responsible for administering the drug.
   2. The person designated as responsible for dispensing the medication must be present when the child takes the medication.
   3. Careful attention must be given to the instructions provided with the medication to ensure that the drug is correctly administered.

C. Storing medication
   1. Storage of medication should be included in the written policy of the school.
   2. Medication should be stored in a locked, limited-access space in either the office of a full-time registered school nurse or the building administrator's office.
   3. All medication must be clearly labeled with the following information:
      a. Child's name
      b. Physician's name
      c. Administration instructions
      d. Person designated as responsible for administration
   4. Large amounts of medication should not be kept at school. We recommend that only daily doses or, at the most, weekly amounts be stored so that the school is not in the uncomfortable position of having to provide security for large amounts of drugs. Walker and Shea (1980) recommend that all drugs be logged in and out and that one person employed by the school be responsible for maintaining an accurate inventory of the drugs kept at school.

Monitoring and communication. The teacher is in an excellent position to provide information concerning the effects of medication by observing student behavior and performance. We urge the teacher to observe the student for any indications of impact, positive or negative; this information can be valuable feedback to the physician prescribing the medication. To perform the monitoring duties effectively, the teacher should request information concerning the desired effects and possible side effects of medication. We suggest that a form like the one in Fig. 9-4 be completed by the physi-

Student medication report

Student: ______________________________ Date: ______________

Birthdate: __________ Teacher: ________________ Room no.: ________

Physician: ______________________________ Office phone no.: ______

Name of drug: ___________________________ Dosage: ______________

Expected changes in student behavior:

Possible undesirable side effects:

Motoric or behavioral indicators of toxic reactions or inadequate dosage:

Length of time student has been receiving this medication: ______________

Date when medication will be reviewed: ______________________________

Fig. 9-4. Sample student medication form for recording pertinent drug therapy information for use by teacher in monitoring activities.

cian and kept in the student's folder. Parental permission should be secured to share this information with other teachers.

Communication between the medical and educational fields is essential and requires cooperation on the part of all professionals. However, achieving the ideal level of communication has been difficult as indicated in Reinert's review (1980) of a study by Beck (1978). In this study teachers claimed that physicians fail to return phone calls and send information quickly enough and are unsupportive of teacher effort. In the same study, the physicians stated that teachers do not return phone calls, schedule conferences at inconvenient times, fail to provide appropriate assessment information, and appear to give insufficient time to the communication process.

Although effective communication may be difficult to attain, we believe it is possible and well worth the effort. We have some suggestions for facilitating communication between medical and school personnel:

1. Secure the parents' help in establishing communication with the physician.
2. The building administrator or supervisor with direct responsibility for the special education program might contact the physician to initiate communication, with parental permission.
3. Use a drug information form like that in Fig. 9-4 to reduce the need for frequent, direct communication.
4. Take note of the complaints listed previously, and be certain to avoid them as much as possible.
5. Remember that the teacher's role is simply to report behavioral or academic change, not to evaluate the overall appropriateness of drug therapy.

Legal concerns. Teacher liability in conjunction with the administration of prescribed drugs is an increasing concern. The central issue in liability suits is the determination of the meaning of "reasonably prudent action." Axelrod and Bailey (1979) discuss this issue in detail; the following information was summarized from their work:

1. Teachers should check their insurance policy to determine if they have liability coverage in connection with the administration of prescribed drugs. The Educator's Employment Liability Policy provided through the National Education Association (NEA) includes some liability insurance for such coverage. However, Axelrod and Bailey state that *"teachers are completely excluded from coverage if they administer any prescribed medication in a non-emergency situation"* and that this "lack of liability insurance applies even in cases when a teacher is asked to administer drugs because the school does not have a nurse on duty" (p. 548).

2. Members of a local affiliate of the American Federation of Teachers (AFT) have been advised by an attorney not to dispense medication in nonemergency situations.

Teachers should obtain a copy of the written drug administration policy. Our opinion is that the professional has the right to refuse to administer medication if the school does not have clearly stated written policies that include the administration form and storage provisions or if these policies are not strictly followed. Local or state statutes should be examined to ascertain if they contain any specific guidelines prohibiting nonmedical personnel from administering prescribed drugs in school.

General guidelines. The following points summarize the use of drugs in biophysical intervention:

1. The teacher's role is one of support, not direct responsibility.
2. Drug therapy should be accompanied by other strategies such as behavior modification or modification of instructional design.
3. The student should have "drug holidays," or periods of receiving no medication. These may be school holidays, long weekends, or summer vacations.
4. Medical supervision should be continuous.
5. Parental awareness should be maintained throughout the period of therapy. Because

parents are the most direct link to medical personnel, they should observe the following:

a. See that the child has frequent physical examinations.
b. Understand the medication process, including its purposes.
c. Keep the school informed about changes in medication.
d. Communicate frequently with the teacher concerning effects.
e. Comply with all legal requirements associated with drug administration in school.
f. Understand the role of the teacher in drug therapy.

6. Drug therapy should be dictated by the student's needs, not those of the teacher or the school.
7. Teachers should consider the possibility of liability action and take appropriate precautions.

Diet control

The most popular approach within the category of diet control is the Feingold diet, which is based on medical research linking the ingestion of certain food additives and dyes to allergies. The logical conclusion is that the elimination of these items from the child's diet will eliminate certain behavioral symptoms stemming from the allergic reactions. A controversy has evolved over the efficacy of diet interventions, particularly by Feingold diet (Baker, 1980; Feingold, 1976; Harley, Ray, Tomasi, Eichman, Mathews, Chun, Cleeland, & Traisman, 1978; Knapczyk, 1979; Sieben, 1977; Spring & Sandoval, 1976). The National Advisory Committee on Hyperkinesis and Food Additives (1975) reported three major criticisms of the Feingold diet research: (1) empirically controlled studies have not produced results to confirm the efficacy of the diet, (2) no definitive evidence has been produced to link hyperkinesis and allergies to specific foods, and (3) evaluative methods have been primarily anecdotal and subjective in nature. "Although the Feingold diet enjoys considerable popularity among parents and many teachers of hyperactive children, the differential results that have been observed by Feingold and attested to by the parents utilizing the diet may be due to variables other than the elimination of artificial colors and food additives from the diet" (Baker, 1980, p. 34).

PSYCHODYNAMIC INTERVENTIONS

Milieu therapy

Milieu therapy is listed by some experts as a psychodynamic strategy (Reinert, 1980), whereas others list it as an environmental therapy (Walker & Shea, 1980). In either event the definitions given are similar: milieu therapy means treatment through modification or manipulation of the environment of the child. In the strictest sense it is a clinical approach to be used in settings over which the therapist has total control, as in an institution or residential facility. However, professionals such as Lewin (1935), Redl (1959), Redl and Wattenberg (1959), and Rossi and Filstead (1973) related various aspects of milieu therapy to the school setting, and recently published methods books (Newcomer, 1980; Reinert, 1980; Walker & Shea, 1980) include milieu therapy as a possible classroom intervention.

An "ideal" milieu cannot be described, since its determining factors are unique to the individual students and environments involved. However, Redl (1959) identified several aspects that must be examined to attempt to develop the appropriate milieu:

1. Social structure of the environment in which treatment is to be implemented, including the type, nature, and intensity of existing relationships
2. Value system of those around the child
3. Routines, rituals, and behavioral regulations
4. Operant group processes
5. Clusters of traits of the individuals involved
6. Attitudes and feelings of the staff
7. Behavioral interactions with others

8. Activity, structure, and performance
9. Space, equipment, time, and props
10. Outside influences
11. Protection from outside influences and explanation of these influences
12. Flexibility of the program and individuals

In practical terms milieu therapy can mean manipulation of activities and schedules of school personnel involved and others including family members in an effort to reinforce certain behaviors or to avoid rewarding others, as well as to increase the opportunities to support positive feelings in the child. Rossi and Filstead (1973) relate the variables of Redl to the school environment, describing it as a method of organizing the social structure of a setting to build on already existing social relationships and state that any teacher can use such strategies to make the school milieu maximally benefit the child.

The planning grid in Chapter 3 aids the teacher in examining a variety of aspects of the child's personal milieu and that found at school. For example, the grid requires the examination of the personological variables of the teachers involved as well as the instructional strategies employed. Manipulating these aspects of the environment is only one simple application of this broadened concept of milieu therapy.

Life-space interviewing

Life-space interviewing can be considered a strategy that might be employed as a part of total milieu therapy or any other intervention aimed at allowing the child to function within the existing setting. Life-space interviewing received major emphasis in the works of Redl (1959, 1969) as he developed strategies for use in institutions and residential settings and also received his endorsement for use at home and at school. The teacher employing life-space interviewing aims to achieve either an adult, clinical explanation of life events to assist the child in understanding events or an emergency, on-the-spot form of emotional first aid. "The aim of [the first] type interview is to use momentary life experiences to accomplish long-range therapeutic goals, as opposed to the temporary relief" (Newcomer, 1980, p. 327). Table 9-5 lists some components of each of these applications of life-space interviewing.

Regardless of the category, Redl has several suggestions for the teacher using life-space interviewing:

1. *Central theme relevance*. Select the time to employ life-space interviewing carefully; it should not be used too often or in every instance because it will lose its effect.

2. *Ego proximity and issue clarity*. Select clear-cut issues, not those cluttered with subissues that may distract or confuse the child, making the "point" difficult to understand. The teacher may be faced with a situation that would be a good opportunity to employ life-space interviewing but that may be too emotional or threatening for the child to handle. The two considerations must be balanced against each other.

3. *Role compatibility*. The child associates certain behaviors with the role normally performed by the adult (e.g., parent or teacher); these expectations and the role of the adult affect the interview and to some extent dictate the level and type of interview with which both parties are comfortable.

4. *Mood manageability*. Regardless of how "perfect" the opportunity or event might be for conducting an interview, a major factor in a successful interview is mood—that of the interviewer and the student. Sometimes the teacher must allow an opportunity to pass because the parties simply cannot "get into it."

5. *Issues around timing*. The immediacy of this type of interview is a major asset of the technique; this requires that the teacher employ it immediately but also be aware that on some occasions the timing is not right to conduct the interview. For example, it may be impossible or inappropriate to stop and have the interview in the middle of a field trip. Doing so might cause more harm than good.

6. *Impact of terrain and of props*. Unfortunately the need for life-space interviewing never seems to present itself in an ideal setting. There-

Table 9-5. Aspects of life-space interviewing

Subcategory or goals	*Possible strategies*
Emotional first aid on the spot	
Drain off of frustration acidity	Demonstrate empathy and understanding. Agree with and support child. Explain reason for particular stimulus that may have triggered event.
Support for management of panic, fury, and guilt	Remain near the child. Remain calm. Be supportive once tantrum or other extreme behavior is over. Be protective.
Communication maintenance in moments of relationship decay	Keep up dialogue to prevent child from totally withdrawing. Allow child to "save face." Provide broad range of communication topics and opportunities.
Regulation of behavioral and social traffic	Avoid moralizing. Explain rules and expectations of classroom or school. Discuss reasons why these rules might exist for benefit of all.
Umpire services	Use physical intervention in fights. Defuse high-tension interactions. Point out "fair" action. Help child do "right" thing in terms of personal guilt.
Clinical exploitation of life events	
Reality rub-in	To balance child's perception, provide information to child about what really happened. Carefully and kindly point out inappropriate behavior. Point out interpretation of others.
Symptom estrangement	Assist child in giving up inappropriate behaviors. Suggest alternatives. Enlist assistance of others involved with child, asking them to encourage substitution behaviors.
Massage of numb value areas	Use event to point out certain aspects of "fair" behavior. Elicit codes of honor that child espouses. Point out other possible codes.
New-tool salesmanship	Suggest other behaviors child might have exhibited. Explain why these behaviors might have been better. Initiate discussion of possible reactions of others to these new behaviors.
Manipulation of boundaries of self	Try to enhance child's own feelings of self-worth. Point out child's personal assets or talents. Reinforce any evidence of support of others demonstrated by child.

Adapted from Redl, F. *American Journal of Orthopsychiatry,* 1959, *29,* 1-18.

fore, the teacher must be prepared to conduct it in less than ideal physical surroundings.

Morse (1976) presents several useful guidelines in a worksheet on life-space interviewing. Since both Morse (1976) and Redl (1969) suggest that this might be useful in assisting mentally healthy children and disturbed youth, this list of suggestions for using the interview would be helpful to regular classroom teachers as well as special education teachers:

1. *Instigating condition*. The teacher should listen empathically to the child's or group's explanation of what happened; the major focus should be on the child's emotional understanding or perception of what happened.

2. *Examination of depth and spread*. The teacher gently probes for related information, listening carefully for additional facts that may be revealed by the child.

3. *Content clarification*. This important step is often missed by teachers. At this point the teacher discusses the event with the child but *without any moralistic overtones*. The child's opinions or values may be introduced, but not those of the teacher. Discussing the facts and trying to understand the child's perceptions are the major targets.

4. *Enhancement of a feeling of acceptance*. If the child is not able to suggest a practical or realistic solution, the teacher must deal with the feelings, not the inappropriate solution.

5. *Value judgments*. The teacher should convey acceptance of the child's perception of what happened, but it should also be pointed out that others may have a different view or opinion. The teacher should attempt to show how others might feel and try to reveal the "other point of view."

6. *Alternatives or changes*. The teacher and child together try to identify other ways the child might have handled the event, including ways in which it might have been avoided.

7. *Resolution*. The ultimate goal, of course, is that the event not recur. In addition, the child should gain some understanding of the adult view of the event, including concepts about school rules and reasons for them. Also, the teacher may have to explain any future consequences of a repetition of the behavior as information, not as a threat.

Reinert (1980) points out some problems encountered by the teacher employing life-space interviewing: (1) often an aide is not available, so the teacher has difficulties taking the child aside at the proper time; (2) the child may learn to exhibit certain behaviors to gain attention from the teacher in the form of life-space interviewing; and (3) trying to focus on the child in the midst of a hectic schedule and a room full of other children is difficult. One solution is to have a resource teacher or principal trained in life-space intervention to assist all teachers. However, this is often also difficult to implement because it requires that the teacher reach the specialist, communicate the basic information, and follow up appropriately. The immediate effect may be lost, and very little time may actually be saved. Regardless of who conducts the interview, the following suggestions should be taken into consideration:

1. Treat the child politely and with respect.
2. Physically get down on the child's level; do not tower over the youngster.
3. Carefully reveal your knowledge of the situation.
4. Avoid asking "why"; stick to a discussion of what happened or solutions.
5. Encourage the child to talk about the event, and listen carefully.
6. Reduce the child's guilt or shame with statements that support the child, and let it be known that there are solutions.
7. Help the child express feelings without imposing your feelings or values.
8. Remember that a child does not think like an adult.
9. Reduce the anxiety of the moment, and help the child generate ideas or plans to "fix" the situation. Let the child know the situation is not hopeless!
10. Give the child abundant opportunity to ask questions of you.

Crisis intervention

Crisis intervention evolved as a public school strategy rather than being transplanted from a residential setting. Crisis intervention is dealing with the management of *surface* behaviors as well as probing the underlying significance of the event. The typical or traditional approach to a crisis may be to send the child to the principal, a strategy with questionable effectiveness (Morse, 1971). Instead of allowing the child time to "cool off" during the trip to the principal's office, the heat of the moment is used to make a point. In addition, principals often seem to represent authority figures who talk rather than listen, thus eliminating any opportunity the student might have to explore the event and learn from it.

Crisis intervention has several critical elements: (1) immediacy, (2) coping with feelings about the event, (3) exploration of collateral events or behaviors, and (4) total involvement of crisis intervention specialists. The concept of a crisis-intervention teacher is one who is trained in various intervention techniques such as the life-space interview, remedial instruction, or study-skill instruction (Newcomer, 1980) indicative of the direct link between emotional and academic functioning that is supported in such intervention (Morse, 1976). The specialist may be responsible for designing instructional plans that encompass the content, the classroom structure, and a management plan for implementation by all personnel associated with the child.

Reinert (1980, p. 57) describes some common characteristics of the application of the crisis teacher approach: (1) a person, preferably one with both educational training and applied psychology, is hired as the crisis teacher; (2) a small classroom is provided in which the teacher works with one or two children at a time, on either emotional first aid in managing surface behaviors or indepth work; (3) a system is developed through which the crisis teacher is alerted to a potential or occurring problem; and (4) intervention is implemented at the time of the event, not later.

Play therapy

Play therapy is a form of psychotherapy that uses the natural behavior of play to assist the child in gaining insight into and understanding of his or her behavior, recognizing and coping with limits, and learning to solve problems (Axline, 1947). Following are the basic principles of play therapy as summarized from Axline:

1. Allow as much opportunity as possible for self-expression, encouraging the child to express feelings.
2. Develop a strong, warm relationship that encourages teacher-child interactions.
3. Establish limits only where necessary for safety and to comply with school rules.
4. Take note of expressed feelings, and reflect them back to the child.
5. Accept the child.
6. Allow the child opportunities to engage in problem solving, and demonstrate respect for the individual problem-solving attempts.
7. Let the child take the lead in conversation.
8. Realize that affective changes occur slowly.

Ginott (1961) suggests a few guidelines for the teacher planning to use play therapy with groups of children:

1. Group students with different types of problems in the same group.
2. Do not use or allow the use of ridicule.
3. Ensure that the nature of the group generates some tension.
4. Avoid grouping friends and siblings together.
5. Do not include strong hero types who demonstrate undesirable behavior.
6. Include students who exhibit moderate behavior.
7. Form groups of three to five children with an age span of no more than 12 months.
8. Group school-aged children by sex.

The application of play therapy to classrooms has been suggested (Nelson, 1966), especially in cases in which teachers wish to (1) help mildly maladjusted students correct inappropriate behaviors, (2) aid children in maintaining good mental health, and (3) model tolerance and acceptance of others (Newcomer, 1980). In such cases, the teacher may elect to schedule play therapy sessions on a daily or weekly basis, during the course of the regular school day or during "free periods" such as after school, at noon, or during recess. The teacher will have to balance the desire to have students conform to class or school rules, which typically requires teacher direction, with the desire to allow children to actually engage in play, free from adult constraints. Play therapy is not merely allowing the child to play; that is recess! It should be treated as any other instructional activity in which the teacher plays an indirect role. The teacher must be involved and should not be grading papers or working with another child. The following suggestions summarize the application of play therapy:

1. Set aside a corner of the room as a play therapy area.
2. Treat play therapy as a part of the program; do not use it as an excuse not to teach.
3. Allow every child an opportunity to participate sometime during the year.
4. Allow freedom of expression and creativity, or the purpose of play therapy is defeated.
5. Remember that the teacher has an important, indirect role in play therapy.

ENVIRONMENTAL INTERVENTIONS

As might be expected, the strategies subsumed under the category of environmental interventions treat the environment as the source of the child's problem and the site of its solution. The literature contains three major types of environmentally centered interventions: (1) architectural intervention, emphasizing the physical setting and design; (2) family intervention, including family counseling and therapy; and (3) school or classroom intervention. The first two appear to be largely beyond the direct control of the teacher; the third type seems more within reach. The focus on environmental interventions is essential for the accommodation of the mildly handicapped student in mainstream education.

Class meetings

Class meetings lend themselves well to the special and the regular classroom settings. If properly managed, a meeting can provide an excellent means through which problems are solved or avoided, more socially acceptable forms of interaction learned, and understanding of self and others facilitated. Class meetings have several advantages for teachers:

1. They can be conducted easily as part of the regular routine.
2. Many opportunities for modeling are provided.
3. Extensive practice in problem solving can be included.
4. Practical problems can be solved by the group.
5. The meetings can be used for preventive purposes.
6. Opportunities arise for the student to see that others have different ideas or perceptions of events.

Vogel and Smith (1974) have suggested three types of meetings: (1) open meetings in which class members express feelings, (2) problem solving meetings during which the group generates solutions and selects an approach to try, and (3) decision-making meetings that focus on programming concerns in the daily operation and content of the class. In a self-contained classroom it is much simpler to implement a discussion group; the teacher has meetings on either a regularly scheduled basis or a "call" basis. However, the resource room teacher may think that the brief periods comprising the day do not easily allow for such groups. We suggest that the teacher try this approach when group decisions might be made that affect the operation of the program. For example, a special meeting might be called at the beginning of the period on a certain day to address the issue of "disappearing" materials or options in subject matter content to be included the next week.

Classroom environments

One of the most obvious environmental strategies is alteration of the classroom environment. Manipulation of the classroom environment is a concept more compatible with public schools than many of the other, more "clinical" approaches; its components are familiar and already exist within the school. Also, over the years many of the other approaches have become associated with permissiveness and lack of adult direction; in contrast, the strategies focusing on classroom environments are founded on the belief that children with behavioral problems require and need structure (Haring & Phillips, 1962).

Two of the most prominent approaches are Hewett's (1968) *engineered classroom* and Haring and Phillips' (1962) *structured classroom*. In both approaches the teacher plays a major role in the operation of the class, and both emphasize the teaching-learning process, identifying various aspects of presentation that affect student performance, as revealed in Tables 9-6 and 9-7. In these approaches attention is given to the floor plans of the room, type of equipment included, use of space, nature of activities, and general organization of the room.

Newcomer (1980), in discussing classroom organizations, offers another approach: the *open-*

Table 9-6. Educational goals and teaching strategies

Components of learning (educational goals)	*Suggested teaching strategies*
Attention	Use concrete experiences. Emphasize important cues such as color. Eliminate distracting stimuli. Present tasks systematically. Use small steps and tasks.
Response	Exhibit flexibility in accepting responses. Ensure that child experiences success.
Order	Clearly specify behavior expected. Be consistent in expectations. Delineate beginning and ending points of activities as well as steps involved.
Exploratory	Employ activities with wide range of experiences. Emphasize multisensory experiences. Indicate expected behavioral outcomes.
Social	Attend to appropriate social behavior. Allow and encourage interaction with peers and teachers. Structure activities to provide opportunity to learn appropriate social behaviors through modeling and discussion.
Mastery	Emphasize self-care skills related to independent functioning. Plan instruction to aid student in achieving expected levels of academics. Emphasize cognitive development such as problem solving.
Achievement	Provide opportunities for student to select learning task. Emphasize reading skills. Provide strong curriculum. Structure activities to encourage critical thinking. Present wide range of learning activities.

Adapted from Hewett, F.M. *Emotionally disturbed child in the classroom.* Boston: Allyn & Bacon, Inc., 1968.

Table 9-7. Teacher behaviors

1. Teach academic content as soon as the student can cope with it.
2. Use well-defined, specific, concrete instructional tasks.
3. Select materials on the child's developmental level to ensure success.
4. Provide immediate feedback.
5. Provide some means for the student to see the sequential progress as tasks are completed.
6. As progress is noted, allow increased freedom of choice.
7. Be consistent in your expectations.
8. Alter tasks as needed, giving shorter assignments, more specific instructions, and greater supervision.
9. Enforce work requirements, ensuring that the task is appropriate.
10. Prepare consequences that avoid punishment.
11. Limit verbalizations, avoid arguing, and rely extensively on demonstrations and illustrations.
12. Do not overlook inappropriate behavior or misbehavior.
13. Require that the child complete all work, even that assigned during an absence.
14. Remind the child that the ultimate goal is to return to the classroom.
15. Continue to provide assistance and follow-up when the child is integrated into the regular classroom.

Adapted from Haring, N.G., & Phillips, E.L. *Educating emotionally disturbed children.* New York: McGraw-Hill Book Co., 1962.

classroom model. It appears to be an appropriate addition to a discussion of socioemotional functioning because of the underlying principles, which point out that children are unique, learn best if encouraged to explore and experience, and are capable of a good deal of self-direction (Charles, 1980; Dupont, 1975; Rogers, 1969). Knoblock (1975) advocates the use of the model for troubled students because of its humanistic orientation, which allows more flexibility, increases the role of the child in classroom learning, and allows the teacher more time for personal interactions with the children. Although not all professionals are in agreement as to the appropriateness or the practicality of this model, we have summarized some of the areas of benefit that Knoblock believes will accrue through use of this model and the suggested strategies (Table 9-8).

Although most of the classroom environment models offer possibilities for the self-contained classroom, their application to the resource room must be examined in light of the particular setting. That is, certain questions must be answered:

1. How different from the regular classroom would the resource room be if one of the classroom models were implemented?
2. Would the behavioral expectations differ greatly from the regular classroom?
3. Could the students handle the change?
4. Could some of the strategies be suggested to the regular teacher?
5. Is there any chance for implementation in the regular classroom?
6. What is the attitude of the administration toward such models?

Since the underlying factors in mainstreaming are shared responsibility and cooperative planning, compatibility of learning environments is important. However, if the regular classroom is stifling, obviously modeling the resource room along the same lines would be ridiculous. Common sense must prevail when the special educator is considering an environmental model.

We agree with Walker and Shea (1980) when they state that certain variables should be given consideration in planning instruction even though their role in instruction may not have been definitively illustrated. Variables in the classroom environment include comfort, organization (use of space and type of groups used), communications, movement, privacy, size and shape, scale, interest (how interesting is the room?), color, accessibility and usability of materials, and amount of clutter.

Table 9-8. Application of strategies from the open-education model

Area of concern for troubled students	*Suggested teaching strategies*
Conflict with authority	Avoid direct-command situations. Allow increased opportunities for choice by students. Allow peer guidance in lieu of teacher direction.
Movement away from others	Provide opportunities for peer interaction. Structure instructional sequences that allow and encourage involvement. Employ a wide variety of learning materials.
Establishment of adult relationships	Build instruction on student's interests. Avoid comparisons with peers in form of grades and other types of evaluation. Hold daily classroom meetings. Allow extensive opportunities for student-teacher interactions. Reward student-initiated interactions
Feelings of loss of control	Employ activities that emphasize child's talents and abilities. Provide constant support as child attempts more threatening activities. As tension builds in child, provide assistance in examining tension and its causes.
Feelings of inadequacy	Provide wide variety of activities to reduce opportunity for comparisons with peers. Reward broad spectrum of skills and performances. Aid child in taking note of particular strengths and bring them to mind when child appears to lack confidence.

Adapted from Knoblock, P. In H. Dupont (Ed.), *Educating emotionally disturbed children.* New York: Holt, Rinehart & Winston, 1975.

ECOLOGICAL INTERVENTIONS

Project RE-ED

The most widely acknowledged application of ecological theories appears to be Project RE-ED, Re-education of Emotionally Disturbed Children. This demonstrates ecological intervention through emphasizing the integration of all aspects of the child, the environment, and the interactions involved. The approach is flexible enough to include many strategies to treat maladaptive behavior. The ecology of the child is examined, a concept built on concern for the whole child. Project RE-ED addresses emotional disturbances as an educational problem, not an illness, so that interventions employed emphasize relearning and modification of the child's environment and social system. The latter emphasis is based on the premise that, although the conflict is within the student, the problem is being influenced or maintained by inappropriate interactions with the environment. Thus, the treatments focus on improving relationships and interactions among the various components of the environment (e.g., family, school, and community) and the child (Hobbs, 1966).

The primary professional involved in Project RE-ED is the teacher-counselor, with assistance provided by social workers, mental health specialists, and educators. The program itself was developed during 1962 and 1963 at two schools, Cumberland House in Nashville, Tennessee, and Wright School in Durham, North Carolina; the students resided 24 hours a day, 5 days a week at the special schools, returning to their families on the weekends. Thus, the teacher-counselors could exert influence and direction over their charges and communicate specific needs to the support personnel. Hobbs (1974) describes the role of these professionals: "Teacher-counselors work with increasingly well-defined and tested strategies. They are not concerned with psychodynamic formation of a child's problem; rather they are concerned with the behaviors and expectations of those who define his life space here and now as well as in the future'' (p. 156).

Although the students were ''pulled out'' of the normal setting and placed in a residential facility, the goal was to return the student to the regular environment equipped with skills to ensure success there. The basic assumptions underlying Project RE-ED reflect this goal (Hobbs, 1966):

1. *Life is to be lived now.* Every hour is to be filled with purposeful learning.
2. *Time is an ally.* The treatment is brief, since the goal is not to alter personality but to teach the child to adapt and to interact more efficiently.
3. *Trust is essential.* Adults must be shown to be supportive and trustworthy.
4. *Competence makes a difference.* Each child must be taught to be very good at something to enhance self-concept.
5. *Symptoms can and should be controlled.* Surface behaviors receive major attention because they are viewed as interfering with appropriate interaction.
6. *Cognitive control can be taught.* Students are taught to seek solutions to problems and to analyze events and situations.
7. *Feelings should be nurtured.* Expression of feelings and establishment of personal relationships are emphasized in RE-ED activities.
8. *The body is the armature of the self.* Physical activities are included to facilitate understanding of the physical and emotional self.
9. *The group is important to children.* Activities are conducted in groups to capitalize on students' effects on each other.
10. *Ceremony and ritual give order, stability, and confidence.*
11. *Communities are important.* The staff attempts to show the students that various aspects of the community really function to aid the individual and are, therefore, important.
12. *A child should know joy.* Activities are designed to ensure that fun and pleasure are included to motivate students.

The major application of the concepts of Project RE-ED to the public school setting might be the use of teacher-counselors as liaison personnel. Newcomer (1980) suggests that teacher-counselors should have the following competencies: (1) ability to understand the child; (2) knowledge of curricula; (3) ability to design, implement, and coordinate curricula; and (4) communication skills.

The effectiveness of the principles of Project RE-ED as applied to the public schools has not been clearly established, although Hobbs (1974) asserts that the techniques involved were simply good pedagogy. The effectiveness of the project schools was examined by Weinstein (1976) by means of survey responses from referring school personnel, parents, and counselors. The reported results seem to indicate that the improvement of students was maintained a year after their stay at a project school. However, this does not indicate the degree of impact that might be possible within a public school setting.

COUNTER THEORIES

The theorists in this group are homogeneous primarily in the sense that they offer something other than the traditional approach to education and socioemotional programming. There appear to be two major groups of counter theorists: those who wish to alter the approaches used currently (reform group) and those who wish to produce radical changes rather than altering existing models and methods (Gibbons & Tracy, 1978). Theorists from both groups have several commonalities:

1. They appear to have ''all the answers''; they know the ''right way.''
2. Although identified as ''theorists,'' most counter theorists really do not have a theory but instead have prescriptions or methodologies.

3. They reject behaviorism and Freudian theory.
4. They espouse a humanistic approach to education.
5. They advocate much less structure and more freedom of choice.
6. They resist labeling of handicapped students.
7. They have *no common approach* to education.

Two major counter theorists, William Glasser and A.S. Neill, have presented ideas that might offer treatment approaches for use by the classroom teacher. The approaches of these theorists are reviewed briefly here in terms of application to the public school classroom.

William Glasser (reality therapy)

"Reality therapy is an attempt to teach responsible, socially adaptive, realistic behavior" (Newcomer, 1980, p. 311). The teacher employs three basic steps:

1. Achievement of some level of involvement with the child
2. Rejection of inappropriate behavior when exhibited
3. Teaching the child more appropriate ways to fulfill needs

Examples of strategies that might be employed by the teacher using the guidelines from Glasser are having the child make a value judgment concerning his or her behavior, discussing how others view the behavior, explaining consequences of failure to alter behavior, and communicating total, unconditional acceptance of the child. Classroom meetings are advocated and may be of three types: social problem-solving, open-ended, and educational diagnostic. The first allows for discussion of behavior and consequences, the second is designed to promote thinking, and the third focuses on content being studied (Glasser, 1969). Throughout the process employed by Glasser, the emphasis is on behavior and its consequences as well as options for change. Newcomer (1980) reviews Glasser's approach and reports that some success resulted in its application with adolescents, but its greatest potential for success might be with young children or youths in residential settings in which more complete control can be exerted by the environment.

A.S. Neill (Summerhill)

In the Summerhill approach the primary concern is to aid students in becoming healthy persons, and Neill seems to believe that healthy growth comes from allowing the child complete freedom and self-determination. "Learning must arise from the desire for intrinsic rewards, and the role of the teacher is simply to keep in touch with the individual needs of the student and facilitate the growth pattern in each individual" (Neill, 1960, p. 5). The central focus of effort at Summerhill, a residential school in England, was to allow the child to become a happy adult.

Because it was a private residential school, Summerhill allowed Neill the type of total control not possible in public schools. Some critics point out that students there were not "typical" of those found in most public school programs. They were "normal" and selected primarily from middle- to upper-class families. Emphasis on social adjustment and happiness, to the almost total exclusion of intellectual or academic activities, made Summerhill even more different from public schools. The strongest critics refer to it as a myth, a religion, and a fraud (Hart, 1970).

However, some of the principles espoused at Summerhill appear to be compatible with democratic philosophy and public education: (1) one must have a firm belief in the goodness of the child; (2) education must be geared to the capacities of the individual students; (3) severe disciplining of the child should be avoided; (4) freedom is important, but it is a mutual arrangement; and (5) the teacher must always be truthful. However, most of Neill's approach cannot be implemented in a school setting because of incompatible goals and the tendency for the American educator to seek domination of students as a societal imperative.

DISCIPLINE

Media reports such as *Newsweek's* "Why Public Schools are Flunking" (1981) communicate the attitude that public schools are losing the confidence and support of the public for myriad reasons, the most important of which is "lack of discipline." The Gallup Poll conducted for *Newsweek* revealed that the largest group (19%) perceived discipline to be the most important problem facing schools today. The same article reported that the Los Angeles schools have the third-largest police force in the county. Thus, schools are under extreme pressure to reduce the effect of such "horror stories" and to meet the expectations of society. The result can be anticipated to be an increased emphasis on discipline in schools.

The manner in which schools respond to this implied mandate will probably be to develop or alter policies for dealing with deviant behavior. The precise approaches employed will vary among districts because of factors such as values of the community, composition of the school board, level of involvement of various pressure groups, and attitudes of school personnel. Walker (1979) describes four types of responses typical of schools: (1) attempting to fix blame, (2) involving the child or family in counseling or psychotherapy, (3) referring the student for drug therapy, and (4) removing the student from the instructional setting. Because the focus of this text is classroom programming, the latter two points are of greater concern; the third, drug therapy, was addressed previously in this chapter. We will emphasize the use of corporal punishment and exclusion.

Corporal punishment

James (1963) defines corporal punishment as "any process which intentionally inflicts a physical hurt upon any part of a human body for the purpose of punishment or correction of the person or with the hope of deterring the same person, or others, from committing acts which necessitate his being punished or corrected" (p. 304). Typically corporal punishment in schools means paddling, usually with boards, striking the buttocks of the student.

Corporal punishment has a long tradition dating back to the first schools in Western society; its emphasis and prevalence waxes and wanes, but it appears to continue as an approach to handling deviant behavior. Corporal punishment has been retained in schools as a result of public pressure, legislative action, and court decisions. *Ingraham v. Wright* (1977) was a case in which the court supported the use of corporal punishment when it "ruled that corporal punishment in public schools, no matter how severe, does not violate constitutional protections against cruel and unusual punishment" (Smith, Polloway, & West, 1979, p. 264).

Although negative effects of corporal punishment have been cited (Dreikurs, 1971; Erickson, 1978; Martin & Pear, 1978; Youngblood, 1973) and there are recommendations that the practice of corporal punishment in the classroom should be thoroughly examined in terms of effects (Erickson, 1978; Smith et al., 1979), it continues to be a strategy employed in schools. The novice teacher may not be able to appreciate the concern over corporal punishment; however, anecdotal records of such cases as the *Ingraham* cases reveal that the child was held by two adults while the principal hit him 20 times with a wooden paddle, producing injuries that required medical attention and caused the child to miss a week of school. This provides some insight into the seriousness of the practice.

Another issue in relation to the use of corporal punishment and the potential for misuse is its differential application to students from various social classes. One case (Ramella, 1974) included information that the principal used three different sizes of paddles, depending on the social class of the child: the lower the socioeconomic status, the larger the paddle.

The greater propensity to use corporal punishment in some districts, coupled with the fact that handicapped students frequently exhibit more deviant behavior and are often from lower socioeconomic classes, increases the chances that special education students will be subjected more frequently to corporal punishment. "It may therefore be concluded that due to both the nature of several of the exceptionalities as well as the existence of social class inequities in the usage of corporal punishment in the schools the potential that exceptional children will be subjected to this disciplinary technique is elevated'' (Smith et al., 1979, p. 266). These authors recommend a moratorium on the use of corporal punishment until sufficient research can be conducted to document its efficacy; we agree and urge teachers to seek alternative methods of dealing with deviant behavior for humane and scientific reasons.

Exclusion

The Center for Law and Education conducted the first National Institute on Legal Problems of Educating the Handicapped in May 1980, sponsored by *Education for the Handicapped Law Report* in cooperation with the National Association of State Directors of Special Education. One session dealt with school discipline and special education, specifically the practice of exclusion. Disciplinary exclusion, suspending the student from school attendance, is of concern because of the following factors:

1. The nature of some types of handicaps may result in the child exhibiting certain inappropriate behaviors.
2. On the surface, exclusion appears to be an easy method for dealing with ''troublesome'' students.
3. Potentially, exclusion can be popular with administrators and teachers because it ''gets the child out'' but does not involve physical punishment.
4. Exclusion may be viewed as reinforcing for the child and, therefore, actually serve to increase the frequency of undesirable behavior.

The workshop included information concerning the exclusion of handicapped students:

1. Handicapped students who engage in misbehavior and disciplinary infractions are subject to normal school disciplinary rules and procedures as long as such treatment does not abridge the right to free and appropriate public education.
2. The IEP team for a handicapped student should consider whether particular disciplinary procedures should be adopted for the student and included in the IEP.
3. Handicapped students may be excluded from school but only in emergencies, only for the duration of the emergency, and never for more than 10 days cumulatively in a school year.
4. After an emergency suspension is imposed on a handicapped student, an immediate meeting of the student's IEP team should be held to determine the cause and effect of the suspension with an objective of assessing the effectiveness and appropriateness of the student's placement and minimizing the harm resulting from the exclusion.
5. The suspended student should be offered alternative educational programming for the duration of the exclusion.

Consistently the courts have agreed that exclusion of a handicapped child from school may magnify the child's problems and deny basic rights, contrary to the law. According to the National Institute (1980), ''Exclusion is either a change in placement or complete denial of an educational placement'' (p. 7), requiring the involvement of the IEP committee. ''The expectation that handicapped students will be subject to the regular disciplinary processes of the school is tempered by one major exception: in emergencies where a child or others are endangered'' (p. 15).

Assertive discipline

As a result of the growing public demand for discipline in public schools, a new emphasis is being placed on managing the classroom and maintaining ''control.'' One such approach, proposed by Canter and Canter (1976), is *assertive discipline*. The espoused purpose of assertive discipline is to allow the teacher to interact with the students calmly and rationally while exerting control. Following are the basic premises of assertive discipline:

1. Teachers should insist on responsible behav-

ior. This type of behavior is desired by students and the community and enhances education.

2. Teachers have classroom rights such as the right to establish optimal learning environments and to expect proper behavior from the children.
3. Pupils have classroom rights, including the right to have teachers establish behavioral limits designed to aid them in developing appropriate behavior, to have teachers reinforce and support appropriate behavior, and to choose their behavior with full knowledge of its consequences.
4. Complying with these rights is best achieved by the teacher communicating expectations to students and consistently following through with proper actions while maintaining the best interest of the student.

Assertive discipline consists of identifying expectations clearly, recognizing appropriate and inappropriate behavior for the student, using a firm tone of voice, maintaining eye contact, and employing nonverbal gestures in conjunction with verbal statements.

The general idea conveyed in assertive discipline is that the teacher is the boss. The approach is simply to have the teacher take charge and assert direct leadership of the classroom. The teacher employs somewhat punitive techniques in the process. A film entitled *Assertive Discipline in the Classroom* is available for school districts interested in instituting assertive discipline. The Media Review section of *The Journal of the Council for Children with Behavioral Disorders* printed a review of the film (Frew, 1979). The overall tone of the review was one of concern; Frew perceived the film to offer overly simplistic applications of time-worn techniques that, although long lived, have not been shown to be beneficial, such as taking names for misbehavior and keeping the students after school. Some points especially concerned Frew:

1. Assertive discipline is presented as a panacea for teachers.
2. Punitive strategies are employed.
3. Implicit is the belief that students are difficult and must be strongly controlled.

In the review Frew used the film with in-service groups as well as undergraduate classes. Both groups reacted positively, apparently identifying a "quick and dirty way to enforce rules in the classroom" (p. 144). This is unfortunate because some teachers will see this as "the answer" and believe they have a mission to *control* children in the classroom, allowing the teacher to place teacher rights and needs above those of the children. The potential for misuse of power is obvious.

Frew concluded: "This film appears to be so ridiculous that no one, especially seasoned teachers, would take it seriously. However, just the opposite is true. . . . It is our duty as child advocates to help teachers more carefully analyze a program that presents itself as a panacea" (pp. 143-144).

Verbal punishment

Unfortunately there are many instances in which teachers have verbally disciplined students harshly. Reprimands, admonitions, and even lectures may often be heard in public school classrooms; however, our concern is with the excessive use of verbal punishment. For instance, we sometimes hear special educators and students complaining about teachers who humiliate special students in front of the class, embarassing them, criticizing their work, ridiculing the special education program, swearing at them, and calling them abusive names. In one such situation the special education teacher consulted us for suggestions because a student did not want to return to the regular class, with only 3 weeks remaining in the term. The special educator wanted to know whether to try to help the child or the teacher! We devised the following strategies:

1. We worked with the student, trying to reason with him, explaining that to quit now would mean that he had endured such treatment for the entire year for nothing. We practiced with the student, role playing some of the interactions that had taken place; the purpose

was to better equip him to endure the poor treatment from the teacher.

2. We suggested that the special educator, who knew the teacher well, talk about liability and legal concerns of such behavior, approaching it through their personal relationship. We elected to take the approach of "one friend to another, trying to protect each other" rather than the moralistic "you shouldn't treat children that way."
3. We suggested, as a last resort, that the special educator talk with the principal. In this case the principal was a strong leader with a great deal of rapport with the faculty; he also would realize that the situation would have to be addressed indirectly to avoid jeopardizing the teacher's position with the faculty.
4. We planned an in-service training seminar for the entire faculty to deal with this type of behavior. We developed its content for broad application rather than direction at one teacher.

Fortunately, in the preceding example, information consultation about legal concerns of such treatment produced results. In other cases, the special educator may not be so successful. As suggested by Marsh, Gearheart, and Gearheart (1978), an Omega list, that is, a list of teachers with whom students *SHOULD NOT* be placed, may have to be prepared. Use of the planning matrix in Chapter 3 will assist the teacher in identifying such variables as the verbal manner of regular class teacher before placement. In instances in which there is no alternative and the child must be placed in the classroom of an abusive teacher, a plan, such as that presented in the preceding outline, might be considered. Verbal abuse can be as damaging as corporal punishment, or more so, to the development of a child. Special students are likely to be targeted by unprofessional teachers and peers.

Teacher's role

We expect special educators to be well equipped to manage behavior in the classroom through a variety of strategies such as those covered in this text; however, we also expect that a given mainstream classroom may not provide such sensitive handling of special students. The special educator may anticipate that special students will experience more disciplinary problems in the mainstream classroom than other students; thus, becoming knowledgeable about school disciplinary procedures cannot be delayed until all other aspects of the program are in order. The teacher who is newly employed by a district should acquire a clearly written set of regulations on discipline and policies governing student conduct because the special educator may have to assume the following responsibilities:

1. *Bailing out the students*. The special educator may have to "run interference" between the students and regular teachers. Tactful intercession may be required in dealing with students who have difficulties, listening to complaints from other teachers without becoming too defensive of students, and serving as something of a "probation officer" within the school.

2. *Justifying the establishment*. When examined, some school rules do not seem to make much sense. However, the students must accept them and learn to abide by them or at least not get caught breaking them. The special educator may need to explain the rules, the perceived or stated reasons for them, and the consequences of breaking them. A lecturing, moralistic approach probably will not have much effect on student behavior. Instead, we suggest a realistic approach that conveys the idea that, if the student wants to stay out of trouble and "make it," this is the way it must be. For example, many schools have rules prohibiting the chewing of gum by students in the classroom. Typically this rule invites violation. The special educator may not care whether the students chew gum, but it is a rule. Therefore, the teacher may elect to explain that it probably stems from problems maintaining the building and that it must be enforced for all parties, teacher included, to stay out of trouble.

3. *Teaching coping strategies*. The special edu-

cator should thoroughly review all rules and regulations with the students, describing desired behaviors and consequences of inappropriate behaviors. Once the students understand the school's rules and policies, discussions can ensue concerning how to cope with them. For example, if it is a rule that students may not go to the restroom except at appointed times, the special educator needs to assist the students in generating ideas for coping, which might include going to the restroom at every proper opportunity regardless of whether the child really needs to or not. The special educator may actually rehearse proper behavior for particular classes. For example, if Mrs. Volker, the teacher of the mainstream class, has a rule that only materials related to the activity may be on the desk, the handicapped student is drilled on the fact that Mrs. Volker insists on this. Although both teacher and child may tacitly agree that Mrs. Volker's rule is not important, the student must cope with it. Preventing inappropriate behavior might be one of the greatest contributions the teacher can make to the development of the students.

4. *Treating the children as people.* The teacher must operate a classroom as part of the overall system. Therefore, some meshing of school rules and personal policies must take place. Once any differences have been philosophically or literally reconciled, the teacher can proceed to manage the classroom of students. The degree of humor, empathy, reasoning, and control employed will vary with the individual teacher. However, the overall objective is to prepare the children to function in a society which has rules by which they must abide. The rule of thumb is to treat them with dignity; perhaps the golden rule might apply in this area.

Discipline has two dimensions: the school's procedures for handling deviant behavior and the teacher's method for managing the individual classroom. The teacher's discipline is generally affected by previous experiences, knowledge of a variety of strategies, and personal value system. Stress may occur when the teacher's system of discipline conflicts with the philosophy and policy of the school. The teacher who is opposed to the use of corporal punishment as employed in a district may experience extreme anxiety and concern and even face harrassment and the threat of dismissal. The novice teacher who bursts into tears when required to "witness" the paddling of a kindergarten student by the principal may not be able to reconcile this disparity of values.

Common types of behavioral problems

Isser, Quay, and Love (1980) suggest that most reported behavioral deviance can be accounted for by four independent dimensions of behavior, the first three of which appear to be most directly related to classroom behavior:

Conduct disorders
- Overt aggression
- Disruptiveness
- Negativism
- Irresponsibility
- Defiance of authority

Anxiety-withdrawal
- Overanxiety
- Social withdrawal
- Seclusiveness
- Shyness
- Sensitivity

Immaturity
- Preoccupation
- Short attention span
- Passivity
- Daydreaming
- Sluggishness

Socialized aggression
- Gang activities
- Cooperative stealing
- Truancy

Erickson (1978) identifies commonly referred problems as hyperactivity, disruptive behavior, underachievement, and social withdrawal. Blackham and Silberman (1980) describe classroom problems as inattention, forgetting assignments, out-of-seat behavior, chronic misbehavior, hyperactivity, and disruptive noise. Stainback, Stainback, and Dedrick (1979) present a discussion of maladaptive behaviors that includes aggressiveness, withdrawal, self-stimulation, and self-injury. Gardner (1977) lists characteristics including shyness and sensitivity, defiance of authority, immaturity, antisocial behavior, inattention, chronic rule breaking, and excessive attention-getting behavior. Examination of these lists makes it obvious that discussion of types of behavioral problems could be a major undertaking; therefore, we have elected to focus our discussion on two that are found on most lists presented by writers in the field and identified most frequently by teachers involved in our in-service consultation.

Hyperactivity. Hyperactivity is a term that frequently occurs in the literature, especially in relation to learning disabilities and in case studies and diagnostic reports filed in school records. This is interesting because there appear to be several sources of controversy surrounding its use. Following are a number of issues related to hyperactivity as garnered from a review of the literature:

1. *What behaviors constitute hyperactivity?* Among the list of characteristics associated with hyperactivity, compiled from various sources, are excessive motor activity, short attention span, poor concentration, impulsivity, frustration, unpredictability, and irritability. Thus, the statement that a child is hyperactive presents only a general description of behavior exhibited. The basic question underlying the controversy is whether hyperactivity is, in fact, a separate and distinct condition or entity. There has been increasing pressure to reveal the existence of a medically identifiable entity (Grinspoon & Singer, 1973). ''In fact, whether there is such an entity as the hyperkinetic impulse disorder and what its nature and origin are, remain matters for debate'' (Axelrod & Bailey, 1979, p. 544).

Thus, although a term is employed extensively, it may not consistently connote the same type of behavior. The implications are great, but the primary one is that no programming can be built on such nonspecific terminology as hyperactivity. Assigning the label to a child does not really communicate information to the teacher concerning the child's performance; it appears to communicate something negative about the child rather than specific information.

''When a teacher complains about hyperactivity, she may be responding to many factors, such as possible byproducts of the problem, including the child's incomplete work, not attending when she speaks, and the target child's adverse influence on the other children'' (Erickson, 1978, p. 261). The professional attempting to deal with the case could have difficulty in designing treatment based on just the teacher's complaint of hyperactivity, without the knowledge of the specific behavior that the teacher associates with the term.

2. *What causes hyperactivity?* Writers seem to be convinced that hyperactivity, in addition to being more than one type of behavior, is produced by more than one cause (Freeman, 1976; Johnson, 1981; Sandoval, Lambert, & Sassone, 1981; Zinna, 1979). Hyperactivity cannot be treated as an entity with a single causative source; rather, etiological factors may include genetic, organic, psychogenic, and environmental factors or combinations of these (Johnson, 1981).

3. *Are all hyperactive children alike?* Hyperactivity is not a single entity; there appear to be subgroups within the population identified as hyperactive (Williams, Cram, Tausig, and Webster, 1978). Hyperactivity will never be linked solely to one cause, and not all hyperactive children should be treated alike (Sandoval et al., 1981, p. 117). Many professionals believe that each child, rather than being labeled hyperactive, should be viewed individually to provide more accurate and specific information about performance.

Examining the concept of hyperactivity raises more questions than it answers. Although we recognize that use of the term continues, we recommend that teachers consider applying more relevant and informative terms: instead of saying that the child is hyperactive, report that the student completes only 4% of the work in an independent setting, talks to seatmates 91% of the time sampled, never exhibits eye contact during teacher-directed activities, or is out of the seat 47 out of every 60 minutes.

A final note concerning hyperactivity and its use as a label: in addition to being unrelated to specific programming, use of the label can be detrimental in another way. The frequency with which the child demonstrates the targeted behaviors may fluctuate. Thus, to label the child as hyperactive permanently may cause the following problems (Sandoval et al., 1981):

1. Those around the child may group all "problem" behaviors into one cluster and identify them as hyperactitivy.
2. The educator may employ a single treatment approach such as drug therapy rather than a variety of techniques to treat the individual behaviors subsumed under the label hyperactive.
3. The label may divert attention from other aspects of the child's problem, such as learning problems.

Aggressiveness. There appear to be two common types of aggressive behavior that frequently elicit concern from parents and teachers: physical and verbal aggression. The degree of tolerance exhibited by an individual teacher or school system is determined by factors such as a threat to the physical safety of the child and others, the degree to which the behavior is disruptive to the class, and the personal level of tolerance of the teacher. Other than physical injury, no consistent cutoff point appears to separate "appropriate" aggressive behavior from "inappropriate" aggressive behavior. The line of appropriateness seems to be relevant, making the teacher's description of a child as aggressive a very subjective one.

Use of the term aggressive suffers from many of the same problems as the label hyperactive. We recommend that the teacher rely on more specific descriptions of the behavior, such as the number of times the child hits a seatmate each day, the frequency of "talking back" behavior, and the duration of tantrums and yelling behavior. The collection of this type of data will produce better programming strategies and, in turn, more desirable results for the teacher and child.

Once the specific types of aggressive behavior have been identified, interventions such as the following can be designed to treat them:

1. Negative reinforcement
2. "Time-out"
3. Token economies
4. Social reinforcement for competing behaviors
5. Extinction

A review of the earlier portions of this chapter will acquaint the reader with the specific steps for application of these strategies.

BEHAVIORAL PROBLEMS IN THE CLASSROOM

Teachers in the mainstream, as well as the special classroom, are expected to deal with student behavior daily. The implementation of P.L. 94-142 prompted much concern on the part of regular classroom teachers about having to deal with deviant behavior from special students. We agree with Gardner's statement (1977) that "in many school systems, management problems are prevalent" (p. 5). Some students are unmotivated and disinterested, engage in truancy, defy rules, and exhibit other behaviors incompatible with academic achievement. However, handicapped students do not have a "corner of the market" when it comes to these behaviors. The concern expressed by educators about mainstreaming handicapped students and having to deal with "problem behavior" may be based on biased expectations.

Algozzine (1980) reviewed the literature addressing behavioral disturbance as a function of the student's interaction with an ecosystem (environment) (Rhodes, 1967, 1970; Rhodes and Paul, 1978; Swap, 1978) and suggested that "the child's behavior is seen more as *disturbing* rather than disturbed" (p. 112). This is significant for the special educator; it implies that several other factors, for example, achievement level, sex, race, and facial attractiveness, may be operating in the description and determination of problem behavior and in teacher-student interactions (Brophy & Good, 1974). In practical terms this means that teachers react to the same behaviors differently when exhibited by different students, a phenomenon that we have observed in classrooms.

We have conducted investigative research on classroom behavior patterns employing an observational instrument called Coping Analysis Schedule for Educational Settings (CASES) developed by Robert Spaulding. Our observations in classrooms confirm that teachers react differently to different students. We agree with other writers (Algozzine, 1980; Gardner, 1977; Mooney & Algozzine, 1978; Rhodes & Paul, 1978) who believe the focus of efforts directed at correcting "problem behavior" might be placed on the environment or ecosystem. Thus, we propose, as does Deno (1980), that attention be paid to the particular standards of the classroom in which the student is taught and the behavior of peers.

Since no clear descriptions of common behavioral problems such as aggressiveness and hyperactivity are accepted, treatment based on labels seems inappropriate. We believe that treatment based on actual descriptions of the type of behavior exhibited, using the expectations of the teacher and the setting as a standard, produces better results in terms of improved functioning within the classroom setting. The "norm" for behavior appears to differ among individual classrooms as a function of teacher bias or preference for certain types of behavior. It seems beneficial to examine the classroom in which the child is to be mainstreamed, identify the standard for that classroom, and analyze the way the child functions in that environment in comparison with the standard. CASES permits this in the following ways:

1. The observer ascertains the rules or behavioral expectations in the classroom (e.g., having to raise the hand to speak or being allowed to interact with peers).
2. The observer codes the child's behavior in terms of the 19 behavioral categories of the instrument.
3. The observer may also code the behavior of a "nonlabeled" peer.
4. The observer analyzes the data by employing the process suggested with the instrument.
5. The results produced include the following:
   a. Identification of the primary *style* of coping or behavioral interaction
   b. A profile of behavioral patterns exhibited in a teacher-directed group setting
   c. Insight into the relationship between the manner in which the class is managed and the behavior of the targeted student

This information is important because it generates possible treatment interventions focusing on the classroom rather than individual (one-to-one) strategies that do not lend themselves well to group settings in the regular classroom. Table 9-9 contains general information on the types of behavior that are perceived as the most troublesome in regular classrooms and possible environmental modification that could be instituted as treatment approaches.

The approach to behavioral descriptions that takes into consideration the teacher's reactions and preferences, as well as the overall classroom environment, has several distinct applications and advantages:

1. *It aids in selection of a teacher when identifying mainstream placement as recommended in the use of the planning matrix in Chapter 3.* Algozzine's study (1980) produced results suggesting that "regular teachers view certain behaviors as more disturbing than other teachers who may be more receptive to them" (p. 114). Thus, if a child exhibits a certain type of behavior that can be tolerated by one teacher and not by another, placement should be made with this information in mind.

2. *It may allow feedback to the teacher concerning the behavior and the teacher's response to it.* "A teacher who conceives of a child as a trouble-maker may selectively attend to those behaviors which confirm that belief, failing to see the apropriate behaviors which the child also exhibits" (Spaulding, 1980, p. 5). Through extensive inservice training, consultation, and teaching of classes in classroom management, we have observed that feedback can be beneficial. The use of observational data rather than subjective, personal

Table 9-9. Common classroom problems and possible treatment strategies

Description of style	*Possible treatment suggestions*
Aggressive and manipulative Is abusive Is destructive Is physically aggressive	Have student work alone to reduce opportunity to physically attack others. Provide individual or small group instruction; carefully supervise. Use carefully planned time-out procedures to reduce unacceptable behaviors. Use positive reinforcement immediately when desired behaviors are exhibited, rewarding on one-to-one schedule in beginning. Ignore daydreaming, delaying, and attempts to manipulate or control teacher and class.
Resistant and nonconforming Is peer-oriented, talkative Defies authority Is passive-aggressive Is involved in self-selected tasks inappropriate for situation	Build in flexibility and self-selection. Use learning centers, learning contracts, and other types of instructional designs that remove teacher from direct control of class. Reinforce desirable behavior such as on-task behavior. Ignore resistance, delaying, and other passive-aggressive behaviors. Avoid tendencies to "lay down the law" and other types of direct commands, since they invite confrontation and violation.
Withdrawn Avoids involvement Daydreams Withdraws physically	Establish clear-cut routine and schedule. Provide structure and specific task requirements, including procedures to use. Employ concrete academic tasks. Ignore dependent, adult-directed, "clingy" behavior. Instruct individually or in small groups, perhaps grouping with strong but supportive students who are task oriented. Reinforce all attempts at appropriate social behavior.
Peer-oriented Employs off-task behavior Wanders visually Pays attention to activities of others Attends to distractions	Use clearly defined schedules and activities. Avoid large group instruction; plan for individual or small group lessons. In beginning of treatment, have student work alone, somewhat isolated; as on-task behavior begins to emerge, reinforce it strongly, and begin to allow student to work with small group of carefully selected students to serve as models. Use learning centers with specific tasks assigned to allow child to interact with peers *appropriately*. Ignore delaying and dependency on teacher.

Adapted from Spaulding, R.L. *C.A.S.E.S. Manual.* San Jose State University, 1980.

reactions enables a clear picture of behavior to emerge. Teachers trained to collect data on their own students are often surprised that certain children actually exhibit one or more desirable styles a large part of the time. The teacher may change not only an attitude toward the student but also the pattern of interaction with the child.

3. *Identification of behavioral problems in relation to the manner in which the class is operated.* Feedback allows teachers to generate ideas for modifying the structure of the classroom as an intervention. "When the classroom teacher is provided detailed information in regard to curriculum effects on severe forms of maladaptive behavior, he/she will be in a better position to control maladaptive behaviors" (Stainback et al., 1979, p. 111). The teacher who has observational data revealing that less off-task behavior and inappropriate peer interaction occurs when curricular activities such as group work or learning centers are employed can design instructional patterns that reduce such behaviors. The child's "problem behavior" can thereby be treated without direct intervention with the student and without negatively affecting other students; in fact, such alterations in instructional programming positively influence not only the targeted child but also the entire class.

Experiences in in-service training have convinced us that the best way to improve attitude is to improve the teacher's ability to deal with handicapped students. If we provide the teacher with effective, efficient means through which the student can be served in the mainstream classroom, measurable, positive changes are exhibited in the expressed attitude toward mainstreaming. To attack the problem of attitude through awareness training and other such strategies has been shown to produce negative changes in teacher attitudes toward mainstreaming; that is, their attitudes became more negative than before. We explain this by the fact that, once information is acquired concerning the various types of handicaps, the anxiety and feelings of insecurity about the ability to serve children with these handicaps increase. Approaching teachers through concrete, easily instituted group interventions produces much better results.

The implications for this in terms of classroom management are that teachers will feel more at ease serving students when provided suggestions such as those in Table 9-9. As feelings of security increase, there is less likelihood that mildly deviant behaviors will be reported. Algozzine (1980) notes that teachers *identify* a great many children as problems, and they may accept a narrow range of behaviors as a basis for defining deviance. Thus, if the classroom teacher can be equipped with a repertoire of management strategies compatible with the operation of the regular classroom, the range of acceptance can be greatly enlarged. This results in improved chances of success of mildly handicapped students in the mainstream setting, improved instructional design for all students, and increased occurrence of positive experiences for students and teacher.

The special educator who is not trained in CASES or some other type of observational instrument may be at a disadvantage in recommending group interventions for the regular classroom. However, examination of Table 9-9 may provide ideas that can be suggested to the regular teacher using anecdotal records or other types of data collection approaches (Chapter 2). Analyzing the regular classroom and the child's performance within this setting may be difficult; teachers typically are reluctant to have others observe their classrooms for fear the visitors may be critical of their performance. The special educator must be extremely careful not to alienate regular classroom teachers when attempting to examine the learning environment and provide suggestions. Chapter 11 contains specific suggestions regarding consultation that will aid the teacher in performing this role.

The teacher may glean information about the mainstream setting through one or more of the following alternatives: listening in the teacher's lounge, interviewing the students tactfully, observing informally, or asking the teacher about certain aspects of the class. If the teacher complains of difficulties with certain children, the special teacher might then have the opportunity to suggest some alterations in the classroom, such as using learning centers or token economies. However, it is often very difficult to institute any changes in the regular classroom without the initial effort being made by the regular teacher. Desiring to change is the first requirement.

If the special educator has the opportunity to do in-service training in classroom management or to provide individual consultation, the range of suggestions that might be made include all of those covered in this chapter. In addition, Chapter 11 presents group strategies for promoting socioemotional growth; these are directed primarily at assisting the regular classroom teacher in accommodating the mildly handicapped student.

RELATED SOCIOEMOTIONAL PROBLEMS

Drug abuse

Drug abuse is the use of drugs in a manner inconsistent with medical, social, and legal regulations or norms. Previously, this might have been considered a problem indigenous only to high school populations, but current media reports seem to indicate that drug abuse is increasingly becoming a problem in elementary schools as well. Children and youth have experimented with various types of drugs including heroin, cocaine, LSD, and marijuana. Although obviously much of the concern focuses on the teenage population, drug use in elementary school, even in small numbers, must be considered a serious problem by teachers and parents.

The reasons for the use of drugs in our culture are difficult to ascertain. We reviewed the literature on drug abuse by adolescents and younger students and discovered a few common explanations as summarized here:

1. Feelings of alienation, rejection, and isolation
2. Peer pressure
3. Curiosity
4. Self-treatment for uncontrolled drives associated with puberty
5. Family dynamics and stresses

Following are the types of drugs employed, which vary as determined by the personality of the user, popularity of certain drugs among peer groups, availability of types of drugs, and physiological effects produced by different drugs:

Narcotics: opiates such as opium, heroin, morphine, and codeine

Sedatives and hypnotics: tranquilizers and sleeping pills (barbiturates)

Stimulants: amphetamines, cocaine, and diet pills

Hallucinogens: LSD, mescaline, and peyote

Solvents: glue, gasoline fumes, lighter fluid, paint thinner, and cleaning fluid

Cannabis: marijuana and hashish

Drug overdose (drug poisoning) is a serious, potentially life-threatening reaction. Because of the increased use of drugs among schoolchildren, teachers should be aware of types of substances used by students and signs of toxicity. If indicated, first aid or immediate attention of medical authorities is necessary. The teacher should be aware of school policies and procedures pertaining to drug possession and use. Table 9-10 is a list of common street drugs and signs of toxicity.

Alcoholism

Some children begin drinking at an early age, and many have taken a drink before their late teens. According to some estimates, a third of teenagers drink. The degree of abuse of alcohol among children is not known, but reports of a few serious cases are enough to alert us to its presence as a problem related to school performance. Peer pressure figures prominently in the use of alcohol; parent modeling may also be a strong influence.

Once alcohol is used frequently by the student, it can be abused for the same reasons that operate in cases of adult abuse: to avoid stress and disappointment and to reduce anxiety. The teacher confronted with a case of alcoholism must realize that dealing with such a problem requires personnel with specific, professional training. To admonish the child to quit is not only ineffective but may also cause additional emotional stress.

Table 9-10. Common drugs and signs of toxicity

Drug	*Mild toxicity*	*Severe overdose*
Opiates		
Heroin, morphine, meperidine (Demerol), methadone	"Nodding" drowsiness; small pupils; urinary retention; slow and shallow breathing; skin scars and subcutaneous abscesses; duration, 4 to 6 hours (methadone: duration to 24 hours)	Coma; pinpoint pupils; slow, irregular respiration
Depressants		
Barbiturates	Confusion, rousable drowsiness, delirium, ataxia	Stupor to coma; pupils reactive, usually constricted; respiration and blood pressure depressed
Methaqualone (Quaalude)	Hallucinations, agitation, motor hyperactivity, tonic spasms	Coma, occasional convulsions, bleeding tendency
Stimulants		
Amphetamines	Hyperactivity, aggressiveness, sometimes paranoid, repetitive behavior, dilated pupils, tremors	Agitation, assaultiveness, and paranoid excitement; occasional convulsions
Cocaine	Similar to amphetamines but less paranoia, often euphoria	Twitching, irregular breathing
Psychedelics		
LSD, mescaline	Confusion; disorientation; perceptual distortion; distractibility; withdrawal or eruptions; wide-eyed, dilated pupils; restlessness	Panic
Antidepressants Imipramine	Restlessness, drowsiness, sweating	Agitation, vomiting, convulsions, sweating

Adapted from Millman, R.B. In B.B. Wolman (Ed.), *Handbook of treatment of mental disorders in childhood and adolescence.* Englewood Cliffs, NJ: Prentice-Hall, Inc., 1978.

School phobias

A phobia is an unwarranted and uncontrollable fear with two components: an emotional aspect and a motoric or compulsive response. Most phobias are mild and transient in nature, for example, school phobia. School phobia is defined as the refusal to attend school because of fear. In contrast to truancy, the fear of school is so real that it actually prevents the child from attending. Regardless of the lack of a rational basis for the fear, the feeling is strong enough to prevent the student from dealing with it.

Fear of school is misunderstood by the general public and is abused as a clinical concept. Although school phobia is considered rare, Erickson (1978) indicates that the incidence may be as high as 8% of school-aged children, a larger percentage of whom are girls. Some mildly handicapped students find themselves in circumstances that may lead to the development of school phobia, such as repeated failures, lack of feelings of involvement, isolation, peer rejection, and feelings of being different.

Bakwin and Bakwin (1972) recommend treatments that include assistance in gaining peer interaction opportunities, talking about the problem with the child, and providing genuine understanding and support. Preventive tactics can be instituted as part of the special education program, since the special educator may be in a position to develop a comprehensive program that would include interventions directed at such problems.

Stealing

Stealing is a problem that may be observed even in primary-aged students; however, it is often overlooked in very young children and treated as a problem that they will outgrow. The reasons for stealing vary, but only a small percentage of the children seem to steal for economic reasons. Shoplifting accounts for more than $1 billion loss from stores each year and seems to be the most common form of stealing among young people; however, they seldom steal what could be considered items essential to survival. It appears that stealing is more of a challenge and adventure and that the need to succeed, either individually or as a part of a group, is central to the problem.

Teachers who discover that students have been stealing typically react either angrily or very sympathetically. No clear-cut strategies seem to be generated from either response. The first inclination is to punish, but examination of the portion in this chapter on punishment might lead the teacher to select another approach. Regardless of the strategy selected, the ability of the teacher to effectively assist the child who is stealing will depend on factors such as the following:

1. Strength of the relationship between the child and the teacher
2. Amount of respect and trust between the two
3. Degree of peer pressure involved in the stealing
4. Availability of other means of gaining stature and self-esteem

Familial problems

The teacher may discover instances in which familial problems are interfering with the student's school performance and functioning in general. Table 9-11 addresses three major types of familial problems: alcoholism of a family member, abuse

Table 9-11. Professional responses to children from troubled families

	Teacher's responses	
Familial problem	*Educational*	*Other*
Alcoholism of family member	Provide support to child Avoid involvement in family situation Avoid making judgments Obtain assistance of school counselor	Possible referral to Al-Anon* Referral to family service agencies
Abuse/battering of child	Recognize health status Recognize embarrassment Provide support in matter-of-fact manner Avoid overreaction Understand denial	Referral to legal authority Report to school authorities Referral to school counselor
Divorce	Understand temporary emotional trauma Recognize importance of reactions of others Provide genuine support	Referral to counselor if trauma persists Referral to counselor in case of absenteeism

*Referral to external agencies such as Al-Anon or counseling groups for children from broken homes should be handled delicately through proper school channels. The school may not wish to be involved, especially in the case of young children.

or battering of a child, and divorce. In instances in which problems arise, it would be advisable to clear certain actions with the school administration and to contact the school counselor. Typically the teacher is limited to (1) providing support that is noninterfering to the student, (2) providing information and support to parents, (3) requesting support and active involvement of parents, (4) making appropriate referrals and recommendations to students and parents, and (5) reporting incidents to school or legal authorities that involve abuse of a student.

SOCIOEMOTIONAL PROGRAMMING

Social status of mildly handicapped students

How well do handicapped students fare socially in the classroom? The answer to this question seems to differ depending on the research. The nature and degree of difference observed in socioemotional functioning varies from severe rejection (Bryan & Bryan, 1978; Gerber, 1977; Goodman, Gottlieb, & Harrison, 1972; Porter, Ramsey, Tremblay, Iaccobo, & Crawley, 1978; Reese-Dukes & Stokes, 1978) to no measurable differences between children with disabilities and nondisabled peers (Dunlop, Stoneman, & Cantrell, 1980; Kennedy & Bruininks, 1974; Peterson & Haralick, 1977; Schoggen, 1975). Thus, any discussion of socioemotional problems encountered by handicapped students would have to be interpreted in light of each case and setting rather than attributed to all cases. However, the special educator should be aware of some of the types of problems that might be encountered.

Rejection by peers

Group identification seems to be essential to feelings of belonging in school. Once experienced, the pain of not being chosen or chosen last is never forgotten. The parent or teacher who has had a child, handicapped or not, say, "No one wanted to play with me," can understand the significance of group membership. Such experience may also make one aware that some strategies can be employed that will help the child achieve group membership.

Formal group membership. Formal group membership becomes more likely in the upper grades as groups such as cheerleaders, Scouts, sports teams, and clubs develop. Membership in some groups is highly prestigious and desirable; however, membership is based on requirements that may be out of reach of some handicapped students. For example, participation on the sixth-grade soccer team may not be possible because the child simply is unable physically to perform the tasks required.

Since membership in certain formal groups seems to ensure acceptance and peer support, the special education teacher may be able to assist students by helping them achieve membership in some group, even if in the overall scheme of the school it is a low-status group. Membership will provide an opportunity for the development of peer relationships and better social skills. Following are suggestions for the teacher interested in providing such opportunities (Marsh & Price, 1980):

1. Consider social skills training to be an important part of assistance to students.
2. Encourage the participation of students in formal school activities.
3. Identify the types of organizations in the school and examine their nature and functions.
4. Ascertain the requirements for membership.
5. Match up possible groups with talents and abilities or interests of each student.
6. Assist the student to join one or more groups.
7. Provide information and assistance to sponsors of specific groups to facilitate the inclusion of students in organizations they supervise.
8. Recognize that the barrier to membership of students may be based on stereotyped responses or policies of the school that discriminate against them.
9. Actively work to remove unfair and unreasonable policies that restrict the student from active participation in groups.
10. The academic grade point average is likely to be a major hurdle for membership in many groups. This reflects policies that are well intentioned but that should be waived or based on alternative candidacy requirements to accommodate the handicapped. (pp. 58-59)

Table 9-12. Six active strategies in promoting social acceptance

Strategy	*Explanation*
Accommodation to increase academic success	Assisting the child through compensatory teaching will prevent the child from being labeled as "dumb" by peers.
Indirect intervention in the form of assisting in formal peer groups	In upper grades the child may be encouraged to join formal groups such as the Scouts and athletic organizations for positive peer interactions.
Direct intervention in goal setting and social skill training	Children who cannot "read" social situations should be directly taught how to behave in general and in specific situations.
Assistance in accurate observation and assessment of peer behavior	Students with poor social perception may not know why others are popular or why adults approve of certain students. They may see attention as status-gaining behavior.
Assistance in selection of appropriate status-gaining behavior	"Clowning" and other negative behaviors will be extinguished and replaced by more appropriate behaviors that the child may not recognize as status-gaining.
Personal appearance	Accepted modes of dress and cleanliness may not be obvious to the child. Personal appearance consistant with peer codes can enhance acceptance.

Informal group membership. Informal groups are also important, even in elementary school. Belonging to an informal group means that the child fits in or that the behaviors of the individual are appropriate and consistent with group norms. The physical characteristics, popularity, and social status of the person permit group acceptance and enhance esteem through belonging. Sometimes mildly handicapped students do not belong to an informal group, often because of a failure to "read" the subtle requirements for membership. These children may dress differently from the group norm; the recent trend toward designer-labeled clothing for elementary children is testimony to this aspect of conformity. Since special education children may not have reached the same emotional levels as nonhandicapped peers, the possibility exists that they will perform inappropriately at peer gatherings, thus attracting attention to their behavior.

The special educator may wish to help the handicapped students achieve membership in an informal peer group. Strategies directed at achieving such membership include the following:

1. Conducting discussions concerning how the child's behavior may elicit negative responses from peers
2. Pointing out peer behaviors that elicit positive reactions and reinforcement
3. Organizing activities that allow interaction among classmates

Table 9-12 contains six active strategies that are directed at assisting the child in gaining peer acceptance. All of the strategies are subsumed under the special education program and are directed toward improving the social skills of the child, as well as facilitating personal-social growth and development. Strategies appropriate for the regular classroom are listed in Chapter 11.

Poor self-concept

Self-concept may be viewed as dependent on social comparisons (Hyman & Singer, 1971). This means that the important factor in determining self-concept would be the social group on which the comparison is based. If this can be accepted, the implications for mainstreaming a handicapped child would be obvious. Comparisons will be made by the teacher, fellow students, and child; the greater the disparity between the child and the standard, the greater the difference in self-concept. Obviously, if the child feels inferior to the group, a low self-concept may result.

A major implication is the importance of the

selection of the classroom and group for mainstreaming. The child should be placed in a group in which opportunity is available for achieving equal status to maintain a healthy self-concept. A classroom should be selected that allows the child to contribute and feel like a member; schools in which mainstreaming simply means allowing the handicapped child to sit in the regular classroom and do worksheets or color are not only missing the mark set by P.L. 94-142 but also may be negatively affecting the child's self-concept. This could have serious implications for the child's life.

Another important implication of the importance of self-concept is that some *preparation must be made before mainstreaming*. The child previously served in a self-contained classroom who is integrated into a regular classroom is suddenly faced with comparison with a new reference group (Smith, 1979). The integration should be performed after preparation by the special educator that includes the following:

1. Discussing that the class will be made up of students who differ from those found in the special classroom
2. Gradually exposing the child to small amounts of work that may elicit various degrees of frustration
3. Obtaining samples of the work done in the regular classroom so that the child has an opportunity to practice

A third implication of the role of self-concept in performance is that tremendous *support must be given in the special classroom* during the period of mainstreaming. One advantage of part-day integration is the reduction of the negative impact on self-concept (Smith, 1979). The special educator should be aware of the stress involved: "It is incumbent on special educators and psychologists to attempt to understand the social-emotional stresses to which the special class child is subjected in the public school system" (Smith, 1979, p. 34).

Objectives for socioemotional programming

The special educator responsible for designing instructional programming for handicapped students may fall into a trap described in Chapter 3: that of including only academic objectives in the IEP. Even learning disabled students whose major categorical characteristics are academically based have been shown to have had social problems including peer rejection (Bryan & Bryan, 1978). Even for this group, total emphasis on academic performance objectives may not be appropriate. The tendency to include only performance-related objectives is understandable in one respect: these objectives, such as stating that the student will demonstrate 100% accuracy in reading the Dolch 220 word list, lend themselves easily to measurement. On the other hand, socioemotional objectives are not as easily written or measured.

Even with the obvious difficulties involved, students experiencing socioemotional problems are entitled to programming that addresses the areas of deficit, including social growth. If the IEP of a child labeled emotionally disturbed contains only academically related objectives, one of two assumptions might be made: the label is inaccurate, or the program is inappropriate. In either event, scrutiny of the labeling and programming components of services is in order.

Using the planning matrix in Chapter 3 will aid the teacher and the IEP team in identifying the actual areas of need rather than areas that are simple to specify in the document. Objectives reflecting socioemotional programming might include the following:

1. The student will demonstrate the ability to complete assigned tasks 50% of the time.
2. The student will demonstrate physically aggressive behavior as measured by an observational instrument in sampling periods 4% or less of the time.
3. The student will exhibit in-seat behavior 75% of the time in the targeted period, consisting of 5-minute periods every half hour.

Once the socioemotional objectives are identified and included in the IEP, particular strategies should be planned to meet these objectives. In some cases the total intervention will take place in the special classroom; in other instances it will be

Table 9-13. Materials and activities for use in socioemotional functioning

Published materials	*Description*
DUSO (Developing Understanding of Self and Others) (American Guidance Service, Inc.)	Kit Programming for entire year Uses puppets, records, songs, group discussion cards, posters, and stories Kindergarten and primary grades
Child's Series on Psychologically Relevant Themes (Videorecord Corporation of America)	Videorecord (six videocassettes) Based on bibliotherapy Uses stories, illustrations, cassettes, and teacher-lead discussion Preschool and elementary grades
First Things (Guidance Associates of Pleasantville, N.Y.)	Filmstrips and manual Includes activities for classroom Emphasizes concepts in physical and social environment Primary grades
The Adventures of the Lollipop Dragon (Society for Visual Education, Inc.)	Filmstrips and kit Uses coloring book to accompany stories Concepts include sharing, taking turns, and personal property Primary grades
Dimensions of Personality (George A. Pflaum Publisher, Inc.; Standard Reference Works Publishing Co.)	Uses pictures, cartoons, posters, and group activities Fosters understanding of emotional and intellectual growth Fourth through sixth grades
Focus on Self-Development, Stage Two: Responding (Science Research Associates, Inc.)	Audiovisual program with teacher's guide Includes workbook Total guidance program Elementary grades

Classroom materials

Foam bats	Tape recorder	Art materials for free expression
Punching bags	Foam or rubber balls	Soft vinyl mats
Record player	Records with music chosen by students	Rubber-tipped darts and board

Activities

Free art activities for expressing emotions and feelings
Musical activities for emotional release
Quiet time if requested by student
Bibliotherapy
Group discussions about emotions and feelings
Problem-solving activities that emphasize social decisions
Role-playing
Group determination of behavioral standards

necessary to involve the regular classroom teacher and perhaps other personnel such as bus drivers, cafeteria workers, and the principal. The interventions may be designed at the time of the IEP placement and refined later by the teacher.

The special classroom, therefore, may have two responsibilities in socioemotional functioning: direct treatment as outlined in the objectives of the IEP and prevention of difficulties through facilitation of continued sociopersonal growth. The strategies associated with the first have comprised the content of this chapter; the latter task can be accomplished through a number of strategies and the use of a variety of materials. Table 9-13 provides a brief review of some representative materials.

SUMMARY

In this chapter we have presented an overview of many components that might be considered in treatment of socioemotional disorders and have provided specific details for certain approaches, treatments, and personal growth programs. The emphasis of most texts seems to be on control or prevention of behavioral disorders. We have expanded emphases in all areas from prevention through personal growth models. The classroom environment is the context of all educational considerations. The special or regular teacher must consider the interactions of students with each other and with instructors as the basis for all educational endeavors because attitudes, modes of behavior, learning, failure, self-concept, and most other behaviors are acquired through human contact. Unquestionably, the teacher who employs behavioral principles in the design and implementation of instruction will be able to address the needs of handicapped and nonhandicapped students. Although many of the outcomes of student achievement may not necessarily relate directly to the style of teaching or the environment, undoubtedly achievement is related to motivation and reinforcement, factors that may be central to the design of the classroom environment regardless of the teacher's personality.

REFERENCES AND SUGGESTED READINGS

Abidin, R.R. Negative effects of behavioral consultation: "I know I ought to, but it hurts too much!" *Journal of School Psychology,* 1975, *13,* 51-57.

Algozzine, B. The disturbing child: a matter of opinion. *Behavior disorders,* 1980, *5,* 112-115.

Axelrod, S. *Behavior modification for the classroom teacher.* New York: McGraw-Hill Book Co., 1977.

Axelrod, S., & Bailey, S.L. Drug treatment for hyperactivity: controversies, alternatives, and guidelines. *Exceptional Children,* 1979, *45,* 544-550.

Axline, V. *Play therapy.* Boston: Houghton Mifflin Co., 1947.

Baer, D.M., & Sherman, J.A. Reinforcement control of generalized imitation in young children. *Journal of Experimental Child Psychology,* 1964, *1,* 37-49.

Baer, D.M., and Wolf, M.M. The reinforcement contingency in preschool and remedial education. In R.D. Hess & R.M. Bear (Eds.), *Early education: current theory, research, and action.* Chicago: Aldine Publishing Co., 1968.

Baker, A.M. The efficacy of the Feingold K-P diet: a review of pertinent empirical investigations. *Behavior Disorders,* 1980, *6,* 32-35.

Bakwin, H., & Bakwin, R.M. *Behavior disorders in children* (4th ed.). Philadelphia: W.B. Saunders Co., 1972.

Bandura, A. Behavior modification through modeling procedures, In L.P. Ullmann & L. Krasner (Eds.), *Research in behavior modification.* New York: Holt, Rinehart & Winston, 1965.

Bandura, A. *Principles of behavior modification.* New York: Holt, Rinehart & Winston, 1969.

Bandura, A. Psychotherapy based on modeling principles. In A.E. Bergin & S.L. Garfield (Eds.), *Handbook of psychotherapy and behavior change.* New York: John Wiley & Sons, Inc., 1971.

Beck, G. The physician-education team: let's make it work. *Journal of School Health,* 1978, *48,* 79-83.

Biggs, D.A., Orcutt, J.B., & Bakkenist, N. Correlates of marijuana and alcohol use among college students. *Journal of College Student Personnel,* 1974, *6,* 22-30.

Blackham, G.J., & Silberman, A. *Modification of child and adolescent behavior* (3rd ed.). Belmont, CA: Wadsworth Publishing Co., Inc., 1980.

Bolmeier, E.C. *Legality of student disciplinary practices.* Charlottesville, VA: Michie Co., 1976.

Brenner, A. A study of the efficacy of the Feingold diet on hyperkinetic children: some favorable personal observations. *Clinical Pediatrics,* 1977, *16,* 652-656.

Bronfenbrenner, U. Childhood: the roots of alienation. *National Elementary Principal,* 1972, *52*(2), 22-29.

Brophy, J., & Good, T. *Teacher-student relationships.* New York: Holt, Rinehart & Winston, 1974.

Brown, L. Instructional programs for trainable level retarded students. In L. Mann & D. Sabatino (Eds.), *The first review of special education.* Philadelphia: Buttonwood Farms, 1973.

Bryan, T.H., & Bryan, J.H. Social interactions of learning disabled children. *Learning Disabilities Quarterly,* 1978, *1* (1), 33-57.

Burdett, C., Egner, A., & McKenzie, H.P. In H. McKenzie (Ed.), *1968-69 report of the consulting teacher program (Vol. 2).* Burlington, VT: College of Education, The University of Vermont, 1970.

Canter, L., & Canter, M. *Assertive discipline.* Seal Beach, CA: Canter & Associates, 1976.

Charles, C.M. *Individualizing instruction* (2nd ed.). St. Louis: The C.V. Mosby Co., 1980.

Cohen, J. *Operant behavior and conditioning.* Chicago: Rand McNally & Co., 1969.

Deno, S.L. Direct observation approach to measuring classroom behavior. *Exceptional Children,* 1980, *46,* 396-399.

Des Jarlais, D. Labeling theory; sociological views and approaches. In W. Rhodes and L. Paul (Eds.), *Emotionally disturbed and deviant children.* Englwood Cliffs, NJ: Prentice-Hall, Inc., 1978.

Dreikurs, R. *Maintaining sanity in the classroom.* New York: Harper & Row, Publishers, 1971.

Dunlop, K.H., Stoneman, A., & Cantrell, M.L. Social interaction of exceptional and other children in a mainstreamed preschool classroom. *Exceptional Children,* 1980, *47,* 132-141.

Dupont, H. (Ed.) *Educating emotionally disturbed children.* New York: Holt, Rinehart & Winston, 1975.

Eisenberg, L. Behavior modification by drugs: the clinical use of stimulant drugs in children. *Pediatrics,* 1972, *49,* 709-715.

Erickson, M.T. *Child psychopathology: assessment, etiology, and treatment.* Englewood Cliffs, NJ: Prentice-Hall, Inc., 1978.

Feingold, B.J. Hyperkinesis and learning disabilities linked to the ingestion of artificial food colors and flavors. *Journal of Learning Disabilities,* 1976, *9,* 551-559.

Fish, B. The "one child, one drug" myth of stimulants in hyperkinesis. *Archives of General Psychiatry,* 1971, *25,* 193-203.

Freedman, D. The use of stimulant drugs in treating hyperactive children. *Exceptional Children,* 1971, *18,* 111.

Freeman, R.D. Minimal brain dysfunction, hyperactivity, and learning disabilities: epidemic or episode? In J.J. Bosco & S.S. Robin (Eds.), *The hyperactive child and stimulant drugs.* Chicago: The University of Chicago Press, 1976.

Frew, T. Media review: Assertive Discipline in the Classroom. *Behavior Disorders,* 1979, *4,* 143-144.

Gambrill, E.D. *Behavior modification: handbook of assessment, intervention, and evaluation.* San Francisco: Jossey-Bass, Inc., Publishers, 1977.

Gardner, W.I. *Learning and behavior characteristics of exceptional children and youth.* Boston: Allyn & Bacon, Inc., 1977.

Gerber, P.J. Awareness of handicapping conditions and sociometric status in an integrated pre-school setting. *Mental Retardation,* 1977, *15,* 24-25.

Gibbons, S., & Tracy, M. Counter theoretical views and approaches. In W. Rhodes & L. Paul (Ed.), *Emotionally disturbed and deviant children.* Englewood Cliffs, NJ: Prentice-Hall, Inc., 1978.

Ginott, H. *Group psychotherapy with children.* New York: McGraw-Hill Book Co., 1961.

Glasser, W. *Schools without failure.* New York: Harper & Row, Publishers, 1969.

Goldstein, A.P., Heller, K., and Sechrist, L.B. *Psychotherapy and the psychology of behavior change.* New York: John Wiley & Sons, Inc., 1966.

Goodman, L.S., & Gilman, A. (Eds.) *The pharmacological basis of therapeutics.* New York: Macmillan Publishing Co., Inc., 1975.

Goodman, H., Gottlieb, J., & Harrison, R.H. Social acceptance of EMR's integrated into a nongraded elementary school. *American Journal of Mental Deficiency,* 1972, *76,* 412-417.

Grinspoon, L., & Singer, S.B. Amphetamines in the treatment of hyperactive children. *Harvard Educational Review,* 1973, *43,* 515-555.

Gross, M.D. Growth of hyperkinetic children taking methylphenidate, dextroamphetamine, or imipramine. *Pediatrics,* 1976, *58,* 423-431.

Hall, R.V. Training teachers in classroom use of contingency management. *Educational Technology,* 1971, *11,* 33-38.

Hamblin, R.L., Buckholdt, D., Ferritor, D., Kozloff, M., & Blackwell, L. *The humanization processes: a social, behavioral analysis of children's problems.* New York: Interscience, 1971.

Haring, N.G. Application of behavioral modification techniques to the learning situation. In W.M. Cruickshank & D.P. Hallahan (Eds.), *Perceptual and learning disabilities in children* (Vol. 1). Syracuse: Syracuse University Press, 1975.

Haring, N.G., & Phillips, E.L. *Educating emotionally disturbed children.* New York: McGraw-Hill Book Co., 1962.

Harley, J.P., Ray, R.S., Tomasi, L., Eichman, P.L., Mathews, C.G., Chun, R., Cleeland, C.S., & Traisman, E. Hyperkinesis and food additives: testing the Feingold hypothesis. *Pediatrics,* 1978, *61,* 818-828.

Hart, H. (Ed.). *Summerhill: for and against.* New York: Hart Co., 1970.

Hewett, F.M. *Emotionally disturbed child in the classroom.* Boston: Allyn & Bacon, Inc., 1968.

Hobbs, N. Helping disturbed children: psychological and ecological strategies. *American Psychologist,* 1966, *21,* 1106-1115.

Hobbs, N. Personal perspective. In J.M. Kauffman & C.D. Lewis (Eds.), *Teaching children with behavior disorders.* Columbus, OH: Charles E. Merrill Publishing Co., 1974.

Homme, L.E. Contingency contracting with parents. In *Proceedings: Early Childhood Intervention Research Con-*

ference. Institute: Exceptional Children and Adults. Tampa: University of South Florida, 1970.

Homme, L. *How to use contingency contracting in the classroom*. Champaign, IL: Research Press, 1974.

Huntsinger, S. School storm: drugs for children. *Christian Science Monitor,* October 31, 1970, p. 1.

Hyman, H.H., & Singer, E. An introduction to reference group theory and research. In E.P. Hollander & R.G. Hunt (Eds.), *Current perspectives in social psychology* (3rd ed.). New York: Oxford University Press, 1971.

Ingraham v. Wright, 430 U.S. 651 (1977).

Isser, A.V., Quay, H.C., & Love, C.T. Interrelationships among three measures of deviant behavior. *Exceptional Children,* 1980, *46,* 272-276.

James, K.F. *Corporal punishment in the schools*. Los Angeles: University of Southern California, 1963 (Education Monograph No. 18).

Johnson, C.F., & Prinz, R. Hyperactivity in the eyes of the beholder. *Clinical Pediatrics,* 1976, *15,* 222-238.

Johnson, J.A. The etiology of hyperactivity. *Exceptional Children,* 1981, *47,* 348-353.

Keniston, K. A second look at the uncommitted. *Social Policy,* 1971, *2*(2), 6-19.

Kennedy, P., & Bruininks, R.H. Social status of hearing impaired children in regular classrooms. *Exceptional Children,* 1974, *40,* 336-342.

Knapczyk, D.R. Diet control in the management of behavior disorders. *Behavior Disorders,* 1979, *5,* 2-9.

Knoblock, P. Open education for emotionally disturbed children. In H. Dupont (Ed.), *Educating emotionally disturbed children*. New York: Holt, Rinehart & Winston, 1975.

Krippner, S. The influence of consciousness research. *Exceptional Children,* 1978, *44,* 418-426.

Laufer, M.W. Medications, learning and behavior. *Phi Delta Kappan,* November 1971, pp. 169-170.

Lewin, K. *A dynamic theory of personality*. New York: McGraw-Hill Book Co., 1935.

Leyser, Y., & Gottlieb, J. Improving the social status of rejected pupils. *Exceptional Children,* 1980, *46,* 459-461.

Marsh, G.E., II, Gearheart, C.K., & Gearheart, B.R. *The learning disabled adolescent: program alternatives in the secondary school*. St. Louis: The C.V. Mosby Co., 1978.

Marsh, G.E., II, & Price, B.J. *Methods for teaching the mildly handicapped adolecent*. St. Louis: The C.V. Mosby Co., 1980.

Martin, G., & Pear, J. *Behavior modification*. Englewood Cliffs, NJ: Prentice-Hall, Inc., 1978.

Martin, R. *Legal challenges to behavior modification*. Champaign, IL: Research Press, 1975.

McIntosh, D.K., & Dunn, L.M. Children with major specific learning deficiencies. In L.M. Dunn (ed.), *Exceptional children in the school* (2nd ed.). New York: Holt, Rinehart & Winston, 1973.

Merlis, G. The updated hickory stick. *Nation,* 1975, *221,* 425-427.

Millchap, J.G. Drugs in management of minimal brain dysfunction. *Annals of the New York Academy of sciences,* 1973, *205,* 321-334.

Millman, R.B. Drug and alcohol abuse. In. B.B. Wolman (Ed.), *Handbook of treatment of mental disorders in childhood and adolescence*. Englewood Cliffs, NJ: Prentice-Hall, Inc., 1978.

Mooney, C., & Algozzine, B. A comparison of the disturbingness of LD and ED behaviors. *Journal of Abnormal Child Psychology,* 1978, *6,* 401-406.

Morse, W.C. Crisis intervention in school mental health and special classes for the disturbed. In N.J. Long, C.W. Morse, & R.G. Newman (Eds.), *Conflict in the classroom: the education of children with problems* (2nd ed.). Belmont, CA: Wadsworth Publishing Co., 1971.

Morse, W.C. Crisis intervention in school mental health and special classes for the disturbed. In N.J. Long, C.W. Morse, & R.G. Newman (Eds.), *Conflict in the classroom: the education of children with problems* (3rd ed.). Belmont, CA: Wadsworth Publishing Co., 1976.

Murray, J.N. Drugs to control classroom behavior. *Educational Leadership,* 1973, *31,* 21-25.

National Advisory Committee on Hyperkinesis and Food Additives. *Report to the Nutrition Foundation,* 1975.

National Institute on Legal Problems of Educating the Handicapped. *Education for the Handicapped Law Report,* Boston, May 1980.

Nay, W.R. *Behavioral intervention: contemporary strategies*. New York: Gardner Press, Inc., 1976.

Neill, A.S. *Summerhill: a radical approach to child rearing*. New York: Hart Publishing Co., Inc., 1960.

Neisworth, J.T., & Smith, R.M. *Modifying retarded behavior*. Boston: Houghton Mifflin Co., 1973.

Nelson, R. Elementary school counseling with unstructured play media. *Personnel and Guidance Journal,* 1966, *45,* 24-27.

Newcomer, P.L. *Understanding and teaching emotionally disturbed children*. Boston: Allyn & Bacon, Inc., 1980.

O'Conner, R.D. Relative efficacy of modeling, shaping, and combined procedures for modification of social withdrawal. *Journal of Abnormal Psychology,* 1972, *3,* 327-334.

Offir, C.W. A slavish reliance on drugs: Are we pushers for our own children? *Psychology Today,* December 1974, p. 49.

O'Leary, K.D., & O'Leary, S.G. *Classroom management: the successful use of behavior modification*. New York: Pergamon Press, Inc., 1972.

O'Leary, S.G., & Pelham, W.E. Behavior therapy and withdrawal of stimulant medication in hyperactive children. *Pediatrics,* 1978, *61,* 211-217.

Pasanella, A.L., & Volkmor, C.B. *Coming back . . . or never leaving*. Columbus, OH: Charles E. Merrill Co., 1977.

Peterson, N.L., & Haralick, J.G. Integration of handicapped and non-handicapped preschoolers: an analysis of play behavior and social interactions. *Education and Training of the Mentally Retarded,* 1977, *12,* 235-245.

Porter, R., Ramsey, B., Tremblay, A., Iaccobo, M., & Crawley, S. Social interactions in heterogeneous groups of retarded and normally developing children: an observational study. In G. Sackett (Ed.), *Observing behavior*. Baltimore: University Park Press, 1978.

Quarterly analysis of legal developments affecting professionals in human services. *Law and Behavior,* 1976, No. 1, p. 1.

Quay, H.C. Behavior disorder in the classroom. *Journal of Research and Development in Education,* 1978, *4,* 8-17.

Quay, H.C. Classification: immaturity. In H.C. Quay & J.S. Werry (Eds.), *Psychopathological disorders of childhood* (2nd ed.). New York: John Wiley & Sons, Inc., 1979.

Ramella, R. Anatomy of discipline: Should punishment be corporal? *PTA Magazine,* 1974, *67,* 24-27.

Redl, F. Strategy and techniques of the life space interview. *American Journal of Orthopsychiatry,* 1959, *29,* 1-18.

Redl, F. Why life space interview? In H. Dupont (Ed.), *Educating emotionally disturbed children: readings*. New York: Holt, Rinehart & Winston, 1969.

Redl, F., & Wattenberg, W.W. *Mental hygiene in teaching*. New York: Harcourt, Brace & Co., 1959.

Reese-Dukes, J.L., & Stokes, E.H. Social acceptance of elementary educable mentally retarded pupils in the regular classroom. *Education and Training of the Mentally Retarded,* 1978, *13,* 356-361.

Reinert, H.R. *Children in conflict: educational strategies for the emotionally disturbed and behaviorally disordered* (2nd ed.). St. Louis: The C.V. Mosby Co., 1980.

Renshaw, D.C. *The hyperactive child*. Boston: Little, Brown & Co., 1975.

Renshaw, D.C. Understanding the hyperactive child. *Illinois Medical Journal,* 1976, *149,* 351-354.

Rhodes, W.C. The disturbing child: a problem of ecological management. *Exceptional Children,* 1967, *33,* 449-455.

Rhodes, W.C. A community participation analysis of emotional disturbance. *Exceptional Children,* 1970, *36,* 309-314.

Rhodes, W.C., and Paul, J.L. *Emotionally disturbed and deviant children*. Englewood Cliffs, NJ: Prentice-Hall, Inc., 1978.

Ritter, B. The group desensitization of children's snake phobias using vicarious and contact desensitization procedures. *Behavioral Research and Therapy,* 1968, *6,* 1-6.

Roberts, T.B. *Four psychologies applied to education*. Cambridge, MA: Schenkman Publishing Co., Inc., 1975.

Rogers, C. *Freedom to learn: a view of what education might become*. Columbus, OH: Charles E. Merrill Publishing Co., 1969.

Rosenfield, S. Introducing behavior modification techniques to teachers. *Exceptional Children,* 1979, *45,* 334-339.

Rossi, J.J., & Filstead, W.J. *The therapeutic community*. New York: Behavioral Publications, 1973.

Safer, D.J., & Allen, R.P. Side effects from long-term use of stimulants in children. *International Journal of Mental Health,* 1975, *4,* 105-118.

Safer, D.J., & Allen, R.P. *Hyperactive children*. Baltimore: University Park Press, 1976.

Safer, D.J., Allen, R.P., & Barr, E. Depression of growth in hyperactive children on stimulant drugs. *New England Journal of Medicine,* 1972, *287,* 217.

Sandoval, J., Lambert, N.M., & Sassone, D.M. The comprehensive treatment of hyperactive children: a continuing problem. *Journal of Learning Disabilities,* 1981, *14,* 117-118.

Schoggen, P. An ecological study of children with physical disabilities in school and at home. In R.A. Weinbert & F.H. Wood (Eds.), *Observation of pupils and teachers in mainstream and special education settings*. Minneapolis: Leadership Training Institute/Special Education, University of Minnesota, 1975.

Shafer, R.P. *Marijuana: a signal of misunderstanding*. New York: Signet, 1972.

Sieben, R.L. Controversial medical treatments of learning disabilities. *Academic Therapy,* 1977, *13,* 133 146.

Skinner, B.F. *Science and human behavior*. New York: The Macmillan Co., 1953.

Smith, J.D., Polloway, E.A., & West, G.K. Corporal punishment and its implications for exceptional children. *Exceptional Children,* 1979, *45,* 264-268.

Smith, M.D. Prediction of self-concept among learning disabled children. *Journal of Learning Disabilities,* 1979, *12,* 664-669.

Solomon, G.E. Minimal brain dysfunction. In B.B. Wolman, J. Egan, & A.O. Ross (eds.), *Handbook of treatment of mental disorders in childhood and adolescence*. Englewood Cliffs, NJ: Prentice-Hall, Inc., 1978.

Spaulding, R.L. C.A.S.E.S. manual. San Jose, CA: San Jose State University, 1980.

Spinazola, C. Application of the diagnostic teaching model. In M.E. Ward, G.P. Cartwright, C.A. Cartwright, J. Campbell, & C. Spinazola (Eds.), *Diagnostic teaching of preschool and primary children*. University Park, PA: The Pennsylvania State University, 1973.

Spring, C., & Sandoval, J. Food additions and hyperkinesis: a critical evaluation. *Journal of Learning Disabilities,* 1976, *9,* 560-569.

Staats, A.W. *Social behaviorism*. Homewood, IL: Dorsey Press, 1975.

Stainback, W., Stainback, S., & Dedrick, C. Controlling severe maladaptive behaviors. *Behavior Disorders,* 1979, *4,* 99-113.

Stewart, W.A., Goodman, G., & Hammond, B. Behavior modification: teacher training and attitudes. *Exceptional Children,* 1976, *42,* 402-403.

Sulzbacher, S.I. Behavior analysis of drug effects in the classroom. In G. Semb (Ed.), *Behavior analysis and education–1972*. Lawrence, KS: University of Kansas, 1972.

Swap, S.M. The ecological model of emotional disturbance in children. *Behavior Disorders,* 1978, *3,* 186-196.

Tomlinson, J.R. Implementing behavior modification programs with limited consultation time. *Journal of School Psychology,* 1972, *10,* 379-386.

Ullman, L.P., & Krasner, L. (Eds.). *Case studies in behavior modification*. New York: Holt, Rinehart & Winston, 1965.

Unger, R.A. The treatment of adolescent alcoholism. *Social Casework,* 1978, *59*(1), 27-35.

Vogel, J., & Smith, A. Rx for change: the classroom meeting. *Learning,* 1974, *2*(7), 69-72.

Walden, E.L., & Thompson, S.A. A review of some alternative approaches to drug management of hyperactivity in children. *Journal of Learning Disabilities,* 1981, *14,* 213-217.

Walker, H.M. *The acting-out child: coping with classroom disruption*. Boston: Allyn & Bacon, Inc., 1979.

Walker, J.E., & Shea, T.M. *Behavior modification: a practical approach for education (2nd ed.).* St. Louis: The C.V. Mosby Co., 1980.

Warner, R.W., & Swisher, J.D. Alienation and drug abuse: synonymous? In H. Thornburg (Ed.), *Contemporary adolescence: readings*. Monterey, CA: Brooks/Cole Publishing Co., 1975.

Weinstein, L. Project RE-ED schools for emotionally disturbed children: effectiveness as viewed by referring agencies, parents, and teachers. In N.J. Long, W.C. Morse, and R.G. Newman (Eds.), *Conflict in the classroom: the education of emotionally disturbed children.* Belmont, CA: Wadsworth Publishing Co., 1976.

Why public schools are flunking. *Newsweek,* April 20, 1981, p. 45.

Williams, J.I., Cram, D.M., Tausig, F.T., & Webster, E. Relative effects of drugs and diet on hyperactive behaviors: an experimental study. *Pediatrics,* 1978, *61,* 811-817.

Wolman, B.B., Egan, J., & Ross, A.O. (Eds.). *Handbook of treatment of mental disorders in childhood and adolescence.* Englewood Cliffs, NJ: Prentice-Hall, Inc., 1978.

Worell, J., & Nelson, C.M. *Managing instructional problems: a case study workbook.* New York: McGraw-Hill Book Co., 1974.

Yancy, W.S., Nader, P.R., & Burnham, K. Drug use and attitudes of high school students. *Pediatrics,* 1972, *50,* 739-745.

Youngblood, W.L. Recent decisions. *Mississippi Law Journal,* 1973, *44,* 550-555.

Zinna, R. Is there a hyperkinetic syndrome? *British Medical Journal,* 1979, *1,* 685.

Zinzer, O. *Imitation, modeling and cross-cultural training.* Wright-Patterson Air Force Base, OH: Aerospace Medical Research Laboratories, Aerospace Medical Division, September 1966.

10 SENSORIPHYSICAL FUNCTIONING

Planning in the IEP and daily instruction must account for a variety of mild sensoriphysical disorders that may occur singly or in conjunction with other handicapping conditions. Problems such as allergies, asthma, cardiac disorders, diabetes, epilepsy, amputations, arthritis, cerebral palsy, and visual or hearing disorders require some degree of planning, monitoring, and accommodation; this is especially important in the regular classroom. Moreover, regular classroom teachers need to deal with the equipment needs of some children, such as wheelchairs, braces, and crutches.

Due to current trends, some children with more severe conditions such as limited vision and hearing are entering mainstream classes. Although these children are not ordinarily considered to be mildly handicapped, their handicapping conditions are discussed in a special section. This discussion is intended to assist regular teachers in accommodating these children and school-based special educators in coordinating activities or answering questions in the absence of itinerant specialists who would customarily work with these children. In some states, however, multicategorical resource rooms and/or centers employ a service model in which one or more special educators coordinate programming in the same room for all handicapped children, regardless of the degree of perceived severity of the handicap. As technological innovations are made, teachers become better prepared, and attitudes change, it can be anticipated that more of the formerly segregated populations of severely handicapped students will be integrated. This is evident, for example, in the trend of deinstitutionalization in state schools for the deaf and blind.

Although there seems to be professional consensus that the term mildly handicapped usually includes the educable mentally retarded, learning disabled, and behaviorally disordered populations, the definition of severely handicapped children limits the number and types of children who would be regarded as severely handicapped (*Code of Federal Regulations,* 1974):

> Severely handicapped children are those who, because of the intensity of their physical, mental, or emotional problems or a combination of such problems, need educational, social, psychological, and medical services beyond those traditionally offered by regular and special education programs, in order to maximize their full potential for useful and meaningful participation in society and for self-fulfillment. Such children include those classified as seriously emotionally disturbed (schizophrenic and autistic), profoundly and severely mentally retarded, and those with two or more serious handicapping conditions such as the mentally retarded–blind and the cerebral palsied—deaf.*

Thus, by exclusion, it might follow that blindness, deafness, cerebral palsy, spina bifida, muscular dystrophy, and other conditions, unless associated with other severe conditions, are in the mild category. As previous attitudes change and these children succeed in the mainstream, these conditions may be regarded as mild rather than severe.

For the most part, the teacher's responsibility includes presenting sound educational programs for children who have sensory, physical, or health-related problems. Responsibility also includes supporting the activities of physicians and allied health professionals and making necessary space and accommodations to permit effective learning in the classroom. Primary therapy and remediation is handled by specialists.

CHRONIC HEALTH PROBLEMS

Several chronic health problems that occur either as primary or secondary disorders can present major problems for children in school. According to the *Federal Register* (1977), P.L. 94-142 defines "other health impaired" persons as those having "limited strength, vitality or alertness due to chronic or acute health problems such as a heart condition, tuberculosis, rheumatic fever, nephritis, asthma, sickle cell anemia, hemophilia, epilepsy, lead poisoning, leukemia, or diabetes, which adversely affects a child's educational performance" (p. 42478). Although these conditions

*Autism has recently been removed from this category.

are not frequently found in public school classrooms, if they are present, teachers must know what actions are necessary to facilitate accommodation of these children. As with other physically handicapped conditions, children with health impairments create a need for a multidisciplinary team approach. Teachers must collaborate closely with the medical personnel to maximize educational opportunities.

Allergy

An allergy is a condition in which the body reacts excessively to some external stimulus. Allergic reactions take several forms including a runny nose, watery eyes, skin reactions, breathing problems, and sneezing. Various substances cause different reactions in people. The substances that most commonly produce allergic reactions include pollen, dust, grass, smoke, animal dander, drugs, particular kinds of foods, and living plants. Some of these substances are more prevalent during certain times of the year than others. Some individuals have problems only periodically, whereas others suffer allergic reactions almost constantly.

Treatment of allergies is primarily medical. Physicians first attempt to determine the cause of the allergic reaction. Once the cause has been determined, individuals can either be desensitized, take allergy-controlling medication, or attempt to stay away from the substance. Fortunately, most children with allergies can remain in school, and their educational programs require little modification. However, teachers should be aware of certain educational implications.

Educational implications. Many children who have allergies are bothersome to the class. A child's constant sneezing or scratching can be disturbing to the other members of the class. Teachers need to be aware of these reactions and try to understand that the child has no control over them. Once substances that cause allergic reactions in certain children are identified, teachers should attempt to keep children away from these substances. For example, if a child is allergic to animal hair, teachers should not keep pets in the room; if pets are present, teachers should keep the allergic child as far from the animals as possible. Often children will miss school. Efforts should be made by the teacher to have the child's assignments brought home and provide the child with a copy of class notes or other material.

Another implication is reaction to medication. Many children may become drowsy or active as a result of medication to control the allergy. Teachers should be aware of these reactions and expect certain types of behavior during periods of medication. Some children with allergies tire more easily than others. For these children, alternative physical activities should be provided so that participation is possible without undue fatigue.

Asthma

Asthma is a disorder caused by blockage of the bronchial tubes and/or lungs. It is characterized by labored breathing and wheezing. The condition may occur rarely or be present most of the time. It is one of the major causes of school absences (Mullins, 1979). Asthmatic attacks can be mild or life threatening, requiring emergency treatment. These attacks are brought on by specific substances to which the child is allergic, excessive physical activity, or emotional stress. About 2.5 percent of children in this country are affected by asthma (Mullins, 1979).

During acute attacks, the child may be given drugs to relax the muscles. At other times treatment consists of removal of the stimulating agent from the child's environment, prescription of various medications, and reduction of stress.

Educational implications. Teachers should consider the following measures:

1. *Reduce stress.* Many authorities believe stress can bring on an asthmatic attack. Teachers should aid the child in avoiding stressful situations. However, the child should not be allowed to manipulate the teacher.

2. *Be aware of drug side effects.* Teachers should be aware of certain side effects resulting

from medication, including hyperactive behavior, drowsiness, and nausea. If these side effects are noted in children receiving antiasthma medication, teachers should notify the child's parents or physician.

3. *Be alert to substances that bring on asthmatic reactions.* Although medical personnel will probably identify substances that bring on attacks, some substances may not be known. Teachers should be alert to these substances and notify the child's parents if new reaction-causing agents are discovered. For example, if the teacher notices that the child has a reaction after going to the chalkboard, this information should be relayed to the parents.

4. *Provide proper physical activities.* Asthmatic children should be given the opportunity to engage in physical activities, but teachers should check with parents or a physician to determine appropriate physical activities. Inactivity, unless recommended by the parents or medical personnel, should be avoided.

5. *Do not overprotect.* Some asthmatic children take advantage of their condition and manipulate teachers. Teachers should encourage activity and not allow a student to avoid tasks by using the asthmatic condition as an excuse.

Cardiac disorders

Although commonly among adults, cardiac disorders affect some children. The two types of cardiac disorders are congenital and acquired. The congenital type occurs approximately 20 times more often than the acquired. Approximately 6 newborns per 1,000 live births have congenital heart disorders (Baum, 1975). Congenital heart defects include holes in the walls of the heart and problems related to the flow of blood involving valves, arteries, and veins (Best, 1978). In most instances, the cause of congenital heart defects is unknown. Some of the known causes include chromosomal abnormalities, congenital heart defects, and maternal rubella. Whatever the cause, the defect occurs during the first 8 weeks of embryonic development (Baum, 1975). Acquired heart defects usually result from rheumatic fever or hypertension.

Children with heart problems usually have shortness of breath; limited exercise tolerance; cyanosis, or blueness of the lips and fingernails; fainting spells; and chest pain.

Treatment of congenital heart defects is usually surgical. Of the 35 types of congenital heart disease, 20 respond to surgical correction (Apgar & Beck, 1972). Children with uncorrectable heart disease must control their diets and exercise pattern and take medication.

Educational implications. Although heart disease, either congenital or acquired, may affect the physical functioning of children, it should not greatly alter academic potential. The children should be encouraged to take part in activities that do not require a great deal of physical exertion. Early in the child's school career, the teacher should emphasize, through career education, vocations that require limited physical activity. Activity and awareness programs also can be implemented to assist children who suffer from cardiac problems. Way (1981) describes an intervention program that focuses on cardiovascular fitness and knowledge about cardiovascular health. Any program implemented must attain the consent and recommendation of physicians. The role of teachers serving children with heart defects is primarily that of monitoring the activity level. Teachers should also be aware of any signs indicating that the child is having difficulty and bring this concern to the attention of parents and medical personnel.

Diabetes

Diabetes is an inherited disorder of metabolism in which the body cannot break down or store sugar. The disorder is caused by an inability of the pancreas to produce the enzyme *insulin.* Although most instances of diabetes occur in older adults, juvenile diabetes is the most common childhood disorder of the endocrine system; it affects approximately 1 out of every 1,000 school-aged children and accounts for 5 percent of all cases of diabetes in the United States (Katz, 1975). Unlike adult cases of diabetes, in which the pancreas can produce insulin but only in limited quantities, juvenile diabetes is characterized by an almost total lack of insulin production. As a result, oral medication taken by adults to increase insulin production is not effective in children. Diabetic children are treated with injections of insulin.

Children with diabetes manifest classical symptoms including polyuria (excessive urination), polydipsia (excessive thirst), polyphagia (excessive hunger), weight loss, drowsiness, and possible visual problems. Children who exhibit these symptoms should be referred for medical attention, since neglect of medical treatment can have severe effects on the child.

Treatment of children with diabetes includes insulin injections, diet control, and a routine of exercise. Insulin injections are a daily routine for children with diabetes. Unfortunately, unless medical research discovers other treatments, daily injections will be required for the remainder of the child's life. Daily injections seem terrifying to most of us. However, children with diabetes usually adjust well and can take care of this requirement on their own. Wentworth and Hoover (1981) suggest that the child, if willing, should be allowed to demonstrate drawing insulin into a syringe and discuss daily treatments with the class. This should not be promoted by the teacher unless the child wants to discuss the condition. Advice and assistance of the counselor, physician, and parents is necessary; a period of time might be arranged to prepare the class for the activity.

Since there are several varieties of insulin and children require different dosage levels, it is unlikely that any two diabetic children would require the same insulin treatment. In addition to insulin, the diet must be monitored and regulated. Regularity is a key element in monitoring the diet. The amount of insulin needed in the body is directly related to the amount and kinds of food ingested. Therefore, if the regular daily dosage of insulin is to have the desired effect, the food ingested must be regulated. Exercise is the third aspect of treatment. As with diet monitoring, regularity is a key element. Exercise reduces the amount of sugar in the body. If a child is much more active than normal on one day, less than normal levels of insulin will be required; if a child receiving the regular amount of insulin has a significantly increased activity level, the body will have excess insulin. Therefore, children with diabetes, although not restricted with regard to physical activity, should maintain a regular regimen of activity. Variations of this routine must be countered with adjustments in insulin doses.

Educational implications. Teachers of children with diabetes are key members of the treatment team. Since they are with the children much of the time, monitoring the child is vital. The most important aspect for teachers to chart is insulin intake. Teachers must be aware of the warning signs and take the necessary intervention steps if distress is noted. If too much insulin is present, a condition called "insulin reaction" results. This can occur from too much exercise or insulin, too little food, or nervousness. Symptoms include irritability, sudden onset of hunger, excessive perspiration, dizziness, inability to concentrate, and trembling. The required intervention is immediate increase of sugar in the body. This can be accomplished if the child eats a sugar cube, candy, or raisins or drinks juice. Katz (1975) states that if teachers are unsure of whether a child is having an insulin reaction, sugar should be given, "since the administration of sugar will cause no harm, while withholding sugar could have serious consequences" (p. 78). Usually, symptoms disappear within 10 to 15 minutes after the snack; if not, parents and/or the physician should be notified. Many diabetic children are aware of the condition and know to eat or drink something. In these instances, the teacher may not even suspect that the child was approaching an insulin reaction.

The second major danger with diabetic children, too little insulin, might result from the child eating more than usual or eating foods with excessive amounts of sugar, not exercising enough, or failing

Table 10-1. Characteristics of insulin reaction and diabetic coma and required actions of teachers

Characteristics	*Actions*
Insulin reaction (too much insulin)	
Usually develops quickly	Give candy, raisins, sugar, juice or soft drink
Irritability	Call parents or physician
Hyperactivity	
Perspiration	
Hunger	
Lack of concentration	
Dizziness	
Trembling	
Convulsions	
Coma	
Diabetic coma (too little insulin)	
Usually develops slowly	Call physician immediately
Heavy breathing	Keep child warm
Dry, flushed skin	Keep child still
Headache	Give nonsweet liquids
Nausea	
Vomiting	
Increased thirst	
Increased urination	
Fruity odor to breath	
Coma	

to take the prescribed amount of insulin. Insufficient insulin causes diabetic coma. Indicators include dry skin, sweet or fruity odor to the breath, deep breathing, nausea, vomiting, and excessive thirst. As with insulin reaction, children vary in symptoms manifested. Treatment for diabetic coma is immediate administration of insulin. Table 10-1 summarizes the characteristics of insulin reaction and diabetic coma and the required actions of teachers.

If the child's diabetes is well managed, insulin reaction and diabetic coma will not occur. In addition to monitoring the child for these critical reactions, teachers should take the following preventive measures:

1. Find out from the parents if a midmorning snack or early lunch is required.
2. Prevent the child from engaging in strenuous activities before lunch, since this will quickly reduce any remaining sugar in the child's system.
3. Keep candy and other edibles available at all times.
4. Inform substitute teachers of the child's condition and the actions to take during a critical situation.
5. Do not panic because the class contains a diabetic child (Gearheart & Weishahn, 1980).

Epilepsy

Epilepsy is a condition that indicates an underlying neurological problem. It is not a disease, but rather a behavioral manifestation. During a seizure, abnormal electrical firings in the brain cause an individual to lose control of certain voluntary muscles. Approximately 0.5 percent of the population in the United States is affected with epilepsy, with the highest incidence in the range of 0 to 5 years, and the lowest in the range of 20 to 70 years (Berg, 1975). Anything that causes neurological damage can lead to epilepsy, including tumors, prenatal and postnatal infections, metabolic disorders, high fever, and anoxia.

There are many types of epilepsy. The three most common are *grand mal, petit mal,* and *psychomotor*. Of these types, the most serious is grand mal. *Grand mal* seizures are characterized by loss of consciousness and uncontrolled jerky movements of the body. Most grand mal seizures proceed through a sequence of stages. The first stage, called the *aura,* is a strange feeling or sensation that precedes the convulsion. This has been described as sensing a strong odor, feeling nauseous, or feeling fearful. Although aura is not experienced by all epileptics, those who do experience it learn to expect the more active parts of the seizure. The aura is followed by the *tonic phase*. During this stage, the muscles stiffen, consciousness is lost, and the individual usually falls. This is followed by the *clonic phase* in which the muscles jerk and move uncontrollably (Berg, 1975). The entire seizure usually lasts only a few minutes.

Since the episode can be exhausting, children will frequently rest or sleep following a seizure.

Petit mal seizures are much less intense than grand mal episodes and usually have the appearance of daydreaming. The student, usually for periods of 5 to 10 seconds, stares and appears to be out of touch with what is going on. Although short in duration, these seizures can occur many times each day. During the seizure, the student appears to stare without actually focusing. The eyes may show a slight movement or flutter, and the student may appear pale. After the seizure, the child will continue with a task as if nothing had happened. In fact, the child probably is not aware that the seizure has occured. Because of the difficulty in identifying this type of seizure, children with petit mal problems are often accused of being lazy and daydreamers.

Psychomotor seizures, like petit mal episodes, are difficult to identify. These seizures are characterized by ticlike behavior including lip smacking, chewing movements, repetitive behavior, or purposeless activities. Children who manifest these behaviors are frequently accused of being attention seekers and exhibiting acting-out behavior.

Whereas the grand mal seizure is unmistakable, petit mal and psychomotor types are often viewed as negative behavior. According to Gearheart and Weishahn (1980), teachers should be alert for students who frequently display behaviors such as "(1) head dropping, (2) daydreaming or lack of attentiveness, (3) slight jerky movements of arms or shoulders (ticlike movements), (4) eyes rolling upward or twitching, (5) chewing or swallowing movements, (6) rhythmic movements of the head, (7) purposeless movements or sounds, and (8) dropping things frequently" (p. 101). It is unlikely that children will express all of these behaviors, but, if several behaviors are noticed on a recurring basis, teachers should refer the child for further diagnosis.

Treatment for epilepsy consists of medication and actions to take during seizures. With proper medication, 60 to 80 percent of seizures can be

Table 10-2. Anticonvulsant drugs and possible side effects

Medication	*Description*	*Side effects*
Phenobarbital	Effective for grand mal seizures	Skin rash, irritability, lethargy
Diphenylhydantoin (Dilantin)	Effective for grand mal seizures	Nystagmus, ataxia, slurred speech, mental confusion, dizziness, insomnia, nervousness, twitching, headaches, nausea, vomiting, constipation, skin rash
Trimethadione (Tridione)	Effective for petit mal seizures	Nausea, vomiting, abdominal pain, gastric distress, drowsiness, fatigue, malaise, insomnia, vertigo, headache, bleeding gums, skin rash, hiccups, weight loss, hair loss
Primidone (Mysoline)	Effective for grand mal and psychomotor seizures	Ataxia, vertigo, nausea, anorexia, vomiting, fatigue, irritability, nystagmus, drowsiness
Ethosuximide (Zarontin)	Effective for petit mal seizures	Anorexia, nausea, vomiting, cramps, weight loss, diarrhea, drowsiness, headaches, dizziness, hiccups, irritability, hyperactivity, lethargy, fatigue, ataxia, swelling of tongue and gums
Diazepam (Valium)	Effective for multiple grand mal seizures and petit mal seizures	Drowsiness, fatigue, ataxia, confusion, depression, double vision, headache, nausea, skin rash, slurred speech, tremor, vertigo, anxiety, hallucinations, rage, sleep disturbances

Based on data from the *Physician's desk reference*. Oradell, NJ: Medical Economics Co., 1979.

controlled (Mullins, 1979). The type of medication used is determined by the type of seizures experienced and other pertinent medical information about the individual. Also, the dose required varies from person to person and occasionally has to be changed. Although many different medications are prescribed for seizure control, phenobarbital is the most effective and inexpensive drug for controlling grand mal seizures. Diphenylhydantoin (Dilantin) is also frequently used for grand mal attacks. The drug of choice for petit mal seizures is ethosuximide (Zarontin) (Berg, 1975). These drugs, as well as others, frequently cause side effects in persons. Table 10-2 summarizes the side effects associated with certain anticonvulsant drugs. Although all children will not manifest these side effects and many children will only exhibit a few of them, teachers should still be aware of the possible side effects.

Educational implications. Children with epilepsy are capable of the same academic work as other children with similar intellectual ability. The only modification that should be made is to protect the epileptic child from dangerous situations. For example, one should never let the child swim alone or climb to tall heights. If seizures occur in these situations, the implications for harm are obvious. For children who experience grand mal seizures, teachers must know the proper steps to take during these attacks:

1. *Remain calm.* Panic on the part of the teacher can only add confusion to the situation.
2. *Help the child to a horizontal position if he or she has not fallen.* The best position is to have the child lie on the side. If possible, keep the child's head turned to the side for saliva drainage.
3. *Do not attempt to restrain the child.* It is unlikely that injury will result from the contractions.
4. *Move any objects away from the child that might cause injury.*
5. *Do not force objects into the child's mouth.* Never insert your fingers into the mouth, since the child may bite down. Also, hard objects inserted into the mouth can cause the child injury.
6. *Loosen tight clothing about the child's neck if possible.*
7. *If the child sleeps immediately after the seizure, let the child stay where the seizure occurred.* If a period of consciousness follows the episode, allow the student to go to the nurse's room or a quiet place to rest.
8. *Inform the child's parents and/or physician of the seizure.* Immediate notification is not necessary unless the seizure is followed by a second seizure or lasts for a prolonged period (more than several minutes).
9. *Following the seizure, turn the entire episode into a learning experience if it is the first occurrence of the seizure.* Class members should be told what epilepsy is, and what it is not (i.e., it is not contagious) and be made to understand the importance of not making fun of the child. Proper procedures for handling an attack might also be discussed.

There is no reason to call a physician or send the child home unless there are specific instructions to do so. However, under the following conditions the teacher should always notify medical authorities (Anspaugh, Gilliland, & Anspaugh, 1980):

1. If there is no history of seizures and this appears to be the first
2. If the seizure lasts for more than 10 minutes
3. If the child goes from one seizure to another without regaining consciousness
4. If the child has breathing complications

In addition to management of grand mal seizure episodes, teachers should be alert for signs of the other types of epilepsy; children who consistently seem to daydream may be experiencing petit mal seizures. Since memory may be affected in children with petit mal and psychomotor seizures, teachers might want to review or summarize a lesson with a child they believe has experienced these seizures to ensure that important information was not missed during attacks. Teachers should assist children who are taking medication in following

Table 10-3. Low-incidence health disabilities

Disorder	*Description*	*Educational implications*
Hemophilia	Hereditary condition primarily affecting males in which blood clots slowly or not at all (Myers, 1975).	Children should not participate in contact sports or activities in which they may be hit by an object. Since exercise is necessary to maintain strong muscles and joints, safe activities include hiking, swimming (no diving), and safe calisthenics. Teachers should be aware if child limps or has discolorations of skin (Mullins, 1979).
Leukemia	Form of cancer of bone marrow that causes extreme overproduction of white blood cells. No known cause; usually fatal in children. Symptoms include pallor, fever, weight loss, joint pains, excessive bruising, and fatigue (Myers, 1975).	Chemotherapy treatment for leukemia may cause side effects including moon face, truncal obesity, and loss of hair (Myers, 1975). Child's tendency for developing infections and required treatment causes child to miss great deal of school. Teachers should assist child in home assignments and have positive but realistic outlook.
Sickle cell anemia	Hereditary blood disorder mostly affecting black Americans in which red blood cells are shaped like a sickle. May cause death; no known cure.	Children should not participate in physical activities that require increase of oxygen, for example, running (Leavitt, 1975). Frequent absences will occur requiring home assignments.
Cystic fibrosis	Most common cause of death from genetic disorder in United States, it affects approximately 1 in 1,500 live births (Harvey, 1975). Condition causes excessive secretion of mucus by all secreting glands; pancreas, liver, and lungs are most affected. Average age of death is 14 years old (Harvey, 1975).	Children should be allowed to cough, since this helps clear lungs. Because of metabolic problems, these children may have increased appetites and require frequent bowel movements. Teacher should be aware of any special diet the child is on, allow visits to bathroom as needed, and plan physical activities that do not require excessive physical exertion.
Muscular dystrophy	Progressive genetic disorder of voluntary muscles that frequently leads to death. Most common type, Duchenne, primarily affects boys and is usually detected by age of 6 (Gearheart & Weishahn, 1980). Children are usually in wheelchairs by age of 10, with death usually occurring 10 to 15 years following diagnosis.	Teacher should encourage child to stand and be as active as possible, since this slows muscle deterioration; allow frequent rest periods; and have optimistic attitude toward child, since, as with any terminal and progressive illness, emotional problems are likely to emerge. Teacher should become familiar with any special equipment that child may need, such as braces and standing tables.
Spina bifida	Condition affecting approximately 3 in 1,000 live births (Myers, 1975). Birth defect results from improper closing of neural tube during first 30 days of embryonic development (Bleck, 1975c). If outpouching contains nerve tissue, paralysis will result.	Since mobility is a major problem, teacher should make programs accessible and not expect child to go great distances to reach classes. Teacher should also be alert for pressure body sores and have child change positions frequently. Medical attention should be sought if child indicates shunt problems such as being drowsy or irritable; complaining of headaches (Mullins, 1979); or having urinary infections, indicated by increased temperature, flushed skin, and excessive perspiration (Gearheart & Weishahn, 1980). Teacher should assist child with bowel and bladder control by a preestablished schedule and medical appliances.

their medication schedule, and should allow them to go out of the room for water if needed to take medication. It is important for children to take all doses on schedule.

Other disorders

In addition to health impairments already discussed that might be present in school children, several other disorders occur in children, although with much less frequency. However, teachers who have children with these disorders also need to know what steps to take to accommodate for the health condition. Table 10-3 summarizes some of these impairments. Teachers who have dealings with these children might want to consult additional sources for a more complete description of appropriate and inappropriate treatment and seek professional assistance.

MUSCULOSKELETAL IMPAIRMENTS

Many problems are associated with the muscular and skeletal systems of the body. We will discuss only those which are most likely to be present in children in public school programs. These include amputations, arthritis, and cerebral palsy (although considered a neurological disability, it will be included because it is primarily manifested through problems of muscle control). Most children who have one of these musculoskeletal conditions will experience it as a single special education problem, whereas others will manifest these disorders in conjunction with other handicaps. Regardless of the extent of the condition, strategies to accommodate for mobility and muscle control problems are required if these children are to be successfully served in public school programs.

Terminology

Terminology used to describe these children is primarily medically oriented, using anatomy as a basis. Table 10-4 defines terms frequently associated with these disabilities. Although teachers will not use these terms often they should be acquainted with them because educational intervention with these types of disabilities frequently includes participation from many professions including communication disorder specialists, social workers, school psychologists, school principals, school counselors, vocational rehabilitation counselors, physical and occupational therapists, pediatric neurologists, orthopedists, recreation therapists, and community agency representatives (Sirvis, 1978). To understand diagnosis, treatment plans, and professional reports, these terms must be in the vocabulary of teachers.

Table 10-4. Terminology used with musculoskeletal impairments

Term	*Body area affected*
Type of limb involvement	
Monoplegia	One limb
Hemiplegia	Both limbs on same side of body
Paraplegia	Lower limbs
Diplegia	All four limbs, with lower limbs more affected than upper
Triplegia	Three limbs
Quadriplegia	All four limbs
Double hemiplegia	Upper limbs more affected than lower
Location of involvement	
Anterior	Front
Posterior	Back
Medial	Nearest to middle
Lateral	Farthest from middle
Superior	Nearer to head
Inferior	Farther from head

Amputations

Amputations, the total or partial absence of limb or limbs, can either be congenital or acquired by an accident or surgical procedure. In children younger than the age of 16, 75 percent of the impairments are congenital (Mullins, 1979). Congenital amputations result from a failure of the limb to develop properly in the first trimester of pregnancy (Bleck, 1975a). The causes for improper development are

Table 10-5. Disabilities associated with various amputations

Location	*Result*
Upper-limb absence	
Above the elbow	Less functional than below the elbow
	Intact upper limb usually used to maximum
	Prosthetic limb frequently discarded as "in the way"
Below the elbow	More functional than above the elbow
Lower-limb absence	
Above the knee	Allows child to walk well
	Limits ability to compete in sports except skiing and swimming
	Causes many children to become overweight because of limited physical activity
	Bilateral impairments create severe disability; usually requires a wheelchair
Below the knee	Allows child to walk well with prosthesis
	Allows child to engage in most sports
	Bilateral prostheses may allow child to walk well
	Allows child to compete in swimming; fins can be attached to residual limbs

unknown in many cases, but possible causes are exposure to radiation, viruses, and chemicals. In the late 1950s in Europe the drug thalidomide was prescribed for pregnant women to reduce nausea, and it has been linked to the occurrence of congenital amputations. Causes of acquired amputations range from traumatic accidents (e.g., automobile and machinery accidents) to the effects of diseases (Best, 1978).

Although amputations can occur in more than one limb, 85 percent of the impairments in children are unilateral, with twice as many occurring in the upper extremities as in the lower extremities (Mullins, 1979). Treatment includes being fitted with artificial limbs (prostheses) and trained in their use (Bleck, 1975a). The following considerations must be made in prescribing a prosthesis: (1) age of the child, (2) type and level of amputation, (3) psychological adjustment of the child to the disability, (4) support of the family, and (5) actual need for the device. The type and fitting of the prosthesis is determined by the type of amputation and the function of the limb that the device replaces (Best, 1978). Although prosthetic devices for children in the past were modified adult devices, specially designed prostheses for children are currently available.

The degree of disability present in children with amputations varies considerably depending on the limb involved, location of the amputation (e.g., above or below the knee), and degree of adaptation to the prostheses. Table 10-5 summarizes the effects of various types of amputations.

Educational implications. Children with acquired amputations usually have more emotional problems than those with congenital impairments. Teachers must be supportive of the child and accepting of the handicap. A positive attitude not only makes the child with the amputation more comfortable, but it also affects children in the classroom. Specifically designed educational programs are rarely warranted. Some children in this group are below and others are above average academically, but the majority should be in the middle academic range. Environmental modification must be a consideration for these children. Following are some basic factors that should be considered by teachers.

General information concerning prostheses. To effectively monitor the usefulness of prosthetic devices, teachers must have a working knowledge of them. This should include an understanding as to how the device should function, fit, and be maintained. Teachers should have prosthetic specialists train them in these areas. This is important because teachers who see the children on such a frequent basis can closely monitor the device. Children grow at a fast rate during the elementary years; prosthetic devices need to be constantly monitored to ensure that lengthening bones and enlarging joints do not make the prosthesis less effective.

Proper exercise. Many children with amputations become overweight because of limited physical activity. Teachers should encourage these children to participate in physical activities and should organize activities suitable for student involvement. Other feasible forms of recreation for these children need to be discovered. Carr, Friedman, and Swinyard (1969) suggest the following guidelines in developing recreation programs for children with limb deformities:

1. The program must be tailor-made for each child.
2. The program should provide the child with pleasure or participation, as well as therapeutic experiences.
3. The child's physician or physical therapist should be consulted before implementing the program.
4. The program should assist the child in integration into activities of the family and peers.

Physical care. Teachers need to ensure that children with amputations do not develop poor posture. This is important because certain amputations and prosthetic devices lend themselves to poor postural development. Proper care of the limb stump is also important. This includes frequent removal of the prosthetic device to enable the stump to be free from constriction and pressure. This most often occurs in the home, but teachers should be aware of the need and monitor the condition, especially if parents are negligent.

Adaptive equipment. Some students will require modified pencils, special seating, book holders, and other adaptive devices to aid them in academic functions.

Curriculum modifications. Although not required in many classes, modifications are needed in some classes. For example, students might be taught typing using one hand, mechanical drawing using procedures varying from normal practice, or woodworking using some mechanical assistance.

Acceptance by peers. Children with amputations arouse the curiosity of classmates. In cases in which prostheses are used, teachers might have the child demonstrate the device and explain its operation to the class. This practice should assist these children in assimilating into the class by satisfying the natural curiosity of classmates concerning the "strange-looking contraption" used by the amputee.

Rheumatoid arthritis

Arthritis is an inflammation of the joints and surrounding tissue; it is mainly thought of as a disorder of adults, but it can strike at any age beginning as early as 6 weeks. The type that most often affects children is rheumatoid arthritis, an inflammation of the lining of joints. Approximately 100,000 to 300,000 children in the United States suffer from arthritis (Miller, 1975). Affecting more girls than boys, the disease most likely begins between the ages of 1 to 4 and 9 to 14 years (Mullins, 1979). Although it can last only a few weeks and may not cause serious problems, rheumatoid arthritis can be chronic for up to 10 years (Myers, 1975). Sixty to 70 percent of arthritic children are free from active symptoms after 10 years (Miller, 1975).

The cause of rheumatoid arthritis is unknown. Suspected causes include infectious organisms, hypersensitivity disorders, inherited disorders, hormonal abnormalities, metabolic defects, nervous ailments, personality problems, emotional stress, diet, climate, and physical injury. Currently it is theorized that abnormal antibodies in the body attack normal tissue; what triggers these antibodies is unknown.

There is no known cure for the disease. Treatment usually consists of rest, drugs, and exercise of the arthritic joints. Aspirin is a mainstay in medication, with a large dosage of approximately 1½ tablets per day for every 10 pounds of body weight being administered in four or more doses given at regular intervals (Miller, 1975).

Children who have rheumatoid arthritis have periods of remission and acute inflammation; these extremes may change rapidly. During acute periods, joints swell, stiffen and ache and movement is restricted. Children are often irritable because of the pain.

Educational implications. Children with rheumatoid arthritis manifest the condition with various degrees of severity. Actions required by the teacher to accommodate these children varies greatly, depending on the age of the child, severity of the condition, and stage of the disease. Problems presented by the disease and accommodation strategies include the following:

Problem	*Action*
Fatigue	Allow frequent rest periods for children.
Stiffness	Allow and encourage children to move about room as necessary.
Restricted mobility	Provide extra time for children to move from one class to another, schedule classes close together, and do not schedule activities that require climbing stairs.
Hearing loss	Since large doses of aspirin can cause high-tone hearing loss, take appropriate steps to ensure that students receive information given orally.
Visual problems	One complication that occurs in some children is inflammation of eyes, which can lead to glaucoma and/or cataracts (Calhoun & Hawisher, 1979). If children complain about their eyes, notify parents and school to set up ophthalmological examination.
Morning stiffness	Schedule activities requiring movement (fine and gross) later in day
Restricted fine motor movement	Avoid lengthy written assignments, allow extra time for written assignments, assign someone to help take notes, provide copy of class notes, and give tests orally.
Frequent absences	Arrange for take-home assignments, and provide copy of class notes.
Need for physical exercise	Individualized physical activity program with physical therapist or physician; avoid contact sports, but encourage swimming
Need for aids	Obtain necessary writing aids such as pencils and paper; use electric typewriters if possible.

Cerebral palsy

Cerebral palsy is a nonprogressive disorder caused by damage to the brain that affects movement and posture. The major aspect of the condition with which teachers must deal is the way the brain damage affects movement and posture, not with the brain damage or its cause. Incidence estimates for children ages 5 to 15 range from 0.6 to 2.4 per 1,000 children, with slightly more males than females being affected (Capute, 1975). Severity and types of manifestation vary greatly.

Cerebral palsy can be classified according to limb involvement and movement. The classification of limb involvement describes the number of limbs involved and their location. This method of classification was previously discussed. Classifying according to movement is unique to cerebral palsy. Six basic categories and their characteristics are described in Table 10-6.

Children with cerebral palsy frequently have associated disabilities that may present more of an educational problem than motor involvement. These include mental retardation, learning disabilities, emotional problems, seizures, visual impairments, auditory impairments, and speech defects.

Table 10-6. Classification of cerebral palsy by movement function of limbs

Movement function	*Description*
Spasticity	Limb muscles are tight and contract with sudden attempted movement or stretching; a slight touch can make muscles shorten. It accounts for about 50 percent of all cerebral palsy.
Athetosis	Limbs have involuntary, purposeless movement. It includes about 25 percent of cerebral palsy.
Rigidity	Severe form of spasticity that usually affects all four limbs; movement of limbs is extremely difficult.
Ataxia	Primarily balance problem; falling occurs frequently.
Tremor	Shakiness of involved limb; may be noticed only when movement of affected limb is attempted.
Mixed	Usually quadriplegic, with combination of spasticity and athetosis.

Adapted from Bleck, E.E. In E.E. Bleck & D.A. Nagel (Eds.), *Physically handicapped children: a medical atlas for teachers*. New York: Grune & Stratton, Inc., 1975. (b)

These conditions compound the educational problems associated with motor and posture control and frequently can be considered the primary handicapping condition.

Services for cerebral palsied children differ greatly from one case to another, depending on the severity of the condition and the type of involvement. An interdisciplinary approach should be used and should involve physical and occupational therapists, educators, speech pathologists, orthopedic surgeons, neurosurgeons, pharmacologists, and pediatricians (Capute, 1975). Without collaboration among these professionals, these children are not likely to experience the maximum benefit from medical and educational intervention. The treatment program includes one or all of the following: occupational and physical therapy, being fitted with braces, orthopedic surgery, and drugs (Bleck, 1976b). Although teachers are not directly involved in much of the treatment program, they must be aware of the total program and know their role is assisting other team members in carrying out the intervention plan.

Educational implications. Beyond assisting with the total program, teachers should be concerned about the following particular problems encountered by children in the classroom:

Convulsive disorders. Know what steps to take if a child has a grand mal seizure in the class.

Proper positioning. In preventing physical deformities, the position in which the child sits/or lays is critical; consult with physicians and physical therapists to learn proper positioning for each child.

Physical transfer. Some children are not able to transfer themselves from wheelchairs to bathroom facilities or from a sitting to a supine position; obtain advice from other professionals on the best method to assist in these transfers.

Dressing. Some cerebral palsied children have difficulty in areas such as dressing themselves and putting on coats; assist in these activities as necessary.

Eating. Depending on the type and severity of the impairment, some children need assistance in eating. An aide may be assigned to provide this assistance, or peers may help; however, do not assign other students to do this if they do not want to help. At times, students' arms must be restricted in some manner to prevent involuntary movements from overturning trays and plates. Allow students to feed themselves whenever possible.

Handwriting. Because of involvement in the upper extremities, some children have difficulty in writing. It may be necessary to obtain special writing aids, allow extended periods of time for the student to complete the assignment, or give tests orally and permit assignments to be turned in orally or taped. Fellow students might be enlisted to write assignments for cerebral palsied children.

Speech. Many cerebral palsied children manifest speech difficulties. If the child has this difficulty,

(1) stimulate the child with sounds, (2) teach the child to follow simple oral directions, (3) encourage any sounds the child makes, (4) imitate the child's sounds (this encourages the child to imitate other sounds), and (5) see that word approximations are rewarded (Trombly, 1969). Remember that inarticulate speech is not an index of the child's intellectual ability.

Special materials. To assist these children in academic activities, some special materials might be required, including the following:

- Pencil holders
- Adapted typewriters with a keyboard guard to prevent involuntary movements from striking undesired keys
- Communication boards, both mechanical and electronic
- Page turners
- Weights for hands and wrists to limit extraneous movements
- Book holders
- Paper holders
- Stand-up tables

Alternative methods of communication. Many cerebral palsied children have speech deficits. These can be corrected and circumvented by developing alternative methods of communication including sign language, typewriters, and communication boards. Communication boards can be either mechanical or electronic. In designing a communication board, consider the status of vision, range of voluntary upper-limb movement, and arrangement of specific communication elements. These individual characteristics should be of primary concern, not the needs of observers or how the device conforms to the physical environment (Anderson, 1980).

Orthopedic aids

Numerous orthopedic aids assist children in the classroom, including wheelchairs, braces, prostheses, walkers, crutches, and canes. According to Venn, Morganstern, and Dykes (1979), "the primary role of the teacher regarding ambulation devices is daily observation of the student's use and care of his or her equipment" (p. 54). With mobility capabilities, many of these children can function well in regular school programs.

Wheelchairs. The primary function of wheelchairs is to increase mobility. However, these devices also (1) enable the child to assume responsibility for certain aspects of daily living; (2) encourage and permit the child to become involved in recreational, vocational, and academic programs; and (3) reduce the psychological effect of being totally immobile (Mullins, 1979).

The most common type of wheelchair has four wheels, a seat, a backrest, and footrests. A handrail is also present to enable the child to propel the device. Although this describes the basic chair, numerous additions are also available, depending on the needs of the child. The five basic chair sizes are small (for children 2 to 6 years old), large (for children 6 to 12 years old), junior (for larger children and small adults), adult (for average adult sizes), and oversize (for large and heavy individuals). Usually, chair sizes are based on the size of the individual, not actual age. In addition to size of the individual, the other factors considered in chair selection include the user's capacities, requirements of the operating areas, and chair's collapsibility, weight, dimensions safety and durability, appearance, and type of upholstery (Kamenetz, 1969).

For children with weak muscles or upper-extremities paralysis, motorized chairs are available. These will not be used unless absolutely necessary because manually propelled chairs provide a means of physical activity and exercise for the child. The teacher must be alert for worn parts, loose screws, general poor functioning of the chair, and changing needs of the child as a result of growth. A key role for teachers is safety management. Accidents with children in wheelchairs are primarily caused by runaway chairs and chairs that are pushed too fast by other children. Calhoun and Hawisher (1979, p. 163) provide some safety rules that should always be followed by students in wheelchairs.

1. Apply brakes when transferring from the wheelchair to the desk or other location.
2. Take turns leaving and entering a room.

3. Stay close to the wall when moving down the hall.
4. Look in all directions before turning or going backward.
5. Push yourself whenever possible.

Probably the most important rule for teachers to follow is to always lock the wheels when the chair is stationary. Since even small objects on the floor easily stop chairs, floors should be free from clutter and objects. Ramps should be available to permit accessibility to the entire school, and doorways should be wide enough for passage.

Braces. The three types of braces are corrective, control, and supportive. Corrective braces prevent and/or correct deformities during the rapid growth period of the student. Control braces prevent or control involuntary movements such as those found in athetosis. Supportive braces provide support for standing and walking. In monitoring braces for problems, teachers should note excessive wear, torn or worn leather parts, missing hardware, and any rubbing caused by the device (Gearheart & Weishahn, 1980).

Crutches. Crutches assist students in standing erect and/walking. They support part of the student's weight that weak or paralyzed legs cannot carry. Although little can go wrong with crutches, teachers should ensure that the crutches' rubber tips are not missing, the height is properly adjusted, and handholds are tight.

Environmental modifications. Teachers can take several steps to accommodate children in their classrooms who have musculoskeletal disabilities. Since each child manifests these conditions to different degrees, individualization is always a consideration. General considerations for the group as a whole include the following:

1. *Safety considerations.* Teachers should ensure that children with orthopedic disabilities are never left unattended during fire and tornado drills. Peer assistants should be assigned and exit routes rehearsed to ensure that plans are implemented. Floors should be free from objects that might make children on crutches fall or wheelchairs stop.
2. *Special equipment.* Special desks, chairs, and tables might be necessary for some students. For children who use crutches, chairs with wheels facilitate movement in the classroom. Teachers should consult with physical therapists to determine individual needs.
3. *Academic accommodations.* Since some children with disabilities work slowly, teachers should give them extra time to complete assignments and examinations. Oral rather than written responses might be necessary, and some children should be given an opportunity to use communication boards.
4. *Travel accommodations.* Travel is a problem for many of these children; therefore, teachers should allow extra time for movement from classroom to classroom.
5. *Seating location.* To prevent children from having to get up and go to their lockers for books and other materials, the teacher should provide an area near desks to store all necessary items. One idea is to use two desks for one student, providing extra storage and desk-top space.
6. *Desk aids.* The teacher should tape the student's paper to the desk top and tie the pencil to a string. This keeps these items from being dropped out of reach and allows for easy retrieval. Paperweights could also be used to stabilize notes and other papers.

MORE SEVERE CONDITIONS

Because of the trend for children with low-vision and hearing disorders to be mainstreamed, a special discussion of these disorders is included. Although the major responsibility for special education needs may be in the hands of itinerant specialists or building-based experts on vision and hearing, the regular classroom teacher and the resource room teacher (ordinarily concerned with educable mentally retarded, learning disabled, or behaviorally disordered populations) will need basic information to assist children in the mainstream. In some programs, such as the learning resource center, several types of special educators may share responsibility for a broad range of students in a multicategorical room. It is anticipated that growing numbers of such children will be placed, to some extent, in mainstream settings.

Visual deficits

Many children in public schools have visual deficits that range from mild (children who see a great deal and need little accommodation) to severe (totally blind children who require more intervention strategies). Although visually impaired children were once thought to be the most difficult to integrate into public school programs, it is currently recognized that these children are among the easiest to include in regular school classrooms if appropriate accommodations are made. A totally blind child may be thought of as severely handicapped, but many have been placed in regular classes successfully.

Aids. Various aids are available for visually impaired children, ranging from simple prescriptive lenses to elaborate electronic devices. The important factor is that with the proper aid many visually handicapped children need little additional accommodation by the teacher.

Glasses. Many schoolchildren wear prescriptive lenses to accommodate for mild visual disorders. Since the majority of visually impaired children have refractive errors, eyeglasses may be the only required accommodational device. In addition to ordinary glasses that are prescribed for many children, special prescriptions are sometimes required, including bifocals, prisms, contact lenses, and tinted lenses for light-sensitive children. Teachers should be prepared to assist children in the proper use and care of glasses, keeping the following considerations in mind:

1. *Know the child's needs.* If children should wear glasses at particular times during the day or during particular types of activities, ensure that the glasses are worn at those times. Also be aware of occassions in which glasses need *not* be worn if they are not necessary. Just because a child has glasses does not mean that they should be worn at all times (Lowenfeld, 1973a).

2. *Keep cleaning equipment available.* Glasses are ineffective if they are dirty. Have tissue and solvent available to clean dirty lenses. The proper solution for cleaning can be obtained from optometrists or ophthalmologists and usually is provided by parents. Because some children often forget to clean their glasses, occasionally check to see if they need to be cleaned.

3. *Check for proper fit.* Since glasses occasionally become bent and misshapen, monitor them for proper fit. Some lenses lose effectiveness if the fit is altered. If you suspect that glasses have been damaged and are not properly fitted, inform the parents and/or school nurse.

Magnifiers. Children whose vision cannot be corrected only with glasses often require prescriptive magnifiers. The three types of magnifiers are hand-held magnifiers, fixed-focused stand magnifiers, and focusable stand magnifiers. The advantage of stand over hand-held magnifiers is that some children's motor control is such that hand-held magnifiers cannot be held steady or for long periods. Teachers should be familiar with magnifiers to assist children in proper focusing and in maintenance of the devices. These skills can easily be acquired from local ophthalmologists or optometrists or as a part of in-service training.

Microscopic and telescopic aids. Some children will benefit from magnification devices that are *attached* to glasses. These are of two types: microscopic, used for close work, and telescopic, used for distance vision. Microscopic devices provide better binocular correction in higher power and with a greater working range than glasses (Faye, 1976a). For individuals performing tasks such as typing, playing a musical instrument, or certain types of schoolwork, microscopic devices are ideal. Telescopic aids have been used in travel assistance and even in permitting individuals to drive automobiles. Since these devices are usually expensive and difficult to fit, teachers should not attempt to adjust or provide maintenance. The role of the teacher is to gain information concerning the proper use of such aids. If these devices are suspected of malfunctioning, teachers should inform the child's parents, school nurse, or ophthalmologist.

Bookstands. To obtain the best lighting of materials and enable students to sit at the optimum distance from printed matter, bookstands can be beneficial. These can be mounted on the desk or floor. The adjustment range of the stand allows visually handicapped students to tilt the material to the most readable position.

Fiber-tip pens. Fiber-tip pens that make a larger and darker line than regular ink pens are preferred for some children with visual deficits. Teachers should experiment to determine which color and breadth are optimum for students.

Special paper. Special paper with lines darker than those found on ordinary paper assists students in writing assignments. This paper is readily obtainable, or regular paper can be modified by teachers to fit the needs of these children. Paper that reduces glare is important for some children who are sensitive to light.

Reading lamps. Some children only need increased illumination to accommodate for their disability. Adjustable reading lamps are effective because they can be moved to the proper distance and location to provide ample lighting without glare.

Typoscope. Another method of reducing glare is the typoscope, which is a black plastic or cardboard card with a cutout that enables students to see only one of a few words at a time. These devices can be constructed or purchased (Faye, 1976b).

Sunvisors. Another device for glare reduction is the sunvisor. It can be fitted to the head or to glasses.

Acetate. Acetate placed over print will usually darken and make it more readable for some children. Yellow acetate usually works best (Corn & Martinez, undated).

Large print and braille textbooks. Many children who cannot read regular print, even with the use of aids, can function well with large print textbooks; a few children with more severe disorders must read braille books. For children who require these materials, teachers should ensure that the necessary books are available at the beginning of the school year. Ward and McCormick (1981) provide the following sources for these materials:

American Printing House for the Blind
1839 Frankfort Ave.
Louisville, KY 40206

Braille Institute of America
741 N. Vermont Ave.
Los Angeles, CA 90029

Clovernook Press
Clovernook Home and School for the Blind
Cincinnati, OH 45231

Howe Memorial Press
Perkins School for the Blind
Watertown, MA 02172

Recording for the Blind, Inc.
215 E. 58th St.
New York, NY 10022

Tactual aids. Aids and devices previously discussed are primarily used by low-vision students—those who have enough residual vision to function visually; tactual aids are primarily used by children with more severe visual disorders, including those who are totally blind with no light perception. These aids allow students to function in the "sighted world" using the sense of touch. Since teachers should have assistance from itinerant specialists, they need not be skilled in the use of these devices.

Braillewriter. A major mode of communication for totally blind individuals is braille. Developed by Louis Braille in the early 1800s, braille is a method of reading and writing that uses a six-dot cell, consisting of two three-dot columns. Variations of dots within this six-dot cell represent letters, words, punctuation, numerals, and even musical notation. The braillewriter is a mechanical device similar to a typewriter that prints braille. The most well-known mechanical braillewriter is the Perkins Brailler, developed in 1950 at the Perkins School for the Blind (Lowenfeld, 1973b). Since braillewriters are somewhat noisy, teachers should place children who use these devices in areas in which the noise will be least distracting to other students. However, teachers should remember that blind children need to be located near the teacher to use their hearing skills.

Slate and stylus. For students who prefer not to use a braillewriter or who do not have access to one, a slate and stylus may be used to print braille by hand. The slate is a metal frame with openings through which dots are punched onto braille paper with the stylus. The slate and stylus is compact and can be carried in a shirt pocket. Although it is more easily carried and quieter to use, children write much slower with the slate and stylus than with the braillewriter.

Raised-line drawing board. The raised-line drawing board is a rubber-covered board that, when covered with acetate and drawn or written on with a pointed object, allows the child to feel the lines that have been drawn.

Abacus. While teachers in elementary grades frequently use the abacus as a teaching tool in mathematics instruction, this device can be equally effective with blind students. The abacus allows students to move objects, thus making mathematics a concrete experience.

Templates. Templates guide visually handicapped children in writing. Many visually handicapped adults use these as signature guides. In the school setting, they can be used in all written exercises, assisting students in keeping their writing within a confined space.

Models. Models are being used more often in instructing blind children in various subject areas. The area most adaptable to the use of models is science. The American Printing House for the Blind has developed 19 models of representative species of the major invertebrate phyla and component structures of flowering plants (Franks & Murr, 1978). Teachers who do not have access to these models can construct their own. Wright (1978) describes the use of glue to make models of microscopic pictures for a botany class. Cooperman (1980) describes methods of constructing models for a wide range of science topics including cell structure, meiosis and mitosis, and genetics. The construction of models can also facilitate instruction in areas other than science such as social studies maps.

Raised-line paper. Writing paper, graph paper, and other forms of paper used by elementary students is available in raised-line format. These "guides" allow visually handicapped students to write, make graphs, or perform other actions in the appropriate space.

Technological aids. With the rapidly advancing field of electronics, there is a significant increase in the number and type of technological aids available to visually handicapped persons. Ranging from mobility devices to closed-circuit television, these aids have revolutionized some of the capabilities of the visually handicapped person. Following are some representative types.

Talking calculator. Similar in size to a hand-held calculator, the electronic talking calculator "speaks" each calculation entry and result. Any calculation performed by a standard calculator can be accomplished by the talking calculator.

Optacon. The Optacon transforms print into letter configurations using 144 small tactile stimulators. The person using the machine must be trained in translating these sensations of touch into letters and words.

Closed-circuit television (CCTV). CCTV is just now being used to its fullest capacity with visually handicapped children. With CCTV, visually handicapped children can enlarge printed material to a size that is readable and change the polarity from white-on-black to black-on-white type as necessary. A student is able to move the tape at any rate to read from the screen.

Microfiche. The use of microfiche as an aid for visually handicapped children is currently expanding and has proved to be a positive complement to other reading aids (Andersson, 1980). Once printed material is converted to microfiche, local schools that serve visually handicapped children make available the needed printed materials for particular classes. Unlike large print textbooks, which can take several months to obtain, microfiche can be developed relatively quickly if the necessary equipment is available.

Tape recorders. Visually handicapped children can benefit greatly from the use of tape recorders; they assist the children in note taking, understanding directions, and responding to an assignment. McCulloch (1979) describes the use of tapes as "tutor tapes," since they can assist visually handicapped persons in practicing or completing assignments.

Microprojectors and microslide viewers. Microprojectors and microslide viewers allow visually handicapped children to view microscope slides, which they would be unable to view with the regular microscope (Ricker, 1981).

Electronic mobility devices. One of the greatest limitations for visually handicapped children is mobility—getting from on location to another. Recently some electronic mobility devices have been developed that greatly facilitate the independence of visually handicapped persons. The *Sonicguide* is an ultrasonic device mounted in a spectacle frame that provides feedback in three ways: intensity, pitch, and timbre. Intensity and pitch provide the main cues to determine direction and distance of objects (Welch, 1977). This device is to be used as a secondary mobility aid in conjunction with another mobility aid. Once the student has learned to respond appropriately to feedback, mobility independence is facilitated. The *Laser Cane* is a modified long cane that provides feedback to the subject auditorily and tactually. Different frequency sounds indicate whether an obstruction is low, medium, or high in height.

Environmental modifications. Although teachers are involved to varying degrees with the aids previously discussed, either involvement is much greater in the area of environmental modifications. Many visually handicapped children can function well in regular school programs with only environmental modifications; for others, environmental modifications in conjunction with other aids provide the necessary accommodations.

Seating. For many childen with visual handicaps, modifications in seating arrangement make a significant difference in ability to function in the classroom. Visually handicapped children should be encouraged to move around the room to take advantage of the best possible seating. For example, if the teacher is using the blackboard, the student may need to move close to it or move to a location in which glare from the blackboard is minimized. Students should not be made to feel self-conscious but rather should be encouraged to move to the location that maximizes their residual vision. Seating should be arranged to take advantage of the child's special lighting needs. For some children, this means allowing them to sit next to windows; for others, this means providing a location in which a lamp can be easily used.

Location of teacher. Teachers should be aware of their location in the room. If visually handicapped children need to be near the teacher during demonstrations, the teacher should not constantly move about. Also, teachers should avoid standing in front of a bright lighting source because this causes the low-vision student to look directly into the light. Teachers should also be aware of glare on the blackboard and should write on the portion of the board where glare is lowest.

Color contrast. Some low-vision children can see dark objects on a light background better than light objects on a dark background. Other children have the opposite need. Teachers should experiment with various color contrasts to determine the best combination for particular children. Every opportunity should be taken to modify the color of objects to suit the particular color-contrast needs of individual children (Sicurella, 1977).

Note taking. Several modifications that aid note taking can be implemented by teachers. These include using tape recorders, establishing the "buddy" system, or making a copy of the teacher's notes for the student. If classes present a vital need for note taking by students, some accommodations must be made for the visually handicapped students to perform well.

Examinations. Teachers need to make modifications in their examinations used with visually handicapped children. These modifications can include giving tests orally, having fellow students read the test, recording test questions with pauses for answers on tapes, or giving a low-vision student extra time to effectively use magnification aids. Many children are capable of reading regular and large print if they can hold the reading material extremely close to the eyes. This does not harm the eyes.

Open and closed doors. Doors that are partly open present a hazard for visually handicapped children. Therefore, teachers should ensure that doors are either completely open or closed; a routine should be established.

Physical arrangement of room. Teachers often like to rearrange the classroom. If this is done when a visually handicapped child is in the room, the child should be reoriented to the new arrangement. This prevents injury to the child or embarrassment resulting from bumping into things.

Storage and shelf space. Because large print textbooks, tape recorders, and other equipment used by visually handicapped students are bulky, considerations should be made for storage and shelf space for these students. Providing a particular shelf or a mobile storage cart can fill this need.

Noise level. Since many visually handicapped children rely on their hearing for information, teachers should keep the noise level in the class room at a moderate level during important activities. Loud and continuous noise will affect the visually handicapped child's ability to employ listening skills necessary for functioning and learning. Noise level is an important factor only at points when information is disseminated, instructions are given, or explanations are offered; in this sense, it is no less important for other students.

General considerations. In addition to environmental modifications that can facilitate a visually handicapped child's functioning in a regular school program, there are some general considerations about working with a visually handicapped child. Corn and Martinez (undated) suggest the following considerations for teachers:

1. Feel at ease using words such as "see" and "look." These words are in the visually handicapped child's vocabulary and are commonly used to describe experiences idiomatically. For example, blind persons say they watch television, whereas, in fact, they listen to it.
2. Introduce visually handicapped children to the class as you would any student. It is likely that the child's handicap will create questions from other students. If the visually handicapped child is comfortable with and accepting of the handicap, encourage the child to respond to questions; consequently the other students in the room will better understand the nature of the disability.
3. Include visually handicapped children in all activities such as physical education. Although modifications may need to be made for some activities, it is much better to include than have the child "sit on the sidelines" during the activity.
4. Encourage the visually handicapped child to assume leadership roles. Most children, at times, like to be the leader and center of attention; visually handicapped children should be given an equal opportunity.
5. Apply the same disciplinary rules to visually handicapped children that apply to the rest of the class; as much as possible, these children should be treated in the same manner as all children in the class. Treating them differently encourages negative attitudes by the other children in the class.
6. Since all children are sensitive to peer acceptance and criticism, be a model of acceptance for visually handicapped students. Fellow students readily acquire teachers' attitudes, making it necessary for you to portray a genuine acceptance of the visually handicapped child. This is an especially powerful model in the early grades.
7. When approaching a visually handicapped child, identify yourself. This, of course, is not necessary if the child has considerable residual vision; however, if the child cannot

recognize persons, introductions must be made. Likewise, inform the visually handicapped child if you are leaving the room. It is an embarrassing situation if a child continues talking to someone after the room is emptied.

Mobility. Mobility is a vital component of the curriculum for visually impaired students. According to Suterko (1973), the objectives of orientation and mobility training include that the person will (1) remain oriented while walking on foot in either familiar or unfamiliar environments, (2) be able to travel safely with a minimum amount of reliance on others and with reasonable ease of movement and physical freedom, (3) develop efficient techniques of physical search and visual scanning, and (4) develop correct techniques for the use of optical and mechanical aids for travel without also developing an incongruous or uncomfortable gait or posture. Travel skills are important if students are to be well adjusted and independent. The three primary modes of mobility for visually handicapped persons are (1) the sighted guide, (2) the long cane, and (3) the dog guide.

The *sighted guide* is the method used by most children in public schools. In this method, the child takes the arm of a sighted person. Acting as a guide, the sighted person should not hold or push the child from behind; this does not provide ample cues for travel and encourages anxiety. By holding the arm of the guide, the child can gain the required information to travel efficiently. Teachers of visually impaired students should have various students practice sighted-guide techniques and assign students, preferably on a rotating basis, to act as the guide.

The *long cane* provides more independence for visually impaired children than the sighted guide because there is no dependence on another person. Individuals with good cane skills can travel independently almost anywhere incuding city streets and rural and residential areas. Acquisition of cane skills requires the child to practice for long periods of time with an orientation and mobility specialist. Although few public schools would employ such an individual, these services are usually available through state departments of education and state agencies serving the blind.

Dog guides are rarely used by elementary children. Their use is more suitable for older adolescents and adults.

Summary

Visually impaired children can function well in public schools. The trend during the past 20 years has been to limit their placement in residential schools and provide educational services in public school programs. With aids and environmental accommodations, many of these children can function well in the mainstream. The role of the classroom teacher is not greatly complicated if support from specialists is available. If the needs of the child are determined, the classroom teacher, special educator, and others can secure the necessary equipment, materials, and strategies to accommodate the child.

Auditory deficits

Children with auditory deficits are usually classified as either hard of hearing or deaf. Those classified as hard of hearing frequently have enough residual hearing to benefit from aids and may function in regular school programs with accommodation. Although needing more extensive accommodation, children who are more severely impaired may be capable of benefiting from some regular school programming. Many hearing-impaired children have been primarily served in residential schools; however, public schools have increased these programs and the amount of time used to integrate hearing-impaired students into regular school classes (Gearheart, 1980). As a result, regular teachers must be familiar with the aids and measures necessary to effectively teach these students in public school programs and school-based special education classes. In many schools assistance from a resource room teacher may be needed in coordinating services with an itinerant specialist.

Aids. Teachers of hearing-impaired students

have various aids available to facilitate educational programming. These range from sophisticated electronic devices such as hearing aids to written scripts for filmstrips.

Hearing aids. For many hearing-impaired students, hearing aids are sufficient for accommodation. Although they do not enable children to hear normally, hearing aids amplify sounds to a level that can be perceived with residual hearing. Several types of hearing aids are available. The two primary categories are personal (wearable) aids and group aids (Bess & McConnell, 1981). Unless several hearing-impaired children are to be served in the same classroom, the personal aid is the type most likely used. Personal aids are worn either on the body or at ear level. The on-the-body aid has a microphone, battery, and amplifier that are attached to the clothing or worn in a harness and a thin wire that is connected to an earmold. Ear-level aids are either attached to glasses, worn over the ear, or worn in the outer ear. There are many advantages and disadvantages to each type. The on-the-body type produces more amplification than ear-level aids; whereas the in-the-ear variety produces less amplification (Webber, 1981). The role of educators is to assist the child with the aid that is prescribed.

Assistance by the teacher entails maintenance of the aid and "troubleshooting" if the aid appears to malfunction. Bess and McConnell (1981) suggest that a traditional troubleshooting kit should include the following items:

Drying agent for removing moisture
Pipe cleaners
Battery test
Hearing-aid stethoscope
Pencil-style typewriter eraser
Spare batteries
Extra cord
Extra receiver

Hearing aids should be examined by parents and teachers. Even if parents methodically check the aid in the morning, the teacher should repeat the examination at school. If an aid does not function for even part of the day, the child may fall behind in academic work and social acceptance.

The daily check includes these steps (Hanners & Sitton, 1974):

1. Check the controls to ensure proper external setting.
2. Clean the microphone aperture with a bristle brush.
3. Check for cracks in the the receiver.
4. Examine the earmold for rough edges, cracks, or buildup of ear wax.
5. Examine the battery contacts for corrosion or dirt, and clean if necessary.
6. Check the battery voltage for proper installation.
7. Listen for distortion, static, or noise while someone is speaking.
8. Wiggle the cords while listening to determine if they are broken or have a loose connection or a short in the connection.
9. Check the earmold and/or tubing for feedback with the aid in place.
10. Check the earmold for a proper seal by increasing the volume to cause feedback and placing a finger over the aperture. If a good seal is present, the feedback will stop.

Table 10-7 lists some common problems of hearing aids and the steps that may be taken to correct them. Although teachers can assist in the daily check and troubleshooting, major repairs should not be attempted. If aids do not function after normal troubleshooting attempts, they should be removed and sent to a service center for repair.

Auditory trainer. The auditory trainer is a group amplification device frequently used if several hearing-impaired children are in the same room. Many audiologists and educators have maintained that group amplification is more efficient and less likely to have mechanical breakdown than personal aids. Teachers who work in classrooms that use group amplification systems need to become familiar with troubleshooting methods and daily maintenance actions required to keep the system functional. This information can be obtained from

Table 10-7. Common problems of hearing aids and required actions

Problem	*Action*
Aid produces squealing or feedback (high-pitched noise), which may occur if child's head is moved or may be constant noise.	Be sure earmold is placed correctly in ear and is proper size. With body aids, check that earmold is snapped firmly to nub of receiver. With ear-level aids, be sure hollow plastic tube from earmold fits tightly over receiver opening.
Aid does not work or works only intermittently.	Replace battery. Make sure that positive and negative ends of battery are placed correctly in battery compartment and that battery is firmly in place.
Aid produces weak, distorted, or scratchy signal.	Change battery even if it is new or checks out as good. With body aid, try another receiver. Turn volume up and down and listen for scratchiness or dead spots. Make sure tone control is set properly.

Adapted from Blackhurst, A.E., & Berdine, W.H. *An introduction to special education*. Boston: Little, Brown & Co., 1981.

the company that manufactures the system used in the school.

Captioned films and filmstrips. Many films and filmstrips are captioned for hearing-impaired students. When ordering films and filmstrips, teachers with hearing-impaired students should check to determine which media materials are captioned. The captioned versions are exactly like noncaptioned ones, except that with words are added at the bottom of each frame. This accommodation enables hearing-impaired students to benefit and enjoy films and filmstrips along with nonhearing-impaired students.

Scripts for films. If teachers do not have access to captioned films and filmstrips, scripts may be necessary. Often scripts are available from the company in which the materials are rented or purchased. If scripts are not available from these sources, teachers can develop their own scripts. Teachers may do this themselves, or they may have this done by students as special projects. School service clubs, honorary associations, retired teachers, or other groups could perform these activities as group projects.

Overhead projectors. Although available at most schools, teachers frequently overlook the use of overhead projectors as a valuable teaching tool for hearing-impaired students and other students. For teachers who use the lecture format regularly, overhead projectors can be beneficial for hearing-impaired students. With the material projected visually, these students are able to take notes, pick up cues to assist residual hearing, and become active in the learning process. Without this accommodation, hearing-impaired students are frequently frustrated in classes that rely on lecture.

Environmental modifications. In addition to available aids that assist in the integration of hearing-impaired students in regular school programs, some environmental modifications can be made in classrooms that will accommodate for hearing-acuity deficits.

Seating. Hearing-impaired students need seating in which they can take best advantage of their residual hearing and speechreading skills. The better ear, if there is one, should be turned toward the teacher and the class. Hearing-impaired children should be encouraged to turn around and face other children in class who may be talking or reporting. They also should be encouraged to move about the room, as necessary, to better use their hearing and visual skills. Since a great deal of stimulation must be received visually, seating should be such that they can see all classroom activities.

Position of teacher. Since many hearing-impaired children gain information from speechreading, visual clues, and residual hearing, the position of the teacher in the room is extremely important. Teachers should be near these children when talking and aware of the following "dont's":

1. Talking with the back to the class
2. Talking while looking down
3. Talking with a book, object, or hand in front of the face

Teachers who frequently move about the room should try to face the hearing-impaired child when talking, and encourage the child to turn or move about to be in a better position for hearing. An effort should *always* be made to be near these children when giving important information and instructions or to see that a peer provides assistance.

Articulation of teacher. Teachers should speak naturally when hearing-impaired children are in the class. The teacher should not overemphasize words by exaggerating lip movements; this only complicates the ability of hearing-impaired children to "read" lips. "Distinct articulation is more helpful to the hearing impaired student than speaking louder" (Gearheart & Weishahn, 1980, p. 52), and natural speech is always better than attempting to modify articulation.

Positive attitudes. Teachers' attitudes toward any child or group of children will likely be modeled by other students; therefore, it is imperative that teachers have an accepting attitude toward any hearing-impaired student in the classroom. Teachers need to regard these students as those who require circumventive strategies to allow them to benefit optimally from instruction. Methods the teacher can use to facilitate positive attitudes of other students toward hearing-impaired students include the following:

1. Presenting a positive attitude
2. Encouraging hearing-impaired students to participate in all activities of the class including social and nonacademic endeavors
3. Ensuring that hearing-impaired students fill some leadership roles in the room
4. Emphasizing things the hearing-impaired students can do well, not the limitations associated with hearing deficits

Visual aids. A great deal of information in most classrooms is learned using the auditory modality; unfortunately, many children with hearing deficits cannot learn through this sense without supplemental input. The obvious supplementary mode would be vision. If teachers would take advantage of visual aids, many hearing-impaired children would be able to benefit greatly in regular class programs. The following suggestions relate to the use of visual aids to assist hearing-impaired children:

1. *Use the chalkboard.* This visual aid is found in nearly all classrooms and can be invaluable for hearing-impaired children. In using the board, teachers should remember to talk while facing the students, not the board, and to place information on the board that provides basic facts and information vital to the lesson.
2. *Use captioned films and filmstrips.* If captioned media are not available, the teacher should make a script.
3. *Use written instructions.* Most children in school do not require written instructions, since they can hear instructions verbalized by the teacher. For hearing-impaired children, however, failing to hear auditory instructions can cause failure. If teachers want to enable hearing-impaired children to perform at a maximum level, they must guarantee that these children receive proper instructions.
4. *Use the overhead projector.* Overhead projectors have all the advantages of chalkboards, and, in addition, teachers are less likely to talk with their backs to the students. If overhead projectors are used properly, teachers are able to provide visual stimulation even though they are not facing the students. Overheads can be used with either

prepared transparencies or blank transparencies that are completed during the lesson.

5. *Use visual models.* Whenever feasible, teachers should use visual models to enhance the learning potential of hearing-impaired students, for example, using the "Invisible Man" (a clear plastic model) for discussions of the human body, maps and charts for the teaching of history and geography, and written examples of proper sentence structure for the teaching of writing skills.
6. *Use demonstration and modeling.* Hearing-impaired students learn efficiently from demonstration and modeling of processes. Teachers should attempt to use demonstrations as often as possible when hearing-impaired students are in the classroom, for example, demonstrating rather than just talking about proper writing strokes. These approaches may also benefit nonhandicapped students.

Note taking. Regardless of the accommodational strategies used by teachers to circumvent hearing loss, some material is best presented through the lecture format. In these instances, teachers should provide hearing-impaired students with an alternative method of gaining information, since they probably will not be able to make copious notes. Such alternatives include (1) allowing hearing-impaired students to copy notes from other students in class, (2) providing hearing-impaired students with a copy of the teacher's notes, and (3) assigning different students to copy notes for these students on a typewriter or using carbon paper.

"Hearing helper." During some activities, assigning a "hearing helper" to those with hearing losses may be effective. This might be appropriate if notes are not required to be taken, but directions need to be understood by the handicapped students. For example, during an assembly a hearing helper could communicate some of the dialogue of the assembly to the hearing-impaired student. To enable hearing-impaired students to participate during physical education classes, a hearing helper could tell the student when to bat and what position to play, what line of the relay race to get into, and so forth.

Speechreaders. A common misconception is that speechreaders can understand most of what is said simply by reading lips. Only a small portion of what is said can be directly understood by speechreaders. Teachers can facilitate speechreading by considering the following points:

1. *Position of the student.* Students who read lips need to be able to see the person who is talking. They should be sitting near the speaker, preferably within 5 to 10 feet (Gearheart & Weishahn, 1980), but not so close that they constantly have to look up. When other students in the class are speaking, they should be encouraged to speak to the hearing-impaired student, and the hearing imparied student should be encouraged to turn around in the chair, if necessary, to look at the speaker. In addition, the child should be seated near the front of the room and to the side to see both the teacher and other students. Finally, students should not have to look into a light source while observing speakers, since this may prevent adequate lighting of the speaker's face.

2. *Position of the teacher.* As mentioned previously, the position or proximity of the teacher is important for instruction. The teacher should always return to the same place to read the next question or make another point. To prevent students from having to look into light, teachers should not position themselves in front of windows or other light sources.

3. *Delivery by the teacher.* Teachers should not exaggerate gestures but rather use them naturally. Gesturing, as with articulation, should be distinct but not overemphasized. Overemphasis of words or parts of words make it more difficult for speechreaders to ascertain the words spoken.

4. *Appearance of the teacher.* Facial hair on male teachers makes it difficult for students to follow intricate movements of the lips. Teachers who wear beards should keep them trimmed as much as possible to enable students to see the outline of the

lips. Teachers who choose to outline the lips with lipstick assist speechreading by making it easier to follow lip movements.

5. *Presentation of spelling and vocabulary.* In administering spelling tests, words should be used in context or presented along with the object or a picture of the object if possible. All meanings of words with multiple meanings should be presented.

General considerations. Following are some general considerations for teachers of hearing-impaired children. First, teachers should treat these children like other students in regard to class assignments, disciplinary rules, and general expectations. Children who have this handicap should be treated differently only to circumvent the disability of a hearing deficit. When aids are prescribed for children, teachers should enforce their use. Second, teachers can promote acceptance of these children by presenting a good model for the other children in the class and accepting the hearing-handicapped child as a normal child who happens to have a hearing problem. Third, teachers should attempt to stimulate interaction between hearing-impaired students and peers. Naiman (1977) describes one method of facilitating interaction using cameras. Students are taught to take photographs and encouraged to show them to each other and talk about them. There are many other creative ways to bring about interaction. Fourth, teachers may need to assist students in seating arrangements. Many hearing-impaired students, when comfortable with moving, automatically adjust their seating to take advantage of a position for better hearing and lighting; however, some children will have to be assisted in moving to the most advantageous position.

SUMMARY

The purpose of this chapter was to provide practical information for classroom teachers and special educators who are not specialized in managing the related needs of children with sensory and physical disorders. Many children with physical, health, and sensory problems attend regular classes; in many districts special educators are expected to assist in the educational program of these children, even though they may not have primary training in dealing with such disorders. Many children with visual and hearing disorders adjust well to regular classroom placement if proper accommodations are made through a variety of aids, instructional procedures, and supportive strategies.

Various responsibilities of the teacher concerning the problems of musculoskeletal disorders were discussed. The major recommendation was that teachers must adjust the physical environment. Many of the teaching procedures used with nonhandicapped children can be used with most physically handicapped children.

Health disorders of many children are of particular concern, either because children do not feel well enough to benefit from school, or because life can be threatened. Some children with terminal diseases cause special problems for teachers who must cope with the inevitability of death of a student.

Many classroom teachers have found that children with a variety of problems may be included comfortably in regular classrooms if proper planning, support, and consultation are established. As this trend continues, the acceptibility of children with sensoriphysical disorders will increase and the classroom teacher will regard the teaching responsibility for these children as a normal course of events.

REFERENCES AND SUGGESTED READINGS

Anderson, J.D. Spatial arrangement of stimuli and the construction of communication boards for the physically handicapped. *Mental Retardation,* 1980, *18*(1), 41-42.

Anderson, T. Microfiches as a reading aid for partially sighted students. *Journal of Visual Impairment and Blindness,* 1980, *74,* 193-195.

Anspaugh, D.J., Gilliland, M., & Anspaugh, S.J. The student with epilepsy. *Today's Education,* 1980, *69,* 78-86.

Apgar, V., & Beck, J. *Is my baby all right? A guide to birth defects.* New York: Trident Press, 1972.

Baum, D. Heart disease in children. In E.E. Bleck & D.A. Nagel (Eds.), *Physically handicapped children: a medical atlas for teachers.* New York: Grune & Stratton, Inc., 1975.

Berg, B.O. Conclusive disorders. In E.E. Bleck & D.A. Nagel

(Eds.), *Physically handicapped children: a medical atlas for teachers*. New York: Grune & Stratton, Inc., 1975.

Bess, F.H., & McConnell, F.E. *Audiology, education, and the hearing impaired child*. St. Louis: The C.V. Mosby Co., 1981.

Best, G.A. *Individuals with physical disabilities: an introduction for educators*. St. Louis: The C.V. Mosby Co., 1978.

Blackhurst, A.E., & Berdine, W.H. *An introduction to special education*. Boston: Little, Brown & Co., 1981.

Bleck, E.E. Amputations in children. In E.E. Bleck & D.A. Nagel (Eds.), *Physically handicapped children: a medical atlas for teachers*. New York: Grune & Stratton, Inc., 1975. (a)

Bleck, E.E. Cerebral palsy. In E.E. Bleck & D.A. Nagel (Eds.), *Physically handicapped children: a medical atlas for teachers*. New York: Grune & Stratton, Inc., 1975. (b)

Bleck, E.E. Myelomeningocele, meningocele, and spina bifida. In E.E. Bleck & D.A. Nagel (Eds.), *Physically handicapped children: a medical atlas for teachers*. New York: Grune & Stratton, Inc., 1975. (c)

Bleck, E.E. Poliomyelitis. In E.E. Bleck & D.A. Nagel (Eds.), *Physically handicapped children: a medical atlas for teachers*. New York: Grune & Stratton, Inc., 1975. (d)

Calhoun, M.L., & Hawisher, M. *Teaching and learning strategies for physically handicapped students*. Baltimore: University Park Press, 1979.

Capute, A.J. Cerebral palsy and associated dysfunctions. In R.H.A. Haslam & P.J. Valletutti (Eds.), *Medical problems in the classroom: the teacher's role in diagnosis and management*. Baltimore: University Park Press, 1975.

Carr, A.C., Friedman, L., & Swinyard, C.A. Essentials of a recreation program for children with limb deformities. In D.D. Peterson (Ed.), *The physically handicapped: a book of readings*. New York: M.S.S. Information Corp., 1969.

Code of Federal Regulations (Title 45, Section 121.1). Washington, DC: U.S. Office of Education, Bureau of Education for the Handicapped, 1974.

Cooperman, S. Biology for the visually impaired student. *The American Biology Teacher*, 1980, *42*, 293-294.

Corn, A.L., & Martinez, I. *When you have a visually handicapped child in your classroom: suggestions for teachers*. New York: American Foundation for the Blind, Inc.

Faye, E.E. Characteristics of near vision aids: convex lenses, telescopic loupes, and closed circuit television. In E.E. Faye (Ed.), *Clinical low vision*. Boston: Little, Brown & Co., 1975. (a)

Faye, E.E. Special categories of accessory aids. In E.E. Faye (Ed.), *Clinical low vision*. Boston: Little, Brown & Co., 1976. (b)

Federal Register. Washington, DC: U.S. Government Printing Office, August 23, 1977, p. 42478.

Franks, F.L., & Murr, M.J. Biological models for blind students. *Journal of Visual Impairment and Blindness*, 1978, *72*(4), 121-124.

Gearheart, B.R. *Special education for the '80s*. St. Louis: The C.V. Mosby Co., 1980.

Gearheart, B.R., & Weishahn, M.H. *The handicapped student in the regular classroom*. St. Louis: The C.V. Mosby Co., 1980.

Golub, S. An R.N. refresher: Muscular dystrophy. In D.D. Peterson (Ed.), *The physically handicapped: a book of readings*. New York: M.S.S. Information Corp., 1969.

Hanners, B.A., & Sitton, A.B. Ears to hear: a daily hearing aid monitor program. *Volta Review*, 1974, *76*, 530-536.

Harvey, B. Cystic fibrosis. In E.E. Bleck & D.A. Nagel (Eds.), *Physically handicapped children: a medical atlas for teachers*. New York: Grune & Stratton, Inc., 1975.

Kamenetz, H.L. *The wheelchair book: mobility for the disabled*. Springfield, IL: Charles C Thomas, Publisher, 1969.

Katz, H.P. Important endocrine disorders of childhood. In R.H.A. Haslam & P.J. Valletutti (Eds.), *Medical problems in the classroom: the teacher's role in diagnosis and management*. Baltimore: University Park Press, 1975.

Landon, C., Rosenfeld, R., Northcraft, G., & Lewiston, N. Self-image of adolescent with cystic fibrosis. *Journal of Youth and Adolescence*, 1980, *9*, 521-527.

Leavitt, T.J. Sickle cell disease. In E.E. Bleck & D.A. Nagel (Eds.), *Physically handicapped children: a medical atlas for teachers*. New York: Grune & Stratton, Inc., 1975.

Lowenfeld, B. History of the education of visually handicapped children. In B. Lowenfeld (Ed.), *The visually handicapped child in school*. New York: The John Day Co., 1973. (a)

Lowenfeld, B. Psychological considerations. In B. Lowenfeld (Ed.), *The visually handicapped child in school*. New York: The John Day Co., 1973. (b)

McCulloch, J. Tutor tapes. *Journal of Visual Impairment and Blindness*, 1979, *73*, 287-289.

Miller, J.J. Juvenile rheumatoid arthritis. In E.E. Bleck & D.A. Nagel (Eds.), *Physically handicapped children: a medical atlas for teachers*. New York: Grune & Stratton, Inc., 1975.

Mullins, J.B. *A teacher's guide to management of physically handicapped students*. Springfield, IL: Charles C Thomas, Publisher, 1979.

Myers, B.A. The child with chronic illness. In R.H.A. Haslam & P.J. Valletutti (Eds.), *Medical problems in the classroom: the teacher's role in diagnosis and management*. Baltimore: University Park Press, 1975.

Naiman, D.W. Picture perfect: photography aids deaf children in developing communication skills. *Teaching Excepional Children*. 1977, *9*(2), 36-38.

Physicians' desk reference. Oradell, NJ: Medical Economics Company, 1979. Ricker, K.S. Optical media bring biology to visually impaired students. *The Science Teacher*, 1981, *48*, 36-37.

Sicurella, V.J. Color contrast as an aid for visually impaired persons. *Journal of Visual Impairment and Blindness*, 1977, *71*, 252-257.

Sirvis, B. Developing IEP's for physically handicapped students: a transdisciplinary viewpoint. *Teaching Exceptional Children,* 1978, *10*(3), 78-82.

Suterko, S. Life adjustment. In B. Lowenfeld (Ed.), *The visually handicapped child in school.* New York: The John Day Co., 1973.

Trombly, T. Pre-speech training for the cerebral palsied child. In D.D. Peterson, (Ed.), *The physically handicapped: a book of readings.* New York: M.S.S. Information Corp., 1969.

Venn, J., Morganstern, L., & Dykes, M.K. Checklists for evaluating the fit and function of orthoses, prostheses, and wheelchairs in the classroom. *Teaching Exceptional Children,* 1979, *11*(2), 51-56.

Ward, M., & McCormick, S. Reading instruction for blind and low vision children in the regular classroom. *The Reading Teacher,* 1981, *34,* 434-444.

Way, J.W. Project superheart: an evaluation of a heart disease intervention program for children. *Journal of School Health,* 1981, *51,* 16-19.

Webber, M.S. *Communication skills for exceptional learners.* Rockville, MD: Aspen Systems Corp., 1981.

Welch, J. Timbre analysis of the Sonicguide. *Journal of Visual Impairment and Blindness,* 1977, *71,* 309-314.

Wentworth, S.M., & Hoover, J. The student with diabetes. *Today's Education,* 1981, *70,* 42-44.

Wright, R.B. Laboratory exercises for visually handicapped botany students. *Journal of Visual Impairment and Blindness,* 1978, *72,* 67-68.

11 ACCOMMODATION

IEP requirements 1. Documentation of current level of ed. peformance
2. Annual goals & objectives
3. Documentation of sp. ed & related services
4. Indication of time in reg. class
5. Projected dates for iniated services
6. Evaluation procedures

The major responsibility of content-area teachers, especially in the upper elementary grades, is to teach knowledge in a variety of specific areas, not to teach basic skills. This is evidenced by the fact that approximately 85 percent of reading skills are taught by the end of third grade (Bloom, 1978). Few teachers who are involved in departmentalized and upper-grade instruction have programs including instruction in the skills of basic literacy. The academic survival of handicapped students depends greatly on the efforts of the special educator, who must encourage support for students attending the mainstream classes of the school. The special educator is faced with the two-fold tasks of directing remedial instruction and attempting to provide support for students attending mainstream classes. Instructional practices of the school may not provide optimum learning opportunities for mainstreamed students; however, instructional changes may not be easily negotiated between the special educator and mainstream teachers because teachers may be unsympathetic, uncooperative, or bound by traditional attitudes toward grading.

The purpose of this chapter is to present major types of accommodation that may be used in the mainstream classroom as well as in the special class. Although compensatory models are generally conceived for students labeled as learning disabled, it is certain that most of the approaches apply to all handicapped as well as nonhandicapped students. The typical service model employing accommodation is the resource room, but practical experience with the consulting teacher role provides evidence of the applicability of these strategies in a variety of instructional settings.

REMEDIATION AND ACCOMMODATION

Remedial programming is considered a common purpose of special education; it is conceived as *training in basic academic subjects or in underlying psychological processes that are thought to be important for learning.* Remedial programming for handicapped students may have many variations, depending on the setting, basis for student classification, and particular orientation of the teacher. The goals of most school-based remedial programs appear to be as follows (Marsh & Price, 1980):

1. To assist students toward normal achievement in the acquisition of basic skills
2. To promote "functional literacy" as a minimum level of competency in lieu of satisfactory remediation

Programs emphasizing remediation focus on the particular deficits of the individual student and include remedial strategies directed at eliminating or minimizing the effect of the deficit. The following two basic types of remedial programs are available to special educators:

1. Approaches that focus on lack of skill or competence in basic-skill areas and that utilize some specific approach to remediate or improve functioning in that area
2. Approaches based primarily on the remediation of an underlying process; perceptual deficit; receptive, integrative, or expressive language disorder; or some known or inferred organic dysfunction that is assumed to be the basic cause of the learning problem

The poor results of training in areas such as perception, attention, and memory should indicate the need for educators to exercise considerable caution in choosing between process-training and direct approaches. The training-benefit outcome is likely to be greater and more relevant to students if approaches are chosen emphasizing remediation of basic-skill deficiencies.

The value of remediation as the only effort of educators for handicapped students may be questioned on the grounds that it may not be successful. In addition, remediation diminishes in importance with the age of a student. The inverse relationship is explained by the relevance of such instruction in the life of the student on a daily basis and whether it contributes to immediate needs. It is also explained by the fact that most seriously disabled students, according to current evidence, cannot be

Objectives: who is doing something (Audience)
what is to be done (Behavior)
To what is it to be done (conditions)
How is it to be done (Degree)

expected to make significant gains with known techniques. Students who are poor readers in elementary school tend to remain poor at the secondary level. Reading failure is a persistent, chronic problem with no easy cure (Muehl & Forell, 1973-1974). Spectacular successes of students at the secondary level are rare, isolated instances. Therefore, focusing *only* on remedial techniques with elementary-aged students may not produce results that could be considered significant in terms of the overall success and progress of the student in the school system. Another problem identified by teachers is that some students make great strides in basic skills but fail in mainstream classes. This is also a matter of concern to regular classroom teachers. Combining remedial strategies with accommodation may prove more fruitful because of the impact on students and teaching techniques.

Accommodation may be considered as any of a variety of methods of adapting and adjusting school organization, curricula, or instructional methods to the learner that is part of a circumventive effort for students. As such, it is not a particular approach but a collection of strategies to help the learner cope in a setting in which the major barrier to learning is inflexibility of instructional procedures. Printed matter is one way of recording information, and reading is one medium of gaining access to it. According to Marsh and Price (1980), the fact that printed matter may comprise as much as 75 percent of instructional activities of students does not mean that other avenues of learning, circumvention, and coping cannot be employed.

The relationship between remediation and accommodation in an elementary special education program is dictated by several factors including the following:

1. *Unique characteristics of the student*
   a. *Age*. The age of the child and, therefore, the grade in which mainstreaming is proposed must be considered; typically, as the child gets older, the content and operation of the regular classroom change, and higher academic performance is required of the student. The amount of remediation may diminish as more effort is directed toward assisting the child in meeting the daily challenges of the regular classroom.
   b. *Ability*. The ability of children to benefit from remediation is variable. If the student is showing significant gain in performance, obviously the return on the time invested in remediation should be considered acceptable. However, if progress is poor, the decision to continue the same remedial efforts year after year should be questioned.
2. *Setting in which the child is served*. The degree to which students are mainstreamed dictates the relationship of remediation and accommodation. If students are served almost totally in a self-contained classroom, remediation might take precedence over accommodation. On the other hand, if students are expected to function in mainstream classes, it is unrealistic to expect them to do so without some support from the special educator.
3. *Goals of the special education program*. The special education program that is evaluated in terms of months of gain on individual achievement tests would be expected to be primarily a remedial program because it is implicit that the major goal is remediation or improvement in deficit areas. The program that is evaluated in terms of improvement in grades, performance in the regular classroom, or socioemotional adjustment would encompass accommodation as a major component.
4. *Relationship between the special and regular classroom*. The special classroom, located in a system in which regular teachers and administrators expect students to improve in performance in regular classes as a result of special education, must, of necessity, address the issue of accommodation. If the program

is considered an isolated element of the school, to focus on remediation might be more appropriate.

ACCOMMODATION TECHNIQUES

Accommodation of the learning environment is any of a variety of methods of adapting the school organization, curriculum, or instructional methods to the learner. The focus of accommodation is the environment as it affects the learner; elements of the environment, rather than the learner, are targeted for change. A number of techniques may be considered, but not as a total programmatic approach for all students; rather, they should be conceptualized as a series of possible strategies that might be applied to a specific student. Following is a discussion of the major components of accommodation—the administration, regular classroom, and special classroom. (See Fig. 11-1 for a graphic representation of the major classification scheme.)

Administration

Change in a school system typically occurs as a direct result of major policy decisions in the administrative sector. Persons who have authority and power can quickly and dramatically alter important aspects of the school, such as instructional arrangements, goals, purposes, and general learning conditions. The degree of power and influence over the entire system decreases downward in the sytem; administrators at lower levels have a more limited impact on the functioning of the system. Mainstreaming seems to have been more completely implemented and readily accepted in those districts in which school boards, superintendents, and principals received in-service training and were assisted in making important policy decisions about integrating the handicapped. The degree of administrative support that is given to a specialist involved in serving handicapped students varies greatly among districts according to attitudes and expectations.

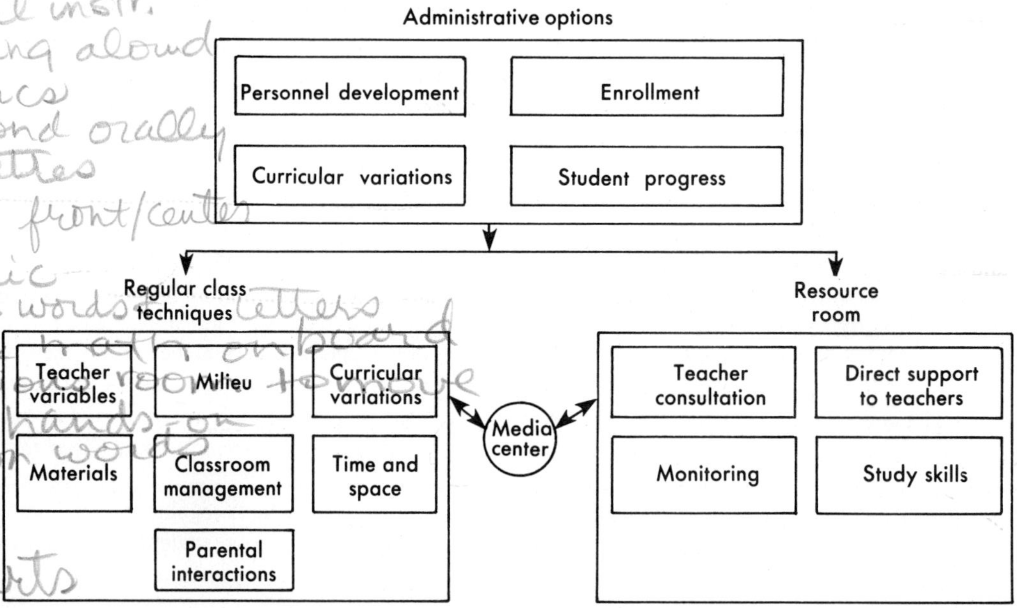

Fig. 11-1. Components of accommodation.

If the administration is supportive of the concept of accommodation, some major administrative innovations can be implemented, including personnel development, enrollment, pupil progress, and curricular variations (Fig. 11-1). *Personnel development* can include important subcomponents such as in-service training for teachers and release time to participate in planning activities. Administrative innovations are important because personnel development cannot occur without a formalized, concerted effort by the institution to bring about change in the attitudes and behaviors of teaching personnel and administrators. *Enrollment* procedures can be varied to aid the handicapped student in mainstreaming. For example, a change in administrative policy in one district allowed the counselors to enroll learning handicapped students in particular sections staffed by faculty interested in working with them. Other scheduling was done by computer, but personal assistance was allowed for these handicapped students. Another example is enrollment alterations in a district that were departmentalized at the upper elementary level. Consideration was given to the floor plan of the building when enrolling handicapped students. The administration moved some classes and selected particular sections based on the potential difficulties that might be encountered by handicapped students during room changes. *Pupil progress* can involve such strategies as allowing modifications in the testing (achievement) program, the report card system, and the number of parental conferences. The administrative component of the school has the power and authority to change the rules to aid students, teachers, and parents in confronting the issue of grades. The subcomponent of *curricular variation* can include strategies such as allowing class substitution, allowing the use of materials not on the state adoption list, and supporting the use of alternative methods within the regular classroom. Some states may have laws pertaining to some of these topics that should be carefully examined before making recommendations about a particular administrative strategy.

Regular classroom

The most salient feature of accommodation in the regular classroom is adoption of the characteristic pattern of the circumventive strategies that permits the handicapped learner to achieve, commensurate with the common expectation for all students or at a lower level of expected achievement. One or more actions that may be employed to bypass student disability also serve to assist the student toward the goal of learning about our culture and our world; in this capacity, accommodation is only one part of a total effort to educate the individual in conjunction with other actions such as remediation. The use of accommodation in regular classes by mainstream teachers is of utmost importance. Most will not assume primary responsibility for improvement of basic skills, but they can be instrumental in circumventing basic-skill deficits. Cooperation, mutual responsibility, and open exchange between the special and mainstream teachers are imperative.

The most crucial element in accommodation is successful implementation of various techniques in mainstream classes. Although the administration may adopt progressive policies and the special educator may be eager to consult with and support mainstream teachers, little progress can be expected if the classroom door is shut to cooperation and mutual responsibility. The ability of the special teacher to elicit cooperation with mainstream teachers is the decisive factor in program change; the teacher must patiently establish rapport with teachers, develop commonly accepted practices to assist students, and strive to influence mainstream teachers to implement and refine circumventive teaching strategies. The more these practices become systematized by being reduced to standard operating procedures, the more likely they will become permanent programmatic features with long-term benefits.

It should be reemphasized that the most important consideration is to avoid, in appearance or reality, intensification of daily teaching and clerical burdens for mainstream teachers. The more

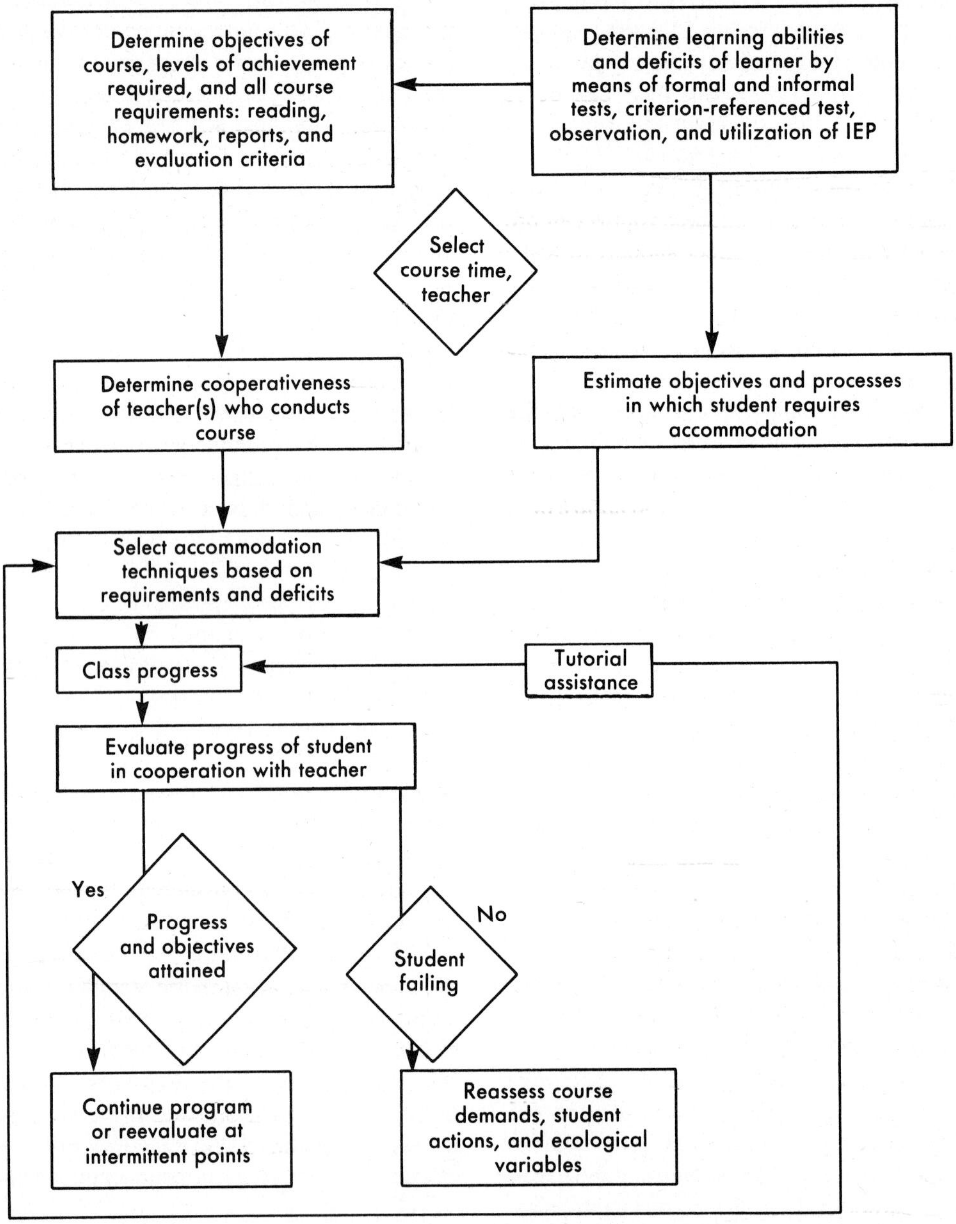

Fig. 11-2. Sequence of events for entry and exit in resource programming. (From Marsh, G.E., II, & Price, B.J. *Methods for teaching the mildly handicapped adolescent.* St. Louis: The C.V. Mosby Co., 1980.)

that accommodational techniques reduce the teachers' anxieties and work load, the more likely that accommodation of handicapped students will be accepted and implemented. Properly organized and planned, the work load can be reduced.

Special classroom (resource room)

The special classroom (resource room) can provide teacher consultation, direct support to teachers, monitoring of students, and study skills.

Teacher consultation. The development of a strategy for teacher consultation is vital to any accommodational approach that is to be shared by professionals. Three aspects in teacher consultation are considered part of the accommodation process: *learner characteristics and needs*, *curriculum of the regular classroom*, and *nature of the regular teacher* (Fig. 11-2). Specific information about the abilities and problems of the individual student must be considered in making decisions about accommodation. The resource room teacher must be able to interpret information about the learner and translate it into an estimate of the likelihood of student success in the regular class. Consideration must be given to individual learner characteristics including the following:

1. *Academic functioning.* The resource room teacher should utilize formal and informal assessment data collected during the placement process, as well as performance information from contact with the student.

2. *Behavior.* The manner in which the student interacts with the external environment is typically of equal importance in predicting classroom success. The observational sampling of behavior required for the assessment process can provide valuable information in examining the student's coping or interactional patterns. CASES, described in earlier chapters, provides useful information in identifying and describing behavioral patterns in the classroom setting.

3. *Study habits.* Organizational skills and study habits should be evaluated as part of the preparation for accommodation. The manner in which students approach the task of studying varies tremendously. Some classes require that students have specific skills to survive, and the resource teacher must acknowledge this requirement.

4. *Motivation and interest.* Students with a particular interest or desire to participate in a class have an increased chance of being successful. If the teacher possesses good rapport with special students and has insight into their interests, this information can be considered in making program decisions.

Curricular demands vary among classes, making it necessary for the special educator to become familiar with the various subjects being considered as part of the accommodation process for an individual student. Attention should be given to subject content and class structure, including the following factors:

Course objectives
Level of achievement required
Topics and skills in grade
Number and types of tests and assignments required
Modes of instruction used
Evaluation criteria

The personality and attitudes of the regular teacher are extremely important in accommodation and must be examined realistically. Fig. 11-3 describes the teacher consultation process, including cooperative and circumventive efforts.

The specialist has skills and abilities as a technician and change agent in the learning environment that should transcend the present scope that is a heritage of the clinical teaching approach. Clinical teaching is an acceptable method of instruction for children in a one-on-one situation, but the role of special education teachers can extend their influence in many ways throughout the system.

ACCOMMODATION IN THE REGULAR CLASSROOM

The challenge of accommodation is to find ways that allow the student to participate in the regular

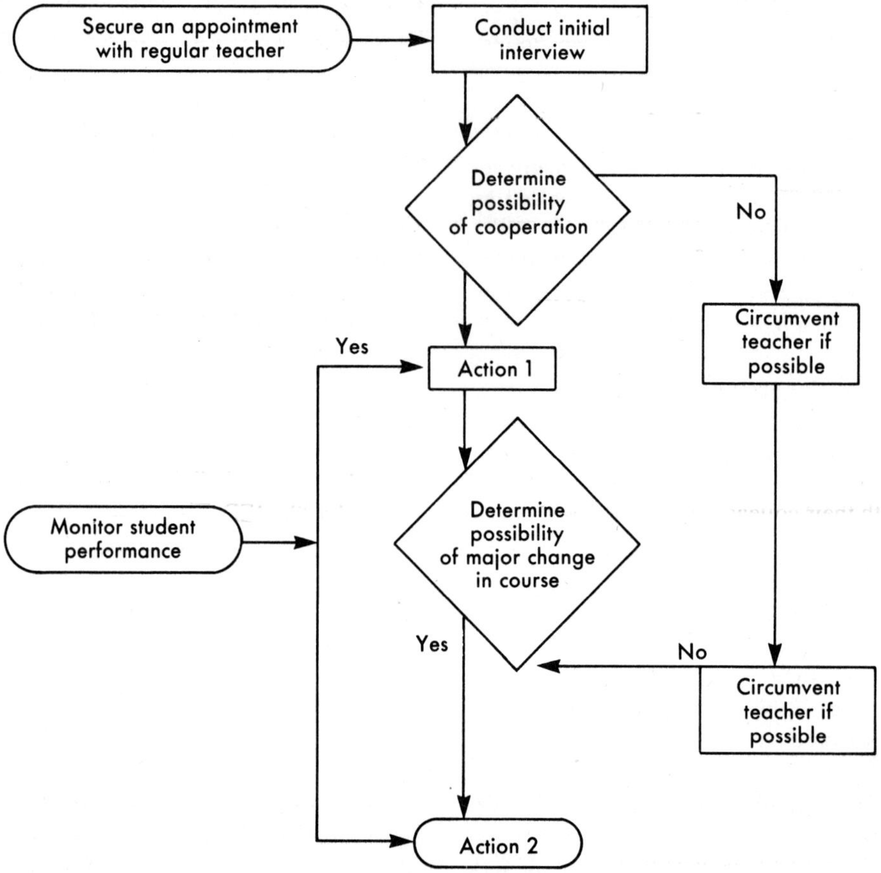

Fig. 11-3. Actions in considering the nature of the regular teacher in accommodation. (From Marsh, G.E., II & Price, B.J. *Methods for teaching the mildly handicapped adolescent.* St. Louis: The C.V. Mosby Co., 1980.)

(mainstream) classroom and to demonstrate competency in the subject matter of the class; the methods used must accomplish this without lowering the goals of education. For this to happen the special educator must serve as an advocate and provide support for students who attend the school's mainstream classes. Fulfilling this obligation may require the special educator to approach teachers with suggestions for accommodating the mildly handicapped students. These suggestions *must* be extremely practical and easily implemented; otherwise, there is little hope that modifications recommended by the special educator will be attempted. In addition, if the special teacher makes recommendations that are useless or impractical, credibility and the opportunity for future cooperative work may be jeopardized. However, special educators have much to learn from regular educators about the mainstream classroom before they can presume to offer them advice about how to teach. This is part of the problem in gaining acceptance for inclusion of students in the mainstream class. Special educators act in an instructive (consultative) role with their colleagues and must be knowledgeable.

Information flow and information processing

A major aspect of the operation of the regular classroom is information flow and information processing, the process by which information is acquired and processed as required by the regular class. For handicapped learners to perform adequately, particularly those with deficient reading skills, a variety of methods must be used to stimulate the flow of information. The goal of such efforts is the transmission of information that the student might otherwise be cut off from as a result of individual deficits and instructional practices of the school. The following points elucidate the need for and uses of accommodation:

1. In keeping with the concept of the least restrictive environment, mildly handicapped students may be expected to participate, as much as possible, in the regular curriculum of the school and attend classes with their nonhandicapped peers. In these classes they will be expected to learn the content as prescribed by the curriculum and presented by various teachers.

2. Learning is the act of acquiring *skills* or *knowledge*. The majority of upper-grade teachers emphasize the acquisition of knowledge such as factual information and concepts. In the early elementary grades, stress is placed on the acquisition of skills such as reading, arithmetic, and writing. The focus begins to shift in the middle grades as students begin to develop cognitive structures that allow abstraction.

3. A major barrier to the acquisiton of knowledge is the interruption of the information flow, which is caused by the student's lack of basic skills and a lack of alternatives to reinstate the flow of information (Marsh & Price, 1980). Fig. 11-4 depicts the learning process, graphically illustrating the information acquisition–information processing flow.

4. Adjusting instruction for handicapped students depends on individual needs and should be reflected in the IEP. Thus, students with *only* academic deficiencies may benefit from instruction that reduces the demand on basic skills to acquire knowledge, students with serious cognitive limitations require a reduction in achievement expectations commensurate with their lower capabilities, children with behavioral disorders may not require significant adjustments if behavioral management is employed, and children with a variety of sensoriphysical handicaps may or may not require accommodation, depending on individual characteristics caused by their conditions in addition to superimposed cognitive, academic, and behavioral problems they may exhibit.

For the purposes of this discussion, certain assumptions are made about the curriculum in most school districts. Curriculum varies among school districts, but most predominant patterns in upper elementary grades through high school invoke some type of specialization or centering on subject areas. In this part we are more interested in the organization of knowledge in curricula. Since the

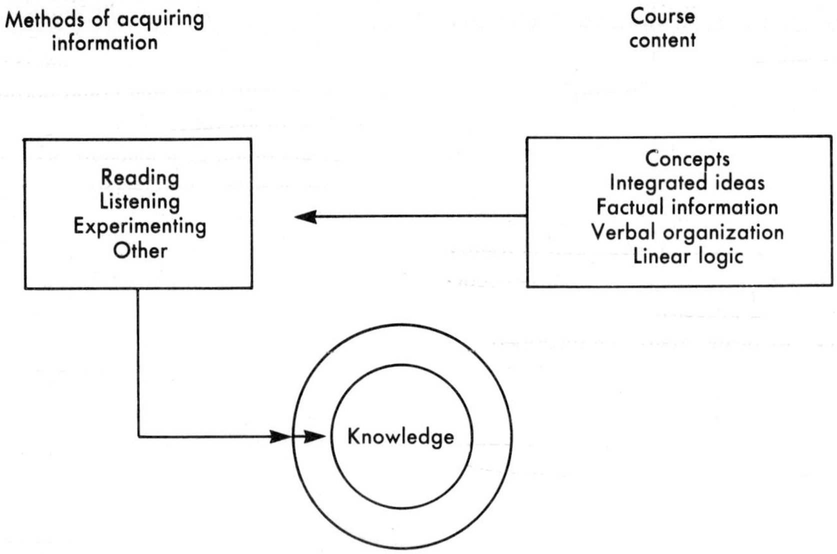

Fig. 11-4. Acquisition of knowledge as a product of information flow. The learner must have the cognitive ability to assimilate abstract concepts, which may result in reorganization of cognitive structures or accommodation to new structures.

1960s curriculum planning has been based on knowledge as the element for design (Hass, 1977). The relationships among a body of facts and concepts are organized sequentially and hierarchically; since all areas are conceived in this manner, the curriculum can be thought of like a lattice. Knowledge is classified, categorized, and assigned to particular subjects. Obviously, there are many criticisms of this approach, but a certain efficiency in this procedure exists because each discipline organizes its own knowledge and arranges it according to superordinate concepts, subordinate principles, and the structure of content around which learning activities are designed.

A major task of the learner in the upper elementary grades and secondary school is to *acquire knowledge*. The ability to demonstrate that knowledge has been acquired is proved on examinations. Although it may appear to be an oversimplification, the greatest deficiency of most handicapped students is not the inability to develop concepts or acquire knowledge; rather, it is an inability to receive information necessary for learning and concept development in the disciplines. This inability to receive information may be thought of as an *individual* and *ecological* variable. There will be differences in the disruption of information flow to individuals because of the severity of academic achievement or cognitive functioning that varies with the individual and differences in school settings that result from varying institutional flexibility in accommodation of individuals.

If the cognitive structures of the learner are intact and an ability to assimilate abstract concepts exists, the learner is capable of acquiring knowledge. According to Bloom (1980), students with low cognitive ability may be expected to achieve at a high standard. Most students have the capacity, theoretically, to attack any discipline or body of knowledge. The limiting factor in the educational process is that the learner may not be able to read efficiently, produce acceptable written responses to class assignments, perform mathematical calculations or symbolize them, or achieve motivation. The learner is excluded from the information flow that leads to knowledge acquisition. Similarly, blind students are excluded from the information flow, but they are accommodated in a variety of other ways that permit knowledge acquisition. Unfortunately, similar considerations have not been allowed for most other handicapped students. The obstacles to learning created in and by the environment are institutionalized. These obstacles cannot be readily overcome unless remediation is totally, spectacularly effective. Accommodation is needed to begin the learning process.

In summary, to bring many handicapped students into the learning arena, diminish their frustration and anxiety, and permit them to succeed in many areas currently closed to them, the educational system must allow them to learn in classes despite their skill deficits.

General approaches to individualization

Individualization is a timeworn word in education, but it has never figured more prominently than in the age of the IEP. Implicit in the IEP is the need for individualized instruction, that is, instruction designed specifically for a particular student. Unfortunately individualized instruction and the individualized education plan are not synonymous. The IEP may specify the objectives, learning activities, and evaluative criteria for an individual student, but all learning activities must be planned in accordance with variables controlled by mainstream teachers, unless, of course, many of them are to occur in the resource room. Individualization in the mainstream setting must account for organization of the learning environment, delivery of efficient instruction, coordination of classroom activities, and simultaneous instruction of a number of pupils who may have different needs and problems (Glicking, Murphy, & Mallory, 1979).

Individualized instruction is said to occur more frequently in elementary schools primarily because children are engaged in individual seat work 25 to 45 percent of the time (Adams & Biddle, 1970; Gump, 1967). However, seat work is not necessarily individualized instruction, especially if each child is sitting independently while working on the same page of a workbook as the rest of the class. Despite this, at least a time frame is established in the mainstream class that could permit individualization with alteration of teaching style.

Any alteration of a teaching style is radical because the teacher, who has total control, inevitably loses some degree of control with any change, except that of removing the student from the class to remain for a period of time in the resource room. Although the student may progress with the aid of accommodation techniques in the mainstream class and support from the resource room, the best efforts of the specialist would be the communication of concepts that will reorganize the learning environment of the mainstream class, enable the mainstream teacher to coordinate activities and deal simultaneously with a number of students and their accompanying problems, and individualize instruction.

The status quo affords comfort to the mainstream teacher; the routines of the day are clear, and covering predetermined quantities of work through lectures or group lesson plans meets the expectations of administrators. Having the handicapped student attend the resource room provides an expedient solution for the teacher. There is really no sense of sharing in the solution of educational problems of the student because the responsibility is shouldered by the resource teacher. If the resource teacher provides remedial reading instruction for the student, the mainstream teacher might be oblivious to the activities of the resource room. If individualization is to be effective, it must plan for the coordinated response of the school in special and regular classes.

Talmage (1975) has identified the following components of traditional and individualized instructional systems:

Traditional	*Individualized*
Fixed outcomes for all learners	Criterion-referenced outcomes
Fixed entry points	Variable entry points
Fixed time and pacing	Variable pacing
Limited decision-making role of learner	Active decision-making role of learner

Traditional	*Individualized*
Large group instruction	Peer or individual group instruction
Norm-referenced evaluation of learner	Criterion-referenced evaluation of learner

The reader can easily contrast the two systems of instruction and see the obvious advantages inherent in the individualized approach. However, the reader will readily notice that the preferred system, individualization, may not be easily accomplished in the traditional regular classroom.

Specific approaches to accommodation

Development of the following accommodation strategies and competencies for classroom teachers grew out of our conceptualization of the actual and needed services in public schools to meet mainstreaming requirements. A systems framework was used to identify important functions and interactions. An analysis of interactions was conducted to determine what was happening in public schools and what might be implemented most easily and inexpensively to better meet the needs of handicapped students by changing the activities and responsibilities of regular and special educators. The focus was clearly on the classroom, except for the possible interaction of administrative personnel and the impact of administrative policies. A number of approaches to aid mainstreaming have been developed, many of which rely on published materials and certain types of systems that must be purchased. It was deemed necessary to develop a system that could alter the structure of the school somewhat and change the interactions of personnel without causing a major change at the level of the principal or higher administrative levels. The reason for this was that funds were not available to conduct massive in-service projects for training administrators, the needs of children were largely classroom needs, and administrators were less interested in adopting massive changes to facilitate programming for a relatively small number of children.

Much of the work was accomplished through use of the accommodation strategies with classroom teachers over a period of 4 years under an in-service grant funded by the Bureau of Education for the Handicapped. Field testing was accomplished by having classroom teacher receive primarily skill-related training, develop contracts with project personnel, implement various approaches, and provide feedback. As a result, several hundred contracts and critiques were obtained; a large collection of materials and programmatic concepts were created by regular educators over a period of 4 years. Currently it is the consensus of the program staff that attitudes of classroom teachers change after they develop skills to deal with handicapped students. The following part of the text describes competencies and the associated strategies that have evolved from the in-service training programs conducted with mainstream teachers.

Knowledge and skill competencies in mainstreaming

The two major categories are knowledge and skill. Five clusters of knowledge competencies have evolved through in-service projects and practical experience, as described previously:

1. Learning characteristics and implications for teaching
2. Shared responsibility
3. Assessment
4. Classroom management
5. Administrative procedures

A complete listing of the competencies included in the knowledge clusters is presented on pp. 367 and 368. These *knowledge competencies* provide a foundation on which accommodation might be built. However, practical experience with regular teachers has proved that faster and more gratifying results are produced by focusing on skill competencies first. While appearing contrary to logic at first examination, the teachers' preference for and receptiveness to skill competencies can be easily explained by the following points:

1. The teachers' most immediate concern is not the acquisition of general knowledge, but, instead, the acquisition of a skill or skills that

will assist them in solving a particular problem anticipated or encountered in serving handicapped students.

2. The skill competencies present practical strategies for which the teachers can see immediate applications, unlike the knowledge competencies that require teachers to make the transition from knowledge to application.
3. The skill competencies are more obviously and directly related to the classroom and its operation; they are couched in terminology that is familiar and acceptable to teachers.
4. Employing one or more of the skill competencies can result in immediate changes in the classroom. This means that teachers see immediate results.
5. The skill competencies focus on classroom strategies that not only benefit the handicapped student but also other low-achieving,

KNOWLEDGE COMPETENCIES ASSOCIATED WITH MAINSTREAMING

Learning characteristics and implications for teaching

1. Teacher lists the major areas of exceptionality.
2. Teacher lists the major characteristics for each area as described in professional literature.
3. Teacher identifies the population included as mildly handicapped.
4. Teacher identifies some general learning characteristics associated with handicapping conditions that are pertinent to regular classroom instruction.
5. Teacher specifies specialized instructional strategies appropriate for implementation in classrooms in which handicapped students are integrated.

Shared responsibility

6. Teacher lists and describes the three main mandates of P.L. 94-142.
7. Teacher lists and describes the major components of due process.
8. Teacher lists the rights of parents and schools in due process hearings.
9. Teacher describes the role of special educators and counselors in referral and placement conferences and proceedings.
10. Teacher lists strategies that might be implemented in the classroom to address socioemotional needs.
11. Teacher describes the role of the regular educator in the following aspects of education of the handicapped:
    Referral process
    Placement conference
    Development of the IEP
    Evaluation and monitoring
12. Teacher identifies some major issues related to the education of handicapped students that concern the regular educator, including grades, graduation requirements, and group expectations versus individualized instruction.
13. Teacher identifies the three major components of accommodation and the subcomponents of each.

Continued.

KNOWLEDGE COMPETENCIES ASSOCIATED WITH MAINSTREAMING—cont'd

Assessment

14. Teacher defines the validity and reliability of the tests and whether they are criterion-referenced or norm-referenced tests.
15. Teacher contrasts norm-referenced with criterion-referenced assessment.
16. Teacher identifies three advantages of informal tests.
17. Teacher distinguishes between rating scales and checklists.

Classroom management

18. Teacher describes the difference between classical and operant conditioning.
19. Teacher demonstrates knowledge of commonly used schedules of reinforcement in operant-conditioning techniques.
20. Teacher defines the following elements of conditioning:
    Successive approximations
    Principles of reinforcement
    Contracting
    Observation
21. Teacher lists guidelines for employing contracting in the classroom.
22. Teacher lists advantages and disadvantages of collecting behavioral data in the natural setting.
23. Teacher identifies at least three major uses of behavioral data in student programming.
24. Teacher demonstrates knowledge of the basic characteristics and uses of behavioral rating instruments designed for classroom use.

Administrative procedures

25. Teacher lists the sequence of events that should be followed to identify and place handicapped students in special classes.
26. Teacher describes the required forms and how these forms provide for accountability and due process rights.
27. Teacher lists the steps involved in referral, evaluation, placement, and follow-up.
28. Teacher describes the role of volunteer programs to help aid the integration of handicapped students.
29. Teacher identifies ways in which community resources might be located and use to help with school activities and problems

unmotivated students; teachers perceive these additional benefits as increasing the returns on the time given to implementing accommodation techniques.

The *skill competencies* are divided into the following eight clusters:

1. Teacher-controlled variables
2. Classroom management
3. Curricular variations
4. Materials development and modification
5. Milieu
6. Time and space modifications
7. Human resources
8. Parental interactions

Table 11-1. Teacher-controlled variables

Skill competencies	*Possible classroom strategies*
1. Teacher identifies major strategies that can be implemented to aid in communicating major concepts and facts within regular classrooms. 2. Teacher demonstrates application of one or more accommodation strategies in regular classroom. 3. Teacher illustrates contrast between accommodation instruction with alternative special curricula and "watered down" curricula. 4. Teacher analyzes daily instructional plans for points at which teacher-controlled variables might be altered without altering content or curricular sequence.	Topical outline Study guide Technical vocabulary or glossaries Advance or cognitive organizers Summaries of concepts Audiovisual aids: Charts Media Transparencies

The following parts discuss each cluster and include a general description of the strategies, examples of their applications, and suggestions to the special educator concerning ways in which the strategies might be instituted. Tables 11-1 through 11-8 provide a complete listing of the competencies comprising the skill clusters.

Teacher-controlled variables (Table 11-1). Each teacher is trained in a discipline, and many classes, especially in departmentalized programs, are founded on disciplines having a knowledge base; the task of teachers is to use these teacher-controlled variables to communicate knowledge to students in the form of facts and concepts. The state curriculum guide, local curriculum guide, course syllabus, and commercial materials are uniformly tied to the framework of each discipline. The following general observations may be made about classes/disciplines:

1. Although the nature of learning activities may vary from class to class, the knowledge content of similar courses is based on invariant *key concepts* and *principles*.
2. Each discipline contains several broad concepts linked together to form the structure of the discipline.
3. This structure contains subordinate concepts and facts that comprise the substance of lectures and reading or other assignments.

By extracting the key concepts and principles from the disciplines, the mainstream and special teachers can identify the precise targets of course work, the general structure and format of content, and the relationship of units, lectures, and assignments. The special educator is not expected to be specialized in any particular discipline, but an understanding of the general organization and goals of each enable teaching personnel to work together cooperatively, since they can communicate about a common purpose.

If the specialist and mainstream teachers have an understanding about the general nature of subject matter by identification of key concepts and principles, it is possible for the specialist to assume a more active role in directing and managing accommodation techniques, assisting in mainstream class activities, and directing resource room activities related to survival in the mainstream. It should be recognized that many resource teachers who work in middle and elementary schools which are departmentalized must deal with subject matter specialization (language arts, science, etc.). The strategies included in this cluster, teacher-controlled variables, deal with accommodational techniques, that may be conducted by the mainstream teacher to more efficiently communicate information.

Topical outline. The mainstream teacher may prepare a topical outline of the course that reflects the general flow of course content. This would be predicated on key concepts and principles and the anticipated accomplishments of students as determined by the local curriculum guide. Some teachers do not provide students with a syllabus or other direction in the class, relying on daily assignments. Topical outlines would benefit all students, not just the handicapped student and the resource teacher, and they should be easy to supply.

The advantage of a topical outline is that it assists upper elementary students in attempts to organize thoughts, notes, and information into a meaningful record to be used in directing them to the acquisition of course outcomes. The provision of a simple outline related to class lectures and intermediate objectives of units can be indispensable as a guide for study because it imposes order on factual information and data of daily lessons. A simple outline on the blackboard has been beneficial in daily classes.

Study guides. A more formalized and demanding procedure than a topical outline is a study guide, which may be designed with specific objectives, assignments, and evaluative criteria. An elaboration of the study guide may be a written *learning* contract that clearly identifies the major concepts to be outlined through study of specific content. Once such instruments are completed, they may easily be used with some modification for each student who subsequently takes the class. After the initial burden of developing a comprehensive study guide or learning contract is completed, it requires much less labor in subsequent efforts with other students.

The study guide might include the following sections:

1. Specific objectives to be accomplished
2. Period of time during which the learning activities will be completed
3. Specific products of study such as book reports and experiments (Examples should be put on display for student review.)
4. Specific reading assignments (or negotiated alternatives) and other learning activities
5. Evaluative criteria (Sample test items should be provided.)

Technical vocabularies and glossaries. Many nonhandicapped students encounter considerable difficulty in reading assignments and understanding discussions in many classes because terminology, jargon, and unfamiliar concepts must be learned and internalized before becoming meaningful. The curious aspect about reading in content areas is that it is tied to a writing style unlike that of recreational reading or instructional materials used to teach reading. It is expository in nature, replete with major sections, subsections, changes in size and style of print, numerous graphs, and peculiar words and concepts. As a student enters a new subject area, words appear with great frequency that are unfamiliar or have different meanings than those of the vernacular.

In addition to varying degrees of ability to decipher new terms, most students will experience difficulty in learning terms and concepts. It is not necessary to "read" a term to learn its meaning and be able to use it. Lists of terms available in glossaries may be used by tutors or placed on tape to simplify for students the definitional process involved in acquiring a body of knowledge. If the only manner by which a student may learn a new term such as "plateau" or "water table" is by reading it, it is apparent that many students will fail. If the task is altered so that knowledge may be acquired by circumventing the deficit, education can proceed despite the limitations of the learner to gather information from printed matter. Mainstream teachers can be taught how to introduce and reinforce the understanding of new terms as a function of teaching reading in content areas.

Advance organizers. Asubel uses the term *advance organizer* to describe a process of mastery learning in curriculum areas. This term has also been adopted with a similar purpose by some reading instructors. Prereading questions are provided to learners before they are induced to cover a reading section in a book. Presumably, the reader is cued to certain information that is required from the passage, such as, "What countries make up Latin America?" Such questions reduce the task of the student to handling specific bits of information, shorten the reading time required for the student to complete an assignment, and eliminate floundering about in a sea of paragraphs without a sense of purpose and with no expectations of subsequent responsibility for the information. Most persons agree that textbooks are not stimulating to read and that their major purpose is to present facts and concepts to the reader about a particular body of knowledge. Why not simply short-circuit the process for the slow reader? If a student learns that timber resources provide a renewable supply of fuel in a world with diminishing oil reserves, it should not concern us how the student learned it.

Use of advance organizers in a unit of study is incredibly simple and can be related to traditional reading assignments, compressed reading matter, or tape-recorded passages for students unable to read efficiently or for blind students. For example, organizers of major concepts for a unit concerning gravity in an upper elementary science class might include the following:

1. What is gravity?
2. How is gravity important to us?
3. How is gravity related to travel to the moon?
4. What are two examples that illustrate the effects of gravity?

Summaries of concepts. Another aid to students would be to provide summaries that are related to the major concepts of a unit or chapter. Frequently teachers tend to be more interested in certain topics and emphasize some aspects more than others. The textbooks and other printed matter may not embrace these emphases, hence the student may be at a disadvantage. It is also true that the most complex, abstract points of a unit are sometimes not understood by students. The complaint of a teacher that "We covered that in class!" is often surprising to students who attended more to the concrete aspects of the material than to the subtle, abstract qualities appreciated by the teacher. The ability to compare and contrast knowledge at highest levels of conceptual attainment requires nurturance and assistance that may be partly provided by the dissemination of summaries.

Audiovisual aids. The variety of audiovisual aids available in schools to assist the learning process is staggering. It is surprising that few teachers use anything more than a piece of chalk. Some factors which might explain this are that some teachers do not know how to use equipment, others cannot interrelate it with class activities that may predominantly surround a lecture, and still others consider it to be a lot of trouble when lecturing will suffice.

The teacher should examine inventories to identify and locate what equipment and materials exist and endeavor to employ them in learning activities.

Audiovisual aids provide additional input that can greatly impact the handicapped learner by emphasizing certain aspects of the topic or by providing another medium through which information is presented. Simple aids such as *charts* or *transparencies* listing major points or illustrating central principles increase the likelihood that the handicapped student understands the concept. These provide a visual organization around which the student can mentally organize information. *Films* and *filmstrips* may be used to elucidate primary points or to reinforce concepts; students with attentional problems often react with increased attention when such media materials are interspersed throughout classes.

In summary, learning, can be facilitated for handicapped students when audiovisual materials are utilized in one or both of the following ways:

1. As a substitute for the more traditional lecture/reading assignment approach to instruction.
2. As enrichment to underscore the most important points the instructor wishes to communicate.

Comment. As total master of instructional design, the teacher can implement one or more of the simple accommodation strategies and, as a result increase the likelihood that mildly handicapped students will succeed in the regular class setting. An interesting by-product that has been observed is the clarification of course content and performance expectation for all students *and* the teacher. If the teacher concentrates on the content and identifies key concepts for inclusion in an outline or guide and/or specifically states desired competencies, a great deal of extraneous and often detracting information is deleted. The more precise

Table 11-2. Classroom management

Skill competencies	*Possible classroom strategies*
5. Teacher defines reinforcers.	Token economy
6. Teacher gives examples of "free reinforcers" available in regular classroom and/or school.	Learning contracts
7. Teacher defines tokens.	Complete contracting system
8. Teacher gives examples of tokens that might be used in classroom.	"Time-out" system
9. Teacher identifies potential difficulties associated with implementing a management system.	
10. Teacher suggests strategies for dealing with these difficulties or avoiding them.	
11. Teacher designs and implements contracting system for one subject area or period of time in daily schedule.	
12. Teacher develops and maintains list of references and resources for dealing with emotionally disturbed students, including resource personnel.	

and clear the direction the teacher wishes the course to take, the easier for all involved, students and teacher, to devote efforts toward achievement of goals.

Classroom management (Table 11-2). Regular classroom teachers frequently resist having handicapped students in the mainstream class because of behavioral problems that students may exhibit. Even though some handicapped students may not exhibit problem behaviors any more or even as much as other students, the teacher may notice the behavior of handicapped students more frequently. Although, obviously, the special educator cannot accuse the teacher of such a bias, some strategies can be recommended that may assist the teacher in dealing with student behaviors *and* provide the mainstream teacher with some methods for accurately perceiving behavior of all students.

The teacher who uses behavioral strategies such as those listed in Table 11-2 attends to the immediate antecedents and consequences of the student's behavior (Rosenfield, 1979). Focusing attention aids the teacher in analyzing the atmosphere of the classroom, the nature of the lesson, and overall learning environment. Redirecting attention produces side effects such as anticipating, avoiding, or increasing the likelihood of events occurring. The teacher notices behaviors of students that would have otherwise gone unnoticed. Self-examination on the part of the teacher and the altered view of the student's behavior and performance are important benefits derived from the use of management strategies (Abidin, 1975; Rosenfield, 1979).

The special educator should have sufficient training in behavioral management to apply a management system to the special classroom and assist interested mainstream teachers in implementing basic systems such as a token economy or contracting process (Marsh & Price, 1980; Stewart, Goodman, & Hammond, 1976). The information in this text (Chapters 2, 9, and 12) should assist the special educator both in ensuring the responsibility for handling behavior in the special class and consulting with the mainstream teacher in an effort to implement one or more of the accommodation strategies of classroom management.

Curricular variations (Table 11-3). The regular classroom teacher must ensure that the content conforms to the curricular expectations of the district. However, the teacher does have some latitude in organizing the curriculum without losing the integrity of the content or scope of the sequence. These curricular variations might include

Table 11-3. Curricular variations

Skill competencies	*Possible classroom strategies*
13. Teacher identifies major components of course descriptions.	Alternative responding
14. Teacher writes accurate and behaviorally stated descriptions for course content or grade or selects appropriate behavioral goals from existing curricular literature.	Classroom test analysis
15. Teacher identifies basic types of performance required of student in classes.	Preparation of course description
16. Teacher analyzes types of evaluation techniques employed in classroom.	Profile of instructional modes used
17. Teacher examines personal preference for instructional mode as well as feasible alternatives.	Profile of student responses desired

alternative responding, classroom test analysis, course descriptions, profile of instructional modes, and analysis of student responses required.

Alternative responding. Typical performance demands on the learner are verbal responses in class, written responses, oral reports, and tests. Students receive grades for the quality of their responses, with greatest emphasis on tests. The inability to read, speak, or write proficiently hampers many handicapped students. Accommodation procedures that have been recognized as important by national testing bureaus, initially for blind students, are also recommended for other handicapped students. Students should be permitted to supply tape-recorded responses or dictated transcripts for such assignments as book reports and be permitted to have readers/writers for examinations.

If a resource teacher becomes involved in alternative testing, it is necessary to assure the teachers that cheating will not occur and that the test "won't get out." There is, of course, a real danger of this unless procedures are established that prevent tests from being compromised. However, the results are worth any effort expended by the teachers. Alternative testing consistently allows handicapped students to score one or two letter grades higher than with traditional forms of testing.

Classroom test analysis. The tests that teachers use in the mainsream classroom can often compound the problems confronted by the handicapped student. Two important aspects of the classroom test should be examined: *format* and *content*. Following are factors considered in examining the format of the classroom test:

1. Spacing of items on the pages
2. Space allowed for responses
3. Margins
4. Readability of the test
5. Test length
6. Test organization
7. Test instructions
8. Item type

The first four items in the preceding list determine the general appearance of the test. Many students have recounted experiences in which they "panicked" at the sight of the test because it appeared awesome. Items that are squeezed between margins of the page can have a negative impact on all students, not just those who are handicapped. The readability of a test, the degree to which reading the questions is stressful, and maintaining one's place on the page should be manageable. The next three items—test length, organization, and instructions—address the structure of the test. Does the teacher include items simply to make the test last 45 minutes, or are they included because they sample some sphere of knowledge considered important? Practices such as sequencing items to have one or two true-false items, a couple of multiple choice, and another true-false item complicate responding. All items requiring the students to perform the same process (i.e., true-false or fill-in-the-blank) should be clustered together so that the student does not have to ''shift gears'' constantly. Test instructions should be very clear to the readers, such as ''select the *best* answer,'' or ''list two reasons.'' The teacher must be certain that the items request the information desired. Varying the item type seems to be a common practice. Tests employing several types of items may provide the handicapped student a little better chance than those which use only one approach.

The following factors should be considered in examining the content of classroom tests:

1. Repetition of items
2. Clarity of vocabulary terms
3. Distribution of item content
4. Level of response required of students

As indicated earlier, some teachers determine test length by the amount of time that students have to be ''kept.'' However a better approach is to include items that directly test concepts covered without using a great deal of repetition to lengthen the test. The teacher should be encouraged to examine the test and to identify any unnecessary repetition. Clarity of vocabularly terms should be verified, and only content-related terms from course material used. Also, testing terms such as ''compare and contrast'' and ''list and illustrate'' should be explained. The phrasing of the test item should be constructed carefully. One good suggestion stemming from in-service training on test analysis is to have a teacher from another discipline read over the test to see if the items convey the intent of the developer. The test should reflect the various concepts or units of information covered in the period of time. Tests that consist of 25 percent of the items relating to a topic which represents 3 percent of the instructional time may not accurately reflect the emphases of the unit; that is, the number of items for a particular concept should approximate the importance given to that topic in the unit of study. This aids the handicapped to prepare for examinations and can be planned in accordance with the relative importance of the topic.

The final aspect of content, the level of response required of students, should reflect the taxonomy of educational objectives described by Bloom (1956). Although daily instruction tends to focus on level one (knowledge), some classroom tests employ items at level three (application). Students must perform above the level of daily class instruction. For example, a social studies teacher discovered that she had been talking to the class about facts: the daily lesson consisted of people and dates in the Civil War. However, one test item was, ''How would the world have been different if the South had won?'' The implications for handicapped students, as well as others who may have difficulty imposing order on information, are apparent; it is difficult for children, most of whom function at a concrete level, to address this kind of open-ended question.

Teacher consultation in this area can take the form of individual assistance in reviewing classroom tests, which definitely requires a great deal of personal rapport between teachers and faculty in-service training, during which teachers *voluntarily* review their own examinations. A good approach is to secure a consultant to conduct sessions of about 30 minutes that review the two major aspects of tests and then allow teachers to work individually or in groups to examine their own tests and make changes. As a result, a gain in letter grades may be expected by the handicaped students; the improvement in grades by nonhandicapped students makes test analysis a permanent strategy used by some classroom teachers.

Course descriptions. A simple strategy that can be used by upper elementary teachers in subjects such as social studies is the preparation of a course description. A course description can be prepared that describes the general goals of the course and the particular topics to be covered. Items that should be included are titles of books from the library that cover the topics, samples of tests items, and a listing of topics to be covered. Topical outlines and study guides (described earlier) might be used as components of a complete course description. The major advantage of a course description is that it can be used by the resource teacher, parents, or others interested in helping the student to present the goals and objectives of the course and other pertinent information. Teachers who are developing a course description might use the teachers' manual and curriculum guide of the district to determine the information to be included.

Instructional mode profile. Teachers interested in examining their curriculum should consider the types of instructional modes employed in communicating information. An in-service activity that we and other teachers have found helpful is the analysis of instructional mode preference. Teachers are asked to brainstorm and collectively identify all possible modes of presenting and communicating information to students. These modes are listed on the board, and teachers then rank, from highest to lowest, their uses of each mode and estimate the percent of time they are involved in each mode in a typical day. The purpose of the activity is to demonstrate that no particular mode is necessarily better; rather, it is hoped that teachers will examine their own styles objectively and choose to retain or alter them.

Teachers who are interested in the teaching process have altered their teaching styles, adding various types of activities that they had not used before. The two staples in the teachers' "bag of tricks"—group activities and lecture—can be augmented with the use of audiovisual aids, demonstration, and other strategies.

Student response profile. Sometimes teachers find that they are requiring students to perform in particular ways to the exclusion of other types of responses. For instance, one teacher discovered that he was requiring students to recall information for 91 percent of the class time. Once it was pointed out that other types of performance such as speech, discrimination, manipulation, and problem solving might be used, he was able to greatly vary the type of student responses required in the sixth-grade science class. He had merely become accustomed to a habitual pattern. The results showed that all students demonstrated more interest and motivation because of the variety introduced. Analysis of either instructional mode or student response can be accomplished as part of formal in-service training or individually between fellow teachers. In either event, we have found that by presenting the information with a general note that there is no *best* way and that it is an individual decision, many teachers have become interested and have engaged in altering one or both of these aspects of teaching.

Materials development and modification (Table 11-4). The materials development and modification cluster includes strategies that are easily implemented, such as taped lessons, compressed texts, games, learning packets, and "talking books." As pointed out in Chapter 2, since teachers typically have a lot of interest in materials,

Table 11-4. Materials development and modification

Skill competencies	*Possible classroom strategies*
18. Teacher demonstrates use of games and approaches, thereby reducing emphasis on reading while presenting content consistent with classroom objectives.	Taped lessons
19. Teacher demonstrates use of learning packets.	Compressed texts
20. Teacher describes process of developing compressed texts and its application to classroom.	Games
21. Teacher demonstrates use of taped material using audiotapes.	Learning packets
22. Teacher identifies ancillary equipment needed to realize potential of technology.	Talking books
23. Teacher identifies major ways in which recorded lessons might be employed in accommodation of mainstream class.	

especially games, so these strategies are readily received by them. Specialists who work with mainstream teachers might consider suggesting the strategies in this cluster or demonstrating their use with content covered in regular class.

Taped lessons. The special educator might consider recommending that the tape recorder be used to assist the student in meeting standards of the content class. Taped material can be used in a number of ways to provide assistance to the student involved in regular classes, but four methods of use appear to be most popular. Each application seems to have different conditions for use, including advantages and disadvantages, and these uses are briefly covered in the following:

1. *Taped lectures.* Taping lectures as a substitute for note taking has been found to be of limited value for most students. Students have a tendency to listen less attentively in class because of total reliance on the machine. Also, studying with tapes is unwieldy because it is possible to tape as many as 20 to 25 hours of instruction in a single week. Students who have difficulty sitting through class in the first place are not likely to benefit much from sitting through it again. Although this is a fairly common approach that some teachers employ initially, few have found it useful on a continuing basis.

2. *Lecture summaries.* The teacher might be approached about preparing a lecture summary to be placed in the media center, library resource room, or some other location that could be used by *all* students. A lecture summary should be brief, emphasizing the major points or concepts encompassed in the lecture. These summaries can be prepared by the mainstream instructor as the unit or class progresses or in advance of the unit. Another approach is for the instructor to prepare the summary outline but to utilize a voluntary or honor student to actually prepare the tapes.

3. *Taped textbooks.* Taping textbooks or other reading assignments in their entirety is one possible use of the recorder, but one that must be approached with some planning. The effectiveness of direct taping can be enhanced by the following suggestions:

Units or chapters should be put on separate tapes to conform with anticipated reading assignments.

The reader must have "pleasant" reading voice as well as good reading style.

The printed material should be available so that the listener may follow along if desired or necessary.

4. *Paraphrased material.* A paraphrased assignment on tape is another modification of taped textbooks. A tape may contain some entire reading passages, whereas others can be paraphrased to reduce listening time without compromising the content. The advantage of adding direct quotes, if important to the purpose of the tape, is that the listener has an opportunity to hear the particular writing style of the author.

5. *Preparation of tapes.* The technical aspects of making tapes deter teachers from using them. Making a tape is not a complex process, but it does demand some planning if it is to result in a quality, reusable tape. Following are some suggestions for the preparation of tapes:

1. Use a standard format so that the student understands how to use the tape each time and does not repeatedly require assistance. (A suggested format is shown on p. 377.)
2. Check the equipment carefully before taping to ensure that time is not wasted because of faulty equipment.
3. Prepare the tapes in a quiet place; extraneous sounds may "creep" into the tape.
4. Store the tapes carefully and in some organized manner. Properly storing and labeling tapes for easy access increases the life and use of tapes and reduces frustration on the part of the teacher and student. (Some general suggestions for storing tapes are listed in Fig. 11-12.)
5. Identify a group of volunteers such as social clubs, professional groups, or even retired teachers who can prepare tapes for teachers. Teacher time should be spent planning the tapes rather than actually providing the manpower to prepare them.

Compressed texts. Special texts with a "watered down" vocabulary are generally available for

TAPED LESSONS

Suggested standard format

1. *Identify general topic, tape number, and specific skill:* English, E-27, grammar (plurals).
2. *List materials needed to complete the lesson:* notebook paper, pencil, worksheets EG-27a and EG-27b.
3. *Identify all parts of the lesson:* This lesson will consist of a taped instructional segment reviewing worksheet EG-27a, providing examples of plural forms, and presenting instructions for worksheet EG-27b.
4. *Clearly specify instructions*
   a. On a piece of notebook paper write your name in the upper right-hand corner, list the date under your name, and list the tape number, EG-27, on the third line.
   b. Along the left margin of the paper number vertically from 1 to 10. Listen to the following sentences on the tape. If the sentence contains a plural, write an X; if the sentence does not contain a plural, write a 0. (For example, the sentence, "The boy is involved in a game of basketball" would be marked with an 0, since it does not contain a plural.)
5. *Provide definite instructions when the taped segment has ended:* Complete worksheet EG-27b independently, use the grading key to check your own work, record the score on your English graph on the wall, turn off the recorder, and store earphones in the proper place.

Storage of taped lessons

1. Label tape clearly, indicating general topic, tape number, specific skill, and length of tape.
2. List all materials required.
3. If tape is to be permanent, take precautions to ensure it is not accidentally erased.
4. Store tapes by instructional sequence and in order of use.

certain subjects. However, implementing them is difficult. Some students would rather not use them because of the connotation associated with them. Many courses do not have alternative materials available. We recommend the use of *compressed* material that is the distillation of materials into key concepts and principles, important words, and summaries.

The objective of compression is to reduce each two or three pages of a written text to one half or one page of reading matter. This need not be done by the teacher; students or volunteers may supply the labor to compress the major textbooks of several courses. The amount of work presented to a student with compressed reading matter does not seem as overwhelming. Compressed material eliminates a lot of tedious work and improves attitudes toward reading; it aids tutors in tutoring sessions, and the material is easily adapted to audiovisual materials and programmable learning machines.

Games. Mainstream teachers should consider the use of games to teach the basic concepts of a particular subject area. Games have several advantages for handicapped students, not the least of which is the reduced emphasis on the ability to read. Specialists should encourage the use of commercial and teacher-made games both for instruction and for evaluation in the classroom.

Learning packets. Learning packets (manila envelopes, boxes, etc.) contain game sheets and worksheets specifically designed or selected for handicapped students. Some teachers have taken skill lists or curricular guides and searched for activities that address each skill or objective. Worksheets are put in a folder or packet for the child; in this way the child gets the content, but through materials modified to suit an individualized lesson plan. This same approach, described in detail in Chapter 12, may be used with other students; once the teachers find that it is effective in circumventing certain reading problems, it may replace other styles of teaching. As a group, teachers have demonstrated that they are very creative in preparing "homemade" materials. An advantage of these packets is that they can be used in the resource room as well as part of any tutoring efforts included in programming.

"Talking books." Talking books and other services for the blind are available to "learning disabled" students in some states in which a psychologist is willing to certify these students as dyslexic. The services are not very helpful because of delays in getting materials and the fact that many materials of importance in course work must be prepared at the local level to be maximally effective.

Milieu. (Table 11-5). Milieu is a variable in learning that interacts with other facets of teaching, making it difficult to measure its importance and effect in isolation. Milieu should be viewed as interwoven with teacher attitude, techniques, curriculum, teacher training, and teacher personality. The relationship of these factors to the environment as fostered by the teacher should be obvious. Change in teacher behavior cannot be accomplished solely through manipulation of milieu, but environmental factors should be considered in the accommodational process. Environmental factors include the definition of a "good" student, classroom rules, student-teacher interaction, student interaction, and physical space.

Definition of a "good" student. Teacher values and expectations set the tone for the classroom environment. The type of student desired by the teacher as a "product" of the program is probably the major determinant of the classroom atmosphere. The definition of a "good" student is related to the teaching style and the way in which the room is operated. Teaching styles have long been

Table 11-5. Milieu

Skill competencies	*Possible classroom strategies*
24. Teacher lists four major factors within classroom environment, or milieu, that can be manipulated to accommodate individual learning characteristics.	Development of specific description of behaviors representative of "good" student
25. Teacher identifies aspects of teaching styles that can be examined to more specifically define "good" student.	Development of specific description of classroom rules
26. Teacher clarifies following aspects operating within classroom milieu: Definition of "good" student Classroom rules Student-teacher interactions (frequency and nature) Student interactions (frequency and nature)	Analysis of differences and similarities between perceptions of above items on part of students and teachers Process for reaching consensus on rules and definition of "good" student
27. Teacher identifies means through which information concerning milieu of classroom can be communicated to students and special educator, if necessary.	Analysis of amount and type of interaction Plans for altering frequency and type of interactions

known to produce definite effects on students, including the following results (Flanders, 1951):

1. Teacher behavior characterized as directive, demanding, deprecating by the use of private criteria, and, in general, supporting of the teacher elicits student behaviors of hostility toward self or the teacher, withdrawal, apathy, aggressiveness, and emotional disintegration.

2. Teacher behavior characterized as receptive, problem oriented, evaluative or critical by way of public criteria, and, in general, student supportive elicits student behaviors or problem orientation, decreased interpersonal anxiety, integration, and emotional readjustment.

Research results have indicated that several types of teachers and students exist and teacher effectiveness is enhanced by matching certain teacher "types" with certain student "types" (Bush, 1954; Heil, Powell, & Feifer, 1960). Echoing a belief long held by educators, Bush states that "a certain type of student tends to work successfully with one, rather than another, type of teacher" (p. 170). If a teacher's style or personality cannot be changed, students should be selectively placed.

Research in the quantitative measurement and identification of teacher behaviors continues, but this knowledge has not yet been used by practitioners responsible for teacher evaluation and student placement. Decisions concerning section or grade are still based on policies and subjective, impressionistic reactions of administrators. The Omega list (Marsh, Gearheart, & Gearheart, 1978) is an example of operational recognition of the effect of teacher behavior and expectations in placing students. Under certain conditions, some teachers should not have handicapped students in their class. The following dimensions of the process of classroom interaction, identified by Spaulding (1965), should be considered in making placement decisions:

1. Manner in which approval and disapproval are conveyed
2. Manner in which teachers use their authority with students
3. Emotional tone of the classroom
4. Means by which teachers prefer to receive student information
5. Types of student behavior that elicit approval or disapproval

Classroom rules. Behavioral standards are rarely consistent among classrooms even if general guidelines for classroom rules are dictated by school policy. The range of student behaviors observed reflects varying tolerance for student interaction, social expectations, and standards for performance. Students typically can identify definite standards or rules for each class, even if they are unwritten.

Classroom rules and teacher behavior affect student behavior. The teacher's attitude toward and treatment of students create a climate that relates to learning. Teachers who have "double standards" create an unhappy environment. The number and nature of classroom rules, as well as the manner in which they are enforced, must be considered in evaluating milieu and in determining accommodation of the student.

Student-teacher interaction. The type and amount of student-teacher interaction is an important aspect of milieu. It is not unrealistic to expect students with academic and social problems to function better in a learner-supportive climate fostered by positive interaction with the teacher. Student-teacher interaction can result in increased or decreased anxiety on the part of both parties, thus affecting performance as well as attitude. Depending on the situation and the student, interaction with the teacher should be positive and consistent with treatment of other students. Being overly solicitous of a student can be detrimental and interfere with student performance just as much as lack of attention or rejection.

Student interaction. The studies supporting the use of peer tutors illustrate the point that students learn from each other (Cloward, 1967; Erickson, 1971; Thomas, 1972). Spaulding (1965), the developer of CASES, has identified a behavioral category called integrative social interaction. It is described as mutual give-and-take, cooperative behavior, and studying or working together in a situation in which participants are on par with each other. This type of behavior appears to be positively related to learning and motivation, making integrative social interaction among students a desirable educational goal.

Unfortunately many teachers neither allow nor foster peer interaction in the form of tutoring or group learning. The traditional classroom is teacher centered, with little or no provision made for student interaction. When planning for accommodation in the mainstream placement, the teacher should consider the amount and type of student interactions. Classroom visitations, student observations with an instrument such as CASES, and interviews with regular students provide useful insight into the amount and quality of student interaction in a classroom.

Comment. Typically if regular classroom teachers are approached with the possibility of mainstreaming mildly handicapped students, their most immediate concern is with the course content and the materials to be used. Generally the regular teacher may employ a wide range of teaching strategies. However, an important aspect of mainstreaming is the atmosphere of the classroom, or its milieu.

To a great extent, certain "types of teachers" and "types of students" may be matched. By examining milieu, an accurate description of the learning environment of the regular classroom can be achieved, which aids those involved in improving the mainstreaming process. That is, the regular teacher examines the environment in which students are expected to function and is able, therefore, to make some adjustments in that environment as required by the various learning characteristics of the student. In addition, requirements for success in the mainstream class can be communicated to the special education teacher and the student, enabling them to concentrate on behaviors that are required to function successfully.

Therefore, examining the specific aspects of milieu can result in accommodation on the part of the student, since he or she can now modify behavior to fit a clear pattern expected by an individual teacher in the regular classroom. Also, the mainstream teacher can accommodate the handicapped student through slight modifications in milieu that facilitate learning and individual learning characteristics.

Teachers interested in examining the milieu of a classroom and in making changes can easily accomplish the task by engaging in activities such as the following:

1. The teacher prepares a written list of classroom rules so that a definite commitment, rather than a nebulous expectation, is made about classroom policies. The teacher may ask the class to list the rules of the classroom; in comparison, the two lists may appear quite different. This provides the teacher with feedback about the accuracy of the rules enforced, and the teacher may elect to retain the stated or implied set of rules or alter either one.

2. The teacher writes a definition of a "good" student without using names of particular students. The specific desirable traits to be exhibited by a "good" student should be identified; then, these can be communicated to the class and the resource teacher, if desired. Surprisingly the trait list may include items such as "always puts name on paper," "asks questions at the right time," and "brings supplies to class!" As this list demonstrates, some behaviors of a "good" student can be taught in the resource room.

3. The teacher keeps a tally sheet on the types of interaction demonstrated by students, such as asking questions about subject matter, asking questions about material other than subject matter, talking to peers, and requesting assistance from peers. This tally sheet provides a profile of the amount and type of interaction that can be maintained or altered, as desired by the teacher.

Time and space modifications (Table 11-6). The cluster of strategies termed time and space modifications focuses on the type of instructional schedule followed in the classroom and the use of classroom space. These strategies are easily described to teachers and have been well received in teacher consultation and in-service programs.

Table 11-6. Time and space modifications

Skill competencies	*Possible classroom strategies*
28. Teacher accommodates mildly handicapped students by altering instructional sequence in daily planning.	Learning centers
29. Teacher plans and implements learning centers.	Interactional model
30. Teacher designs and implements interactional model within a specific content area or period of time.	Modular or flexible scheduling
31. Teacher alters instructional sequence to allow fixed learning, but at variable rate.	Alternative seating arrangements

Learning centers. The teacher who is willing to use learning centers finds mainstreaming much less taxing than the teacher with preferences such as having straight rows of desks and limited student interactions. Learning centers facilitate accommodation for the following reasons:

1. Allowance for individual rates and levels of performance is more easily maintained.
2. Student differences in performance are much less noticeable to peers.
3. A wider variety of activities are employed without drawing attention to individual students.
4. Opportunity for the occurrence of peer learning is increased.
5. Interactional learning models are used more effectively.
6. Responsibility of the teacher to be a "ringmaster" is eliminated.
7. The environment imposes a natural control on behavioral problems because students are actively engaged in learning activities.

Specialists who encourage teachers to use learning centers should provide assistance in setting up centers so that any additional work is shared. Ideally the resource teacher also employs learning centers in the special classroom for the same reasons as listed previously (the use of learning centers is covered more fully in Chapter 12). Following are some general guidelines that the teacher should remember when establishing learning centers:

1. Begin with only one center, and gradually add centers as management skills improve.
2. Use a wide variety of materials; do not simply put worksheets at every center.
3. Be sure that the student understands how to operate any equipment involved. It is best to introduce the equipment to the entire group; it saves explanation time as each group progresses through the centers.
4. In the group meeting, review the specific requirements of each center to reduce confusion.
5. Have students take only the materials (e.g., pencils) that are required at a particular center. Many teachers have pupils bring a little plastic Ziploc bag for carrying the basic set of equipment to each center.
6. Have a specific place at each center in which worksheets and other mateirals are left for grading, collect these after each group finishes, and, if possible, grade them quickly and return them. Some teachers use the assistance of peers in grading.
7. Expect some cheating in the beginning. Do not directly address the behavior or call attention to the students involved. Instead, reward individual effort and be tolerant of varying levels of performance. As one teacher said, "At least Jeff is now interested enough to copy the work; before learning centers were used, he never did anything in my class!"

Modular or flexible scheduling. The basic premise in accommodation is that the learning environment is altered to match or accommodate the particular learning characteristics of the handicapped student. Several obvious elements within the regular classroom are readily identified as areas of accommodation, such as materials and methods used. However, the sequencing of instruction or scheduling is an avenue of accommodation not often recognized by regular educators.

Many students demonstrate some disorganization in their approach to a task as well as difficulty in organizing instructional materials. Labels applied to students do not seem to consistently reflect the presence of any definite characteristics; in other words, two students identified as learning disabled may, in fact, demonstrate different learning characteristics. For this reason, individual students should be described by particular descriptive statements rather than categorical labels; this provides a much sounder basis for accommodation.

When specific learning characteristics of the student have been identified, the regular teacher, perhaps with the aid of the special educator, can scrutinize the sequence of instructional events to isolate scheduling factors that can be modified to mesh with student characteristics. For example, if a student seems to have difficulty maintaining attention within a large group for an entire period or unit of time, an alternative would be to change the schedule and provide for small group instruction. This same change would accommodate the student whose major source of interaction is with peers; rather than trying to compete with the peers for attention, the teacher provides an appropriate time for peer interaction.

The following exemplifies how teachers have altered the sequence of instruction or time block to accommodate particular student characteristics. The examples reflect a different approach to scheduling, but each is an application of an approach to instruction in which learning characteristics interact with the instructional sequence utilized.

Example of an interactional model. A fourth grade–social studies teacher was having difficulty integrating handicapped students, even though the students appeared capable of handling the information. Examination of the 45-minute period revealed that four instructional blocks were included by the teacher—vocabulary, reading of assignment, worksheets, and discussion with all students in one large group and directed by the teacher. Observation of the handicapped students indicated that one student had major difficulty in identifying what was expected behavior and kept "doing the wrong thing at the wrong time" such as reading the book when he should have been attending to the teacher. Another student had a problem with either short attention span or lack of interest and a desire to be moving around the classroom.

Rather than changing the content to be taught or the instructional block or activities, the following scheduling changes were implemented:

Block 1—vocabulary. Students were instructed together in vocabulary.

Block 2—reading. Students were divided into four groups, each with seven students, and asked to move into groups in the four corners of the room, and, by taking turns, read the assignment orally.

Block 3—worksheets. All students returned to seats to individually work on sheets.

Block 4—discussion. Students returned to the four groups in the corners of the room to participate in a discussion led by the teacher.

Student performance improved because the schedule acknowledged the learner's needs, rather than attempting to change behavior. The schedule allowed student movement, student interaction, and additional opportunity for teacher-student interaction as the teacher moved from group to group in blocks 2 and 4. The only variable that was changed in this approach was the schedule, yet the effect was great.

This same approach can be implemented in a self-contained regular classroom as well as in a departmentalized classroom. The teacher would examine the time period during which student performance and behavior is perceived as a problem or an anticipated difficulty, identifying specific instructional sequences. These could then be varied to reflect the learning needs of the students.

Alternative seating arrangements. A predominant practice in school seating assignments has been the "T" pattern; favored students, those with whom the teacher has most interaction, sit down the center and across the front of the classroom forming a pattern like an inverted "T". This becomes common practice in upper elementary grades and secondary school in which seating is traditional. Teachers may discover that some students are only noticed at roll call. Other teachers may notice "troublemakers" who sit around the back or outside edges of the group. The typical response is to bring such students up to the front of the class, near the teacher; unfortunately this sometimes provides the "controlling student" a bigger audience, making him or her the focus of attention rather than the teacher.

One simple time and space strategy is to alter the floor plan of the classroom. A traditional plan can be altered by the teacher to change both instructional modes used and student behavior patterns exhibited. This strategy allows the teacher to interact with more students, increases the opportunity for modeling among peers, and causes the students to break up previous behavior patterns. In classes containing one or more resistant controlling students who compete with the teacher for attention and control of the class, grouped seating makes it difficult for these students to get an audience. In classes with several small groups functioning in a variety of activities, it is more difficult to gain the attention of the whole group, unlike with the traditional seating plan in which the student can become the center of attention merely by making a few crude noises! This is a popular strategy for upper grade teachers who employ the unit or project approach to content classes.

Human resources (Table 11-7). This cluster of strategies emphasizes human resources and provides assistance to the regular classroom teacher who is confronted with the task of mainstreaming. Paraprofessionals, peer tutors, and volunteers can provide instructional support and clerical assistance. Some districts have such groups, but more likely human resources available to teachers are limited. The regular classroom teacher, the special educator, and perhaps others such as the counselor and principal may have to discover sources of supportive manpower. The counselor may coordinate peer tutors as part of the counseling program, whereas the principal may be in a position to enlist the aid of community groups such as service sororities and philanthropic organizations.

Specific steps in implementing support programs, including selection of personnel and training procedures, are vital to the success of such programs. Details for developing and implementing human support programs are included in Chapter 12.

Table 11-7. Human resources

Skill competencies	*Possible classroom strategies*
32. Teacher identifies sources of manpower for assistance that might be considered in particular situation or setting.	Paraprofessional program Peer-tutoring program Volunteer-assistance program
33. Teacher identifies pertinent information to be considered in selecting paraprofessionals, peer tutors, and volunteers.	
34. Teacher outlines information to be included in manual for assisting personnel.	
35. Teacher outlines orientation and training program to be conducted for assisting personnel.	
36. Teacher provides examples of types of tasks (clerical or instructional) for which assisting personnel might be used.	
37. Teacher plans and implements peer-tutoring program.	

Table 11-8. Parental interactions

Skill competencies	*Possible classroom strategies*
38. Teacher maintains file containing specific information on student and parental rights as related to due process and programming.	Resource information file Conference preparation plans Conference guidelines
39. Teacher identifies parental organizations that can provide information and support for parents of handicapped students.	
40. Teacher lists major considerations in planning for parental conference for parents of mildly handicapped students.	
41. Teacher specifies major considerations in conducting parental conference for parents of handicapped students, including the following: Conference site Materials Conference structure Termination of conference	
42. Teacher identifies means by which records of parental contacts might be maintained.	

Parental interactions (Table 11-8). Regular classroom teachers sometimes complain about difficulties in dealing with parents of handicapped students, describing some parents as militant and interfering. Preparing for the parent conference has sometimes been anxiety provoking for teachers because of concern over student rights, feelings of parents, and their own inability to convey any "good news." For these reasons, suggestions for conducting parental interactions have evolved as part of the accommodation skill clusters. The special educator should consider sharing the information concerning *planning* and *conducting parent conferences,* as was presented in Chapter 5; the regular teacher and special educator should develop some means of communicating and *reporting on the conference.* This is an important aspect of parental interactions because the parents may relate differently to each teacher, making it necessary for all parties to be aware of any communication to ensure that information is consistently reported. A sample conference report form is presented in Fig. 11-5; using this or other forms of written reporting can aid in maintaining an accurate record of parental interactions.

A strategy that might aid in parental communication is the *resource information file.* This file has been recommended by regular classroom teachers who are involved in mainstreaming efforts and who have frequent contact with parents of handicapped students. The file might consist of the following items:

1. Information concerning membership in parental groups, both national and local, (e.g., the Association for Children with Learning Disabilities or the Association for Retarded Citizens)
2. List of names of contact persons in the local area for these or other advocacy groups
3. Pamphlets concerning parental and student rights available from the state department or other local sources
4. Copies of any school policies concerning handicapped students
5. A curriculum guide or general list of skills covered in the particular grade or subject area
6. An explanation of the grading policy for the district and information concerning the grading of handicapped students in particular

The special educator should also maintain a par-

Conference summary

Special education teacher:____________________ School:____________________

Conference date:____________________ Student:____________________

Purpose of conference:

Conference outcomes:

Conference participants:

Comments:

Fig. 11-5. Sample parental communications form.

ent information file that might consist of packets, for distribution to those teachers wishing to have them available for reference.

Altering instructional environment

Accommodation and teaching process. (Table 11-9). The relationship of the teaching competencies to the teaching variables that were introduced in Chapter 1 and reviewed in Table 11-9 can be understood by examining each of the competencies in terms of which variable is addressed. The 12 variables simply provide a general framework for including what might be an infinite list of teacher and learner variables in the instructional setting. In the broadest possible terms, the 12 variables provide the classroom teacher with generic approach to any handicapped student. The individual characteristic of the learner may point out a need for alteration in the manner in which information is presented by the teacher, the type and level of information selected, the way in which the child is situated in the classroom, types of materials and devices used, and numerous other considerations. The rule of thumb seems to be for the teacher and/or consultant to examine the needs of the student, which should be confirmed through direct observation, in terms of how the teacher presents information, how the student responds, and what the teacher should do to improve instruction. Some simple kinds of activities can be conducted to measure improvement in terms of expectations. The teacher can ensure that the student is not given materials that are clearly beyond his or her level; can examine in what type of setting the student performs best, such as with a small group or instructional equipment; and can monitor behavior and learning in different aspects of the curriculum. In Chapter 12 the reader will be introduced to the other side of the ledger, the numerous learning theory variables that might be used by the teacher to more specifically tailor teaching and other activities under the three broad headings of direct teacher-controlled variables, curriculum, and ecology of the classroom.

Perhaps the reader may now appreciate the reasons for including instructional approaches that may seem to be simple, if not just obvious. In our experience and that of the project staff who have

Table 11-9. Teaching variables and mainstreaming competencies

Teaching variables	*Mainstreaming competencies*
Direct teaching variables	
Control of student attention and time on task	Teacher-controlled variables
Organizational control of information (input) to be learned with objectives	Classroom management
Redundancy of instructional cues	
Alternative informational access	
Alternative responding	
Reinforcement and feedback	
Ecological variables	
Environmental climate of classroom	Milieu
Time and space utilization	Time and space
Participation-interaction of students	Human resources
	Parental interactions
Curricular variables	
Sequence and rate of presentation of skills to be learned	Curricular variations
Uses and adaptation of materials and equipment	Materials development and modification
Accommodation and compensatory teaching	

worked with classroom teachers for several years, we found that nothing should be taken for granted. Many classroom teachers, those experienced or new to the teaching field, develop a teaching style that is primarily based on lecture and seatwork. This can be seen as early as the first grade, and it is almost universal among secondary and college instructors. No amount of reading materials, lectures, or films during in-service training will create better learning conditions for students than actual intervention in the classroom and changing the manner by which the teacher presents information to a child, provides reinforcement and feedback, alters the instructional space, permits interactions between students, or alters the curriculum or expectations. Many classroom teachers may wish for a simple and direct approach in the form of a "magic kit" that would change the learner dramatically but not change the classroom structure or teaching style; this is not possible. As was presented in Chapter 1 and will be presented again in Chapter 12, the most comprehensive research that currently exists demonstrates that teacher effectiveness deals primarily with such simple notions as clarity of presentation, explanations, and feedback. This is the essence of good teaching in the classroom. If it cannot be expected that many learning characteristics can be dramatically changed, elements that can be changed are teaching behaviors and expectations for conformity to a group of expectations.

It should also be obvious that if the special educator as a consultant can influence the classroom teacher to do one or more of the activities or develop one or more of the competencies listed previously, an impact will have been made on the instructional environment of the school. Depending on the teacher, this impact can be very small or significant.

Example of consultation process. The subtleties of the consultation process may be difficult to grasp with little prior experience. Often the best ingredients for consultation are common sense, courtesy, and the ability to put oneself in the other teacher's position. The importance of these factors can best be illustrated with the following example.

The special education supervisor routinely provided each classroom teacher with three referral forms at the beginning of the school year. Instructions were provided concerning how to refer students and describing the purposes of the program. During the second week of the fall term, Ms. Rogers, a fourth-grade teacher, sent the following note to the new special education teacher:

> Mr. McRae only gave me three referral forms; I am going to need at least four more this week. My class this year is totally impossible; many of them are siblings of former students, so I know what I am up against. The whole class is slow and just not up to fourth-grade work, so they will have difficulty all year. These seven students obviously will not be able to keep up with even this slow group, and, with 32 students in the class, there isn't any time to pull them out into a slow group each day. Please send the additional referral forms immediately because these kids need to be in your class all the time. Mr. McRae said in the meeting that your program is wonderful and designed to help us with these problem kids. I want you to have them immediately!

Shown on pp. 388 and 389 are two responses to this note; the differences between them, as well as the long-term impact that might be created by each, should be obvious.

Guiding thoughts in developing individualized instruction

The reader has been presented with an extensive list of accommodation techniques for use in the regular classroom to aid the handicapped student. These have been recommended because principles of laboratory-based learning systems are difficult to apply in large group instruction; moreover, the nature of the school organization poses significant problems to the specialist. These reasons explain why some practitioners have elected to limit their involvement in mainstreaming. However, if they do, the special education program will be jeopardized. We have stressed the importance of engineering a system to support the student and the classroom teacher in the mainstream setting to maximize the effectiveness of accommodation

EXAMPLES OF SPECIAL EDUCATION TEACHER'S RESPONSES

Response 1

Dear Ms. Rogers,

It seems like you are feeling overwhelmed with this class. Perhaps with our support you can deal with your class in some alternative ways. I am not able to come and take all of your behavior problems, but I am willing to help you set up some individual behavioral programs that may lessen the acting out behaviors that bother you.

Mr. McRae and I will screen the seven children you referred. They may not all be high-risk cases, and those we refer back to you, we will assist you with.

As for your comment on the class being "slow," perhaps you could use a topical outline and describe what the children will expect to learn in fourth-grade classes. Then make each class exciting by using various media methods to reach all modes of learning.

Also, don't expect too much of yourself or your students. Do the best you can and realize that they are not *all* going to learn everything you teach in fourth grade. By modifying your expectations, you'll ease the pressure of success on you and your students.

Please feel free to consult with us on any other management problems you have. We will give you specifics for each child you need help on. Good luck!

COMMENTS

Appears condescending (lines 1, 4, 5, and 13 to 16)

Implies superiority of experience, knowledge, and position (lines 2 to 5, 7, 17, and 18)

Implies that the class is poorly taught (lines 9 to 12)

Imputes teacher's ability to spot "problem" students (line 7)

Contains poorly structured sentences and poor word choices such as "refer back to you" (line 7)

Invites future consultation (line 17) when in fact no consultation has occurred or can be expected to occur as a result of this note because it has been a monologue (i.e., why believe there will be any assistance in the future, since none seems eminent in this exchange?)

techniques. We also suggested that the specialist may be of assistance by supporting educational concepts in the mainstream class.

A variety of approaches may be used ranging from major programs that must be adopted by an entire school system to more likely possibilities such as the development of alternative learning units and restructuring selected regular classroom environments. The major programs of individualization are useful because they can guide the development of individual instructional techniques in special education. Teaching is a complex process that involves the learning environment, style of teaching, motivation and style of the learner, and interaction of the student with the subject matter. More needs to be learned about these variables.

EXAMPLES OF SPECIAL EDUCATION TEACHER'S RESPONSES—cont'd

Response 2

Dear Ms. Rogers,

In responding to your memorandum, I feel that between the two of us we can work out some possible solutions. If we can detect the specific skills that the children are lacking, then through alternative procedures and extra help, the children can catch up enough to function at grade level.

I could, with your permission, observe your class and obtain more information about the nature of the problems. After identifying the problem in more detail, we can decide on some accommodation techniques that might be implemented in both your room and mine, if they are assigned to my class. Some possible strategies that we might both try would be rearranging seating, developing topical outlines, using audiovisual aids, and providing study tapes. Some instructional grouping might also be done based on my observations and your experience with the group. We can at least meet and generate a few ideas without having to wait until Mr. McRae can complete the process to determine whether these students can be assigned to my class.

Let me know when we can get together, and I will help in any way I can. Together, we might come up with some solutions!

COMMENTS

Communicates a feeling of equality or peer relationship (lines 1, 2, 5, 7, 9, 11, 12, and 16)
Avoids attempting to find "cause"
Identifies problem as possibly within the child, not the teacher (lines 3, 4, 6, and 7)
Offers to share responsibility (lines 2, 5 to 9, 11, 12, and 17)
Invites future consultation (lines 16 and 17)
Provides possibilities for specific strategies to be tried (lines 9 to 11)

However, we can find direction and support from existing approaches.

Bloom (1980) has discussed three constructs about learning capabilities of students that should have some bearing on the issues of individualization and may be helpful to planners. These constructs are as follows:

1. There are both good and poor learners.
2. There are both fast and slow learners.
3. When provided with favorable learning conditions, most students can become similar in their learning ability, rate of acquiring knowledge, and motivation for further learning.

In considering these three constructs, Bloom makes the point that the correlation between measures of school achievement at grades 3 and 11 is about +.85, which reveals that over an 8-year period the relative ranking of students in a class or school remains almost perfectly fixed. This should impress special educators who think that continued remediation, as a single effort, will be very fruitful. Although Bloom indicates that this relationship may be broken, it will be done by programming or instruction that is adapted to each student's *needs* and under conditions in which students believe a new school situation is one in which they can start afresh, no matter how poorly the past record has been. Therefore, poor learners who apparently learn more "slowly" may achieve at high levels through *mastery learning* under conditions in which instruction is tailored to their needs and presentation is unique and fresh.

SUMMARY

In this chapter an approach for assistance of handicapped students in mainstream classes was recommended under the general heading of accommodation. In general, accommodation is any method of changing the instructional environment and expectations of the learner and any instructional approach that compensates for deficits for the learner rather than remediates them. The three general areas of accommodation techniques are the administration, regular classroom, and special education classroom. A teacher consultation process, which requires the cooperation of the mainstream teacher, provides an effective implementation of strategies recommended by the special education teacher.

Regardless of the type of handicap, most students are primarily limited by traditional practices in the classroom. Knowledge and skill competencies permit individualized instruction by regular classroom teachers; the relationship between these strategies and special education programming is important.

REFERENCES AND SUGGESTED READINGS

Abidin, R.R. Negative effects of behavioral consultation: "I know I ought to, but it hurts too much!" *Journal of School Psychology,* 1975, *13,* 51-57.

Adams, R.S., & Biddle, B.J. *Realities of teaching.* New York: Holt, Rinehart & Winston, 1970.

Bloom, B.S. (Ed.). *Taxonomy of educational objectives: the classification of educational goals* (Handbook 1: *Cognitive domain).* New York: David McKay Co., Inc., 1956.

Bloom, B.S. New views of the learner: implications for instruction and curriculum. *Educational Leadership,* 1978, *35,* 563-576.

Bloom, B.S. The new direction in educational research: alterable variables. *Phi Delta Kappan,* 1980, *61,* 382-385.

Bush, R.N. *The teacher-pupil relationship.* New York: Prentice-Hall, Inc., 1954.

Cloward, R.D. Studies in tutoring. *Journal of Experimental Education,* 1967, *36,* 25.

Erickson, M.R. *A study of tutoring program to benefit tutors and tutees* (University Microfilm No. 71-16914). Ann Arbor, MI: University of Michigan, 1971.

Flanders, N.A. Personal-social anxiety as a factor in experimental learning situations, *Journal of Educational Research,* 1951, *45,* 100-110.

Gagne, R.M. *The conditions of learning* (2nd ed.) New York: Holt, Rinehart & Winston, 1970.

Glicking, E.E., Murphy, L.C., & Mallory, D.W. Teachers' preferences for resource services. *Exceptional Children,* 1979, *45,* 442-449.

Gump, P.V. *The classroom behavior setting: its nature and relation to student behavior* (Final Report, Project No. 2453). Lawrence, KS: Midwest Psychological Field Station, University of Kansas, 1967.

Hass, G. *Curriculum planning: a new approach.* Boston: Allyn & Bacon, Inc., 1977.

Heil, L.M., Powell, M., & Feifer, I. *Characteristics of teacher behavior related to the achievement of children in several elementary grades.* Washington, DC: Office of Cooperative Research Branch, U.S. Department of Health, Education, and Welfare, 1960.

Hoetker, J., & Ahlbrand, W.P. The persistence of the recitation. *American Educational Research Journal,* 1969, *6,* 145-167.

Marsh, G.E., II, Gearheart, C.K., & Gearheart, B.R. *The learning disabled adolescent: program alternatives in the secondary school.* St. Louis: The C.V. Mosby Co., 1978.

Marsh, G.E., II, & Price, B.J. *Methods for teaching the mildly handicapped adolescent,* St. Louis: The C.V. Mosby Co., 1980.

Muehl, S., & Forell, E.R. A follow-up study of disabled readers: variables related to high school reading performance. *Reading Research Quarterly,* 1973-1974, *9*(1), 110-123.

Rosenfield, S. Introducing behavior modification techniques to teachers. *Exceptional Children,* 1979, *45,* 334-339.

Spaulding, R.L. *Achievement, creativity, and self-concept correlates of teacher-pupil transactions in elementary school classrooms.* Hempstead, NY: Hofstra University, 1965. (Available from Institute for Children Development and Family Studies, San Jose State University, San Jose, CA.)

Stewart,W.A., Goodman, G., & Hammond, B. Behavior modification: teacher training and attitudes. *Exceptional Children,* 1976, *42,* 402-403.

Talmage, H. Instructional design for individualization. In H. Talmage (Ed.), *Systems of individualized education.* Berkeley, CA: McCutchan Publishing Corp., 1975.

Thomas, J.L. Tutoring strategies and effectiveness: a comparison of elementary age tutors/college age tutors. *Dissertation Abstracts International,* 1972, *32,* 3580A.

12 COMPREHENSIVE PROGRAMMING

The focus of this chapter is on direct instruction of students: models of instruction, learning theory, and a management system. Direct instruction regardless of the content, consumes more of the special educator's time than any other activity (Sargent, 1981). It is complicated in cases in which mainstreaming demands coordination between special and regular class activities. This chapter is designed to assist the teacher in the delivery of direct instruction in the development of management strategies for effective and efficient instruction of handicapped students.

MODELS OF INSTRUCTION

Theoretically, a teacher in the regular classroom may draw on a wide variety of instructional models. In special education many instructional approaches may also be considered. Tailoring them for effective integration of the regular and special classrooms requires a management system. Many models of instruction can be used in the regular classroom; however, most teachers probably develop a personal style that draws on the elements of several models. The common, or "genus," classroom is ordinarily characterized by group instruction, a considerable amount of seat work, and a teacher-centered approach. The special educator should be aware of the general approaches that might be used by the regular educator for effective planning even though a particular teacher will most likely be eclectic in practice.

General education approaches

Although numerous educational models are recommended for use in general education and a wide variety of arrangements and adaptations exist, four basic families of models are suggested by Joyce and Weil (1980): information-processing, personal, social interaction, and behavioral.

Information-processing models. Information-processing models tend to emphasize the intellectual functioning of the student and mastery of information. The teacher is concerned with how to efficiently present information to the learner and the learner's ability to deal with problem-solving tasks in terms of input, organization, and output. Concept development in various disciplines is stressed. Examples of information processing include inductive thinking (Taba, 1966) and concept attainment (Brunner, 1967).

Personal models. Personal models are especially concerned with emotional development and the ability of the individual to develop a strong identity and adjust to the environment. Self-awareness, self-understanding, and personal development are stressed. Examples are nondirective teaching (Rogers, 1971) and classroom meeting (Glasser, 1965).

Social interaction models. Social interaction models are concerned with the relationship of the individual to larger groups and to society; teaching the individual to relate to others and to become a member of society is stressed. The best-known example is that of social inquiry (Massiaias & Cox, 1966).

Behavioral models. Behavioral models, thoroughly described in Chapter 9, are a major influence in education. The basic approach is behavioral theory, which deals with stimulus control and reinforcement, and Skinner (1953) is the best known theorist.

As Joyce and Weil (1980) point out, the classroom teacher may find a variety of instructional models more useful than specialization. The type of preparation, nature of the teaching assignment, and other factors dictate the nature of a district's curriculum; the type of commercial materials available may define or restrict the type of instructional approaches to be used. However, most teachers probably have a great deal of flexibility and freedom of choice. When the classroom door is closed, the teacher's domain is mostly under his or her control. The teacher's choices should depend on the types of students and their needs, content to be taught, and available resources.

Special education approaches

A number of special education models seem to stand out; some have developed as specific approaches to be used with certain diagnostic categories. Due to the fact that special and regular educators use elements of various approaches, each approach is significant in its potential for use, regardless of the population for which it may have originally been intended.

Mercer (1979) cites several authors who suggest that there are at least two general instructional approaches in special education (Quay, 1973; Stephens, 1977; Yesseldyke & Salvia, 1974); these approaches may be referred to as *ability* and *skill* training models, and they have different theoretical orientations.

In ability training the presumption is made that something is wrong with an underlying process that is essential for learning. Training is devoted to correcting the process, such as in motor, perceptual, and psycholinguistic programs. Skill training deals with erecting an approach to teach specific skills with clearly defined outcomes. The learner is not necessarily considered as the source of difficulty or the reason for failure.

Many teachers combine approaches from each area, a method which is recommended by Smead (1977). Smead criticizes each model and contends that combining them is necessary for diagnostic-prescriptive teaching because each approach, singly, is ineffective, despite their theoretical inconsistencies.

It is important to reemphasize that the diagnostic-prescriptive approach to teaching, whether it is guided by ability or skill models, is only as precise as the validity of the diagnosis and the reliability of the treatment prescribed. If process theories cannot be supported by research, or if skill sequences are inaccurate, diagnostic-prescriptive teaching is of limited value. Thus, diagnostic-prescriptive teaching is complicated by the difficulty of educators to analyze within both domains, for example:

1. There is a lack of precision in the analysis of tasks and subtasks of a skill-model approach if the skills are sequenced inaccurately or if a particular learner must learn skills in a sequence different from the curriculum that is prescribed. This matter deserves much more research, especially with scaling techniques.
2. There is an inability to analyze tasks and behaviors in processes that lack an apparent skill sequence and have an unknown relationship of a process to academic skills (e.g., perceptual-motor development).

Practically, the teacher is discouraged from attempting to use any process training approach because research has been consistently unsupportive. Knowledge of abilities, based on tests with poor validity, does not lead to sufficient information for educational intervention. On the other hand, unless it is clear that natural hierarchies of skills exists in various areas or school subjects, and unless it can be determined that most children should be expected to progress in a stage theory pattern of development, the usefulness of the skill model may also be diminished.

The variety of instructional approaches used in special education can be classified in many ways. For example, they may be classified as ability or task-analytic approaches, special education categorical approaches (e.g., for the emotionally disturbed or learning disabled), or as theories (e.g., a perceptual-motor theory). Research pertaining to most of these topics has been presented in earlier parts of the text. The teacher who selects an approach, or a combination of them, should do so with a knowledge of the current and emerging research in each area and in terms of apparent appropriateness for a particular student.

Psychological process approaches. A variety of ability approaches, termed psychological process approaches, have been developed primarily for learning-disabled children, although they are also used with children classified with other labels. The basic contention is that improvement of an underlying psychological process results in improved academic performance. Notable in this category are the approaches based on the work of Ayres (1972), Delacato (1959), Frostig and Maslow (1973), Kephart (1971), and Kirk, McCarthy, and Kirk (1968). Using the diagnostic-prescriptive teaching approach in this area, the teacher attempts to identify the process weaknesses of the student and remediate them. A number of critics state that these approaches are unfounded because of the following reasons:

1. There is no clear understanding of the nature of psychological processes or their relationship to academic learning; few tests can reliably provide information with which a teacher can make educational decisions.
2. Results of training programs based on these theories have not been significant (Hammill, Goodman, & Weiderholt, 1974; Hammill & Larsen, 1978; Newcomer & Hammill, 1976).

Whether or not a child engages in motor training, eye-hand coordination exercises, or activities to improve psycholinguistic skills may be important decisions of the special educator. If the decision is made to attempt process remediation, it will be necessary for the teacher to restrict the amount of time the student is engaged in other learning activities, especially if the child is mainstreamed. There can be little assurance that improvement in academic functioning will ensue.

Aptitude-treatment/multisensory approaches. Aptitude-treatment/multisensory approaches emphasize a system based on a learning style or bombardment of sensory channels. A theorist might acknowledge the importance of a process weakness but would not necessarily attempt to improve its functioning. Rather, a "strong" process would be used for input of information, or several channels would be used to circumvent problems encountered in ordinary instructions. Examples here include the multisensory systems of Fernald (1943), Gillingham and Stillman (1960), and Johnson and Myklebust (1967). The diagnostic-prescriptive approach here would be to identify the best style of learning.

Direct-skill training. Approaches that primarily emphasize the skills to be learned are best known as behavioral (e.g., precision teaching and applied behavioral analysis). However, behaviorism is content free; it is a process of teaching. The major emphasis, as a teaching approach, is on the direct instruction of skills a teacher wishes a student to acquire. Thus, mastery learning and system approaches would also be placed in this category. The best special education examples are the works of Lovitt (1975) and Lindsley (1964), which have been imitated by many others. Diagnostic-prescriptive teaching in this category would be concerned with determining what level of achievement a student has reached and presenting skills in a logical sequence.

Instructional planning

Regardless of the instructional strategy that may be selected, the IEP must serve as the basis for planning in special education. Diagnostic-prescriptive teaching may be used along with, or in addition to, the IEP. It should be remembered that the IEP and DPT are not synonymous. The IEP is, or should be, a dynamic document that guides instruction during specific periods of time. Instructional planning for daily or weekly periods should follow a structure adhering to the following steps:

1. *Statement of lesson objectives.* Specific objectives are developed for the lesson and stated in behavioral terms.These objectives deal with discrete outcomes that might be anticipated for the instructional period covered in the plan.

2. *Behaviors of the teacher.* Implicit in the lesson plan is the behavior of the teacher, which consists of acts such as describing, explaining, illustrating, modeling, and inquiring. In the learning model described elsewhere in this text, teaching behavior is referred to as presentation.

3. *Selection of courseware.* To execute the plan, the teacher selects any of a variety of courseware, such as commercial materials, games, teaching machines, media aids, pencil-and-paper activities, and blackboard activities.

4. *Identification of instructional setting.* The child may be placed in the special classroom, in the regular classroom, in a small group, or in a large group or engaged in independent work or some interaction with teaching machines or another person.

5. *Identification of student behaviors.* As the student attends, the task will require some response such as writing, watching, listening, or talking.

Beyond these steps, which the teacher can easily control, other types of student responses might be considered, such as mediating responses examined in learning theory research. However, the most promising learning theory variables are attention, memory, and transfer because they are most directly related to classroom instruction. They offer areas for the teacher to consider the overlap between the teaching behavior, the curriculum, and practical student needs.

LEARNING THEORY AND INSTRUCTION

Several bodies of research in special education that may be used by the teacher in the design and implementation of instructional strategies are based on learning theory. Theory guides practice and enables an investigator to test possibilities, evaluate and reevaluate positions that might explain behavior, redefine basic constructs, and find practical solutions to problems.

There are many learning theories; no attempt is made here to present a comprehensive view of each theory, cover all possibilities, or relate recommendations to specific categorical types. Whether specific approaches apply to a given individual depends on the individual in question. Any given approach may or may not be suitable for a particular student; this will have to be determined in the instructional setting. The reader should consult original sources and interpret emerging research in terms of their implications.

A few texts attempt to provide the teacher with practical applications of research results. One example is the impressive work of Mercer and Snell (1977) who summarized the learning theory research of mental retardation and made recommendations to give the teacher a conceptualization of how research findings might be practically applied. Perhaps such a text would be useful to teachers who deal with mildly handicapped children, although the amount of such research is probably not as great as in areas in which research can be conducted on an intact, available group of subjects (e.g., in an institution).

Operant conditioning (e.g., applied behavioral analysis, precision teaching, and behavior modification is not specifically included in the following sections because it was considered in Chapter 9, and piagetian stage theory also is not reproduced. Concerns here are traditional areas that have been popular in special education literature and methodology: attention, memory, and transfer.

Attention

Attention has been examined by many investigators, and there are many theories and notions about the variables that might affect it. Thus, motivation, attractiveness of a stimulus, fatigue, drive states, level of development, and many other concepts might be used to study and understand attention. For the teacher, attention is an important classroom variable in the learning and teaching process; without attention, nothing else is possible.

Teachers usually think of attention or ''paying attention'' to mean that a child is watching and listening to the teacher and generally staying on task. As a psychological variable, attention can mean attending to relevant stimuli, being able to distinguish relevant stimuli from among unimportant ones, and sustaining attention sufficiently to complete a task. Children who do not pay attention are characterized as being hyperactive, distractible, bored, lazy, unmotivated, defiant, or immature.

In the field of special education, a considerable amount of research has been conducted under the general headings of *attention* and *selective attention*. The classical work was done by Fisher and Zeaman (1973) House, Brown, and Scott (1974) Ross (1976), and Zeaman and House (1963).

Children may have difficulty attending to instruction, which can be controlled by the schedule of reinforcement used by a teacher. Attentional problems may also be thought of as related to task difficulty. Some children are not able to determine the relevant or important cues among stimuli. They do not know what to pay attention to. This relates to previous learning and how tasks are presented.

Children who perform poorly on the Digit Span

subtest of the WISC–R, Auditory and Visual Sequential Memory subtests of the ITPA, and other similar tests are often said to have an attentional and/or memory problem. They lack a plan of attack or strategies to solve a problem. This may be explained as an inability to select or attend to proper stimuli or an inability to manage several analyses at the same time without prompting and structure.

In any learning task, some children may be helped significantly by having irrelevant or extraneous information removed from elements such as the general classroom environment and irrelevant cues in a specific learning activity. Such information is distracting and may invite attention to the wrong set of cues. Discovery learning is difficult for some children because they are unable to sort out the important information. Color, shape, size, and pictures can be irrelevant and distracting; for example the attractiveness of colored letters can be confusing, unless there is a purpose to the color and the child is aware of cue distinctiveness. Colored letters and numbers and attractive pictures can be detrimental to learning if used haphazardly.

Cue distinctiveness can be enhanced for a specific purpose by colored or darkened letters, words, and numbers which can later be faded to ordinary properties. Teaching children to attend specifically to important stimulus properties (phoneme/grapheme relationships) is important and cannot be left to chance. Color should have a constant relationship; for example, each process sign in arithmetic should have a distinctive color (e.g., blue for addition).

Although clustering or categorizing stimuli aids in learning, this process should be avoided in certain circumstances. Grouping things together on the basis of similarity can be confusing for certain tasks, such as in distinguishing the letters b, d, p, and q. Initial introduction of these letters should be done with higher contrast cues to focus attention specifically.

Changing cues rapidly or switching to an entirely different learning task without careful preparation is devastating to some students. For example, shifting from addition $\begin{array}{r}2\\ \underline{+2}\end{array}$ to multiplication $\begin{array}{r}2\\ \underline{\times 3}\end{array}$ as in the case of mixed problems on a worksheet may result in error because the student tends to ignore the new cue; also classifying objects by color and then by shape may result in error. These examples refer to what psychologists call intradimensional and extradimensional shifts or transfer-stimulus generation.

A teacher can improve attention and enhance learning by introducing novelty and oddity cues in learning situations. Presenting letters, words, and numbers in a different way; putting surprises in the middle of a learning activity; and doing unusual things will attract attention! Having children verbalize tasks as they perform them also seems to reinforce attention.

Attention is an important matter; the choice of stimulus information used to teach students to decode words or do other tasks may be only as effective as the attending behavior of students during initial learning.

Memory

A major consideration in special education assessment and teaching has been memory, especially short-term memory. Most of the research has concerned the learning disabled and mentally retarded populations and has been based on the number of digits or images a person can immediately recall after an auditory or visual presentation. The major foundation for this research is the work of Ellis (1970) who proposed a multiprocess theory of memory. In this process, any stimuli presented to the attending subject are processed first in primary memory (PM)—encoding. PM is not able to handle much information, since it is rapidly replaced by newer incoming data, and information that is held in PM will quickly decay—forgetting. In order to put information into secondary memory (SM) or tertiary memory (TM) storage, the subject must rehearse and organize the information in some form—storage.

Except as a research tool in a task on the WISC–R or the ITPA (digits) or as a device to remember someone's phone number, the memory of digits is a useless activity. Having children practice the rehearsal of digits may improve their ability to remember digits somewhat, but it does not transfer to other tasks.

In research with mentally retarded and learning-disabled subjects, there is a consistent tendency for subjects to remember fewer digits overall and a tendency not to rehearse, although the long-term memory of these students is similar to that of nonhandicapped students. Of course, we are interested in individuals and not labeled groups. It can be hypothesized that an individual will have difficulty with short-term memory, as indicated by Digit Span of the WISC–R. Depending on the point of view, and if there is validity in any of the viewpoints, this deficit can be alternatively explained not as a short-term memory disorder but rather as a deficit of attention, organization, or metamemory (described later).

Working with the assumption that a child may have a short-term memory deficit, what are the implications for the teacher? Drawing on findings from group research that may or may not apply to a specific individual, a number of possibilities can be considered. Much of the research indicates that memory can be improved by clustering bits of information and organizing input for the learner (Spitz, 1973). One example is paired associate learning, the process of presenting pairs repeatedly and later asking the subject to provide the other part of the pair if only one cue is given. This is of limited usefulness in classroom learning but has application for some purposes.

Color and shape are attractive to young or lower-functioning children. If a child persists in confusing letters, for example, b and d, the task

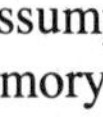

can be altered by using shape and/or color to make it more discriminable. A colored or darkened letter in the middle of a word tends to improve memory for serial learning, such as in spelling, because it gives the learner organization for storage and recall.

Retention is better if practice is spread out over a long period of time in small amounts (massed versus spaced practice). Too much information during a short period is unmanageable. Requiring all students to complete the same number of problems on a worksheet during a time period may be "democratic," but it is unreasonable for those who cannot handle that much information. The amount, rate of presentation, and relevance of information are variables affecting learning and memory. Presenting too much information too fast can be frustrating. Some students are not able to process information as quickly as others; therefore, adjusted rates should be considered. Of particular importance is the relevance of information; it should be based on previous learning and not exceed the learner's experience or capacity for processing.

Encouraging children to verbalize or make stories about content can enhance memory. Visual imagery is also useful; having children tell stories or envision objects improves storage and recall. Letters, words, and other stimuli can be associated with pictures or made to look like animals to aid in memory storage. Talking through a problem, algorithm, or sequence is an intermediate step between concrete experiences and representation. Constructing mental images and rhymes are useful techniques for a variety of activities. Specifically concentrating on what is to be learned, rather than requiring students to impose order on disorganized cues, also enhances learning, especially if extraneous stimuli are removed from the central task.

Studies showing differences between children labeled as mentally retarded and normal have always implicated a problem in short-term memory, or encoding, as causing poorer performance of the mentally retarded groups. Interestingly this has also been found among learning-disabled groups (Bauer, 1979). Elaborative encoding or rehearsal strategies either are not used or are used incorrectly. The student may attend to information, store it in short-term memory, and recall information from long-term storage; however, proper rehearsal is necessary first. These strategies can be taught to students and the problem reduced by properly organizing and structuring information for learning.

Cognitive organizers and prequestions are important for any learning activity and aid in structuring a lesson, presenting information, probing, encouraging feedback, and restructuring after the lesson is completed. If the teacher provides a classification scheme before teaching, uses the scheme to teach, and uses the scheme for testing, the responses of students will be better than if no structure is used or if a different structure is used for testing.

Overlearning, or drill, is an effective means of teaching children to recall information from long-term storage. Unfortunately, the teacher will have to teach beyond the point of mastery on criterion. Since this can be boring, children will need to have many varied activities for drill so that the same activities are not used. Some students will not attend, make proper (selective) cues the point of focus, or rehearse. An important procedure in any learning activity is to reduce cue selection so that attention and rehearsal can proceed, rather than, in effect, requiring the student to impose order on a confusing array of data.

Memory has been investigated primarily by means of visual or auditory spans for short-term memory and serial or paired associate learning for long-term recall. In psychological assessment, auditory digits or visual strings of some sort typically are used. These tasks are affected by environment and anxiety. However, in a practical sense, it is necessary to evaluate all aspects of memory to determine if there seems to be a problem, although this is not commonly done. In summary, the research indicates that children may have a problem in three areas: storage deficit disorder, retrieval deficit, and encoding deficit.

If the research on attention and memory is considered, the problems of many children result from the way in which information is presented (i.e., type, amount, rate, and organization) and the non-use of strategies to attack and remember the information. Memory can be affected by alterations in the way in which information is presented by the teacher and by instruction in how to use rehearsal strategies.

The work of Tarver, Hallahan, Kauffman, and Ball (1976) indicates that some handicapped students may attend to different cues than those attended to by students who are successful in recall tasks. This tendency relates to central and incidental stimuli, and it underscores the need to focus attention of learners on the stimuli of importance.

Metamemory. A relatively new field of endeavor is known as *metacognition,* which is literally defined as awareness or knowledge of one's own cognitive processes. The individual considers how he or she thinks, attacks problems, and remembers information. Different strategies are intentionally employed, depending on the task. *Metamemory* is subsumed under the rubric of metacognition and may be defined as introspective knowledge of one's own memory functioning. Those who have investigated metamemorial processes have been interested in finding out what children know about their memories and how this information may be used to improve learning (Brown, 1975; Torgenson, 1978). In general, the variables of metamemory may be listed as follows:

1. *Person metavariables:* the individual's awareness of his or her own memory abilities and limitations including how much information can be retained and for how long.
2. *Task metavariables:* the demands of the task on the individual, such as recognition, recall, and generalizations.
3. *Item metavariables:* the type of stimulus—namely, visual, auditory, size, and shape—and whether or not it can be correlated with other data and classified.
4. *Strategy metavariables:* all strategies, mnemonics, rehearsal techniques, writing behavior, "mental lists," and any other practices the person uses to remember.

In fact, a teacher can assist children immensely by attempting to determine how each of these variables affects learning; suggestions under other topics in this section would be appropriate. If the teacher knows that a student does not employ rehearsal strategies, has difficulty with a type of task such as recall, functions better with one type of item or combination of items, and can be encouraged to remember by using a specific strategical approach, the learning task can be individualized far beyond the individualized conceptualizations inherent in most IEPs.

Performance in the classroom requires deliberate, intentional learning. Most children enter school with a great deal of knowledge that is acquired primarily by means of incidental learning. Learning how to learn in the classroom is a task that most children accomplish. The development of metamemory is evidence of a child's emerging ability to learn in the school. It appears that this development is stage related; older children tend to have a wide variety of memory skills and are aware of what they are doing as they learn. This appears to be fairly well developed by age 8. Many handicapped learners are deficient in metamemorial development. However, if children know the tasks, are given an approach for categorizing information, and are coached on how to relate information to previous stores of knowledge and how to retrieve it, their achievement can be improved dramatically. Thus, knowing what is important, realizing that rehearsal is important and necessary, understanding that organization of information for processing is important, knowing elaborative strategies, and intentionally ignoring non-relevant information are important aspects of metamemory. The teacher can control the task and items and promote the use of strategies by using some of the following considerations:

1. The teacher should determine what the learning tasks require a student to do. If teaching is predicated on simple recall questions given daily but tests and other evaluations require application skills, the child will not perform well.

2. The teacher can control factors that influence learning, such as rate, type, and total amount of information presented. Many learners who experience confusion are frequently bombarded by information that is meaningless to them. They do not know what is important, how to organize the task for learning, or how to relate it to previous learning. Considering that immense amounts of information are introduced in the first three grades, it does not take long for such a disadvantage to turn into a long-term deficit in achievement.

3. Five-year-old children do not employ strategies of rehearsal and have difficulty doing so even when the behavior is modeled. If older handicapped children present the same lack of ability, educational approaches will have to be limited to a more concrete level of training.

4. Six- to 8-year-old children can verbalize as they learn and be taught to verbalize after seeing a learning activity (task). They will model the behavior also. Although they may not employ the strategy spontaneously, they will do so if asked and reminded by the teacher. For handicapped children who present the same level of development, it is important that the regular and special teachers remind these children to "talk through" tasks to facilitate learning.

5. Labeling and naming stimulus items aids in learning. This is something that can be done with the most activities, and it provides mental hooks for organization of information.

6. Clustering stimuli is best for young children, labeling information is useful for 6 to 8 years olds, and children who are 10 or older ordinarily employ a wide variety of strategies voluntarily. Various strategies can be observed as they are "invented" by the learner. Anyone who has watched children take the Visual Sequential Memory subtest of the ITPA will note that many children invent names for peculiar geometrical shapes in order to process them verbally.

7. Very young children cluster items based on sounds (rhyming). Most school-aged children, beginning in kindergarten or the first grade, have a tendency to cluster according to concrete categories (e.g., animals, flowers, big, or small). If categories are pointed out to children, objects or items are put into categories, or children are given a classification scheme and asked to put items into the existing structure, performance will improve.

8. Many of the study skills taught in reading, as

well as and the teacher-controlled variables listed earlier in the text, are actually devices for imposing order on information. Children need to be deliberately led through the process of recognizing certain relationships in order for them to grasp the order. In fact, to aid retention, categorization of information and prompting can be superior to reinforcement alone.

9. Phonics instruction seems to be a suitable practice with most children because young children are able to use strategies based on sound. They have a spoken language and have acquired rules that may be applied or transferred in the process of intentional learning.

10. Visually presenting information in reading, using discriminable items, clustering by sound, and using the patterns or "word families" approach seem to be supported by metamemory stages.

11. Students who have command of the vocabulary can recall sentences better if they are segmented or broken into phrases. This approach may help in comprehension and later recall of a passage. Most poor readers cannot independently identify important and unimportant topics, ideas, or passages in written materials; the teacher must deliberately point out and organize the information in some way for the significance to be apparent.

12. Of particular importance for classroom lecturing and discussion is the fact that poor and good readers are able to process, comprehend, and recall information that is organized for them. If the teacher's lecture is organized, points are clearly made, and each step is related to the next, the poor reader is able to receive the message as easily as the good reader. However, if the lecture is unstructured and there is no sense of organization, better readers are able to impose order on the lecture, something that they can also do during reading, but the poor reader is lost (Oaken, Weiner, & Cromer, 1971).

Transfer

An early and contemporary concern of psychology has been transfer of learning. This is of particular concern to the educator for obvious reasons, and it should be of specific interest to special educators who use task analysis and skill sequences in training because transfer is essential. In planning, educators are interested in determining what skills a student has and then in arranging learning experiences for skills that follow. Connecting the skills is transfer—relating old knowledge to new situations.

It is worth noting that aptitude, ability, or intelligence test scores are highly correlated with *beginning* instruction but not so highly correlated with the *end* of training, a fact established many years ago through the extensive research of Woodrow (1938, 1946) and recognized today in the mastery learning approach (Bloom, 1980). Although children may have initial problems in learning a task, ultimate achievement may be a relatively independent result of initial ability. This means that, as a measure of prior experience, tests indicate that certain people do well on one measure of transfer (initial ability) and can be expected to perform well on other transfer tasks during instruction. However, persons with lower initial scores can be taught the tasks effectively. The better they perform throughout training, the more likley they will also acquire transfer sets.

Therefore, ability tests should be accepted as a measure of readiness for instruction at beginning performance; one who scores high may be expected to continue to do well, but others may also be expected to reach criterion. Students who score high on entering ability may be able to proceed with little assistance from the teacher because they can rely on past experience and transfer to achieve. However, handicapped students need to have a knowledge of their performance, immediate feedback, and reinforcement in order to succeed.

A finding of Zeaman and House (1963) is that intelligence is related more to attention than to learning. The implication is that, if the teacher can engineer the attention of students to relevant cues and cue dimensions, learning can proceed rapidly. Many children have insufficient and narrow experiences with which to equip themselves for the routine school curriculum; lack of experience means they cannot transfer from previous experience to new situations. The options for the teacher are to improve the experiential background of students, change the nature of the task, or illuminate the important cues in attention and learning sets. The success of Head Start can be attributed to improvement of experience. The success of DISTAR and similar programs is partly explained by the fact that children are deliberately taught specific information to the mastery level. Experiences are planned, and teaching techniques are highly specific, focusing on the relevant dimensions of learning tasks. An attempt is also made to equate whatever experiences the children have had to instruction, an easier accomplishment with middle-class children who have more readiness experiences.

The fact that some students have so much trouble with certain subjects may be partly explained by the arrangement of the content and the type of teaching they receive rather than the difficulty of the subject. The more similar the elements the easier the transfer. This becomes a teaching problem and a learning problem. Spelling, arithmetic, reading, and other school subjects are difficult for particular students because they have not been led carefully from concrete to symbolic experiences, have not been given sufficient time to overlearn before a new task is introduced, and have not been provided with teaching that promotes generalization and transfer.

McLeskey (1980) notes that reading-disabled students tend to use different strategies in learning to read. McLeskey's research found that the good reader is more flexible, is willing to take risks, and has a wide range of response patterns. The poor learner is not only less flexible but is also unwilling to take chances and will repeat an incorrect response after receiving negative feedback. The problems that such children have may be explained by transfer difficulty. It might be argued that these differences would be noticed in these children anyway because of variances in their abilities. The argument would follow that their differences in reading performance are only indicative of their differing abilities. However, research indicates that learning to learn, or transfer, can be improved or damaged by the types of experiences the learner has. These experiences are controlled, to a great extent, by the teacher and the nature of instructional design.

Learning styles

One of the approaches of special education has been to teach according to learning styles. This is most notable in the learning disabilities literature and has spread to other areas of handicaps. It has also become a popular trend in regular education. In its basic form it means that certain children have a preferred learning style—a certain affinity for encoding and processing information in a particular way. Some children are said to be visual learners, some auditory learners, and others haptic learners. Although it may be true that some children have abilities and interests that affect their approaches to schooling and school subjects, there is less evidence for the existence of learning styles than for process deficits. Attempting to teach children by limiting information to one channel or another (visual or auditory) is not necessarily a reasonable technique, even if it were possible. Learning style pertains primarily to initial input preferences, not necessarily to internal mediation.

Learning-style theories that have a research base can be traced primarily to the work of Witkin (1954), who conducted research with subjects responding to different perceptual tasks. Based on results of a number of studies, persons would be classified according to a *cognitive style* as field dependent and field independent. The field-dependent person is one who is passive and has low self-esteem, poor impulse control, and a need for structure and direction. The field-independent person is the opposite, being self-reliant, assured, and able to approach a learning task from a unique and flexible point of view. These theories have been elaborated over the years, extended by others, and stripped of negative connotations. Computer programs are used to determine if a person is field dependent or independent, based on a variety of tasks and questionnaires. In theory, a subject's cognitive style can be used to plan educational experiences, type of instruction, and kinds of examinations. Whether a learning style is learned, developmental, or idiosyncratic is an important distinction for future research.

Other emerging learning- or cognitive-styles theories (e.g., Dunn & Dunn, 1978; Keefe, 1979) postulate that all children have learning styles which can be determined reliably with specific instruments. After knowing the style, a teacher need only arrange the learning environment in accordance with the child's preferences. Although this is an interesting assumption, no extensive research demonstrates the efficacy of this approach; it has all the earmarks of a new educational fad that will be widely discussed. Interestingly, special education has already used this approach, albeit in a different form, and special education teachers are much more likely to be cautious about devotion to an appealing, popular theory.

If there are learning styles, they relate to internal mediational states where information is processed. Although some children may actually have "deficits" of internal mediating process components, for most it is plausible that external presentation of information (encoding) and reinforcement contingencies can affect processing.

There is an indication in the research that types of information processing, or learning styles, are actually age or stage related and may be highly influenced by experience and training. To this extent, teachers may search for preferred modalities of students in order to plan teaching units and to *change* the learning style so that it will be more efficient. However, currently there is little reason to believe that learning styles can be reliably identified. Even if they are, a substantial change in the conduct of education would have to ensue before such knowledge about the learner could be used to good advantage. Given the limited amount of available information, the following general points can be made (Mills, 1956; Stephenson & Gray, 1976):

1. Children of low socioeconomical status tend to prefer or use visual and motor learning.
2. Young children use auditory processing, which shifts to visual processing as they mature, learn to read, and become adept at formal learning.
3. Generally, there is no clear pattern for handicapped children, except for those who are limited by impairment of one channel or another.
4. Gifted students tend to have no preference, using all inputs efficiently (this may show the necessity for encouraging children to employ all strategies available to them).

Learning characteristics as alterable variables

Bloom (1980), in speaking of alterable variables in the new generation of educational research, refers to the creation of favorable learning conditions that can enable virtually all students to learn to high standards. He states that the old generation of research dealt with variables which could not be changed substantially, such as the amount of time available during the day, the age or personality of the teacher, and the IQ of the student. Alterable variables are ones that can be changed, and that may make a difference in achievement. A few examples Bloom lists are time-on-task (the amount of time a student is actively engaged in learning), cognitive entry (the specific knowledge a student has before being introduced to a learning task), formative rather than summative testing, teaching approaches, and behavior of the parents instead of their status. It is Bloom's contention that by searching for more alterable variables, learning can be changed by moving from an emphasis on prediction and classification to a concern for causality and the relations between means and ends in teaching and learning. Many of the variables in learning theories may be included in this list. Searching for reasons why children fail or succeed in the teaching-learning context of the classroom may be much more fruitful than traditional practices in special and regular education.

Classroom planning

To consider the learning theories just presented, a structure should be imposed on the teaching-learning events that are supposed to occur in the regular or special classroom. The teacher can have formal assessment data, significant amounts of in-

Table 12-1. Example of classroom planning

Teaching events	*Problems*	*Strategies*
Attention	Child is nonattending, is off task, distracted, talks to peers, daydreams, is withdrawn, and sleeps.	Reinforce attending Use audiovisual equipment, machines Highlight stimulus cues Use novel stimuli Check complexity of task
Presentation	After presentation, child is confused, hostile, outer-directed, crying, and apathetic.	Check difficulty of task Check clarity of directions Check rate and amount Check type of stimuli Check cognitive entry
Response	Child has no opportunity to show response, is outer-directed, makes errors, and is off task.	Improve monitoring system Use self-recording system Use daily probes Use peer checking system Use programmed materials
Feedback	Child either receives no feedback, or feedback is lavish or negative, delayed, or not given with reward.	Use self-correction Implement intermittent reinforcement schedule Develop feedback strategy Use self-recording system

formal and observational data, hypotheses about which materials and methods to use, and the IEP as a structure. However, execution of the plan depends on the application of scientific principles of learning, identification of a skill sequence, and monitoring of daily behavior and responses. Daily data collection is absolutely essential. Implementing the IEP requires that the teacher be sensitive to existent and emerging learning-theory research, domains that cannot necessarily be tapped by existing tests. The teacher has to use an experimental, trial-and-error approach to elicit information about what goes awry in the sequence of teaching events and in the ecology of the classroom. This process is conceptualized in Table 12-1.

Table 12-1 is only an example of a technique that may be developed and expanded by the teacher who wishes to ascertain what variables may be affecting learning in the classroom environment. Observation of students is essential, but it is also necessary for the teacher to make hypotheses about what may be causing problems that were identified by observation. Generally, the child may be uninterested, be confused by a task, not understand what is expected, have difficulty with the rate of information, or not be able to selectively attend to important cues. The major responsibility of the teacher is to ensure that presentation is appropriate to the learner and that feedback is adequate.

In previous chapters, 12 important variables have been considered under the headings of direct teaching, ecological, and curricular. The emphasis was on identifying broad, common variables that would apply to various teaching environments. The teaching behaviors, learner behaviors, and environmental factors should be arranged around the curriculum to maximize learning. The most important responsibility is clarity of presentation, clarity of the instructional process, and reinforcement. In fact, the editors of the newsletter *Phi Delta Kappan* have reported on a synthesis of relevant research about what is necessary for instructional clarity. The major findings concerning research trends on teacher effectiveness reported by them are summarized in the following (Practical Applications of Research, 1981):

1. *Structuring*
   Teacher emphasizes key terms and ideas to be learned.
   Teacher explains work to be done and how to do it.
   Teacher asks students if they know what work needs to be done and how to do it.
   Teacher takes time when making explanations.
   Teacher provides students with standards and rules for satisfactory performance.
   Teacher specifies content and shares overall structure of a lecture or discussion.
2. *Process*
   Teacher explains and then pauses so students can think.
   Teacher prepares students for what is to follow.
   Teacher repeats questions and explanations.
   Teacher allows students to ask questions.
   Teacher answers questions.
   Teacher synthesizes and demonstrates real-world examples.
   Teacher adjusts teaching to the learner and the topic.
   Teacher reduces nonessential content.
   Teacher makes clear transitions.
   Teacher avoids vague terms and fillers.
   Teacher continuously monitors learning.
   Teacher uses step-by-step teaching.
   Teacher uses a variety of demonstrations and materials.
   Teacher creates an environment in which students can process information.
3. *Output*
   Teacher provides feedback.
   Teacher provides reinforcement and redirection.

A teaching perspective

In one sense, learning is the process by which a student makes increasingly more accurate discriminations as a result of practice. In simple discrimination research, even with animals, it is clear that learning how to learn increases with successful experience (Harlow, 1959). Maximum performance is correlated with the number of problems the learner encounters; in other words, practice on successive problems increases improvement. In the school setting, the more failure a child has and the less practice, the less likely he or she is to achieve on a daily basis. The teacher must ensure that the child is given tasks that are appropriate, that practice is provided, and that flexibility is created for learning. The experiences of many handicapped children after the first or second grade are much different from the ideal. They are often unable to receive activities appropriate for them because the rest of the class is more advanced, dealing with content that is much too difficult for them; they receive fewer success experiences and do not learn how to learn.

Learning may also be viewed as a process of eliminating the strengths of incorrect choices. It may be a difficult task for the teacher to get a student to understand that something is incorrect and know why. Incorrect choices create bonds that must be broken; it is necessary to reduce the number of incorrect choices. Color, shape, placement, and other factors may capriciously influence a student in early learning and cause the learner to be farther off track each day. Thus, the major difference between gradual, continuous learning curves and those which seem to jump depend, in great measure, on the amount of learning already acquired before a new task. This is used to explain anticipated benefits of mastery learning by Bloom (1980). The amount of time-on-task and relevant learning experiences of the learner can create a store of successful experiences that will increase learning. The nature of instruction in many schools prevents the handicapped student, who may also be deprived of a basic experiential base at school entry, from progressing. The curriculum continues to advance, individualization does not occur, and the learner's progress is stymied because of poor educational planning and instructional procedures.

As children gain success, they also increase in the ability to develop mediating response acts (thinking) as a linkage of different inputs and outputs. The most likely explanation of this ability is verbal mediation (Kendler & Kendler, 1968). As this is acquired, the child's conscious thinking and talking can be employed in learning and problem solving, thereby bringing about the emergence of metacognition, or self-awareness of memory, and problem-solving abilities. Success in learning experiences fosters confidence in the child that school problems can be attacked and solved; continuous failure does not.

An excellent teaching model which employs principles of learning theory appropriate for direct instruction is based on the recommendations of Mercer and Snell (1977), who summarized the work of Denny (1966). Denny's work was concerned with creating optimum learning conditions. The following principles are found in detail in Mercer and Snell (1977, pp. 147-150):

1. *Prevention of incorrect responses and eliciting as many correct responses as possible in early learning*. This entails the use of fewer choices, since they invite error; physical prompts; interruption of errors; redundancy of cues; matching instructional choices to sample cues; modeling; and cuing.

2. *Providing immediate knowledge of results*. Although this has been discussed in detail at other points in the text, it is important to note that, even in simple discrimination learning, subjects learn something about the stimuli that can be transferred to new situations. Thus, learning is not simply a matter of stimulus-response bonds. A type of central coding process (Lawrence, 1963) can function to mediate and improve learning in a new situation. Providing immediate feedback serves at least two important purposes: it assists the student in achieving mastery of the content presented by the teacher at the time, and it also forms the basis for future learning experiences, or learning to learn.

3. *Differential feedback*. When appropriate, the teacher should use particular kinds of feedback that relate to the learning task at hand to emphasize the concept being learned. These may be situation specific and not apply to other learning tasks. Differential feedback involves talking and moving the child through operations rather than just accepting a correct response or permitting an incorrect response to occur. For example, rather than just talking about the action, the teacher can actually put a ball in the child's hand, move the hand to the box, and release the ball. Sights, sounds, and motor movements give cues to provide stronger feedback inputs. This is similar, conceptually, to the VAKT approaches to learning.

4. *Stimulus generalization, randomization, and positive transfer*. The principle here is to teach a child to specifically use a learned response in new situations to form the basis for transfer and generalization. Generalization involves teaching the same concept in different contexts. Randomization refers to the elimination of irrelevant stimulus cues (e.g., position, size, shape, and color) that have nothing to do with the task.

5. *Distributed repetition and positive transfer*. This principle is generally well known and means that learning occurs more efficiently if practice is spread out over time (e.g., cramming versus studying throughout the semester).

6. *Motivation*. If the learning task is interesting, motivating, attracts attention, and results in reinforcement or reward, learning will be improved.

7. *Sequential building*. This principle involves the process of developing a response sequence in clearly identifiable steps that are related to what has been learned previously. Mastery learning and task-analytic approaches are based on this principle. The purpose is to permit positive transfer to build for application to more difficult concepts.

The seven steps listed previously can incorporate most of the learning theory research, even those that seem to be somewhat contradictory. They may also be used as a framework for including process-training and skill-training models, at least theoretically. Pragmatically, they provide a general direction for instruction of handicapped students in the elementary grades.

To summarize the review presented here and resolve it with the 12 teaching variables listed previously, the following statements are presented.

Control of student's attention and time-on-task learning. In any teaching event, the most important initial act of the teacher must be to secure the attention of the learner. Many youngsters are involved in off-task behavior much of the time during an instructional period. It is absolutely crucial that children not be permitted to attend to noninstructional cues or to withdraw: they must remain on task. Moreover, it is important for the teacher to consider the manner in which cue dimensions are presented, as indicated in the review of learning theory. For many students, planning and reinforcement can correct the lack of attention. Some teachers seem to be content to permit nonattending behavior if students are not disruptive. The special educator can be of great assistance to regular classroom teachers by assisting with classroom organization, teaching strategies, and other activities devoted to securing the attention of children. Obviously, technological devices may be of great importance to this end.

Organizational control of information (input to be learned with objectives). By using a structural sequence of skills, task analysis, behavioral objectives, and applications of appropriate teacher-controlled variables, the teacher can convey information or skills to students in an effective and efficient presentation. Students should not be expected to impose their own order on information if they cannot do it. The organization should be clear and obvious; extraneous cues should be removed.

Redundancy of instructional cues. Redundancy of instructional cues involves drill, overlearning, and organization for efficient information processing. Students must be given sufficient distributed practice in skills to master them; they must also overlearn basic skills beyond the criterion level for long-term retention. Cues should be presented in sufficient redundancy during a lesson to permit encoding of information.

Alternative informational access. The tasks of many children, their daily instruction and major assignments, are presented in written form or in spoken language may not be clear. Any task should be completely described. Students who do not understand should be given sufficient support until they do. They should be provided with numerous external cues including charts and models mounted on the desk or fixed in the room. They should also be able to model the behavior of other students. Any task that is written should be read to students or otherwise simplified if the task is not specifically designed to teach reading.

Alternative responding. It is common practice to permit latitude for children with hearing, vision, or speech disorders. Other handicapped students should also be permitted alternative modes of responding on daily assignments and on tests and examinations.

Reinforcement and feedback. Students who are daily required to learn specific skills and to process information should be given feedback about their responses in learning. Their tasks should be reasonable, and moderate failure should be expected to occur, since this is the case for most learners. Lavish, unwarranted praise or continuous failure should be avoided. Appropriate rewards should be paired with feedback.

Environmental climate of the classroom. The physical comfort and arrangement of the classroom are obviously important factors. Students should also feel secure in the classroom; they should not be threatened by the teacher or peers. Students should feel free to seek assistance and have a sense of direction through efficient arrangement and uses of physical space.

Use of time and space. The teacher has primary responsibility for making efficient use of the time and space available for children. Fixed time can be managed by avoiding large group instruction and employing a wide variety of small group and individual activities. The physical space can be manipulated for these purposes.

Participation/interaction of students. Students can effectively serve each other in the learning tasks of the school day. A variety of aproaches have been suggested to include modeling and peer tutoring. The interactions of students, if they are not rigidly controlled in a hostile environment or totally unmonitored, can be the basis for cognitive-academic learning and socioemotional development. This is especially important to handicapped students.

Sequence and rate of presentation of skills. It is absolutely essential that a skill sequence exist in the curriculum. This permits the identification of objectives, learning activities, and appropriate evaluation; it also permits communication between educators about the sequence and achievement of a student. This enables the school to evaluate students in terms of their progress against the scale, rather than in terms of rank among peers or normative groups. The rate of presentation is important for handicapped students, many of whom are not given sufficient time or are introduced to skills before they have overlearned the prerequisites.

Uses and adaptation of materials and equipment. Ideally, each classroom would be equipped generously with materials and equipment. Because of the lack of resources, the teacher should wisely purchase supplementary materials and equipment and exercise good judgment in the uses of such materials to support the major learning activities planned in the curriculum. The teacher should have a command of the proper uses and limitations of materials and equipment and should remain current with new technological advances.

Accommodation and compensatory teaching. Surrounding the regular classroom and special education program are systems components that have an impact on the education and adjustment of handicapped students. These lie outside the influence of classroom teachers. However, a number of adaptations to the traditional curriculum and instructional approach of the classroom have been addressed in this text. The major goal is to meet the needs of students despite their disabilities or the inability of the school to remediate them.

MANAGING THE PROGRAM

Comprehensive programming must allow for *individual* and *individualized instruction.* It is necessary to make a distinction between *individual instruction* and *individualized instruction.* Many teachers provide individualized instruction but not necessarily individual instruction. *Individualized instruction is instruction specifically planned for a particular student.* The teacher matches instructional materials to the learning objectives of the student. This could mean assigning the student to work in a group or selecting the appropriate workbook page. The student who is taught in a discussion group may be said to be receiving individualized instruction if the student's needs were examined and it was determined by the teacher that this group would provide the required instruction. However, if the same student is placed in the group merely to simplify scheduling, this is *not* individualized instruction. *Individual instruction is teaching that is one-to-one.* This instruction can be provided through tutors, aids, and technological supports as well as by the teacher personally. If a teacher instructs a group of seven students in a particular concept or skill that each student needs, indvidualized instruction is taking place; if each of the seven students is taught separately, individual instruction has been used.

This may appear to be a matter of semantics and unrelated to the coordination of the program. However, when the outcomes expected of programs are examined, it becomes apparent that this is not an artificial distinction. Two of the outcomes generally expected are that individual students will exhibit increases in academic performance and behavioral change and that a certain number of students will be served each day in the program. Therefore, the teacher must structure the program in such a manner as to provide both individualized and individual instruction to meet expected outcomes. It is the same problem regular classroom teachers have always had: "What do you do with the others while providing individual instruction?" If teachers could function in a clinical setting, individualized and individual instruction would be synonomous, since there would be one student at a time for whom instruction would be personally designed and delivered. As one new teacher said, "I know how to provide individualized instruction, but my professors forgot to show me how to do it for a room full of students at one time."

Comprehensive programming is an effective and

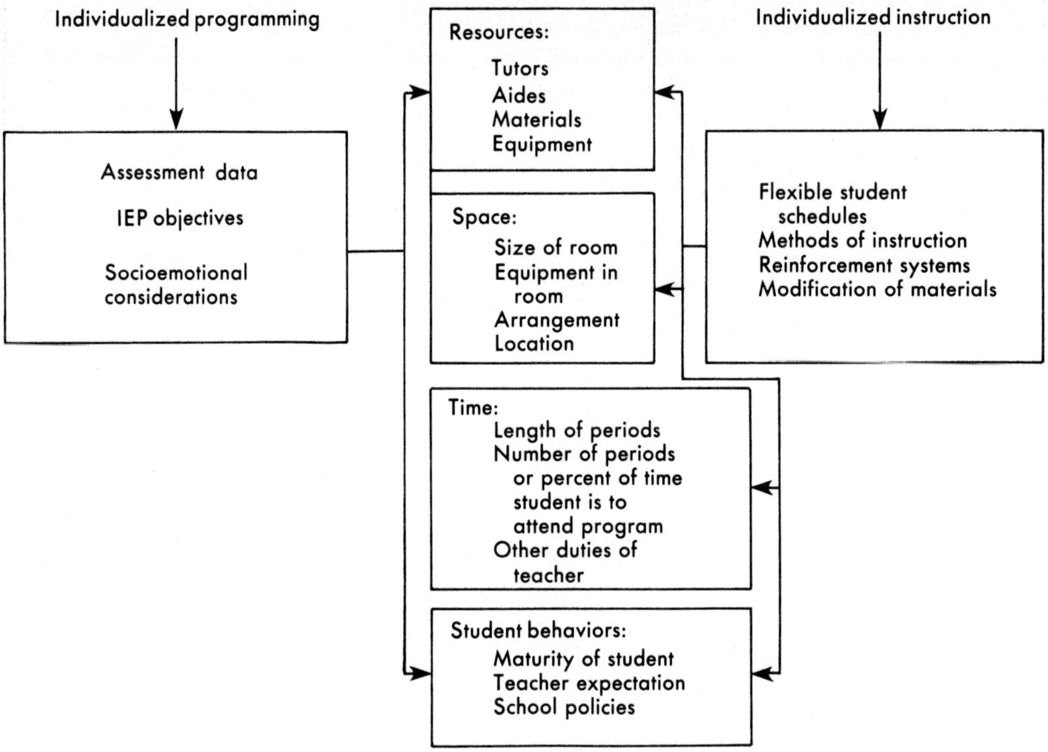

Fig. 12-1. Comprehensive programming plan.

practical way to provide appropriate instruction and a solution to the problem of group versus individual instruction. Daily and long-term planning acknowledge the ecology of the class and employ all available support services, including various methods of instruction, aides, or volunteers, various types of technology, modified materials, and modular scheduling. Comprehensive program planning, depicted in Fig. 12-1, provides the means for converting the special education room into a total service model and prevents it from becoming simply a room in which the instructional groups are smaller than those in the regular classroom. The variables listed under individualized planning (e.g., assessment data, IEP objectives, and socioemotional considerations) have been addressed elsewhere. The following examines critical components of *individual education:* flexible daily scheduling, approaches to instruction, reinforcement systems, and instructional materials.

Flexible daily scheduling

Comprehensive programming may require that students receive services through any of the service models, including the resource room and self-contained classroom. In most models, students may be integrated into the regular school environment, requiring the organization of the classroom to accommodate outside class schedules. The resource room in particular must conform to the organizational pattern of the school; students must be scheduled to maximize the impact of the resource room and to minimize conflict with the mainstream classes. As Thurman and Lewis (1979) note, the concept of educational ecology of the handicapped encompasses new settings. For this reason, assign-

Table 12-2. Organizational and grouping strategies

Strategy	Description	Sample schedule			
		Time	*Student*	*Grade*	*Activity*
Grade- or age-level groups	Same age- or grade-level students scheduled for same time period Typically, schedule fixed by total school plan	Monday 8:30-9:00	Anna	2	Sullivan readers
			Kama		Sullivan readers
			Meredith		Counting objects and worksheet
			Jake		Listening tape and worksheet
			Susan		Language experience chart
			Marilyn		
			Jim B.		
Subject area groups	Accommodational programming Based on area of curriculum in which instructional assistance is needed	Monday 8:30-9:00	Jim F.	4	Arithmetic
			Mary	4	
			Tommy	5	
			Donna	6	
			Ada	6	
Remedial area groups	Based on specific skill requiring remediation Typical of programs emphasizing remedial programming Frequent changes needed, since skill groups will reflect student change	Monday 8:30-9:00	Fred	2	Handwriting
			Jack	2	
			Donnie	3	
			Sammy	3	
			Elizzie	3	
			Gary	3	

ing students and organizing the special classroom have become more complex tasks, requiring the special educator to balance individual student data, mainstream schedules, and resource room constraints when setting up groups or period schedules.

The special educator must schedule each student's day individually while attempting to make direct instruction time efficient from the teacher's point of view. Presented in Table 12-2 are several organizational frameworks that might be considered. Regardless of the organizational structure, the special educator must design a daily schedule. The daily schedule consists of two components: a schedule that determines which students attend and when and an instructional schedule within each period reflecting what each student does. The first component must receive immediate attention when the year begins because of its interrelationship with the rest of the school. Hawisher and Calhoun (1978) identified several factors that should be considered by the teacher when initially establishing the daily schedule, including the following:

1. Degree of remediation or severity of the deficit in academic performance
2. Size of the resource room group into which the child will be placed
3. Socioemotional characteristics of the student

At the beginning of the year, the special educator should develop a temporary schedule rather than attempt to immediately institute a permanent schedule. The temporary schedule should be developed with consideration given to the following characteristics of the school:

1. Regular classroom schedules for art, physical education, and library, since students should not be scheduled into the instructional activities in lieu of these classes
2. Daily classroom schedules for reading, arithmetic, and other subjects that are developed by the individual teacher
3. Preferences of the teacher (Ask the teacher to complete a schedule sheet indicating the *best* and *worst* possible times to schedule students in and out of class.)
4. Lunch and recess schedules

The other side of the coin in organizing class schedules is the strategy employed in selecting mainstream assignments. As Valett (1981) points out, "most exceptional children have been mainstreamed with their chronological age peers in traditional grade-level classes." We agree with Valett when he states that special education children may be different from their age cohorts in terms of academic performance, ability, and maturational stages; therefore, it does not seem particularly logical to *automatically* assign the handicapped student to the regular class based on chronological age. Although in some instances this may be appropriate, the following possible alternatives might be considered (Valett, 1981):

1. Grouping by sex
2. Grouping by maturational development
3. Grouping by functional achievement level

The schedule of students is important to the success of the special class within the system, but the true effect of the class is determined by the *instructional schedule* (i.e., what each student does from 9:00 to 9:45 while in the resource room or self-contained classroom). The instructional schedule should reflect the following variables:

1. Instructional objectives for the individual student
2. Socioemotional characteristics of the student
3. Learning profile of the student (i.e., the ability to employ memory strategies, make knowledge transfers, etc.)
4. Type of materials used by the student

Blocks of 45 minutes appear to offer sufficient time for instruction and "housekeeping" details. Daily instructional schedules should include both group and individual instruction, if required by student needs. Group instruction within the resource room is important to the student because training in group behavior may be important preparation for participation in the mainstream class (Demers, 1981); group instruction may also be significant for the teacher because of the time-saving potential involved. However, the special educator must remember that groups may evolve rather than needing to be "forced" in order to complete a schedule. A properly coordinated special education program should make scheduling an individual matter, allowing the teacher to accept students at a time most convenient for the student.

Fig. 12-2 is a lesson plan that should be considered an example of the way in which a teacher might write the instructional plan for a special classroom. The teacher can modify it to fit a particular format or lesson plan book. The important aspects of the plan are the components rather than the organization:

Listing of students
Instructional activities
One-to-one instructional block (individual instruction)
Group activities
Instructional objectives addressed
Materials required

Another approach to daily planning is to use learning centers (the content and application of learning centers is covered in this chapter, while the focus here is on daily planning). A lesson plan for a classroom using learning centers might look like the one presented in Fig. 12-3. This approach allows the teacher to use centers equipped with multilevel materials and tasks as a means of providing individualized instruction as well as facilitating a one-to-one period of individual work with each child.

The information included in both daily lesson plan examples (Figs. 12-2 and 12-3) allows the teacher, a member of a monitoring team, or an administrator to see at a glance the relationship

Time	Students	Behavioral objectives	Procedures	Materials
9:00-9:15	Heather Larry	1 3	Play game with math cards, sums 1 to 10	Math cards Recording sheet
	Jason Robert Amy	1 2 4	Work in reading workbooks from regular classroom	Workbooks
	*Marvin	3	Review sound decoding and complete decoding task	Decoding list
9:15-9:30	*Heather *Jason	2 2	Introduce cursive writing, letters y and z	Charts with letters Writing paper
	*Larry	1	Complete science lesson from regular class with help from sixth-grade tutor	Science worksheet Science kit from regular class Response sheet
	Marvin Robert	1 4	Use math kits to complete assigned demonstrations of grouping	Math kits of rods, beads, buttons, etc. Cards with numbers to be illustrated with objects
	Amy	2/3	Copy experience chart in cursive	Experience chart from yesterday Penmanship paper
9:30-9:45	*Robert	3	Work on reading comprehension activities with tutor	Library books
	Heather Marvin Larry	3 2 2	Complete worksheet on comprehension from yesterday's chart	Chart Worksheet
	Jason	3	Read assigned story from regular class into tape recorder	Tape recorder Reader from regular class
	*Amy	1	Drill vocabulary	Vocabulary cards

Fig. 12-2. Sample lesson plan for the period from 9:00 to 9:45. ***Asterisk,*** **Student involved in period of individually or personally directed instruction.**

Week: October 12-16
Day: Monday

Time slot	Students	Behavioral objectives		Station assignments
9:00-9:45	Amy	1/3	1; 2; 5	NOTE: The teacher works individually or in small groups with the students at Center 7. In this time period, four students have received 10 to 15 minutes of 1:1 or 1:2 instruction. The other students complete the assigned tasks at the centers listed. The centers contain task cards specifying various levels and types of tasks that allow multilevel instruction at each center, as a later description will indicate.
	Bill	2/3	1; 7; 6	
	Tom	2/3	3; 4; 7	
	Ann	1/2	2; 5; 6	
	Bob	1/3	7; 4; 5	
	Sarah	3/4	4; 7; 3	

Fig. 12-3. Lesson plans using learning centers 1 to 7. *1*, Mathematics; *2*, measurements; *3*, writing; *4*, reading (decoding); *5*, reading (comprehension); *6*, spelling; *7*, individual (one-to-one or small group instruction with the teacher). Analysis of each weekly schedule reveals that students are involved in minigroups, independent activities, and one-to-one instruction.

between the daily activities and the objectives of the IEP. This serves as a constant reminder that the IEP is a process, not a form to be completed; teachers employing such lesson planning approaches may develop a more positive attitude toward the development of the IEP.

Other activities. Scheduling must include activities such as physical education, library, art, and other classes provided within the school. *Physical education* is defined by P.L. 94-142 as one of the services that must be considered in programming for handicapped students; in this law physical education includes physical and motor fitness; fundamental motor skills and patterns; skills in aquatics, dance, games, and sports; special physical education; adaptive physical education; movement education; and motor development (*Federal Register,* 1977). The IEP may include programming for *art,* primarily to provide an opportunity for handicapped students to participate in mainstream classes and experience successful creative activities.

Integration into mainstream activities such as physical education and art can be successful on the basis of a good plan for selecting and assigning students to classes—scheduling these classes as a means of "keeping students busy" is unacceptable. These activities should be pleasant, contribute to the student's feelings of self-worth, and be related to the overall goals for the student. Following are some suggestions for designing and implementing this type of programming for handicapped students (Rider, 1980):

1. Level of ability should be ascertained through observation of standardized assessment.
2. The educator should place two, three, or four handicapped students in a class; placing only one student may cause that child to be the focus of the whole class, whereas more than four students may be too many.
3. In the case of moderately retarded students, a class should be selected of children with motor ability commensurate with that of the handicapped pupils, but not so much below their level that great physical differences become obvious.
4. Social integration into the group should be considered in placement decisions.
5. Activities should *not* be competitive.
6. The special educator and regular class teacher should monitor the child's reaction and cooperatively make changes needed.

One particular approach to mainstreaming and physical education that might be generalized to other activity classes was employed and evaluated in Project PRIME. The project, funded by the Bureau of Education for the Handicapped and conducted by Tennessee Technological University, demonstrated the merits of a peer tutor approach in aiding handicapped students who participate in mainstream physical education. Although the project focused on physical education, the following tutoring program might be instituted in other areas. A list of the major aspects of the peer tutor program follows (Folio & Norman, 1981), and additional information may be found in other parts of this chapter.

1. Upper elementary children served as tutors (peer teachers) and were selected on the basis of the following:
   a. Leadership
   b. Acceptance and tolerance
   c. Maturity
   d. Motor ability (outstanding ability was *not* required)
   e. Ability to follow instructions
2. Miniworkshops were conducted for the peer teachers covering the following:
   a. Skills to be taught
   b. Simple use of praise and rewards
   c. General information on types of handicapping conditions
   d. Overview of strategies to be used by the instructor of the class to which peer tutors were assigned

Approaches to instruction

Two basic types of instruction occur in classrooms: direct teaching and independent child activities (Charles, 1980; Pasanella & Volkmor, 1977). Direct teaching appears to use either group or individual instruction, whereas independent child activities appear to consist of seat work, learning packets, and other activities planned but not directly supervised by the teacher. Therefore, the task of the special educator in planning daily instructional periods is to orchestrate the classroom to provide both opportunities for direct teaching and independent student activities consistent with the goals and objectives of the IEPs.

Selecting an organizational approach to provide individual and individualized instruction within each time slot may appear extremely complex at first, considering the number of approaches described by various writers. For example, Charles (1980) reviews methods of individualized instruction, using the following organization:

Behavior-referenced approaches	Diagnostic-prescriptive Modularized Nonformal Learning centers Commercial
Experience referenced	Open experience Learning centers (nonbehavioral) Nonformal (stressing experience)
Combination	Activities based on behavioral objectives and experience

Dunn and Dunn (1977) review several methods that they consider to be responsive to individual styles and learning characteristics, including instructional packages, task cards, learning circles, and contract activity packages.

Swift and Spivack (1975) identify several types of classroom organization and instructional "approaches" as part of their approach to structured teaching, including the following:

1. *Open classroom.* This term refers to both the instructional pattern used and the physical environment. This approach requires (a) independent student work, (b) well-planned activities, (c) proper selection of materials, (d) free movement of students, and (e) thorough monitoring strategies to check student progress.

2. *Team teaching.* This approach involves teachers working as teams to achieve complete planning, preparing, and teaching. This model (a) allows teachers to focus on a particular aspect of the curriculum, (b) requires specifically stated objectives, (c) requires clearly stated responsibilities of all team members, and (d) necessitates highly integrated curricular activities.

3. *Discovery learning.* Materials used allow the student to deduce or discover facts or principles rather than passively receiving the information from the teacher. This approach (a) requires that the students have the required skills to employ discovery learning; (b) depends heavily on the materials included, since they must make the desired "discovery" possible; and (c) emphasizes the need for various discovery strategies to be taught.

Turnbull and Schultz (1979) state that "several techniques that have proved to be effective with handicapped children are peer teaching, learning centers, contracts, and learning activity packets" (p. 109). Following are some of the methods common to these lists that appear to be among the most frequently used organizational patterns in classrooms.

Learning centers and learning packets. These two approaches to planning and delivering individual instruction have found wide application in both regular elementary and special education classrooms. Following are some of the several commonalities between the two strategies:

1. Allowances are provided for student interest in selecting activities.
2. Ability levels of materials and activities allow for individual differences in ability.
3. Competencies or content are held constant, but rate or pace of the learner can be varied.
4. Individual differences among students become less obvious than in group instruction.
5. Independent student work can be designed to reflect the particular objectives of each student's IEP.
6. Students have an opportunity to learn self-discipline.

Table 12-3. Learning centers: an approach to individualization

Components	Objectives Directions Descriptions of activities (task cards) Samples and models Media Recording materials Scheduling devices (shows which students are assigned at each time)
Management	Introduce the center to all students and include pertinent information on equipment, schedules, rules, products, and purposes. Schedule students using method that allows students to monitor and maintain schedule without teacher supervision. Organize all materials and have them in the center; if students are to bring particular materials to the center, post that information. Troubleshoot as needed, usually in response to equipment failure or student performance problems. Monitor the center from a convenient location in classroom.
Possible evaluation strategies	Examination for accuracy or amount of work completed at the center Observation of students Student interviews Testing over content taught in the center
Steps in developing learning centers*	1. Choose topic. 2. Identify objectives. 3. Select variety of instructional activities that are varied in terms of ability required, performance required, and materials used. 4. Collect materials. 5. Prepare activities, including samples, task cards, and worksheets to be used. 6. Select method for scheduling students into the center. 7. Prepare record forms needed to record student participation and results.

*Adapted from Charles (1980).

7. The activities develop the student's ability to follow directions.
8. The relationship between activities and objectives is more obvious to students.
9. Peer interaction is encouraged or at least allowed.
10. The learner assumes more responsibility for the learning task than in traditional teacher-directed instruction.

A brief description of *learning centers* that reflects the basic components, suggestions for management, and evaluation strategies is given in Table 12-3. Through use of learning centers, students can be scheduled for direct (one-to-one) instruction and independent activities, as indicated earlier in Fig. 12-3. Teachers using *learning packets* can achieve the same results (Table 12-4).

Although there are, no doubt, other strategies or methods of instruction, learning centers and learning packets have particular merit for use in special education programs, including students involved in mainstream classes. As the following reasons

Table 12-4. Learning packets: an approach to individualization

Components	Prerequisites Goals or objectives Preassessment Learning activities Postassessment
Management	Arrange room to provide areas in which students may perform particular activities associated with each packet or module. Decide exactly what objectives are to be addressed in packet. Decide if there are any prerequisites; if so, specify those. Development preassessment and postassessment activities; these typically are tests of knowledge, demonstrations of skill competency, or exhibitions of products. Select learning activities; these may include reading particular selection, examining model, assembling product, using media, and completing worksheet. Assemble all components; if learning activity requires using something that is not feasible to actually include, be sure that instructions are included that clearly indicate location and other details of use. For packaging, consider using folders, shirt boxes, file pockets, or other storage. Be ready to trouble shoot. Monitor student who is working with packets.
Possible evaluation strategies	Product can be critiqued. Tests can be developed based on postassessment. Postassessment tasks and activities can be accepted as evaluation. Students can be observed. Students can be interviewed. Data might be collected reflecting number of modules or packets completed correctly. Amount of on-task time exhibited by students can be recorded.

suggest, both of these approaches are compatible with instruction that is delivered in the regular classroom:

1. Materials from the regular classroom can be incorporated into the packets or the centers.
2. Curricular objectives from the mainstream class can be addressed through alternative methods including strategies that circumvent the need to read efficiently.
3. Independent behavioral patterns can be fostered that aid the student in functioning in the regular classroom, such as assuming responsibility to complete tasks, following instructions, and performing independently.

Unit teaching. One other approach to instruction that is employed occasionally by teachers is the unit-teaching approach. Meyen (1976) describes the use of unit teaching as a basis of curriculum design and instruction, both in the regular and special classrooms. He states that "unit teaching is a highly generic instructional approach which allows skills and concepts to be couched in the context of themes meaningful to students" (p. 3). A brief overview of unit instruction including major components and evaluation strategies is presented in Table 12-5.

Commercial materials. Several writers (Charles, 1980; Hawisher & Calhoun, 1978; Turnbull & Schultz, 1979) mention instructional programs based on commercial materials. These writers point out that, although many of the programs are sound and certainly beneficial, their use

Table 12-5. Unit teaching: an instructional approach

Components	Purposes or goals Vocabulary Objectives Learning activities Enrichment materials and resources
Management	Identify relationship between curriculum and unit. Specify goals, objectives, and vocabulary. Select learning activities to be included, such as assignments, projects, media, and participatory activities. Identify enrichment activities that can be optional to unit. Design unit, including the following: Period of time Group assignments Introductory session Overview for students Materials Evaluation strategies Daily lesson plan (see below)
Possible evaluation strategies	Tests of knowledge competency Demonstrations of skill competency Examination and critique of product Observation of student performance Student surveys or interviews Progress in related curricular area Inventory of checklist of accomplishments—objectives (Meyen, 1976)

Suggested daily lesson plan*

Scope of lesson:

Objectives of unit (lesson)	*Activities*	*Materials*	*Experience chart*

*Adapted from Meyen (1976).

as a means of structuring and delivering instruction is somewhat limited for the following reasons:

1. Most commercial materials, especially those offering comprehensive content and activities, are expensive.
2. Some "individualized" materials are for group use, and, as Charles (1980) states, "their only claim to that name (individualized) is that they contain instructions so students can work on their own" (p. 211).
3. Complete or so-called total curricular packages may produce a menu of instructional content that the resource teacher has difficulty reconciling with the activities and skills of the mainstream classrooms.

The special educator is better advised to purchase

materials using the objectives of the classroom as reference than to attempt to invest in a "set" or kit on which the individualized curriculum is based.

Reinforcement systems

Managing behavior in a classroom is a task required of all teachers, not just special educators. Problems may arise within any classroom; academic achievement may lag or students may exhibit disruptive behavior. As Sloane, Buckholdt, Jenson, and Crandall (1979) point out, "for relatively typical students the existence of problems suggests some failure in the current teaching procedures that can be remedied by the use of social reinforcement, the design of teaching tasks, or the pacing, planning, scheduling, or manner of presentation" (p. 209). The teacher should not automatically assume that the solution to academic or behavioral problems is to develop an extensive reinforcement system such as a token economy or contracting system. Initially, the teacher should examine the classroom in light of the following components:

1. To what extent has social reinforcement been used? How effective are social consequences in impacting student behavior?
2. Is it possible that low academic performance results from the assignment of inappropriate learning tasks? Are the tasks clearly specified and adequately planned?
3. Could low academic performance and what appears to be lack of motivation result from student's inability to perform the tasks?
4. Are behavioral problems related to insufficient planning that leaves the student confused or reluctant to engage in the desired activity?

Swift and Spivack (1975) offer extensive suggestions for altering the instructional design and classroom instructional patterns as a means of addressing student behaviors. Strategies such as those of Swift and Spivack and others covered in earlier parts of this chapter focus on the ability of the teacher to alter instructional variables to effect student behavior and performance change. When problems are observed in the areas of academic performance or behavior, teachers should explore the possibility of manipulating the instructional variables as a treatment of the problem. Even in a resource room for special education students, the teacher has great potential for effecting change in students without directly treating the children. To immediately institute one of the specific reinforcement systems, token economies, or contracting without first attempting to find solutions within their own instructional design may mean that treatment has been directed at symptoms rather than causes. The results of such efforts may fall short of those desired by the teacher.

If performance or behavioral problems persist after experimentation and alteration of the instructional variables, the teacher may consider using one of the common classroom management strategies. The special educator dealing with particularly disturbed children may need to institute behavioral management techniques as a basic part of the program. Behavioral management techniques should be developed as part of the special educator's professional training (Stewart, Goodman, & Hammond, 1976). The amount of training needed to reach proficiency in use of behavioral management has not been clearly defined (Hall, 1971), but all special educators should have sufficient instruction and basic experience in application to implement a management system within the special classroom. Behavioral management techniques can be used that reflect a teaching philosophy as well as aspects of a controlled science. Unless involved in research, the teacher may use behavioral management techniques without meticulous collection of base-rate data (Tomlinson, 1972). If the behavioral data are to be used for evaluative purposes such as program evaluation or completion of IEP objectives, the collection of base-rate data might be imperative to show change. The special educator should make this decision based on program goals and the uses of the data to be collected.

Several advantages seem to accrue as a result of the exposure of teachers to behavioral strategies and classroom systems, including the fact that (1) the attention of the teacher may be directed away from certain behaviors and result in awareness of previously unnoticed positive behaviors, (2) the teacher may become more aware of antecedents and consequences of behavior (Rosenfield, 1979), (3) the teacher may engage in self-examination and attitudinal change in regard to the student's behavior and performance (Abidin, 1975; Rosenfield, 1979), and (4) the teacher may become more aware of the impact of the environment on the behavior of the child (Buckley & Walker, 1980).

In classes with students having more disturbed behavior, a complex system of behavioral management will be mandatory. With most mildly handicapped students, however, token economies and other less complex systems are adequate. The use of one-to-one, laboratory-based behavioral programs with sophisticated, expensive equipment will be neither necessary nor appropriate; the teacher can be equipped with basic behavioral techniques that will allow the maximization of the learning environment (the classroom) (Buckley & Walker, 1980). Two of the most common classroom systems are token economies and contracting.

Token economies. Sloane, Buckholdt, Jenson, and Crandall (1979) describe token economies as follows: "In a classroom token economy, children receive tokens upon completing specific social or academic activities, and the tokens are then periodically exchanged later for goods or activities (called backups), which themselves are reinforcing" (p. 205). The tokens have no real value but can be exchanged for the backups in much the same way that money or trading stamps are used in society. The basic components of a token economy are summarized in Table 12-6.

Contracting system. The basis of the contract-

Table 12-6. Summary of components of a token economy

Component	*Description*
Tokens	Any item with no value in and of itself but that can "purchase" desired privileges or items, for example, poker chips, points, stars, stamps, play money, squares or slips of paper, or check marks. Not available outside of classroom economy; "economy" can be inflated by students who have access outside of classroom!
Targeted behavior and "alerting" system	Specific behavior for which tokens will be given; "being good" is not specific enough (see earlier chapters). "Alerting" system lists or states precise behavior targeted; it formally "notifies" students of ways to earn tokens.
Rewards or "store"	Rewards that can be "purchased" with tokens—these may be privileges (e.g., free time, time in gymnasium, exemption from desk cleaning, time with equipment) or items (e.g., toys, gum, pens, stickers)—or system of dispensing rewards, such as using a "store," locker, shelf, or box.
Reward menu	*Posted* listing of *rewards* and *cost* (in terms of tokens); listing should be changed frequently to maintain its rewarding appeal.
Management system	System for dispensing tokens, including the following: Time period when it will operate Method by which tokens will be given Recording system of tokens awarded, if necessitated by token selected or period of operation System for dispensing rewards, including the following: Shopping time Redemption periods when privileges can be taken Monitoring system

Table 12-7. Summary of components of a contracting system

Components	*Description*
Contracting parties	Teacher and student participating in contract
Period of contract	Beginning and ending dates
Targeted behavior	Behavior student must demonstrate, precisely described so that all parties understand requirement
Criterion	Amount or degree of behavior specified so both parties know when contract is ''done''
Rewards	Privileges, items, or other reinforcers that student will ''earn'' on completion of contract
Conditions	Any specific information concerning terms of contract, such as particular materials, locations, or other details pertinent to contract
Signatures	Element needed for completed written contracts

ing system is the agreement made between teacher and student that specifies the task or behavioral goal and the rewards earned on completion of the contract. Contracts using student input seem to increase student motivation to reach goals; students can ''negotiate'' with the teacher concerning the various components of the contract in an effort to reach a mutually beneficial contract. Following are other advantages of contracting (Walker & Shea, 1980):

1. The method is a positive one.
2. Personal responsibilities are identified for the student.
3. The teacher collects progress or evaluation data reflecting student progress.
4. The data can be used for program evaluation and alterations.
5. The child's interests, needs, and abilities can be acknowledged in developing the contracts.
6. Planning and instruction may proceed more systematically.

Sloane et al. (1979) point out that many students perceive contracting to be an ''adult'' procedure, which may partially explain its particular appeal and potential application with older students who are uncooperative and resistant (Bristol & Sloan, 1974; Lovitt, 1975).

The components of the contracting system are briefly summarized in Table 12-7. Homme, Csanyi, Gonzales, and Rechs (1970) provide the following contracting system:

1. Provide the reward immediately.
2. Allow for and reward approximations of the targeted behavior.
3. Frequently give rewards.
4. Reward accomplishments rather than obedience.
5. Make sure that the reward follows the targeted behavior.
6. Establish a contract that is fair for both parties.
7. Make the requirements of the contract and reward clear to both parties.
8. Ensure that the contract is honest.
9. Create a contract that is positive, contracting for the occurrence of a desired behavior.
10. Conduct contracting systematically and consistently as a part of the operation of the classroom.

Negotiating the contract is integral to its success. Shea, Whiteside, Beetner, and Lindsey (1974) suggest a negotiation procedure for the novice teacher initiating a contracting system; the following summarizes some of the steps:

1. Establish and maintain good rapport and communication with the child.
2. Explain the purpose of the meeting.
3. Define the contract and how it is to be developed mutually.
4. Discuss tasks and reinforcers to be included.
5. Fairly and honestly negotiate the ratio of task to reinforcer.

CONTRACT

This contract between ____________ and ____________ has been developed for the following purpose(s): ____________________________

____

During the period ____________ to ____________ the student ____________

____

____

The contract will be considered completed when ____________________

____

____________________ and the rewards will be: ____________

____

Special conditions of this contract include: ____________________

____

____________________ ____________________ ____________
(Signature) (Signature) (Date)

6. Agree on the time allotted for the task.
7. Identify the criterion for completion.
8. Discuss evaluation procedures for meeting the criterion.
9. Negotiate delivery of the reinforcer.
10. Prepare the final contract (in writing if desired and appropriate).
11. Review the contract and modify if necessary.
12. Sign the written contract—verbal agreement may be sufficient.

Written contracts may be prepared for older students. Preparing standard forms for these written contracts may save the teacher time and may be appealing to some students (see above). Verbal contracts are equally effective in some situations. Determination of the type of contract must be based on student characteristics, preference of the teacher, and the schedule and structure of the classroom.

Cautions. Following are some general reminders for the teacher who is considering implementing a token economy or contracting system:

1. The rewards (tangibles) should be accompanied by social reinforcements; the nature of the social reinforcement varies with the individual personality of the teacher as well as that of the pupil. The teacher must communicate to the student that it is important to achieve the objective of the contract and that the student has done well in attaining that goal.
2. There will be times when the system may not work properly; tasks may be too easy or diffi-

cult. Modifications will have to be made in the targeted task or behavioral objective.

3. Sometimes the system fails because the rewards have lost their reinforcing effect; this requires that the teacher, with input from students, alter the rewards.
4. Good organizational skills on the part of the teacher help in developing and implementing a system; teamwork with another teacher may help "debug" the system.
5. Flexibility is a must; manipulating the various components of the system may be required frequently as the teacher evaluates the effectiveness of the system.
6. Nothing replaces sound teaching.

Instructional materials

The selection of instructional materials is one of the major tasks associated with instruction. The teacher should make decisions concerning materials based on factors such as existing materials, budget constraints, program rationale, instructional approaches associated with the particular materials, quality of the product, and desired student outcomes.

Existing materials. Many teachers overlook available materials and, instead, concentrate on new purchases, an approach that may even be less viable in the future because of reduced budgets in most schools. Materials available within the special education program and the regular classroom should be examined for possible application in special programming. Following are some suggestions for evaluating the availability of materials:

1. Secure an inventory of materials assigned to the special and regular classes with which there might be interaction; these may be available from the principal for review.
2. Examine the basic supplies provided by the school (e.g., paper, staples, glue, and ditto paper)
3. Examine the school or building inventory that lists support materials such as models, kits, maps, and instructional media.
4. Informally contact any regular classroom teacher to locate teacher-made instructional aids that are available on loan. (This must be done carefully, especially for new teachers; it might be desirable to delay until rapport has been established.)
5. Examine the basic texts and instructional supports such as workbooks assigned to regular classrooms.
6. Scout storage rooms and other areas for used materials.
7. Request a list of free films that are available through the state education department, nearby universities, or other agencies.
8. Check local libraries and professional organizations for materials or funds that could be used.
9. Explore local stores and industries for discarded display materials or for purchases. (Such purchases are tax deductible as professional deductions.)
10. Peruse sources of free materials*
11. Contact local or national instructional materials centers such as Special Education Instructional Materials Centers and Regional Materials Centers (SEIMC/RMC) that acquire, catalogue, and loan materials to educators free and at minimal costs (Table 12-8).

Budget constraints. The amount of money each teacher has to spend on classroom materials varies among districts and may have been decreased to an even lower level in recent years because of economic problems confronted by public schools. Following are some suggestions for collecting and using budget information in making decision about materials.

1. The teacher should request specific information from the supervisor or principal, including the following:

   Is there a line item budget for special education classes and, if so, how much?

**Free and Inexpensive Learning Materials*
Norman R. Moore, Editor
Division of Surveys and Field Services
George Peabody College for Teachers
Nashville, TN 37203

Table 12-8. Special Education Instructional Materials Centers and Regional Materials Centers (SEIMC/RMC)

Region	*Areas served*	*Addresses of centers*
1	Alaska Hawaii Idaho Montana Oregon Washington Wyoming Guam Samoa Trust Territory	Northwest ALRC University of Oregon Clinical Services Building, Third Floor Eugene, OR 97403 (503) 686-3591
2	California	California ALRC 600 Commonwealth Ave. Suite 1304 Los Angeles, CA 90006 (213) 381-2104
3	Arizona Colorado Nevada New Mexico Utah Bureau of Indian Affairs	Southwest ALRC New Mexico State University Box 3 AW Las Cruces, NM 88003 (505) 646-1017
4	Arkansas Iowa Kansas Missouri Nebraska Oklahoma North Dakota South Dakota	Midwest ALRC Drake University 1336 26th St. Des Moines, IA 50311 (515) 217-3951
5	Texas	Texas ALRC University of Texas at Austin College of Education Building 1912 Speedway Austin, TX 78712 (512) 471-3145
6	Indiana Michigan Minnesota Wisconsin	Great Lakes ALRC Michigan Department of Education P.O. Box 30008 Lansing, MI 48909 (517) 373-9443

Continued.

Table 12-8. Special Education Instructional Materials Centers and Regional Materials Centers (SEIMC/RMC)—cont'd

Region	*Areas served*	*Addresses of centers*
7	Illinois	ALRC Materials Development and Dissemination Specialized Educational Services Illinois Office of Education 100 N. First St. Springfield, IL 62777 (217) 782-2436
8	Ohio	Ohio ALRC 933 High St. Worthington, OH 43085 (614) 466-2650
9	Connecticut Maine Massachusetts New Hampshire New Jersey Rhode Island Vermont	Northeast ALRC 168 Bank St. Hightown, NJ 08520 (609) 448-4775
10	New York	New York State ALRC 55 Elk St., Room 117 Albany, NY 12234 (518) 474-2251
11	Pennsylvania	Pennsylvania ALRC 573 N. Main St. Doylestown, PA 18901 (215) 345-8080
12	Delaware District of Columbia Kentucky Maryland North Carolina Tennessee Virginia West Virginia Virgin Islands	Mid-East ALRC University of Kentucky 123 Porter Building Lexington, KY 40506 (606) 258-4921
13	Alabama Florida Georgia Louisiana Mississippi South Carolina Puerto Rico	Southeast ALRC Auburn University at Montgomery Highway 80 East Montgomery, AL 36117 (205) 279-9110, ext. 258

Are there specific periods during which the money must be spent?
Is an amount allotted to the building as a whole?
Does equipment (e.g., record players, listening posts, and special cutting scissors) come from the materials budget for the class?

2. If an amount is allotted to the program, the teacher needs to know the chain of approval required before purchase (i.e., who approves the request?).
3. In the event the amount is insufficient, some teachers have also found that good documentation of need can result in additional funding from the administration. This justification should include the following elements:
   Intended use of materials
   Number of students to use materials
   Period of time materials are used
   Cost of materials
   Life expectancy of item purchased

Program rationale. Program goals affect all aspects of the special education program, including the selection of materials. For instance, a program with the major emphasis on remedial instruction will require extensive remedial materials, programs incorporating affective goals will select materials for developing socioemotional objectives, and accommodational emphases within special programs will require that materials be selected with the mainstream classroom and curricula as a point of reference. Keeping program goals in mind aids teachers in selecting appropriate materials.

The rationale of the program should be reflected in the criteria and general bases for evaluation of the program. The measures of success of the program must be taken into consideration because materials must be acquired and used that will produce the particular results desired.

Instructional approaches associated with the materials. The particular strategies required to use the materials must be examined with regard to the *population* to be served; factors to consider include the following:

1. Age of students
2. Previous educational experiences of students
3. Presence of any additional handicapping conditions
4. Special interests of the group
5. Reinforcement systems used effectively with this population

It may be necessary for the teacher to delay final selection of any new materials or the modification of existing ones until there has been some opportunity to interact and observe. The number of students to be served should also be considered.

The *format* of the materials must be carefully examined for compatibility with organizational patterns of the classroom and instructional needs of the students; aspects to be considered include the following:

1. Size of print
2. Need for accompanying supplies (e.g., special pencils)
3. Clarity of information presented
4. Organization of materials
5. Appropriateness of format for age groups
6. Presence of any indication of grade level
7. Storage requirements
8. Hidden costs (e.g., updating, service, and repair)

Other considerations related to use of materials are *level of difficulty, level of independent functioning required,* and *number of students who can use the materials at any one time.* The *amount of teacher supervision required* is a major aspect that should also be considered in evaluating the strategies for using the particular material. Manufacturers may not provide adequate or accurate information concerning this particular feature of the product.

Durability. The initial cost of materials should only be considered part of the expense of the item; other costs may include consumable items required with the materials, availability of replacement parts or consumable items, and amount of maintenance required. In addition to possible future costs, the item should be examined for its general construction. For example, a recording should be evaluated not only in terms of content and use but also durability of the cover. Books should be made of durable materials and quality paper and be well bound to last for some time. One major factor in the decision to purchase a kit is the storage case, since it is integral to the durability of the kit.

Desired student outcomes. Student outcomes expected from the program directly result from the goals selected for the program. Student outcomes may vary from an emphasis on improving reading to achieving passing grades in mainstream arithmetic. The nature of these outcomes and the relationship of the special education program to the total school program are important considerations in selection of materials. The IEP and teaching approaches designed to implement the IEP should receive much consideration in purchasing or modifying materials. Review of the IEPs for students may also reveal some common goals that could be addressed by a type of material not currently offered in a program.

Equipment. Individual and individualized instruction and the amount and quality of each program are affected by the availability of equipment for augmenting instruction. Following is an equipment inventory that could greatly aid a teacher in designing instructional programs:

Essential equipment
Tape recorders
Ear phones and listening posts
Audiotape storage units
Typewriters

Desirable equipment
Record player
Overhead projector
Blackboards (preferably portable on stands)
Worktables
Study carrels
Filing cabinet (at least one)
Bulletin and pegboards
Storage cabinets for large equipment and models
Film and filmstrip projectors
Microcomputer

Examine the various types of listening posts and earphone connections that are currently available. The following selection represents a wide variety of factors that might be considered in selecting earphones and controls:

1. Individual volume controls are best because students may have different hearing levels, which makes volume adjustment difficult from the central control.
2. "Wireless" sets, using batteries or a ceiling loop for transmission, offer more student mobility and options for setting up rules for the listening centers.
3. Earphones offering easy adjustments of the headset are more versatile and accommodate a broader range of ages and sizes.

Typewriters should also be considered necessary equipment for a special education room. The best model depends on the particular circumstances, such as amount of money allotted, number and age of student typists, and frequency of use. The school administrators can probably identify a reputable sales company if a new machine has to be selected, or an approved list may exist.

Following is a list of equipment to which the special education teacher should have access within the school system:

Duplicator
Copier
Opaque projector
Film projector (16 mm)
Slide projector

Resources

As indicated in Fig. 12-1, comprehensive programming must be designed to take full advantage of the human resources available within the ecology of the special education classroom and school. The special educator's role is sometimes conceptualized as that of a "program manager" (Brown, Elliott, & White, 1977); teachers who embody this concept of manager find that support such as aides, tutors, and volunteers is critical to a total program. Although the prevalence of paraprofessionals may be somewhat limited, there are other sources of assistance in peer tutors and volunteer programs. Following are some general suggestions concerning these groups.

Selection. If no paraprofessionals are included within school personnel, the teacher must begin to identify possible sources of assistance such as parents, school organizations, community groups, and student groups. Parents may be considered as a possible source of clerical personnel and for academic tutoring of students other than their own (McLoughlin, Edge, & Strenecky, 1978; Poper, 1976). School groups such as Future Teachers of America (FTA), Key Club, and other service groups may have student members that are interested in providing volunteer time to the special education program. Special education programs located near universities or colleges may be able to use students from courses requiring that a specified number of observation or volunteer hours be completed as a course requirement. Groups within the community, such as the Jaycettes or Lions Club, may be able to provide some volunteer time for particular activities.

Groups of retired teachers in some areas contribute extensively to school programs. Buffer (1980) suggests that retired persons may be contacted through sources such as directors of retirement communities, nursing homes, and Retired Senior Volunteer Programs (RSVP); many of these organizations have numbers listed in local phone books.

The next step in selection is identifying individuals who might be able to fulfill the needs of the teacher in a particular situation. It may be a task requiring a great deal of tact, since some of the most eager volunteers may not be well suited to the tasks or the situation. The following factors should be considered in selecting paraprofessionals or volunteers as well as peer tutors:

1. Work schedule: the number of hours and exact time periods when the person would be available
2. Experience: special talents or experiences
3. Personality: the disposition and social skills of the person
4. Personal interest: relationship to students
5. Motivation: reasons for volunteering
6. Expectations: what is expected from the experience

Teachers often express reluctance in using aides or volunteers in the classroom, saying, "They are more trouble than they are worth," "They are just in the way," or "I just don't feel comfortable with a stranger in the classroom." One of the most vital ingredients in making the volunteer or aide program work is the rapport between the teacher and the support person. Therefore, a good rule of thumb is for teachers to select persons with whom they feel rapport and in whose presence they feel comfortable!

Training. Whether paraprofessionals are provided by the district or volunteers are secured within the community, training should be carefully planned and conducted. This allows all parties to understand what the job requires and what the responsibilities are for all persons involved. Training should include the following aspects:

1. *Manual.* A manual should be provided by the teacher for the aide or volunteer to keep for later reference and should include the following:
   - School calendar and schedule listing activities
   - Phone number to call if the person is unable to attend
   - Program philosophy emphasizing confidentiality, commitment, and cooperation
   - Map of the school including important locations such as the principal's office, nurse's workroom, library, media center, restrooms, and storage rooms
   - List of equipment that the aide or volunteer might use
   - List of student's names for each time period
   - Description of classroom rules and specific behavioral expectations
   - Any relevant school policies
2. *Orientation and training session.* Planning

and conducting an orientation session for aides and volunteers requires time on the part of the teacher, but the 1-hour session can save time throughout the semester because it reduces the amount of individual orientation and training required. The orientation session might include the following:

Tour of the building
Explanation of the nature of the special education program and overview of the type of students served
Goals of the program
Discussion of confidentiality
Discussion of the importance of dependability, with instructions given about reporting when absences are necessary
Identification of area designated for volunteer or aide's use to store materials, leave messages, and so forth.
Orientation to and demonstrations of equipment
Introduction to materials such as glue and paper and their location

Individuals unwilling to make the commitment to attend this single training session or those too ''busy'' are probably not going to work out as volunteers or aides for the same reason!

Supervision and communication. Cunninggim (1980) reports the following suggestions given by the National School Volunteer Program (NSVP)* in regard to using volunteers in the classroom:

1. Assess which needs or duties require the help of a volunteer.
2. Request a volunteer through the principal or volunteer coordinator; list duties to be performed and specify days and times.
3. Provide an orientation program for the volunteer.
4. Establish a system for communication.
5. Share progress information.
6. Show appreciation.

*A nonprofit group governed by a national board of directors, with headquarters at 300 N. Washington St., Alexandria, VA.

These suggestions, basically emphasizing communication, apply to paraprofessionals, either paid or nonsalaried. However, in the midst of attempting to orchestrate multilevel learning for a variety of students and coordinate mainstreaming interactions, such communication may not be easily achieved by the special educator. The teacher should not have to stop each time an aide or volunteer enters the room; instructions should be communicated easily through some system devised by the teacher. One popular approach is to use a ''mailbox'' for each aide or volunteer. As the teacher thinks of things to be done the next day or week, instructions can be outlined and left for the aide. Examples are shown on p. 429.

Selecting the particular type of task appropriate for aides or volunteers may require some teacher time. There are no clear limits as to the nature of the task other than the teacher's ability to structure and the aide's ability to understand what is expected. Following are common categories of tasks:

1. *Clerical tasks* such as making bulletin boards, making graphs, locating materials, duplicating worksheets, and grading papers
2. *Instructional support tasks* such as conducting drill sessions, showing films and doing follow-up activities, tutoring following a teaching script developed by the teacher, and monitoring learning centers

Supervision of aides and volunteers should mean providing feedback concerning their performance. Reinforcement for a job well done should receive as much attention from the teacher as an error. Straightforward feedback related to problems and mistakes may also be required. The ultimate responsibility for the program rests with the teacher, and this must be kept in mind in evaluating the effectiveness of an aide or a volunteer program.

Peer tutors may be a special source of assistance for some classrooms. Jenkins, Mayhall, Peschka, and Jenkins (1974) provide data lending considerable support to the concept of cross-age peer tutors; the results were significantly greater than those produced by small group teacher instruction.

COMMUNICATIONS WITH AIDES, TUTORS, AND VOLUNTEERS

Example 1: Clerical task

Date: 8/28

Review library holdings, including filmstrips, related to the following list of units:

1. Seasons of the year
2. Animal habitats
3. Types of housing around the world

Preview the materials for appropriateness for this class.

Prepare a list of materials you deem appropriate, and list them under each topic; identify them as books, models, media, and so forth.

I need these materials by September 4.

Example 2: Instructional support task

Date: 11/10

Plan to conduct a 15-minute drill–review session daily for 5 days concerning writing alphabet in cursive for the following six students: Meredith, Jake, Kama, Matt, Anna, and Wendy.

The week-long review should include the following:

1. Capital and small letters
2. Cursive writing
3. Correct pencil position

Plan activities such as the following:

1. Copying
2. Tracing
3. Original work
4. Demonstrations

Conduct the sessions in the review center at the other end of the classroom from 11:00 to 11:15 during week of November 19.

Therefore, the special educator should explore the possibility of using cross-age tutors within the program, with the possible by-products including availability of role models and increased understanding of the program among members of the school population.

Space

Space is a related aspect in comprehensive programming that may be addressed in state plans for special education because specific requirements may be stated regarding the number of square feet of classroom space required per student. The special education room should resemble other classrooms considered typical in characteristics that include size, appearance, electrical systems, and ventilation. Although the number of students served at any one time may be low, the spatial needs cannot be determined by the size of the group. Physical space requirements may be affected by factors such as the following (D'Alonzo, 1979):

1. A broader scope of materials may be needed because of the great diversity of students.
2. IEPs may require individual and independent work through strategies such as learning cen-

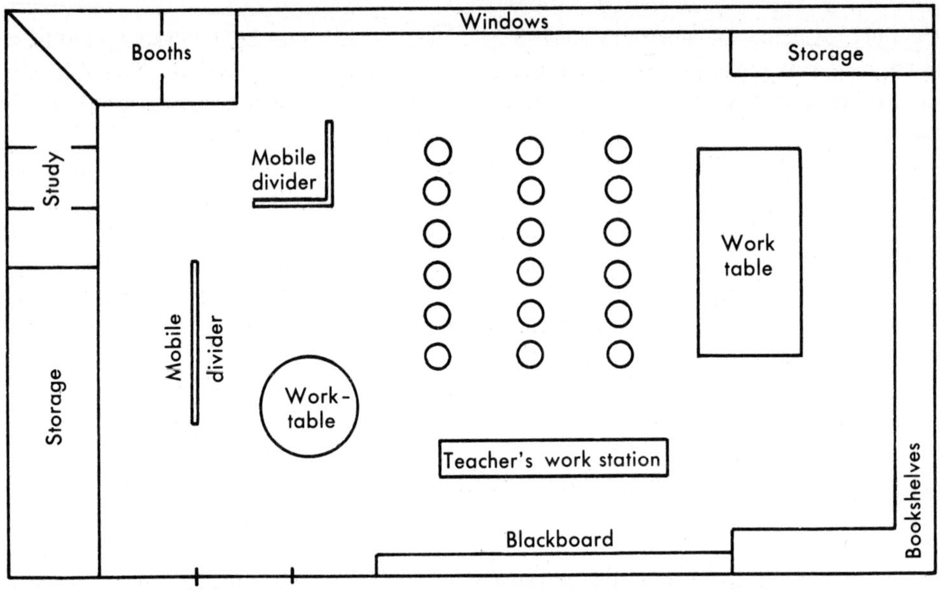

Fig. 12-4. Floor plan example 1. ***X,*** **Teacher;** ***circle,*** **earphones/recorder or record player;** ***square,*** **audiovisual equipment such as filmstrip projector and film projector. (From Marsh, G., II, & Price, B.J.** ***Methods for teaching the mildly handicapped adolescent.*** **St. Louis: The C.V. Mosby Co., 1980.)**

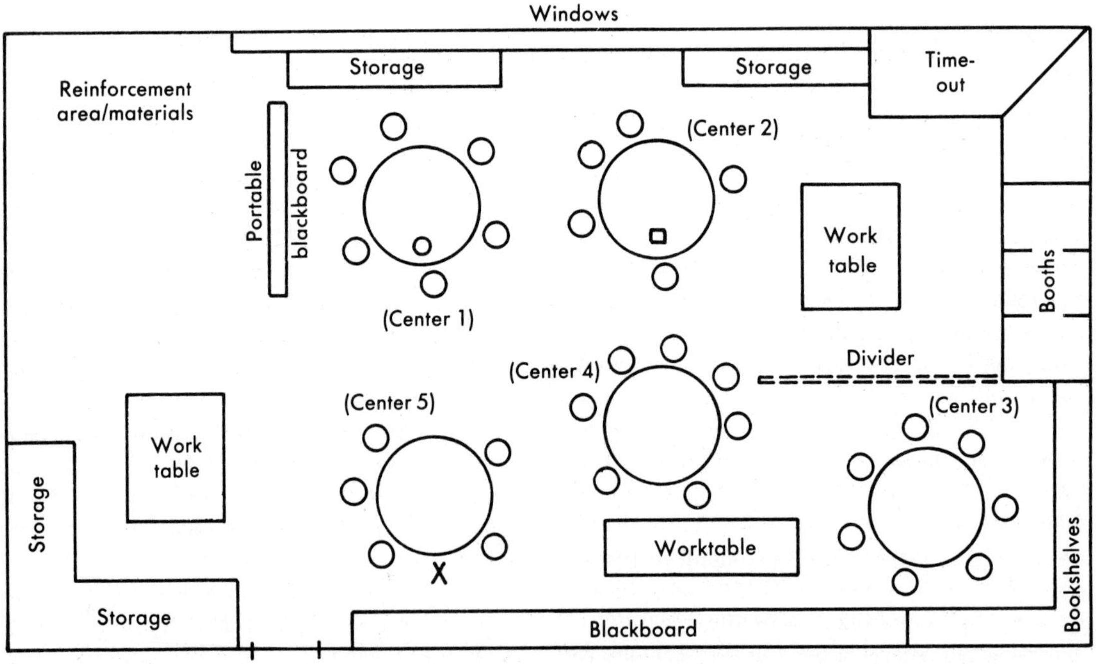

Fig. 12-5. Floor plan example 2. (From Marsh, G., II, & Price, B.J. ***Methods for teaching the mildly handicapped adolescent.*** **St. Louis: The C.V. Mosby Co., 1980.)**

ters, thus requiring the same physical space for the center as for any classroom although only one student may be in the center at any one time.

3. A reinforcement or time-out area may be required.
4. Study carrels or booths should be available.
5. There must be adequate space for students to move freely about the room.
6. Privacy should be provided to facilitate teacher-pupil communications and conferences.
7. The classroom or an adjacent area should include office space for the teacher.

The floor plan established by the teacher will be affected by the physical characteristics of the room, teacher preference, equipment, and planned activities, not to mention the amount of power wielded by night custodians Figs. 12-4 and 12-5 present two examples of floor plans; one represents a more traditional plan, whereas the other reflects the use of learning centers.

There are some general considerations in regard to the location of the classroom within the building. It should be in a central location close to other support services used in conjunction with the program. Mainstreaming may present one mundane type of problem—student conduct in the halls while enroute to and from the regular classroom. Any preparation of the student to participate in mainstreaming should include some awareness of the behavioral expectations in the hall and the precise route to be taken. Depending on the nature of the handicapping condition, particular attention must be given to this related concern in training.

Program evaluation

Once the special educator has achieved a satisfactory plan for planning and implementing individualized instruction, additional considerations should be addressed in managing the program. Program evaluation must be viewed as a management tool useful in daily programming as well as in measuring the annual effects of the program. For this concept of daily evaluation to become reality, the teacher must be involved in or at least aware of the evaluation procedure. The following factors must be considered in monitoring and evaluation (Marsh & Price, 1980, pp. 218-219):

1. State and federal guidelines and requirements
   - Has the program followed the specified guidelines for placement?
   - Have all procedures regarding due process been followed to guarantee rights?
   - Have parents been involved as prescribed in legislation?
   - Has the IEP been developed to ensure appropriate educational services for the student?
2. School policies
   - Are the procedures followed in the program consistent or at least compatible with school policy?
   - Have the teacher and the program fulfilled all of the roles or responsibilities expected by the school administration and/or dictated by school policy?
   - How do other teachers view you and your program?
   - Has the room met specifications for physical environmental factors determined by school policy?
   - Have materials and other resources been used maximally and in accordance with school policy?
   - Is the cost of the program in line with expectations?
3. Student outcomes
   - Have goals stated in the IEPs been achieved?
   - Have program goals been achieved in terms of general student outcomes?
   - Is the program successful and appealing to the consumers (students)?
   - Does the program assist the students in functioning in the real world?

Grading students. Hawisher and Calhoun (1978) state that in the event the elementary schoolchild attends the regular classroom for various content areas, "the assignment of grades is the regular classroom teacher's responsibility" (p. 148). If the mainstream teacher is hesitant to assume this responsibility, and if the child has received instructional support in the content area in the resource room, the special educator and mainstream teacher might consider cooperative grading. This would necessitate a conference to ensure that communications to parents concerning the grade are consistent and accurately presented by both teachers.

In some instances state and district policies dictate the specific grading procedure to be used with special education students. The special educator should request a copy of the policy, if it exists, to correctly comply with the procedure. If the policy is that the grades are to be given by the special educator, some attention must be given to the following factors:

1. Curricular objectives for the content area courses for which the special educator must provide a grade
2. Specific objectives in the IEP
3. Any evidence of progress that might be reflected in knowledge competencies, skill competencies, or products

The awarding of grades by special educators may present a number of problems among parents and administrators as well as other teachers. Obviously, there may be some concern regarding the special educator's ability to understand the school's curriculum well enough to assign appropriate grades. Grraduates from teacher preparation programs that include both elementary and special education training are not as susceptible to such criticisms. Another concern, more prevalent in middle and high schools, is the "lowering" of standards and "grade inflation"; the special educator who is able to demonstrate progress in regard to curricular objectives may be more secure in engaging in the assignation of grades in subject areas.

A common practice seems to be reporting student progress in socioemotional areas, study skills, and organizational skills. The special educator may be asked to provide feedback to the student and parents concerning these variables; the reporting may be in the form of a checklist, modified grade card, parental letter, and/or parental conference.

SUMMARY

The purpose of this chapter was to concentrate attention on teaching methodology as an important variable in the teaching-learning paradigm for instructional design. Too frequently educators have tended to emphasize population-specific commercial materials or popular theories of remediation without examining basic environmental conditions, learning behaviors, and teaching acts. The chapter provided a review of learning theories with practical suggestions and a section of management of the program.

THE FUTURE

The purpose of this text was to provide the practitioner with a practical reference to education of handicapped children. It was noted in the first chapter that the emerging delivery are increasingly based on noncategorical or generic arrangements as a result of social, legal, and professional influences emanating from many sources. In the future it seems that economic conditions of the nation, conservative political trends, public attitudes toward education, and related factors will have an impact on the schools and special education. It seems apparent that diminishing enrollment, diminishing resources, poor salaries for educators, limited resources for the purchase of materials, and competition from private schools, especially if voucher systems are approved, will undermine public education. Special education, as a part of public education, may have a future predicated on these same issues. There will be less funding for research, limited resources for salaries and materials, and continuing litigation pertaining to the rights of the handicapped. A negative backlash may arise among parents, politicians, and professional educators as financial resources dwindle and other interest groups seek a larger share. A conflict over resources may develop as the needs of the gifted child are pitted against those of the handicapped. The regulations and laws that now govern special education may be challenged or altered as the "control of education is returned" to the states.

The immediate future of special education is clouded by economic and political realities. The demand for accountability means that it will be necessary for special educators to deliver truly realistic and practical programs for handicapped children. Noncategorical programs and mainstreaming will also become more prominent, if for no other reason than they are less expensive.

Therefore, it is imperative that special education personnel plan to address their responsibilities effectively. The following considerations are made concerning the future of special education:

1. Special educators must be willing to work across categorical lines.
2. The school curriculum must be conceptualized as being the guiding document for special education rather than a preoccupation with specialized curricular that may not address the needs of children or the demands of society.
3. The impact of technology, especially the computer, must be permitted to change teaching.
4. The teaching method must be given a more significant role in meeting needs of children, rather than focusing on test data or special method-oriented aproaches.
5. The goal of special education should be to enable handicapped children to assume adult roles in society; this will be more difficult in the future because technology and the economy will impact vocations by eliminating many jobs and creating new, highly technical occupations.

In the final analysis, the cost efficiency of special education will be used to judge the quality of programming. If special education is markedly more expensive and not effective in its ability to meet the real-world needs of children and regular educators, it will be curtailed. The critics who currently wield the budget-cutting axe are already questioning the need for P.L. 94-142, the regulations, and the expense of special education.

REFERENCES AND SUGGESTED READINGS

Abidin, R.R. Negative effects of behavioral consultation: "I know I ought to, but it hurts too much!" *Journal of School Psychology,* 1975, *13,* 51-57.

Ayres, J. *Sensory integration and learning disorders.* Los Angeles: Western Psychological Services, 1972.

Bauer, R.H. Memory, acquisition, and category clustering in learning-disabled children. *Journal of Experimental Child Psychology,* 1979, *27,* 365-383.

Bialer, I. *Conceptualization of success and failure in mentally retarded and normal children.* Ann Arbor, MI: University Microfilms International, 1960.

Bloom, B.S. The new directions in educational research: alterable variables. *Phi Delta Kappan,* 1980, *61,* 382-385.

Blumenthal, S.H. A study of the relationship between speed of retrieval of verbal information and patterns of oral reading errors. *Journal of LP,* 1980, *13,* 568-570.

Bristol, M.M., & Sloan, H.N. Effects of contingency contracting on study rate and test performance. *Journal of Applied Behavior Analysis,* 1974, *7,* 271-285.

Brown, A.L. The development of memory: knowing, knowing about knowing, and knowing how to know. In H.W. Reese (Ed.), *Advances in child development and behavior* (Vol. 10). New York: Academic Press, Inc., 1975.

Brown, E.C., Elliot, D., & White, R. *ASSIST: Associate instructional support for teachers* (Program 2). Bloomington: Developmental Training Center, Indiana University, 1977.

Bruner, J., Goodnow, J.J., & Austin, G. *A study of thinking.* New York: Science Editions, Inc., 1967.

Buckley, N.K., & Walker, H.M. *Modifying classroom behavior.* Champaign, IL: Research Press, 1980.

Buffer, L.C. Recruit retired adults as volunteers in special education. *Teaching Exceptional Children,* 1980, *12,* 113-115.

Charles, C.M. *Individualizing instruction* (2nd ed.). St. Louis, MO: The C.V. Mosby Co., 1980.

Cromwell, R.L. A social learning approach to mental retardation. In N.R. Ellis (Ed.), *Handbook of mental deficiency.* New York: McGraw-Hill Book Co., 1953.

Cunninggim, W. Citizen volunteers: a growing resource for teachers and students. *Teaching Exceptional Children,* 1980, *12,* 108-110.

D'Alonzo, B.J., D'Alonzo, R.L., & Mauser, A.J. Developing resource rooms for the handicapped. *Teaching Exceptional Children,* 1979, *11,* 91-96.

Delacato, C. *Treatment and prevention of reading problems.* Springfield, IL: Charles Thomas, Publisher, 1959.

Demers, L.A. Effective mainstreaming for the learning disabled student with behavior problems. *Journal of Learning Disabilities,* 1981, *14,* 179-188.

Denny, M.R. A theoretical analysis and its application to training the mentally retarded. In N.R. Ellis (Ed.), *International review of research in mental retardation* (Vol. 2). New York: Academic Press, 1966.

Dunn, R., & Dunn, K. Educational accountability in our schools. *Momentum,* 1977, *8*(3), 10-16.

Dunn, R., & Dunn, K. *Teaching students through their individual learning styles: a practical approach.* Reston, VA: Reston Publishing Co., Inc., 1978.

Ellis, N.R. Memory processes in retardates and normals. In N.R. Ellis (Ed.), *International review of research in mental retardation* (Vol. 4). New York: Academic Press, Inc., 1970.

Federal Register, August 23, 1977, *42*(163), 42481.

Fernald, G. *Remedial techniques in basic school subjects.* New York: McGraw-Hill Book Co., 1943.

Fisher, M.A., & Zeaman, D. An attention-retention theory of retardate discrimination learning. In N.R. Ellis (Ed.), *The international review of research in mental retardation* (Vol. 6). New York: Academic Press, Inc., 1973.

Folio, M.R., & Norman, A. Toward more success in mainstreaming: a peer teacher approach to physical education. *Teaching Exceptional Children,* 1981, *3,* 110-114.

Frostig, M., & Maslow, P. *Learning problems in the classroom: prevention and remediation.* New York: Grune & Stratton, Inc., 1973.

Gillingham, A., & Stillman, B. *Remedial training for children with specific disability in reading, spelling, and penmanship.* Cambridge, MA: Educators Publishing Service, Inc., 1960.

Glasser, W. *Reality therapy.* New York: Harper & Row, Publisher, 1965.

Hall, R.V. Training teachers in classroom use of contingency management. *Educational Technology,* 1971, *11,* 33-38.

Hammill, D.D., Goodman, L., & Weiderholt, J.L. Visual-motor processes: Can we train them? *Reading Teacher,* 1974, *27,* 469-478.

Hammill, D.D., & Larsen, S.C. The effectiveness of psycholinguistic training: a reaffirmation of position. *Exceptional Children,* 1978, *44,* 402-417.

Harlow, H.F. Learning set and error factor theory. In S. Koch (Ed.), *Psychology: a study of a science (Vol. 2). New York: McGraw-Hill Book Co., 1959.*

Hawisher, M.F., & Calhoun, M.F. *The resource room: an educational asset for children with special needs.* Columbus, OH: Charles E. Merrill Publishing Co., 1978.

Homme, L., Csanyi, A.P., Gonzales, M.A., & Rechs, J.R. *How to use contingency contracting in the classroom.* Champaign, IL: Research Press, 1970.

House, B.J., Brown, A.L., & Scott, M.S. Children's discrimination learning based on identity or difference. In H.W. Reese (Ed.), *Advances in child development and behavior* (Vol. 9). New York: Academic Press, Inc., 1974.

Jenkins, J., Mayhall, W., Peschka, C., & Jenkins, L. Comparing small group and tutorial instruction in resource rooms. *Exceptional Children,* 1974, *40,* 245-250.

Johnson, D., & Myklebust, H. *Learning disabilities, educational principles and practices.* New York: Grune & Stratton, Inc., 1967.

Joyce, B., & Weil, M. *Models of teaching* (2nd ed.). Englewood Cliffs, NJ: Prentice-Hall, Inc., 1980.

Keefe, J.W. School applications of the learning style concept. In J.W. Keefe (Ed.), *Student learning styles: diagnosing and prescribing programs.* Reston, VA: National Association of Secondary School Principles, 1979.

Kendler, H.H. & Kendler, T.S. Mediation and conceptual behavior. In K.W. Spence & J.T. Spence (Eds.), *Psychology of learning and motivation (Vol. 2). New York: Academic Press, Inc., 1968.*

Kephart, N. The slow learner in the classroom. Columbus, OH: Charles E. Merrill Publishing Co., 1971.

Kirk, S., McCarthy, J., & Kirk, W. *Illinois test of psycholinguistic abilities: examiner's manual* (Exp. ed.). Urbana, IL: University of Illinois Press, 1968.

Lawrence, O.H. Acquire distinctiveness of cues (Pt. 2). Selective association in a constant stimulus situation. *Journal of Experimental Psychology* 1950, *40,* 175-188.

Lawrence, O.H. The nature of a stimulus: some relationships between learning and perception. In S. Koch (Ed.), *Psychology: a study of a science* (Vol. 5). New York: McGraw-Hill Book Co., 1963.

Lindsley, O.R. Direct measurement and prosthesis of retarded behavior. *Journal of Education,* 1964, *147,* 62-81.

Lovitt, T.C. Applied behavior analysis and learning disabilities (Pt. 1). Characteristics of ABA, general recommendations, and methodological limitations. *Journal of Learning Disabilities,* 1975, *8,* 432-443.

Marsh, G.E. II, & Price, B.J. *Methods for teaching the mildly handicapped adolescent.* St. Louis, MO: The C.V. Mosby Co. 1980.

Massiaias, B., & Cox, B. *Inquiry in social studies.* New York: McGraw-Hill Book Co., 1966.

McLeskey, J. Learning set acquisition: problem solving strategies emloyed by reading disabled and normal children. *Journal of Learning Disabilities,* 1980, *13,* 557-562.

McLoughlin, J.A., Edge, D., & Strenecky, B. Perspective on parental involvement in the diagnosis and treatment of learning disabled children. *Journal of Learning Disabilities,* 1978, *11,* 291-296.

Mercer, C.D. *Children and adolescents with learning disabilities.* Columbus, OH: Charles E. Merrill Publishing Co., 1979.

Mercer, C.D., & Snell, M.E. *Learning theory research in mental retardation: implications for teaching.* Columbus, OH: Charles E. Merrill Publishing Co., 1977.

Meyen, E.L. *Developing instructional units* (2nd. ed.). Dubuque, IA: William C. Brown Co., Publishers, 1976.

Mills, C.W. *The power elite.* New York: Oxford University Press, Inc., 1956.

Newcomer, P., & Hammill, D.D. *Psycholinguistics in the schools.* Columbus, OH: Charles E. Merrill Publishing Co., 1976.

Oaken, R., Wiener, M.C., & Cromer, W. Identification, organization, and reading comprehension for good and poor readers. *Journal of Educational Psychology,* 1971, *62,* 71-78.

Paper, C.C. *The relationship of socioeconomic status, sex, and ability group to learning styles among eighth grade students.* Unpublished thesis, Old Dominion University, 1973.

Pasanella, A.L., & Volkmor, C.B. *Coming back . . . or never leaving.* Columbus, OH: Charles E. Merrill Publishing Co., 1977.

Practical applications of research. *Phi Delta Kappan Newsletter,* March 1981.

Poper, L. *A handbook for tutorial programs.* Brooklyn, NY: Lab, Inc., 1976.

Quay, H.C. Special education: assumptions, techniques, and evaluative criteria. *Exceptional Children,* 1973, *40,* 165-170.

Rider, R.A. Mainstreaming moderately retarded children in the elementary physical education program. *Teaching Exceptional Children,* 1980, *12,* 150-152.

Rogers, C. *Child centered therapy.* Boston: Houghton Mifflin, Co., 1971.

Rotter, J.B. Generalized expectancies for internal versus external control of reinforcement. *Psychological Monographs,* 1966, *80* (1, Whole No. 609).

Rosenfield, S. Introducing behavior modification techniques to teachers. *Exceptional Children,* 1979, *45,* 334-339.

Ross, A.O. *Psychological aspects of learning disabilities and reading disorders.* New York: McGraw-Hill Book Co., 1976.

Sargent, L.R. Resource teacher time utilization: an observational study. *Exceptional Children,* 1981, *47,* 420-425.

Shea,T.M., Whiteside, W.R., Beetner, E.G., & Lindsey, D.L. *Contingency contracting in the classroom.* Edwardsville IL: Southern Illinois University, 1974.

Skinner, B.F. *Science and human behavior.* New York: Macmillan, Inc., 1953.

Sloane, H.N., Buckholdt, D.R., Jenson, W.R., & Crandall, J.A. *Structured teaching.* Champaign, IL: Research Press, 1979.

Smead, V.S. Ability training and task analysis in diagnostic/prescriptive teaching. *The Journal of Special Education,* 1977, *11,* 113-125.

Spitz, H.H. Consolidating facts into the schematized learning and memory system of educable retardates. In N.R. Ellis (Ed.), *International review of research in mental retardation* (Vol. 6). New York: Academic Press, Inc., 1973.

Stephens, T.M. *Teaching skills to children with learning and behavior disorders.* Columbus, OH: Charles E. Merrill Publishing Co., 1977.

Stephenson, B., & Gray, W. Psycholinguistic abilities of black and white children from four SES levels. *Exceptional Children,* 1976, *38,* 705-709.

Stewart, W.A., Goodman, G., & Hammond, B., Behavior modification: teacher training and attitudes. *Exceptional Children,* 1976, *42,* 402-403.

Swift, M.S., & Spivack, G. *Alternative teaching strategies.* Champaign, IL: Research Press, 1975.

Taba, H. *Teaching strategies and cognitive functioning in elementary school children* (Cooperative Research Project 2404). San Francisco: San Francisco State College, 1966.

Tarver, S.G., Hallahan, D.P., Kauffman, J.M. & Ball, D.W. Verbal rehearsal and selective attention in children with learning disabilities: a developmental lag. *Journal of Experimental Child Psychology,* 1976, *22,* 375-385.

Thurman, S.K., & Lewis, M. Children's responses to differences: some possible implications for mainstreaming. *Exceptional Children,* 1979, *3,* 468-470.

Tomlinson, J.R. Implementing behavior modification programs with limited consultation time. *Journal of School Psychology,* 1972, *10,* 379-386.

Torgenson, J.K. Performance of reading disabled children or serial memory tasks: a selective review of recent research. *Reading Research Quarterly,* 1978, *14,* 57-87.

Turnbull, A.P., & Schultz, J.B. *Mainstreaming handicapped students.* Boston: Allyn & Bacon, Inc., 1979.

Valett, R.E. Mainstreaming exceptional children by functional achievement group. *Journal of Learning Disabilities,* 1981, *14,* 123.

Walker, J.A., & Shea, T.M. *Behavior modification* (2nd ed.). St. Louis, MO: The C.V. Mosby Co., 1980.

Witkin, H.A., et al. *Personality through perception.* New York: Harper & Row, Publishers, Inc., 1954.

Woodrow, H. The relation between abilities and improvement with practice. *Journal of Educational Psychology,* 1938, *29,* 215-230.

Woodrow, H. *The ability to learn.* Psychological Review, 1946, *53,* 147-158.

Yesseldyke, J.E., & Salvia, J. Diagnostic-prescriptive teaching: two models. *Exceptional Children,* 1974, *41,* 181-185.

Zeaman, D., & House, B.J. The role of attention in retardate discrimination learning. In N.R. Ellis, (Ed.), *Handbook of mental deficiency.* New York: McGraw-Hill Book Co., 1963.

Zigler, E. Research on personality structure in the retardate. In N.R. Ellis (Ed.), *International review of research on mental retardation* (Vol. 1). New York: Academic Press, Inc., 1966.

INDEX